ARTHUR HUGH CLOUGH

Towards a Reconsideration

ARTHUR HUGH CLOUGH

Towards a Reconsideration

—

ROBINDRA KUMAR BISWAS

OXFORD
AT THE CLARENDON PRESS
1972

Oxford University Press, Ely House, London W. 1

GLASGOW NEW YORK TORONTO MELBOURNE WELLINGTON
CAPE TOWN IBADAN NAIROBI DAR ES SALAAM LUSAKA ADDIS ABABA
DELHI BOMBAY CALCUTTA MADRAS KARACHI LAHORE DACCA
KUALA LUMPUR SINGAPORE HONG KONG TOKYO

73 15509
820 CLO

821|CLO

PRINTED IN GREAT BRITAIN
AT THE UNIVERSITY PRESS, OXFORD
BY VIVIAN RIDLER
PRINTER TO THE UNIVERSITY

To

BRONWEN

*who will, I hope, be surprised
and pleased*

Acknowledgements

My thanks are due, first, to Miss Katharine Duff. She not only gave me permission to quote freely from unpublished material, but also encouraged me to look at the Clough material in her possession and was a charming hostess when I did so. I am indebted to the Master and Fellows of Balliol College, to the Keeper of Western Manuscripts in the Bodleian Library, to the Provost and Fellows of Oriel College, and to Mr. Kittermaster and Rugby School for letting me have access to their collections. Harvard College Library has kindly given me permission to quote from materials there. I thank the following presses for permission to quote from published sources: the University of Auckland Press (*The New Zealand Letters of Thomas Arnold the Younger*, ed. J. Bertram), the Clarendon Press (*The Poems of Arthur Hugh Clough*, ed. H. F. Lowry, F. L. Mulhauser, and A. L. P. Norrington, and *The Correspondence of Arthur Hugh Clough*, ed. F. L. Mulhauser), the Oxford University Press (*The Letters of Matthew Arnold to Arthur Hugh Clough*, ed. H. F. Lowry), and the University of Alabama Press (*Selected Prose Works of Arthur Hugh Clough*, ed. B. Trawick).

Among more personal debts my first is to Professor Douglas Grant, who was a wise, compassionate, endlessly patient teacher and supervisor. His death was as tragic as it was sudden. Professor John Jump was a gentle and encouraging examiner when I presented a version of this study as a thesis at Leeds University, and his comments were uniformly valuable. My acquaintance with Professor Frederick Mulhauser is relatively recent. I am indebted to him not only for extended conversations about Clough but also for letting me look at Clough's Oxford journals. Sir Arthur Norrington has been unfailingly helpful and constructive. His generous response in the first place and his careful rereading of the typescript were both encouraging and salutary. The book has benefited immensely from having passed through his experienced hands. To my colleague, Professor Hugh Parry of York University, Toronto, I owe thanks for his help with Greek and Latin. I need hardly add that the responsibility for errors and misjudgements is wholly mine.

My debt to three people in particular can only faintly be acknowledged here. Michael Millgate has been an affectionate and faithful friend, always understanding and helpful towards a junior colleague. He was the first to read drafts of roughly half the chapters here, and he read with a characteristic thoroughness and discrimination. I regret not having had the opportunity to show him the complete draft, since his comments and suggestions resulted invariably in improvements. Although Bryan Wilson is not directly connected with this book, it is unlikely that without him it would have been written. He has never been in any formal sense a teacher, but I have learnt more from him than from any other single person. Finally, my debt to my wife is vast—but she would be the last person to recognize or admit it; hence the Dedication.

I must also thank Leeds University for its award of a Scholarship which enabled me to begin thinking about Clough, the Foyle Trust for helping out when things were difficult, and the Canada Council for enabling me to spend six weeks in British libraries. York University, Toronto, has always been generous with assistance. A year on sabbatical leave has allowed me to devote part of the time to getting this book finally ready for the press. Lastly, I would like to thank the Warden and Fellows of All Souls College for their hospitality to a Visiting Fellow during this year and their care in providing everything possible to help him get his work done.

February 1971

Contents

x　　　　　　　　　　　CONTENTS

Abbreviations

AND NOTE ON REFERENCES

Catalogue Richard M. Gollin, Walter E. Houghton, and Michael Timko, *Arthur Hugh Clough: a Descriptive Catalogue* (New York Public Library, New York, n.d.)

Chorley Katharine Chorley, *Arthur Hugh Clough: the Uncommitted Mind* (Oxford, 1962)

Corr. *The Correspondence of Arthur Hugh Clough*, ed. F. L. Mulhauser (2 vols., Oxford, 1957)

Houghton Walter E. Houghton, *The Poetry of Clough: an Essay in Revaluation* (New Haven, Conn., and London, 1963)

Lowry *The Letters of Matthew Arnold to Arthur Hugh Clough*, ed. H. F. Lowry (London, 1932)

Poems *The Poems of Arthur Hugh Clough*, ed. H. F. Lowry, F. L. Mulhauser, and A. L. P. Norrington (Oxford, 1951)

PPR *The Poems and Prose Remains of Arthur Hugh Clough*, ed. by his Wife (2 vols., London, 1869)

Trawick *Selected Prose Works of Arthur Hugh Clough*, ed. Buckner B. Trawick (Alabama, 1964)

References to manuscript letters give the library call number, followed in parentheses, wherever possible, by the letter number from Mulhauser's 'Catalogue of All Known Letters' (*Corr.* ii. 622–49). References to twentieth-century scholarly and critical journals adopt the abbreviations used by the Modern Language Association of America.

Introduction

CLOUGH is an important poet, a poet whose stature and significance have, after a long period of neglect, only relatively recently begun to be acknowledged—and it is as a poet that he is important. In stressing the primacy of his poetry I am not, of course, denying his significance as a figure who belongs to the intellectual and spiritual history of his times. Clough's is a significant Victorian mind, but the significance, subtlety, and distinction of that reacting mind, its full historical implications, emerge clearly only in his finest poetry. In that poetry alone do we get a full sense of the play of outstanding capacities, discern an independent, alert, completely engaged intellect and art, discovering and responding to a complex and problematic experience. And yet, in order to arrive at an adequate sense of his achievement, and of the centrality of his poetry in that achievement, it is necessary to follow attentively the whole history of a mind and personality. A context has to be established as well as a claim. One has to try and make sense of the notorious 'phenomenon' of Clough.

The dominant description of that phenomenon used to be the one which Mrs. Clough gave to the world in her memoir of 1869, and which her husband's friends took up and developed, since it confirmed their own valuations of him. She was by no means his best or most perceptive friend as far as his intellectual and literary life was concerned. Her apologetic portrait was that of a gifted, high-minded, personally lovable, but also curiously weak, failure. The clash between Rugbeian values and the Oxford Movement figured largely in this picture of wasted promise, and Clough became for posterity a dolefully instructive case-history in the spiritual turmoil of the nineteenth century. Clough still remains a fascinating case-history in the intellectual and spiritual life of the period—but not quite the same case-history as presented in older descriptions. As a result of the scholarly and critical attention he has attracted since the publication in 1951 of a careful edition of the poems and in 1957 of the correspondence, the need for revising our portrait and our valuation has become evident. Enough material in the way of manuscripts, editions, and reinterpretations is available now to support an attempt at a fresh and comprehensive description.

The poetry on which I base my claims for Clough issues, however, from an extraordinarily limited period of his life, a period which extends roughly from 1847 to 1852—to whenever, that is, he stopped working on *Dipsychus*. Further distinctions can be made within this time-span, but at this point it is sufficient simply to note this oddly constellated creative output. Prior to this we have only a handful of outstanding lyrics; subsequently, the long poetic silence which followed his engagement to Blanche Smith. That silence is broken only—and often with acutely embarrassing results—by the short lyrics written in America. It terminates with the *Mari Magno* stories and his death in 1861. The traditional explanation for this strange distribution of Clough's creative energies, first advanced by his wife, does not take us very far. She maintained that her husband needed rest and time before he could create. As she pointed out, the bulk of his poetry was written during vacations. The explanation depends for its satisfactoriness on her estimation of the *Mari Magno* stories. For her they were clear evidence of a newly found maturity and profundity. It is unlikely that many readers today will concur in her judgement. For them, as for me, her explanation will leave untouched the crucial question of quality.

The questions raised by this unevenness in Clough's poetry extend into his whole life. Some of the answers I have suggested were first hinted at in a provocative essay which Humbert Wolfe contributed to a volume, edited by John Drinkwater and entitled *The Eighteen-Sixties*, which appeared in 1932. The broad features of the area in which I have looked for my understanding can be indicated briefly here. The most casual glance through the list of correspondents in the second volume of Frederick Mulhauser's edition of the letters reveals how closely Clough was in touch with the middle-class establishment which was beginning to emerge in the middle of the century, and which Noel Annan described in his book on Leslie Stephen. Clough's upbringing and education, with their ultimate roots in Evangelical values, his friendships, the connections he established through his marriage, place him in a particular stream of Victorian culture and achievement. It is a stream which flows confidently

in channels of public service, its course marked by bishoprics
and deaneries, by headmasterships in public schools, by eminence
in the universities, by recognized place in the civil service. Yet
Clough, who seems so obviously to belong in it, is half in and
half out of this stream. The incipient amphibian image is appropriate. It suggests the central characteristic of his wider relationship to his age: its ambiguousness. This ambiguousness, which
involves every aspect of his life, displays itself at the deepest and
most personal level in terms of the troublesome question of
authority. The psychological reading, stressing the importance of
Clough's relationship with his mother and of the shock of his
early separation from her, advanced in Katharine Chorley's
biography, is obviously relevant in this connection. I have attempted to interpret Clough's career in the light of his shifting
relationships with, and attitudes towards, more varied kinds and
locations of authority.

My attempt, then, is twofold. Through a close scrutiny of the
poetry I have tried to discriminate its quality and furnish grounds
for my claims on its behalf. I have also attempted to support the
portions of this study devoted to the poetry with an extended
consideration of a developing mind and personality. In order
to solve some of the difficulties inherent in such a dual attempt I
have resorted to a compromise that I hope is not altogether unsatisfactory although it has certain consequences, the criticism
being slanted in a biographical and intentional direction, the
history of a personality tending to pre-empt the history of a mind.
As far as possible I have kept the discussion of the life and the
poetry distinct from one another. Instead, however, of separating
the study into two main sections, one dealing with the life and the
other with the poetry, I have adopted the somewhat clumsy
procedure of dividing the life roughly into the chronological
blocks which have become more or less traditional with biographers of Clough. In each of these sections a study of his general
development is followed by an examination of the poetry he
wrote during the period. One advantage of this arrangement, I
hope, is that it brings the two strands of inquiry close enough
to one another to enable us to follow and relate parallel processes
of development. Perhaps it may enable the reader also to maintain a necessary separateness between the two.

This effort at separation, however, breaks down obviously at

some points. In dealing with the shorter poems of 1849 I have
resorted to more straightforward methods, reading the poetry
for its 'content' and for the biographical illumination it can
provide. I have also thought it necessary to break the chronological
sequence in the chapter on Clough's poetics—although I have
tried to suggest there the importance of chronology even in this
limited area. To disperse the consideration of Clough's mature
attitudes towards poetry over the appropriate chronological
periods would be confusing rather than instructive.

The question of chronology introduces special problems into
a study of Clough. With the exception of *The Bothie of Tober-na-
Vuolich* and the *Mari Magno* stories, it is virtually impossible to
ascribe a definite date to any of his long poems. We know when
they were begun, but cannot be absolutely sure how long he was
actively working at them. Yet the significance of these poems—
the dating of which can only be surmised—is enormous. The
shorter poems, too, often present awkward problems. I have
invariably adopted the earliest date, because the chronological
overlappings are not likely to have been extended enough to
destroy the significance of sequence, and also because my essential
aim has been to isolate the dominants in a single evolving
experience. The ideas of development and succession must be
balanced by notions of simultaneity; the chronological approach
is convenient because it separates out the most important emphases
and interactions in a phenomenon which is continuous and, in
several senses, coexistent. Clough's ambiguousness itself is a source
of confidence in facing the problem of chronology in this manner.

Biographically, I have concerned myself not with a full-scale
'Life' but with an attempt to discover those emphases in Clough's
personality and experience which can lead to a fresh—and perhaps more accurate—understanding. The factual and narrative
portions of this study, therefore, are not evidences of ingratitude
to previous biographers; they are simply attempts to provide an
adequate and self-complete framework for the biography of
a personality and a mind. In dealing with the larger intellectual
and cultural life of the period I have simply tried to point out some
of the obvious connections with the larger movements of thought
in the period which help to place Clough intellectually. Further,
I have seen these movements as filtered through my subject:
Early-Victorian England is a landscape viewed through the

coloured and individually rippled glass of Clough's own interests and conflicts and endeavours. The glass is of singular transparency but it is not a colourless one.

Finally, we come to the vexed question of Clough's failure, and, as with most of the large questions he raises, the answers can never be unequivocal. In so far as the charge amounts to no more than that he was a failed Eminent Victorian the answer is easy enough: we have learnt to recognize other kinds of success. The other main charge, that he was a failure as a poet, is not completely true. A poet who can awaken fresh speculations about the nature of poetry and who can, in his own way, call in question some of the achievement of Tennyson and Matthew Arnold cannot be written off as a failure. But it is equally important to recognize that it is chiefly in one poem, *Amours de Voyage*, that Clough confidently fulfils his potential as a poet. His success is not wholly confined to this single work, but nowhere else does he achieve this same kind of distinction. His failure, then, is to be measured by his success. This is a rather different thing from the versions of failure which have customarily been alleged against Clough. To locate his success principally in *Amours de Voyage* and, to a lesser extent, in some of the poems which surround it chrono-logically, to recognize the heterodoxy, the irony, the satire, the bitterness, the uncompromising self-consciousness which give many of these poems their distinction, and to remember then his subsequent lapse as a poet is to introduce the possibility of another kind of failure—the failure of self-betrayal. Clough cannot be exempted completely, but a consideration of the other main aspect of his activity, his life as a 'thinker', is necessary before the charge can be fairly estimated.

Clough himself regarded poetry as only part of his vocation, which, in so far as it was literary at all, he tended to envisage in very much more extensive terms. He saw himself essentially as a potential leader of ideas and his ambitiousness in this respect was extraordinary: in a sense what he undertook to create was nothing less than a new gospel for his fellow men, a gospel which re-integrated man's experience. He succeeded in muddling and terrifying himself by his own honesty, and he ended up in an impoverished and stoically circumscribed personal adjustment—but it is difficult to see how anyone could have accomplished what he set out to do. He is unique because he had courage and intellectual penetration enough to arrive at the roots of the Victorian dilemma and to recognize his own involvement in that dilemma. He entered as an adult into a world unsheltered by the confidences of final truth or absolute certainty. He held out as long as he could before his own unevasive and disinherited vision, but he finally panicked: he had to choose and he chose, in Blanche Smith, the reassurance of the conventional. It is more than likely that in his own eyes he was a failure, since he never arrived at his own impossible goal. But in his confusion and his clarity, in the courage with which he undertook his re-examination of the basic premises on which his life was built, he takes us closer—and more directly—to the heart of Victorian darkness than many of his more renowned contemporaries. He also takes us to the edges of a new kind of light. His journey is a sad one, both because of its achievement and because of its surrender; but it is neither an unimportant nor a fruitless one. It is also a very human journey and, in its unyielding, solitary way, heroic. Like some of the finest things in Clough, that heroism, too, makes no claims for itself—and it renders the question of failure irrelevant.

It is that minor key, finally, that seems to me Clough's exact note. I see in him an important poet who needs to be drawn into the main-stream of discussion about poetry—and yet, thinking imagistically rather than analytically, I find something peculiarly apt about the traditional place he has been assigned in literary history, especially when we consider him in the general context of Victorian poetry. He is a footnote that is crucial, substantive, and intransigent, the kind of footnote which challenges the main text, which is absorbing in its own right, which illuminates not a local reference but a major argument. He is a footnote we should not overlook.

*   *   *

Clough is not the neglected figure he used to be twenty years ago. The attention he has attracted in recent years—and continues to attract—makes one self-conscious about venturing on yet another general, proselytizing, and, in many ways, introductory study: one feels at moments that one is preaching to an audience that is not only already converted but also extremely knowledgeable. I suspect, however, that the revival of interest is not quite as widespread as it might be, that Clough is still insufficiently recognized, that much of the discussion is a discussion among specialists; and, while I hope that I have been able to contribute something to that discussion, it is for the general—or perhaps, more accurately, the marginally interested reader—that much of this book is intended. A great deal of it therefore is of an introductory nature—sometimes, as in Chapter III, blatantly so. Necessarily, too, there is much rewriting of what is already fairly well known.

I have tried to be scrupulous in acknowledging my indebtedness to the work of others. I should like here to record my debt to some specific works. Walter Houghton's *The Poetry of Clough: an Essay in Revaluation* was for me an exciting and revelatory study. Although I disagree with many of Professor Houghton's interpretations and valuations his influence should be obvious to any reader. Richard M. Gollin's 'Arthur Hugh Clough's Formative Years: 1819–1841' is a fine study, unfortunately still unpublished. My debt to him is less extensive but no less real. Perhaps it is unnecessary to point out that I found Katharine Chorley's *Arthur Hugh Clough: the Uncommitted Mind* enormously helpful as a framework—even if, frequently, one to construct my disagreements on.

CHAPTER I

Liverpool, Charleston, and Rugby
1819–1837

I. CHILDHOOD AND SCHOOL-DAYS

THE Cloughs were an old family. They traced themselves as far
back as the sixteenth century and they had long been connected
with Denbighshire land. Their politics were Tory, their class
affiliations clearly gentry, but with the passing years younger sons
were finding it increasingly difficult to linger on in traditional
shelters. James Butler Clough at the beginning of the nineteenth
century elected to go into commerce. He was the third of ten
children, the first in the family to leave the neighbourhood of the
ancestral home in Wales. He moved to Liverpool and set up as
a cotton merchant. In 1806 he sailed for America as a cotton ex-
porter, but returned to Liverpool in 1810 when his house, along
with several others, failed as a result of the lifting of the embargo
on cotton. He went into the corn trade for a while, but, with the
close of the Napoleonic War and the promise of brisker trade,
returned to cotton in 1816. The same year he married Ann Perfect,
the daughter of a Pontefract banker. The couple lived in Liverpool, at 5 Rodney Street, and there, on New Year's Day 1819,
their second child, Arthur Hugh, was born.[1] Charles Butler had
been born two years earlier, Anne Jemima was born in 1820,
and their last child, George Augustus, in 1822.

James Butler Clough does not appear to have been very well
equipped, either by temperament or upbringing, for the competitive life of nineteenth-century commerce. He was too easy-
going, too sanguine; his sense of honour was too fine. He must
have flourished for a while, since his family seems to have lived
spaciously enough, but, as his wife recalled later, in August 1825
'the grand stop' to their 'apparent greatness' occurred (*Corr.* ii. 386).

[1] Minutes of Ordinary Meeting, *Proceedings of the Literary and Philosophical
Society of Liverpool*, liii (1899), xxiv–xxv. Other details about Clough's childhood
are taken from the Memoir in *PPR* i, and B. A. Clough, *A Memoir of Anne
Jemima Clough* (London, 1903).

Things got worse, and by 1841 he had decisively proved himself a failure. The fact of this steady decline in his family's standing is an important component in Arthur Hugh Clough's early experience.

The social heritage James Butler Clough handed on to his children was divided and uneasy. They were, of course, unambiguously middle-class, but within this widely accommodating social perimeter their position was one which encouraged a certain self-consciousness. From one angle they were clearly gentry and could claim by social right the attitudes and values of that class; from another, their origins were as clearly mercantile. Socially their place was ambiguous, financially they had to learn relatively early in their lives the embarrassing lessons of straitened means.

In December 1822 the Cloughs removed from Liverpool to Charleston in South Carolina. Although Arthur was to live in Charleston for the next six years, and his mother and father and Anne for the next fourteen, the children were never allowed to forget that they were merely sojourners in an alien land. 'Home' was in England: that was where they were to return eventually, that was where English children naturally went to school. The Cloughs did not make many friends; those they did make tended to be English. Few contacts with Charleston reality were permitted to intrude into the segregated and self-sufficient rhythms of family life, and it was a painful dismemberment when James Butler Clough left on a visit to England and took Charles with him to start his schooling in Chester.

Ann Clough seems in every way to have been a contrast to her genial, optimistic, openly affectionate husband. She was a much more inward person, more intellectually inclined, critical of others but herself rather indolent. Timid in general society and, no doubt largely because of her timidness, contemptuous of it, she could appear to her children slightly severe and somewhat remote. Actually, she was a very shy, quiet, but strongly affectionate and very dependent woman. When her husband left she retired even further from society and drew her children even more tightly together into a staunch flag-waving Englishness. He was away for almost a year, and she turned for understanding and companionship to her beloved second son. Arthur had always been the petted and spoilt one, and now, at the age of seven, was the acknowledged 'genius' of the family. He became, in his father's absence, his mother's constant companion, and, according to his sister, she poured out to him the 'fulness of her heart'. Together they read the novels of Scott and parts of Pope's *Iliad* and *Odyssey*, they read history and biography and poetry. Ann Clough's literary tastes were firmly controlled by her moral values. As her daughter later put it,

In her tastes and habits she was rigidly simple; this harmonised with the stern integrity which was the foundation of her character. She was very fond of reading, especially works on religious subjects, poetry and history; and she greatly enjoyed beautiful scenery, and visiting places which had any historical associations. She loved what was grand, noble, and enterprising, and was truly religious. She early taught us about God and duty, and having such a loving earthly father, it was not difficult to look up to a Heavenly one. She loved to dwell on all that was stern and noble. Leonidas at Thermopylae, and Epaminondas accepting the lowliest offices and doing them as a duty to his country; the sufferings of the martyrs, and the struggles of the Protestants, were among her favourite subjects. There was an enthusiasm about her that took hold of us, and made us see vividly the things that she taught us (*PPR* i. 9).

The moral syllabus of enthusiasm is a familiar Romantic one. It derives from an ethic predicated on purity, on the basic nobility of human nature, and it appeals more to sensibility than to conscience. The ethic interprets the moral life in terms of noble emotions vitally and worthily mobilized in the service of high ideals. God presides as a benevolent father over the ethic which Ann Clough communicated to her children, an ethic strongly other-directed in service and self-regarding only in so far as it cultivated contact with the inspiring and elevating aspects of external nature and human history. The highest good in its ideal of selfhood was the noble loss of self in abnegation, suffering, and service.

For Arthur the lessons were fleshed out with the demanding, isolating, cherishing love of a shy and lonely woman, and in those lessons, as in the whole relationship, was laid down an irremovable basis. His future life was to be a series of solitary and never fully comprehended battles with and submissions to the heritage of this early, intimately enclosed, special relationship. Yet one can detect strains and anomalies even in this hermetically sealed childhood.

In his relationship with his mother he was required to fill a role which was out of all proportion to his years. He was invited to hold before him an ideal of self-immolation and self-forgetfulness, and yet, at the same time, it was made abundantly clear to him that he held a special place in the life of the family: he was encouraged simultaneously to lose himself and prize himself. Understandably, the 'beautiful boy, with soft silky, almost black hair, and shining dark eyes, and a small delicate mouth' (*PPR* i. 4), developed at an early age a strong streak of independence, even of stubbornness. His sister recalled that 'he was said to be very determined and obstinate', that he 'would always do things from his own choice, and not merely copy what others were doing' (ibid.). When the others went paddling on the curlew-haunted sands of Sullivan's Island, the fastidious Arthur steadfastly refused to take off his shoes. In the hot afternoons he would withdraw to the privacy of his bedroom to pore over the *Universal Traveller* and *Captain Cook's Travels*.[1] Perhaps significantly, travel was to become an important metaphor in his mature poetry, the condition of travel to become a symbol expressive of man's spiritual state. His own life was shortly to become distressingly migratory.

In 1828 Arthur was judged ripe for school and in June the whole family sailed for England. In November, after installing him in the private school in Chester where Charles had been enrolled earlier, his parents returned to Charleston with Anne and George—but he himself had seen the last of that city. England, the promised home across the Atlantic, proved unexpectedly difficult to adjust to. The clustering relatives in Wales and in Yorkshire were bewildering, the boisterous cousins who dragged him into their noisy games puzzled and disconcerted him. Almost predictably, Uncle Charles, a widower with a quiet vicarage at Mold, became a favourite; so did Uncle Alfred, who was a Fellow at Jesus College remembered by Tom Mozley for his distinction in being the 'tallest, longest-legged man in Oxford'.[2]

[1] In 'A Long Talk', an account of the education in poetry of a fictitious 'Willoughby Moreton', which Clough published in *The Rugby Magazine*, he made a significant comment about his own early reading: 'Our old nursery books, the tales of Jack the Giant Killer, and so on, are too much despised in our times. . . . I cannot claim any great acquaintance with them myself, for I remember being told that they were foolish things, and as such I never saw them much . . .' (*Trawick*, p. 44).

[2] T. Mozley, *Reminiscences, Chiefly of Oriel College and the Oxford Movement* 2 vols. (London, 1882), i. 26.

With the departure of the rest of the family for Charleston, Arthur, now almost nine years old, was thrown back even more on his own resources. His existence was not exactly an unhappy one. There was activity and interest and kindness enough. There were always new things to do and to see. He wrote elaborate and dutiful letters home, touching in their mixed precociousness and *naïveté*, their intent, laboriously correct, solemnity. At least on the surface he was getting used to being shunted from relative to relative, and when he learnt that he and his brother were to go to Rugby in 1829 he accepted the news as passively as the intimation that they were to spend their Easter vacation with Uncle Charles at his vicarage. Katharine Chorley has remarked that he was learning to keep his balance by keeping his centre within himself.[1]

Emotional and spiritual centres are, however, as difficult to maintain as they are to find. Too often they prove illusory. New forces, new recognitions, new loyalties—and old insecurities—alter the pattern and commit one to a fresh start. This, essentially, was the major problem which Clough had to face. He came firmly to believe in the possibility of a centre, and he tried with all the fortitude he could muster to wait till he found a valid one. But he needed that centre desperately, and the need, which gave emotional solidity to the belief, was generated in the wandering and insecure circumstances of his childhood. The image of man and the moral life contained in the lessons he learnt from his mother offered one possible source of inner balance; Rugby, under its new headmaster, was to deepen and extend those lessons.

In 1829 Dr. Thomas Arnold had been headmaster for one year and, although some steps had been taken, the celebrated refashioning of Rugby was still an unrealized ideal. Arnold has been described by one of his successors, Dr. Percival, who later became Bishop of Hereford, as a special version of the Victorian prophet—the prophet as schoolmaster.[2] The description is apt: it puts us in touch immediately with the true scope of the dictating urgencies behind Arnold's endeavours as head of a great public school. For he brought to Rugby not only a prophet's sternness and zeal, but a vision, a historical understanding of his task, which was nothing short of prophetic. A massive energy, an inexhaustible

---

[1] Chorley, p. 12.
[2] Quoted, J. Fitch, *Thomas and Matthew Arnold* (London, 1897), pp. 108-9.

industry, a galvanic personality, and a vigorous intellect, were all informed and fused in him by the central power of complete moral certitude. A pugnacious and ready fighter who delighted in fluttering established dovecotes, he encountered at Rugby considerable opposition—from masters, from trustees, from the middle-class public, from the press—but he wielded his authority both confidently and effectively. By the time of his death in 1842 at the age of forty-seven he had become a towering legend in the school, his identity and that of the institution had become indistinguishable from one another. As Arthur Penrhyn Stanley, one of his most illustrious pupils, put it, 'Throughout, whether in the school itself, or in its after effects, the one image that we have before us is not Rugby, but ARNOLD.'[1]

We cannot share today the absolute reverence of a Stanley. Arnold, for us, is too laboriously the Headmaster, too self-consciously the Interpreter of Destiny, too unremittingly the Flogger of Evil. Many of his doctrines are repellent and even vicious. We have learnt to question much in the legacy he left to British education. The inflation and insensitivity of his rhetoric often make him ludicrous. Giants, however, are seldom gifted with a sense of proportion—and in his way Arnold was a giant, noisily impatient of the smaller, finer, more human motions and gestures. The scale is preposterous, but despite the heavy breathing it is undeniably impressive. Arnold is a crucial formative figure in Victorian culture. The acuteness of some of his insights and the range of his relevance to the developing liberalism of nineteenth-century England command respect. In fact, the extraordinary feeling for the relevant which he consistently displays supplies the single most useful clue to the nature of his importance—just as in another way it indicates the nature of his limitations. Without being a subtle or even strikingly original thinker, he had an unusual capacity to transform the insights he gained from his teachers (among whom Hooker, Bishop Butler, Burke, Coleridge, and historians like Vico and Niebuhr are prominent) into an intensely sensed, living tradition, a tradition which enabled him both to locate and identify the maladies of the age and to propose, broadly, a remedial programme of action. The energy of the transformation often generated only a confusing

[1] A. P. Stanley, *The Life and Correspondence of Thomas Arnold, D.D.*, 2 vols. (London, 1844), i. 102.

heat, but Arnold was too urgently practical to pause for long over such problems. It was left to more sensitive, more intellectually and emotionally scrupulous beings, like Arthur Clough, to work their own way through the dilemmas and inadequacies of Arnoldism. But Arnold was an exciting teacher, and even to such beings he gave a stamp, a habit of concern, a way of looking at themselves and the world, the impress of which never faded. It is worth pausing at this point to reconsider, however baldly, some of the main outlines of Arnoldism.

'The object . . . of every public writer at this moment should be to calm and to enlighten the poor; to interest and to arouse the rich', Arnold declared in a letter, one of a series on the condition of England addressed to the editor of the *Sheffield Courant* in 1831 and 1832.[1] His avowed role in these letters was that of an educator. Light and guidance were desperately needed. Reform—in men's values and beliefs, in their economic, political, and social relationships, in the institutions and procedures of society—was imminent and necessary, but if society was to survive it was absolutely imperative that reform should be truly enlightened, truly progressive, organically continuous. England could not afford to misread the clock of history: the threat from the 'wretches' and 'madmen', as he called them in another letter to the same paper, who were eager to throw into the crucible 'every law and every principle' which civilization had evolved, was too grave.[2] Arnold's attempt at Rugby to transform the public schools into something other than the 'seats and nurseries of vice' which John Bowdler said they were (and Arnold fully agreed that they were) has to be seen in the context of the larger educational preoccupations which these letters to the *Sheffield Courant* suggest. Rugby was simply the point at which responsible change began; it was to become the nursery from which a distinctive strain of schoolboys could be transplanted into the world, schoolboys who had learnt the lessons of stewardship, who realized fully the enormous significance of the role which they, as members of the middle class, were to play as custodians of the future.

Arnold's motivating energies derived ultimately from the religious revival which marked the later years of the eighteenth

---

[1] *The Miscellaneous Works of Thomas Arnold* (London, 1845), p. 175.
[2] Ibid., p. 203.

century. Basically Evangelical, he was clearly aware, nevertheless, of the shortcomings of the general Evangelical orientation, of the narrowness of its horizons, and its lack of intellectual force. As a Fellow of Oriel College he had been absorbed into the life of the most intellectually alert and progressive common-room in the Oxford of the time. He rapidly shed the Toryism of his undergraduate days and became closely associated with the 'Noetics'—the informal group of liberal, non-dogmatic, reforming theologians and Fellows who were largely responsible for the distinction of Oriel particularly, and the awakening of the University as a whole from its eighteenth-century slumbers. Cast in the mould of eighteenth-century rationalism, Aristotelian in temper, the Noetics—who included men like Copleston, Davison, Whately, Milman, and Hawkins—aimed at saving the cause of religion by stripping Christianity of doctrinal encumbrances, submitting it to the scrutiny of logic, and establishing its broad, essential principles. Instead of repudiating change or resisting unsettling inquiry, these men welcomed it: if Christianity was to survive in an altering society it needed to be redefined and re-organized. But Arnold, although he valued open discussion and respected the capacities of reason, displayed an unwavering aware-ness of the limitations of intellect. As a young man he had had intellectual doubts, specifically about the Doctrine of the Trinity, but these he put down, under Keble's advice, by 'main force'; he had cured himself 'not by physic, *i.e.*, reading and controversy, but by diet and regimen, *i.e.*, holy living'.[1] This early and, by all appearances, completely successful application of a moral remedy to an intellectual difficulty seems to have confirmed for him a scale of value the certainty of which sustained him through-out life. 'All societies of men, whether we call them states or churches, should make their bond to consist in a common object or a common practice, rather than in a common belief: in other words, their end should be good rather than truth.'[2] 'O that we would know and remember to search the Scriptures not for truths but for lessons', he exclaimed in one of his sermons,[3] and, in sermons and letters alike, his warnings against an 'ex-clusive and corrupted love of truth' were recurrent. His intense

---

[1] Stanley, op. cit. i. 22.
[2] T. Arnold, *Introductory Lectures on Modern History* (London, 1874), p. 39.
[3] T. Arnold, *Sermons*, 6 vols. (London, 1878), iii. 395.

sense of actuality and of the necessity for action absorbed, without evidence of unease, this cleavage between two values normally regarded as inseparable. As Basil Willey has pointed out,[1] for him the concept of God was important morally, not meta-physically, and in his cultivation of moral consistency he was cheerfully willing to yield up the consistency of logic and doctrine. His grasp on moral affirmatives was so firm that intellectual negatives held no terrors and the onslaughts of German scholar-ship found him invulnerable, since he countered them with a clear distinction between 'questions of religion' and 'questions of criticism'—and of the relative unimportance of the latter he had no doubts. This dichotomy between moral and intellectual value, encouraged by Keble's advice, left, as James Martineau observed, a 'speck . . . on his intellectual clearness',[2] and herein, for less assured minds, lay the fundamental weakness of the Arnoldian position.

Arnold's distrust of the unchecked intellect and his emphatically activist sense of the difference between truth and good were not, of course, merely quirks derived from his own personal experience of difficulties about the Trinity. Shaping his response to those difficulties was the habit of a mind trained in the school of Butler and Coleridge. In his Rolls Chapel Sermons, particularly, Butler had distinguished between the fallible reason and the infallible moral sense, the conscience, which God had implanted in man. The conscience was not, as Lockean and post-Lockean empiricism would have it, simply the product of habit and association; it was an absolute epistemological organ, which, either directly or through the workings of remorse, intimated with unmistakable and unwavering authority the purposes of a providential God and the nature of moral reality. The voice of conscience was the voice of truth and law. Coleridge admired Butler profoundly, and the influence of Butler's moral epistemology can be traced in the distinctions he drew, in modified Kantian terminology, between the Understanding, which operates discursively on data delivered by the senses, and the Reason, which is a 'direct aspect of truth', 'an inward beholding, having a similar relation to the intelligible or spiritual, as Sense does to the material or

[1] B. Willey, Nineteenth-Century Studies (London, 1949), p. 58.
[2] J. Martineau, 'Dr. Arnold', Essays, Reviews and Addresses, 4 vols. (London, 1890–1), i. 61.

phenomenal'.[1] Reason, for Coleridge, was divided into the Speculative and the Practical, the Speculative concerned with formal abstract truth, the Practical with what he called 'actual (or moral) truth'. Coleridge's 'Practical Reason', the means by which the Kantian categorical imperative is perceived, is, like Butler's 'conscience', the 'sole fountain of certainty'.[2] Arnold's habit of discriminating between the 'lower' and 'higher' forms of intellectual activity had its basis, then, in a general Butlerian and Coleridgean temper. He, too, insisted on the primacy of conscience, of 'higher reason' or 'moral reason', in matters of faith and morality. 'The moral reason acting under God' was a 'telescope of faith' revealing objects which were too distant for the 'naked eye' of intellect to discover.'[3] Conscience was 'the Holy Ghost, or Holy Spirit of God', by which 'is meant God speaking to men in such a language that no man can mistake who it is that is speaking'.[4] Like Butler, too, he recognized the existence of vitiated and therefore unreliable consciences, the result of corrupt living. A distinctive Arnoldian development, however, was the manner in which he confronted what can be called the historical problem: men who were considered good in their own time have often displayed qualities which were accounted vicious in later periods. How, then, could conscience be accounted authoritative? Arnold found his solution in an evolutionary and relativistic theory of history. In any single age the difference between right and wrong was absolute. In a wider historical perspective, however, when one compared one age with another, right and wrong were relative. It was impossible, for instance, to attach to the injunctions of the Decalogue in the nineteenth century the same interpretation and weight as they originally had for the Jews: the Ten Commandments were still relevant, but their relevance had to be newly stated. Morality, therefore, was historically contingent. Conscience enabled a man to discern absolutely only in his own age, to act morally at a given moment in history. In historicizing the concept of conscience Arnold readmitted in a special way the

[1] S. T. Coleridge, *Aids to Reflection*, 2 vols. (London, 1848), i. 175. I am indebted extensively for the substance of this paragraph to R. M. Gollin's unpublished Ph.D. dissertation, 'Arthur Hugh Clough's Formative Years: 1819–1841' (University of Minnesota, 1959).
[2] S. T. Coleridge, *Table-Talk and Omniana* (London, 1907), p. 407.
[3] Stanley, op. cit. ii. 52. Cf. Coleridge, *Aids to Reflection*, i. 277.
[4] Arnold, *Miscellaneous Works*, p. 120.

validity of intellect and of knowledge of the external world. An accurate discrimination of the historical moment was essential to the working of Arnoldian conscience. In the light of history alone could the dictates of conscience be discerned. Given such a function, that light for him necessarily shone with a moral colouring.

The insights of the historian and the faith of the Christian pietist co-operate in unifying Arnold's manifold and widely deployed energies. The influence of his vision of history is pervasive. It penetrates all his values and beliefs, it colours his thinking as headmaster, as moralist, as social and political analyst, as religious controversialist. History for him was virtually queen of all sciences. If one could discover the right method of historical analysis one would possess, in effect, nothing less than a key to the true movement of the world. Defending his favourite study in a lecture he delivered in Oxford as Regius Professor of Modern History (an honour conferred on him the year before he died), he said,

If historical testimony be really worth nothing, it touches us in one of the very divinest parts of our nature, the power of connecting ourselves with the past. For this we do and can do only through knowledge which we call historical. . . . Without such knowledge . . . our life would be at once restricted to the space of our own memory; nay, I might almost say to the span of our own actual consciousness.[1]

The historian, however, if he was not to become a mere antiquarian, a babbling and irrelevant memory, had to combine with his knowledge of the past a wide acquaintance with the present. Only out of such a union could grow both the ability to assess what part each period had played for good or for evil in the drama of the world's history, and the faculty of discerning the direction of historical flow and determining the extent to which nations were fulfilling their appointed end—the end of 'setting forth God's glory by doing His appointed work'.[2] History, for Arnold, was not random. The laws which dictated the rise and fall of states were discoverable and were as little

---

[1] Arnold, *Lectures on Modern History*, pp. 282–3. Clough's *Amours de Voyage*, with its radical suspiciousness about the historical act, its despair at the lack of any perceived connection between memory and consciousness, becomes a crucial document when it is seen from this Arnoldian angle.

[2] Ibid., p. 13.

open to dispute as the laws of morality. Moral judgements, in fact, were inseparably involved in the study of history: the historian's impartiality was not to be confused with moral indifferentism.

The distinction between modern history and ancient, he argued, was not significantly a matter of chronology. The question of modernity was to be decided by an investigation of the institutions and experience of a society, of the political and economic forces at work within it. Greek and Roman history could, in some phases, be nearer the realities of nineteenth-century England than the chronologically and nationally closer English Middle Ages. This, in fact, was the most important argument in favour of studying the history of Greece or Rome or Palestine, for here one discovered the simplified but essential and recurrent patterns of historical process. Indebted to Vico and influenced by Niebuhr, Arnold's account of historical change carried with it a peculiar, urgent tonality. In the earliest stages of society an aristocracy of blood or conquest prevails. As society develops and its economic life becomes more diverse and complicated, wealth rather than blood becomes the decisive factor, political and social power redistribute themselves along the new economic lines. In the third and final stage numbers begin to assert themselves. The conflict between aristocracy and the principle of wealth is replaced by that between wealth and the democratic force of numbers. This conflict, in direct contrast with the first, occurs when the gap between the opposing forces is most extreme. The many in their poverty struggle against the few with their wealth in a situation of crisis and alarm. Clearly England in the nineteenth century was in this situation.

The note of desperate urgency in Arnold's historical analysis arises when another aspect of his sense of modernity combines with this account of the development of states. Modern history differed from ancient in the fact that modern periods combined into themselves the total previous experience of the human race. States had risen and fallen, progress and civilization had passed from Greece and Palestine to Rome, and now, in the nine-teenth century, were in the hands of the Germanic races. The fund of racial, national, institutional, linguistic experience and development was in the present entrusted to people like the English, 'whose race and language are now overrunning the earth from one end of it to another'.[1] If the lapse into primitive barbarism which marked the end of the Viconian cycle was to be avoided, the responsibility of the modern age was awesome. In the imagination at least, the nineteenth century, marked by Germanic dominance, could see itself as 'not only *a* step in advance of ancient history, but *the* last step; it appears to bear the marks of the fulness of time, as if there would be no future history beyond it'.[2] He hesitated to press this view, but could declare, nevertheless,

But without any presumptuous confidence, if there be any signs, however uncertain, that we are living in the latest period of the world's history, that no other races remain behind to perform what we have neglected or to restore what we have ruined, then indeed the . . . importance of not wasting the time still left to us may well be called incalculable. When an army's last reserve has been brought into action, every single soldier knows that he must do his duty to the utmost; that if he cannot win the battle now, he must lose it. So if our existing nations are the last reserve of the world, its fate may be said to be in their hands —God's work on earth will be left undone if they do not do it.[3]

Arnold had a special affection for the military metaphor, with its emphasis on ranked discipline, on corporate and strenuous endeavour against a clearly discerned enemy.

It was with this anxiety of living in the eleventh hour that Arnold surveyed his own age. Haunted by the spectres of revolution and collapse, he refused, however, to retreat behind the barriers of the *status quo*. 'We see around us', he observed,

one vast and fearful struggle going on between the friends of things as they are and the advocates of change. Not in England only, but all over Europe, this contest is raging, and no man who loves his country or mankind ought to remain neutral in it. . . . Who can wish success to that blind ignorance which cannot see that all things are and must be forever changing?—that it is worse than kicking against the pricks to oppose our vain efforts to an eternal and universal law of God's providence; and that by striving against change we do not prevent it from coming, but only render it more violent and injurious, when it might have been natural and beneficial?[4]

Change was the law of things, inescapably necessary in a turbulent epoch, change, however, which was closely obedient to the laws of Providence.

[1] Arnold, *Lectures on Modern History*, p. 23.   [2] Ibid., p. 28.
[3] Ibid., p. 31.   [4] Arnold, *Miscellaneous Works*, p. 116.

His respect for class and the institution of property firmly controlled Arnold's vision of society. 'Equality', he maintained, 'is the dream of a madman, or the passion of a fiend.'[1] The Chartists were a 'mere curse to the human race'. 'Entitled to no compassion and no respect', their leaders deserved fully 'the heaviest punishment of law'.[2] The Owenites and Saint-Simonians who attacked the institution of private property were 'a set of political fanatics'. For Arnold, as for Burke, there was an almost mystical sanctity about property and the political and civil institutions founded on the principle of property: 'An institution so sacred, and so essential to the elevation of our nature, is and ever has been deeply valued by all freemen who have been more than savages.'[3]

Conservative, paternalistic, frequently condescending, Arnold's meliorism has its obvious limitations. Yet it would be a mistake to allow a sense of his shortcomings to obscure his genuinely humane and liberal outlook. His sympathy for the poor and the disinherited, his sense of injustice done and dignity appallingly outraged, the very fact of his concern, are rare enough in his time; certainly, in this respect, he stands alone in his day as an educator of middle-class youth.

. . . [Richard] Carlile tells the poor that they and the rich are enemies, and that to destroy the property of an enemy, whether by fire or otherwise, is always lawful in war—a Devil's doctrine, certainly, and devilishly applied; but unquestionably our aristocratical manners and habits have made us and the poor two unsympathizing bodies; and from want of sympathy I fear the transition to enmity is but too easy when distress embitters the feelings and the sight of luxury in others makes that distress still more intolerable. This is the plague spot to my mind in our whole state of society, which must be removed or the whole must perish.[4]

Sensing appalling and imminent crisis, he reacted bitterly against the Tories. In their self-engrossed enjoyment of privilege they were as much enemies of order as working-class agitators. The two were simply allotropes, aristocratic and democratic, of that pernicious spirit of individual self-will which set itself stubbornly against the light. Both were forms of Jacobinism—and 'it is waste of time to talk of wickedness to a Jacobin, for it is the very essence

---

[1] Arnold, *Miscellaneous Works*, p. 182.   [2] Ibid., p. 476.
[3] Ibid., p. 493.   [4] Stanley, op. cit. i. 285.

of his nature'.[1] Like Carlyle, whom he resembles in so many
ways, Arnold saw in the doctrines of *laissez-faire* an inhuman
systematization of selfishness.[2] Obviously there was a measure of
truth in the teachings of political economy, but the truths were
those of the specialist, to be respected, but, finally, subordinated
to the larger vision of the 'statesman'. In the absence of such
correction *laissez-faire* replaced community by mere congrega-
tion, human relations by purely commercial ones, substituted
a murderously unequal, thoroughly selfish race for a collective
march towards the common good. And for the common good
Arnold was willing, even, to encroach on the sanctity of property.
It was the business of civil society to defend property: it was no
less its business to limit any exorbitant excess of its power. No
man had the right to do what he wanted with his own. Property
was a trust not to be abused, and he admitted, violating the most
cherished convictions of his class, 'I suppose the Government may
entrench upon individual property for a great national benefit.'[3]

Although he brushed aside the dream of equality as an outrage
against reason and the will of God, Arnold maintained that
'extreme inequality' was no less a 'folly and a sin'. 'But an inequality where some have all the enjoyments of civilized life,
and none are without its comforts,—where some have all the
treasures of knowledge, and none are in ignorance, that is a
social system in harmony with the order of God's creation in the
natural world.'[4] The physical image of social health was to be
encountered not in the manufacturing towns, where the choking
slums obscured all sense of a varied, justly proportioned and
regulated community, but in the traditional towns and villages
of England. Here one encountered dwellings of every description
and size, all grades of society were represented, and 'although the
houses of the poorest class are the most numerous, yet their number
does not so much exceed that of the houses of the richest classes,
as wholly to dilute . . . that social influence which every class of
society ought to exercise upon the rest'.[5] The task of reinstating
this model of harmonious degree and infusing it with vitality
was, quite simply, 'the most difficult problem ever submitted
to civilized man'.[6] In notes which awakened eager echoes in the

[1] Arnold, *Miscellaneous Works*, p. 189.   [2] Ibid., p. 453.
[3] Stanley, op. cit. i. 69.   [4] Arnold, *Miscellaneous Works*, p. 182.
[5] Ibid., p. 458.   [6] Ibid., p. 478.

hearts of his most responsive listeners—and Clough was preeminently responsive—he issued his call:

> What Bible or Missionary Society can propose to itself an object so great as the redemption of the labouring population of England from its present wretched state . . .? And if the work is to be done by combined efforts, will no society be formed for this highest and holiest of all purposes? If it is to be accomplished by individual energy, will there be no new Howard, or Clarkson, or Fry to lay bare the evil in all its enormity, and to resolve with God's help that it shall no longer remain unremedied?[1]

Sceptical, like Carlyle, of the effectiveness of single measures, Arnold believed that nothing short of 'one great system, clearly and comprehensively devised, and steadily and perseveringly executed' would answer present needs.[2] The system he devised was certainly vast; his disciples were to discover that it was not quite as clear or workable as they might have wished. For them it dwindled from a programme to an attitude. The two sources to which their master looked for salvation were the aristocracy and the Church. He knew that radical surgery was needed, but he was also convinced that in these institutions alone were to be found 'nobility and religion', the twin instruments for 'elevating and purifying' mankind and lifting it out of Utilitarian self-interest.[3] Knowledge, refinement, liberality, courtesy, feudal responsibility—mixed in with its arrogance, self-preoccupation, and extravagance, the aristocracy possessed the traditions necessary to a national culture, and it was essential that these purified and purifying traditions should be preserved and disseminated. Here the middle classes, because of their mediate position socially and economically, played an indispensable part. They were a vital link in unifying society and its culture, in humanizing and, ultimately, Christianizing it. They had to educate themselves to be real and not merely nominal gentlemen, influencing society by their example as committed participants in an integrated, truly Christian culture.

The Church was, of course, paramount in the Arnoldian scheme—but, as he wrote in 1832, 'the Church, as it now stands, no human power can save'.[4] The re-emergence of Christianity as a living social and spiritual force could be assured only through

---

[1] Arnold, *Miscellaneous Works*, p. 478.   [2] Ibid., p. 188.
[3] Ibid., p. 214.   [4] Stanley, op. cit. i. 317.

drastic overhaul. The traditions of eighteenth-century orthodoxy were bankrupt, but there were other enemies as well. Sacerdotalism, now asserting itself in the Tractarian movement, and the Evangelical readiness to surrender to Caesar all temporal concern were alternatives of the same betrayal. Both sundered what God had put together, separated body from soul, secular from spiritual. 'Every act of a Christian is at once secular and spiritual;—secular, inasmuch as it is done in the body, in time, and on earth;—spiritual, as it proceeds from the mind and the heart, and therefore affects the soul, and reaches on to eternity'.[1] Logically it was a short step to his vision of an Established Church which was united with the State. Only out of such a sovereign union could grow power comprehensive and creative enough to contain the political, intellectual, and spiritual ferment of the age. The spirit of Sectarianism—unruly, fissive, acrimonious—was, obviously, a major obstacle, as in itself it was one of the most shameful features of the development of Christianity. It was the counterpart in English religious life of that unregenerate and wilful Jacobinism, that refusal of centrality, which in secular life manifested itself in the organization of working-class unions. Sectarianism, in Arnold's view, could be effectively countered by enlarging and liberalizing the Establishment, by taking the stress off doctrine and doctrinal differences (these, after all, were simply matters of 'opinion'), and by laying down a broad basis of essential Christian belief to which all could subscribe. What was needed above all was that Christians (Quakers, Roman Catholics, and Unitarians, Arnold admitted, posed a problem here) should sink their disagreements: it was imperative that the only battle-lines of the future be drawn between Christians and non-Christians.

Rugby, as has often been pointed out, was a rough working-model of Arnold's idea of the Christian State. Like the State, the school was to be primarily a moral and spiritual force, a training-ground where youth could learn not only the nature of truly responsible citizenship, but also its ultimate allegiance, the allegiance Arnold himself professed to 'the party of Christ against wickedness'.[2]

His universe was sharply and rigidly divided. Across a tortuous but decisive line, good and evil, God and the Devil, the principle of light and life and the principle of darkness and death, waged

[1] Arnold, *Miscellaneous Works*, pp. 473–4.   [2] Stanley, op. cit. i. 195.

unceasing war. 'We are in a world where evil exists within us, and about us; we cannot but know it . . . this noisome wilderness of weeds, this reeking swamp.'[1] Evil was a historical fact and part of the historical process; the progressive triumph of good was involved in the unrolling of God's design in human history; meanwhile, the personal struggle of the individual was an inescapable duty of co-operation in the grand design. Arnold was a man haunted by the reality of Evil and Sin; relentlessly watchful, the Devil stalked visibly through his moral world. He shuddered in moral pain at the least glimpse of wickedness. When his wife once remarked on the innocent appearance of a new boy, 'he checked her quite imploringly: "Oh, my dear, do not speak of it. You know how it pains me to think of it, when I think how soon the devil will put his filthy paw upon him and mar it all." '[2] He exhorted his schoolboys to constant watchfulness against the trifling act, the heedless thought, which, sowing the seed of sin, eventually flowered into a corruption of the whole moral frame. His struggle was fierce and unceasing; as he remarked of his task as headmaster, '. . . it has all the interest of a great game of chess, with living creatures for pawns and pieces, and your adversary, in plain English, the Devil: . . . It is quite surprising, to see the wickedness of young boys. . . .'[3]

Strictly and wholly transitional between innocent but ignorant childhood and aware manhood surrounded by the fearful forms of sin, boyhood, especially in the context of the mischievous social and personal relations encouraged by school life, had no redeeming virtues whatsoever in Arnold's eyes. Convinced of the 'evil of boy nature', he pounded into his pupils a sense of the momentousness of this period in relation to adult life and, beyond that, to eternity. In these years the soul first came in contact with the reality of the world and of evil, and, he warned his charges, 'A character will be formed, whether you watch and pray, or whether you do neither; but the great point is what this character may be. If you do not watch the process, it will surely be the character of death eternal.'[4] Clearly only the 'manly' could face such responsibility. Shortly after his election to Rugby he declared,

[1] Arnold, *Sermons*, iv. 202–3.

[2] R. E. Prothero, *Letters and Verses of Arthur Penrhyn Stanley, D.D.* (London, 1895), p. 73.

[3] Stanley, op. cit. i. 259.   [4] Arnold, *Sermons*, iv. 83.

'[M]y object will be . . . to form Christian men, for Christian boys I can scarcely hope to make.'[1] His procedure was to hasten the process of maturation. Examining this solution in two sermons entitled 'I put away Childish Things', he concluded that it was 'sin' to retain the 'imperfections' of childhood, when it was not only desirable but possible to hasten the change to 'manliness' without injury to body or mind;[2] the dangerous consequences of moral distension seem not to have occurred to him.

We can conveniently separate three main lines of approach to Arnold's goal of an awakened moral sense—an ethic of enthusiasm, an ethic of personal responsibility and consequence, and an ethic of moral earnestness. Though to some extent these were separate and successive stages in the growth to manliness, they were coexistent and co-operative in the most fully developed moral natures.

To a pupil who thought he had offended him, Arnold wrote:

I had observed, with some pain, what seemed to me indications of a want of enthusiasm, in the good sense of the word, of a moral sense and feeling corresponding to what I knew was your intellectual activity. . . . [T]here seemed to me a coldness on religious matters, which made me fear lest it should change to sneering, as your understanding became more vigorous: for this is the natural fault of the undue predominance of the mere intellect, unaccompanied by a corresponding growth and liveliness of the moral affections, particularly that of admiration and love of moral excellence, just as superstition arises, where it is honest, from the undue predominance of the affections, without the strengthening power of the intellect advancing in proportion. . . .[3]

Clearly aware of the dangers and limitations of enthusiasm, Arnold saw it, nevertheless, as a basic motivating force in man's spiritual and moral life. To arouse the admiration of the young and direct it towards human models of virtue and nobility, he advocated the use of history books illustrated with 'vivid prints' which 'should contain as much as possible the poetry of history; the most striking characters, the most heroic actions, whether of doing or suffering'.[4] The highest model and the goal of all striving was, of course, Christ. 'One name there is, and one only; one

---

[1] Stanley, op. cit. i. 81.   [2] Arnold, *Sermons*, iv. 8-15, 16-22.
[3] Stanley, op. cit. i. 358.
[4] T. Arnold, 'Rugby School', *Quarterly Journal of Education*, vii (1834), 246.

alone in heaven and in earth; not truth, not justice, not bene-
volence, not Christ's Mother, not His holiest servants, not His
blessed sacraments, not His very mystical body, but Himself
only, who died for us and rose again, Jesus Christ, both God and
Man.'[1]

The ethic of punishment and consequence, too narrowly prudential and self-regarding for the fervent love of good and abhorrence of evil he wished to arouse, is not stressed heavily in Arnold's
teaching. He could, nevertheless, on occasion remind his hearers
in fearsome phrase of the awful judgement of God. In a school
sermon, preached after the death of one of the boys, he recalled
the pains and terrors of that inevitable visitant: 'It is fearful to
go from light to darkness, from all that we have ever known and
loved, to that of which we know and love nothing. But if death,
when thus stingless, is yet full of horror, what is he with his
worst sting beside, the sting of our sins? What is he when he is
taking us, not to nothingness, but to judgment?'[2] Taking the
terrible fulfilment of Elisha's curse on the children who jeered
at his baldness as his theme, he elaborated on the infinite consequences of what unheeding youth was too apt to regard as
trifling follies. God was as 'angry with the faults of young persons
as with those of grown-up men . . . and he punish[ed] them as
heavily'.[3] It was fatally easy for schoolboys to lose sight of eternity.
'[I]f you displease God, which you know you do by every fault,
the evil of your conduct is infinite, and its consequences are
infinite; not doing injury here but doing far greater injury—
injury to your immortal souls, ruin to your immortal happiness.'[4]
In speaking in this vein, he hastened to add, he was using the
'language of the law more than that of the Gospel' not because
he thought it 'in itself the best and highest instruction', but because
he was afraid that his young hearers 'could not understand profitably any other'.[5]

'The predominant characteristic of Arnold's mind, and that
for which above all others we honour him, was his *earnestness*',
wrote W. R. Greg in 1844. '. . . Life, in his view of it, was no
pilgrimage of pleasure, but a scene of toil, of effort, of appointed
work—of grand purposes to be striven for—of vast ends to be

---

[1] Arnold, *Sermons*, iv. 154.   [2] Ibid., p. 52.
[3] T. Arnold, *Sermons Preached in the Chapel of Rugby School* (London, 1847),
p. 58.   [4] Ibid., p. 62.   [5] Ibid., p. 88.

achieved—of fearful evils to be uprooted or trampled down—
of sacred and mighty principles to be asserted and carried out.'[1]
Even his contemporaries, it would appear, were impressed by the
intensity of this quality, for which Arnold has become notorious.
For him, the carelessness of schoolboys was, ultimately, an indifference to the moral issues that were delicately balanced in
every act and moment. In overlaying the moral nature, such
indifference resulted in a culpable existence at second-hand, in a
dulled state in which men's real and best selves, their consciences,
were unengaged. What he desired in his schoolboys was a moral
thoughtfulness and a moral stature which was independent of
the herd-instinct. 'To be in earnest', he said in a sermon,

is indeed with most of us the same as to be good; it is not that we love
evil, but that we are indifferent both to it and to good. Now, many of
us are very seldom in earnest. By this I mean that the highest part of
our minds, and that which judges of the highest things, is generally
slumbering or but half-awake. We may go through a very busy day,
yet not be, in this true sense, in earnest at all; our best faculties may,
as it were, be all the while sleeping or playing. . . . It has been but a
skirmishing at the outposts; not a sword has been drawn in the main
battle. . . .[2]

This strenuous ideal of continual moral engagement led to his
Jehovah-like descent on the slightest sign of 'levity' or, in his
inimitable phrase, 'what St. Paul calls *revelling*'.[3] He continued
the sermon just quoted:

[T]his habit of never being in earnest greatly lowers the strength of
our feelings even towards the good which we praise and the evil
which we condemn. It was an admirable definition of that which
excites laughter, that it is that which is out of rule, that which is
amiss, that which is unsightly, . . . provided that it was unaccompanied
by pain. . . .

Here, then, we have the secret of vice becoming laughable; and of
things which are really wicked, disgusting, hateful, being expressed
by names purely ludicrous. . . . The evil that does not seriously pain or
inconvenience man, is very apt to be regarded with feelings approaching to laughter, if we have no sense of pain at the notion of its being
an offence against God.[4]

[1] W. R. Greg, 'Review of Stanley's *Life*', *Westminster Review*, xlii (1844), 380.
[2] Arnold, *Sermons*, iv. 127-8.   [3] Stanley, op. cit. i. 170.
[4] Arnold, *Sermons*, iv. 129-30.

It is not surprising that he could hardly bring himself to read Aristophanes till 1835 when he was forty, and that his 'strong moral disapprobation always interfered with his sense of the genius both of that poet and Juvenal'.[1]

Having awakened their 'earnestness', Arnold pointed out to his charges that it was a principle validating itself only in unceasing scrutiny and appraisal. 'Men crave a general rule for their guidance at all times, and under all circumstances; whereas life is a constant call upon us to consider where one general rule, in the particular case before us, is modified by another, or where one rule should be applied, and where another.'[2] Substantive good was something that could be definitely pin-pointed only in a few particulars—work, for instance, or self-denial. For the rest, the struggle against the enemy demanded an ever-renewing search and fresh recognition, a constant, conscious, independent dissection and recreation of the self in its altering environment. It involved a naked encounter between the stripped conscience and moral reality. It was, no doubt, to facilitate such encounters that Arnold sought, unsuccessfully, the permission of the trustees to introduce solitary confinement as a punishment.[3]

Temperamentally disinclined to radical change, Arnold adopted at Rugby much of the existing machinery of public school discipline and administration. One remarkable innovation, however, was the complete trust he accorded to his schoolboys: as the saying went, 'it was a shame to tell Arnold a lie—he always believes one'.[4] An entirely novel educative approach, this assumption of reliability aimed, by eliciting the individual's willing moral response, at replacing the barriers between masters and pupils by the sense of a shared participation in common values and purposes. This trust found its fullest expression in Arnold's treatment of the sixth form, the praepostors, the conception and working out of whose function is the most commonly known aspect of his work as headmaster. He pinned his highest hopes on these aristocrats of the little state of Rugby: 'When I have confidence in the Sixth,' he told them, 'there is no post in England which I would exchange for this; but if they do not support me, I must

---

[1] Stanley, op. cit. i. 143–4. *Corr.* i. 55, showing Clough's eagerness to make an acquaintance with Juvenal, suggests that this poet was definitely *not* read in Rugby.   [2] Arnold, *Sermons*, iv. 247–8.
[3] W. H. D. Rouse, *A History of Rugby School* (London, 1898), p. 228 n.
[4] Stanley, op. cit. i. 179.

go.'[1] Their status was only slightly below that of the masters and no argument against them was tolerated. They were expected to weigh their every action and utterance with care, to set by their maturity an example to the rest of the school, to train themselves through the principled exercise of trust for their future as leaders in a troubled world. They possessed, Arnold pointed out, enormous powers for 'good or for evil' and, given the authority, it was up to them to seek out opportunities for exercising their influence beneficially. The Rugby Sixth were never allowed to forget that they were not simple mediators of the headmaster's line; earnestness required from them a dynamic and independent role—they were not merely custodians but creators of moral health.

Possibly Arnold had no very significant or enduring influence on the average schoolboy; it is impossible to doubt his impact on the more receptive. Dr. Moberly, Headmaster of Winchester, remarked on the discernible difference in Rugbeians when they came up to Oxford. Here was a new breed, 'thoughtful, manly-minded, conscious of duty and obligation', who impressed by their 'immense improvement . . . in respect of morality and personal piety'.[2] A concern for character was not, however, Arnold's only legacy. Intellectually, he was for his best pupils an exhilarating agent of deliverance. Apart from some significant changes in the teaching of history and the addition of modern languages the Rugby curriculum did not differ substantially from that of other schools. It continued in the liberal-humanist educational tradition rooted in the classics, but in Arnold's hands that tradition freed itself from the usual pedantic grind and came alive. Morally, he encouraged his schoolboys to think for themselves, to stand four-square on their principles; intellectually, he demanded from them originality and independence. He made them work hard but he also inspired them by the breadth of his vision, his infectious sense of larger ends. He laid before them his impressive resources as a historian, put them in touch with the most recent and forward-looking developments in continental theology, gave to all their studies the excitements of relevance and reality.

Nothing can indicate more forcibly the reverence which the Doctor was capable of inspiring—and, of course, the kind of

---

[1] Ibid., p. 171.   [2] Ibid., p. 183.

guilt a backsliding child of Rugby was liable to—than the enskied
and sainted figure who towers over his hapless successor, Tait,
in the remarkable letter Stanley sent on hearing of the election.
Stanley, incidentally, had strongly supported Tait's candidacy.

My DEAR TAIT,—The awful intelligence of your election has just
reached me. . . . I have not heart to say more than that I conjure you
by your friendship for me, your reverence for your great predecessor,
your sense of the sacredness of your office, your devotion to Him
whose work you are now more than ever called upon to do, to lay
aside every thought for the present except that of repairing your
deficiencies. . . . Read Arnold's sermons. . . . Alter nothing at first.[1]

Tait was generally considered a failure as headmaster.

From his eleventh to well over his eighteenth year Clough
breathed this intense Rugby air, and, as Stanley wrote, 'Of all
the scholars . . . in the time when Arnold's influence was at its
height, there was none who so completely represented the place
in all its phases. . . . He received . . . into an unusually susceptible
and eager mind the whole force of the electric shock which
Arnold communicated to all his better pupils.'[2] Initially, the
Doctor's attention must have been arrested by this pupil's
outstanding scholastic abilities. Starting by winning the only
scholarship open to boys under fourteen and a half years old,
he picked up every single prize the place offered, ending his
career in a blaze of glory with a Balliol Scholarship performance
which broke all records and left the dons glowing in enthusiastic
admiration over his English essay.[3] Thanks to his childhood
training, Rugby found in him, too, an apt and willing moral
being, sensitively enough organized to respond eagerly to demanding ideals.

Lonely, acutely aware of his distance from home and from his
family, Clough saw far more of Arnold than most other boys.
He was a member of Arnold's own School House, and Mrs.
Arnold, who noticed his somewhat delicate health, developed
a great liking for him. Tom Arnold, Dr. Arnold's second son,
remembered that 'his gentleness, and that unwonted *humanity*

[1] R. T. Davidson and W. Benham, *Life of Archibald Campbell Tait, Archbishop of Canterbury*, 2 vols. (London, 1891), i. 113–14.
[2] A. H. Clough, *Poems*, with a Memoir (London, 1862), p. v.
[3] C. E. Mallett, *A History of the University of Oxford*, 3 vols. (London, 1927), iii. 354 n.

of nature which made him unlike the ordinary schoolboy, caused him to be a welcome guest in her drawing-room'.[1] There and at Fox How, the Arnolds' holiday home in the Lake District, Clough shared in the rich, relatively unrestrained holiday life of the family, saw and marvelled at the great man's unbuttoned presence—'I cannot indeed conceive anyone calling "the Dr" Tom even at Fox-how', he wrote in 1836 (*Corr.* i. 50). For his part, he repaid these kindnesses with passionate gratitude. 'Thank God for Arnold, and his kindness of which I am most unworthy indeed', he wrote in his private journal in the second week of the Lent Term of 1838 after he had left Rugby for Oxford.[2] On one occasion when Arnold visited his study, he was so excited afterwards that he could hardly look at his trigonometry.[3] In his veneration he adopted, almost completely, the chief Arnoldian positions. One can watch the master's views percolating unadulterated into the letters he wrote. Arnold's position on the indivisibility of Christian responsibility, for instance, is faithfully mirrored: 'Is one Christian bound by any laws which another is not obliged to obey? If you were to say so you would not have the clergy better, but the laity worse' (*Corr.* i. 14). In another letter to his sister, a long discussion centres on the question of Church Establishment and its relationship to the State. The letter proceeds through Arnoldian views on the desirability and necessity of Establishment and Church–State unity, and arrives at the conclusion that the Christian State could be achieved by admitting 'all such sects as are Christian sects, and believe in the *essentials* of Christianity, meaning by essentials, those points without which no one can be saved' (*Corr.* i. 33). In thrilled excitement he followed the fortunes of his hero's Liberal party in its row with the Newmanists about Renn Dickson Hampden.

Do you know that Arnold has written a Hampden defence pamphlet? . . . which Price and Grenfell say gives the Oxford people the most thorough and regular thrashing that can be conceived. . . . What glorious fellows those Proctors are for stopping that furious Convocation, and as Price says doubtless these High-Church Newmanitish people will try and get their Proctors' power of a veto done away with. . . .[4]

[1] T. Arnold, Jr., 'Arthur Hugh Clough: A Sketch', *Nineteenth Century*, xliii (Jan. 1898), 106.   [2] Quoted, Lowry, p. 2.   [3] Ibid., p. 3.
[4] *Corr.* i. 42. In 1836 Lord Melbourne, at the head of a Whig Government, appointed Hampden, a theological Liberal, to the Regius Professorship of

Aware of the public stir Arnold was causing by his firmness, he sent off a reassuring letter to his parents:

[I]f any rumours of ill-conduct as headmaster have crossed the Atlantic, I believe they have got a great way through the Times and John Bull newspapers; I might as well tell you that the Trustees of the School met last week in London, all being present except 3 of the 12, and wrote a letter to the Dr. saying that they had the most complete confidence in him, that the school was going on as well as could be expected, and that the discipline was perfectly humane (*Corr*. i. 43).

His family, when they returned to Liverpool in 1836, found their Toryism mildly scandalized by the 'radical' Arnoldian views he had imbibed and which he expounded so freely. They vaguely regretted not having sent him to Shrewsbury instead and consoled themselves with the thought that this was only a passing youthful phase.[1]

His immersion, finally so nearly complete, was a gradual one; each succeeding year brought fresh responsibility which he undertook willingly and gratefully. He sought out like-minded friends and was in turn cultivated by them—all older than himself, all committed members of the Rugby elect. Stanley and Vaughan and Lake, the brilliant triumvirate of first-generation Arnoldians, were more distant objects of admiration and flattering acquaintance, high examples to be followed, than intimates. Gell and Simpkinson, belonging to the next generation, were his particular friends, especially the latter, and it was from them that he took over full responsibility. In the winter half of 1835 Simpkinson left for Cambridge and Clough became head of School House —'an office of considerable trust and great difficulty', as he wrote to his brother (*Corr*. i. 21). He faced two years of lonely responsibility, responsibility made heavier by his consciousness

Divinity at Oxford. Going counter to the recommendations of the Archbishop of Canterbury and supporting those of Whately, Bishop of Dublin, and Copleston, former Provost of Oriel, the appointment was generally unpopular with Oxford orthodoxy. It aroused, particularly, the theological—and personal— animus of the Tractarians. As a gesture of insult an attempt was made to deprive Hampden of some of his privileges as Professor, chiefly his vote in the nomination of Select Preachers to the University. The Statute was defeated at its first submission to Convocation in March 1836 by Proctorial intervention. It was reintroduced in May and carried by 474 votes to 94, new Proctors having assumed office in the interval.

[1] B. A. Clough, op. cit., p. 17.

(shared by Arnold) of a decline in the general tone of the upper school. 'My oldest and only friend Simpkinson', he wrote to his sister,

is just gone to Cambridge; and there are also two or three more gone whom I knew and loved better than the rest; so that I am now quite alone, and am doomed so to remain for two long years. . . . [T]here is a deal of evil springing up in the School, and it is to be feared that the tares will choke much of the wheat. There is a great deal of good in the top of the School, but then it is what may be called disagreeable good, having much evil mixed with it, especially in little matters. So that from these persons, good is disliked. I am trying if possible to show them that good is not necessarily disagreeable, that a Christian may be and is likely to be a gentleman, and that he is surely much more than a gentleman. It is a weary thing to look around and see all the evil, all the sin and wickedness of those with whom one must daily associate. . . . *I know the work is appointed for me and I for it, and woe to me if I do not do it* (*Corr.* i. 19–20, my italics).

The priggishness is odious, but the sense of duty and moral responsibility out of which it grows is frightening. The issues at stake, and Clough's conception of his place in the struggle, are clearly indicated in a letter to Gell: 'I sometimes think that the last two years were given me to make me strong and discipline me for this time, and it is very painful to think how neglected they have been—more particularly if through that neglect the balance will be decided in favour of evil' (*Corr.* i. 24).

During these years he took upon himself, too, the task of supervising his younger brother's unhappy progress through King William's College in the Isle of Man, and, after that, Mr. Prince's private school in Liverpool. In a series of epistolary sermons, evoked by George's piteous cries for spiritual and moral succour, he cajoled and exhorted his brother to greater effort, warning him against indolence (allegedly a Perfect trait), pointing out to him the infinite suffering of Christ and His sustaining mercy, reminding him of his duties as a Christian. Repellent and hectoring though these letters are, there is something oddly moving in their desperate, myopic innocence, their worried scrupulousness, in the eagerness with which they welcome the stark shelters of moral absolutism and missionary duty.

No, George, you should remember that even the most trifling things are ordered by God, and I doubt not that he has sent you to this school for his own good purposes to give light to these poor boys who are walking in sin and darkness. You are now in a very important situation; you are the only one it seems of a set of boys, who knows God, and wishes to serve him. So that you are in some manner responsible; I mean you will have to answer for some of their sins, if you do not exert yourself in their behalf, to make them better (*Corr.* i. 18).

His two objects, he wrote to George, were, '1st, the improvement of the School. 2nd, the publication and telling abroad of the merit of the School by means of the Magazine' (*Corr.* i. 19). He was among the pioneers when this journal was begun in 1835, and in his last year he became its editor. It was, from its inception, one of his most anxious, time-consuming concerns. As he wrote to Gell, 'apathy won't do for R. Mag.' (*Corr.* i. 42). It was a sacred trust to be taken up with prayer, self-dedication, gratitude—and without a single thought for personal glory.[1] For the gravely enthusiastic Arnoldians who maintained it this journal was no mere school magazine; it was a message to the unconverted, a shining light set on a hill for all the world to see. 'But did I say', Clough wrote in the article which introduced the first number,

that our motive for writing was to give amusement and knowledge? Our motive, we trust, is a higher one. It is one of love and gratitude; it is to pay our debt to the mother who has fostered and is fostering our young intellects; nor, we trust, our intellects alone: it is to raise her still higher than she is raised, or at least to maintain her on her present elevation. We might be pardoned, even though we did pluck the blossoms of our youth, if we plucked them to weave a chaplet for the brows of our Alma Mater.[2]

Not surprisingly, the bulk of the material within the high-minded covers of *The Rugby Magazine* impresses by its stubborn indigestibility.

As his school-days drew to a close Clough's thoughts turned increasingly to the prospect of a University career, and a debate about the relative merits of Oxford and Cambridge becomes prominent in his letters. His strong, Arnold-inculcated sense of work to be done, and of himself as a chosen vessel, drove him to

---

[1] Cf. the prayer of self-dedication Clough composed for the occasion, which is printed in Lowry, p. 12, and G. Levy, *Arthur Hugh Clough, 1819–1861* (London, 1938), pp. 20–1.
[2] 'Introductory', *The Rugby Magazine*, i (July 1835), 13.

decide in favour of Oxford. His reasoning would strike anyone but a total Arnoldian as quaint. In 1836 he wrote to Simpkinson: 'One may fancy Cambridge a very excellent and useful big place of education, but Oxford is the place for the education of statesmen and great political men, and the influence of Oxford and its place in relation to the Commonwealth is far higher, for good or evil' (*Corr.* i. 49). He had absorbed completely Dr. Arnold's conception of public service as being, primarily, a moral one. The nature of his immediate task at Oxford was clear to him: he had to propagate with like-minded Rugbeians the spirit of Rugby, and so 'leaven the whole lump' (*Corr.* i. 38) of that ancient seat of learning.

On looking more closely, however, one discovers that this faultless, completely committed, fearfully priggish Rugby front covered, in fact, a personality painfully taut with emotional tensions and self-questionings. A separation between an official Rugby Clough and an unofficial one is facile and misleading. It can obscure the constant mutuality between the two, the complicated dialectical play of fulfilment, recoil, anxiety, reassurance, release, and guilt. Nevertheless, the separation is convenient, and if the official Rugbeian shows us the burden of values, purposes, and roles which the boy so eagerly willed on himself, the unofficial shows us the strain of carrying that burden—and that strain contains the germs of positive independent growth, of the individual and private sensitivities and apprehensions which, sharpened and clarified, Clough later shaped into his best poetry.

The outward circumstance of the lack of a fixed home was accompanied by a consequent uncertainty. Early in Clough's life money became a real concern. At the age of sixteen we find him writing to his sister in America, 'The matter I wrote about to my Father [the letter was lost in a shipwreck] was this—I mentioned at length the various expenses caused by the uncertainty of where the money to pay my expenses was to come from, nobody knowing where to send the bills and so on. . . . Secondly D. Williams has left Uncle C. and where to find him je ne sais pas, so that source is no use' (*Corr.* i. 14). Uncertainty caused by the indefiniteness of his financial sources, and the difficulties of communication, developed within a year into uncertainty about his family's resources. Winning the Balliol Scholarship, he pointed out, meant not only honour but an income of £30 a year; this, together with an Exhibition, would all but pay his way at Balliol, which was about £20 or £30 cheaper than any other College (*Corr.* i. 44). Self-denial, one of the most frequently commented-on traits of Clough's mature personality, and developed early into an independent moral value, was encouraged, of course, by Arnold, but it also bore the impress of real economic necessity.

Rugby, as has been frequently pointed out, was Clough's home in these years, a stable point in the restless pattern of his holiday life. The moral and intellectual assent he accorded to its values was strengthened by emotional ties, both of love for Arnold and the school, and of the need for stability. Wholehearted support and loyalty were essential for his existence, for without them he belonged nowhere. Yet strangely enough, his being, soaked through with attachment for the place, longed for respite. The bonds he thought so strong, the character he thought so fixed (unlike Etonians, 'our character is fixed before we go to College', he observed),[1] were subject to guilt-generating change. The process of change involved inevitably—and disloyally—distressing shifts in one's feeling and desires. After Simpkinson's departure for Cambridge Clough wrote to his sister:

> The nights . . . are getting quite long, . . . so that I have a great deal of time in my study,—and am almost more by myself than I wish. Sometimes when I am thus alone I long very much indeed to have you all over again; for before Simpkinson left, Rugby was almost like home to me, and now I feel the want of a home far more than I ever did before. . . . *Even the holidays without you seem now a thing to be looked forward to very much*, which they never did before except last half-year when I was unable to work. I am very tolerably well now, and think I have recovered altogether from that attack, though I verily believe I shall not be able ever again to fag so much; indeed I shall never wish to do so in the same way (*Corr.* i. 20, my italics).

This is the first indication we have of the loosening bonds, an almost involuntary turning away from the pressures of loneliness and of the intensive work—intensive almost to the point of breakdown—undertaken, partly, as a means of self-forgetfulness. We have noticed how Clough's thoughts turned, with laudable anticipations of apostleship, towards Oxford in his later years.

---

[1] *Corr.* i. 35.

Unavoidably though, however hard he tried to cast his forward-looking thoughts in the Rugby mould, the present ties loosened perceptibly, and his references to the University indicate increasingly an autonomous and therefore not wholly pure anticipation. In May 1836 we find him aggressively denying Simpkinson's charge that he had lost interest in the School: 'Indeed this ["that I am too fond of Balliol and too little fond of—was it Rugby, or the fellows now at Rugby?"] is a foul and calumnious accusation, and I must try and undeceive you' (*Corr.* i. 45). For Clough, loving Arnold and Rugby, it would seem, meant loving the school dog as well. Later that year, after winning the Balliol Scholarship, he frankly admitted that the ties had slackened— the phrasing of the admission reveals the ambivalent movement between guilt and something suspiciously like relief: 'I am so glad Burbidge is coming next half; it is just the very thing I wanted so grievously and this Scholarship has made me feel so much less closely attached and joined to the School that I was almost beginning to lose interest in the fellows and th[eir] ways, and leave off concerning myself about them.'[1]

Akin to this uncertainty within himself about his real relation to the school is the uncertainty revealed in his personal relationships with others, his notorious shyness. Rugby earnestness, directed away from the instinctual, from acceptance of the unexamined 'given', demanded an intense self-consciousness. At the same time, in alliance with enthusiasm, it condemned self-cultivation. The tension of this opposition was, for Clough, basic in an unpatterned conflict of cross-weaving moral, spiritual, and emotional claims. Friendship in one aspect was only instrumental, not a value in itself but a matter of 'associating with . . . fellows for their good' (*Corr.* i. 25). Popularity and the desire for it was a snare, for, as he told George, '[R]emember always, that to be liked is not the thing we should wish for on its own account, but only because it will make [it] more easy for us to do good, namely to those who like us' (*Corr.* i. 21). The wish to be liked required to be suppressed severely, to withhold one's friendship was a moral obligation—it was one's duty to be 'very kind to but not intimate with' all one's fellows (*Corr.* i. 46).

---

[1] *Corr.* i. 57. After winning the Balliol Scholarship Clough stayed on in Rugby till 1837 in order to win an Exhibition.

Some of the dangers besetting personal relationship are given clearly shaped, because impersonal, expression, in an article on 'School-Society' Clough contributed to *The Rugby Magazine*:

[T]here appear to be two dangers, the first lest a boy should associate with too many, the second lest he should associate with too few. It happens, however, generally, that both these terminate in the same point, namely, selfishness, a heedlessness of the love of others,— that scepticism of the affections which in its full development, we call misanthropy. . . . The timid one is more likely to make true and abiding friendships, for his reserve may serve him in the stead of judgment. There is, however, here too danger,—there is the danger of that most evil habit which concentrates every thing on self, so that even those we love most dearly should be but the lesser stars that revolve around that sun. At the same time it need not be accompanied by the common outward symptoms of selfishness—these are often wanting; nay, self-love may even go so far as to suppress, still from selfish motives, aught that might betray the evil within: and a character for good nature, kindness, generosity, is but too little inconsistent with deep and engrossing self-love.[1]

Against this judicious, formal statement we can place profitably his agonized, self-lacerating appraisal of himself in a letter to Simpkinson written a few months later:

I hope . . . I shall not be cold or balancing or utilitarian, . . . but I know at the same time that I am running into the same extreme as Stanley, namely that of almost swallowing up all individual affections in hopes and fears and resolutions and struggles for the good of a greater number. I feel this creeping upon me very often, more particularly because I am so apt to get full of high thoughts of my own importance to the School etc. Indeed after two years of constant and unthought of, and unreproached indulgence in my burning thirst for praise, do not think me affected or wild in saying that there seems to be an atmosphere of conceit around me enveloping my whole frame like the body does the soul, and that however pure and good my thoughts are when they spring in my heart they cannot come out without passing through and being infected with that. I do hope and pray that my heart is not the slave of those wicked feelings, but it seems like a punishment for so long indulgence that they should still hold the apertures of my heart, and seize all that comes from thence, infecting them and breathing upon [them] the accursed thought, 'Shall I get praise for this.' Sometimes under the influence of strong feeling the

1 *The Rugby Magazine*, i (Jan. 1836), 209.

spell is broken and for this reason it is that I have written this so immediately after receiving your letter and yet even now the thought has arisen once or twice, 'Is not that a good thought, etc., etc.,' 'will he not have a better opinion of me for this', and I am forced to cry every moment for God to save me. . . . It has sometimes been quite dreadful to feel one's prayers for aid, whilst they were being breathed to God, infected with this loathsome disease. Sometimes however I felt quite triumphant in the consciousness that it could not touch my heart, that that was sanctified for a temple of God's spirit, and that the evil spirit had no power there (*Corr.* i. 39-40).

The sleepless conscience, relentlessly committed to absolute purity, pursues motive to its last guilty covert, and only two defences remain—pure and uncomplicated and spontaneous feeling, and the conviction of an inviolable sanctuary of spiritual self-possession. Ironically and agonizingly, the fulfilments offered by Arnoldian achievement—the fulfilments of academic distinction and missionary labour—were undermined by the terrifying vigilance of Arnoldian conscience. The needs of the shy schoolboy continually mocked and infected the aspiring enthusiastic will.

The deep emotional capacities he brought to his friendships, the jealous hunger for attachment, and also the lonely struggle to control these, are clearly attested to in an unpublished passage from one of his letters to Simpkinson:

. . . I mean giving up more of one's time to a new friend; though it is no doubt a trial to one's old ones—and in the strong feeling of this I am sure I can sympathize with you—for it was just the same last Easter with you and me—I felt quite sure, though it cost me two hours' sitting by myself in my study to gain that security, that you did not love me less though you were so much more often with Walrond and tho' he was enjoying what I longed for so much, the happiness of being alone with you. . . .[1]

Hungering for emotional contact, he was, nevertheless, tormented by a sense of the inadequacy of communication, of his painful efforts to utter 'what [he] really felt in really true words' (*Corr.* i. 48). His awareness of the gap between emotion and expression led to an uncertainty about the authenticity of expressed relationships. Writing to Simpkinson about Henry Walrond, he said:

[1] 1 Jan. 1837, Bodleian MS. Eng. Lett. c. 189, fol. 105 (54).

I can never be sure either that my own feelings towards him, or his to me are really and genuinely our own, and not a reflection of yours. And till people are convinced of the reality of their own affections and the affections of the other party to them, why it is only an εἴδωλον of friendship, and not good true substantial flesh and blood (*Corr.* i. 45).

This sense of exclusion from the real and living emotional centres of those around him explains his better-known statement that his reserve was caused, not by fear of ridicule, but by 'never being accustomed to be among those who I was sure love me' (*Corr.* i. 24).

Clough's inclination to trust strong feeling as a solution for the dilemmas and complexities of personal relationships was under-cut, however, by a more radical uncertainty, a suspicion of feeling itself. It was too liable to blur the edges of actuality and truth:

I hardly know what I said in the first page and I am afraid to read it again, and I hope you will excuse it if there is anything foolish, which I am always afraid there is, however much truth may go along with it, when I speak anything about myself, for the feeling carries me away beyond all rule of common-sense. Indeed I believe this is the great difficulty, that for a certain distance pleasure and feeling take the same path as duty and understanding, then they gradually split; and how is one to hit just the right moment for turning ourselves with the one and keeping out of the other? (*Corr.* i. 25–6.)

He later attempted to resolve this particular set of problems by a stern-willed adherence to minimal and incontrovertible fact.

Spiritual necessity, no less than moral claims and emotional uncertainties, contributed to his reserve. 'Have been a good deal excited—intellectually—little spiritually—living much too fast', he recorded in his diary in August 1835.[1] In addition to the excite-ments and agitations of his more intimate friendships, there was the emotional and physical drain of working hard and of setting a moral example. His nerves reacted strongly to such excitement; his letters refer more and more frequently to headaches and nervous 'fevers'. Often the strain of living an unslackening life of engagement left him prostrate. After winning the Balliol Scholarship he wrote to Gell from Rugby: 'I suppose I am very weak, for Burbidge's short visit the other day quite upset me and

---

[1] Quoted, Lowry, p. 8.

brought me back feverish sleepless nights and headaches once more, and Vaughan and Stanley, who are staying together at Arnolds have effected something of the same kind today' (*Corr.* i. 56). All this had to be curbed, as well as the excitement of trying to make sense of his whirling and conflicting thoughts and impulses. As Dr. Arnold had warned, such an existence was only a 'skirmishing at the outposts' which left the best self unengaged. In such living the essential spiritual self was starved and in danger of atrophy. Self-preservation demanded withdrawal.

Against this background of anxiety, self-doubt, and self-isolation we must place Clough's repeated self-accusations of guilt and sinfulness, of ceaseless falling away from ideals which, as we have seen, were not always compatible with one another. The fissures, the strained efforts to bridge them, the guilt consequent on his failures, explain this passage in a letter to his mother:

I wish I could get rid of this humour-rule, but there are times when I feel so utterly weak both in intellectual and moral power that I half fancy myself crazed. Again there are other times when I feel so strong that I could do anything; and then I can look back and judge rightly of what is past. . . . The truth is I have been in one continued state of excitement for I think at least the last 3 years, if not more, and now comes the time of exhaustion.—But I must take care now also, and stop this talk, for egotizing comme ça is very exciting indeed, and I feel my face getting hot and my mind confused. . . . [A]fter all I believe that the excess of thinking about one's self is very ruinous indeed (*Corr.* i. 16).

By the time he wrote that, the habit of introspection had become an inalienable part of himself—but, by the time he left Rugby, he was also beginning to learn that he could live—if only intermittently—at a lower pitch of intensity, that he could be cool, detached, even amused about himself and his beloved school, without dramatically violating his conscience or his integrity. It was an important discovery.

Loved by Arnold, loaded with academic honours, popular among his schoolfellows, Clough departed for the University in the radiance of full success. Even after the disaster of his failure to get a First he remained an object of awed admiration in the school.[1] Yet it is impossible to regard him as the complete,

[1] For a fictional representation of this veneration see A. G. Butler, *The Three Friends* (London, 1900), pp. 104-5. For the general trustworthiness of Butler's

entirely coherent Rugbeian, going forth into the world with
untroubled gaze to confront uncertainty for the first time in the
intellectual and spiritual ferment of Tractarian Oxford. Oxford
challenged some hitherto unexamined basic convictions and
values, Oxford was in many ways radically unsettling, but if he
yet had to taste intellectual uncertainty and its consequences
when he left Rugby, he already knew emotional uncertainty
and its resultant guilt.

Although he never entirely left Rugby and Arnold behind
him, we have Lake's testimony that Clough frequently lamented
'bitterly' the overstrain of his school years,[1] and from one point
of view his life may be regarded as a progressive surrender of
Rugby-fostered positions and habits of thought. Certain limitations in Arnoldism are particularly relevant to Clough's career.
The vulnerability of the basic adjustment on which Arnold's
values were founded has already been noticed—that between
the claims of truth and good, with the balance tilted continually
toward the latter. Another equally important limitation was one
later noticed by Clough himself. 'There are men—such was
Arnold—too intensely, fervidly practical', he wrote in a review
of Francis Newman's The Soul, 'to be literally, accurately,
consistently theoretical; too eager to be observant, too royal to be
philosophical, too fit to head armies and to rule kingdoms to
succeed in weighing words and analysing emotions; born to do,
they know not what to do.'[2] Arnoldism was inadequate, for, in
its Hebraic emphasis on doing, it left unregarded large segments
of man's moral experience which lay outside action. Further,
Arnold's activism, we have seen, demanded from the schoolboy
an independent generation of moral values, and within the clearly
articulated structure of school society such activity was relatively
easy: the centres of authority were conveniently defined and easy

picture see 'Rugby 1850: Arnold, Clough, Walrond, and In Memoriam', in
G. and K. Tillotson, Mid-Victorian Studies (London, 1965).

[1] K. Lake, ed., The Memorials of William Charles Lake, Dean of Durham (London,
1901), p. 13.
[2] Trawick, p. 278. Clough's other criticisms of his Rugby experience are in:
(i) the prose Epilogue to Dipsychus (Poems, pp. 295–6), where the criticism of
Arnold's effect on schoolboys' consciences is equivocal, because in dramatic form;
(ii) A Passage upon Oxford Studies (PPR i. 407; Trawick, pp. 326–7), where, by
implication, he includes his own experiences in condemning the intellectual
overstrain and competitiveness in Public Schools; (iii) a letter to Blanche Smith,
in which he laments the absence of any real boyhood in his life (Corr. ii. 310).

to locate, the general lines of behaviour laid down, the broad demarcation of good and evil already made. Too often the responsible schoolboy tended to forget that his authority was wholly delegated and existed within a particular social unit only. Some of the first problems the sensitive Rugbeian had to face in the University were those of realizing that there was no one central authority—intellectual or moral or religious or disciplinary—in this more complex society, that a morality geared so completely to action was compelled to face its own inadequacy when confronted by plurality—that, in fact, the University, like the world, differed in kind, not degree, from Rugby. Arnold had taught his schoolboys to regard themselves as leaders in an enterprise which, for all its vastness, had about it a final military simplicity. They saw themselves marching by the light of conscience and intellect through a majestically unrolling, progressive landscape of history towards the final overthrow of evil. Just as they had to discover that conscience and intellect did not always shine with a uniform Arnoldian light, they had to learn that the map of history they were provided with was open to challenge, that the configuration of the actual landscape of their century was more confused and perturbing than they had been led to expect.

2. EARLY POETRY

As a child, Clough was 'perpetually writing verses, not remarkable except for a certain ease of expression and for a power of running on, not common at that early age' (PPR i. 10). At least two specimens of this fledgling verse survive.[1] The first, written

---

[1] The first is copied in a letter to his mother from Pontefract dated 12 July 1850, Bodleian MS. Eng. Lett. c. 189, fol. 11. The second is in Bodleian MS. Eng. Poet. d. 129, fol. 79. A letter to Clough's widow from Edmund Ffoulkes, dated 4 Apr. 1862, states that the second was written by Clough 'during a rainy afternoon, whilst spending the day from school, when only twelve years old, on Snowdon' (Bodleian MS. Eng. Poet. d. 129, fol. 76). In a second letter, dated four days later, Ffoulkes, a nephew by marriage of Clough's uncle Alfred, Fellow of Jesus College, Oxford, wrote, 'I had read it originally in a copy which my aunt had made long since. I now see by the date of the original that it must have been written at Oxford not Chester' (Bodleian MS. Eng. Poet. d. 129, fols. 77–77ᵛ). The two letters have understandably caused some confusion—Ffoulkes's prose is not a model of clarity. The Bodleian catalogue lists the poem as written when Clough was either twelve or eighteen years old. Catalogue (p. 14), which prints four lines, concludes that the poem was written while Clough was staying with his uncle during the summer just before going up to Oxford. A consideration of the style and substance of the lines, and the handwriting, makes

at the age of eleven, is a patriotic effusion occasioned by the death of George IV and runs to twenty-two lines. The second is a more extensive topographical-mythological-pietistic piece on Snowdon written the following year. Two passages, the first six lines of the first and the concluding section of the second, are sufficiently illustrative. I have preserved Clough's punctuation.

> O Muse of Britain teach me now to sing
> In verses sad of our late noble king
> Teach me in notes of sorrow to proclaim
> To all the world our noble Prince's fame
> Teach me O Muse to tell in mournful strains
> Of all his deeds and all his dreadful pains

The young poet fortunately lacked the knowledge or stamina to complete this particular design.

> How beauteously the sunny smiles of Joy
> Play o'er the waters of Beaumaris Bay
> How venerably rising from the green
> Penrhyn thy turrets grey adorn the scene
> But further see where yon stupendous pile
> [Joins?] across coast to Mona's sacred isle
> Sublimely great, majestically still
> A lasting monument of human skill—
> Stranger, enraptured though thou be, depart
> Leave scarcely scanned the works of human art.
> Pass by them all—and thither turn thine eye
> Where yon proud mountain stands in conscious majesty.
> No time-worn tow'r no chiselled stone is there
> No forest green completes a landscape fair
> Not there the works of art that nature ape
> All, all is nature on her [illegible word] shape.
> Leave then the works of mortal man behind
> Works there superior far to his you find.
> Man formed this pile but that th'almighty nod
> Of God himself—of Man's Creator God.

This prim and dutiful—but undeniably fluent—verse, clearly influenced by later eighteenth-century models, displays equally

this conclusion difficult to accept. The lines are dated 'Jesus College, July 10', and Ffoulkes's second letter is obviously concerned with correcting the impression that the lines were written while Clough was at school in Chester. Clough frequently spent his holidays with his uncle Alfred—some of them in Oxford. The 1831 watermark would seem to support the date I have chosen.

clearly the imprint of Mrs. Clough's pietistic literary values.
Rugby took up, developed, and in many ways complicated, those
values.

It has been argued—notably by James Osborne in his *Arthur
Hugh Clough*[1]—that the Rugby experience, as far as Clough's
life as a poet was concerned, was quite straightforwardly a
crippling one. Usually such a judgement is closely bound up
with preconceptions about poetry which do not and cannot
comprehend Clough's distinctive qualities as a poet. The nature
of the conjunction is made clear in Howard Lowry's assertion
that during his school-days Clough did not have 'sufficient time
for that "wish-thinking" which is the making of the creative artist.
Young Marlowe amid the jewelled pageantry of Canterbury,
Shelley seeking his ghosts within a starlit wood, and Tennyson
listening to the mystical cadences of his own name are without
question nearer to the muse that fires the passion and the sensuousness of verse.'[2] If ghostly dream, wish-thinking, mystical cadence,
and sensuous fire are the only begetters of poetry, Clough is only
doubtfully a poet. His achievement lies elsewhere: Dryden,
Pope, some of Byron, furnish more relevant criteria; and Rugby
can be seen, in effect, as a contributory force directing his service
away from the simple, sensuous, passionate—and triumphantly
post-Romantic—muse celebrated in Lowry's roll of honour.
Similarly, the journal-entry (was it entirely *au sérieux*?) which
figures prominently in the indictment of Rugby, 'Instead of
turning to God last night I wrote a sonnet, and poetized till
10 o'clock. Composed 2 more in bed',[3] should be placed beside
another sentiment, contained in an unpublished letter to Gell,
'It may be rather extravagant but I never sit down to write an
article, except poetry, without feeling very strongly that I am
doing something unfitting and unbecoming.'[4] The oscillation
between guilt at leaving sterner duties unattended and an irrational sense of rightness, indicating as it does a doubleness in
Clough's Rugby-conditioned responses, suggests that the situation was psychologically—as it was from a more purely literary
point of view—more complicated than the charge against Rugby
usually allows. In tethering Clough's mind to present fact and

[1] J. I. Osborne, *Arthur Hugh Clough* (London, 1920), pp. 25–9.
[2] Lowry, p. 9.   [3] Quoted, Lowry, p. 8.
[4] 20 Feb. 1836, Bodleian MS. Eng. Lett. c. 189, fol. 65ᵛ (34).

moral responsibility, in restraining romantic imagination, the
school strengthened the basis of some of his most valuable poetry.
The positive contribution of the Rugby experience is apparent,
however, only when it is conjoined with qualities developed
much later in Clough's life—wit, incisiveness, irony, and flexibility of outlook. In narrower and more obvious ways Rugby
was, unquestionably, an unfortunate influence, fostering qualities
which have notoriously bedevilled Clough's poetry—though
never quite so thoroughly or pervasively as popular misconcep-
tions would believe. Encouraging an earnest, drearily toneless
moralism, encouraging a too-ready confusion between literature
and life, encouraging also a distrust of the necessary artifice of
art, Rugby set him problems as a poet for which he never really
found stable solutions.

Forgivably derivative and only fitfully disclosing an authentic
talent, Clough's Rugby poems are significant mainly as early
documents in his search for an appropriate medium, an appropriate
subject, an appropriate manner. His contributions to the school
magazine reveal a variety of literary influences—Macaulay, for
instance, whose 'fourteeners' in 'The Battle of Ivry' he praised in
a review[1] and imitated in his own 'Count Egmont',[2] and Carlyle,
whose urgently kaleidoscopic narrative-descriptive historical
style he reproduced with some skill in the descriptive prose
passages of a piece entitled 'Two Autumn Days in Athens'.[3] The
dominant, although not very profoundly assimilated, influence
on the poems, however, replacing his earlier models, is that of
Wordsworth and, to a lesser extent, Coleridge.[4] The themes of
alienation and guilt, of the search for and finding of spiritual

---

[1] 'Macaulay's "Battle of Ivry"', Trawick, pp. 29–38.
[2] *The Rugby Magazine*, i (Oct. 1835), 160–2.
[3] Ibid. ii (Nov. 1837), 348–58.
[4] Clough's account of 'Willoughby Moreton's' education as a poet provides
an illuminating footnote: Moreton 'had not . . . been very well reared at first in
the gentle nurture of poetry; he had read Pope's Homer very early, and this
gave him, for a long time, a greater delight in good verse than in real poetry.
But after a while this passed away, in a great measure, and I do not ever remember
to have seen any progress so rapid as that he made in one year. . . . There was
awakened a craving appetite for beauty, which was continually searching for,
and feeding on, the loveliness of outward things' (Trawick, p. 46). Clough
tacitly identifies himself with 'Moreton' in 'Meditations After Fourth Lesson',
The Rugby Magazine, i (Apr. 1836), 398. The attempt to exhibit an adequately
'craving appetite for beauty' accounts for some of the most serious flaws in
Clough's adolescent—and even subsequent—poetry.

health, which figure prominently in the more personal poems, seemed to Clough at this stage of his career to house themselves naturally in the kinds of poetry these men had written—or at least in that poetry as filtered through Rugbeian interpretations.

The Doctor himself approved of both Wordsworth and Cole-ridge—rather more of the former (a close neighbour at Fox How) than of the latter, whose unending speculativeness caused him unease. In 1831 he supplied an Introduction to a volume of selections, *The Poetry of Common Life*, put out particularly for the common man by his friend, Platt, editor of the *Sheffield Courant*. The Introduction is, in effect, a simplified and coarsened version of some of the major arguments in Wordsworth's Preface to the *Lyrical Ballads*. The common man, Arnold believed, was like M. Jourdain: he had 'most certainly been many times in a state of mind completely poetical' and had uttered poetry without being aware of it. Poetical speech was, in fact, the most natural utterance of man; only an accidental tradition had rendered it artificial, had debased it into the idle toy for the rich which men like Cobbett castigated.[1] Arnold's point—like Wordsworth's before him—has an important though indirect bearing on Clough's developed practice as a poet, on his exploitation of 'anti-literary' diction, syntax, idiom, rhythm. The function of poetry, indeed its essence, Arnold went on, was to embody and elicit 'poetical feelings', 'the highest and purest feelings of our nature', to lift us out of 'our common temper . . . which is but too cold, selfish and worldly, [and] altogether unpoetical'.[2] The language of poetry, in Arnold's interpretation, was the linguistic exteriorization of this purified and, above all, non-utilitarian, condition of being. The quickened poetical mind caught at every impression and drew it into sympathetic emotional vibration with its ennobled self, rapidly agglomerative imagery and emotive music being the natural exponent of this heightened receptivity.[3]

Arnold's response to literature was emphatically a moral one, and he kept strict surveillance over the feelings and attitudes he was willing to admit into the canon of the 'poetical'. He asked his pupils to 'note in any common work that they read, such judgements of men and things, and such a tone in speaking of them as [were] manifestly at variance with the Spirit of Christ'.[4]

---

[1] Arnold, *Miscellaneous Works*, pp. 251–2.   [2] Ibid., pp. 252–3.
[3] Ibid., pp. 253–4.   [4] Stanley, op. cit. i. 146.

And we find Clough noting dutifully in the margin of his copy of the *Musae Graecae*: 'It is curious and striking how we find in Ritson's collections of songs an immense number quite as bad as this—and this [illegible word] utterly vile and bad—in a country calling itself Christian.'[1] We have already noticed Arnold's dislike, on moral grounds, for comedy in general, and Aristophanes and Juvenal in particular. How deeply Clough absorbed this moral attitude to literature is seen in the earliest surviving undergraduate essay he wrote at Balliol in 1837. The title of the essay is 'On the Effect of Dramatic Representations on the Taste and Morals of a People'.[2]

[T]hrough the Taste it is principally that the Drama acts on the Morals. . . . It is a great matter to have the Spirit of Utilitarianism and of love for Gain suppressed, and to suppress these there is no fitter engine than Taste. A person capable of entering into the Beauties of any great species of Poetry or of Poetical Art will generally have learnt the lesson that there are better things . . . than railroads and Steam-Engines. And again it is a truth and a most comforting one that the use and cultivation of these faculties, which God has given us, for the perception of Beauty and of Truth not only *can* be sanctified to his Glory but moreover *are of themselves* conducive to the health and well-being of our Spiritual Nature.

The love of beauty and truth—which it is the function of literature to serve—exists both as a province of man's spiritual existence and as an instrument for the enrichment of that existence. Aesthetics and morality combine. A cultivated taste is, ultimately, a cultivated moral sense, and literature, by forming and sustaining that sense, elevates man above selfish 'utilitarian' values. Clough then points out that such functions can be assigned to tragedy only; comedy, viewed from this angle, is an intractable phenomenon hardly 'allowable properly in a Christian land', for it conduces to no good, and 'it seems clear that to any sincere Christian mind the contemplation of his Neighbour's Sin cannot but be painful and therefore cannot be truly laughable'. That, we remember, is the voice of Dr. Arnold. Finally, the essay considers drama as a social instrument: 'Something of the kind [i.e. drama] is doubtless very much needed . . . in the Poorer Classes to present some enjoyment great enough to lead them to prefer it to Drunkenness,

[1] Temple Reading Room, Rugby School. The annotation appears on p. 172.
[2] Trawick, pp. 53–8.

and of such a nature as to elevate them into some moral union
with their richer brethren.'

Another important early critical statement, though of a different
kind, is contained in 'The Exordium of a Very Long Poem'
(*Poems*, 438) which Clough contributed to *The Rugby Magazine*.
The machinery of an 'autumn eve', a 'cloudlet', and the 'gem-
like hues' of a 'beaming moon' shining forth 'in perfect purity
of maiden might' prepares us for the main subject:

> Oh, such art thou, whom long my heart hath known,
>   Nay, rather striven to know,—thus pure and bright
> Thou dwellest in the heaven of holy things,
> Of wise and lofty thoughts, and pure imaginings.
>
> Yea, such thou art, O heaven-born poesy,
>   Such in thy solitary grandeur thou;
> Thy varied face, one orb,—and they to thee,
>   To thy embracing power, all yielding now
> Science and Art, and all the lights that be
>   The lesser lights of Truth and Wisdom. How
> Shall man's weak words approach thy holy place?
> Shall man's weak wits set forth thy centred grace?
>
> Yet, blessed Spirit, yet vouchsafe to take
>   Our thoughts and words to dwell thine orb beside;
> Yet let our earthly souls in that bright wake
>   Still, still with fond and springing rapture ride; . . .

Certainly there seems to be no self-doubt in these ardent platitudes. The purity and comprehensive centrality of feeling as a
sacred essence of wisdom, beauty, and goodness are announced
and celebrated unhesitatingly; the distance marked between the
earthly dross of flesh and intellect and the unalloyed spirituality
of 'Poesy' to which the terrestrial 'soul' aspires is an absolute
one. And yet the deprecating 'very' of the title and the editorial
comment which follows the fragment in the magazine—'The
rest is happily wanting'[1]—place the whole statement in a re-
ductively ironic frame. What we have here, in effect, is an early
example of one kind of critical problem Clough poses. On the
one hand there is often in his critical statements a subscription to current 'official' theory, and on the other, a departure
from that theory in his own practice. This explains, in part, the

[1] *The Rugby Magazine*, i (Apr. 1836), 404.

constantly diffident tone in which he spoke of his own poetry; frequently that poetry is a poetry wrily conscious of its own failure to 'measure up'.

Apart, however, from these sly self-puncturing comments on the 'Exordium' and two boisterously valedictory pieces in the final number of the magazine—one recalling nostalgically the exciting 'botheration' of producing the first issue, the other celebrating the hard-living, morally untroubled giants who inhabited the school before its growth from mythological infancy to adult 'history' under Arnold[1]—Clough's Rugby poetry is totally dedicated to the task of measuring up, of fulfilling its obligations as an agent of social, moral, and aesthetic health within the community, of making conscience and the will of Arnold prevail. He seems to have derived from Coleridge (although his understanding of it was neither subtle nor penetrating) a distinction of considerable importance in his search for a poetic; the distinction, that is, between 'subjective' and 'modern-objective' modes. 'Subjective' poetry was poetry written in the first person, its subject, quite simply and inertly in Clough's interpretation, was the state of the speaker's mind. It was 'equivalent, I believe, to egotistical' and was a product of self-preoccupied individualism.[2] 'Objective' poetry, by contrast, was that 'in which we see nothing of the writer's self, . . . he is but the medium through which we view an object; when the reader is the nominative case of the verb, and the thing told the accusative.' As against the individualistic and isolating 'subjective' mode, objective poetry, whether narrative or dramatic, embodied the 'social and domestic' bonds of Christianity. 'Objective' poetry alone, Clough thought, could raise readers to that 'fearful . . . pitch of excitement' at which 'the more unyielding parts of our nature seem to be melted . . . till they will receive any shape and any impression'. In this kind of poetry the reader became 'the poet, the maker, and creator', as the 'collecting and unifying power of the imagination' was exhibited to and 'infused' into him.[3]

Clearly 'objective' poetry, since it most completely served the poetic cause of the good Rugbeian, demanded Clough's preference.

---

[1] *The Rugby Magazine*, ii (Nov. 1837), 394, and 'Effusions of a School Patriarch', *Poems*, p. 433.

[2] 'Macaulay's "Battle of Ivry"', Trawick, p. 30.

[3] Ibid., pp. 30–1, 32, 35.

He contributed several narrative pieces to the magazine which held up edifying examples of self-immolating virtue. 'Count Egmont', for instance, centred on the hero's noble acceptance of defeat, trial, and death in his patriotic struggle against the treacherous and tyrannical Duke of Alba, and on his willed renunciation of the life he had been tempted to preserve—but at the cost of his followers and his country. In 'Rosabel's Dream',[1] which is obviously imitative of 'Christabel', Clough invented his own fiction instead of relying on the framework of an actual historical event. Despite its general narrative aimlessness and its manifold ineptitudes, the poem is an important reference point in his development. It opens up imaginative, psychological, and moral areas which he revisited over and over again to the very end of his career, and, for all the grotesqueness of its adolescent understanding of sin and purity, its disturbed mixture of erotic fantasy and unbending ethical repressiveness remains his first report on the tangled relationship between monk and libertine which never ceased to fascinate and torment him. The poem is set against a medieval background. The lovely and virtuous Rosabel, 'daughter of the Lord Warden', passes a hectic 'day of pleasure'. Quite what these pleasures are we are not informed; they must, at any rate, have been highly potent. She retires to bed glowing with excitement, her blood awakened, her senses urgent. She is, however, 'Pure from stain of purposed ill, / Though wild fancies came between'. She says her prayers and falls asleep, but is tempted in a dream in which a young man offers her his love—the real temptation being the self-gratification which this love offers. Rosabel awakens in perplexity and distress, and Clough comments:

> She was living, struggling still
> In a world of good and ill,
> And things without or things within
> Had tempted her to grievous sin.

Praying earnestly for God's protection from the sin of living selfishly, the girl once more composes herself to sleep. There is little point in detailing the other dreams—tempting to violence and suicide—which assail her. She resists them successfully, and eventually drifts into tranquil sleep while angelic voices celebrate

---

[1] *The Rugby Magazine,* ii (Nov. 1837), 361–74.

her deliverance through God's grace. What is truly extraordinary about the poem is the intransigent austerity of its ethical judgements. Clough refuses to permit any exemptions from moral responsibility; conscience is sleepless: ' 'Tis ill to choose, though but in dream, / What waking conscience dreads as sin', for even in sleep there is—or should be (although obviously for the schoolboy fantasist there was not in this self-incriminating poem)—a whisper, a faint guiding beam, to 'check the grosser instincts of the soul'. The happiest man, the poem announces, is

> he, whom trials long
> Have armed in God's own surest mail,
> Whom, slumbering on secure and strong,
> No evil visions e'er assail. . . .

Despite his theoretical preferences, however, the bulk of the poetry Clough wrote as a schoolboy is, by his own criteria, 'subjective'. Intensely self-conscious and yet at the same time deeply troubled about the diseases of subjectivism, about the dangerous encouragement of self-pride, egotism, introspection, he sought, notably in the poetry of Wordsworth, some formula by which the self as subject could be legitimized. Wordsworth—and also Dr. Arnold—had taught him to value spontaneous upward-reaching emotion as a cognitive faculty which outstripped the slow and often erring calculations of reason, to prize individual experience and response as offering direct, concrete insights into reality. In his own poetry he took pains to display the validity of such emotions and insights as recollected in didactic tranquillity. Invariably the poems set forth the poet's state of mind in an immaculately edifying light: moral instructiveness sanctioned an otherwise culpable preoccupation with self, didactic containment took on a function analogous to that of narrative externality in the 'objective' poems. Thus, in 'An Incident' (*Poems*, 441), Clough recounted his experiences on an excursion to a 'mighty city', and how his heart, initially full of 'fancies sweet', was clouded by the shoddy and unlovely commercialism he witnessed, how every sight he saw, every word he heard, seemed expressive 'of something bought or something sold'. The experience—and the poem—ends, however, with Wordsworthian reassurance in the sight of a little girl walking along holding her brother's hand, a sight which spoke 'Of home and homely duties meet, / And charities of daily life'. Henceforth, Clough declares, whenever he is distressed by thoughts of man's selfishness he will 'call to mind that little pair'.

The familial and domestic content of this therapeutic image is significant: in one form or another a sense of isolation, exclusion, lack of relationship, appears repeatedly in the poems, often to be mastered only by an exigent resoluteness. 'I watched them from the window' (*Poems*, 437), inspired by the sight from a sick-room window of the Arnold children playing in the garden, is a senti-mental but nevertheless moving confession of loneliness, of Clough's awareness of the geographical distance from his family, of his longing to be back in the warmth of Charleston although he had once believed that 'home' was in England. Such a con-fession could not, of course, be allowed to stand by itself; Clough had to reconsider the poem and 'add on a patch' (*Corr.* i. 8) before it came up to the demanding standards of the magazine.

> But when cold strange looks without, and proud high thoughts
>   within,
> Are weaving round my heart the woof of selfishness and sin,
> When self begins to roll a far, a worse and wider sea
> Of careless and unloving thoughts between those friends and me,
> I will think upon these moments, and call to mind the day
> When I watched them from the window, thy children at their
>   play.   (*Poems*, 438.)

The pious resolve accompanies an expansion of the theme of loneliness to a much more widely disturbed level. The 'cold strange looks without' are double-edged: the 'look' of the other, insensitive and self-absorbed, and one's own 'look' that belongs only to the exterior self. Preoccupation with self progressively widens a gap which is more profoundly isolating than geographical distance. The estranging and misinterpreting look is a recurring token of isolation in Clough's poetry, and even in the relatively small body of his Rugby poems there is at least one other parallel, in 'An Incident', where the spirit quails 'under cold strange glances' in the busy, self-interested streets of the city. A variation, giving a cosmic, metaphysical dimension to alienated guilt, is seen in a sonnet of 1835,[1] which can be compared

---

[1] The fourth of five sonnets under the general title 'The Lunar Microscope', *The Rugby Magazine*, i (Oct. 1835), 172. The sonnet is signed 'Z'. For the identi-fication of 'Z' as Clough see *Corr.* i. 28, 34.

with two passages (Scene II, ll. 54–8 and Scene II A, ll. 1–2) in
Dipsychus:

> O heaven, and thou most loving family
> Of sister stars, whose intermingled light
> From the pure blue home of this most quiet night
> Shineth forth aye in conscious unity!
> Why bend ye thus your kind looks still on me,
> That am a wretch, whose passions' ceaseless fight,
> And gnawing thoughts of self—an inborn blight—
> But vex the warmth of your pure sympathy?
> Mine is no cup for you, blest stars, to pour
> The rich draughts of your sympathies therein;
> It mantled once with all the joys of sin,
> And I have quaffed them; now is nothing more,
> Save only dregs of bitterness; and woe,
> That ever comes when self's brief pleasures go.

The 'Spasmodic' strain which some critics have detected in
Clough's poetry manifests itself as a debased Byronism in this
early instance. The acute sense of impurity is embraced, almost
narcissistically, as a mark of alienated distinction. Concentrated
in 'quaffed', the heavy dramatic posture is maintained through
the opaque and tired richness of a literary and utterly conventional
diction. The stars 'bend' their looks, the 'draughts' are 'rich',
the 'cup' 'mantles' with a Shakespearian echo, and only 'the
dregs of bitterness' are left. One readily forgives the cliché-ridden
turgidness of this metaphysical loneliness in a sixteen-year-
old; in a more mature poet it signalizes serious deficiencies—
and Clough was quite capable of perpetrating such lines in later
life. Just as he never entirely grew out of the sense of the world
and of himself in it which informs these lines, he never entirely
lost the habit of writing up to the notions of the poetic suggested
by the sonnet. But as he grew older and developed his characteristic
strengths of irony and detachment, as he developed a finer and
surer sense of what he could do with the language, he also learned
how to turn his 'Spasmodicism' to deft comic use. The early
scenes of *Dipsychus* provide the most obvious example.

    The most characteristic poem of these years, and the one which
shows Clough most clearly straining after his models, is, perhaps,
the one entitled 'Lines' (*Poems*, 439). It is an exercise in combining
the Wordsworth of 'Resolution and Independence' in the first

section of the poem with the Coleridge of *The Ancient Mariner*
in the second. The scene is set in a quiet country lane on an
evening when

> The leaves were shining all about,
>   You might almost have seen them springing;
> I heard the cuckoo's simple shout,
>   And all the little birds were singing. . . .

But for some reason the poet cannot participate in the surrounding simplicity and joy.

> My eyes could see, my ears could hear,
>   Only my heart, it would not feel.

The sensed distance between the inert self and the external world
worries the mind into a search for its cause, and, inevitably, the
poet concludes that he 'must have done some sin'. For Nature is
the Holy Book of God, and those who have 'gazed, and read her
lessons high' of human love and sympathy, can tell, because of
their heightened moral sense,

> When aught has gone amiss within,
> When the mind is not sound and well,
>   Nor the soul free from taint of sin.
> For as God's Spirit from above,
>   So Beauty is to them below,
> And when they slight that holy love,
>   Their hearts that presence may not know.

In the second section the poet turns homeward, 'A guilty thing
and full of shame', when suddenly there comes to him

> . . . the thought of one
> Who on his bed of sickness lay,
> Whilst I beneath the setting sun
> Was dreaming this sweet hour away; . . .

Immediately the truancy is acknowledged the well of sympathy
begins to flow and the burden falls away, albatross-like; the poet
feels 'in truth again / The lovely things that stood before', and
can return home 'More soft and good than when [he] came'.

The poem is interesting because it suggests, both in the explicitness of its statement and in its artistic failure, some of the major
problems Clough faced as a poet: on the one hand a sense of guilt

usable in romantic manner, and on the other a most unromantically precise location of the source and nature of that guilt. The down-to-earthness which a Rugby training only emphasized, coupled with the generalized quality of the language, pulls heavily against any deeply, richly, and precisely imagined notation of the psychological and spiritual situation. The attempt at such a notation results only in the histrionic excess of 'a guilty thing and full of shame', and in the strained perfunctoriness of the last few lines, which with ludicrous deliberateness invite comparison with the disburdening of the Ancient Mariner's guilt (cf. *Corr*. i. 40). This is, quite simply, a reach-me-down poetry, assiduously assembling its platitudes—of language, of feeling, of moral insight. If Clough was to make any significant contribution he would have to choose other masters or break out on his own.

CHAPTER II

Oxford: Balliol, 1837–1841

I. WARD AND THE OXFORD MOVEMENT

IN July 1833 John Keble preached the momentous Assize Sermon on 'National Apostasy' which John Newman was to look back on as the real starting-point of the Oxford Movement. Just over four years later Clough came up to Balliol to begin his career as an undergraduate. In that interval the Movement, which arrayed some of the most remarkable minds of the time under the militant banners of the *via media*, of a Church Catholic, Apostolical, Authoritative, Sacramental, anti-Erastian, and authentically Anglican, had imposed itself firmly on the intellectual and spiritual life of the University. Oxford, as the centre of the upheaval which was for some years to continue to convulse the religious life of the country, was in a state of theological war. Pamphlets were written, charges and counter-charges laid, authorities appealed to. It seemed impossible for anyone, if he was at all serious-minded, to escape the questions which were discussed so earnestly or disputed so fiercely on every side. It seemed a time for standing up and being counted. In his classic account of the Oxford Movement Dean Church recalled the years immediately prior to Clough's arrival at Balliol:

It is hardly too much to say that wherever men spoke seriously of the grounds and prospects of religion, in Oxford . . . the 'Tractarian' doctrines, whether assented to or laughed at, deplored or fiercely denounced, were sure to come to the front. All subjects in discussion seemed to lead up to them—art and poetry, Gothic architecture and German romance and painting, the philosophy of language, and the novels of Walter Scott and Miss Austen, Coleridge's transcendentalism and Bishop Butler's practical wisdom, Plato's ideas and Aristotle's analysis.[1]

John Campbell Shairp, later a close friend of Clough's, came up to Balliol in 1840 as Snell Exhibitioner from Glasgow. He noticed

[1] R. W. Church, *The Oxford Movement: Twelve Years, 1833–1845* (London, 1891), p. 159.

little change. The newcomer, he observed, soon realized that only the oldest members of the University—Heads of Houses and Senior Tutors—and the youngest and most unserious under-graduates appeared to be unaffected. 'But the great body that lay between these extremes, that is, most of the younger fellows of colleges, and most of the scholars and elder undergraduates, at least those of them who read or thought at all, were in some way or other busy with the new questions.'[1] In February of the year after Shairp came up—and three months before Clough went into the Schools—Newman published his celebrated *Tract XC*, which precipitated the most serious crisis the Oxford Move-ment had so far experienced. Roman Catholics, Newman argued, in an attempt to show the insufficiency of existing formularies in defining an Anglican position, could subscribe in perfectly good faith to all of the Thirty-Nine Articles, except the one which pertained directly to the Bishop of Rome. Oxford hummed with excitement; an outraged orthodoxy quickly put the wheels of retribution in motion; the Bishop of Oxford re-proved Newman, and the Tracts—hitherto the main evangelizing weaponry of the Movement—were discontinued. The Examina-tions, of course, went on as usual, and Clough, whose reputation for brilliance was awesome, set a new record. He was the first Scholar of Balliol to fail to get a First.

Interpretations of Clough's career have been dominated by what might be called the catastrophic theory of his experience as an undergraduate.[2] The antagonism between Arnold's Rugby and Newman's Oxford is seen as offering a major clue to the nature of his intellectual and spiritual difficulties and to the causes of his 'failure'. The Tractarian attack, it is argued, was utterly demoraliz-ing. It destroyed his Arnoldian faith but failed to provide a

---

[1] J. C. Shairp, 'John Keble', *Studies in Poetry and Philosophy* (Edinburgh, 1868), p. 270.

[2] The most important single source of this interpretation, and one which has influenced subsequent writers, is the letter of reminiscences which William Ward sent to Mrs. Clough after her husband's death. See Wilfrid Ward, *William George Ward and the Oxford Movement* (London, 1889), pp. 108–10. Parts of this letter appear in *PPR* i. 13–14, 17–19. The interpretation was first challenged, briefly but sharply, by A. W. Benn in *The History of English Rationalism in the Nineteenth Century*, 2 vols. (London, 1906), ii. 47. It was first examined critically, carefully, and extremely ably, however, by R. M. Gollin in 'Arthur Hugh Clough's Formative Years, 1819–1841' (unpublished Ph.D. dissertation, University of Minnesota, 1959).

positive substitute. Between them Newman and William Ward lured him into the deserts of religious controversy and speculation, and left him there, an exhausted, perplexed, and vacillating wanderer to the end of his days. Incidentally, the distractions of Tractarianism also cost him his certain First. The charges against the Oxford Movement are certainly comprehensive and they have had at least two important effects on Clough's reputation. On the one hand, they have ensured for him and his quality of doubt an impeccably laundered respectability—after all, what could be more high-minded, more spotlessly engendered, than perplexities which sprang from such sources? On the other, they have made of him a major casualty in what now seems a minor engagement in the intellectual and spiritual warfare of the nineteenth century. Clough has, in other words, been rendered quaint at best, dull and marginal at worst.

The letters Clough wrote as an undergraduate offer no firm and unmistakable corroboration of this traditional reading of the Balliol years. The poems, too, while they reveal a profound unsettlement, anxiety, guilt, and even exhaustion of spirit, provide no finally reliable support. The evidence, then, is almost wholly external, consisting of the testimony—often by way of hearsay, conjecture, and imputation—of friends and associates, some of whom (like William Ward and Tom Arnold) were themselves seriously affected by the Oxford Movement. Further, as in the case of Ward most obviously, many of these men were calling up memories which floated in a void of lapsed acquaintance. They had no recent knowledge of Clough, no close acquaintance with his later life and work, by which to interpret their recollections. And yet their testimony was accepted.

To call the evidence in question is not, of course, to reject it entirely, or maintain that the Oxford Movement had no impact on Clough. It did. The question, rather, is whether that impact was as catastrophic as it has been made out to be, or whether, in fact, a positive, individual direction did not emerge out of the confrontation between Arnoldism and Tractarianism. Necessarily that question can be answered fully only in the context of his career as a whole.

★   ★   ★

Dr. Arnold's view of the Oxford Movement was clear. Ardently devoted to a practical, non-speculative Christianity,

absolutely convinced of the existence of 'general' Christian
principles which could unite all Protestants, he could see no
possible relevance in a movement so thoroughly committed to
sacerdotalism, so intent on resurrecting and multiplying doctrinal
points, and—as far as he could make out—so completely heedless
of the larger problems of society. He had abused it with energy
in the *Edinburgh Review*.

[T]he fanaticism of the English High Churchman has been the fanaticism of mere foolery. A dress, a ritual, a name, a ceremony;—a
technical phraseology;—the superstition of a priesthood, without its
power;—the form of Episcopal government without its substance;—
a system imperfect and paralysed, not independent, not sovereign,
—afraid to cast off the subjection against which it is perpetually murmuring. Such are the objects of High Church fanaticism—objects so
pitiful, that, if gained ever so completely, they would make no man
the wiser or the better,—they would lead to no good, intellectual,
moral, or spiritual—to no effect, social or religious, except to the
changing of sense into silliness, and holiness of heart and life into
formality and hypocrisy.[1]

Clough, although he shared his master's liberal sympathies,
was open-minded enough—even while he was at Rugby—to
regret that this ill-tempered and unfair article had ever been
written (*Corr.* i. 47). He came up to Balliol, then, as an avowed
but not totally uncritical champion of Arnoldism.

Almost immediately on his entry into Oxford he was snapped
up into the dialectical jaws of William Ward, Fellow and mathematical Tutor of Balliol, and one of the most prominent 'per-
sonalities' in the University. Large, ungainly, untidy, with the
awkward and floppily charming enthusiasm of a Newfoundland
dog,[2] Ward was, visually, an engaging and unmistakable if not
beautiful feature of the University scene. The daring paradoxes
he tossed out, his wit, his brilliant intellect, made him one of the
most talked-about men in his generation. An unrivalled logician,
endowed with an almost grotesquely developed faculty for abstract speculation, 'he had round him perpetually', in the words
of Church,

[1] T. Arnold, 'The Oxford Malignants and Dr. Hampden', *Edinburgh Review*,
lxiii (Apr. 1836), 235.
[2] Cf. Jowett to Stanley, 'You like him as you like a Newfoundland dog. He
is such a large, jolly, shaggy creature.' E. Abbott and L. Campbell, *The Life
and Letters of Benjamin Jowett*, 2 vols. (London, 1897), i, 80 n.

some of the cleverest and brightest scholars and thinkers of the place; and where he was, there was debate, cross-questioning, pushing inferences, starting alarming problems, beating out ideas, trying the stuff and mettle of mental capacity. Not always with real knowledge, or a real sense of fact, but always rapid and impetuous, taking in the whole dialectical chessboard at a glance, he gave no quarter, and a man found himself in a perilous corner before he perceived the drift of the game. . . .[1]

This elephantiasis of abstract speculation unsupported by wide scholarship, his ignorance particularly of history and of its relevance to the religious and theological subjects on which he delighted to exercise his powers, made him, intellectually, something of a splendid throwback. As Church observed, 'If the old scholastic disputations had been still in use at Oxford, his triumphs would have been signal and memorable.'[2]

In his earlier life an avid reader of Jeremy Bentham and James Mill, Ward, in his middle twenties in 1837, had come to be an admirer of Thomas Arnold, finding satisfaction in the latter's union of intellectual independence and high morality. Admiration for their master made him seek out the outstanding Rugby boys in Oxford, and he found them congenial in their own right—independent flesh-and-blood embodiments of their master's teaching. Before he came to know Clough there was Stanley, in whose company, overcoming his repugnance to Tractarian doctrine, he first heard Newman preach. It was with Stanley, too, that he went to the great man's theological lectures in Adam de Brome's Chapel. This was a major turning-point in his life; his mind started to probe at the basis of Arnoldian religion and slowly the fissures and inconsistencies in that foundation were revealed. Arnoldism was characterized, in Ward's view, by its rejection of authority in religion in favour of free inquiry and independent judgement. Yet such independent inquiry, if pushed to its logical conclusion, would end in the horror of no-religion, and Arnoldism was forced, in order to save itself, to turn against its own logic and check the process of inquiry at certain basic points of Christian doctrine. Increasingly dissatisfied with Arnold's brand of Christianity, Ward hurried off to Rugby and badgered the poor Doctor, tired after a hard day's work, with his pitiless logic, and left him to a restless and feverish bed: his questions,

---

[1] Church, op. cit., p. 298.   [2] Loc. cit.

he thought, had been unanswerable.[1] The purely personal
character of Arnold's system weighed most heavily on Ward: it
was Arnoldism rather than Christianity.[2] The future direction of
his religious search followed with the precision of one of his
syllogisms: if atheism was the logical outcome of the free intellect,
refuge lay in the arms of Authority: the voice of Newman was
in his ears. In 1838—Clough's second year at Oxford—he joined
the Movement, and soon became its most unmanageable passenger. The older members did not take kindly to the 'huge
young cuckoo' who sprawled so untidily across the achieved
pattern and for a time divided the leadership. The *enfant terrible*
of the party',[3] his remorseless, goading logic precipitated Newman
and his associates into unprepared positions which they themselves would have preferred to feel their way towards tentatively,
one step at a time. Once accepting the principle of Authority and
Dogma, Ward, the future Ultramontane, was led—by ineluctable
process of logic—to a growing realization of the hazy, unsatisfying, anomalous, and schismatic position of the Anglican Church;
true religious rest and truth lay in the plenitude of doctrine:
the Romeward drift was under way. If Ward's private pushing of
conclusions was disturbing, his reckless public championing of
the cause was embarrassing and, finally, disastrous. In 1841 he
capped the furore caused by *Tract XC* with an aggressive pamphlet in its defence,[4] which resulted in his being deprived of his
Balliol Tutorship. Complete disaster, leaving the whole Movement
disorganized and bewildered, struck in 1845, when the gage he had
recklessly thrown down before the authorities, in *The Ideal of a
Christian Church*, was taken up.[5] On 13 February, at an electric
meeting of Convocation in the Sheldonian Theatre, which
culminated weeks of tense activity on either side, his book was
condemned and he was stripped of his University degrees. Later

[1] For an account of the meeting see Wilfrid Ward, op. cit., pp. 78–9.

[2] Ibid., p. 90. William Ward, 'Arnold's *Sermons*', *British Critic*, xxx (Oct.
1841), 298–364.

[3] 'Huge young cuckoo' and '*enfant terrible* of the party'—Wilfred Ward,
op. cit., pp. 218, 217.

[4] W. G. Ward, *Appendix to a Few More Words in Support of the Tracts for the
Times, in Answer to Mr. Lowe's Pamphlet* (Oxford, 1841).

[5] Ward's challenge was most blatant in the paragraph in which he wrote:
'Three years have passed, since I said plainly, that in subscribing the Articles
I renounce no one Roman Doctrine: yet I retain my Fellowship which I hold
on the tenure of subscription and have received no Ecclesiastical censure in any
shape.' *The Ideal of a Christian Church in Comparison with Existing Practice*, 2nd
edn. (London, 1844), p. 567.

that year he became a convert to Roman Catholicism—a step taken by Newman himself shortly after.

It was during the period of transition, while painfully sloughing off Arnoldian liberalism and growing into Newmanism, that Ward struck up his friendship with Clough, and, on Lake's evidence, the extent to which he 'absorbed' the youth, with whom he became even more intimate than he had been with Stanley, was resented by Clough's friends.[1] Eager and impressionable, Clough must have found it flattering to be singled out by one of the most outstanding men in the University, and initially, at least, it is quite possible that Ward's disintegrating logic had a paralysing effect. But although he continued to see a great deal of Ward (Lake remembered their almost 'daily' after-lunch walks, which continued till 1841),[2] gradually it became clear to him that what he should be defending against Ward's insistent syllogisms was not Dr. Arnold but himself—and, whatever of Arnold he had really absorbed, that the assertion of his own distinctive personality was his only secure defence, that only by an independent search for truth could he see his way between conflicting claims and opposing loyalties.

Rarely, if ever, did Clough and Ward argue on the same intellectual plane. Intellectually they were differently constituted and in that difference lay Clough's most effective defence. 'Ward was always trying', he is reported to have said, 'to put me on the horns of a dilemma; but somehow I generally managed to get over the wall.'[3] A clue to his methods is provided by Ward's own description of Clough's mind: 'Intellectually, he struck me as possessing very unusual independence and . . . straightforwardness of thought. He was never taken in with shams, pretences, and traditions, but saw at once below the surface. On the other hand, he was perhaps less remarkable for logical consecutiveness.'[4] As Bagehot observed of Clough, 'He had by nature . . . an exceedingly real mind. . . . The actual visible world exercised over him a compulsory influence. . . . He could not dissolve the world into credible ideas and then believe those ideas. . . .'[5] Clough's

---

[1] Wilfrid Ward, op. cit., p. 425.

[2] K. Lake, ed., *Memorials of William Charles Lake, Dean of Durham* (London, 1901), p. 26.

[3] Wilfrid Ward, op. cit., p. 111.   [4] Ibid., p. 109.

[5] W. Bagehot, review of Clough, *Poems* (1862), in *National Review*, xv (Oct. 1862), 314–15.

comment on Coleridge in a letter written in 1841 throws an interesting sidelight on the intellectual difference between pupil and Tutor:

I should like much to have heard Carlyle's complaints against Coleridge. I keep wavering between admiration of his exceedingly great perceptive and analytical power and other wonderful points and inclination to turn away altogether from a man who has so great a lack of all reality and actuality (*Corr.* i. 106).

In another letter, written two years earlier, he had said:

Lake's Newmanistic tendencies are, I am afraid, as certain if not as strong as you represent. *He is so determined on having a conscious system* that these tendencies are, I think, not unnatural. I hope you do not think me much perverted. My resistance, when there is occasion for it against proselytizers, is of the most vague, unsystematic kind, resting in the most unstable way on intuitions, idealities, etc., etc. (*Corr.* i. 98, my italics).

The compulsory hold on his mind of the actual three-dimensional world was too powerful for any reduction to formulable system, and his response to Ward's water-tight logic was not merely an escape into the a-logical; it was a counter-assertion. The unshaped truth delivered on the pulses and intuited by conscience was more real, carried more force, than rational symmetry.

After a period of intense and sympathetic discussion and examination, his reaction to the theological, doctrinal, and intellectual aspects of Tractarianism was one of increasing resistance, and finally of bitter impatience. The first extended discussion of this side of the Movement is in a letter to Gell written towards the end of his first academic year at Oxford. To his correspondent, brought up in an Evangelical home, he wrote:

One thing I suppose is clear—that one must leave the discussion of τὰ Νεανθρωπικά κ.τ.λ. all snug and quiet for after one's degree. And it is no harm but rather good to give oneself up a little to hearing Oxford people, and admiring their good points, which lie, I suppose, principally in all they hold in opposition to the Evangelical portion of society—the benefit and beauty and necessity of forms—the ugliness of feelings put on unnaturally soon and consequently kept up by artificial means, ever strained and never sober. I should think very likely too their Anti-Calvinistic Views of Justification were very, if not just, at least useful to lead us to the Truth. I should be very sorry ever to be brought to believe their further views of matter acting on morals as a charm of sacramentalism, and their succession-notion so closely connected with it. All this, and their way of reading and considering Scripture—such a contrast to the German fashions—rests I suppose entirely on their belief in the Infallibility of the Church down to a certain period, to which they are led by a strong sense of the necessity of some infallible authority united with a feeling of the insufficiency of the New Testament. Indeed I think a good deal of what they say as to this latter point is stronger than anything I ever heard against it. Newman is now giving lectures on the Mystical Power of the Sacraments and seems to have stated the objections to it Scripturally in a very fair and candid manner (*Corr.* i. 71–2).

Obviously, behind this attempt at a judicious placing of himself in relation to the newly encountered doctrines there was an extensive background of discussion and examination, shot through with a nagging consciousness of a dereliction of his immediate duties as a student, duties he owed to Arnold, to Rugby, and to himself as a favourite son of Rugby. Tractarian airs had blown strongly through this young mind, challenging its preconceptions and intimating to it the existence of problems and viewpoints which Rugby had never suggested. But the extraordinary circumspectness of the letter is significant: whatever else he might do, Clough was not going to let himself be stampeded out of his fair-mindedness. It was this fair-minded openness, finally, which was to issue in his characteristic 'faith'. Instead of drawing doctrinal lines more closely round him, it encouraged him to broaden the basis of his faith even more liberally than Dr. Arnold had done.

The intensity of discussion in the University was exhilarating for Clough only in so far as it was free-ranging; he had very little time for the bulk of Newmanistic undergraduates and their narrow interests and sympathies; it was, largely, the range as well as the searchingness of Ward's conversation that attracted him. Comparing Oxford with Cambridge, he wrote:

There is I suppose no doubt much more interest in such matters (theological, ecclesiastical, political etc., etc.) here than with you, though the society Stanley sees is much the most *enquiring* at any rate on them of any in Oxford and it is not a very large set. The Newmanistic undergraduates mostly shut their ears and call it blasphemy, but not quite universally; and of course they, though they will not listen to anything else, have a scheme of Church Government etc. which they uphold, not to say anything about understanding or appreciating it. If you were to come here . . . you would at once have Ward at you asking you your opinions on every possible subject of this kind you can enumerate, beginning with Covent Garden and Macready and certainly not ending till you got to the question of the Moral Sense and Deontology (*Corr.* i. 85).

Progressively, however, discussion hardened round specific and narrow theological issues choking this freedom and range of inquiry, and Clough yearned for respite from this aspect of life in what he called, early in 1839, 'the Seat and Citadel of Orthodoxy' (*Corr.* i. 88). By October of that year desire for respite had turned into anxious longing. 'I only hope', he wrote to Simpkinson, 'to escape the vortex of Philosophism and Discussion, (whereof Ward is the Centre), as it is the most exhausting exercise in the world; and I assure you I quite makarize you at Cambridge for your liberty from it. It seems to have a different effect on Stanley and Lake, but I do not think it can be wholly beneficial to anyone. The contrast of home is great' (*Corr.* i. 97). Early the next year the University's seemingly exclusive, claustrophobic preoccupation evoked the exhausted comment, 'Oxford is of course as usual replete with Newmanism and Newmanistic gossip, from which it is one blessing for you that you are preserved' (*Corr.* i. 100).

The threat posed by Ward was not, however, simply an intellectual one. Whatever some of his acquaintances may have occasionally been tempted to think, Ward was not a pure logic-machine. His vivacious conversation, the zest with which he lived out his untidily heaped enthusiasms for music, sermons, opera, mathematics, the theatre, concealed a lonely, morbidly sensitive man, who was so unsure of any affection that he reacted with a pathetic, even ludicrous, eagerness to the smallest show of consideration.[1] Depression and ill health frequently overlaid his sunny extravagance, leaving a restless and darkened mind grinding on its own self-doubts. He turned to Clough, not as any Tutor might to an exceptional pupil, but as a friend, a soul-mate, who would satisfy his own emotional hungers. As he later confessed, with the single exception of Newman, he was not as strongly attracted or attached to any of his Oxford friends as he was to

---

[1] Wilfrid Ward, op. cit., pp. 37-8, 135.

Clough.[1] That Clough responded encouragingly during his first year is evident from the intimate and relaxed tone of the first surviving letter from Ward, dated July 1838. 'I never got on nearly so well in writing to anybody as to you', he confided touchingly (*Corr*. i. 76). But even while Ward was writing that letter Clough seems to have had misgivings about the relationship and the emotional demands Ward was making. For one thing, his native reserve shied away from the uncurbed expressions of affection in his Tutor's letters. His Oxford journals reveal an almost despairing uncertainty as to how to react to these demands: on the one hand, he felt obliged to respect Ward's emotional needs—particularly since he had himself been so heedlessly responsive, on the other, he felt threatened by Ward's invasion. His immediate reaction, to surmise from Ward's letter of 23 July 1838 (*Corr*. i. 80–3), was to send short, impersonal notes to his Tutor, from whom he had been separated by the Long Vacation, confining himself mainly to neutral subjects; it was the impersonality of these letters rather than 'the absence of warm expressions' which Ward found most galling and depressing.

If my reading of them is correct, these two letters of Ward's shed a significant light on the extent to which Clough—at least in the opinion of his Tutor—was attracted to Newmanism in the course of his first year at Oxford. In the first, after praising the Newmanists and recommending some of the articles and reviews which had appeared in the *British Critic*, Ward wrote: 'I have actually not yet written to [Capes?]; I have been so afraid of the annoyance I shall cause him by my vacillation (not yet to call it change)' (*Corr*. i. 76). In the second he observed,

> As to my 'change', I thought I had not used the word; I generally say 'vacillation', which is true to a certain extent of you I think as well as of me. I cordially concur in all that you say of acting up to your present 'instincts' and letting things take their course; though at my age and circumstances I am perhaps called on to do rather more than that. Any way I fully trust I may not 'change' if at all, till you are prepared to do so too. At the same time with me the current is decidedly setting towards Newmanism at present (*Corr*. i. 81).

He went on in this letter to urge the strength of the Newmanistic position as against the Protestant and Arnoldian, both in point of

---

[1] Ibid., pp. 105, 108.

doctrine and as productive of higher holiness. In a few months he openly avowed his adhesion to Newman's cause. It is more than probable that the 'vacillation' and the expected 'change' refer to a vague hope of a joint conversion. Obviously, Ward interpreted Clough's position—with what exact justification it is impossible to say—as a very strong sympathy verging on complete adherence to Tractarianism.

After this first Long Vacation the intimacy between the two continued, perhaps in somewhat maimed fashion, for another term, but sometime during the following Christmas Vacation Clough must have imposed a drastically unambiguous check on it, thus calling forth the close-packed and jealous anguish of Ward's letter of 4 January 1839 (*Corr.* i. 86–8). This pathetic document, in which Ward admitted his affection, his dependence, and his need, and tried to salvage the relationship through an attempted extraction of elaborate promises and resolutions, is too important to quote from selectively, and should be read in its entirety. The letter, in which the distinguishing line between *agape* and *eros* seems remarkably faint, needs to be approached with caution. Whatever our conclusions about its ambiguousness, the letter by any account remains a crucial document in an abnormally highly charged relationship. Clough's association with Ward probably never recovered its original intimacy after this, but the two continued to see a great deal of each other. Neither did their relationship dwindle immediately into a purely formal one; the two were on holiday together in the Lake District in the summer of 1839 and again in that following; and, as the Oxford journals show, although Clough was always uneasy and self-mistrusting about his dealings with his Tutor, about creating false impressions and affections, he often spent hours on end with him.

Not unnaturally, the unbiased attention Clough attempted to give Tractarian claims resulted in a sensitiveness about his reputation at Rugby. Anxiety about the reactions of the school to his attitude towards the Newmanists mingled with irritation at the categorizations that tended to be imposed on persons trying to act freely and independently between two conflicting camps. Early in 1839 (after the severe strain of the crisis in his intimacy with Ward) his bitterness expressed itself as a faint edge in a letter to Gell: 'Among other incidents I have had the pleasure of twice meeting the heresiarch αὐτότατος, namely John Henry Newman, once at a dinner party, and once at a small and select breakfast d[itt]o. I was introduced, and had the honour of drinking wine with him: on the strength of all of which of course, as is one's bounden duty, I must turn Newmanist' (*Corr.* i. 88). After one of his visits to his old school he wrote to Gell: 'I found that at Rugby I had been quite set down among theological gossips as a Newmanist; but the impression was pretty well removed by the time I came away' (*Corr.* i. 90). In the opinion of his more detached correspondent in Cambridge, he was becoming too sensitive. 'I hope you will be able to judge more correctly', Gell wrote, 'of your intellectual than of your theological state, for in spite of your assertions, the impression at Rugby was by no means uncommon that you were no better a Newmanite than you should be' (*Corr.* i. 90 n.).

There was one aspect of the Oxford Movement, however, to which Clough along with Ward reacted with complete admiration, its ethical and moral idealism. According to Dean Boyle, both Stanley and Clough declared that 'the grip which Newman seemed to get on the conscience, was greater even than that of their master Arnold'.[1] The scrupulous Rugby-inherited morality found in this aspect of the Movement an opening out to an ampler, holier, more sanctified, severer ideal. The first mention at any length of the Tractarians in Clough's correspondence, although it still declares his Rugbeian enmity, refers in admiring terms to the quality of their lives and the change wrought in Oxford preciosity by their activity (cf. *Corr.* i. 67). Three months later he read Hurrell Froude's *Remains*, which reminded him of Henry Martyn's *Journals*—both records of the rigorous disciplining of the refractory self, but from diametrically opposed points of the doctrinal spectrum. He found them, he said, 'the most instructive books [he] ever read each in their way'.[2] In Passion Week of the same year (1838) he noted in his journal:

I must keep in mind . . . that many of the most advanced piety and goodness are this week engaged in all sorts of self-denial, and mortification—fasting from food and sleep, amusement and society—Newman for instance, whose errors as we believe them to be must not make

---

[1] G. D. Boyle, *The Recollections of the Very Reverend G. D. Boyle, Dean of Salisbury* (London, 1895), p. 75.

[2] *Corr.* i. 69. *The Journals and Letters* of Henry Martyn, a disciple of Simeon, were edited by S. Wilberforce and published in 1837.

me ever forget how far he is above me in goodness and piety, and wisdom too—tho' in certain points we with less power may by our own advantages be nearer to real truth, and though less wise have more wisdom.[1]

Issuing from their rooted conviction of man's sinfulness and their commitment to an uncompromising sanctity, the ideal of ascetic self-repression in thought, word, and deed that marked these Oxford men, that informed, indeed, and distinguished the whole presence and bearing of a man like John Newman, was an ideal that Clough came into intimate contact with in the person of Ward, beneath whose easy-going and affable buffoonery lay a hard core of self-denying impulse. Froude's *Remains* had been a turning-point in Ward's life.[2] He was attracted to Rugby men largely because of their moral idealism, the conviction of greater sanctity in Newman's way of life was one of the most powerful levers in his conversion from Arnoldism, and a similar attraction to the ascetic record of Roman Catholic hagiology influenced his further conversion. Much of his conversation with Clough was devoted to the question of 'Practical Christianity' and its realization in their own lives. In his letter of 23 July 1838 he wrote to Clough, after discussing the theological strengths of Newmanism and its attractiveness 'as productive of higher holiness',

I wish you especially to write me word if you have changed at all upon matters of practical Xtianity, if you understand me, (e.g. enjoyments and self-denial); they are quite 'instincts' with me by this time and I am as confident of their truth as of the truth of Xtianity itself. . . . I was very glad to find Vaughan apparently fully agreeing in my warm praise of that whole phase of Newmanism (*Corr.* i. 82).

'Purity of intention', according to his son, was the primary value Ward placed before his pupils, teaching them to 'view success in the schools or even in the career each had chosen for life, as quite secondary in comparison with elevating and purifying the character'.[3] Clough responded to this call to unworldliness, Ward thought, with an enthusiasm which even he found exceptional. 'The notion of preparing himself for success in a worldly career was so far from prominent in his mind', he wrote to his former pupil's widow, 'that he might, with some plausibility,

[1] Quoted, Lowry, p. 14.   [2] Wilfrid Ward, op. cit., p. 84.
[3] Ibid., p. 102.

have been accused of not thinking about it enough. But his one idea seemed always to be that he should to-day do to-day's duty, and for the rest leave himself in God's hands. And, as to unselfishness, his self-abnegating consideration for others may be called in the best sense feminine.'[1]

Stimulated by the ethos of the Oxford Movement and nurtured by the personal contact with Ward, the ethical basis of Clough's personality was offered every opportunity of developing naturally and uninterruptedly. To observers his way of life could seem forbiddingly monkish. He lived in cold, fireless rooms in Balliol— 'an excellent plan for keeping out visitors', he is said to have declared.[2] In 1840 (the year before he finally went into the Schools) he moved to lodgings in Holywell, where after a cold bathe every morning he used to read hard all day.[3] Ward remembered that he 'very much abstained from general society', particularly in his later years. 'The opinion', Ward wrote, 'both of tutors and undergraduates undoubtedly was that there was an unusual degree of reserve in his demeanour which prevented them from understanding him; but they all—certainly all the tutors, and, I believe, all the undergraduates—greatly appreciated his singularly high principle and his exemplary spotlessness of life.'[4] Possibly Ward's unwavering preoccupation with the religious difficulties he imputed to Clough renders the chiaroscuro more dramatic than it really was. It is likely, as other evidence suggests, that Clough's conscientiousness was not quite so spartan or so dutiful. But the reputation for asceticism and reserve are important: his withdrawal into silence and austerity was part of his response to, as well as a symptom of, his struggle. He was driving in on himself in his search for a stable self, a clear value, an authentic response, trying to find in himself a solution for warring loyalties and a validation of his choices.

Within the austere limits of his self-isolating reserve he found support in one aspect of Tractarianism which continued and sustained Dr. Arnold's teaching. Influenced by Butler's insistence on the claims of conscience, Newman and his associates asserted the absolute epistemological validity of this organ; through it the spirit within recognized the spirit without. 'Even philosophers, who have been antagonists on other points,' Newman wrote in

[1] Ibid., p. 108.   [2] *PPR* i. 17.   [3] Ibid. 19.
[4] Wilfrid Ward, op. cit., p. 110.

the *Grammar of Assent*, 'agree in recognising the inward voice of that solemn Monitor, personal, peremptory, unargumentative, irresponsible, minatory, definitive.'[1] Ward maintained that 'knowledge of phenomena is obtained by the intellect, knowledge of realities by the conscience.'[2] Clough could accept these men's recognition of the noumenon and their placing of conscience; their further claim, that this inward voice called in unmistakable notes to the authority of the Church, he could not accept: Arnoldian historicism had taught him to be more self-reliant. The place of the individual conscience and the extent of its reliability as a guide to life became in later years, although he never entirely lost his confidence in it, a subject for examination; in the melting-pot of his Balliol years he was too involved in the struggle, too puzzled by his own difficulties, for such scrutiny.

The essays Clough wrote as an undergraduate offer some important insights into his responses to his own developing experience over these years. Broad and general discussions, they reveal his thoughts on such topics as the place of knowledge, the duties of youth, the problem of action. In the light of his own lapse from Rugbeian grace they provide a crucial commentary. The ethical frame is never absent from these essays, and the moral and spiritual norms are unquestioningly Christian ones. As he wrote in an essay on 'Aristotle's View of the Virtues in *Ethics IV*,' 'It were hardly to be expected that a full and duly balanced View of the Virtues should be found in the pages of any heathen Moralist'—the main reason being the absence in Aristotle of the one essential corrective to any estimate of human virtues, 'a due sense of the corruption and continual sinfulness of our Nature'.[3] That sense of sinful, fallen human nature is the continuous basis of the mind revealed in these essays. The essays show a development away from facile moralizing (the first three essays in his first year, for instance, end with scriptural tags and references dragged in by their heels to cap the argument);[4] they show, within a broad Christian framework, a progressive

---

[1] J. H. Newman, *An Essay in Aid of the Grammar of Assent*, ed. C. F. Harrold (new edn., New York, 1947), p. 93.

[2] Wilfrid Ward, op. cit., p. 258.

[3] Bodleian MS. Eng. Misc. d. 513, fols. 41, 42ᵛ.

[4] 'If the salt have lost its savour . . .'; 'I will have mercy, and not sacrifice . . .'; the third essay, on 'Venice', ends by adducing the parable of the unjust steward.

loss of certainty on stable, ultimately reliable and sufficient moral values—an uncertainty most clearly revealed in his treatment of action; but the rooted awareness of his own participation in Christian guilt is unshaken throughout.

The second essay in the 1837–8 collection deals with the effects on literature of the invention of printing, and it concludes, breaking away from the Arnoldian moral bias, by advocating the worth of knowledge in and for itself, and asserting the value of the search for truth, independent of any practical consequences or secondary advantages. The spread of printing has, in Clough's opinion, been accompanied by enormous advantages, but it has also

. . . led to an overweening an dunworthy attention to physics, and a habit of asking in every kind of study what is the use of it? As if the Knowledge of Truth and the Possession of the Power of obtaining it were not in itself 'its exceeding great reward'—and as if God could not be glorified in the Cultivation of the Faculties he has given unless they were put to some practical operations.[1]

This reflects something of Arnoldian anti-utilitarianism, but dissatisfaction with Dr. Arnold's approach to intellectual activity —generated, possibly, by Clough's encounter with Tractarianism —also results in an attempt at altering his lateral moral emphasis, if we may use such terms, into a vertical spiritual dimension: knowledge and the search for truth justified in themselves and in the eyes of God. Assertion of autonomous spiritual entity tends to replace the value of moral instrumentality.

Turning to the duties of youth in another essay, Clough concludes—adopting the military rhetoric which Arnold had made familiar—that these are mainly preparative, at one level to 'fabricate the Arms, to levy, to assemble, to discipline the Army, which after-life's impending Warfare will . . . demand of them'. But there is another 'still higher duty of rooting out evil and cultivating good in our own character though not immediately affecting our performance of those our duties to our neighbour, to at least begin . . . [to acquire] . . . some portion of power over ourselves—of self-government, of self-control and self-guidance'.[2] This primary duty of self-discipline, and the related value of

[1] 'On some of the principal Effects on Literature resulting from the Invention of Printing', Bodleian MS. Eng. Misc. d. 513, fol. 6ᵛ.
[2] 'Examine the Truth of Νέων δὲ πάντες οἱ μεγάλοι καὶ πολλοὶ πόνοι', Bodleian MS. Eng. Misc. d. 513, fol. 19.

asceticism, are illuminated by the ambivalence revealed in his comments on the Stoics:

> The Stoic ... whilst he acknowledged the healthy and pure nature of our original and uncorrupted impulses, strove and struggled to escape the Pleasure that ensued on their indulgence: and was ever writhing and torturing himself to escape what was a component and inseparable part of his human Being. It was as though our mental Perceptions of external objects should induce us to close the eye and shut the ear in the hope that we should see and hear more perfectly than by their aid. An unwise attempt truly, yet an attempt in so far superior to the objects of the Peripatetic Philosophy's as it acknowledged and sought, though but weakly and vainly, to cultivate the seeds of Immortality within us. Without definitely recognizing a future state in theory, in practice it recognized that part of our being whose fruit and full development, whose kingdom and citizenship is not of this world.[1]

Accepting the dichotomy between flesh and spirit, body and soul, and relying on the Christian promise as the sure witness of the non-physical reality of man's nature and the pledge of his divine inheritance, the Stoics' attempt to realize this higher nature wins his admiration; at the same time he is uneasy at the complete rejection and subdual of the flesh, for, together with his acceptance of its separation from the spirit, he is aware of its incontrovertible reality and its epistemological value. The adjustment of this ambivalence between the claims of the spirit and of the flesh, and the allied question of his own relation to Christian guilt, become major subjects of sharpened examination in his later life and poetry.

With an inherited, clearly apprehended moral outlook that placed itself firmly within the framework of action, with a very much more inchoate and groping consciousness of the possible existence of moral and intellectual value dissociated from such a framework, and with an indistinct awareness of the demands of flesh and natural impulse as equally valid as those of spirit, then, Clough approaches the problems inherent in action, in a group of essays which record his early grapplings with a theme which exercised much of his mature attention, and informed the dialectical structure of the bulk of his poetry, notably *Adam and Eve*, *Amours de Voyage*, and *Dipsychus*. The first essay in which

---

[1] 'The History and Influence of the Stoical Philosophy', Bodleian MS. Eng. Misc. d. 513, fol. 32.

he deals with the theme of action, written in 1837–8, lays out the problem in general terms. Two principles, that of Caution or Timidity—the retarding tendency to view everything as a gateway to evil—and that of Confidence—the energizing principle, —operate against each other in shaping human action. Clough is aware of the dangers of paralysis in the excess of caution, but 'the fact is', he asserts,

that men do not err usually from any excess of caution, but from an evil habit of mind which is confident in deciding, and timid in action. We yield ourselves up to our imaginations: and while it is yet in our power to decide for or against, we yield ourselves to the contemplation of the hopeful view: when we have thus thrown ourselves into the midst of the difficulties a reaction at once takes place and we again obey slavishly those gloomy and desponding views with which our imagination now presents us.

This feeling then [of caution which refers us at each step to reason] which under right direction is exalted into Prudence may perhaps be well regarded as the most necessary for us in our present condition of mixed good and evil.[1]

The consciousness of the world as a moral theatre for action is, obviously, the central characterization of the problem. The crucial stage in determining the quality of an act is the flux of moral decision that precedes it, and Clough, writing so soon after his Rugby days, still seems to believe in the possibility of precipitating from that flux a clear, sharply contoured crystal of moral direction.

This general account is extended and modified in the essays written two years later. In one respect, the influence of the Oxford Movement and the teaching of Arnold ran in clearly confluent channels: human life was not only unceasingly effortful but hedged round with relentless laws of consequence:

One field alone there is; for the learner alike and the mature one only world wherein to prepare and wherein to work: and that a world in which with every petty Act effects are bound up eternal and irrevocable. Each rash attempt, each awkward movement of the Novice is indeed no more to be undone, a seed cast once and for ever in the Earth, which may bring forth the bitterest harvest. No playground, no gymnasium has been on man bestowed wherein to

---

[1] '"Etenim nescio quo pacto magis in studio homines timor quam fiducia decet"—Pliny', Bodleian MS. Eng. Misc. d. 513, fol. 27.

prove his undeveloped strength; and learn the laws of Action free from that law of Consequence which governs his maturest labours.[1]

More distinctive in these essays—distinctive, that is, when we think of Rugby—is their evidence of a clearer, more continuous feeling for spiritual purity, a feeling nurtured and encouraged, no doubt, by the Tractarian ideal of perfect sanctity. The dove of Newmanism spiritualizes and consecrates the morality of Arnold; it also creates fresh insights into the personal problem involved in action. Accepted as the law of man's being, action is seen in these essays as a corrosive to spiritual reality, rusting man's awareness of his spiritual birthright, coarsening his perception of the spirit within, overlaying its primal purity. The problem becomes that of preserving unsullied this spiritual core, of how

in the rough unyielding material of action duly to set forth the expression of the lofty ideal within, itself so easily forgotten. And being then thus difficult, at once to retain and to express,—how tempting must it be to surrender one by one to the hard necessity of Circumstance each faintly remembered feature that made up the perfect whole of that high Original. How needful seems it at the time to acquiesce in the second-best: and how short the step when we once acquiesce to pass on to forget ourselves and to deny to others the existence of that higher excellence which we thus at one time consciously departed from.[2]

Man, caught in the necessities of action by the terms of his existence, is also, by the same terms, caught up in the trammels of relation—the reticulation of social and personal connection and dependence, which entangles still further the problem of living actively and at the same time preserving untainted one's individual heritage of purity.

As the actor hurried on the stage with his fellows around him and before him the gazing multitude, as the gladiator thrust out upon the arena, so [man] once set within these bounds of Time and Space is committed to the Work: and as wisely may he shake himself loose from Existence itself as believe that by any effort he can escape the no less wondrous mystery of Relation. . . .

This call [to the task] he must of necessity obey: though the sound

[1] 'On the System of Education pursued at Athens under Pericles', Bodleian MS. Eng. Misc. d. 514, fol. 33ᵛ.

[2] "Τῷ δὲ ὑπερβάλλοντι αὐτῶν φθονοῦντες ἤδη καὶ ἀπιστοῦσιν", Bodleian MS. Eng. Misc. d. 514, fol. 29.

of more than earthly music be ringing in his ears, and the vision of more than material beauty be floating before his eyes; though, worse than this, as he rises to obey the command, the music grow faint and the vision fade into air—He must go forth among his peers; tho' his heart sink within and declare as with oracular assurance that he and those he must be with are creatures depraving and depraved and that as heat passes unseen from body to body so evil radiates invisibly and ever from Soul to Soul. Yet to stand still avails not, nor is possible; —it is useless to close fast the mouth that it speak not and, as it were with hands too thin and small seek to hide the face and eyes that speak no less. And happy they perhaps to whom Earth's call is loudest and least to be mistaken; and who must without shrinking or delaying hurry forth to perform her bidding.[1]

The impulse of withdrawal to the refuge of spiritual isolation and self-cultivation was a painfully real temptation in Clough's own situation. As he said, concluding an essay on Plato,

the philosopher had enough to do to preserve his own mind incorrupt —enough for him would it be, and more than he could easily secure, if in the general tempest he could find some little creek or haven in the which to shelter his bark and look on in sorrowful contemplation: —Madness would it be and worse than madness were he to leave his hard-gained harbourage to join in unequal conflict with the mid sea's winds and waves.[2]

The oscillation between perilous action and philosophic with-drawal appears, in these essays, to be positively resolved in a characteristically strenuous adjustment. Admitting an element of truth in the view that 'one deed is better than many dreams, and that a little achieved is better than much intended', Clough writes:

To forget and strive to forget that for which we are to work can of course be no virtue: but a feeling of half-angry disbelief and rejectance when an object which we deem beyond our power to attain is pre-sented to us may be often deemed an evidence that all we believe ourselves equal to we strive for and will acquit its possessor of the heavier charge of a sentimental indolence which is contented to behold in occasional contemplation, but in action refuses to seek.[3]

1 " ' Ὁ δὲ μὴ δυνάμενος κοινωνεῖν ἢ μηθὲν δεόμενος δι' αὐτάρκειαν οὐδὲν μέρος πόλεως, ὥστε θηρίον ἢ θεός" Arist. Polit. I', Bodleian MS. Eng. Misc. d. 514, fols. 30–1.

2 ' "Capessentibus rem publicam nihilo minus quam philosophis adhibenda est magnificentia et rerum humanarum despicientia"—Cicero', Bodleian MS. Eng. Misc. d. 514, fol. 40.

3 "Τῷ δὲ ὑπερβάλλοντι αὐτῶν φθονοῦντες ἤδη καὶ ἀπιστοῦσιν", Bodleian MS. Eng. Misc. d. 514, fol. 29ᵛ.

But how could one know where and how to seek, in what action, with what virtue? At Rugby the answers were simple. One did one's assiduous best to go about one's master's business, one kept at one's studies and swept the board of prizes—those badges of puissant grace. But the multiform pressures and demands of Oxford blurred those clear perspectives. Looking back on his undergraduate years Clough wrote in 1853, 'I had been pretty well sated of distinctions and competitions at school; I would gladly have dispensed with anything more of success in this kind, always excepting the £200 a year of the Fellowship.' Of the race for prizes and distinctions in general he wrote, 'Surely, after the age of nineteen or twenty, it is really time that this school-boy love of racing, this empty competition should be checked. . . . Examinations are useful things, and the stricter they are the better. . . . Only, of all Senior Wranglers, Medallists, and even "Double-Firsts", let us be fairly and finally rid.'[1] The assurance of this assimilated assessment (and retrospectively perhaps a disingenuous one, since he did try for a number of prizes while he was at Balliol) contains nothing of the anxiety and guilt that sometimes assailed him when he was actually an undergraduate. It conveys nothing of the self-doubt involved in the only partly willing surrender of the identity most readily accessible to the brilliant undergraduate. Clough's reputation was enormous; as John Shairp wrote to his sister, 'he had the reputation of being the best head Balliol has had for years'.[2] Yet, strangely, Clough's academic record was one of persisting failure culminating spectacularly in his Second Class degree. In 1838 he missed the Hertford Scholarship. 'You see', he wrote to his sister, 'I was not successful in my trial at the Latin Scholarship, and as I have not written for either of the prizes, it is quite impossible that by any chance I should be drawn out of my retirement this year' (*Corr.* i. 69). But when Achilles did go forth the outcome hardly followed epic precedent. His attempt at the Newdigate the following year ended in disappointment, as did his further attempt in 1840.[3]

[1] 'A Passage Upon Oxford Studies', Trawick, pp. 325, 327.

[2] W. Knight, *Principal Shairp and His Friends* (London, 1888), p. 45.

[3] For the first of these attempts see E. B. Greenberger, '"Salsette and Elephanta": An Unpublished Poem by Clough', *Review of English Studies*, (hereafter *RES*) xx (Aug. 1969), 284–305; for the second, 'Clough's "The Judgement of Brutus": A Newly-Found Poem', *Victorian Poetry*, viii (Sept. 1970), 127–50.

In the letter of reminiscences which Ward—reviving a thirty-year-old memory—sent to Mrs. Clough, he claimed almost total responsibility for his former pupil's failure. He saw his devastating logic 'prematurely forcing Clough's mind', and the 'intellectual perplexity' thus induced preying 'on his spirits' and issuing ultimately in the Schools disaster.

What was before all things to have been desired for him was that, during his undergraduate course, he should have given himself up thoroughly to his classical and mathematical studies; that he should have kept up . . . the habits of prayer and Scripture-reading which he brought with him from Rugby, but should have kept himself aloof from plunging prematurely into the theological controversies then so rife at Oxford.[1]

The efficacy of the revised prescription put forward so confidently by Ward is, in turn, highly doubtful. For part of Clough's problem at Oxford was to adjust himself to an intellectually undemanding curriculum.[2] No doubt the outstanding and conscientious student soon realized that in order to excel one had to do much more than the bare curriculum suggested; but the standard of common instruction too often made of that curriculum a dismal, old-fashioned slog through a handful of well-worn classics. Clough found himself in his classes in the company of very much less advanced students, forced to go page by page through books he had already mastered as a schoolboy.[3]

He reacted like many other bored but able undergraduates. He relaxed in his working-habits, although he 'did go on, for duty's sake, and for discipline and docility, sadly doing Latin prose; but except in docility, profiting but little'. He also began

[1] Wilfrid Ward, op. cit., p. 109.
[2] For Clough's criticisms of the state of Oxford Studies see the *Report of Her Majesty's Commissioners Appointed to Inquire into the State, Discipline, Studies, and Revenues of the University and Colleges of Oxford* (London, 1852), 'Evidence', pp. 211–16 (Trawick, pp. 303–16). Also see his review of this *Report* in the *North American Review*, lxxvi (Apr. 1853), 369–96, part of which has been printed in *PPR* i. 403–8 and in Trawick (pp. 324–7). For a general corroboration of Clough's estimate see Stanley's reaction to Balliol, as recorded in R. E. Prothero, *The Life and Correspondence of Arthur Penrhyn Stanley, D.D.*, 2 vols. (London, 1893), i. 126–7, and the evidence, for example, of Robert Lowe in the *Report* just cited ('Evidence', p. 12). In his letter Lowe pointed out the danger of underestimating the demands of the Final Schools, to which the more outstanding Public School men were particularly susceptible.   [3] Trawick, p. 310.

to 'pasture freely, following a natural instinct'.[1] Obviously the
issues raised by Tractarianism occupied most of his attention,
but the over-all impression created by his undergraduate letters
is one of expanding mental and personal horizons. The exclusive
and eminently dutiful preoccupations of his Rugby days are
replaced by a widened range and variety of reading, a developing
inquiringness of mind, which made him impatient with the
narrowness which the Oxford Movement too often encouraged.
In 1841 he wryly commented on the Newmanists' reading, 'Shall
I inundate you with Oxford Controversy,—or with Rom.
Cath. books of which French, Germ. and Engl. besides Latin
(e.g. Thom Aquinas, 15 vols. folio) Oxfd. daily becomes fuller?'
(*Corr.* i. 108).

His references to his own reading are not abundant, nor are his
comments on the books he does mention extensive (they never
are in the whole body of his correspondence), but most prominent
in these scattered notices are the names of Goethe and Carlyle.
'I think Tacitus rather like Carlyle, whose Fr. Revoln I have
[been] reading for the first time through, and with increasing
admiration. I have also been reading with my sister, . . . our old
friend, Dorothea and Herman, at least 2 books, and like it much
better, and indeed very much', he remarked in August 1839
(*Corr.* i. 93). Goethe does not seem to have gripped him with
any great intensity at this stage, and the only other book of his
he refers to is the first part of *Werther*, which he read with 'more
satisfaction and admiration than . . . expected—or rather . . .
found all the power and little of the extravagance' he looked for
(*Corr.* i. 98). Much later in life, though, he admitted that he did
not read it through to the end (*Corr.* ii. 389). Carlyle, however,
he refers to with unmistakable enthusiasm:

I have been reading some of Carlyle's Miscellaneous Essays (from the
Edinburgh and Foreign Quarterly etc.) just collected and published
in 4 vols. I think they are very fine, one on Burns and one on Boswell's
Jonsoniad as he calls it, especially (*Corr.* i. 96).

I wish you would recommend me some book which Gell has not got,
to give him before he goes [to Tasmania]. . . . I should not like to
give him anything ephemeral, which is a fault attaching itself I suppose
even to Carlyle's Essays, which are just published, though I admire
him extremely in general and these Essays even more than the Revolu-

[1] Trawick, p. 325.

tion. . . . He is certainly however somewhat heathenish: but that it seems to me is the case with all literature, old and new, English and foreign which is worth calling literature, and comes in one's way (*Corr.* i. 96).

Significantly, the enthusiasm for Carlyle occurs in the same letter as that in which he expresses his weariness with the Tractarian vortex with Ward as its centre. His praise for Carlyle's *Chartism*— 'It is very good, though not quite so eloquent as I expected it to be' (*Corr.* i. 100)—is juxtaposed with his description of Oxford as 'replete with . . . Newmanistic gossip'. The strong, astringent voice of the Scotsman calling away from theologically encumbered Christianity evoked in Clough a positive attitude of rejection towards that form of religion which was to grow stronger in the years which followed. A welcome relief from the clogging controversy surrounding him, Carlyle nourished and directed his independent search. If Ward's logic was mainly negative and destructive, Carlyle broke fresh ground, held out hope to the doubter, suggested value in the rebelling mind.

A notebook in the possession of Miss Katharine Duff[1] provides fairly strong presumptive evidence that even at Balliol—at least towards the end of his career there—Clough was ranging even further, marking out for himself in the process an area of study and speculation which was to become, during his time as a Fellow of Oriel, a distinctive, emphatically non-Tractarian, venture into contemporary social and economic problems, and so provide him for a number of years with an exhilarating role as an Arnoldian reformer. Possibly under the impetus of Ward, the one-time admirer of Mill, possibly on his own initiative, very probably as a consequence of his frequent participation in the meetings of the Decade, a private debating society started by William Lake and Benjamin Brodie as a kind of Oxford counterpart to the Cambridge Apostles, of which, the Oxford journals show, he was an active member even as an undergraduate, he seems to have undertaken a serious study of current economic thinking. The notebook is labelled 'Essays—1841' on its front cover, and on the inside of that cover is written, 'Adam Smith's New Patent Self-Acting Producer/ Coleridge's approved distributor.' It is filled with tables and charts, with jottings and sometimes longish

---

[1] See Appendix A.

extracts from McCulloch, Mill, and Coleridge, and Clough's own reflections on these. On the inside back cover a significant message is scribbled: 'Meanness of the Obj[ec]t: the true thing being to inspire a zeal for some τέλος which w[oul]d make men feel these matters unimportant.' Moving from McCulloch to Mill to Coleridge, the notes show a steady progression—too logically tight to be accidental—away from the doctrines and definitions of *laissez-faire* theory to a more liberalized, more humanly comprehensive conception of the subject. The notebook as a whole anticipates questions Clough raised and positions he adopted in his later writings, most notably in the pamphlet on the Retrenchment Association which he wrote at the time of the Irish Famine. The first entry is dated 'March 5th'; a loose inserted note on private charity is written on the back of an envelope addressed to 'Arthur H. Clough Esqre./ 99 Holywell/ Oxford' and postmarked for 25 October 1841; on fol. 10^v there are some very hastily pencilled notes (of a conversation with Dr. Arnold, who had come up to Oxford to deliver his Inaugural Lecture on 2 December?) headed: 'Arnold Dec[embe]r 6th.' It is possible, therefore, that the material in the notebook belongs to a period after Clough had taken his degree. Another inserted half-sheet, however, suggests that he was working with the notebook while preparing for the Final Schools. On one side of the half-sheet is written, in one column, 'Whately's def[initio]ns/ All [Seniors?] / [All] Lectures/ Herm[an] Merivale's [lectures]/ Vaughan's Essay'; in the other, 'Is the labourer dependent on Consumption?/ If Productiveness be increased so that 10 p[e]r c[en]t less labour be wanted: what is the result in labourers?—/ If there be no increased consumption those who wo[ul]d in that case be the greater consumers will now "take off" = the cond[itio]n of the labourer will not fall.' The first column looks very much like the kind of list of materials to be covered that a candidate for an examination would draw up. One should note that the most significant material in the notebook is on fols. 1^v–10 10, that is before the notes dated 6 December, and it is impossible, therefore, to date it any more precisely than after 5 March. Further, that material itself suggests long and careful thought about the issues involved; Clough's acquaintance with the subject seems neither recent nor unassimilated.

There were, however, other aspects to—and consequences of—

this impulse of Clough's to pasture freely. In the enticing, expansive, lightly supervised atmosphere of Oxford the temptation to drift was dangerously attractive to anyone who had not completely internalized his sense of duty or achieved a state of unassailable grace. Rugby, as we have seen, turned out a persevering but not entirely perfect son, although to observers he may have seemed one. Even before he went up to Oxford he had become aware of his own 'double-mindedness' and 'want of faith', his tendency to spend too much time in friendships which were a 'snare' to him (*Corr.* i. 62). He started at Oxford with faultless intentions. He had to leaven the Oxford lump, of course, but he also looked forward to reading 'diligently' in his first term. He intended to go in for the Ireland Scholarship in the spring and to peg away at his mathematics (*Corr.* i. 64). But the change to Oxford, he soon discovered, 'unsettl[ed] many old habits'. After the 'miserable lack of pleasant society and almost dearth of friends' in his last two years at school, this lonely lieutenant of Arnold's found himself heaped with riches. In his first term he made at least three promising and congenial friendships—with Brodie (in later life Professor of Chemistry at Oxford), with Ward, and with Lake (later Dean of Durham). The newness and strangeness of the first term did not wear off as he thought it would; the days slid by in excited and exciting conversation, spiced with the occasional wine-party, gradually stringing themselves out into a 'proper' first-year of 'great do-nothingness' (*Corr.* i. 72).

Although he persisted in it, he did not live easily with his 'idleness', however. Day after mis-spent day he returned to his rooms at night to wrestle with his conscience and confront his own renegade self in his journals. He excoriated himself for wasting time, for his indolence, for his utter lack of exertion. He was 'careless and pleasure-seeking', a 'wilful rebel and outcast' who needed to keep perpetually in view his 'daily trespass and doublemindedness'. Dependent, impressionable, open, he was profoundly unsettled by his friendships, which, as in the case of Ward, seemed inevitably, because of his own unguarded impulsiveness, to lead him into 'sham' relations, 'sham' feelings, 'sham' intimacies, which he found himself both embarrassed by and curiously loath to extricate himself from. Although invariably his closer friendships became occasions of distress, he

needed those friendships desperately, always reaching out to a
perfect understanding, a perfect sympathy. Even after the 'break'
at the end of his first year, Ward could still excite and disturb.
In 1840 and 1841 Theodore Walrond, who was a schoolboy at
Rugby, and whose brother Henry had once caused him such
heartache about Simpkinson, offered fresh hopes of a companionship which would not sour. 'I am all along resting on the fancy
of affection in Walrond; whereas I have no reason to believe he
cares for me, nor yet could be justified in expressing to him that
I care for him.' The reverse of this almost helpless impressionable-
ness, this dependence which made him slacken his vigilance for
the sake of fraudulent sympathy, and led him to 'do things which
may be the means of ruining me everlastingly', was an 'arbitrary',
wilful independence. Even the Decade meetings were a snare:
they filled him with fantasies about his own brilliance, left him
agitated and in a 'terrible state of vanity'. He had lost command of
himself, impulse and duty seemed to have become completely
dissevered, the voice from within had become muffled. 'I am in a
very bad way utterly wanting in Earnestness for Goodness or for
Truth—and influenced simply by a desire for Praise.' Filled with
despair at his own moral numbness, he recognized in his calloused
conscience the state of spiritual sleep Dr. Arnold had warned
against—'I seem to have lost all notion of sin—I must keep fast
every day to the end of term except Sundays and Holydays or I
shall never keep right.' Only through self-discipline could he
recollect and re-engage his dispersed and errant self. In an entry
which illuminates his whole response to Tractarianism he confessed that he badly wanted 'forms': 'I have not the least real
sense of Uncleanness or of Vanity etc. Cannot I therefore devise
something or other to serve the purpose of these bodily punish-
ments . . . ?' But, looking again into himself, he fell back im-
potently, 'I incline to think that I ought to give up seeking much
about the great Newm[an] Question: for I have little or no real
earnestness.' It was all folly, all merely impressive talk, all show
and insincerity.

His letters, however, tell a different, more unregenerate story.
By April 1838 he had become accustomed enough to his easy-
going ways to write airily about his 'idleness', about his end-
of-term 'liberty to lie in bed, go to the newsroom, read reviews
and novels, learn to skiff', and to reflect with placid cheerfulness

on the 'probable degree of working' which would have given
him the Hertford Scholarship (*Corr*. i. 68). A month later he was
confessing to shame at his lack of the kind of industriousness he
knew himself capable of, and referring vaguely to 'magnificent
plans for reading'—but then hurrying on to discuss in detail
Newmanist matters that clearly occupied more of his attention
(*Corr*. i. 71). After his second Christmas Vacation the 'glorious'
mid-February weather helped to bring on 'the increase of hunting
and boating and the decrease of reading' (*Corr*. i. 88). That
summer brought something of a change; distantly apprehensive
remarks about his mathematics, which hung before him 'like
a great black cloud', began to creep into his letters (*Corr*. i. 93).
He still maintained an airy distance, but the insouciance was
beginning to wear thin. 'I am in excellent health, . . . and hope to
expend some of the stock on Mathematics, which are with me at
present feebly struggling rather to die than to live', he wrote to
Simpkinson early in Michaelmas Term. In his next sentence he
gave in to his anxiety about the 'vortex of Philosophism and
Discussion' in which he seemed to be caught (*Corr*. i. 96–7).
Just over two months later he commemorated his twenty-first
birthday and the beginning of a New Year in another letter to
Simpkinson:

> I wish with all my heart that my ordeal was over, even though it were
> in a failure. I have but little appetite for Work Mathematical or Classi-
> cal, and there is as little compulsion to it and as much enticement
> from it as is possible in our ways of life at Oxford. I would give much
> for the pleasant treadmill routine of school. . . .
> Many happy returns of the day to you, and to me, now entering
> my years of discretion in the most indiscreet and idle fashion possible,
> writing letters namely scarcely an hour after breakfast notwithstanding
> the claims of the lever, the pulley, and the screw all equally ineffectual
> to overcome my vis inertiae (*Corr*. i. 98).

Clough had indeed fallen. Conscience and purpose had deserted
him, leaving in their place a blank apathy—and the remembrance
of a treadmill Paradise. Gathering whatever remnants of duty he
could muster, he returned to Oxford planning to 'work away
diligently I hope till the beginning of July' (*Corr*. i. 99).
   The summer of 1840 he spent reading with Ward in Grasmere,
and then by himself in Liverpool. His hero-worshipping sister
noticed his anxiety. Anne and her brother had grown into an

especially close relationship. The wistfully earnest girl, groping her way awkwardly out of the Victorian dependency of her sex, looked up to her brother as infinitely wise, infinitely good. She hung on his every word. When he used to go away it seemed to her that 'some bright star that shed a lustre round had disappeared'.[1] Probably under the influence of her brother's progressive, Arnold-influenced ideas, she had begun to teach in the Welsh National School in Liverpool shortly after her arrival there in 1836. She also started visiting the poor and conducting a Sunday School. Her brother, when he was at home, often helped with her work, accompanied her on her visits, advised her on her reading, and supervised her studies. But what she most longed for were the quiet, serious walks with Arthur, when she could discuss with him shyly and tentatively her ponderings on subjects like religion, morality, or the place of women in society. But this summer of 1840 he seemed changed and preoccupied. 'Had a walk with Arthur;' she confided to her journal in August, 'he seems very much out of spirits, and fearful about his examination turning out well. He says he has not been well since Easter, but all the time he has been at home he has seldom if ever complained.'[2]

Time was wearing on, the Schools were no longer a distant prospect seen through a sunny glass of society and friendship and talk, and unmistakable signs of stress were showing themselves. His luxuriant dark hair was beginning to thin rapidly, and there were other more familiar symptoms: stocktaking, self-reproach, the attempt to get 'right' in his personal relationships, to discern once again the solitary light of personal rectitude. The Examinations had precipitated a much larger moral and personal crisis. As he had written in his journal, 'I may safely say . . . that before coming to Oxford I never saw that the right way was to get to hate Evil by a faith in Punishment and not try to keep oneself by a love of Good.' Towards the end of August he wrote to Simpkinson:

That I have been a good deal unsettled in mind at times at Oxford, and that I have done a number of foolish things is true enough, and I dare say the change from Rugby life to its luxury and apparent irresponsibility has had a good deal of ill effect upon me. I hardly know what you allude to in the 'self abandonment and misgivings'

<hr/>

[1] B. A. Clough, *A Memoir of Anne Jemima Clough*, p. 42.   [2] Ibid., p. 28.

you speak of; but what you complain of in me has proceeded simply
from my foolish fickleness and forgetfulness of the past united with
the very rare intercourse we have had personally and the fact that I
have had things come across my way at Oxford which could not but
be very absorbing. . . . If the lessons I have been taught at Oxford
do not follow the fate of a good many others before them and evaporate,
I trust at any rate that my sympathy will not be so irregular and indiscriminating as formerly, I fancy, it used to be (*Corr.* i. 102).

In October he moved out of college into his lodgings in Holywell
and a life of rigorous discipline: he had, as he repeatedly wrote in
his journal, *to be by himself.* In this dark and cheerless hour he was
struggling for self-mastery, and for his poetry it was an exceptionally productive period: the vein of self-examination which
had been opened flowed abundantly.

   Feeling that he had not read what he ought to have, he put off
taking his degree till the following Easter. The knowledge of his
family's precarious financial state heaped further fires on his head.
As early as October 1839 he had written in confidence to Burbidge
of the likelihood of his father's business collapsing in the near
future (*Corr.* i. 95). Now, early in 1841, he wrote to his brother
Charles to tell him that he had 'cut his moorings' and was trying
to live solely on the money from his Exhibition and his Scholarship without applying to their father for help. His performance in
the examination had become distressingly consequential—as he
pointed out to Charles, he needed a First if he wanted to be sure of
pupils (*Corr.* i. 104-5). James Clough's business finally failed in
the summer of 1841, and the family had to move to a more
modest house in Liverpool where Anne and her mother took
care of most of the housework. The shamefaced and struggling
gentility to which the family had been brought comes across
movingly in the understated details of the letter, expressing a
touching concern for his son's health and spirits, which Clough's
father sent him early in 1842: a loan from Uncle Charles to be
repaid, an anonymous gift of £10 in an unmarked envelope,
George's holiday paid for by Uncle Alfred, his own withdrawal
from civic life under the shame of commercial failure (*Corr.* i.
114-16).

   In putting off his degree Clough merely prolonged his ordeal.
Remorse drove him early in February to drag up feelings of past
inadequacy and confessions of past ingratitude. He wrote to

Charles about the pain with which he frequently thought of the
way he had 'neglected and made an ill-return to [his] kindnesses
when [they] were elder and younger brother together long ago'.
'This I hope', he said, 'you will always believe of me; whatever I
seem to be' (*Corr.* i. 105). Reality and shadow, appearance and
substance—a week later he was writing to Burbidge in a letter
which included part of the sequence of poems he entitled 'Blank
Misgivings of a Creature moving about in Worlds not realized':

> The truth is that I have got a good deal into loose and foolish ways
> and have been continually afraid of allowing myself in anything like
> that in writing to you. I fear however to a great extent I must have
> done so. I have at any rate done wrong in going on writing to you
> while concealing this. I began so to do as early I think as the first letter
> I wrote after Easter Vacn. Before that though I believe in other ways
> foolish enough, I at any rate did not do or say things which I doubted
> at the time whether I should really go on with and fulfil (*Corr.* i. 105).

The effort to collect himself, to get his work, his obligations,
his past and his present into perspective, to correct old follies
and recover lost ground, was exhausting. As he wrote to Gell
(enclosing some more lines from 'Blank Misgivings' with his
letter), simply to have the examination over would be a blessing,
however it turned out (*Corr.* i. 107).

When the Class Lists finally appeared the consternation was
general. The disaster of this brilliant Scholar's Second cast a pall
over Balliol High Table which only lifted in November, when
Constantine Prichard successfully pulled off his First.[1] Tait, a
Fellow and Tutor of the college at the time, was 'furious' and
went about the University 'loudly denouncing' the stupidity
of examiners who had failed to recognize 'a man of original
genius'.[2] Clough himself was admirably tough-minded; as far as
he was concerned the decision was a perfectly fair one, although
it left his estimate of his own abilities unimpaired. Before the
results were out he had written to his anxious sister, 'I did the
papers much worse than I expected. However you exaggerate
both my labours and suspense very much; for I am not at all
broken down and care less about it than I think I ought to do'

---

[1] E. H. Coleridge, *Life and Correspondence of John Duke Coleridge*, 2 vols.
(London, 1904), i. 93.

[2] R. T. Davidson and W. Benham, *Life of Archibald Campbell Tait, Archbishop
of Canterbury*, 2 vols. (London, 1891), i. 72.

(*Corr.* i. 108). Curiously, the actual trial itself had been cathartic. He emerged from it not scarred by conscience and convictions of failure, but with a strange sense of exemption from expected imperatives. 'As for the causes of this mismanagement, I do not feel very guilty . . . though it is does [*sic*] not therefore follow that I ought not so to feel' (*Corr.* i. 110). It was not his class he had been worried about during the past year, he assured his sister, but 'principally . . . other things altogether' (*Corr.* i. 109). In the calmness of completion his anxiety about these other things seems to have allayed itself: he had confronted the imperfection of his own state and, understandably, all he desired for the present was to get away from Oxford for a while.

He was perfectly aware, of course, that he had been a sad disappointment to 'many whom [he] ought to wish to gratify' (*Corr.* i. 109)—among them, and above all others, Dr. Arnold. Significantly, he decided to walk all the way with no other company but his own thoughts to that unavoidable encounter. Years later Tom Arnold recalled his friend standing in the front court of the School-House 'with face partly flushed and partly pale, and saying simply, "I have failed"'. By himself again, Clough walked back to Oxford through the reassuring country-side of early summer. He chose for the return journey 'quite a new way and far pleasanter than the old' (*Corr.* i. 109).

After a summer spent coaching pupils whom the good offices of Dr. Arnold—and a threatened outbreak of typhus at Rugby which prolonged the holidays—had procured, Clough returned to Oxford in October. In November he went in for a Balliol Fellow-ship, but, although two of his examiners, Tait and Ward, were very decidedly in his favour, he was not elected. Stanley, now a Fellow of University College, wrote to Simpkinson about this fresh reversal which had befallen 'one who was likely to have been the ablest of all the rising generation':

[I]t seemed so great a misfortune that I cannot help venting my lamen-tations over it. But there is this great comfort. Some of his papers were done so splendidly as fully to show that the spring of genius has not yet dried up within him, and therefore I hope that he will get in at Oriel. Not that I ever thought the genius was gone; but I feared that the power of expressing it to the world was gone. What a singular person he is! I, of course, never having been intimate with him, can only reverence him at a respectful distance. But the little I do know of him has always made me think and maintain that he is the profoundest man of his years that I ever saw, or that Rugby ever sent forth. His very misfortunes invest him with a kind of sacredness, for, academically speaking, who ever was so unfortunate—so able, so laborious, and yet so unaccountably failing? How singular a contrast with my own fortunate career, and yet with no apparent reason! But I am full of hope for him. It may be superstitious, but I cannot help thinking that so remarkable a concatenation of disasters has not been without some great end.[1]

It is an interesting letter, revealing in the gossip among friends so much more than intended. Under the generous praise 'there but for the grace of God' relief mingles with sneaking, half-admitted misgiving about the reality of Clough's ability (the 'yet' in the third sentence is curious). Already his friends were beginning to hedge their bets on Clough—of course they did not accept the world's verdict, but nevertheless in future perhaps . . . and if he did continue to fail, there was the world above. The more he failed the more 'sacred' he became. Curiously enough, the more sacred he became, the more he was singled out in the eye of Heaven and justice for 'some great end'. Thus early in Clough's life the trend was set for an increasingly popular activity among his friends, especially those who reverenced him from fittingly respectful distances: the actual reality of the man proving so unsatisfactory, they injected appropriately graduated quantities of 'nobility' into the image. In all fairness to them, however, we should remember Clough's impenetrable reserve, which hid from them the true nature of his struggle and also fed the myth that was gradually growing round him. The insidious pressure towards an imprisoning acceptance of the valuation of himself embodied in the evolving myth—a valuation which flattered and nourished his own strong urges towards self-transcendence— was one Clough had to face more and more frequently and to resist, not always successfully, in the years that followed.

★　★　★

Clough's experience as an undergraduate, diverse—and even confused—as it is, is unified by the emergence of a new independence of outlook. All undergraduates grow into some measure of independence—it is almost an axiom of their state and condition.

[1] R. E. Prothero, *Letters and Verses of Arthur Penrhyn Stanley, D. D.* (London, 1895), p. 65.

Clough's independence was not only in many ways uncertainly and reluctantly assumed, at the cost of considerable personal strain, but was also unusually significant. All the major influences in his life so far can be subsumed under a single word—authority. The authority of his mother, the authority of Dr. Arnold, the authority of Ward, formidable in themselves, summed up the impressive weight of abstract values and imperatives. And he tended to be, as even the single instance of his Schools performance suggests, highly sensitive to the sheer magnitude of surrounding authority and authoritative expectation. His early and prolonged schooling in the ethic of enthusiasm, with its stress on admiration and imitation, fostered the attitude of genuflexion. The deeper problems of identity too, rendered especially acute in his case by the particular circumstances of his childhood and youth, impelled him towards acceptance of the authority whose dimensions, refracted through his own personal uncertainties, assumed such compelling proportions. At Rugby he had resolved his dilemmas by conforming to a coherent, authoritatively upheld structure of beliefs and purposes. Oxford challenged the bases of those beliefs and the logic of that conformity, but the need and the longing for such attachment remained: Ward's use of the word 'feminine' to describe his nature is peculiarly apt—especially when we remember its nineteenth-century associations. His emotions and his dependence urged him in the direction of submission, his personality was strongly drawn towards the sanction and security of the given. Independence, with its consequences in uncertainty, was, for him, an attitude wrung from a personality naturally susceptible to the centralizing claims of authority. His toughness and integrity can be gauged from this particular—and almost omnipresent—tension in his life, for it compelled him to recognize the unsatisfactory and incomplete in these claims, and forced him to vacate, against the temperamental inertia of attachment, positions he would gladly have held.

It would be limiting, however, to confine this struggle wholly within the issues of an individual temperament and psychology, for the terms of Clough's struggle, as they gradually develop, also derive from—and illuminate—the wider intellectual and cultural crisis in which, as a Victorian, he was involved. On leaving Balliol he encountered fully for the first time forces which hitherto had been matters of vague and distant—and always disparaging—report, forces, however, which were central to the life of the century and which impinged directly on his search for an individual vision of truth: rationalism, scepticism, utilitarianism. On the whole he accorded to these—for a time at least—a positive welcome. But always, even in his most enthusiastic moments, his response was counterpoised by the heritage of his upbringing and background. Both Dr. Arnold and the Oxford Movement (and Newman in particular) encouraged a distrust of reason and an abhorrence of utilitarianism, both stressed the importance of conscience as a spiritually individuating and magisterial organ, which not only delivered final moral judgements, but—for Newman and Ward—afforded glimpses of reality beyond the physical world. Inheriting a non-rational epistemology of the validity of which he was convinced, his acceptance of it was troubled by that suspicion of emotionality and subjectivism which made him sympathetic to rationalistic and utilitarian modes of thought. Truth, finally, was the sole authority he was willing to recognize, and in his search for foundations he showed himself a true child of his age: the confident Romantic internalization of authority was no longer culturally viable, one had to look outward into a distressingly heterogeneous and conflicting civilization and somehow achieve a synthesis between outward fact and inner impulse.

2. UNDERGRADUATE POETRY

With the exception of only one poem, 'Truth is a golden thread', all Clough's undergraduate poetry dates from 1839 onwards—dates, that is, from the period when the anxieties about his own spiritual condition which culminated in the crisis of 1840–1 first began to distress and darken his life. The large bulk of this poetry is directly confessional and occupies itself with communicating his inner turmoil, with charting the movement of conscience and consciousness through the baffling tangle of experience towards some ultimate stability, some pure value, the existence of which is unwaveringly believed in, although a deceitful phenomenal world yields only the most elusive and fragmented visions of it.[1]

Biographically, these troubled poems are indispensable in illuminating the stresses and tensions out of which they were

[1] Cf., e.g., 'Truth is a golden thread' and 'Away, haunt not thou me'.

born. The first sonnet in the series of ten poems under the general
title 'Blank Misgivings of a Creature moving about in Worlds
not realized' maps out briefly the sensibility which is amplified
and particularized in other poems:

> Here am I yet, another twelvemonth spent,
> One-third departed of the mortal span,
> Carrying on the child into the man,
> Nothing into reality. Sails rent,
> And rudder broken,—reason impotent,—
> Affections all unfixed; so forth I fare
> On the mid seas unheedingly, so dare
> To do and to be done by, well content.
> So was it from the first, so is it yet;
> Yea, the first kiss that by these lips was set
> On any human lips, methinks was sin—
> Sin, cowardice, and falsehood; for the will
> Into a deed e'en then advanced, wherein
> God, unidentified, was thought-of still.
>
> (*Poems*, 28.)

The urge towards action (most emphatically expressed in Χρυσέα
κλῆς ἐπὶ γλώσσᾳ which was written in July 1841 after Clough
had taken his degree, and may be read as anticipating his efforts
at engagement in his years at Oriel) and the guilty impotence of
lost activating impulse are undercut here, in this first 'Blank
Misgivings' poem, by a suspicion of will and a sense of the sinfulness of the flesh issuing in action—how deep and how radical
in its implications can be seen from the draft reading of the lines
which Katharine Chorley has noted:

> Yea, the first kiss that by these lips was set
> Upon my mother's was methinks a sin.[1]

The sickened awareness of corruption which envelops these
poems is accompanied by an unendurable consciousness of having
lived a lie, of the hypocrisies which not only interpose themselves
between inner life and outer but infect one's inner life itself and
cast a total doubt on the possibility of any substantial self-hood.

> How often sit I, poring o'er
>   My strange distorted youth,
> Seeking in vain, in all my store,
>   One feeling based on truth; . . .
>
> (*Poems*, 30.)

[1] Chorley, p. 353.

The 'buried world' of whole, unfractured being, the fragile and vulnerable spiritual inheritance, not only yearns for authentic expression in living and feeling, but cries out against the hemming dangers of dissipation, in task-work,[1] in the arid fascination of intellection,[2] in false allegiances falsely imposed by false conceptions of duty,[3] or embraced through a weak hungering for rest and ease.[4] The intense distress of the struggle against an inward surrender of mind and spirit issues, on the one hand, negatively in a regressive yearning towards ablutionary purity:

> Sweet streamlet bason! at thy side
> Weary and faint within me cried
> My longing heart,—In such pure deep
> How sweet it were to sit and sleep; . . .[5]

On the other hand, more positively and characteristically, it results, as in the following lines, in a sternly enforced rejection of will in action, and in a soft and humble attitude of expectant openness which attempts to preserve the malleability of the child's spirit:

> Come back again, old heart! Ah me!
>   Methinks in those thy coward fears
> There might, perchance, a courage be,
>   That fails in these the manlier years;
> Courage to let the courage sink,
> Itself a coward base to think,
> Rather than not for heavenly light
> Wait on to show the truly right.

(Poems, 10.)

A poem written in 1839, only part of which has been printed, extends the scope of both these poems and clarifies Clough's

---

[1] 'Blank Misgivings', ix, ll. 71–4.   [2] 'Away, haunt not thou me'.
[3] 'Thought may well be ever ranging'.
[4] 'Blank Misgivings', ii and x; 'So I as boyish years went by, went wrong'.
[5] *Poems*, p. 23. Chorley (pp. 342, 345, 352) presents this poem as an important link in arguing the case for Clough's profound mother-fixation. One should note the additional lines from the 1839–42 Notebook (*Poems*, p. 467) for Clough's enlargement of the statement which advocates work—even the most 'poor mechanic task'—as the means to a recovery of that blissful pristine state of purity. The close association between the attitude towards work as a remedy for the ills of mind and spirit and deeply rooted psychological trauma which the complete poem suggests, neatly focuses some of the central features of the 'Clough problem': the further he moved away from a fairly homogeneous complex of values— Work, Duty, Purity, Self-Sacrifice—the more acute became the psychological strain, the more powerful the inner compulsion to resubscribe those values.

attitude to the ideal of childhood. Against the Evangelical emphasis on the universal Fall and the innate depravity of children, he places Platonic–Wordsworthian remembrance, the innate knowledge of the One, and out of this opposition he builds the synthesis of his belief, which, typically, rejects neither view outright:

Thou bidd'st me mark how swells with rage
    The childish cheek, the childish limb,
How strongly lust and passion wage
    Their strife in every petty whim;
Primeval stains from earliest age,
    Thou say'st, our glorious souls bedim;
Yet not, though true thy Wisdom says,
Will I love less the childish days.

Thou askest, ask it as thou wilt,
    How thus I dare to praise the State
Of Adam's child, an heir of guilt,
    And sin, original, innate;
And why the holy blood was spilt
    If sin at last were not so great:
'Tis true, I own; I cannot tell;
Yet still I cherish childhood well.

Perchance, though born 'twixt good and ill
    To join in warfare through his life,
His heart is in the garden still,
    With Eden thoughts his spirit rife,
And therefore conquering Passions fill
    His struggling breast [heart?] with fiercer strife:
It may be—doubtful Wisdom says,
And lets me love the childish days.

With sin innate, that still descends
    On Adam's children one and all,
Perchance innate remembrance blends
    Of Adam's joys before the Fall;
His sinful heart to us he sends
    And we with him his bliss recall:
And so, a truer wisdom says
Go cherish still the childish days.

We go our worldly ways, and there
    Our Eden thoughts we lose them quite;
Only the quiet Evening air,
    Or dewy Morn or starry night

Remind us of the Vision fair,
   Or bring it back in living might,
And offer to our tearful gaze
The Paradise of childish days.

Such be the Cause, or be it not,
   Believe, and let the causes go;
New love may every day be got
   So long as here we dwell below;
Of more the heart is ware, I wot,
   Than philosophic systems know;
So heed thou not what thy Wisdom says,
But cherish thou the childish days.[1]

Considered as poetry rather than as biographically or intellectually illuminating material there is a great deal that can be dispensed with in these undergraduate poems; only rarely do we encounter a craftsmanship or an inspiration which is truly distinctive or arresting. Yet the uneasy and awkward conventionality of this poetry—like its occasionally experimental qualities—raises important points about Clough's development as a poet. In his search for an authentic artistic personality he follows a path closely paralleling that which can be discerned in his biography generally. One notices the same inertia and hesitancy in questioning prevailing conventions about the nature of poetry and the qualities of the poetic, and, eventually, the same dissatisfaction with throwing himself into acceptable and expected postures.

An obvious problem he faced in his undergraduate poetry was that of finding some alternative poetic which could justify his fall from the didactic and 'objective' grace of his Rugbeian verse into a nakedly self-involved and confessional mode. An exchange of letters in July 1838—before, that is, virtually all his undergraduate verse was written—may very well have helped in providing him with such a poetic. Burbidge's *Poems, Longer and Shorter* had just been published, and Clough wrote:

All poetry must be the language of Feeling of some kind, I suppose, and the imaginative expression of affection must be poetry: but it seems to me that it is both critically best and morally safest to dramaticize your feelings where they are of a private personal character—e.g.

---

[1] 1839–40 Notebook. Bodleian MS. Eng. Poet. d. 126, fols. 9ᵛ–10ᵛ. The poem also appears in an unpublished letter to Burbidge dated 16 May 1839—Bodleian MS. Eng. Lett. c. 189(80). The fifth stanza has been printed in *Catalogue*, p. 14.

in case of affection for a brother to write a poem like Wordsworth's 'Brothers' or to suppose your brother dead and write a 'My Brother's Grave' ἐκ φαντασίας. Persons however of more passionate natures and less fearful of or prone to affectations may I dare say without any harm morally to self or intelligent readers write straight de rebus et personis ipsis. Thus much I would grant, but critically I should think these would be inferior, just as portraits are to ideal paintings.[1]

As the rest of the letter shows more clearly, Clough had most prominently in mind the moral—and secondarily aesthetic—inferiority of the identifiable depiction of other persons in expressing 'private and personal' feelings. His particular objection to Burbidge's practice in this respect, however, is contained in a critical and personal tendency to prefer oblique and generalized expression of feeling—grounded partly in his awareness of the danger of 'affectation', and also, no doubt, in his own natural reserve.[2] Gell replied with a persuasive 'treatise on the publication of private feelings in poetry', in which he argued for the unclothing of the poet's psyche, because, apart from the consideration that 'to one who studies the natural philosophy of the mind, (as for instance a poet, pursuing his art,) the private feelings of any mind are worth having', 'the private feelings of a superior mind are well worth knowing, and do a great deal of good to many others'. 'To Leviathan', Gell concluded, 'the poet can only presume to offer an account of his private feelings, as being more acute, comprehensive and cultivated than those of ordinary

---

[1] *Corr.* i. 73–4. The letter betrays an interesting mixture of critical attitudes. The half-unwilling concession that poetry is 'the language of feeling' is a concession to post-Romantic doctrine—most forcefully asserted, of course, by John Stuart Mill. At the same time, the contrast between 'ideal paintings' and 'portraits', while it is by no means specifically anti-Romantic, suggests neo-classical habits of preference, and thus gives some historical depth to our understanding of the generality and abstraction of much of Clough's verse.

[2] The danger of 'affectation' was double-edged. On the one hand, it made one acutely conscious of insincerity in directly self-revelatory expression; on the other, it also made one uneasy about the implications of role-playing. The rudimentary attempts at disguising himself behind aliases in *The Rugby Magazine* suggest that Clough was drawn towards the freedoms offered by oblique presentation early in his literary career. As he wrote to his sister, 'Z means nothing at all, except that I don't want to be so openly known, or rather, it is a bore having to support the character of Clayton throughout' (*Corr.* i. 28). The tension between the impulse of direct, completely precipitated self-confession, and the urge towards more tangential modes becomes increasingly important as Clough develops as a poet, and is stabilized most characteristically—and successfully—in his self-ironic satire.

mortals.'[1] Clough seems to have come round, although reluctantly, to something like his friend's way of thinking, and the case for subjective and expressivist art urged by Gell would have been strengthened by an article on poetry in the *British Critic* of which Clough wrote in October 1838: 'There is a very good article . . . involving a Theory of Poetry, in the last no. of the British Critic, . . . by a man . . . called Rogers' (*Corr.* i. 85). 'A *poetical* way of viewing things', Frederic Rogers wrote in this article, 'is that which is opposed to a matter-of-fact one; it is poetical so far as it does not rest in the mere phenomena which it handles, but aims at informing them with something spiritual, ideal, unearthly; and any object or thought is ordinarily called poetical so far as it refuses to be appreciated except through this medium.'[2] 'Poetry is essentially an aspiration', Rogers concluded, since its main characteristic was 'elevation of tone'.[3] Conceding that this last characterization was somewhat vague, he maintained that 'while it leaves the poet truth as his subject, it gives him the privilege of not being taken *quite* literally. He is allowed to place his thoughts and feelings before others, not *exactly* as he thinks and feels them, but with a certain golden colouring.'[4] Pressing the case for subjective art, he argued that such art enabled the reader to recognize the minute fluctuations of his own thoughts and emotions; further, this discovery of shared experience could help to soften the 'sense of insulation and peculiarity by an intelligent expectation of a wider communion with others'.[5] From the poet's side, the legitimate inspiration of such expected sympathy could save him from pure egotism. Intensely conscious of the loneliness and isolation of his struggle in these years, Clough must have found this last argument especially appealing, and, as Walter Houghton has observed, it is very likely that this article combined with the influence of Gell in strengthening the element of direct reportage in Clough's subjective poetry.[6] Introspection, nurtured by Arnold and the Oxford Movement, was given artistic justification.

The artistic problem, implicit in the coupling of a conception of

[1] *Corr.* i. 76, 77. Houghton, p. 58, has drawn attention to the importance of these letters.

[2] 'Poems by Trench and Milnes', *British Critic*, xxiv (1838), 277.

[3] Ibid., p. 278.   [4] Ibid., p. 279.   [5] Ibid., p. 281.

[6] In the preceding two paragraphs I am indebted extensively to Houghton, pp. 58-9.

poetry as 'a poetical way of viewing things . . . as opposed to a matter of fact one' with a mode involving the direct transcript of the results of introspection, boiled down to the question of sincerity and spontaneity (or, as Clough would say, the absence of 'affectation'). Inevitably these central criteria of thorough-going expressivism shaded off into moral questions—especially when, as so often with Clough, they were blurred by the failure to distinguish firmly enough between artistic and personal sincerity and spontaneity. How, in short, could one view oneself 'poetically' and yet be absolutely truthful?

Though much of his poetry was written from within these expressivist assumptions and betrays an inability to resolve such basic dilemmas, we should note that, even at this early date, Clough showed some reservations about the more extreme consequences of expressivism. One of these was that poetry was a window into the personality of the creative artist, and that there was a direct qualitative correlation between the two. Clough's passing remark on Milton is illuminating—*Paradise Lost* would be 'unsaleable' in Tractarian Oxford, he feared, 'Were it not for the happy notion that a man's poetry is not at all affected by his opinions or indeed character and mind altogether' (*Corr*. i. 88–9). Writing of some of his own verses in 1841, he said, 'I am afraid that there may be something of affectation in them or at any rate of calling things by wrong names and better names than they deserve, which I seem to detect in all the things I wrote in the Magazine' (*Corr*. i. 107). He had put his finger directly on the problem he faced, often unsuccessfully, of being both scrupulously precise and, at the same time, 'poetical' in the poems in which he attempted to exteriorize his inward states. In pruning the moral implications of 'affectation' into 'calling things by wrong names and better names than they deserve', he showed a realization that this was an artistic problem fundamentally, a question of precision and fidelity of language, rather than a moral one. The 'golden colouring' advocated by Rogers as signalizing an appropriate 'aspiration' and 'elevation' could be an artistic as well as a moral pitfall.

Certainly, the precisely poised epigrammatic enactment of perplexity in the lines, written in Grasmere in July 1841 after he had taken his degree, and printed for the first time by the Oxford editors, is exceptional in the directly subjective poems of these years:

Would that I were,—O hear thy suppliant, thou,
    Whom fond belief still ventures here to see,—
Would that I were not that which I am now
    Nor yet became the thing I wish to be!
What wouldst thou? Poor suggestion of today
    Depart, vain fancy and fallacious thought!
Would I could wish my wishes all away,
    And learn to wish the wishes that I ought.

                                          (*Poems*, 49.)

The thought evolves in a firm uncluttered flow, but yet conveys
the complex movement of emotional reaction and the shifting
ambiguities of response. Depending for its achievement on the
syntactical rather than the vocabular resources of the language,
it looks forward to Clough's most characteristic achievement in
poetry. The rhythmic impetus of the initial appeal, checked by a
lightly broken phrase which underscores the ambivalent attitude
to belief in the second line, carries the thought—thus qualified
and deepened—into the swift rejection of the third and fourth
lines. Substantially the same pattern recurs in the next four lines
where pause and variation of pace are used to undermine personal
competence. The confidence of the opening phrase, 'Would that
I were', dwindles to a question, 'What wouldst thou?', and
ends in the completely bewildered and deflated uncertainty of
the last two lines. Austere, intellectual, precisely ordered in its
command of movement and tone, the pleasure of complete and
final precipitation which this verse offers is distinctively Cloughian.
Too often in these poems, however, the colloquial and muscular
strength of the terse, plunging beginnings—'Well, Well,—
Heaven bless you all from day to day!', 'Yes, I have lied, and so
must walk my way', 'So I, as boyish years went by, went wrong'
—is smothered by a flabby and automatic phrasing. Here is an
example:

            ——Roused by importunate knocks
    I rose, I turned the key, and let them in,
    First one, anon another, and at length
    In troops they came; for how could I, who once
    Had let in one, nor looked him in the face,
    Show scruples e'er again? So in they came,
    A noisy band of revellers,—vain hopes,
    Wild fancies, fitful joys; and there they sit

In my heart's holy place, and through the night
Carouse, to leave it when the cold grey dawn
Gleams from the East, to tell me that the time
For watching and for thought bestowed is gone.

('Blank Misgivings', VII; *Poems*, 30–1.)

Competent, undistinguished verse, where the central image is
furbished up with poetic archaism ('anon', 'carouse') and con-
traction ('e'er') and cliché ('a noisy band of revellers', the 'heart's
holy place', the 'cold grey dawn gleams from the East', 'the time
for watching and for thought').

The unevenness of many of these poems can be traced to two
other chief causes, both related to Clough's efforts to 'poeticize'
and give a 'golden colouring' to his communication. Number
VI of 'Blank Misgivings' is an example of one source of failure—

———Like a child
In some strange garden left awhile alone,
I pace about the pathways of the world,
Plucking light hopes and joys from every stem,
With qualms of vague misgiving in my heart
That payment at the last will be required,
Payment I cannot make, or guilt incurred,
And shame to be endured.

(*Poems*, 30.)

The Byronic attitudinizing is unsatisfying largely because of the
falsification involved, the lack of grip on the working out of the
embodying imagery, indicated, for instance, in the bringing
together of 'child' and 'pace'. Again, can the 'qualms of vague
misgiving' of the poet have any serious content, can the payment, the shame, and the guilt be so grievous, if the equivalent
to his situation is that of an unattended child doing some mild
damage in a garden? As Henry Sidgwick, one of Clough's most
sympathetic Victorian critics, observed, 'He becomes unpoetical
chiefly when he becomes less eagerly intellectual'—not when he
is not feeling intensely.[1]

If Clough fails in these poems because of his attempt at height-
ening through the use of a would-be poetic language and a worn
currency of inadequately thought-out imagery, he also fails at
times because of his retreat—dictated, no doubt, by a similar

[1] Review of *PPR. Westminster Review*, xcii (Oct. 1869), 367.

impulse—to the ready-made poetry of his literary models. He confronts his subject at second-hand, through a literary and dated haze that blurs and dissipates any attack. Wordsworth and archaism together give us:

> ——so at whiles
> Lights have descended, hues have been,
> To clothe with half-celestial grace
> The bareness of the desert place.

('Blank Misgivings', IX, 27–30; *Poems*, 32.)

All these allied weaknesses appear in the blatant badness of the following lines, in which Clough, Wordsworth, and Milton play catch with 'poetical' sentiments and phrases:

> Oh well do I remember then the days
> When on some grassy slope, what time the sun
> Was sinking and the solemn eve came down
> With its blue vapour upon field and wood
> And elm-embosomed spire, once more again
> I fed on sweet emotions, and my soul
> With love o'erflowed or hushed itself in fear
> Unearthly, yea celestial, once again
> My heart was hot within me, and meseemed
> I too had in my body breath to sound
> The magic horn of song, I too possessed
> Upwelling in my being's depths a fount
> Of the true poet-nectar, whence to fill
> The golden urns of verse.

(*Poems*, 46.)

Worried speculation and stark self-introspection dominate Clough's undergraduate poetry—but they are not the only sources of inspiration. In an essay on 'The Moral Effect of Works of Satire' written in 1839–40 he maintained, citing Juvenal and Persius as masters of the mode, that satire,

being then as in its highest form it is, the means whereby a love of Virtue and Excellence in circumstances of general depravity has best found vent, we cannot doubt its efficiency as a moral engine in the service of this feeling. Numbers too careless to heed, and too hardened perhaps to appreciate the more usual and universal admonitions, are by the keen edge of Satire roused to a sense of their folly and baseness.[1]

[1] Trawick, p. 63.

This newly acquired sense of the potentialities of satire can be traced in some of Clough's own undergraduate verse, in which the moral sense bequeathed to him jointly by Dr. Arnold and the Oxford Movement feels its way towards an alternative mode of expression. The volume of Clough's satirical poetry in these Balliol years is meagre and most of it displays the dependency and awkwardness of the fledgling. The attack on competitive, myopically mercantile and ostentatious London in 'To the Great Metropolis' (*Poems*, 48) is a well-turned variation on the 'Westminster Bridge' sonnet. Weighty capitalized abstractions invoking the high-Wordsworthian manner combine with images of shoddy, emptily busy, and purely utilitarian activity to revoke the Wordsworthian vision of 'a mighty nation's heart'. Standing too close to his moral judgement, too passionately engaged, he loses grip on his criticism in 'Duty—that's to say complying' (*Poems*, 27), although, from a technical point of view, the exploitation of expressive rhythmic disintegration from an initial, monotonously conforming automatism is not without interest. Attempting a Juvenalian indignation, Clough's angry denunciation of the tyranny of conventional notions of duty, important as it is biographically as an early manifestation of his exasperation, explodes into a spectacularly ineffective show of bad temper. The satirist, in Humbert Wolfe's words, beats 'his hands in vain against the iron doors of Victorian insensibility'[1]— and, aesthetically, the clangorous spectacle is less than engaging. The incoherent rhyming of the first sections matches the shrillness and splutter of a protest which subsides, in the concluding lines, in complete, name-calling collapse:

> 'Tis the blind non-recognition
>   Either of goodness, truth, or beauty,
> Except by precept and submission;
>   Moral blank, and moral void,
>   Life at very birth destroyed,
> Atrophy, exinanition!
> Duty!—
> Yea, by duty's prime condition
>   Pure nonentity of duty!

(Poems, 28.)

[1] 'Arthur Hugh Clough', in *The Eighteen-Sixties*, ed. J. Drinkwater (Cambridge, 1932), p. 35.

Sometimes, however, Clough's gaze, usually so unremittingly and despairingly fixed on himself, turned outward on the world in fugitive moments of detached, lightly mocking social observation. One such moment is recorded in the letter he wrote to Gell in 1839 inviting him over to Oxford for Commemoration Day:

> You will also have the opportunity of seeing Conybeare Pater issuing fulminatory condemnations of the Fathers at the heads of astonished Newmanists from St. Mary's pulpit: himself in shape, conformation and gestures most like one of his own icthyosauri and his voice evidently proceeding from lungs of a fossil character. Again you will see Chevalier Bunsen, Poet Wordsworth, and Astronomer Herschell metamorphosed into Doctors of Civil Law, a sight worthy, especially in the second case, of all contemplation. Furthermore there will be boat races with much shouting and beer-drinking, a psychological study of great interest (*Corr.* i. 91–2).

This feeling for social comedy had to wait, as Houghton has remarked,[1] till 1848 for its developed expression in Clough's art: he was too preoccupied elsewhere to devote much time to its cultivation. But even in these early years the vein is not entirely unworked. In 'Look you, my simple friend, 'tis one of those' (*Poems*, 25), written in 1840, his satiric impulse finds a more perfectly controlled and structured form through its exploitation of comic distance. The poem is an early example of Clough's device of juxtaposing different manners and voices to increase the range and flexibility of his effects. The light he had elsewhere turned so bleakly on himself here plays from a much more freely moving pivot. In the first section he weaves twenty lines of effective pastiche, effective because reductive of itself and moving with his satiric purpose—self-criticism as much as social, since the animal anatomized is also partly himself:[2]

> Look you, my simple friend, 'tis one of those
> (Alack, a common weed of our ill time),
> Who, do whate'er they may, go where they will,
> Must needs still carry about the looking-glass
> Of vain philosophy. And if so be
> That some small natural gesture shall escape them,
> (Nature will out) straightway about they turn,

---

[1] Houghton, p. 70.
[2] See especially lines 10–13 of 'Enough small Room,—tho' all too true' (*Poems*, p. 48).

> And con it duly there, and note it down,
> With inward glee and much complacent chuckling,
> Part in conceit of their superior science,
> Part in forevision of the attentive look
> And laughing glance that may one time reward them,
> When the fresh ore, this day dug up, at last
> Shall, thrice refined and purified, from the mint
> Of conversation intellectual
> Into the golden currency of wit
> Issue—satirical or pointed sentence,
> Impromptu, epigram, or it may be sonnet,
> Heir undisputed to the pinkiest page
> In the album of a literary lady.

The unhurried movement, qualifying, turning back on itself, sustained by the periodic amplitude and the studied ceremoniousness of the diction, underscores the slow deflation. The poverty of the reward so assiduously pursued is noted briefly and with equally deceptive ceremony in lines 11 and 12, and then more elaborately in the figure of laborious refinement and coinage which flows into the sharply turned irony of the last two lines.

The second section, setting the governing centre of the satire firmly and abruptly against this, exhibits a complete shift in tone. The poem develops into a close and demanding structure of argument.

> And can it be, you ask me, that a man,
> With the strong arm, the cunning faculties,
> And keenest forethought gifted, and, within,
> Longings unspeakable, the lingering echoes
> Responsive to the still-still-calling voice
> Of God Most High,—should disregard all these,
> And half-employ all those for such an aim
> As the light sympathy of successful wit,
> Vain titillation of a moment's praise?
> Why, so is good no longer good, but crime
> Our truest, best advantage, since it lifts us
> Out of the stifling gas of men's opinion
> Into the vital atmosphere of Truth,
> Where He again is visible, tho' in anger.

Except for the slightly troubling patness of 'longings unspeakable' and 'lingering echoes', the whole movement is firm and precise. The explicitly analogical control of the images, the unadorned denotativeness of the language, and the tight habit of antithesis contribute towards a clarity of logical evolution which easily sustains the final paradox towards which the whole poem moves. As Houghton has argued, the Victorian ear was not attuned to the pleasures offered by this kind of poetry.[1]

The bulk of Clough's undergraduate verse is undistinguished and depressing. Drab, unashamedly earnest and finger-wagging, chronically inattentive to verbal surface in its single-minded effort to say things, it beats with a listless and sub-poetic pulse. Its energy is usually only a fitful stridency, its occasional attempt at enrichment a patchwork of dead ornament. But many of the features which mar this verse so seriously—its frequent second-handness, its tendency towards generalization and abstraction, its thinness of verbal texture—in themselves contain possibilities for distinguished achievement. As the few successes indicate, they can produce a peculiarly satisfying, precisely—and even com-plexly—articulated poetry of ideas, firm in its outlines and subtly controlled in its movements and tonalities. For the really significant deficiency is not so much a matter of local failures in technique—although these are important and, sometimes, decisive. It is, rather, the deeper and more embracing failure of inspiration. Over and over again in reading this verse one senses the absence of any real organizing and directing artistic purpose. Somehow, somewhere an impulse, a cause, an energy has evaporated, leaving behind only a limp and dispirited evidence of perhaps having once been. Clough is a significant poet only at those moments in which he achieved full possession of his purposes: fortunately for English poetry, as he grew older those moments became more frequent—and more consecutive.

[1] Houghton, pp. 12–13.

CHAPTER III

Oxford: Oriel, 1842–1848: The Question of Religion

[T]here is hardly to be found in England an individual of any importance in the world of mind, who (whatever opinions he may have afterwards adopted) did not first learn to think from one of these two . . . Jeremy Bentham and Samuel Taylor Coleridge—the two great seminal minds in England in their age.

J. S. Mill, 'Bentham', *Dissertations and Discussions*, vol. i.

It was an era of new ideas, of swift if silent revolution. . . . To those who inquired with open minds it appeared that things which good and learned men were doubting about must be themselves doubtful. Thus all round us, the intellectual lightships had broken from their moorings, and it was then a new and trying experience. The present generation which has grown up in an open spiritual ocean, which has got used to it and has learned to swim for itself, will never know what it was to find the lights all drifting, the compasses all awry, and nothing left to steer by except the stars.

In this condition the best and bravest of my own contemporaries determined to have done with insincerity, to find ground under their feet, to let the uncertain remain uncertain, but to learn how much and what we could honestly regard as true, and believe that and live by it.

J. A. Froude, *Carlyle's Life in London*, vol. i.

None of the ways in which . . . mental regeneration is sought, Bible Societies, Tract Societies, Puseyism, Socialism, Chartism, Benthamism, etc.—will *do*, though doubtless they have all some elements of truth and good in them.

J. S. Mill, letter of 1842 to R. B. Fox, in C. Fox, *Memories of Old Friends*.

'It is the trial and mystery of our position in this Age and Country, that a religious mind is continually set at variance with itself; that its deference to what is without contradicts suggestions from within; and that it cannot obey what is over it, without rebelling against what is before it'—Br. Cr. lxii, 401. In this state of non-adjustment, Obedience becomes conformity, conventionality, . . . and sham, while Non-Conformity leads into Passion for Passion's sake, fancy for fancy's sake, that perpetual semi-consciousness of rebellion which leads into rebellion. We are tempted at one time to give our faith in semblance, where we do not feel it reality,—to [therefore] at another to [*sic*] fasten upon that which we know to be an object of faith only by a proud assumption of our own. Seeing nowhere extant the truly adequate object, we attach ourselves to that which so far as we know is inadequate, by an arbitrary assumption in the one case of pride, in the other of cowardice.

Arthur Hugh Clough, *1842 Journal*.

Those are indeed happy who can still hope for England, who can find, in identifying themselves with our political or social institutions a congenial atmosphere, and a suitable machinery for accomplishing at last all that they dream of. Of such sanguine spirits, alas! I am not one. . . . Our lot is cast in an evil time; we cannot accept the present, and we shall not live to see the future. It is an age of transition; in which the mass are carried hither and thither by chimeras of different kinds, while to the few, who know the worthlessness of the chimeras, and have caught a glimpse of the sublime but distant future, is left nothing but sadness and isolation.

Tom Arnold to Arthur Hugh Clough, 16 April 1847,
The New Zealand Letters of Thomas Arnold the Younger.

IN choosing to lecture on Heroes and Hero-worship Carlyle was appealing to one of the most deeply rooted responses of his age. Troubled by self-consciousness of a kind which had never been known before, acutely aware of the forces of change, of its own state of crisis and dissolution, the age projected its achievements and its virtues, its desires for stability and reassurance, on to the gigantic images of itself and its leaders that it created. There were, undoubtedly, giants in the land: only demi-gods could allay the unease and anxiety of this radically disturbed society. The nurture of demi-gods started early. Where else, except in the pages of nineteenth-century memoirs, does one encounter the schoolboy Hercules? In what subsequent period can one uncover such glowing accounts of prodigious victories wrested from University Examiners, of Firsts and Double Firsts? What other period could match that superb story of J. B. Mozley's Fellowship Examination at Oriel, when, after a full day's silent contemplation of the essay paper for which he was allowed till dusk, he threw himself down on the floor to catch the fading light of the embers in the fireplace, and finished his ten lines, ten prize-winning lines of unbelievable distinction, 'ten lines . . . such as no other man in Oxford could have written'.[1]

The titan's part had been assigned to Clough early in his life, and, despite strain and occasional misgiving, he had filled it with conspicuous aptitude at Rugby. At Balliol he had been less

---

[1] R. W. Church to H. P. Liddon in M. Church, *Life and Letters of Dean Church* (London, 1895), p. 19.

exemplary; he had become regrettably entangled in religious controversy, he had allowed himself to drift and had been a universal disappointment in the Schools. Painfully and slowly, however, he was learning the ways of independence. Less than three months after his election to his Oriel Fellowship tragedy struck with sudden paralysing force. On 11 June 1842 Dr. Arnold died. Clough was stunned; on hearing the news he took himself off to Liverpool and went walking alone in the Welsh mountains. His leader, the titan and begetter of titans, had been struck down. He was on his own. Two clear trends emerge from his career as a Fellow at Oriel. On the one hand he developed to a full, far-reaching, and adult engagement with the manifold questionings and anxieties of the forties, especially with the contention between the forces of religion and secularism, trans-cendental idealism and rationalistic positivism. On the other, he emerged from that encounter with the flattering—though not altogether respectable, and, in fact, rather troublesome—reputa-tion of a Carlylean idol-breaker and—his friends hoped, rather uncertainly—very possibly the prospective Carlylean sage.

A re-reading of the evidence reveals Clough's response to the new and troubled world which opened out to him in his years at Oriel as a complicated pattern of wide-ranging and often radical questioning of the bases on which contemporary life was ordered. Religion and morality, the organization of society, the dogmas of economics, the problems of industrialism, University reform—these were some of his concerns. It is the biographer's task to connect and relate diverse strands, but in Clough's case the very intricacy of his lived criticism, the inter- and often counter-acting relatedness of his intellectual and emotional life, threatens to prove embarrassing. The working of his mind has been compared with John Newman's.[1] Clough, like Newman, insisted on the movement of the 'whole man': the description of an integrated development can readily degenerate into an incoherent tangle of interrelationships and qualifications. In attempting to unravel the major lines in Clough's development over these years I am concerned primarily, not with evaluating Clough's conclusions or lack of conclusions, but with describing the nature and direction of that development and the kinds of emotional and psychological reassurance and stress it created.

[1] Review of *Corr.*, *Times Literary Supplement*, 6 Dec. 1957, p. 738.

'All [Clough's] religious needs, hopes, aspirations remaining the same,' Henry Sidgwick wrote in 1869, 'a new view of the universe, with slowly accumulating force impressed itself on his mind, with which not only the intellectual beliefs entwined with these needs and aspirations seemed incompatible, but even these latter fundamentally incongruous. And thus began a conflict between old and new that was to last his life. . . .'[1] As more recent studies, notably by Michael Timko,[2] have demonstrated, the element of paralysis has been too frequently overstressed; Clough is not quite so thoroughly the undecided figure presented in older accounts. It is possible, too, to lay too much emphasis on his religious preoccupations. But to denude his response of the fine dialectic of uncertainty, of the sensitive interplay in it of tradition and emancipation, of its perplexed but courageous provisionality, is both radically misleading and reductive: Clough becomes a bland and effortless—and ultimately un-interesting—figure. Positiveness of belief in itself guarantees no distinction. Sidgwick's description, outlining as it does the wider cultural terms and conditions of Clough's quest, is both sensitive and central. In his way Clough is as complete and inclusive a cultural symbol of his time as Teufelsdröckh is, and if he did not complete his journey with a resonating Carlylean arrival, it is because he looked further and more minutely than his literary counterpart did into the world which, as Matthew Arnold put it, 'was struggling to be born'. In venturing outwards intellectually he admitted not only heterodox ideas but emotions, acknowledged in himself responses which simply refused to accommodate themselves in traditional moulds or submit to his own provisional formulations—and those formulations could only be provisional: the logic of adherence, both intellectual and emotional, was too strong to allow a final severance. The honesty of his inquiry into his own nature and that of the world around him wins our admiration, but the very nature of that honesty was limiting in strictly intellectual terms. It insisted on a lived rather than merely theoretical inquiry, in the face of his own sensitivity to isolation

---

[1] H. Sidgwick, 'The Poems and Prose Remains of Arthur Hugh Clough', *Westminster Review*, xcii (Oct. 1869), 370.

[2] Cf. M. Timko, 'The "True Creed" of Arthur Hugh Clough', *Modern Language Quarterly* (hereafter *MLQ*) xxi (Sept. 1960), 208–22. The article has been reprinted in a revised form in the same author's *Innocent Victorian* (Columbus, Ohio, 1966).

it drove him to become an outsider, but the personal consequence, the sheer exigencies of living, of having friends and being loved, weighed heavily in the final balance.

However much of an outsider he might have felt—encouraged as he was by the socially ambiguous position of his family, the 'foreignness' of his early life in America, the distance he discovered within himself from the values and assumptions of his friends, his own persisting exclusion from professional success—he belonged clearly in a particular cultural and historical stratum of society; his education, his class allegiances, his social codes put him there. In other words, extensive as his questioning was, radical as his experience of the diseases of modernity was, he was an Early-Victorian of the middle class submitting Early-Victorianism to a critical scrutiny, and the particular balance of acceptance and rejection which that scrutiny displays gives it an individual and special value. One example will illustrate the nature of this particular tension. The 'Long Vacation Pastoral' in hexameters, *The Bothie of Tober-na-Vuolich*, which he wrote on leaving Oxford, was read, at the level of social criticism, by the more reactionary among his Oxford contemporaries as a radical attack on existing society that deserved the rather vague but definitely reprobative epithet 'communistic', with all its contemporary associations of flagrant immorality and wild-eyed egalitarianism (*Corr.* i. 240). Yet a twentieth-century critic writes of the same poem: 'It is incredibly evocative of a day that has gone: when gentry were gentry, and everyone else merely people. When Clough wrote "The Bothie", though he liked to think he was in flaming revolt against the accepted values, it is perfectly clear that he was still in his heart accepting them.'[1] Both judgements, so dependent on historical perspective, are 'true', but though they conflict, neither cancels the other out: a final 'placing' must accommodate both. Biographically, the more relevant point is contained in the first reaction: how it felt to live as a reputed radical.

By his election to an Oriel Fellowship on 31 March 1842 Clough retrieved his academic fortunes and allayed his friends' doubts about his abilities. Oriel's Fellowship examination was still regarded as one of the best tests of intellectual power in the University, even though the college had lost to Balliol the

[1] M. Bishop, 'Thyrsis; or the Importance of Not Being Earnest', in *The Pleasure Ground*, ed. M. Elwin (London, 1947), p. 72.

pre-eminence acquired earlier in the century. The decline of
the college was generally traced by observers to the election as
Provost in 1830 of Edward Hawkins. In his earlier days Hawkins
had been numbered among the Noetics, had been a companion
in logic and liberalism with Arnold and Whately, but under the
cares of Provostship, that liberalism had subsided into a settled
and obstinate orthodoxy. He had become, as Max Müller put it,
a thoroughgoing 'representative of Old Oxford', whose chilling
formality earned him among his Fellows the nickname of 'the
East Wind'. He played up to that sobriquet with his forbiddingly
exact discriminations of social station—'He had a very peculiar
habit; when he had to shake hands with people whom he considered his inferiors, he stretched out two fingers. . . .'[1] He lived
by rule and statute and form. One story about him maintains that
when an undergraduate fell to his death in the quadrangle from
an upper-storey window, he lingered punctiliously to don cap,
gown, and bands before venturing from his lodgings to view the
body of the unfortunate youth.[2] And yet, in his intermittent but
extended correspondence with Clough about the latter's religious
difficulties this quaint, inflexible, unimaginative incarnation of
outdated certainties exercised an almost endless patience, made
genuine though bewildered efforts to understand the nature of the
difficulties which seemed to have taken possession of this new
generation. Erect, perplexed, obsolete, he nevertheless emerges
from that exchange of letters with a freshened dignity, a striking
humanity.

The comparative freedom from worry of the months immediately following Clough's election was short-lived, and doubts
and questions revived with fresh relevance as the time for taking
his M.A. approached. Essential if he wanted to stay on at Oxford,
an M.A. required a re-Subscription to the Thirty-nine Articles.
The question of his M.A. raised a further spectre: unless he took
orders his Fellowship would expire at Easter in 1849. In October
1845 he wrote to tell Gell, possibly only half-seriously, that he
was 'ruminating . . . a precipitate flight from Oxford' in order
to escape being put down as an adherent of the 'Puseyite' camp
or, for that matter, any other doctrinally embattled one. He liked
his work as tutor, he had no idea where he would go or what he

[1] Müller, F. Max, *My Autobiography* (London, 1901), p. 241.
[2] D. W. Rannie, *Oriel College* (London, 1900), pp. 188-9.

would do if he left Oxford, but he was restless. He had had enough of the niceties of doctrinal condition and was beginning to feel a 'large amount of objection or rather repugnance to sign "ex animo" the 39 Articles'. It was not, he assured Gell, that he had definite and particular objections to specific points; rather, his repugnance stemmed from a 'general dislike to Subscription and strong feeling of its being after all, malgre Guy's Hospital Maurice [i.e. Frederick Denison Maurice], a bondage, and a very heavy one, and one that may cramp one and cripple one for life' (*Corr.* i. 124). Perhaps under the pressure of financial necessity quite simply, he shelved these doubts, however, subscribed the Articles later that month, and took his M.A.

Difficulties about the Thirty-nine Articles were not at all uncommon in Clough's day, but his position—which led him ultimately to resign his Fellowship—was not distinctive simply by virtue of a quirky scrupulousness and intransigence. Even the most cursory consideration of a broad historical movement in which utilitarians like Bentham, theological liberals, and Tractarians were alike involved, gives us a clear idea of the significance of his stand in a crucial issue in the liberation of the intellect from ecclesiastical authority. The Feather's Tavern Petition of 1772, presented to Parliament by about two hundred liberal Christians, urging the replacement of Subscription to the Thirty-nine Articles by a general declaration of belief in the Bible, may be regarded as the beginning of a movement which in the eighteenth century included Paley, who questioned the logic of a test imposed by a Church which made no claim to infallible authority, and Richard Watson, Bishop of Llandaff, who based his objection on the damnatory clauses of the Athanasian Creed.[1] In 1775 the University of Cambridge abolished Subscription at matriculation, and, though Subscription remained compulsory for Fellows, for Bachelors of Arts the Articles were replaced by a deliberately ambiguously worded declaration.[2] The nineteenth century brought a fresh spate of objections and difficulties. Dr. Arnold, for instance, was troubled especially (like his pupil Stanley later) by the VIIIth Article and its connection with

[1] V. F. Storr, *The Development of English Theology in the Nineteenth Century, 1800–1860* (London, 1913), p. 92.
[2] E. Halévy, *A History of the English People in the Nineteenth Century*, trans. E. I. Watkin and D. A. Barker, 4 vols. 2nd edn. (London, 1949), i. 547.

the Athanasian Creed. In Cambridge, Frederick Denison Maurice, though he eventually returned to the Anglican fold and took orders in 1834, was excluded from his degree and a Fellowship because of his refusal to subscribe. In 1835 Dr. Hampden wrote a strong pamphlet urging the abolition of Subscription at matriculation in Oxford, but the measure he initiated was defeated in Convocation that May. One of the numerous pamphlets provoked by Hampden's was entitled *Subscription No Bondage* and signed 'Rusticus'. 'Rusticus' was none other than the recently converted Maurice, and in his pamphlet he upheld the Articles not as tests and confessions of faith, but as 'conditions of thought'.[1] In the late thirties and early forties Tractarians and Liberals alike came up against this uncomfortable set of doctrinal formulas, and resolved their difficulties by stretching their interpretations— in the direction of Rome and 'non-natural' Subscription in the one case, or in the other, of elaborate liberalizing qualification. Jowett tackled the Gordian knot by refusing to make Subscription an issue involving personal integrity, and implying in his signature only the most general assent.[2] And so the controversy continued till 1871, when, inspired by Clough's example twenty-one years earlier, Henry Sidgwick resigned his Cambridge Fellowship. Largely because of the impact of this resignation Subscription for Fellows at both Universities was finally abolished.

One can see, then, that where most objectors stumbled on specific doctrinal points and involved themselves in complexities of interpretation and qualification, Clough based his dislike, as the letter to Gell quoted above shows, and his further correspondence on the subject confirms, on fundamental principles. If he examined himself in detail about the Articles, he wrote to Hawkins in 1848, he would probably find that his objections to particular points were substantive and not subordinate, but he was unwilling to undertake such an examination, and his 'objection in limine to Subscription' was that it was 'a painful restraint on speculation' (*Corr.* i. 196). In adopting this attitude he took up a position in direct opposition to Maurice's equally fundamental, and exceptional, stand on the other side. Involved in any more particular objections Clough might have had was an opposition to the principle of Subscription as such, to the im-

---

[1] R. W. Church, *The Oxford Movement* (London, 1891), pp. 135–6.
[2] G. Faber, *Jowett* (Cambridge, Mass., 1957), p. 153.

position of the Articles as 'conditions of thought', as an unexamined
set of conditions containing all intellectual inquiry. For him this
question ran into the allied one of the precise extent and validity
of the University's authority as a final court of Ecclesiastical Law.

Gell replied to Clough's letter with the sensible man's plea for
conformity: 'Pray why not sign the XXXIX Articles; you must
sign something, unless you mean to have nothing to do with
anybody. Where will you find a more sensible set of clerical
regulations?' (*Corr.* i. 128 n.) By the time Clough received
Gell's letter it was October and Ward's book, *The Ideal of a
Christian Church*, was already a couple of months old. The outrage
it had caused was gathering the momentum which resulted finally
in the events of 13 February 1845, when the author was declared
guilty of bad faith and stripped of his degrees. In the highly
charged atmosphere of incipient conflict Clough wrote a long
and important reply to Gell's remonstrance. He had, he said,
laid aside the questionings of a year ago, submerging them in
'the thoroughly terrestrial element of college tutorism, not to
speak of Mendicity Societies and the like'. But buried though they
were in routine, and the demands of social conscience, the old
scruples would have to be confronted someday.

My own justification to myself for doing as I am doing is I fear one
which would be as little approved of by you as my objections on the
other hand. However it is simply that I can feel faith in what is being
carried on by my generation and that I am content to be an operative—
to dress intellectual leather, cut it out to pattern and stitch it and cobble
it into boots and shoes for the benefit of the work which is being guided
by wiser heads. But this almost cuts me out of having any religion
whatever. If I begin to think about God, there [arise] a thousand
questions, and whether the 39 Articles answer them at all or whether
I should answer them in the most diametrically opposite purport is
a matter of great doubt. If I am to study the questions, I have no right
to put my name to the answers beforehand, nor to join in the acts of
a body and be to practical purpose one of a body who accept these
answers of which I propose to examine the validity. I will *not* assert
that one has no *right* to do this; but it seems to me to destroy one's
sense of perfect freedom of enquiry in a great degree, and I further
incline to hold that enquiries are best carried on by turning speculation
into practice, and my speculations no doubt in their earlier stages
would result in practice considerably at variance with 39 Article
Subscription. Much as I like, fond as I am of Oxford and much as I

should hate the other element undisguised, I verily believe that as
a preliminary stage it would be far better to be at Stinkomalee (the
London University acknowledges that agnomen I believe does it not?)
... [H]ere what religion I have I cannot distinguish from the amalga-
mations it is liable to, and I am, right or wrong, as matter of fact,
exceeding averse to act on anything but what I have got from myself....

   Without the least denying Xtianity, I feel little that I can call its
power. Believing myself to be in my unconscious creed in some shape
or other an adherent to its doctrines I keep within its pale: still whether
the Spirit of the Age, whose lacquey and flunkey I submit to be, will
prove to be this kind or that kind I can't the least say. Sometimes I
have doubts whether it won't turn out to be no Xty at all. Also
it is a more frequent question with me whether the Master whom I
work under and am content to work under is not carrying out his
operations himself elsewhere, while I am as it were obeying the directions of a bungling journeyman no better than myself. . . . Thou
however, in thy wisdom, consider the sad scruples and perplexities
that encounter said Flunkey amidst all the most flunkeyish occupations
of his Flunkeydom, and in the hope that at this time year he will still
be engaged in these same occupations transmit to him advice and good
counsel as to those same scruples and perplexities. In the meantime he
must dress and put on his livery for dinner—*Exit Flunkey* (*Corr.* i.
140–1).

The letter is important for a variety of reasons, not all of them
obvious. Indicating the line along which Clough was thinking
about the immediate subject of Subscription, and something also
of the quality of his mind generally—strongly desiring independence, insisting on turning 'speculation' into 'practice'—the
letter also reveals his ambivalence about the professional problem
which was so intimately connected with the religious and intellectual one. Disclosing that Clough had, even at this early date,
considered London as a possible neutral ground, removed from
the theological clutter of Oxford, the letter reveals at the same
time his emotional attachment to his own University and the
strong element of disdain with which he viewed the academic
and social pretensions of 'Stinkomalee'. The Carlylese of the
imagery generally, and the buried but specific reference to *Past
and Present* in defining himself as a 'flunkey',[1] acknowledges the
powerful influence of the Sage of Ecclefechan. Clough's comparison of his own position to a flunkey's rather than a hero's

---

[1] See especially *Past and Present*, Chapter IV, 'Hero-Worship'.

establishes, too, a characteristic reaction to the larger forces of the *Zeitgeist* within which the more specific problems of his Oxford position presented themselves. In attempting to hold at an adequate distance the clamouring ideas, opinions, beliefs, and panaceas of his age, he saw himself reduced, unavoidably, to the status of an 'operative' dressing 'intellectual leather', doing the immediate and humble duty he could clearly discern as his own.

By the time Clough had completed his letter, the opposition to Ward's book was gathering distinct head, and the line of action to be taken against him by the authorities gradually emerging from the welter of gossip and rumour and surmise. 'It looks likely however', Clough wrote in this same letter five days later, 'that they intend to banish him—a power which the Statutes no doubt accord to the Vice Chancellor and indeed I believe they empower him to expel pro arbitrio. But such a power the Heads would hardly venture to conjure up in the present day' (*Corr.* i. 142). In the event, the Hebdomadal Board did pursue a course very similar to banishment. In reviving an antique legal justification against the whole weight of advanced opinion, they made clear their harsh and reactionary attitude. As Stanley wrote bitterly after Ward's degradation, '[H]ad it been in the sixteenth, instead of the nineteenth, century, just the same men, with just the same arguments, would have been voting, not for degradation, but for burning.'[1] By their conduct towards one another these disputatious zealots for doctrinal purity were making increasingly clear to Clough the possible superiority, morally, of 'practice considerably at variance with 39 Article Subscription'.

This autocratic assertion of *de jure* authority led, naturally, to the question of Convocation's competence as judge. On 31 December 1844 Clough wrote:

The matter is clearly judicial and ecclesiastical; the Convocation is not a court of justice, nor an ecclesiastical body. What right have our MA's to say whether statements x, y, z agree or not with the Articles, or say in what sense the University, which imposes the Subscription simply as a Church of England body, understands the Articles? If the Church does not settle it, the University has no business to do so (*Corr.* i. 143).

[1] R. E. Prothero, *The Life and Correspondence of Arthur Penrhyn Stanley, D.D.*, 2 vols. (London, 1893), i. 341.

This was the argument he used against Hawkins in refusing to vote against his 'misguided friend', as the Provost called Ward. In answering Clough, Hawkins, who had played some part in the measures taken against Ward, made a fairly strong legal case for the 'obsolete functions' of the Vice-Chancellor's Court, 'which *is*, or at least *was*, an Ecclesiastical Court' (*Corr*. i. 144). He refused, however, to take up Ward's challenge to the authorities to declare the meaning of their own law. At the same time, somewhat illogically, he urged Clough to vote in favour of the third measure against Ward originally proposed by the Heads of Houses but later abandoned through an access of good sense. This measure required the subscriber to declare that he took the Articles in the sense in which 'they were both first published and were now imposed by the University'—a sense which, literally, no one could define.

By the end of 1845 the doubtful honesty of retaining his own position in Oriel, especially after Ward's degradation, turned Clough's thoughts definitely outward, and he made his first decisive attempt at quitting Oxford. In November he had his name submitted to Sir James Graham, the Home Secretary, for a post in one of the proposed non-sectarian colleges in Ireland. The scheme, however, came to nothing, since the colleges were not actually established until 1849, when Clough had already been appointed at University Hall. Probably because he expected further developments in Ireland, Clough left the whole question of his position at Oriel in abeyance for almost a year, and during that time it must have become obvious that he could hardly look in that direction for a speedy resolution of his difficulties. It is likely too that during this period he fell in love,[1] and that this added a further element of uncertainty to the problem of a career. Celibacy was one of the conditions of a Fellowship; if Clough married he could not remain a Fellow, nor could he marry without reasonable employment. Towards the end of the Long Vacation in 1846 he wrote to Hawkins from Scotland inquiring whether it would be possible to share his Tutorship with someone else. Since it was unlikely that he would be entering orders, he felt that he could most profitably make use of the remaining three years of his Fellowship by devoting himself to independent reading

[1] See Chorley, pp. 91–4. The question of this probable love affair is discussed in greater detail in Chapter IV.

and study in order to prepare himself for regular work, probably
as a private tutor. He was willing to have his emoluments reduced,
and he thought that the arrangement could very well benefit the
college by increasing his efficiency as a teacher. Hawkins did
not agree to the proposal and Clough did not press the matter.

No further discussion about the subject of Subscription seems
to have occurred between the two till the following December,
when in the course of conversation Hawkins remarked that the
duties of a Tutor included that of instructing undergraduates in
the Thirty-nine Articles. Clough thought the point over, and sent
his Provost a note saying that in his position and holding his
views he did not feel himself qualified for such an office. In the
intricate correspondence which ensued, and in which Clough
only very gradually disclosed the basic nature of his objections,
Hawkins was unfailingly helpful, unfailingly courteous. His
position was a delicate one and he was both puzzled and distressed.
He wanted to be scrupulously conscientious about his responsibilities as Head of a College and administrator of University
Statutes; at the same time he wanted to do everything possible to
help Clough and to avoid, if this could be managed in any way,
the necessity of his resignation. Certainly in this particular case
he did far more than extend the two well-known and distant
fingers. In his notes he repeatedly spilt over into concerned italics:
he was 'not', he assured Clough, 'for hurrying anyone into difficulties,
or premature decisions' (Corr. i. 196). He wanted to give the
younger man ample time to resolve the questions which troubled
him. There was, he pointed out, no need for Clough himself
actually to teach the Thirty-nine Articles, since there were three
other Tutors in the college, and Clough could, if he chose, take up,
at least as a pro tem step, the vacant lay Fellowship in Medicine—
but once he had come to a decision about the state of his belief
he would have to act on it. To add to his embarrassment he felt
at times that the distinctions the young man was drawing between
'negative acquiescence' and positive Subscription were less than
completely honest: it was a case, he pointed out, 'to be settled
rather in foro conscientiae' than in the Vice-Chancellor's Court
(Corr. i. 195). He might reasonably have felt, even, that Clough
was courting public trial, challenging him to a dramatic imposi-
tion of a fresh Test—and he was sensitive about being known as
a martinet: 'If I have been ever supposed to have been imposing

new Tests, the reverse has been the fact. I . . . have only sought to
ascertain, where my office required it, that our existing Tests
were honestly subscribed' (*Corr.* i. 196). When Clough finally
made known his objection to Subscription as 'a restraint on
speculation', he took kindly advantage of his seniority and
position to remonstrate with his junior—disclosing as he did so
his horror at anything remotely resembling religious scepticism.

. . . I take a real and personal concern in all that you have been led to
disclose to me. I am very sorry to see whereabouts you stand. I am
afraid of unrestrained speculation tending to general scepticism—a
very unhappy state, and one for which God did not design us.

In truth you were not born for *speculation*. I am not saying a word
against full and fair inquiry. But we are sent into this world not so
much to speculate as to serve God and to serve man.

. . . I do indeed most earnestly desire that you may not pursue speculation so as to omit action, and neglect the fulfilment of your practical
duties towards God and man, and working out, through grace, your
own salvation (*Corr.* i. 197–8).

Thoughts of his own salvation did not, perhaps, trouble Clough
unduly at this stage of his career, but Hawkins's exhortation to
service and action, reinforcing as it did the voice of Carlyle and
echoing that of Dr. Arnold, was a telling barb.

That letter of Hawkins's was written on 24 January 1848. On
the 31st Clough wrote to Tom Arnold, who had left for New
Zealand, informing him that he had intimated to the Provost
his intention of relinquishing his Tutorship at Easter.

I feel greatly rejoiced to think that this is my last term of bondage in
Egypt, though I shall, I suppose, quit the fleshpots for a wilderness,
with small hope of manna, quails, or water from the rock. The
Fellowship, however, lasts for a year after next June: and I don't
think the Provost will meddle with my tenure of it, though I have
let him know that I have wholly put aside adhesion to 39 Articles. . . .
I am not quite sure, my dear Tom, how far you would think me honest
in my correspondence with him—and you being away, I don't know
who to ask. . . . Perhaps when old Shairp comes up, . . . we will talk
over the thing together (*Corr.* i. 199).

Perhaps it is significant that Clough should have turned for advice
to that idealistic and radical liberal, Tom, on the one hand, and,
on the other, to the cautious and conservative Shairp. As Easter

drew nearer, he looked forward more eagerly to his emancipation. In mid March he wrote to Shairp:

Another three weeks will see me at the end of these tutorial. . . . what shall I call them?—wearinesses, now at any rate. But whither the emancipated spirit will wing its flight, can't be guessed, Paradise, or purgatory or. . . . .? The limbo of meditation, the penal worms of Ennui, or the paradise of. . . . .?

VANITAS VANITATUM

OMNIA VANITAS

(*Corr.* i. 202, Clough's dots.)

In May he went to Paris. He stayed there for five weeks to observe at first-hand the state of Revolutionary France. His visit overlapped with Emerson's and the two met daily through-out the latter's stay. Perhaps the joint influence of the infectious Parisian air and Emerson's company turned his thoughts seriously once again to his position in Oxford and helped to decide his immediate course. In July he wrote to tell Tom Arnold that now that he had given up the Tutorship, he was seriously thinking of surrendering the Fellowship as well—at the very latest in October. When October arrived he took the decisive step and wrote to Hawkins asking him to accept his resignation: 'I can have nothing whatever to do with a subscription to the xxxix articles—and deeply repent of having ever submitted to one. I cannot consent to receive any further pecuniary benefit in consideration of such conformity' (*Corr.* i. 219). Hawkins replied with an extraordinarily generous letter, in which he suggested that since their professional positions had hitherto prevented any full discussion of Clough's difficulties, they might now examine the position more closely and, if possible, prevent the necessity of resignation. But here he came up against the younger man's glacial and sometimes sardonic reserve:

I assure you that I am very sensible of the kindness of your offers to assist me in examining my difficulties. But I believe it will be best for me, if you will allow me to retire in silence.

However little I may anticipate any such result I can safely say that my only chance of a recurrence to orthodox conviction or acquiescence will be found in taking the step which I propose to take in the manner in which I wish to take it. Those who estimate most highly the im-portance of such an ultimate recovery will I hope not be least inclined to make allowance for that only immediate course which could possibly lead to it (*Corr*. i. 220).

Hawkins, unwilling to give up hope, reluctant to push Clough into any decision, deferred proposing Clough's resignation to the College till February the following year, and, in a series of personal interviews with him, tried to get to the root of his difficulties.

Concluding his notes of a conversation he held with Clough on 18 October, Hawkins wrote: 'A. H. C. had little or no money —had saved something—had no intention to marry,—and thought he could support himself as a single man by taking pupils . . . he certainly wished me to declare his Resignation at once . . . (*Corr*. i. 222). When Clough resigned he had no prospect of permanent employment. His brother, George, had died in 1843, his father the following year, and when his remaining brother Charles married in 1846, the whole burden of supporting his financially straitened family devolved on him.[1] Although by Christmas he had been invited to stand for the headship of University Hall, London, in October there were only the vaguest of prospects, none permanent and none of which matured—of taking a pupil abroad, of a tutorship at Esher with a son of Lord Lovelace, who lived there with his grandmother, Lady Noel-Byron, and of another in the family of William Rathbone Greg which offered a meagre £150. A Co-Examinership in the Education Office with W. R. Lingen, offering £500 a year 'and no oaths', was a much more suitable possibility which Matthew Arnold suggested—but, Arnold added, the work was very hard and it was 'possible' that 'Lingen might wish a less extraordinary colleague'.[2] Since the possibility came to nothing, neither Clough's capacity for hard work nor Lingen's reactions were seriously tested.

Clough's anxiety about the consequences of his resignation were compounded by his apprehensiveness about possible social repercussions. Rigid and intolerant Oxford, he felt, could easily have decided to ostracize him. When James Froude published *The Nemesis of Faith* early in 1849, he was cut by his friends, he was forced to resign his Fellowship at Exeter, his book was semi-publicly burned by an especially outraged Fellow, and he

[1] For details of Clough's financial circumstances at the time of his resignation see Chorley, pp. 89–90.　　　　　　　　　　　　　　[2] Lowry, p. 89.

was compelled to leave Oxford. The rancour of his opponents pursued him even outside its cloisters, and their determined efforts finally secured a revocation of his appointment to a headmastership in Tasmania.[1] Clough's was an altogether more pallid exit, but genuine relief—and possibly a hint of disappointment—betrays itself in the letter he wrote to Tom Arnold early in November 1848 from his lodgings in Holywell: 'I am extremely jolly meantime, rejoicing in my emancipation. I stay up here; it is now 3 weeks within 24 hours since I resigned; and people don't cut me at all. I dine at some high tables and generally ... I am treated as a citizen' (*Corr.* i. 223). As always, the timidity of the emotionally insecure wove into Clough's refusal to conform.

Hawkins continued his patient efforts to rescue Clough. He visited him in his lodgings and notes continued to pass between them. The nature of their encounters can be judged from some unpublished notes Hawkins made after he went to see Clough on 12 November, in response to a letter of farewell which he had received.

Called on Clough in answer to his letter of Nov. 11th [Cf. *Corr.* i. 224] —allowed that he need not withdraw from University—he had not withdrawn himself from the Church of England, nor placed himself in an attitude of hostility to her, nor wished to do so—there was no other communion he proposed. . . .

As to his opinions, doubts &c, I gained nothing further from him. He was apparently grateful, and candid towards me, but still as reserved as ever. . . .

I inquired if he was studying anything in a manly way to remove his difficulties—No, he was not—The subject was in his mind—but he read nothing about it. I inquired whether he was familiar with N.T. Yes, he knew the Greek Test. while in the 6th form at Rugby! . . .[2]

Restraining his exasperation, Hawkins wrote to Clough at length eight days later, advising '*a course of serious study*, with a view to your getting a firm hold of the *elementary principles* of Religion' (*Corr.* i. 225). He proceeded to prescribe an appropriate regimen of study—Paley, Butler, Grotius, Lardner, and an armful of others, good solid stuff in its day, but the authority and relevance of which a newer age had learnt to question radically.

[1] W. H. Dunn, *James Anthony Froude*, 2 vols. (Oxford, 1961-3), i. 130-50.
[2] Oriel Papers, Letters -/8-/ 701-800, no. 734.

Hawkins's utter inability to even begin to understand the forces which had led to his young correspondent's resignation is underlined, not without a certain grave and antediluvian charm, in his attempt to furnish sufficient intellectual artillery to combat the rationalism which, no doubt, was the root of the trouble: 'I suspect, however, that many of your difficulties turn upon the O[ld] Test[amen]t. They can scarcely be of such a character that Watson's Apology for the Bible would meet them; for, if I recollect rightly most of T. Paine's Objections were built upon sheer ignorance. Yet you would admire Watson's answers both to him and to Gibbon . . .' (*Corr.* i. 226). Returning to the subject of the Greek Testament, on which Clough had been particularly uncooperative, he wrote patiently:

. . . I had in mind such a study of these writings as you could not be competent to pursue at School. For you could not then judge for yourself of the strong internal marks of genuineness which you would now, I trust, discover in a serious study of St. Paul's Epistles—and if these are genuine, so are the Acts, and the Xtian Revelation generally.—And so, I should trust, would a serious study of the teaching and character of Christ in the 4 Gospels, convince you of the genuineness, or rather authenticity, of these books, and of the fundamental truths of Christianity (ibid.).

Clough delayed his answer to Hawkins's letter for two months, by which time he had been appointed at University Hall. Informing the Provost of his new position, he added, 'Though I confess I do not fancy the books which you speak of exactly fit to meet the doubts with which young men now are familiar, of course I shall bear them in mind' (*Corr.* i. 234). Finally, on 28 February Hawkins wrote to tell Clough that the College had accepted his resignation. He also mentioned *The Bothie of Tober-na-Vuolich*, which had been published late in 1848 under its original title, *The Bothie of Toper-na-Fuosich*. He found, he said, parts of the poem indelicate (as he had been told by others he would), and he regretted especially the 'frequent allusions to . . . or rather parodies of Scripture' which Clough had seen fit to publish. 'You will never be secure from misbelief, if you allow yourself liberties of this kind', he added sternly. He also asked, since Clough had said that he did not feel that the books he had suggested were suitable for present-day needs, 'Will you do me the favour, some time or other, to tell me what class of difficulties, according to your observation, most perplexes young men at present' (*Corr.* i. 247-8). Perhaps because he was stung by the uncomprehending criticism of a poem which was very much a vindication of his resignation from Oxford, Clough was prompt with an ironically understated reply in which he indicated that possibly there were worse things than the 'misbelief' which so worried Hawkins: 'I submit to wiser judgments in the matter of the Poem you speak of. I could wish several things altered. But do not plead guilty to any graver charges than those which you make. I do not think I have sinned against morality' (*Corr.* i. 248). He went on to make a brief statement about the religious difficulties which faced men of his own generation. The furore caused by *The Nemesis of Faith* was less than a week old, and he took care to point out that the author, whom Oxford orthodoxy had rejected, was a friend of his:

To your last question I will endeavour to give what answer I can at once. A book just published by a friend of mine, Froude, once of Oriel afterwards of Exeter, contains a good deal of what I imagine pervades the young world in general, though at Oxford there is great apathy and incuriousness, to the best of my observation, among undergraduates and even bachelors. Elsewhere I think there is a general feeling that Miracles are poor proofs. The doctrine must prove them, not they the doctrine. Can we be sure that anything is really a miracle? . . . Again books like Strauss's life of Jesus have disturbed the historical foundations of Christianity. And people ask further what has History to do with Religion? The worth of such a doctrine as that of the Holy Ghost as the Lord and Giver of Spiritual life is intelligible: but what is the value of biographical facts?—External Evidence is slighted: but I think the great query is rather as to the *internal* Evidence. Is Xtianity really so much better than Mohometanism, Buddhism (a more extensive faith) or the old heathen philosophy? Are those virtues and graces, which are our religious and moral tradition, really altogether Christian? is there not a good deal of Homer and Virgil in them? Nay, if the loftiest of them belong to Christianity, are they exclusively Christian in matter of fact, or necessarily Christian in matter of philosophy?

I don't think young men are at all inclined to part with Christianity, absolutely: but they have no Christian ideal, which they feel sure is really Christian, except the Roman Catholic. And [Any?] middle term is felt to be a sort of mixed Christianity; and whence that admixture comes they are not careful to enquire, nor in what quantity it may be admitted:—but they have a growing sense of discrepancy.—

This is an extremely crude description; but such as it is I must leave it: and trust to your discernment to give meaning to its incoherencies (*Corr.* i. 248–9).

Several important points emerge from a review of Clough's difficulties about the Thirty-nine Articles. Subscription was a specific issue, but it was not an isolated one. The whole question of religion was involved in an extensive pattern of questioning and investigation, the nature of which is best indicated briefly at this point by quoting James Froude:

[E]specially in Clough I found strong sympathy in my general uneasiness. Clough, like myself, had been attracted first by Newman, then repelled from him as the goal of the Movement became more visibly Rome. He had come, as I had done, to a sense that there was uncertainty where the ground was supposed to be fixed as a rock. . . . He too at this time had passed under Carlyle's influence, and shared Carlyle's horror at the very appearance of insincerity. . . . We had read Rousseau and Louis Blanc and George Sand.[1]

Clough's growing curtness in his correspondence with Hawkins is one clue to the sharpening of his attitudes. Considered solely against Hawkins's concern and goodwill, it appears inexplicably boorish. Seen against the chasm which separated the old, traditional Oxford from the intellectual and spiritual turbulence which men like Froude and Clough were attempting to cope with, that almost calculated offensiveness underlines Clough's exasperation with these constricted, satisfied, self-sufficient cloisters. As he remarked to his sister in April 1848:

Up here at Oxford I keep, in general company, very quiet, insomuch that . . . people not infrequently take me for some little time after introduction to be no less than a Puseyite: but all the same time I could sometimes be provoked to send out a flood of lava boiling-hot amidst their flowery ecclesiastical fields and parterres. Very likely living in this state of suppressed volcanic action makes one more exasperated than one should be when any sort of a crater presents itself. Natheless, there is wisdom in withholding (*Corr.* i. 203).

Hawkins, unenviably, seems to have been a crater through which some of that repressed pressure could be released.

Clough was not exaggerating the oppressiveness. 'The Oxford of 1848 was still the Oxford of the Heads of Houses and of the

---

[1] Quoted Dunn, op. cit. i. 95–6.

Hebdomadal Board. . . . Seldom has a University passed through such a complete change as Oxford has since the year 1854',[1] Max Müller remarked, and that view can be amplified with details from Mark Pattison's *Memoirs*. Newman's conversion to Rome in 1845, following closely on the heels of Ward's, was, for Pattison 'a deliverance from the nightmare which [had] oppressed Oxford for fifteen years'.[2] A lull followed on Newman's conversion, and 'the railway mania of 1847 was the first material that rushed in to fill up the vacuum. . . . Then came the railway crash, a new and still greater interest, as so many fellows of colleges lost their savings in it. Finally, in 1848, the universal outburst of revolution in every part of the Continent. It seemed incredible, in the presence of such an upheaval, that we had been debating any matter so flimsy as whether England was in a state of schism or no.'[3]

Railways and revolution; the mid nineteenth century, and the irrepressible and alarming intellectual, social, and political forces from which the powers that ruled Oxford resolutely averted their eyes:

If any Oxford man had gone to sleep in 1846 and had woken up again in 1850 he would have found himself in a totally new world. In 1846 we were in Old Tory Oxford; not somnolent because it was as fiercely debating, as in the days of Henry IV, its eternal Church question. There were Tory majorities in all the colleges; there was the unquestioning satisfaction in the tutorial system, *i.e.*, one man teaching everybody everything; the same belief that all knowledge was shut up in the covers of four Greek and four Latin books; the same humdrum questions asked in the examination; and the same arts of evasive reply. In 1850 all this was changed as if by the wand of a magician. The dead majorities of heads and seniors, which had sat like lead upon the energies of young tutors, had melted away. Theology was totally banished from the Common Room, and even from private conversation. Very free opinions on all subjects were rife; there was a prevailing note of dissatisfaction with our boasted tutorial system. A restless fever of change had spread through the colleges—the wonder-working phrase, University reform, had been uttered, and that in the House of Commons.[4]

In an Oxford so clearly divided into a hard reactionary crust

---

[1] Müller, Max, op. cit., pp. 226, 235.
[2] Pattison, *Memoirs* (London, 1883), p. 236.
[3] Ibid., pp. 235-6.   [4] Ibid., pp. 244-5.

and a murmuring, progressive, youthful substratum, Clough's position was that of a leader on almost every front of revolt and criticism.[1]

Ward and Tractarianism had led Clough into a *cul-de-sac*—but they had also created the unrest, uncertainty, and dissatisfaction, the awareness of a need to find a fresh basis for himself, out of which the whole organic body of his criticism and inquiry grew. He found himself involved in a re-examination of a total world view: not only points of doctrine but the whole integrated concept of man, of nature, and of society embodied in traditional Christianity came under scrutiny. Further, inevitably, that scrutiny widened out to include a whole inherited cultural matrix and all the conceptions of value, order, purpose, morality it contained. But although Clough's reappraisal was so extensive, and although he never arrived at any doctrinal certainty, the dissolution of his belief was only partial. He never forsook the attitude of belief. His hold on certain large values and concepts—God, Truth, Faith, Law—remained unwavering, although he denied the possibility of any final knowledge or definition of these.

Although Clough travelled far from religious conformity, the force behind his reinvestigation of the world and of man, the force behind his rebellion against orthodox Christianity, derives its basic energy and direction from a religious need and a religious impulse. A necessary, though not sufficient, condition of religion is that it should provide a coherent frame of beliefs and values which is comprehensive enough and detailed enough to cover all areas of living. In this sense, and in the further sense that Clough tried to relate his findings to some transcendental version of reality, the search for an adequate and viable synthesis, to which he was committed through the loss of his hold on the certainties of traditional Christianity, was basically a religious one. The search for such a synthesis, for what Carlyle would call a 'Life-Philosophy', makes Clough very much a child of his time. His

[1] Charles Kingsley described Clough as 'one of the leaders' of 'Young Oxford' in a letter to J. M. F. Ludlow: *Charles Kingsley: His Letters and Memories of His Life*, ed. by his wife, 2 vols. (London, 1877), i. 181. F. T. Palgrave described Clough as conspicuous 'as one of the earliest who battled for just freedom of opinion and speech, for liberation from archaeological formulas, for more conscientious fulfilment of duty towards students'. 'Hence', he went on, 'all who longed for that truer University of which they have since seen the beginning, looked upon Clough as among their leaders....' 'Arthur Hugh Clough', *Fraser's Magazine*, lxv (Apr. 1862), 528.

distinction—and his problem—in this respect is that he refused
to take—despite the pressure of his own desires and the expectations of others[1]—the final step which would, disingenuously for
him, round off and complete any system.

He was not vaguely leaving open the possibility of unhampered
speculation when he refused to subscribe to the Thirty-nine
Articles; his refusal reflected actively the influence of a wide
background of European thought to which his experience of
Tractarianism made him especially receptive. Diverse, and at
points contending, as these intellectual currents were—and Clough
was in time to discover the difficulties of that contention—
they were united in a common end: an erosion of the bases of
orthodox historical Christianity. For convenience three main
areas of this intellectual background can be separated out: the
growth of historical studies (together with its ancillaries in
historical criticism and comparative religion), the growth of
the scientific outlook generally, and certain key developments in
philosophy.

The growth of a feeling for history has been seen as, quite
possibly, the most important single development in the intellectual
life of the nineteenth century;[2] even science was, in a sense, subordinate. As Noel Annan has observed, 'It was not science itself,
but science interpreted as history, which upset the orthodox
cosmology.'[3] The historical approach which had been born in
the eighteenth century with Lessing and Herder gradually established in the nineteenth the sovereignty of the idea of evolution.
Truth could no longer be seen as an absolute and philosophically

---

[1] An example of the pressure of expectation on Clough can be seen in Morley's
account of his part in the 1847 election, in which he supported Gladstone as the
Oxford candidate. Clough's support, Morley said, was as influential among
younger men as Hallam's was among older. 'Mr. Northcote described Clough to
Mr. Gladstone as a very favourable specimen of a class, growing in numbers and
importance among the younger Oxford men, a friend of Carlyle's, Frank
Newman's, and others of the stamp; . . . just now busily taking all his opinions
to pieces and not beginning to put them together; but so earnest and good that
he might be trusted to work them into something better than his friends inclined
to fear.' J. Morley, The Life of William Ewart Gladstone, 2 vols. (London, 1950),
i. 329.

[2] Cf. V. F. Storr, The Development of English Theology in the Nineteenth Century,
1800–1860 (London, 1913), p. 1. I am extensively indebted to this work and to
L. E. Elliott-Binns, Religion in the Victorian Era (London, 1936) for my account
of the general philosophical and theological background.

[3] N. Annan, 'The Strands of Unbelief', in Ideas and Beliefs of the Victorians,
with an introduction by H. Grisewood (London, 1949), p. 151.

static entity; it was relative, involved in an evolutionary historical
flow. As a historian Dr. Arnold not only stood at the forefront
of developments in the discipline in his own country, but
communicated his enthusiasm to his schoolboys. He venerated
Niebuhr, the commanding father of modern historiography, and
was a close friend, correspondent, and companion in endeavour,
of the Chevalier Bunsen, Prussian Minister in London and poly-
mathic disciple of Niebuhr. Niebuhr himself had applied the
methods of 'scientific' historical criticism to the early history of
Rome, and had concluded that it had little basis in fact and
represented only an accretion of legendary and literary material.
Reviewers of Hare and Thirlwall's translation of Niebuhr in
1829 were quick to point out the dangers to faith involved in the
application of his methods to the scriptures, but Arnold, like
Bunsen, was unmoved: historical inquiry would never shake
a faith which was 'centred' 'in moral and spiritual truths'.[1] The
development of historical criticism to the point at which, in the
conclusions of Strauss and Baur, it impinged most dramatically
on Clough's belief, requires, for its understanding, some sense
of concurrent developments in romantic philosophical and theological thought. Clough's active acquaintance with certain of these
developments can be inferred from some notes on religion he
made in 1845 in the 1849 (Roma) Notebook.[2]

Two tendencies in Fichte's doctrine of the Absolute Ego—
which he developed out of Kant's idealistic emphasis on the
contribution of mind to experience—came to their full development in Schelling. The first of these was to substitute humanity
for Christ, to make the Incarnation an eternal fact or process.
The second was to set aside the historical person of Christ in
favour of a speculative theory of the relation of man to God.
In his exploration towards an objective ground of reality which
he named the Absolute, Fichte had begun with man, with
the moral setting of the Finite Ego. Schelling began with the
Absolute, the existence of which, he claimed, men grasped by

[1] A. P. Stanley, *The Life of Thomas Arnold, D.D.*, i. 409.
[2] See Appendix B. Dean Boyle reported that in his day Tutors in Oxford were
in the habit of recommending Coleridge's *The Friend* and *Aids to Reflection* to
undergraduates reading for Honours: G. D. Boyle, *The Recollections of the Very
Rev. G. D. Boyle, Dean of Salisbury* (London, 1895), p. 81. Clough was reading
Coleridge fairly early in his life, and he would have been acquainted with the
leading ideas of German Transcendentalism from this source.

intellectual intuition. In Schelling's view the central truth that
man and God are one had been wrapped round by the Christian
Church, which attached as much importance to the husk as to the
kernel, with a covering of historical narrative. Two broad lines
of development can be traced from this idealistic position. One,
as developed in Schleiermacher's purely speculative romantic
theology, did not have any immediate effect on the growth
of historical criticism. The other, in Hegel's dialectic,[1] gave,
through its philosophical vindication of the concept of evolution,
immense power and authority to the historical critics. Schleiermacher, defining religion as a 'taste for the infinite', contended
that religion was based on intuition and feeling and was independent of all dogma; he saw its highest expression in a sensation of
union with the infinite. Starting with the fact of Christian consciousness (of which he saw the person of Christ as source and
cause), he held that religious experience was prior to and independent of intellectual constructions in creed or dogma. Hegel,
setting out to translate Christian truth into its pure philosophical
form, reduced it to an intellectual scheme which prepared the
way for Strauss and the Tübingen School. Strongly critical of
Schleiermacher's emphasis on feeling, he attempted to be severely
realistic in evolving a logic which embraced the whole universe,
a logic not of being but of becoming, which stressed the ideas of
development and evolution through the dialectical process of
thesis, antithesis, and synthesis.

All these related strands in the development of historical,
philosophical, and theological thinking, which converged to an
interiorization of Divine reality, were woven into the book
which seems to have finally dissevered Clough's connection with
orthodox historical Christianity—the *Leben Jesu*. In writing this
book Strauss aimed, first, at reconciling Christian theology with
Hegelian philosophy, next, at destroying all belief in the supernatural or miraculous, and, finally, at producing a work which

---

[1] Clough's very probable acquaintance with Hegel can be inferred from the
letter which Tom Arnold wrote to him on 18 Nov. 1847, just before leaving
for New Zealand, about the incendiary literature he was carrying with him
across the Equator—'Rousseau! Spinoza!! Hegel!!! Emerson!!', *New Zealand
Letters of Thomas Arnold the Younger*, ed. J. Bertram (Wellington, 1966), p. 12.
The 'Equator Letters' Tom wrote to Shairp give an account of his intellectual
and religious development to the date of his departure for New Zealand which
throws considerable light on Clough's development over the same period. Ibid.,
pp. 207-19.

should conform to the canons of 'scientific' historical criticism. At the same time, however, following his philosophic antecedents, his purpose was not purely destructive. While on the one hand he aimed at emptying historical Christianity of its supernatural contents, on the other he attempted to assert the philosophical truth of the Christian revelation. 'The supernatural birth of Christ, his miracles, his resurrection and ascension, remain eternal truths, whatever doubts may be cast on their reality as historical facts.'[1] Strauss rejected the historical basis of all the supernatural elements in the Gospels, although he did not deny the existence of a historical being called Jesus. These supernatural elements he assigned to an unintentionally creative legend which developed between the death of Christ and the writing of the Gospels in the second century. During this interval the collective myth embodied in the Gospels had been evolved, Strauss maintained, out of the powerful impression of a great personality on his disciples and the Messianic belief and hope of an oppressed people. The growth of primitive Christianity, Strauss further maintained, was to be understood through the principles of the Hegelian dialectic. In his treatise on the Pastoral Epistles, Baur, the leader of the Tübingen School, saw this growth of second-century Christianity in Hegelian terms, as the synthesis of the ideas and tendencies of two conflicting groups within the Church. The narrow Ebionite Judaism which was the earliest form of Christianity Baur regarded as representing the principle of particularism which came in conflict with the universalism of St. Paul. The history of the primitive Church thus became the history of the triumph of that universalism, helped by the Logos doctrine of the Fourth Gospel.

George Eliot's translation of the *Leben Jesu* in 1846 exploded with shattering force on the religious mind of mid-nineteenth-century England, and we have seen the important place Clough assigned to Strauss's attack in his last letter to Hawkins. Nevertheless, Tom Arnold's statement, 'Strauss, the Hegelian critic, clad in armour seemingly of proof, of Pantheistic philosophy and cool all-questioning logic, had destroyed for him the faith in Christ overcoming death',[2] is both exaggerated and

---

[1] D. F. Strauss, *The Life of Jesus*, trans. G. Eliot (London, 1898), p. xxx.

[2] T. Arnold, 'Arthur Hugh Clough: A Sketch', *The Nineteenth Century*, xliii (Jan. 1898), 112.

over-simplified. Strauss was important in Clough's religious life, important enough to elicit a poem, but, thanks to his Rugby training, Clough was also a willing follower of developments in historical criticism before he encountered Strauss. From Arnold he had learnt to respect German (the language of infidelity and Luther, according to the Tractarians) and German scholarship.[1] In 1839 he had written to Gell, 'I hope you will carry out with you or send home for a good Germanized Cambridge Scholar or Historian; as that (next to Paley's Horae Paulinae and Rationalistic Divinity) is the great bulwark against Newmanism' (*Corr*. i. 92). The notes he made in the 1849 (Roma) Notebook reveal, for instance, an acquaintance with the ideas of De Wette. His attitude towards religion in these years draws heavily on the philosophical background to Strauss. What the *Life of Jesus* did then, it seems, was to draw together into a decisive edge a body of ideas which Clough had been acquainted with for some time.

The comparative study of religions, a branch of inquiry related in some ways to historical criticism, was still in its early infancy in the 1840s. The Deists had toyed with the subject, Schleiermacher had touched on it and had taught that there was truth in all religions, the peculiar glory of Christianity being that its truth was inclusive of whatever was true and vital elsewhere. F. D. Maurice devoted his 1846 Boyle lectures to *The Religions of the World*, and in them he took substantially the same line. Elliott-Binns has dated the real beginnings of the comparative study of religions to the lecture on Mahomet which Carlyle delivered on 8 May 1840 and later published in *Heroes and Hero-Worship*.[2] Carlyle's sympathetic account of the founder of a religion which was traditionally seen as a notorious enemy of Christianity struck out on a new line—and, in thinking about the major world religions, the younger Oxford men followed the lead of 'amateurs' like Carlyle and Emerson.[3] They asked questions like those that Clough posed in his letter to Hawkins: 'Is Christianity really

[1] J. S. G. Simmons, 'Slavonic Studies at Oxford: I. The Proposed Slavonic Chair at the Taylor Institution in 1844', *Oxford Slavonic Papers*, iii (1952), 125–52, throws a fascinating and generally little-known light on this area of contention between Tractarians and Liberals. I am indebted to Mr. Simmons for drawing my attention to this article.   [2] Elliott-Binns, op. cit., p. 178.

[3] When James Froude brought his religious difficulties to Emerson, he was advised to read the Vedas. In 1848 Clough himself, on the recommendation of Matthew Arnold, read the Bhagvad-Gita, but without any great satisfaction. Lowry, pp. 69, 71.

so much better than Mahometanism, Buddhism (a more extensive faith) or the old heathen philosophy? Are those virtues and graces, which are our religious and moral tradition, really altogether Christian?' The second question hinted at the kind of problem which Francis Newman enlarged on in his book, *The Phases of Faith*, which appeared in 1850. Christianity, it was claimed, had effected a moral miracle—and yet, Newman pointed out, it had countenanced slavery. As early as 1839, however, Clough, as has been recently shown,[1] had acquainted himself with Friedrich von Schlegel's *Essai sur la langue et la philosophie des Indiens*. Attempting to protect the claims of Christian revelation and at the same time honestly confront the evidences of religious truth he had discovered in India, Schlegel advanced the hypothesis that there was an original form of Hinduism, traces of which are discernible in the laws of Menu, in which Brahma was identifiable with the God of Judaeo-Christian tradition. Divine truth had been revealed to the Hindus just as it had been to the western world, but that original—and shared—revelation had become obscured. Creation is an emanation from God, but the universe is a descent, a degradation, a continual falling away, and Evil inevitably entwined in the process. Schlegel's speculative account of the history of religious truth seems to have gripped Clough's imagination strongly. Not only did he utilize it explicitly and extensively in 'Salsette and Elephanta', his Newdigate Prize attempt of 1839, but its influence can be traced in poems like '*Epi-Strauss-ium*' and, more strongly, 'Uranus', and in his attitude towards the nature of revelation generally.

The comparative consideration of different religions operated in a twofold manner in its influence on religious belief. On the one hand, it tended to undermine the authority of Christianity as a religion peculiarly sanctified and authenticated. On the other, by revealing the almost universal diffusion of the religious consciousness, it gave historical validity to—provided, so to speak, 'scientific' corroboration of—that consciousness as posited by transcendental philosophers and theologians.

Although the educated man's acquaintance with the leading scientific developments of his time can be gleaned from Clough's letters and his writings generally, science as a set of specific

[1] E. B. Greenberger, '"Salsette and Elephanta": An Unpublished Poem by Clough', *RES* xx (Aug. 1969), 289.

findings seems to have had little influence on Clough's religious belief.[1] The mechanistic views of Laplace and Herschel awakened in him a sense of their inadequacy, but also troubled him with a sense of their possible rightness.[2] Mechanism was a spectre which he was horrified by, but always attempted to disprove. He was much more sympathetic towards, and at home with, pre-Darwinian concepts of evolution, geological and biological, which supported, as they were supported by, the evolutionary ideas of the philosophers and historians. In 1844 he remarked on the *Vestiges of the Creation*, and its revival of 'The theory that the human race is a distaillation of the monkey-kind' (*Corr.* i. 148), and he could hardly have remained unaware of the small tempest in reviews, in pulpits, and, if Disraeli is to be believed, in salons that the book created on its appearance.

As a general attitude, however, what we may loosely call the scientific outlook exerted a strong hold on his mind. Ever since he bought a book on 'The Newtonian System of Philosophy' while he was still at school in Chester, he showed, especially when compared with Matthew Arnold, a marked interest in and respect for science and scientists. As late as 1857 he was reporting on a 'remarkable lecture' by Faraday on the 'Conservation of Forces' which he had attended in the Royal Institution, and speaking of the 'good lectures' that Owen was giving on 'Fossil Mammalia' (*Corr.* ii. 526). Describing to Tom Arnold the 'impression of perfect intellectual cultivation' which Emerson created, he said that it was as complete as that given by 'any great scientific man in England—Faraday, or Owen for instance, more in their way perhaps than in that of Wordsworth or Carlyle' (*Corr.* i. 215). The frequent analogies and images drawn from science one encounters in Clough's prose and poetry alike are indications of a general interest and respect which reflect a basic habit of mind. To relate all experiences, all speculation, back to a factual, objective, basis was for him an intellectual and temperamental imperative—an imperative which had a direct bearing on the history of his religious beliefs.

[1] For an extended discussion of Clough's attitudes towards science see F. W. Palmer, 'The Bearing of Science on the Thought of Arthur Hugh Clough', *Publications of the Modern Language Society of America* (hereafter *PMLA*) lix (1944), 212–25.

[2] Cf. 'When Israel Came out of Egypt' (*Poems*, 16) and 'Notes on the Religious Tradition' (Trawick, pp. 289–90).

More specifically connected with Clough's rejection of the Thirty-nine Articles and Christian orthodoxy than this general 'scientific' interest, however, were the ideas of three thinkers especially—Spinoza, Comte, and Mill—who not only reinforced the attack of historical criticism but opened up new ranges of thought. Spinoza,[1] whose real impact as a philosopher dates from the nineteenth century, had developed in his pantheism a system of thought which, although few could accept it in its entirety, contained the elements of an exciting liberation of outlook. Denying both free will and a personal God, Spinoza saw God as creative energy, nature as 'Natura Naturans'—not dead and inert but a creative force of which man was part, the whole living universe finding moral justification in self-fulfilment. By viewing man *in* nature and not in terms of the man–nature opposition of traditional theology, Spinoza struck a blow at the concept of Sin. As James Froude, who was especially strongly influenced by Spinoza in the direction of determinism, put it in the words of Markham, the fictional hero of *The Nemesis of Faith*, '[T]he spectre which haunted the conscience is gone. Our failures are errors, not crimes—nature's discipline with which God teaches us; and as little violations of his law, or rendering us guilty in his eyes, as the artist's early blunders, or even ultimate and entire failures, are laying store of guilt on him.'[2] Clough's own movement towards such a liberation we shall examine later.

[1] Clough's acquaintance with Spinoza may be inferred from Tom Arnold's letter of 18 Nov. 1847 (p. 133 n. above), from '*Natura Naturans*', and from a fragment of verse in the 1849 (Roma) Notebook:

> As one who shoots an arrow overhead
> Straining in vain to follow with his eye
> Looks down and sees it by him, on the earth.
> As one who posts and hurries in his dream,
> Wakes suddenly and finds himself in bed
> So swarth Magellan through the Indian seas/main
> Pressing he knew not whither nor how far
> Sick, fainting with the sense of endless space before
> O for daily [illegible word] return, one morn looks forth
> And finds himself where he started from.
> That moment
> Through the ripe brain of human kind was sped
> A new vibration,—while in Amsterdam
> Sat one who knew and said
> The finite is the infinite, Man God   (Balliol MS. 441, fol. 25ᵛ.)

[2] J. A. Froude, *The Nemesis of Faith* (Chicago, 1879), p. 108.

Auguste Comte's *Cours de la Philosophie Positive* (1830–42) was widely discussed in the Oxford of the 1840s, and Clough's respect for Comte may be inferred from Matthew Arnold's letter of 8 March 1848, in which he chaffed his friend about his excessive regard for the Frenchman.[1] Comte added a further dimension to evolutionary, secularizing thought—one we may call, loosely, sociological. Spanning his whole system of Positivism, and the elaborations of 'the religion of humanity' which were acceptable to only his most committed disciples, was the famous law of three stages—the theological, the metaphysical, and the 'positive'—which he saw as constituting the phases of the development of the human race as a whole as well as that of its individual members. Whereas in the theological and metaphysical stages the human mind sought a cause or essence to explain phenomena, the third stage confined inquiry to observable, 'positive' facts and their relations, and eschewed all considerations of ultimate issues. Clough could never yield up a consideration of ultimate issues, but Comtism not only confirmed him in his rejection of theological inquiry but provided a modernist validation for his empirical temper.

John Stuart Mill's *System of Logic* ably and extensively supported this temperamental and philosophic disposition of his. In 1843 he remarked that he had been reading 'a grand new Philosophy-book, Mill on Logic—very well written at any rate, and "stringent" if not sound' (*Corr.* i. 126)—an opinion which reflected both his affinity with and respect for the tradition of Locke and Hume, and his unease at Mill's complete rejection of *a priorism*. Although in his book Mill was not directly involved in a quarrel with the theologians, that rejection, since it denied the existence in the human mind of any independent source of knowledge, amounted in effect to an attack on doctrine that had been traditionally favourable to religious belief.

Perhaps even more important, when we consider Clough's struggles with the sense of sin he had been bred into, was the way in which Mill supported Spinoza's rejection of transcendental evil. The implications for religious morality of the law of universal causation, which was the basis of Mill's theory of scientific induction, were far-reaching. It was entirely consistent with this law that moral responsibility between man and man should be

[1] Lowry, p. 74.

recognized, and that conscious human acts should be subject to the ethical judgement of the community. But it was irrational to believe that over and above these sanctions there existed a transcendent responsibility to the Cause of the universe, the non-fulfilment of which involved the infliction of useless and eternal penalties. Such a belief was irrational, because it would have to assume that a free intelligence had set the machinery of unconditioned sequence in motion—but such a supposition transferred the whole weight of responsibility on to the Creator. Further, universal causation excluded the possibility of super-natural intervention in any shape. Such interventions would break the causal sequence: as Clough wrote to Hawkins, young men of his generation considered miracles poor evidence, since they could well be the result of as yet unknown natural law (*Corr.* i. 249). The only alternative would be to make God him-self part of his creation and interweave his volitions into the chain of consequence, make him, that is, a finite and conditioned being.[1] It is impossible on the basis of a single mention to say how carefully Clough considered the *System of Logic* and its implications, but if he read it with an attention which matched his enthusiasm, it would have been clear to him that if God were to survive he would have to be rescued from the formulations of traditional historical Christianity, and particularly from the traditional eschatology.

Even these hurried suggestions of the kinds of intellectual inquiry to which Clough had become attentive explain the interest which, swinging away from both Tractarianism and Arnoldism, he developed during his Oriel years in Unitarianism. In 1845 he read the recently published *Life* of Joseph Blanco White, and found this moving account of the author's transition from Roman Catholic priesthood in Spain through a crisis in religious belief to Anglican orders in England, and then, through a recrudescence of doubt, to Unitarianism, 'strong meat' which 'almost . . . persuaded [him] to turn Unitarian—that is, for the moment' (*Corr.* i. 155). He recommended both White's *Life* and the Unitarian *Prospective Review* to his sister, but Anne, while she felt that the book 'had a tremendous effect on her',

---

1 I have drawn heavily on A. W. Benn, *A History of English Rationalism in the Nineteenth Century*, 2 vols. (London, 1906), i. 427–34, for this account of the implications of Mill's *Logic*.

could not help feeling 'horrified' at the extremes to which White went in his views on the authority of the Scriptures and on the evil effects which Christianity had had on the human race.[1] About the same time, in June, she had a conversation with her brother on the subject of baptism, 'which he seemed greatly inclined to regard merely as a sort of form which had been instituted as a sign of admission into the early Christian Church'.[2] Clough had indeed moved a considerable distance from any Tractarian sympathies he might have felt at one time. In August he wrote to Anne vindicating White, and the terms of his defence could well be significant about his own responses at Oxford. '[W]ith the Inquisition hanging over him,' Clough said, '. . . he could not but fancy . . . that he was being bullied into a sham belief.' He remarked, however, that he was convinced that 'there is a vicious habit of poking into intellectual questions for the fun of it, or the vanity of it', although he did not feel, he added, that this habit was quite as prevalent as that of comfortably uncaring acquiescence (*PPR* i. 97). Meanwhile, during this Long Vacation, he was seeing quite a lot of the Liverpool Unitarians, towards some of whom he was beginning to feel 'no common attraction' (*Corr.* i. 155). During the Christmas Vacation he was in Liverpool again and in January went to the Unitarian Chapel there to hear Martineau preach—but he was disappointed, since, instead, he had to endure a 'Brummagem' preacher offering a 'mere rechauffé of Carlyle and Emerson, dished up in Brummagem ware' (*Corr.* i. 168). 'An evening or two' later he 'met Martineau accidentally at a small party chez mon seul ami Unitarien', and was taken with both the man's conversation and his countenance, which had in it a great deal of the 'rough hewn mountainous strength which one used to look at when at lesson in the library at Rugby, not without trembling' (ibid.).

The generally non-dogmatic and intellectually free-ranging character of Unitarianism obviously explains why Clough was attracted. The special nature of mid-nineteenth-century Unitarianism, however, provided some more specific points of support for his speculations and convictions. English Unitarianism had developed considerably since the days of Priestley. Reviewing that development in a sermon, James Martineau marked out three

---

[1] B. A. Clough, *A Memoir of Anne Jemima Clough*, p. 56.   [2] Loc. cit.

phases. The initial intellectualist stage, when the influence of Priestley was paramount and the doctrine of universal necessity generally accepted, was followed by a reaction which Channing heralded. Channing preached the gospel of human freedom, but at the same time emphasized the claims of conscience. Man's ethical life became sharply contrasted with the necessities of external nature. In the third stage, developed out of Channing through the influence of Martineau himself, the religion of the Spirit was supreme, the voice of conscience, as with Butler, was the voice of God. Religious fulfilment and religious direction came from within.[1] Martineau's ethical theism offered to Clough not only a variant of the divine fact within man which thinkers like Strauss and the Romantic philosophers generally had asserted, but appealed strongly to his inherited acceptance of conscience.

R. W. Church, reviewing Clough's *Poems* in 1863 in the *Christian Remembrancer*, observed:

The author, we fear, renounced Christianity and became a kind of Deist. . . . We have before us the spectacle of a mind of singular conscientiousness, purity, and philanthropy, which was subjected to the influence of two great waves of thought, Arnoldism and Tractarianism, and which, after being sensibly affected by both, deserted both for a vague scepticism.[2]

Regrets of this kind are less relevant in the twentieth century than they might have been in the nineteenth—yet their influence has persisted. The nineteenth century has handed down to us an image of Clough as a kind of archetype of mid-Victorian doubt, 'destitute of faith and horrified at scepticism', clinging vaguely to the remnants of early religious belief. Among nineteenth-century critics only John Symonds and Henry Sidgwick showed any sympathetic understanding of the positive nature of Clough's refusal:[3] because of his honesty Clough is a man on whom has been laid an unfair burden of uncertainty and timidity. The religious attitude which was formed in these Oriel years, and which provides the basis for all Clough's future thought on

---

[1] Cf. Storr, op. cit., pp. 457–9.

[2] [R. W. Church], 'Clough's *Poems*', *Christian Remembrancer*, xlv (Jan. 1863), 71, 73.

[3] J. A. Symonds, 'Arthur Hugh Clough', *Fortnightly Review*, x (Dec. 1868), 591–7; [H. Sidgwick], 'The Poems and Prose Remains of Arthur Hugh Clough', *Westminster Review*, xciii (Oct. 1869), 363–4.

the subject, is fairly indicated in two letters. The first, to Hawkins,[1] sets out some of the objections to traditional Christianity he had to face. The second, written to his sister two years earlier in May 1847, outlines the positive content of his religious belief:

My own feeling certainly does not go along with Coleridge's in attributing any special virtue to the facts of the Gospel History: they have happened, and have produced what we know—have transformed the civilization of Greece and Rome, and the barbarism of Gaul and Germany into Christendom. But I cannot feel sure that a man may not have all that is important in Christianity even if he does not so much as know that Jesus of Nazareth existed. And I do not think that doubts respecting the facts related in the Gospels need give us much trouble. Believing that in one way or other the thing is of God, we shall in the end know perhaps in what way and how far it was so. Trust in God's Justice and Love, and belief in his Commands as written in our Conscience stand unshaken, though Matthew, Mark, Luke, and John or even St. Paul, were to fall. The thing which men must work at, will not be critical questions about the scriptures, but philosophical problems of Grace and Free Will, and of Redemption as an Idea, not as an historical event. What is the meaning of 'Atonement by a crucified Saviour'?—*How* many of the Evangelicals can answer that?—

That there may be a meaning in it, which shall not only be consistent with God's Justice—that is, with the voice of our Conscience, but shall be the very perfection of that justice—the one true expression of our relations to God, I don't deny;—but I do deny that Mr. McNeile or Mr. Close, or Dr. Hook, or Pusey, or Newman himself quite know what to make of it: the Evangelicals gabble it, as the Papists do their Ave Mary's—and yet say they know; while Newman falls down and worships *because* he does not know and knows he does not know.

I think others are more right, who say boldly, We don't understand it, and therefore we *won't* fall down and worship it. Though there is no occasion for adding—'there *is* nothing in it—' I should say, Until I know, I will wait: and if I am not born with the power to discover, I will do what I can, with what knowledge I have; trust to God's justice; and neither pretend to know, nor without knowing, pretend to embrace: nor yet oppose those who by whatever means are increasing or trying to increase knowledge (*Corr.* i. 182).

The letter is of central importance. In relation to the intellectual movements we have been surveying, it reveals Clough's religious attitude not as a merely negative scepticism or an attempt to retain

---

[1] Quoted above, pp. 127–8.

some vague grasp on faith, but as a positive assertion based, as Michael Timko has pointed out, on a careful consideration of the 'available evidence'.[1] Clough brought to his examination of this 'evidence' an evolutionary and dialectical habit of mind which compelled him to reject any procedures which might result in an immobilization of truth. He brought, too, a stern and scrupulous refusal to suppress either the reality forced on him by the logic of facts or that urged on him by the deep-seated desires and dictates of his religious nature. And yet the attempt at a total vindication of Clough against the customary charges of ineffectiveness and failure, even in this special area of belief, falters when confronted by his life as a whole. There is about Clough a special kind of failure, a special kind of ineffectiveness, an accurate sense of which can be arrived at only when the complete life has been surveyed. A beginning can, nevertheless, be made here in considering the crucial subject of his religious beliefs.

Even in this confident letter outlining his convictions, a significant doubleness betrays itself. The primary emphasis is on the interior conviction and interior illumination achieved through the conscience. Equally important, however, is the implicit insistence that the intimations of conscience are also subject to verification by the finite and rational understanding. Dovetailed into Clough's trust in conscience is a radical distrust of it as an epistemological instrument: the Arnoldian belief in necessary correctives to conscience is taken to its extreme. The tension between the sceptical impulse and the will to believe is not really resolved; the condition of tension is written ineffaceably into the belief. Other stresses in Clough's religious belief as an inhabited state, rather than as a set of propositions capable of abstract formulation, render that belief less complete and less satisfying than such formulation might suggest. Intellectually, Clough was thinning out the soil in which, emotionally and psychologically, he was rooted— a healthy and liberating activity only so long as he could provide for himself other sources from which his psyche could draw sustenance and energy, when, that is, his religious speculation was accompanied by an active and creative exploration of other areas of experience and investigation. In the absence of this other activity he lapsed into passiveness, repeating over and over

[1] M. Timko, 'The "True Creed" of Arthur Hugh Clough', (*MLQ*) xxi (Sept. 1960), 214.

again the lonely impartial convictions which he had won for himself in his years at Oriel. While he was at Oriel, however, and in the years immediately following, he was far from passivity. His religious convictions were fresh and vigorous, and intimately involved with his investigations into other areas of man's life. We must now consider some of these areas.

CHAPTER IV

Oxford: Oriel, The Wide World Outside

I. CARLYLE AND EMERSON

IN 1841 Matthew Arnold came up to Balliol as a Scholar. His younger brother, Tom, came up to University College in 1842, the year of Clough's election to his Fellowship. Theodore Walrond—whom Clough had tutored successfully for a Balliol Scholarship the previous summer—had come up a year earlier. Within the larger circle of his friends (which included in these years men like Shairp, Jowett, Stanley, Lake, Conington, Temple, Prichard, Palgrave, and Froude) Clough formed with these three young men a special, extremely closely knit 'interior company'. The four met almost daily. They made a habit of breakfasting together every Sunday in Clough's rooms in Oriel. Together they went skiffing on the Cherwell or on the channels that interlace the meadows of Iffley and Sandford. Together they explored the countryside which Matthew was to make unendingly memorable in 'The Scholar Gipsy' and 'Thyrsis'. These were the years of young manhood when wits ran fresh and clear, when one talked endlessly into all hours, when one turned the whole world over in one's head—and for Clough the world was new and exciting and multiple. Mrs. Humphry Ward, writing of her father's life between 1842 and 1846, when Tractarianism in Oxford was in its last convulsive phase, observed that he, Matthew, Clough, 'and a few other kindred spirits, lived in quite another world of thought. They discovered George Sand, Emerson and Carlyle, and orthodox Christianity no longer seemed to them the sure refuge that it had always been to the strong teacher who trained them as boys.'[1]

Although Carlyle and Emerson played a crucial part in forming Clough's religious views, their influence—like George Sand's rather more subordinate one—worked in far more diversified and extensive ways. Intellectually, they resumed and confirmed for him many of the ideas, attitudes, and questions we have

[1] H. Ward, *A Writer's Recollections*, 2nd edn. (London, 1919), p. 12.

been considering; morally, they provided sources of strength and decision, helped him to define his own stance in relation to his convictions. His experience of them was living, creative, personal —living because it was a shared enthusiasm fed by close discussion with like-minded friends, creative because it inspired a comprehensive engagement with the conditions of contemporary existence, personal because they were living, accessible, personally encountered beings who breathed the same disturbed nineteenth-century air. Emerson was a visitor whom Clough entertained in Oxford and saw a great deal of in Paris. Carlyle, although it is impossible to say when exactly Clough first met him, was someone who was continually present in one's thoughts, someone whose literary life was growing visibly and excitingly before the eyes of young admirers, to be talked about and reported on as one expectantly awaited the latest fruits (cf. *Corr.* i. 153, 166). He was a man to whom one was moved to send tokens of one's regard, as Clough did in December 1845 (*Corr.* i. 166). When Matthew visited Paris, George Sand was one of the people he made a special point of visiting.

Looking back from the settled perspectives of the eighties, James Froude evoked vividly Carlyle's impact in these earlier years: 'Amidst the controversies, the arguments, the doubts, the crowding uncertainties of forty years ago, Carlyle's voice was to the young generation of Englishmen like the sound of "five hundred trumpets" in their ears.' In his writings 'dogma and tradition had melted like a mist, and the awful central fact [of the reality of God and His moral law] burnt clear once more in the midst of heaven'.[1] The admiration for Carlyle which Clough had developed as an undergraduate deepened into near-discipleship in his years at Oriel. The 'five hundred trumpets', he was to discover in time, shrilled an unclear and often contradictory message, but theirs was an inspiriting stridency; Carlyle awakened aspiration, he directed one's attention, he moralized and fortified one's existence. Above all—like Emerson—he presented to one's view a fresh and compelling vision of the City of God.

Heavily indebted to German Romanticism and Transcendentalism, Carlyle presented himself in a dual role: he was both Destroyer and Preserver. Deriving from Herder and Goethe the notion of palingenesis—cultural death and rebirth—he saw in

[1] J. A. Froude, *Carlyle's Life in London*, 2 vols. (London, 1890), i. 313–14.

his iconoclasm the constructive purpose of clearing the way for renewal and growth. Launching a massive attack on contemporary society, its religion, its values, its culture, and its institutions, he waged unceasing war against sham and cant and hypocrisy. In doing this he regarded himself as co-operating— as he exhorted his readers to do—in the 'World's Eternal Tendencies', in the ultimate, irresistible, 'triumph of Truth'. He included in his rejection of cant and sham the traditional but now outdated forms of Church Christianity, of 'Hebrew old clothes' as he called them. At the same time, fervent in his anti-self-consciousness theory, he held up as an ideal the religious belief of men like Jocelin of Brakelond, who

have as yet nothing of 'Methodism'; no Doubt or even root of Doubt. Religion is not a diseased self-introspection, an agonizing inquiry: their duties are clear to them, the way of supreme good plain, indisputable, and they are travelling on it. Religion lies over them like an all-embracing heavenly canopy, like an atmosphere and life-element, which is not spoken of, which in all things is pre-supposed without speech.[1]

If nineteenth-century Christianity was outworn, mechanism, the scientific and materialistic spirit, was for Carlyle the spirit of death itself. He repudiated entirely the tradition of English empiricism. The 'enlightened Scepticisms of the Eighteenth Century' were the marks of 'a haggard epoch, with its ghastly Doctrines, and death's-head Philosophies'.[2] Utilitarianism, though it possessed at least the grace of freedom from cant, was only a diabolical revival of this blighted spirit, its philosophy was one simply of self-interest, the highest human motive it could discover was hunger. Against the inert, materialistic, and reductive philosophies of life which had resulted in the nineteenth-century 'gospel of mammonism' Carlyle pitted his torrential assertions of the reality of Spirit. 'All visible things are emblems; what thou seest is not there on its own account; strictly taken, is not there at all. Matter exists only spiritually, and to represent some Idea, and *body* it forth.'[3] Teufelsdröckh's despair and unbelief had been born in the deserts of mechanism. It was only through his passionate protest on the Rue Saint Thomas de L'Enfer,

---

[1] T. Carlyle, *Past and Present*, in *The Works of Thomas Carlyle*, Centenary Edition, 30 vols. (London, 1897), x. 60.   [2] Ibid., p. 241.
[3] Carlyle, *Sartor Resartus*, in *Works*, i. 57.

when his whole being had risen up to assert its freedom, and his
further passage through the Centre of Indifference, where he had
learnt annihilation of self, that his eyes had been unsealed and he
had been prepared for the Everlasting Yea, the perception of
the vital cosmos 'wherein all contradiction is solved': 'like soft
streamings of celestial music to my too-exasperated heart, came
that Evangel. The Universe is not dead and demoniacal, a charnel-
house with spectres; but godlike, and my Father's.'[1] And
Teufelsdröckh's journey was type and symbol of the cyclic
periodicity of Carlyle's view of history itself: 'If our era is the
Era of Unbelief, why murmur under it; is there not a better
coming, nay come? As in the long-drawn systole and long-drawn
diastole, must the period of Faith alternate with the period of
Denial. . . .'[2]

Central in Carlyle's spiritual vision was the emphasis on what
he called 'natural supernaturalism'. The spiritual was a fact of
everyday life, the gap between spirit and matter was wholly
illusory, sanctity invested the meanest particle. 'Sooty Manchester,
—it too is built on the infinite Abysses; overspanned by the
Skyey Firmaments; . . . Go or stand, in what time, in what place
we will, are there not Immensities, Eternities over us, around us,
in us?'[3] In human terms, Carlyle's was a powerful assertion of the
dignity of individual man. Socially, man was part of that essential
spiritual and moral community which the nineteenth century
(which placed its highest good in making money and whose only
hell was 'the hell of not succeeding') had entirely lost sight of.
For Clough, however, Carlyle's assimilation of spirit and matter
set special problems. The teacher was untroubled—for him the
spirit was triumphant and real; it transformed all matter, but
Evil in his tough Calvinist vision remained Evil, and Good,
Good: the gap between them was immeasurable. The pupil was,
in time, to discover a central despair—what if matter, in fact,
swallowed up the spirit, completely overturned moral and
spiritual categories, completely erased higher and lower?

Carlyle, like his Martin Luther, was 'a bringer-back to reality',
and the reality to which he strove to bring his contemporaries
back was, on the one hand, that of the spirit and, on the other,
the harsh fact of England in the 1840s. He confronted his readers
with the squalor, the greed, the misery, the spiritual and social

---

[1] Ibid., p. 150.   [2] Ibid., p. 91.   [3] Carlyle, *Works*, x. 228.

illness of the age, and though he was unable to make anything for them out of the experience, that enforced confrontation was in itself invaluable. The dignity of man and of labour, the need for moral heroism, the gospel of duty, the gospel of work, these are the only clear directions that emerge from his Eternities and Immensities ; his advocacy of emigration and elementary education are the only workable suggestions in the whole body of his social criticism. Vitriolic in his scorn for all the efforts of his contemporaries to cope with the problems of a stricken society, he rejected almost every single instrument—social, political, intellectual—which had been forged. But if the positive content of Carlyle's social teaching was unclear, if his effect was mainly destructive, he did jolt—violently—the complacency of his readers. Embedded in his transcendental assertions was the overwhelming message of his sociological realism: man's relationship to man was as important as his relationship to God. He forced on his sensitive readers an awareness of rottenness, of the need for examination, of the unrealness and immorality of an exclusive preoccupation with the heavenward view, with the subtleties of theological belief, or with the intricacies of Romantic self-consciousness.

Carlyle himself failed ultimately as a teacher, and the nature of his failure helps to illuminate both Clough's career as a thinker and life as a man. Carlyle failed partly because of the very nature of his attempt. He was trying to be, as H. V. Routh has pointed out, a realist in ideals, but he could not substantiate his ideals.[1] Battling mechanism and science and the depersonalization of an industrial society, he was unable to comprehend either the magnitude or the nature of his enemies. He set out to renovate entirely the lives of his countrymen; he ended by reinforcing some of their dominant values. His intensely willed assertion of the living soul that should and ought to penetrate the social organism foundered, ultimately, on the treacherous rock of authority. His dangerous attachment to the heroic and individual ideal only made it easier for him to confuse might and right, the violence of his opposition came to rest finally in an acquiescence in the achieved locations of power: the Captains of Industry absorbed and nullified Carlyle's attack.[2]

[1] H. V. Routh, *Towards the Twentieth Century* (Cambridge, 1937), p. 135.
[2] Cf. R. Williams, *Culture and Society* (London, 1958), Chapter IV.

An often-recounted story maintains that while Clough was
seeing Emerson off on the *Europa* in Liverpool in 1848, he complained that the American's departure would leave the youth of
England leaderless, since Carlyle had 'led [them] all out into the
desert, and . . . left [them] there'. Emerson, the story continues,
placed his hand on Clough's head, announcing that he thereby consecrated him 'Bishop of all England'. Clough was commissioned
to go 'up and down' the desert, gathering in the wanderers and
pointing out to them the way to the Promised Land.[1] Emerson's
gesture was only a light-hearted piece of mummery—at least, so
one hopes—but it summarizes perfectly the role which devolved
on Clough in these Oriel years. The elder prophet had failed,
his Pisgah-sight had proved illusory, but he had pointed something of the way, and there were among the younger men leaders
who would in time become prophets of the new dispensation.
Clough willingly accepted the part; it engaged all his highmindedness, his aspiration, his dedication to the idea of service.
But this, too, was imprisonment—imprisonment in a sanctioned,
conditional nonconformity—and, as his subsequent career shows,
his most exciting, most alert, most individual contributions were
made only on those occasions when he could hold aloof from
this last temptation of Titanism. Emerson, although he extensively
reinforced Carlyle, also encouraged the development of that
aloofness, that private and non-sanctioned heterodoxy.

In the England of the forties Emerson's was a name which
aroused very mixed feelings. The *English Review*, High Church
and Tory in its sympathies, viewed the 'Emerson mania' with
undisguised apprehension. The reputation this 'Transatlantic
thinker', this 'setter forth of new gods', enjoyed, and which the
widespread publication of his writings attested to, was a matter
for 'grave reflection'. Particularly disturbing was the fact
that he had gained 'many readers and admirers amongst the
youth of our Universities'.[2] Years later one of these admirers
was to recall with nostalgic eloquence the voice from America
which had once sounded in his ears, 'a clear and pure voice which
. . . brought a strain as new, and moving, and unforgettable' as
the voices of Newman and Carlyle and Goethe, a voice of 'soul
and genius' which spoke so effectively 'that from that time forth

[1] E. E. Hale, *James Russell Lowell and His Friends* (London, *c.* 1899), pp. 136–7.
[2] 'The Emerson Mania', *English Review*, xviii (Dec. 1849), 546.

Boston Bay and Concord were names invested to my ear with a sentiment akin to that which invests for me the names of Oxford and Weimar'.[1] Carlyle worked powerfully on the minds and hearts of young men like Clough, but his was essentially a pessimistic vision, turning away from a stark and unmanageable present to a heroic past and the myths of order, purpose, conviction, to be discovered in the monastery of Saint Edmundsbury. Emerson, while he furnished no key (he did not set out to), did offer a general attitude of hopefulness.

Clough's Oxford journals show that he was reading Emerson's *Essays* as an undergraduate. He must have recommended them to his sister, for she was reading them in 1845,[2] and when Emerson came to England in 1847 she met him in Liverpool at Samuel Bulley's house. As part of the entertainment on that occasion passages from Clough's pamphlet on the *Retrenchment Association* were read out to the distinguished visitor.[3] On 26 November Clough wrote to him inviting him to Oxford. There were, he said, among the junior men at Oxford 'not a few that [had] largely learnt' from his writings who would welcome him, although his name would not be exactly 'a passport in a society fenced about by Church Articles' (*Corr.* i. 186). At the end of March 1848 Emerson visited Oxford, but stayed only 48 hours,[4] and on the day of his departure breakfasted with Clough at Oriel. '[T]ruly', he declared, 'I became fond of these monks of Oxford', some of whom, he found, were 'prepared and decided to make great sacrifices for conscience sake'.[5]

For one of these 'monks', Clough, Emerson developed an especial liking, which was to grow over the years into a deep and constant friendship based on mutual respect. In April 1848, when Emerson was contemplating a new journal to establish a Transatlantic intellectual link, the name of the young Oxford don naturally suggested itself to him as that of a worthwhile collaborator.[6] That May the two were together in Paris, where Clough, Emerson reported, was full of 'interest in life and realities, in the state of woman, and the questions so rife ... through Com-

[1] M. Arnold, *Discourses in America* (London, 1896), pp. 145–6.
[2] B. A. Clough, *A Memoir of Anne Jemima Clough* (London, 1903), p. 56.
[3] Cf. *Corr.* i. 186 n.
[4] *The Letters of Ralph Waldo Emerson*, ed. R. L. Rusk, 6 vols. (New York, 1939), iv. 48. *Corr.* i. 215 says, however, that he stayed three days.
[5] Emerson, *Letters*, iv. 48.   [6] Ibid., p. 56.

munism, and through the old loose and easy conventions of that city for travellers'. The younger man also talked 'so considerately of the grisette estate' that Emerson found him 'the best *pièce de resistance*, and tough adherence, that one could desire'.[1] Clough returned to London from that trip especially to hear Emerson lecture, and he was with the American again in Liverpool to say his good-byes personally at the end of the latter's English visit. The day after Emerson left he wrote a long account of him for the benefit of Tom Arnold, now in distant New Zealand. What impressed him most, he said, was that he was 'much less Emersonian than his Essays. There is no dogmatism or arbitrariness or positiveness about him' (*Corr.* i. 216).

Emersonian transcendentalism, fed from the same German springs as Carlyle's, was, like Carlyle's, a faith more than a philosophy. Its mode was oracular and affirmative rather than speculative or questioning, and the kind of assent a mind like Clough's could give to it was strictly limited. His realism, his respect for the empirical tradition in British philosophy, permitted him to go only part of the transcendental way with Emerson. But he found in Emerson, as both man and writer, an important source of confirmation and strength. As a personal friend Emerson offered him the kind of understanding and sympathy, the room to expand, that he badly needed. As a thinker Emerson's most obvious support was in his rejection of organized Christianity: 'We have contrasted the Church with the Soul. In the soul then let the redemption be sought. Whenever a man comes, there comes revolution. The old is for slaves. When a man comes, all books are legible, all things transparent, all religions are forms. He is religious.'[2] Emerson had acted out his assertion in resigning his Boston pastorship—but he had lost neither faith nor optimism. His call to independence, to a nonconformity that amounted almost to anarchism, came as a clear summons to the ears of younger men, steeling the nerves of their resolution, giving them courage in their opposition: 'Trust thyself: every heart vibrates to that iron string.'[3] 'Society is a

[1] Quoted, R. L. Rusk, *The Life of Ralph Waldo Emerson* (New York and London, 1947), p. 347.
[2] R. W. Emerson, 'Divinity School Address', *The Works of Ralph Waldo Emerson*, Standard Library Edition, 14 vols. (Boston and New York, 1883), i. 141–2.
[3] Emerson, 'Self-Reliance', *Works*, ii. 49.

joint-stock company . . . . The virtue in most request is non-conformity. Self-reliance is its aversion. . . . Whoso would be a man, must be a non-conformist.'[1] Emerson provided a counter-poise to Britain's own transcendentalist. He balanced his optimism against Carlyle's gloom, his quietism against the Scotsman's stridency. The cast of his mind was one especially congenial to Clough, showing as it did such a diversity of approach, such an insistence on the principle of polarity in confronting reality, such a reluctance to entrench itself in the fixity of a position. Finally, and perhaps most important in connection with Clough's social thought, Emerson's was *the* voice from America.[2]

A distinct streak of utopian hope runs through Clough's thinking in these years. It manifests itself in *The Bothie of Tober-na-Vuolich*; it shows itself, in a variant form, in the romantic primi-tivism of his ideas on 'democratic' sexual love; according to Froude, Clough had often and seriously discussed with him the conviction that they had no business to be 'gentlemen', and had spoken of going out to New Zealand as a farmer.[3] That hope, it is true, was always curbed and qualified for Clough by his vigilant realism, but it was well enough known among his intimate friends. When Alfred Dommett, the Colonial Secretary, suggested starting a liberal college in Nelson, Tom Arnold, who had gone out to New Zealand at the end of 1847, immediately thought of Clough as a co-operator in this enterprise.[4] To Clough himself Tom, the incurable idealist, wrote:

> Fancy if Shairp and you and I were working together here, living in the light of a common faith, and united by the affection which we already bear one another,—do you not think we might make a glorious onslaught on the great kingdom of Darkness, and do somewhat to-wards speeding the coming of that day, when King-craft and Priest-craft shall be among the things that were, and Love shall bind up the wounds of this bruised and suffering Humanity? (*Corr.* i. 222–3 n.)

Clough had just given up his Fellowship and, though he appears briefly to have toyed with Tom's idea, he settled finally for

[1] Emerson, 'Self-Reliance', *Works*, ii. 51–2.
[2] Cf. C. Gohdes, *American Literature in Nineteenth-Century England* (New York, 1944), p. 145.
[3] W. H. Dunn, *James Anthony Froude*, 2 vols. (Oxford, 1961–3), ii. 527. See also i. 96.
[4] *New Zealand Letters of Thomas Arnold the Younger*, ed. J. Bertram (Wellington, 1966), p. 55.

London and University Hall. In February 1849 he wrote a revealing letter to Tom. The Revolution in France had run its course and he observed, both about it and his new position:

I am not . . . so clear as you are of the rottenness of the poor old ship here—Something I think we rash young men may learn from the failure and discomfiture of our friends in the new Republic. The millennium, as Matt says, won't come this bout. I am myself much more inclined to be patient and make allowance for existing necessities than I was. The very fighting of the time taught one that there were worse things than pain—and makes me more tolerant of the less acute though more chronic miseries of society—these also are stages towards good— or conditions of good. Whether London will take my hopefulness out of me as it did yours, remains to be seen. Peut-être.

. . . Not but that thou wert right, my Tom, . . . but for thy departure I should perhaps be still lingering undecided in the courts of conformity —nor will I affirm that I am right in giving myself unto Stincomalee— but quit the country for altogether is not, so far as I can tell, my vocation. This may be Ur of the Chaldees or even Egypt, but no angel hath as yet spoken to me either in dreams by night or in any burning bush of the desert (*Corr.* i. 243).

For these overstrained young men, bred into an old and oppressive society burdened by history, America was a symbol of hope, of freshness and newness. Clough himself, because of his childhood, had a special relationship with America, but as he grew older he matured into a deep interest in the working out of a vigorous and youthful society.[1] That interest culminated in his visit to America in 1853, and Emerson represented for him the most outstanding and inspiriting example of what the New World had made of its opportunity.

2. THE PROBLEMS OF SOCIETY

As early as 1897 F. R. Statham, writing in the *National Review*, suggested that the 'true key to Clough's work and character' was to be found not in his religious preoccupations but in 'his deep and at times almost painful appreciation of the inequalities and unrealities of social existence'.[2] Yet, until relatively recent

[1] In 1844, for instance, he was reading *The Lowell Offering*, the magazine published by the girl operatives in the woollen-mills in Lowell, Massachusetts, which attracted international attention among students of social and economic problems. Cf. *Corr.* i. 130.

[2] F. R. Statham, 'Arthur Hugh Clough', *National Review*, xxxix (Apr. 1897), 207.

years strangely little attention has been paid to this side of Clough's life.[1] Here, as in so many other areas, we are only beginning to get him into focus.

The depth and seriousness of Clough's concern with the problems of society appear unexpected and even astonishing when we consider the previous emphases in his career. That concern, however,—as I suggested about the notes on political economy he made late in his career at Balliol or shortly after—is intimately involved with his earlier religious and ethical anxieties. His new interest was part of an expanding search for purpose, service, reality, a widening out, ultimately, into an Arnoldian engagement with history. If Clough developed at Oriel a lively and extensive interest in economic and social questions, he developed, as well, a sympathy for democratic movements which went far beyond Dr. Arnold, and which his contemporaries found both exceptional and disturbing. Richard Church thought there was 'room for more dread about' Clough's 'chartism' than about the fashionable radicalism of many other people at the University, because he was in such deadly earnest about his convictions.[2] Stanley, who himself was considered an outstanding liberal by his contemporaries, felt nevertheless that Clough's sympathies for the poor 'may have led him . . . into excessive regard for the democratic and socialistic tendencies of opinion, both here and in France'.[3]

Carlyle's, quite obviously, is an influence which can be detected both in the details and in the larger patterns of Clough's social thinking. Yet, although the attitudes and conclusions of the two men so frequently coincide, it would be seriously distorting to see in Clough an image of passive discipleship. Some of his most characteristic attitudes and endeavours can be traced back through Carlyle to Rugby and to Dr. Arnold, who, one might say, handed him on to Carlyle. From Arnold, initially, Clough derived not only the social conscience but the moral

---

[1] F. W. Palmer, 'Was Clough a Failure?', *Philological Quarterly* (hereafter *PQ*) xxii (Jan. 1943), 58–68, and M. Timko, 'The "True Creed" of Arthur Hugh *MLQ* xxi (Sept. 1960), 218–22, contain fairly detailed accounts of Clough', Clough's social and political attitudes, but from a different angle from mine. The second of these has been reprinted in revised form in the same author's *Innocent Victorian* (Columbus, Ohio, 1966).

[2] [R. W. Church], 'Clough's *Poems*', *Christian Remembrancer*, xlv (Jan. 1863), 68.

[3] R. E. Prothero, *Life and Correspondence of Arthur Penrhyn Stanley, D.D.*, 2 vols. (London, 1893), i. 390.

concern which informs and contains all his thinking, the conviction of the need to humanize and elevate a selfish, mammonistic,
impersonal society. To Arnold, too, can be traced both his sense
of middle-class responsibility and his middle-class conservatism,
his sense that the regeneration of society was to be achieved
through the infusion of moral responsibility into the structure
of society more or less as it existed, through the infusion of
spiritual and social meaning into the petty, fragmented tasks that
industrialism imposed on people, rather than through a radical
reordering. And quite apart from Arnold there were figures like
George Sand. We must return later to her liberating influence on
traditional ethics; at this point she is important as a social thinker,
powerfully mediating through her novels the doctrines of the
French Socialists, whose ideas about the organization of labour,
especially, Clough eagerly embraced. Like Clough, George
Sand was disillusioned by the outcome of the Revolution of
1848, and in July of that year we find her writing to Tom
Arnold with obvious respect about the three articles on 'religion,
dogma and worship of France' which she had recently published
in the now suppressed *La Vraie République*, 'The dogma very
boldly eliminating everything miraculous from the Gospel
History, leaving personality with prophetic and exalted physical
power to Xt. Yet retaining a Liberty–Equality–Fraternity Gospel
as Xty.' (*Corr.* i. 216.)

The religious question and the social and political one, as I
have said, were for Clough interwoven. The Christianity he
had inherited had provided a total reading of man's life, spiritual
and secular, individual and social, and it had frequently enough
been invoked to justify given social and political structures. In
questioning some of the basic premises of that Christianity
Clough was also committed to a reconsideration of the social and
ethical superstructure which he saw as founded on them. The
conviction of injustice here strengthened, in turn, his rejection
of the religious foundation. Shairp protested:

The life and character of Christ,—I do not see why it should not
belong to the future and enter into all its developments even more
fully than ever yet into the past.

I think if we could look stedfastly at these, they would seem not at
all compromised by past forms. Though Christianity has passed through
many systems both political and dogmatical now outworn, there is

nothing in it specially congenial with divine right of feudalisms—
monarchies, aristocracies—nor with bygone creeds, confessions,
priesthoods (*Corr.* i. 218).

This source of dissatisfaction with Christianity as it had hitherto
existed was important in determining the quality of Clough's
concern with social problems. In June 1844 he wrote to Burbidge:

. . . I do believe that [the labourer] has not his proper proportion, that
capital tyrannizes over labour, and that government is bound to
interfere to prevent such bullying; and I do believe too that in the
some way [*sic*] or other the problem now solved by universal competition or the devil take the hindmost may receive a more satisfactory
solution. . . . It is surely not wholly Utopian to look for some system
which will apportion the due reward to the various sets of workmen
and evade this perpetual struggle for securing (each man to the exclusion of his neighbour) the whole market (*Corr.* i. 126–7).

The verbal echoes declare the Carlylean parentage of the general
attitude, but, whereas Carlyle had dyspeptically dismissed the
whole business of political economy as 'vague janglement',
Clough, although he attempted to combat some of the ruling
economic dogmas of his time, displayed considerable interest in,
and respect for, political economy. In this he went even further
than Dr. Arnold. In July 1844 he declared, 'I am considerably
inclined to set to work at Political Economy, for the benefit of
the rising generation;—and to see if I cannot prove "the Apostle
of Anti-laissez-faire"' (*Corr.* i. 130). The self-conscious reference
to his role *vis-à-vis* the 'rising generation' shows clearly one
kind of hopefulness with which he embarked on this new inquiry:
he was answering his headmaster's call for a new Howard or
Clarkson or Fry to lay bare the evil that lay at the heart of
industrial society, and to resolve by God's help that it should no
longer remain unremedied. For Clough political economy was
basically a handmaiden to morality; his interest was distinctly
coloured by an attempt to find some extra-personal moral
imperatives to replace discarded religious foundations. Repeatedly
we find him pressing a particular interpretation of economic
law into the service of his own Evangelically based moral sense.
As he put it in a letter to the editor of *The Balance*, a short-lived
liberal weekly, political economy was a 'science most needful for
Christian men'. It provided the essential 'arithmetic' of justice

without which all the 'ignorant generosity' in the world would be useless. One could, he assured the editor, combine 'the supremest contempt for considerations merely pecuniary' with a lively sense of the value of that arithmetic. Society was contractual; social and economic relationships depended on the division of labour and the exchange of its results, and from a study of these alone could 'proceed a right appreciation of those relations, and a knowledge of our duties in them'. It was true, he conceded, that the 'pure laws of economical science' had been applied rather to the 'low practical question' of making money than to the 'high practical imperative' of doing justice to one's neighbour, but, he asserted, 'numerous moral applications may be found; numerous cases occur where moral guidance would be given by principles of political economy; numerous actions are daily done . . . whose evil is justified by those principles misunderstood, and, were they rightly understood, would, perchance, be corrected'.[1]

Some notes Clough made in 1845 in the 1849 (Roma) Notebook indicate the lines along which he thought about man's economic life, particularly about the issue of wages, which the Chartists had made central. He started with a Labour theory of value which he formulated as 'Labour or Difficulty+Utility generate value',[2] and which, incidentally, tended to provide 'scientific' authority for the ideals of work and service he had been educated to uphold. Yet, although Clough started with this basic proposition of classical economics, he was uneasy about the consequences drawn from it in the Ricardian theory of wages and in the laws of supply and demand. The notes show him trying to feel his way towards some form of organized protection for labour against unrestricted competition in the fixing of wages:

Competition—
    Given a thousand labourers with no present subsistence;—you have a stock of corn,—clearly it is your duty to divide the corn and the labour requisite for the reproduction of it equally amongst them. . . .
    Granted:—but what people do is not this—They do not give work and pay to all—but put up the work at auction for the lowest contractor.
            . . .
Clearly the value of the article to the purchaser does not alter by the

           [1] 'Political Economy', Trawick, pp. 211–12.
           [2] Balliol MS. 441, fol. 3.

fact that there are four or five labourers anxious to produce it, where there were two or three before. . . . If there is no other occupation for the supernumerary seampstresses, the only fair way is to divide the work and pay, both alike, between them all; clearly it is no fair way at all to give the whole work and the half pay to a portion of them.[1]

Convinced of the unfairness of unchecked competition as an economic principle, he considered the feasibility of establishing, within a capitalist economy, some collective and regulative mechanism to fix wages and profits on the basis of adequate living standards:

The Natural Price of Labour, viz., the cost of rearing and maintaining, underlies the market price.—Is not this settled in a manner by Legislation, viz., the Poor Law? . . . Might not this minimum be otherwise fixed and regulated?—It is on a moral ground that the law interferes, I suppose, not on the economical ground of keeping a corps de reserve for possible demand in the labour market—and why not carry that principle further?—Supposing an Englishman and an Irishman equally skilled and equally ready to work—might not the law protect the former in maintaining his standard of wages—in refusing to go barefoot and filthy? But how? By saying You must, if you take the Irishman, pay him Englishman's wages? or at any rate may not the law insist on Schools being kept up—habits of a certain nature adopted—and the Master (manufacturer or otherwise) still more so.

Could a Chamber of Commerce settle for ea[ch] y[ea]r on the gr[oun]d of there being so many orders, so many labourers and so much capital, what the rate of wages and profit should be, independent of daily higgling?[2]

In the letters which he wrote to *The Balance* the following year Clough developed one of his central economic tenets— the 'undoubted principle' that on *economic grounds* saving was more beneficial than spending, that the 'capitalist' who saved his money and invested it in 'reproductive enterprise' did more good to the country than the consumer.[3] In a subsequent letter he allowed certain exemptions from this condemnation of luxury consumption. Such consumption was justified in the cause of education, in the encouragement of the arts, in the laudable 'expression of kindly and affectionate feeling'. He had no quarrel, he said, with 'investments, whose return is moral and spiritual,— investments, of all, the most truly reproductive'. Apart from these

---

[1] Balliol MS. 441, fols. 6–7.   [2] Ibid., fol. 9ᵛ.
[3] 'Political Economy', Trawick, pp. 212–13.

exceptions, however, he mounted a full attack on the idea that luxury-spending justified itself on economic grounds, that it justified itself by creating employment. In the economics of consumption the labour of 'milliner, sempstress, spinner, weaver, merchant, and shopkeeper' simply ran to waste. Instead of such sterile and spendthrift expense of labour, he advocated 're- productive' investment in mills, farming improvements, mining companies, canal and railway projects, and, finally, assisted emigration, or, as he put it, 'reproductive' transport of labour.[1] The programme at first sight appears just another document in the nineteenth-century dream of material progress, and, to a certain extent, it doubtless is that. Secure in his own abstemious personal morality he could sense no moral dangers or difficulties about the vast, impersonal flood of goods his own schemes would release. But uppermost in Clough's mind was not the wealthy society, but the just and humane one. 'Yet economists', he wrote, con- cluding with an attack on the opponents of protective legislation,

who against this high consumption say not a word, profess that the Ten Hours' Bill is a robbery from the labourers—that the workmen's long time and short wages are simply indispensable for laying up a stock for his future employments. . . . Verily, if this be so—if to limit the hours of labour be to rob the coming generation of the stock that should be laid up for them—a far greater and more guilty robbery do they commit who . . . diminish that stock by consuming for consumption's sake only.[2]

Thrift, investment, 'reproductive' labour—the cluster of related 'goods', like the frequently hectoring manner, betrays how closely Clough's moral purpose entwined with his argument. His attempt to formulate the Protestant conscience as a set of hard, objectively derived economic imperatives is, obviously, a variant of the Victorian habit of extrapolating social, moral, and even cosmological significance from discovered 'law'. In making such an attempt Clough, who more customarily rejected such pro- cedures, reveals a crucial ambivalence in his sense of truth. If, on the one hand, he was convinced of the evolutionary and relative nature of truth, he was, on the other, deeply and irre- movably attached to the idea of Truth as unitary, immutable, comprehensive. The tension of that ambivalence became in- creasingly important, and difficult to endure, as he grew older.

[1] 'Expensive Living', Trawick, pp. 218, 219, 220.
[2] Ibid., pp. 220-1.

The confusions inherent in this quasi-scientific attempt could be cleared up only by an honest declaration of value-priorities and a frank admission of the distinct levels that must somehow be accommodated in single discourse. In his sixth and final letter to *The Balance* Clough made such a declaration. It was, he said, 'a fundamental misconception pervading . . . mercantile practice' and theory that the 'common rules of trade' constituted in themselves 'the laws of fairness and honesty'. In reality these rules required the constant intervention of higher principles, such as equity. They were merely expedients, instruments demanding 'perpetual superintendence'. They were like a 'ruthless inanimate steam-engine, which must have its driver always with it to keep it from doing mischief untold'. In yielding up in this way some of his previous claims Clough cleared the ground for an immensely more real, more authentically supportable, frame of reference. The gain is discernible even in this last letter to *The Balance*. The declared priorities controlling the argument give it a new authority, a more confident and responsible flexibility. Taking his stand on the basic principle of fairness, Clough maintained that the uses of economic theory were to increase wealth, multiply production, accumulate capital—but 'in at least equal measure' they were also to ensure that 'the labourer "who is worthy of his hire" may receive it. Partly, no doubt, that money may be made; but greatly, also, that work may be paid.' The kind of flexibility I have referred to appears in the manner in which, by shifting the emphasis from production to wages, this argument for moral *laissez-faire* (only 'the labourer who is worthy of his hire' is provided for) is turned into a flanking attack on unrestricted economic competition:

I am not to regard myself as engaged in a petty warfare with all those for whom I work or who work for me. . . . We are not adventurers, soldiers of fortune, each man for himself, and chance for us all. . . . True it is, at first sight it seems otherwise: as in ancient warfare, so now in modern trade, each man is ordered to fight for himself. But the army is not therefore disbanded; we are still under orders. And as in modern warfare it has been found that organized co-operation is, if less stimulant of individual energy, nevertheless more effective of general success, so may it be in future days with modern trade. But . . . whatever the tactics, whatever the commands, we are still to all intents fellow-soldiers, a single army engaged for the common good against a single enemy, the earth, which we have to 'subdue', the elements, whose resources we must force.[1]

The strenuous undertones, the puritan energy behind the material vision of redeemed Hobbesian man, even the military image, are familiar manifestations of the Victorian economic will; the energy and the image recall the voices of Dr. Arnold and Carlyle, and Clough's concluding call to the aristocracy and the land-owning gentry in this letter suggests the pattern of Carlyle's thinking. Carlyle's tone, however, had been often denunciatory and always threatening. Clough preserved an even more open regard for the class as a class than Matthew Arnold did. The great landholding class would be obliged soon to enter trade, and it was essential that when they did so, they should refuse to 'adopt, as a matter of course, this commercial spirit as it is'. It was imperative that they should 'impregnate trade with their own ancestral feeling of service owed and duty to be done to the country, with that hereditary sense of honour which, in its rightful Christian phase, is but "the finest sense of justice"'.[2]

One of the most interesting aspects of these letters to *The Balance* is the way in which they modify, soften, qualify themselves, until the initial 'radical' ambitiousness comes to rest finally in a containing moral conservatism. The evident revision and correction over such a brief span of time (the letters were published between January and March 1846) indicate not only the rapidity with which Clough's ideas were forming and settling, but the amount of attention he devoted to these subjects. During these years he was also a prominent member of the Decade, the debating society which had caused him so much soul-searching as an undergraduate. The membership of the Decade was distinguished. It included men like Benjamin Jowett, John Duke Coleridge, James Riddell, Richard Church, Frederick Temple, John Conington, and John Shairp. But in the eyes of some observers at least, Clough, particularly when he managed to break through his reserve, was the most able and distinguished speaker in the group.[3]

---

[1] 'The Spirit of Trade', Trawick, pp. 223–4, 224, 224–5.
[2] Ibid., p. 225.
[3] Cf. T. Arnold, 'Arthur Hugh Clough: A Sketch', *Nineteenth Century*, xliii (Jan. 1898), 107, and [R. W. Church], 'Clough's *Poems*', *Christian Remembrancer* xlv (Jan. 1863), 65.

The Decade meetings, like the correspondence columns of *The Balance*, provided Clough with an opportunity for clarifying his ideas on contemporary social issues, and surviving reports of speeches he made show him testing out in this forum as well some of the ideas and positions we have already encountered. Tom Arnold, for instance, remembered Clough's support of a proposal he had moved in favour of Lord Ashley's 'Ten Hours Bill' for the 'marvellous insight' and 'at the same time . . . strict moderation and conscientiousness' with which he 'combated the doctrines of *laissez-faire* and the omnipotence of the action of supply and demand, then hardly disputed in England'.[1] John Shairp recalled another speech on the subject, 'That the character of a gentleman was in the present day made too much of'. Not surprisingly, when we remember the concluding remarks in his final letter to *The Balance*, Clough 'spoke neither for nor against' this particular motion. Instead, for nearly two hours,

he went into the origin of the ideal, historically tracing . . . how much was implied originally in the notion of a 'gentle knight'—truthfulness, consideration for others (even self-sacrifice), courtesy, and the power of giving outward expression to these moral qualities. From this high standard he traced the deterioration into the modern Brummagem pattern which gets the name. These truly gentlemen of old time had invented for themselves a whole economy of manners, which gave true expression to what was really in them, to the ideal in which they lived. These manners, true in them, became false when adopted traditionally and copied from without by modern men placed in quite different circumstances and living different lives. . . .

One expression I remember he used. . . . 'I have known peasant men and women in the humblest places, in whom dwelt these qualities as truly as they ever did in the best of lords and ladies, and who had invented for themselves a whole economy of manners to express them. . . .'[2]

Dr. Arnold's aim had been to turn out 'Christian gentlemen', and, in the pupil's attempt to define the true nature of gentlemanliness, we see exactly how much the teacher had contributed to the concerted nineteenth-century redefinition of the term. That the redefinition, while it disengaged the idea of the gentleman from the old aristocratic connections, firmly connected it with the

---

[1] T. Arnold, 'Arthur Hugh Clough: A Sketch', 107.
[2] *PPR* i. 26–7.

social and cultural values of a soberly moral middle class, indicates a significant limitation in Clough's 'radicalism'. His
contempt for the 'Brummagem' gentleman was at once democratic
and rooted in class assumptions.

The qualifications in that 'radicalism' become more apparent
when we consider his part in a debate held on 14 February 1846.
The Corn Law agitation had passed a critical point, Sir Robert
Peel had just announced the change in his policy, and the motion
on this occasion was, 'That means ought to be adopted by the
Legislature for recognizing formally the social and political
importance of the manufacturing interest'. John Conington
recalled the occasion.

[T]hose of us who were on the movement side were naturally . . .
enthusiastic in favour of the manufacturers, who appeared to us as
winners of a great social victory. My proposal . . . was to the effect
that they ought to be made peers just as great landowners were. In
this the bulk of the members present . . . do not seem to have concurred
with me; but I had Mr. Clough's support. . . . I can recall . . . the stately
serene tones in which he delivered a kind of prophecy of the new era
which in a few days was to be inaugurated, and told us that 'these
men' (the manufacturers) 'were the real rulers of England'.[1]

The diagnosis of the emerging structure of political, social, and
economic power is acute, and clearly it owed a great deal to
Carlyle. In the perspective of the forties the industrialist could
legitimately be seen as a champion of the reformers and of the
oppressed rural workers; Clough could, quite sincerely, voice
his sympathy for popular causes. Church remembered him in
the same speech electrifying 'some even of those among his
audience who were by no means ultra-Conservative' by the
vehemence of his expressed feelings about 'the claims of the poor,
the duties incumbent upon holders of property, and such like
topics'.[2] In showing this faith in 'master-manufacturers', and the
part they could play in shaping a new and less unjust England
(cf. Corr. i. 243), however, Clough was succumbing to the same
authoritarian temptation Carlyle had—he was throwing in his
lot with the ascendant class. Unlike John Stuart Mill, neither
man saw that the crucial problem was that of setting up a multiple
and balancing set of power-groups. Carlyle had exhorted the

---

[1] Ibid., p. 31.   [2] [R. W. Church], 'Clough's *Poems*', 65.

Captains of Industry to become heroes; Clough was attempting to persuade them to become gentlemen. Like Matthew Arnold—although he never even remotely approached the subtlety, penetration, and scope of Arnold's analysis—he saw class-characteristics as a kind of abstract human fund, available to all men, from which one could draw the appropriate qualities as required. Like Arnold, he failed to see that without self-interest there would be no class.

In the light of the kinds of extended thinking we have been considering, Clough's pamphlet on the *Retrenchment Association*, which enjoyed some celebrity (although of a very minor kind) in its day, appears not as a quixotic engagement with tangled issues but as a deeply serious and long-pondered argument. Written in 1847 at the height of the Irish Famine, it derives its energy and its rather dated effectiveness primarily from Clough's moral indignation, but the Carlylean rhetoric of concern also encompasses a seriously held theory of economic life. The articulation between the moral and the economic argument in Clough's condemnation of luxury-spending becomes fully clear only in the context of his letters to *The Balance* and the speeches he made before the Decade. The pamphlet also provides a clearer sense of the more truly 'radical' elements in his position.

Addressing a privileged Oxford audience, Clough proceeds from a call to austerity on both moral and economic grounds to a consideration of the part the traditionally privileged should play in a society rapidly moving away from a rigidly stratified, land-centred economy. He concedes the absolute necessity of cultural traditions, the vital importance of the great heritage of 'law, and thought, and religion' in the nation's life. He concedes, too, that 'there are things worse than starving', but then goes on to outline sardonically the actual concern for cultivation shown by the Oxford gentleman.

And as this our English aristocracy draws its recruits almost exclusively from the newly rich, what, may we ask, is the most fitting lesson it should inculcate upon them, what discipline and what drill should it place them under? Shall it meet them half way with the precept of, Expense and ostentation? Shall it say, Your business as a member of the best part of the English nation is to entertain, to give good dinners, and see the world, to have houses larger than you want, . . . carriages more than you use, horses more than you have work for? Is this to be the talismanic tradition handed down from chivalrous days to the new generation; is this the torch of wisdom and honour which our feudal aristocracy transmits to the new one that succeeds it? . . .

A leisure-class is possibly indispensable to the welfare of the nation (one of Clough's sentences about men 'who, though thousands and tens of thousands perish by starvation, stoically meanwhile' occupy themselves 'in books and in study, in reading, and thinking, and travelling' yields a peculiarly ambiguous tonality), but can one invoke such necessary exemptions, when for the traditions of leadership, service, and self-dedication, of pioneering 'the route of the armies of mankind . . . to the citadel of truth', is substituted an unendingly appetitive leadership in a 'pilgrimage to the Palestine of Cockaigne'? '[H]owever essential be these higher classes, still there remains the question, is there not a holier land than Cockaigne . . .?'[1]

The nature and extent of Clough's 'radicalism' in this pamphlet has not always been appreciated. Katharine Chorley, for instance, has written that Clough is 'arguing the case, not for a new social dispensation, but for a responsible use, both on moral and economic grounds, of the existing private property basis of society'.[2] The final position is fairly represented, but to leave it at this ignores the lengths to which Clough goes in questioning established assumptions. Speaking in the House of Lords on the subject of the Irish Famine on 23 March 1846, Lord Brougham had maintained that it was the landlord's undoubted right to 'do as he pleased, and if he abstained he conferred a favour and was doing a kindness. . . . [P]roperty would be valueless . . . if it were not acknowledged that it was the landlord's undoubted, indefeasible and most sacred right to deal with his property as he list. . . .'[3] 'Some one, I fear,' Clough wrote, 'might be found to look up your title-deeds, and to quote inconvenient Scriptures.'

The Institution of Property, he might urge, is all well enough as a human expedient to secure its reward to industry, and protect the provident labourer against the careless or idle. But for half-a-million-per-annum fortunes, fifty-mile-long estates, and may-I-not-do-what-I-please-with-my-own proprietors, some other justification, it would seem, must be sought. Sought and found. Found it must be by owners, or looked for it will be by others.

[1] Trawick, pp. 234, 235–6.   [2] Chorley, p. 135.
[3] Quoted, C. Woodham-Smith, *The Great Hunger* (London, 1962), p. 72.

Such an inconvenient Bible-quoter might ask about the origins of hereditary property: one's father or grandfather, one hoped, at some stage 'in time past, did service to receive [such property]; worked for it; earned it'—'for by begging, stealing, or serving, all men live, said Mirabeau'. It was the earth, finally, which gave him that work to do, 'And "the earth hath He given to the children of men". Not, says the Scripture, to the children of the rich, or of the noble, or of those who have had it hitherto; not to the well-bred and well-educated—rather, it might seem, to the children of those by the sweat of whose brow it is subdued.' And, Clough maintains, it is far nearer the truth—although it is not the whole truth—to declare that 'whoever is born into the world has a just claim to demand therein and therefrom work and wages for work' than to assert the unlimited right of property. '[E]ven as in some Alacran shipwreck; each new-comer . . . may be called upon to share in the toils, and may demand to share in the food; and no old citizen of the rocks shall dare to say, We may monopolize the work alike and the pay.'[1]

Intentionally, perhaps, Clough seems to have gone to some trouble to cover himself. The hypothetical third person called in to utter the more radical sentiments shifts some of the responsibility. The implication that the existing distribution of wealth represents, substantially, the results of fairly rewarded industry (although the quizzical reference to Mirabeau casts some doubt here) softens the radical intent. Indeed, Clough's moral criteria of social justice, drawing on Carlyle and the doctrines and slogans of Saint-Simonianism and Chartism, also lead to an alternative justification of private property.

Nor need we fear to acknowledge this principle [that all men have a right to demand work and wages] freely. There is enough sense of fairness in the world to let the sacred institution of property find itself a basis secure and unassailed in that other great principle: 'If a man will not work, neither let him eat.' . . . And, as it is, when we punish the starving man who steals the loaf, it is not because either the baker or we have an exclusive right to it, but because society at all hazards must avoid putting a premium on laziness.[2]

Yet, despite the qualifications, Clough's insistence on the right to work and to be paid fairly amounted, in its day, to a vigorous and startling onslaught.

[1] Trawick, pp. 232–3.   [2] Ibid., p. 233.

[P]roperty is scarcely, by law or gospel, that inalienably personal, individual thing, which we that have it would believe it to be. . . . [I]n calamities and horrors the old laws of *meum* and *tuum* shrink to nothing, while a loftier principle reveals itself, and no man gainsays it.

The sons of deceased public servants—yea, the living workers themselves—possess no indefeasible title to those lands, and goods, and monies, which they call their earnings. Their lands come to them saddled with indefinite rent-charges, reservations, and reversional interests—the poor and the needy that are, and that shall be, have a lien on their monies and their chattels.[1]

That, after all, is Clough's last word in this pamphlet, and its effect can be estimated from the long remonstrating letter which Bonamy Price, who had taught him at Rugby and who was to become in 1868 Drummond Professor of Political Economy at Oxford, wrote to him.[2] Arguing a liberal but conservative case based on orthodox *laissez-faire* principles, the letter not only makes clearer the nature of Clough's radicalism but suggests also the secularizing direction in which he had moved from Arnoldian theocentricity in his social and political attitudes. Clough appeared to be discarding, Price thought, the 'old position' which proclaimed the duties of all men towards God and their fellow humans, the duties of fully utilizing one's talents, 'of humanity, kindness and the like'. Instead, he seemed to be asserting certain 'rights which the poor have towards the rich, and their being justified in themselves, at certain times, carrying those rights into execution'. He was making the 'law of property' contingent, 'subject to conditions', and therefore in cases of abuse 'liable . . . to justifiable revolutions'. Such views were dangerous undoubtedly—but were they true? Everyone, admittedly, had the right to be protected from starvation, but Clough seemed to 'mean more', for he adopted the 'operative's cry, "fair day's wages for a fair day's work"'. Only a 'socialist' or 'communist' would argue that such an economic arrangement was 'most calculated in the long run to maintain the largest number of men in comfort and abundance'. He himself was convinced that, once property-owners were made to feel that they had to share their wealth compulsorily with the masses, all incentive would be paralysed, since such coercive procedure would violate the

1 Ibid., p. 236.
2 Bodleian MS. Eng. Lett. c. 190, fols. 109–16 (252).

desire implanted in all men by God to 'improve their condition'
and enjoy to the full 'the fruit of their labour'. Unjust laws,
laws which gave 'unequal chances in the race of life' were
politically unjust, and 'political injustice may justify revolution:
but this proceeds on a very different principle from any attack
on property as badly, wastefully, or inefficiently used'. The
present circumstances of national crisis were to be met by 'direct
calls on the government and by appeals, *moral* appeals to indi-
viduals—not by challenging particular use of property made by
anyone'. Nothing was to be gained by interfering with the rights
of property. Human legislation could never improve the general
economy 'founded by God'. The poor man was to be taught that
'the misconduct of the rich man does not give *him* a right to
correct it—that the rights of the poor were not co-extensive
with the obligations of the rich'.

In the clouded and ominous forties, there were, besides the
Irish Famine, other grave issues to engage the attention of concerned young men. At home in England Chartism rumbled ever
more threateningly. From France came reports of swelling
political activity among the discontented masses. From his
insider's position Matthew Arnold, who had been appointed
Lord Lansdowne's secretary in 1847, kept Clough abreast with
the latest news about both Chartism and France. Oxford, however, for the most part remained splendidly untouched; it had
preoccupations of its own. 'Meantime . . . we go on in our usual
humdrum way. The ecclesiastical world agitated by all manner of
foolish Hampden-rows: of the confused babble about which all
quiet people are infinitely tired.'[1] By the time Clough took up
this letter to Tom Arnold again, on 25 February, revolution had
broken out in France. His comments generally—especially
when we remember the wild enthusiasm displayed by some of
his friends[2]—were cool, even sceptical. From the beginning
he seems to have suspected the nationalistic and militaristic

[1] *Corr.* i. 198. The proposed appointment of Dr. Hampden to the Bishopric
of Hereford had awakened the ire of the enemies of theological liberalism.

[2] Froude, for instance, was so elated that he set a band to play the Marseillaise
under the Vice-Chancellor's window: W. H. Dunn, op. cit. i. 98. Clough might
have been rather more enthusiastic than his letters suggest. According to Froude,
he spent much of his time in Paris talking to the workers. Froude also reported
that he received letters from Paris in which Clough signed himself 'a heathen man
and (Re)publican'. Ibid. i. 99, 98.

fervour that interwove with the revolutionary aspirations of the French.

The chances of going abroad will very likely be cut off, for we may shortly see *Europam flagrare bello*, the Austrians driven out of Lombardy by French bayonets. *Alter erit tum Lodi* and another Arcola shall crown *delectos heroas* with, we will hope, a better-used victory. But the French armies are not quite apostolical, nor do I put much faith in Michelet's holy bayonets as preachers of any kind of Gospel (*Corr.* i. 200).

At the beginning of May he set off for Paris to see for himself the state of revolutionary France. The letters he sent back to England reveal an alert eye for everything that was going on around him, and particularly for anything which touched on the question of Socialism or the organization of labour. Initially, at least, they reveal, too, a clear sense of elation and expansion— but, as Katharine Chorley has remarked, they do not show 'deep personal engagement'.[1] One should be careful here, however, of misinterpreting either Clough's 'radicalism' or this particular revolution. Clough had some genuinely radical sympathies, but the city he dreamed of and hoped for was not really an earthly city. Like Tennyson's dream city it was a city 'built to music, therefore never built at all, and therefore built for ever', and there were strict limits to the amount of political reality his vision could bear. Further, his radicalism was of a fundamentally qualified kind, balancing itself, ultimately, against an ingrained respect for traditional social order: he preached revolutionary doctrine only in a melioristic cause. Politically he had an assortment of attitudes rather than a settled, coherent, closely thought-out philosophy, and his visit to Paris should be seen not as a search for confirmation but as an attempt to look into the evidence. And the evidence of 1848 in France offered little scope for any profound engagement—especially to someone who combined with a genuine concern for the poor the eagerness of a theoretical Socialism. This was a muddled, confusing, and—viewed through the hopes of both workers and intellectuals—ugly revolution.

Fired by Louis Blanc's cry, 'The right to work', it started in aspiration, but, as its course unfolded, the weaknesses in the way in which the socialists and the workers had organized themselves were revealed. Insidiously the ascendancy of the bourgeoisie was

[1] Chorley, p. 145.

reasserted, and, finally, violently confirmed in the bloody 'four days' of June. The complicated political manœuvres involved in this process of attenuation, the false political declarations, the jealousies and betrayals, the shifts in allegiance and power, made it impossibly difficult for the contemporary observer to arrive at any clear understanding. When disillusion came, it was gradual, diffuse, and dull. For Clough an experiment had failed, a promise had faded, and that failure and waning made impossible his earlier idealistic trust in the solutions offered by social and political organization.

In a letter he wrote to his sister on 14 May Clough clearly indicated the direction of his sympathies and the aspects of the revolutionary programme which held most interest for him.

I don't expect much good will come of this present Assembly.—It is extremely shopkeeperish and merchantish in its feelings, and won't set to work at the organization of labour at all, at all. But will prefer going to war to keep the people amused, rather than open any disagreeable social questions. . . . The Socialist people are all in the dumps (*Corr.* i. 204).

The same day he wrote to Stanley about Lamartine's decline in popularity:

But some say that the Bourgeoisie, to shirk the Organization-of-Labour question, are eager for War, and La Martine, having proclaimed Paix a tout prix, is therefore thought an obstacle. On all hands, there is every prospect, on dit, of War. . . . The Socialists, i.e. the leaders, for the most part lament this extremely—the People of course are excited about Poland; and either are indifferent to the Socialist Ideas or are blind to the certainty of these questions being then indefinitely adjourned. The boys . . . of the Garde Mobile are infected with bourgeoisistic loyalty, also the new members of the National Guard. The Socialists simply deplore the whole result;—regard the whole thing as at present a failure, a Bourgeoisistic triumph. Mais attendons (*Corr.* i. 205–6).

In another letter to Anne he reported the excitement of the 15th, when the Assembly was invaded under pretext of the Polish question, and the real revolutionary left-wing leaders, Blanqui and Barbés, made their abortive snatch for power. Barbés even managed to read a proclamation in the Hôtel de Ville, declaring a new provisional government, before he was arrested and dispatched to prison, where he was joined a fortnight later by

Blanqui. This was the closest view of violence Clough had during his stay, and it tested his revolutionary ardour. His comment on a demonstration which left the workers leaderless is illuminating: 'There was no firing and scarce any fighting. The whole thing is put down, for the present, and I am glad it is, on the whole' (*Corr.* i. 205). Dismissing 'Citizen Blanqui' and his 'hang-dog, conspiratorial aspect', he turned an ironic eye on his own non-participation, on the middle-class observer detached from everything but his own timidity.

I do little else than potter about under the Tuileries Chestnuts and here and there about bridges and streets, pour savourer la republique. I contemplate with infinite thankfulness the blue blouses, garnished with red, of the garde mobile; and emit a perpetual incense of devout rejoicing for the purified state of the Tuileries, into which I find it impossible, meantime, to gain admittance. I growl occasionally at the sight of the aristocratic equipages which begin to peep out again, and trust that the National Assembly will in its wisdom forbid the use of livery servants. . . . Gen'lly one can not better express the state of Paris in this respect than by the statement that one finds it rather pointed to be seen in the streets with gloves on (*Corr.* i. 206–7).

By the 19th the revolutionary waters had quietened sufficiently for the rich to venture out openly. February had become a faded promise, and Clough sent off an account to Stanley which deliberately echoed Carlyle's voice:

Ichabod, Ichabod, the glory is departed. Liberty, Equality, and Fraternity, driven back by shopkeeping bayonet, hides her red cap in dingiest St. Antoine. Well-to-do-ism shakes her Egyptian scourge to the tune of Ye are idle, ye are idle; the tale of bricks will be doubled, and Moses and Aaron of socialism can at the best only pray for plagues, —which perhaps will come—paving stones for vivats, and emeutes in all their quarters.
Meantime the glory and their freshness of the dream is departed. . . . The voice of clubs is silenced: inquisitors only and stone walls of Vincennes list the words of Barbés; . . .
Wherefore—
Bring forth, ye millionaires, the three-months-hidden carriages; rub clean, ye new nobles, the dusty emblazonries; ride forth, ye cavalier-escorted amazons, in unfearing flirtation, to your Bois de Boulogne: the world begins once more to move on its axis and draw on its kid gloves (*Corr.* i. 207).

Curiously, only the lost cause—or the impossibly distant one—seemed to elicit such confidently committed rhetoric from Clough. On the 21st the French finally held their twice-postponed fête in honour of the new Republic. Emerson was an enchanted spectator. In his optimistic eyes the enormous crowd which thronged the Champ de Mars was 'like an immense family'.[1] 'It was easy to see', he wrote, 'that France is far nearer to Socialism than England and it would be a short step to convert Paris into a phalanstery.'[2] He would, perhaps, have been rather rudely shaken had he discovered that most members of the Assembly had taken the precaution of secreting a dagger or pistol on their persons before committing themselves to the 'Feast of Concord, Peace and Labour'.[3] Clough, although a frequent companion of Emerson in Paris, was much less impressed. Beneath the fastidious sneer of the account he sent to Stanley there was a keen political awareness. He was becoming adept at exposing the sophistry of surfaces:

There was a great deal of confusion, marching and countermarching, and there was a full half hour's interval in the procession before le Char came up; and it was an ugly affair, when it did come; the jeunes filles looked pretty in their white dresses, with the tricolor streaming from the left shoulder and (artificial) oak-wreaths in their hair, pretty en masse, but individually not by any means remarkable either for face or figure. Moreover they were de-classicized by their use of parasols. I don't think they and the char got fairly to their work's end till 1 o'clock. I passed, and proceeded to the Champ, where a little after 12 went up the tricolor balloon but in a rather disorganized condition. . . . [T]he perpetual gunfiring gave me a headache and I retired early. The illumination in the evening in the Champs Elysees was extremely pretty. . . . The crowd was enormous. It was funny in the afternoon to see the classical virgins walking about with their papas and mamas, people of the under-shoemaking and back-street-shopkeeping class (*Corr.* i. 208–9).

In the letter he wrote to his sister the following day he showed how little deceived he was. Although there was no immediate prospect of disturbances, since the old leaders were either in hiding or in prison, he had no doubt that within three months

---

[1] Emerson, *Letters*, iv. 76. [2] Ibid. p. 77.
[3] P. Robertson, *Revolutions of 1848*, paperback edn. (Harper Torchbooks, New York, 1960), p. 83.

there would be another *émeute* (*Corr.* i. 210). The prediction, in fact, did not have long to wait for its fulfilment.

The 'four days' of June, when workers protesting against the closure of the revolutionary National Workshops were savagely put down by Cavaignac's troops, awakened in him the sadness of a man who was now facing brutal realities, but who had, in his first fortnight in Paris, 'walked about Jerusalem and told the towers thereof with wonderful delight' (*Corr.* i. 214).

I confess I regard it in the same light as a great battle—with, on the whole, *less* horror and, certainly more meaning than most great battles one reads of. However, there is no doubt that France's prospects are dubious and dismal enough, and one is almost inclined to think that the outbreak was premature; with their ideas so far from ripe the French had better, if possible, have endured a little longer the immorality of L. Philip's [*sic*] government. But yet on the whole one accepts the whole thing with gratitude. It will, I think, on the whole accelerate change in England; and perhaps, my dear Tom, you may yet live to see some kind of palingenesy effected for your repudiated country (*Corr.* i. 215).

The reiterated 'on the wholes' echo forlornly as they sound the retreat from the confidently unrolling panoramas of Arnoldian history. Next year, in February, he wrote again to Tom Arnold,

Today, my dear brother republican, is the glorious anniversary of the great revolution of 48, whereof what shall we now say? Put not your trust in republics nor in any institution of man. God be praised for the downfall of Louis Philippe. This with a faint feeble echo of that loud last year's scream of *a bas Guizot* seems to be the sum total. Or are we to salute the rising sun with Vive l'Empereur and the green liveries? (*Corr.* i. 244.)

Matthew Arnold, who 'was at one time really heated to a very fervid enthusiasm' by the revolution (*Corr.* i. 215), remarked after the June uprising, 'If one had ever hoped any thing from such a set of d——d grimacing liars as their prophets one would be very sick just now.'[1] Clough had been among those who had hoped.

3. THE QUESTION OF MORALITY

In rejecting orthodox Christianity, Clough found himself involved in an attempt to find alternative definitions and bases for

[1] Lowry, p. 84.

his sense of social justice and morality. Also and inevitably, he was committed to a re-examination of the individual moral life, of the implications of being human, of the nature of good and evil. Froude's hero, Markham, responding to naturalistic currents and to Spinozistic doctrines especially, had declared himself emancipated from the tyranny of Evil. A roughly similar tendency can be detected in Clough—a tendency only, not an achieved emancipation, a reaching-out, not a finished conviction. The line of his growth towards this area of freedom was neither clear nor confident; it was constantly blurred by the thwarting sense of guilt and corruption which impelled him constantly to embrace more conventional understandings of moral purity. Here, as elsewhere, the pull of his moorings against the new tide was perpetual, the dialectic unending. He had discarded the machinery of theological doctrine, but the mills of puritan conscience ground relentlessly on. The consciousness of depravity, which Rugby had instilled in him and Balliol exacerbated, had entrenched itself ineradicably in his psychology: his attempt at redefining the concept of sin was, at the most personally significant level, an intense search for release.

The notes on religious subjects which he made in 1845 in the 1849 (Roma) Notebook show him probing at the theological and philosophical implications of the problem of Evil when set in the context of an unhistorical idealism.[1] Two years later he told his sister that he had 'quite given up' his belief in eternal punishment.[2] In discarding the traditional Christian eschatology, he had also jettisoned a vital generative source of personal morality. Evil had to be redefined, fresh terms had to be made with sin, and the most obvious possibilities for such redefinition lay in the direction either of naturalism or of the ethic of social responsibility and consequence. A letter he wrote to Anne early in 1847, in response to her complaints of petty pilfering among her school-children, indicates how far he had travelled from the ironclad moral sense of earlier days when he had agonized over the 'evil' he had neglected to combat in Rugby.

Sad indeed it is to hear of the evil doings of the children, and what you are to do with them I really can't say. However I wouldn't exaggerate either the sin or the evil. With the education (so to call it!) that these children get at home, what is to be expected from them?

[1] See Appendix B.   [2] B. A. Clough, op. cit., p. 67.

And really in some children pilfering is a matter of mere fancy or habit—a sort of trick like biting their nails, or shaking their legs. Of course it is necessary they should know that the thing *is* wrong, and also *why* it is wrong; the former is not much use without the latter. I am convinced it is very bad for children to be *frightened* into believing themselves to have done wrong and to be very wicked. But you might easily show them that people can never live with each other in the world without respecting the rules of property, that it would come otherwise to the strongest or the cunningest taking away what other people had earned by their own hard work, and *that* they would see to be really wicked . . . (*Corr.* i. 176–7).

The obverse of this rational attempt to cope with what Dr. Arnold had called 'the evil of boy nature' was, obviously, the task of redefining good. A letter written to Clough in January 1849 by Constantine Prichard furnishes a clue here. 'It did not need more than the little I have known of you the last year or two,' Prichard wrote,

to teach me that any doubts—or more—of the truth of the Xian System which you might feel, were grounded on what you say of its not satisfying your ideal of man's nature. . . .
It is possible that a freer and less shackled development of all impulses might do for some: but it would not, I feel convinced, for more than the golden few. And Xy is not for the few but for mankind. Those who feel the ingrained evil of their own hearts most deeply are perhaps most conscious of this.—This is my objection to your 'moral philosophy'—that I do not agree with your mode of cutting the knot of the world-old difficulty concerning 'law' and 'impulse' (*Corr.* i. 239).

Even as an undergraduate Clough had begun to realize that there was room—even need—for questions regarding the kind of recognition to be granted to flesh and impulse, that the rigid Evangelical dichotomy between flesh and spirit was unnaturally constricting, and that there were crucial difficulties involved in the attempt to balance the felt claims of the animal against the intuited reality of the spiritual. The need for a fresh adjustment became a more pressing personal concern in his Oriel years, edged with the sharpness of adult self-recognition. As he wrote in the 1849 (Roma) Notebook:

What used to disgust me so was the sight of a man looking up in this way into . . . vacuum, seeking and claiming Spiritual en-reportité with Angels and Archangels and all the company of heaven at the same time that his nether parts were not en-raportité only but in actual active combination with Elementa terrestria vel pudendi prima. This is the hypocrisy hated of Men.[1]

The sickened awareness of man's 'nether parts' forms an anguished undercurrent to Clough's search for a saner balance. At the same time it makes particularly urgent his receptiveness to influences which pointed toward a new orientation. Devil-ridden Carlyles, though they impelled one to face facts, were of little help here— they merely nourished the disease, and it was to the tradition of romantic naturalism that Clough looked for guidance—to Spinoza and, among contemporaries, to optimists like Emerson who had erased Evil and defined it as purely privative. 'No law', Emerson had also declared, 'can be sacred to me but that of my nature. Good and bad are but names very readily transferable to that or this, the only right is what is after my constitution, the only wrong what is against it.'[2]

This general impulse of Clough's towards a less rigorous moral scheme reveals itself most sharply (and inclusively) in his attempts to come to terms with the fact of sexuality. Some of the dominant elements in his response to sexual experience can be seen clearly in the poems on sexual love which he wrote during these years, poems which scrutinized, at times with delicacy and perceptiveness, the complexities of the relationship between man and woman. We should, however, attempt—without pressing this poetry too heavily into service—to establish a background for this side of his development, recognize it as an individual effort, and also see it as part of a broader historical and cultural movement.

Emersonian man found his highest good in self-fulfilment, but it was strictly as spiritual essence that he did so; somehow in man's ascent towards this particular heaven of realized divinity his animality rarefied itself out of existence. The gentle Emerson could take one only part of the way; two other writers proved franker, more realistic guides. Clough shared the enthusiasm of his discovery of both Goethe and George Sand with the two Arnold boys,[3] and Matthew later recalled the impact on them, particularly, of Goethe, 'the greatest voice of the century', who 'came to us in those youthful years through Carlyle'. 'The large,

---

[1] Balliol MS. 441, fol. 39, Clough's dots. The jotting follows the draft of a passage from *Adam and Eve*, Scene III. It appears to belong, therefore, to a period after 1847.   [2] 'Self-Reliance', *Works*, ii. 52.   [3] H. Ward, op. cit., p. 12.

liberal view of human life in *Wilhelm Meister*, how novel it was
to the Englishman in those days! And it was salutary, too, and
educative for him, doubtless, as well as novel.'[1] Carlyle had
introduced Goethe, but Clough read him in the original and not
only in Carlyle's severely bowdlerized translations. This is a
point of some importance, for only in the original could he feel
the full power of Goethe's insistence on the clear, harmonious
development of all human faculties, of that unashamed acceptance
of man's earthiness and sexuality that opened a new, sunlit world
of guilt-free possibility.[2]

Clough's sympathies with the Socialist programme and his
interest in its theoretical bases would have acquainted him with
the extreme radical doctrines of what used to be called 'free love'.
These doctrines, formulated and extended by successive Utopian
Socialists, from Godwin and Mary Wollstonecraft to Saint-
Simon, as a protest against the institution of marriage as it stood,
had developed, in Enfantin and the later Saint-Simonians, into
the 'principle of the rehabilitation of the flesh' against centuries
of Christian disparagement, and they had found in George Sand
a passionate literary propagandist.[3]

Clough's response to George Sand appears to have been
ambivalent. He obviously respected her political activity. In
some moods he was also attracted by the 'amorality', the frank

---

[1] M. Arnold, *Discourses in America*, pp. 143–4.

[2] This was pointed out by J. Brewster, 'Arthur Hugh Clough: His Thought
and His Art', unpublished M.A. thesis (University of London, 1951), p. 93.

[3] J. Killham, *Tennyson and 'The Princess'* (London, 1958), contains a detailed
study of the feminist movement which provides a useful background to Clough's
own position in this respect. Through his sister he had formed an early acquaintance with the 'Woman Question', although, naturally, he was most exercised
about the problems of unmarried women. That spinsters presented a problem
had come to be fairly generally recognized among the progressive-minded by the
late 1840s. Married women were an altogether different matter, and, apart from
a few dissenters, the age was substantially in agreement with the Arthur Freelings
and Sara Ellises, whose pious manuals exhorted wives to a fitting subservience
by stern reminders of the sacramental promise of obedience. Clough appears to
have read enough of George Sand and been sufficiently exposed to French
doctrines, however, to have acquired a particular interest in the most radical
doctrines. In Paris he was especially interested—apart from the questions of
Socialism and the organization of labour—in the divorce Bill which had been
introduced to the Bureaux (cf. *Corr.* i. 211, 213). He went to a feminist meeting
at the Club des Femmes, where the new proposals were to be discussed by
women. He was appalled by the discourtesy and grossness of the males present,
and showed a fine sense both of a woman's right to be heard, and of the difficulties she faced merely by the fact of being a woman.

admission of flesh and desire, which she represented. Perhaps this
was what Matthew Arnold was getting at in referring to
Tom's enthusiasm: 'And whilst my misguided Relation exchanges
the decency God dressed his Features in for the déshabille of
an Emotee, we, my love, lovers of one another and fellow-
worshippers of Isis, while we believe in the Universality of Passion,
as Passion, will keep pure our Aesthetics by remembering its
one-sidedness as doctrine.'[1] At the same time, a puritan shadow
seemed to interpose continually, cutting him off from an untroubled acceptance of spontaneous gaiety. When he visited
Shairp's home in the Long Vacation of 1845, he was uneasy about
the 'gaieties perpetual' of his host's sisters and wondered that
'they are not worse than they are, with them' (*Corr.* i. 152).
He was taken to the ballet and if he had been disturbed about the
sisters, he was now utterly scandalized.

> Last night what thinkest thou? I saw—whom thinkest thou? Taglioni!
> May I never see her again, were but a foolish ejaculation, for she is
> leaving the stage. But may I never be carried again to the ballet!
> It is really strange that matrons and maidens delicately nurtured, not
> to speak of daughter-delighting-in papas, should patronize such sights.
> However so it is: and is likely to be for many years to come no doubt.
> We went πανδημεί; and I had the honour of projecting a tender
> virgin's bouquet at the feet of this callida surarum ostentatrix (ibid.).

And yet, lurking beneath the outrage there is the hint of a leer:
puritanism and prurience are not always totally unrelated.

When, therefore, for the benefit of Thomas Burbidge, an
extremely important friend in this connection, he attempted to
form an opinion of George Sand, the conflicts between his
impulse towards moral relaxation and his unease at any actual
evidence of impropriety, made him tightly guarded though
generally sympathetic. 'I have . . . found time in the last three
days to read "Jeanne, par George Sand", the most cleanly French
novel I ever read, and not cleanly only but pure. What one has
heard of the actual life of Mad. Dudevant is certainly, so far as
it goes, agst. her in this respect. Howbeit I incline to believe her a
Socrates among the Sophists' (*Corr.* i. 159). This particular novel,
embodying in the frank and pious character of its heroine George
Sand's faith in the vitality of the peasantry, appealed as much to

---

[1] Lowry, p. 59, where this is seen as a reference to Tom's interest in Roman
Catholicism. I disagree tentatively.

Clough's social idealism as it did to his search for frankness in confronting human life, and the story of Jeanne's encounter with a sophisticated hunting party of three friends, all of whom are impressed by her simplicity, industry, and strength of character, and—naturally—fall in love with her, may very well have influenced his own poem, *The Bothie of Tober-na-Vuolich*.

Clough was not isolated, of course, in his concern with the problem of human sexuality. He was sharing in a general anxiety which the visible weakening of religious belief and the influx of new doctrines had created. Unless the very basis of moral and social order was to disintegrate, an adequate accommodation for sexual energy would have to be discovered. An elaborately and assiduously cultivated ethic of purity, quite obviously, was the broadest, most characteristic Victorian response to the threatening forces of carnality—but the flesh was a cunning adversary, its containment demanded a continuing reinterpretation of 'purity'. As Houghton has observed, in the 'literature of love' written during the forties and fifties a note of 'reconstruction' is persistent.[1] Tennyson, Kingsley, Patmore, are obvious names here. Tennyson on the whole was conservative. Kingsley, with his 'woman worship', his muscularly Christian laudation of the body, his assertions of the purity of fleshly impulse when expressed within the legitimized pale of Christian Sacrament, and Patmore, with his erotic-mystical idealization of womanhood, attempted alternative solutions. Both, however, represented a broadly Christian adjustment. For more secular, more strictly humanistic, attempts we must look to later figures—to Gissing and *The Unclassed*, for instance, and to Meredith and his doctrine of the 'triad'. Historically, then, Clough occupies a significant position in a pattern of development which culminates in Lawrence and leads on to modern understandings of sexuality. His attitudes often coincide with Kingsley's, and almost as often with Patmore's, but not infrequently they bypass both Kingsley and Patmore and reveal their affinities with later orientations.

History, however, happens inside people, and the pressure of intensely personal needs and impulses can be detected in Clough's preoccupation with the problems of sexuality and sexual ethics. The 'singular purity and spotlessness' of his life that his friends

[1] W. E. Houghton, *The Victorian Frame of Mind* (New Haven, Conn., 1957), p. 375.

testified to, was, in a sense, a façade; the composed self-possession he presented to the world concealed a struggle which, to judge from the evidence, was as fierce as it was persistent, a struggle which extends up to the period of *Dipsychus*, but stops, significantly, after his marriage. The evidence appears in the poetry itself, especially in cancelled passages and fragmentary lines, and it occurs again and again in his prose. This evidence, in conjunction with the austerity so abundantly testified to by Clough's contemporaries, suggests a repression exceptionally severe in its stresses. His austerity was not only a commitment to intellectual and spiritual self-possession; it was primarily a tense struggle to come to terms with the demon of realized carnality.

A Latin dialogue which he wrote at some point in his Oxford career is of particular relevance here. Entitled *Addenda ad Apocalypsin Secundum Interpretationem Vulgatam*, it derives from Plato's *Symposium* (180–1), and the distinction drawn there between the common or vulgar Aphrodite (Eros Pandemos) and the heavenly Aphrodite.[1] In its semi-facetious treatment of the war between body and spirit the dialogue faintly anticipates something of the tone of the earlier scenes of *Dipsychus*. The daring use of Scripture and the frankness in describing Pandemia suggest a significant relaxation of puritan watchfulness. The spirit appears in a dream saying, 'I am spirit, that is, nothing, body, that is, substance, I have not.' She introduces her sister Pandemia, 'who has body and flesh and limbs and substance', and commands, 'Come take her and lie with her, for to lie with me is impossible.' Pandemia, in presenting herself, declares,

... I am Pandemia for whom you are looking. Behold, I am not spirit; I have body and flesh and limbs and substance. Happy are they who lie with me. ... I am the life, the way and the truth. He who possesses me does not walk in darkness. He is whole and dares to do neither good nor bad. Those who are with me are in the world and are not overcome by the world. He who is afraid to come to me does not know where he is and does not even know whether he exists.

The dreamer, however, weeps out his protestations. He is spirit and cannot be with body and flesh. He cries to God, his creator, to help him, but is answered only by silence, and the woman once again says, 'Try and see.' The heavens and earth are silent

---

1 Bodleian MS. Eng. Misc. d. 512, fols. 1–6, and *Catalogue*, p. 47, where the dialogue is dated tentatively as 1841–2. A later date is not improbable.

once again, no direction issues from them. Then, towards evening, the dreamer looks up once more and beholds a woman
dressed in white, who takes him by the hand and announces herself his 'fellow-servant', 'the servant of the most high'. 'Come,'
she invites, 'let us be servants together'. The dreamer looks into
her face and asks whether she is not Pandemia, whom he had
previously spoken to—but she avoids the question: 'I am your
fellow-servant, the servant of the most high; let us serve together
you and I, Come.' The ending is ambiguous; as Clough declared,
'This is the great mystery, Happy are they who have ears and
hear.' But the resolution in the third term of service is significant:
love, as Clough later came to define it, was 'fellow-service'.

He brought, it is evident, a growing recognition of the sexual
forces within himself to the reflections about love and marriage
which occupied him extensively over these years. The general
theme had, of course, always been a topic of conversation between
him and his sister, but that his interest was not altogether an
academic one may be seen from his comments on a draft of
'When panting sighs the bosom fill' which he enclosed in his
letter of 2 November 1844 to Burbidge:

> You will duly observe I trust that this is wholly and solely a Loquitur
> quidam composition: I, you will remember am only *twenty-five*: so
> that if I should marry within the year of course I shall not fall within
> the scope of the Poem. . . . You will please not to show these even to
> Simpkinson. I think I had rather not, as I do acknowledge a *certain*
> sympathy and understanding with the quidam who loquitur in
> them.[1]

By November 1846 he had almost certainly fallen in love seriously
enough to at least consider the possibility of marriage. On the
18th he wrote to his sister:

> As for her whom I hope someday to see your sister it is very true
> that it won't be in a moment that you will quite understand each
> other—but there is no fear in the end. She is very slow to advance—
> and I almost think that the visit to Ambleside, pleasant as it was, was
> *too* much an advance. If you can, let all advances come from her, and
> don't be afraid, that they will.—Shall I tell you, for example, I would,
> were I you, call her by her name as little as possible. I doubt whether
> she is quite up to it, except from Mother. When you write to her,
> it would come best at the end of a bit from Mother (*Corr.* i. 175).

[1] Bodleian MS. Eng. Lett. d. 175, fol. 114 (166).

An exceptionally shy—or extraordinarily punctilious—girl this must have been.

We have no indication, of course, of the identity of this person —or, for that matter, of the precise nature of the relationship. James Bertram has suggested that she was Agnes Walrond, sister of Theodore. Clough met her in the summer of 1845 in Calder Park near Glasgow, home of the Walronds, and had been considerably attracted by her charm, vivacity, and intelligence.[1] It seems difficult, however, to reconcile the outgoing Agnes Walrond with the very unsure, easily embarrassed woman Clough's letter to Anne suggests.

Margaret Symonds, writing of her father's brief and plangent encounter with Rosa Engel, referred in passing to a similar attachment in Clough's life, a real-life version of Elspie, the heroine of The Bothie, and a counterpart to Matthew Arnold's 'Marguerite'.[2] She gave, however, neither details nor evidence. Despite this lack of firm evidence, critics and scholars have continued to suspect an actual experience behind Clough's repeated recurrence to the theme of the 'Highland Girl'—a variant of which can be detected in the figure of Guilt in Dipsychus Continued.[3] A. M. Turner, in examining the relationships between The Bothie and 'The Lawyer's Second Tale', the last of the Mari Magno stories, suggested that the two fables provide alternative imaginary endings—the first idyllic, the second tragic—for an actual love affair, which he assigned to 1847.[4]

The question, obviously, must be left open; one can only conjecture and surmise. One fresh point is possibly worth noting, however. Philip, the Oxford undergraduate of The Bothie, appears in 'The Lawyer's Second Tale' as an Oxford Tutor who has to leave his Highland beloved, Christie, on account of the college audit at which his presence is essential, since he is the Junior Bursar. On 3 May 1846 Clough wrote to his sister, 'Concerning marriage—it is true, my child;—but to fall in love

---

[1] New Zealand Letters of Thomas Arnold the Younger, pp. 222–3.

[2] M. Symonds, Out of the Past (London, 1925), p. 47.

[3] Cf., e.g., A. Huth, Über A. H. Clough's 'The Bothie of Tober-na-Vuolich' (Leipzig, 1911), p. 50; F. L. Lucas, 'Thyrsis', Life and Letters, ii (May 1929), 356 (reprinted in Ten Victorian Poets); M. Bishop, 'Thyrsis; or the Importance of Not Being Earnest', in The Pleasure Ground, ed. M. Elwin (London, 1947), pp. 72–4.

[4] A. M. Turner, 'A Study of Clough's Mari Magno', PMLA xliv (June 1929), 578–80.

without knowledge is foolery—to obtain knowledge without time and opportunity and something like an intimate acquaintance is for the most part impossible—and to obtain time, opportunity etc. is just the thing which somehow or other has never duly befallen me, at least in the cases where I could have wished it most' (*Corr.* i. 170). Clearly he had pondered these questions carefully; clearly, too, his eye had been caught from time to time—no doubt, among others, by Agnes Walrond whom he had met the previous summer. But he does not seem to have fixed his affections definitely. In November he wrote to Anne about the person whom he eventually hoped to marry. It is likely, then, that the attachment ripened—if it was not actually formed—in the interval between May and November, possibly in the Long Vacation of 1846.

Clough spent much of that vacation with a reading-party in Castleton Braemar in Aberdeenshire, and he utilized some of his experience there for important details in his 'Long Vacation Pastoral'.[1] He also seems to have returned to Oxford, via Liverpool, in time for the College audit;[2] but he was never College Treasurer—that position was held from 1844 to 1849 by D. P. Chase, who had been elected to a Fellowship at the same time as Clough.[3] Is it possible, then, that the extraordinarily shy girl referred to in his letter of November to Anne was the 'Highland Girl', and that a juxtaposition of himself and Chase in 'The Lawyer's Second Tale' was the final piece of mystification in this most closely guarded, most frequently reverted to, secret of his life?

The symbolic and imaginative significance of the 'Highland Girl' is, however, of more importance than problematical biographical details. The recurrent motif of a relationship which cuts across social barriers, and links the intellectually sophisticated with the most natural and unspoilt, underscores both the Rousseauistic elements in Clough's social idealism and his shared Victorian thirst for that spontaneous, unthinking, and unconscious knowledge that could be slaked only at the well of inartificial womanhood. But the 'Highland Girl' is for Clough also a dual and uneasy symbol. If she represents an ideal naturalness and purity, the simple daughter of the lower classes is also sexually

---

[1] Cf. *Corr.* i. 171 (for the pool in *The Bothie*, iii. 19–67), and 172 (for the festivities with which the poem opens).   [2] Cf. *Corr.* i. 173.

[3] Cf. G. C. Richards and C. L. Shadwell, *The Provosts and Fellows of Oriel College, Oxford* (Oxford, 1922).

open, vulnerable to her social superiors. Like the prostitutes in
Dipsychus, she is a brutally available symbol of sexuality. Focused
in a single symbol, then, we have some of the central tensions in
Clough's understanding of human nature—is sex emancipating and
natural, or is it foetid death? In his attempt to face such questions
frankly his friendship with Burbidge was of considerable importance.

Thomas Burbidge had always been something of a stumbling-
block to serious-minded Rugbeians. William Ward, too, had
disapproved—and very possibly been jealous—of him, and
Clough, as a sixth-former, had occasionally gone to rather
unctuous lengths of highmindedness to justify his association
with him.[1] Why exactly—apart from Burbidge's tendency to be
flippant—everyone disapproved is not clear, although cryptic
references to his shortcomings are frequent enough in the letters
which passed between Clough and his friends. What is clear,
however, is that Burbidge's unconventionality seems to have
played a significant part in creating the atmosphere of disapproval.
He seems to have been something of a scapegrace, a rather
theatrically disreputable, outspoken, slightly irreverent light-
weight, who curiously fascinated Clough despite his occasional
misgivings,[2] and he must have been a refreshing counterpoise
to the rigours of Rugby. The very fact of his persistent loyalty
to this backslider is additional evidence for the ambivalence in
his response to Rugby during his later years there. At Balliol,
too, the friendship had proved oddly helpful, for when Ward
threatened to smother his individuality, Clough—to Ward's deep
chagrin—fell back on his enthusiasm for Burbidge as one of his
defences.

During Clough's years as a Fellow the friendship became even
stronger, and it culminated in 1849 in their joint authorship of
Ambarvalia. Several elements of mutuality sustained the intimacy.
To judge from the evidence of his contributions to *Ambarvalia*,
Burbidge, too, had strong 'democratic' sympathies, and it is
not altogether impossible that he chose his Italian wife under the
influence of these sympathies.[3] Burbidge's social unconventionality
had always been refreshing, but, while he was at Balliol, Clough

---

[1] Cf. *Corr.* i. 54–5.
[2] 'I fear Burbidge is in some degree a snare to me. . . .' *Corr.* i. 62.
[3] Cf. *Corr.* i. 224.

had had doubts about his friend's unabashed self-exposure in his *Poems, Longer and Shorter*. When Burbidge was criticized for the frankness of some of his *Ambarvalia* poems, however, Clough rounded on the critics with a new aggressiveness. 'I think', he wrote to Shairp, 'you people are making great donkeys of yourselves about Burbidge's freedom of speech. Go to the Bible, thou prude, consider its language, and be wise. Consult also Shakespeare, Milton, Dante also, . . and in fact "all great poets" ' (*Corr.* i. 245, Clough's dots). It is likely that not only did he share with Burbidge an interest in the 'question of sex' but that he and his friend had devoted some attention to the problem of the frank treatment of the subject in poetry.

At least one poetic link between the two supports the likelihood of a background of shared discussion of, and experimentation in, 'erotico-philosophica' as Clough called it.[1] In one of his *Ambarvalia* poems, 'Lilie: A myth', Burbidge had written with more daring than graceful confessional bravado:

> I was a coarse and vulgar man,
> I vile and vulgar things had done;
> And I, as Nature's instincts ran
> Was wont to let them run.[2]

A similar attempt at breaking through Victorian taboos on Clough's part can be seen in an unpublished poem entitled 'Homo sum, nihil humani'. The poem appears only in the proof-copy of the 1850 reissue of his own contributions to *Ambarvalia* where it is placed next to last in the volume,[3] but it is marked for cancellation and does not appear in the edition as finally issued.

The poem, which I have reproduced in full, can be read, beneath its moralistic surface, as a foil to " '*O θεὸς μετὰ σοῦ*" (*Poems*, 38), as a frank, half-ironic recognition of the sexual and social arrogance behind the sentimental tenderness of that poem, with its pious refrain, 'God be with you!'

---

[1] Clough to Burbidge, 2 Nov. 1844. Bodleian MS. Eng. Lett. d. 175, fol. 112 (166). He enclosed with his letter an early version of 'When panting sighs the bosom fill'. The link between Clough's poem and Burbidge's was pointed out by J. Bertram, 'Clough and His Poetry', *Landfall*, xvii (June 1963), 141–55. I am indebted to this article for many of my remarks on Burbidge.

[2] Quoted, Bertram, ibid., 146.

[3] 1850 Reissue (A), pp. 62–4; Bodleian MS. Eng. Poet. e. 88. The first, sixth, and seventh stanzas have been printed in *Catalogue*, p. 17.

She had a coarse and common grace
    As ever beggar showed,
It was a coarse but living face,
    I kissed upon the road.

And why have aught to do with her,
    And what could be the good?
I kissed her, O my questioner,
    Because I knew I could!

And do you do, or good or bad,
    Whatever thing you can?
What's healthy freedom of a lad
    Is licence of a man:

And do you, if you can and will,
    Kiss any on your way?
I know not; be it well or ill
    I did kiss one to-day.

I kissed her, for her carnalness
    It could not come to me;
For I in my containedness
    Was mightier Force than she;

For royal-rich I was of force
    Exuberant of will;
And carnal if she were and coarse,
    She was a woman still.

I kissed, and said,—and piercing-in,
    I looked her through the face,—
I muttered, as I held her chin,
    God give you of his grace!

But whether virtue from him flowed,
    And if it did her good,
He did not question, on the road,
    Who kissed because he could.

And whether heard or not the word,
    And whether understood,
He doth not wis who gave the kiss
    Because he knew he could.

There is no way of telling why Clough should have gone to the
trouble of inserting this poem especially and then have taken it

out. Perhaps, belatedly, he recognized its inferiority. Perhaps the suppression was due to nothing more complicated than an attack of cold feet. Anyway, in his later life Clough seems to have become significantly reticent about this one-time poetic association. Charles Eliot Norton was to make two revealing notes about the veil of silence which the Clough he knew drew over this earlier friendship. The first, made in Richard Trench's copy of the original 1849 volume of *Ambarvalia*, reads, 'Clough was always reticent as to the circumstances which led him to associate himself with Burbidge in the publication of their poems. I think he felt it had been a mistake.' The second is on the title-page of Norton's own copy of the 1850 reissue—'I fancy that Clough saw that his poems had another quality from those of his associate, and were not helped by doubtful companionship.'[1] But this was in 1853. In the late forties Clough was still fresh in hope, fumbling in revolt, eagerly if cautiously open to any influences which might liberate him from puritan rigidity and middle-class conventionality.

It is small wonder, then, when we consider Clough's development at Oriel, that the still spotless Walter Bagehot was slightly dubious when he first met the author of *The Bothie*. He had read the poem recently, and he wrote to Richard Hutton on 1 March 1849, 'Clough you will like very much, I think. He is a man of strong, and clear though not very quick intellect. . . . [H]e unfortunately has been in the Highlands and talks of barmaids and potato-girls, and other operative females there in a very humiliating manner. . . . You would, I think, agree with me in thinking that his mind was defective in severity of moral feeling and in the conception of law generally as applied to morals.'[2] As Alastair Buchan has pointed out, it was soon to become apparent to Bagehot that what Clough was deficient in was not moral feeling, but moral certainty.[3]

4. THE 'SWEET CITY WITH ITS DREAMING SPIRES'

Clough's resignation of his Fellowship must be connected finally with the religious problem, but that connection acquires

---

[1] Both these volumes are in the Houghton Library, Harvard. The comments have been printed by Bertram, 'Clough and His Poetry', p. 147.
[2] Quoted, A. Buchan, *The Spare Chancellor* (London, 1959), pp. 51–2.
[3] Loc. cit.

its real fullness of significance only when it is seen as establishing itself through a whole range of new values and understandings, a new way of looking at the world, created out of a broad, interlinked process of development. He had come to breathe an intellectual and spiritual air very different from that of traditional Oxford. He rejected Oxford's theology and its religious beliefs, he disagreed with its politics, he questioned its conception of society and its interpretation of morality. But it would seriously distort the meaning of his experience if we were to regard his resignation as an unambiguous and outright rejection of the University and all it stood for.

Charles Norton claimed, somewhat dramatically, that 'when Clough left Oxford he had conquered the world'.[1] The courage of his resignation and the sense of victory it brought are indisputable, but what, in human terms, did the act mean to him? What price did 'victory' exact? The totality of relevances Oxford had come to have is involved here: Oxford as an emotional equivalence, Oxford as exasperation and enchantment. '[A]fter all', Clough had declared as an eager schoolboy, 'Cambridge can never be equal to Oxford in the grandness of the idea of it' (*Corr.* i. 49). How did the idea wear in actual experience? Some of the answers to such questions—and their importance extends to Clough's life as a poet—can be approached through an examination of his attitudes towards Oxford education, since in this localized area one can identify conveniently the ambivalences which characterized his whole relationship to the place.

Perhaps it was its spectacular theological disputes that drew public attention to Oxford affairs in the 1840s, but whatever the immediate cause, the eye which the nation turned on the University was not exactly an approving one. When on 10 April 1848 (significant Chartist date) a motion was proposed in Parliament for a Royal Commission of Inquiry into the state of the University, it expressed a general dissatisfaction. Within the University, too, there were stirrings. Among the younger, more progressive dons there was a growing instinct for change, a growing desire for a more relevant kind of education and for more effective methods of teaching. The reforming spirit embraced a wide variety of issues, from the actual machinery of instruction to

---

[1] [C. E. Norton], 'Arthur Hugh Clough', *North American Review*, cv (Oct. 1867), 440.

questions of curriculum and administration, and in every aspect Clough was regarded as a leader.

Convinced of the 'inefficiency of college tuition' (*Corr.* i. 174), he was in the front ranks of those who were dissatisfied with a system that reduced the teacher to a Jack-of-all-trades. Even as late as 1848 he was actively concerned about the need, from both the pupil's angle and the teacher's, for some kind of specialization in instruction. In April of that year Jowett wrote to Lingen outlining a scheme for which he was ready to fight 'tooth and nail', by which the 'nucleus of a Professorial system' would be established. It was proposed, he said, that lectures should be organized in the Schools on 'all principal subjects connected with our present examinations'. He himself would lecture on the history of Greek Philosophy, Stanley on Herodotus, Clough on Livy.[1]

Questions of administrative structure, religious tests, the tenure and distribution of Fellowships, raised fundamental points, and the 'Chartist' programme which Clough drew up for Stanley in a letter from Paris indicates how far-ranging were the reforms he envisaged—'Abolition of Subscription; Reconstitution of Fellowships; New Hebdomadal Board; Extra-collegial matriculation; and Permanent Commission.'[2] By the beginning of 1849 Oxford had begun to make concessions as far as curriculum was concerned. Under the existing system only two Schools—the Classical and the Mathematical—were available to a candidate in the Final Schools. Now a new Statute was proposed (in the drafting of which Clough seems to have had some hand)[3] that aimed at a wider range and greater freedom of choice. The candidate would be required to pass in two of four Schools— Literae Humaniores, Mathematics, Natural Science, Law and Modern History, the examination in Literae Humaniores being compulsory.[4] 'It appears to me', Clough wrote to Hawkins, 'to be the wisest step that has been taken in Education for many years;

[1] E. Abbott and L. Campbell, *The Life and Letters of Benjamin Jowett*, 2 vols. (London, 1897), i. 193.

[2] *Corr.* i. 211. See also the 'revolutionary' broadsheet circulated as a joke in Oxford on 4 July 1848 (doubtless with American Independence in mind), proclaiming 'Liberty! Equality! Fraternity!' and '(Signed) Citizen CLOUGH'. *New Zealand Letters of Thomas Arnold the Younger*, p. 221.

[3] Cf. *Corr.* i. 211.

[4] For further details see the *Report of Her Majesty's Commissioners . . . [on] The University and Colleges of Oxford* (London, 1852), pp. 67–8.

and to embody all the good with little of the evil of modern movements' (*Corr.* i. 242). His comments to Hawkins a little over a fortnight later reflect clearly both his dislike of the persistent theological bias and his conviction of the relevance of more modern, secular studies: '[W]hat I desiderated myself was the separation of the Literae Humaniores School from that of Theology: and to Modern History I would gladly have added the stronger aliment of Political Economy' (*Corr.* i. 248).

Yet manifold as these criticisms are, they are those of someone committed to the idea of Oxford. The only radical change Clough desired was the abolition of Subscription and the elimination of the theological bias; all the others are contained in an overriding assent. Nowhere does he question fundamentally the relevance or the value of Oxford. Even his reference to it as a finishing school for the upper classes in his letter to the Royal Commission[1] is, in its context, not quite the disparaging slogan it has since become. In that closely argued letter the value of Oxford is assumed as given; Clough's concern is to make its liberal leisure-class education available to as many prospective 'solicitors, general practitioners, merchants, manufacturers'[2] as can be done without dilution or vulgarization.

The point is made clearer in the two letters he contributed over the pseudonym 'Alpha' to *The Spectator* in response to a lecture on 'The Relationship of Free Knowledge to Moral Sentiment' which Francis Newman delivered at London University on 13 October 1847. In the first Clough argued that, whereas imposed theological belief was intellectually strangling, a closely regulated and disciplined community life such as that encouraged by Oxford residence yielded, in contrast to 'lecture-room aggregation', substantial moral benefits. The 'complicated subscriptions, . . . stringent exclusions, . . . compulsory sacraments, and all [the] orthodox etceteras' which the authorities at Oxford and Cambridge had imposed were like a loosely hanging surplice on this 'real system or at least . . . real inspiration of the old Universities'. '[M]oral culture . . . in the Universities, need not', Clough thought, 'be Papistically authoritative, or ecclesiastically dogmatical', and he was not convinced that Newman had successfully demonstrated that the 'breath of moral teaching' which the Oxford system infused into instruction simply by 'close

[1] Trawick, p. 304.   [2] Loc. cit.

association in Colleges' was 'intellectually mephitic'. 'Most true it is', he concluded, 'that those who know the place cannot but say, be it in the bitterness of exclusion, or be it in the discontent of conformity, "Oxford, with all thy Articles, I love thee still." Yet, without thy Articles, I think they would love thee quite as well, and serve thee a good deal better.'[1]

'Can a course of general instruction be other than a moral proceeding? Can art and science ignore their relation to human life? Can I talk to the mind without being overheard by the spirit?'[2]—Clough's questions in his second letter raised basic issues of meaning in education. His sense of the essential right-ness of the 'real inspiration of the older Universities' shaped his broad practical solutions. 'The idea of the New University is not surely this unnatural divorce, but education, intellectual alike and moral, freed from the timid intolerance of a worn-out dogmatism.' The example of the older Universities in effecting the necessary conjunction did not deserve to be neglected—rather, it was an example for which the 'country owes them that best of boons assistance or even compulsion to self-reform'. Turning to the future, he declared, 'Far be it from me to shackle young merchants, lawyers, or shopmen, with dishonest subscrip-tions, tedious devotionalities, obtrusive theologics. But both by them and by the London students I believe an organization for culture is needed, whose pattern, as the modern musket in the matchlock, may be recognized in our obsolete machinery here.'[3] The faintly supercilious 'young merchants, lawyers or shopmen' did not exactly promise well for the experiment in Gordon Square which he was shortly to embark on.

Newman, much more boldly committed to radical reform in University education, was perhaps particularly sensitive, but the letter of protest he wrote to Clough when he discovered the identity of 'Alpha' shows a rather more realistic sense of the situation which expanding education faced. He was not being wholly unfair when he remarked of Clough's last letter to *The Spectator*:

Altogether the tone of the whole letter was not that of one who cared to be a cooperator with me or my friends; but rather of those who studiously denominate our institution 'The Gower Street Lecture Rooms': and while it condemns Oxford in theory, it in fact tends to

[1] Trawick, pp. 274–5.   [2] Ibid., p. 275.   [3] Ibid., p. 276.

puff up Oxford men with things as they are, by its eulogy on their 'residence' and on *the moral training* which they give (*Corr*. i. 188).

Running through Clough's sense of frustration and his impulse of repudiation, then, were complicating threads of attachment. For Oxford, over his eleven years there, had invested itself with contrary significances. A fully felt desire for liberation permeated his intellectual dissent; his emotional attachment was strengthened by the assent which, on the whole, he accorded to Oxford as an institution. His resignation was a choice made from within this fundamental polarity in his valuations.

That choice, made as it was at a time when financially he could least afford it, was an act of victorious conviction, and it brought, for a brief spell, the confidence of release and the glow of sacrifice. For his life as a poet it brought a positive and enormously valuable liberation, releasing finally a wholly individual vision, an individually authentic accent. But the sacrifice was also a parching one. Professionally he became a man who had somehow lost his way; Oxford was henceforth to appear as a modest island of achievement in a blank and desolate sea. Further, the loss of Oxford involved him in a loneliness and uncertainty the roots of which penetrated much deeper.

For Oxford, rather like Rugby earlier, had sustained him with identity. In the vivid and outgoing interests of his Oriel years especially he had reached out towards and discovered a delightful and congenial society. The bright webs of relationship he had woven over the leisurely Sunday breakfasts, the stirring causes, the long-remembered debates, the exuberant and hardworking Highland reading-parties—all assured him of a community of values, of sympathy if not full agreement, of understandings that could be relied on. It is not altogether an accident that both his letters to *The Spectator* should have upheld the community aspects of Oxford life. Paradoxically, his absorption in this Oxford ethos can be detected even in the occasional extravagance of his expressions of revolt: his tones are those of the acknowledged *enfant terrible*, his ebullience is that of a person who has a firm sense of his place in the society which he rounds so fiercely on— 'I could sometimes be provoked to send out a flood of lava boiling-hot amidst their flowery ecclesiastical fields and parterres' (*Corr*. i. 203).

Yet the very vehemence of this particular expression of revolt arouses suspicion. Such a self-absorbed, self-conscious sense of volcanic potentiality is excusable, perhaps, in the clever, opinionated sixth-former or undergraduate. In the twenty-nine-year-old Oxford don it betrays a radical immaturity of outlook which, suggesting as it does how completely Clough had come to accept an impossible valuation of himself, points to the pernicious aspects of the identity which his particular circle at Oxford had conferred on him.

As J. M. Newton has suggested,[1] Clough's connection with the Decade set might very well provide a clue to his final ineffectiveness in public life, and to his extraordinary difficulty in finding a fitting vocation for himself. The discontent with the age which Clough shared, of all his friends, most fully with Tom Arnold was a discontent too ambitiously general, too diffused in its scope to be easily channelled into clear and effective leadership. Yet Clough was the widely acknowledged leader; for Tom Arnold he was the 'Hieland oracle' (*Corr.* i. 273), and Shairp was to write in 1851, 'I do think you are meant to teach (whether in prose or verse) men something' (*Corr.* i. 295). The independence into which he had been forced by his experience at Rugby and at Balliol had become 'institutionalized' in his Oriel years. Like his 'originality', it had become an attitude expected of him, a privilege granted to him as a precondition of leadership. Among his friends only Matthew Arnold seems to have had serious, sustained doubts about the quality of this independence. The others might have had their moments of hesitation but those moments were conquered by their larger trust.

Not surprisingly, Clough was radically infected by this flattering expectation. It held out the promise of positives he longed for; at the same time it nourished his cherished independence. Not surprisingly, too, he appears to have been altogether unclear about quite what it was that he expected of himself and how exactly he might go about doing it. In 1848, when he had more or less made up his mind about giving up his Fellowship, his friends—Matthew Arnold especially—pressed upon him the necessity of taking up some work and suggested several possibilities for private tutoring. '[W]hen I resign the Fellowship,

[1] J. M. Newton, 'A Missed Opportunity', *Cambridge Review*, lxxxix (Feb. 1958), 304–7.

which I shall do, I suppose, in October . . . I fear I shall take some tutorship for the sake of victuals', he wrote to Tom Arnold, and he added, 'Is this a dereliction of duty, my dear Tom? I can't see my way clearly about it and don't mean to bind myself to more than a year or two of it and trust that it won't rob me of all my time or *much* of my independence' (*Corr.* i. 217). One wonders what he could possibly have conceived of as his particular 'duty'. Clearly, however, his independence was essential to it and to be guarded jealously as, very probably, the silent and watchful preparation of the Carlylean reforming sage. This belief in the need for consciously withholding himself appears again a few months later in another letter to Tom, in which Clough, who had recently accepted the University Hall appointment, questioned how 'right' he had been in 'giving [himself] unto Stincomalee' (*Corr.* i. 243).

Instead of fulfilling itself in triumphant affirmatives, however, the nonconformity which had been cultivated so hopefully seemed somehow to stop at itself. No new gospel issued for the community; the friends waited in vain. The independence developed, instead, into an estranged and critical privacy, an exceptionally watchful isolation. The positives which emerged from the habit of independence (and there were valuable positives) were beginning to prove embarrassingly intractable. Instead of aligning themselves into a victorious, unambiguous, acceptably 'healthy' resolution, they set themselves up in stubborn opposition—they questioned, they ridiculed, they set up disturbing ironic tensions. Clough's friends had helped to create the nonconforming eye, but neither they nor he himself had expected exactly the mocking, unevasive, subversive vision of the years when his isolation was at its deepest, the years immediately following his resignation. None of them approved of that vision and he himself only partly assented to it. One part of him longed for intellectual and emotional respite, for stable rest in the authorized identity which this other self was so busily undermining.

CHAPTER V

The Question of Poetics

IN 1853 Clough was in America, seeking in the New World the fulfilment which he had been unable to find in the Old. He was confronted, on the one hand, by the radical uncertainty and professional failure into which he had been led by his refusal to conform; on the other, he was in the process of surrendering his isolation, his scepticism, and his 'disengagement' for the warmth of Blanche Smith's companionship, a companionship which, in prospect, made more conventional attitudes than his own appear both more desirable and more valid than they had hitherto. Creatively, this incipient surrender issued in the banal sentimentalities of the 'Songs of Absence'[1] and in the neurotic self-repudiation of *Dipsychus Continued*. The consequences on Clough's literary standards can be seen in the review, 'Recent English Poetry', which appeared in *The North American Review* in July 1853, and which welcomed enthusiastically the turgid, vaguely aspirational outpourings of Alexander Smith's *A Life Drama*. In fact, when we consider how rapidly that enthusiasm for Smith cooled, it is not unlikely that he was more specifically influenced in his opinions by his shock at Blanche Smith's horrified reaction to *Dipsychus* and personal pique at Matthew Arnold.[2] He received his fiancée's letter on 24 May. On 13 April he referred for the first time to Smith: 'Do you know, dear, I am very much taken with Alexander Smith's life-drama—it is really what I have had in my own mind' (*Corr.* ii. 414). On 15 April he wrote, 'You may read Alexander Smith . . . if you

---

[1] For the sake of brevity I have used Mrs. Clough's collective title in *PPR* for the following poems: 'Farewell, farewell! Her vans the vessel tries'; 'Ye flags of Picadilly'; 'Come home, come home!'; 'Green fields of England!'; 'Come back, come back'; 'Some future day when what is now is not'; 'Where lies the land to which the ship would go?'; 'The mighty ocean rolls and raves'; 'That out of sight is out of mind'; 'Were you with me, or I with you'; 'Am I with you, or you with me?'; 'Were I with you, or you with me'; 'O ship, ship, ship'.

[2] S. B. Coulling, 'Matthew Arnold's 1853 Preface: Its Origin and Aftermath', *Victorian Studies*, vii (Mar. 1964), 233–63, contains valuable incidental comments on Clough's review and the differences between him and Arnold.

like; the first half isn't good but the last is, I think' (*Corr.* ii. 415). On 1 May he changed his mind about both Smith and Arnold, whom he criticized in his review, 'If you haven't read A. S. don't trouble yourself; 'tis hardly worth the while. MA's Tristan has been giving me pleasure' (*Corr.* ii. 424). Finally, on 17 May he wrote, 'I am rather sorry I recommended Master Alexander Smith to you' (*Corr.* ii. 434). Clough's review was 'finished or all but finished' by 4 p.m. on Saturday 30 April and was to be sent in on the Monday (*Corr.* ii. 424).

In it he quotes from the last scene, in which Smith's 'Spasmodic' poet-hero, Walter, stands with his beloved, Violet:

> Thou noble soul,
> Teach me, if thou art nearer God than I!
> My life was one long dream; when I awoke,
> Duty stood like an angel in my path,
> And seemed so terrible, I could have turned
> Into my yesterdays, and wandered back
> To distant childhood, and gone out to God
> By the gate of birth, not death. Life, lift me up
> By thy sweet inspiration, as the tide
> Lifts up a stranded boat upon the beach.
> I will go forth 'mong men, not mailed in scorn,
> But in the armour of a pure intent.
>   . . . Our night is past;
> We stand in precious sunrise; and beyond,
> A long day stretches to the very end.

Clough's comment is embarrassingly benedictional: 'So be it, O young Poet; Poet, perhaps it is early to affirm; but so be it, at any rate, O young man. While you go forth in that "armour of a pure intent", the hearts of some readers, be assured, will go with you.'[1] Walter and Violet standing in the hopeful sunrise are painfully like an ideal image of Arthur and Blanche and fresh beginnings. The critical faculty has been clouded by personal anxieties and private visions. To place the passage from Smith here upheld for approval against poems like 'Natura Naturans', 'Easter Day, Naples', 'The Latest Decalogue', 'Sa Majéste très Chrétienne', *Amours de Voyage*, and *Dipsychus* is to see clearly the scope of the recantation.

---

[1] Trawick, p. 153. Cf. Clough's lines, written probably in Jan. 1853, beginning 'Were you with me, or I with you' (*Poems*, p. 100).

That impulse of recantation becomes even more apparent when we consider the strictures in the same review on the poems of William Sidney Walker, who spent 'fifty-one years, mostly in isolation and poverty, shivering upon the brink, trembling and hesitating upon the threshold of life. Fearful to affirm any thing, lest it haply might be false; to do any thing, because so probably it might be sin; to speak, lest he should lie; almost, we might say, to feel, lest it should be a deception. . . .'[1] That bitter image of futility was an image and a valuation of a former self which the reviewer was beginning to recognize. A similar kind of self-recognition, a similar longing for positive affirmations, colours the treatment of Matthew Arnold's poetry in the same review:

But now, we are fain to ask, where are we, and whither are we unconsciously come? Were we not going forth to battle in the armour of a righteous purpose . . . with Alexander Smith? How is it we find ourselves here, reflecting, pondering, hesitating, musing, complaining, with 'A'? . . . Between the extremes of ascetic and timid self-culture, and of unquestioning, unhesitating confidence, we may consent to see and tolerate every kind and gradation of inter-mixture. Nevertheless, upon the whole, for the present age, the lessons of reflectiveness and the maxims of caution do not appear to be more needful or more appropriate than exhortations to steady courage and calls to action. There is something certainly of an over-educated weakness of purpose in Western Europe. . . . There is a disposition to press too far the finer and subtler intellectual and moral susceptibilities.[2]

One can hardly argue, of course, that Clough's judgements in this important essay were determined solely by a special personal situation, and that they were unconnected with any larger framework of convictions about the nature and function of poetry. It is important, however, to stress, at the outset of an examination of Clough's mature views on poetry, the interconnection between lived experience and critical orientation. A practising poet's criticism is organic rather than systematic; it is intimately related to his problems as a poet, the problems of the poet are closely linked with those of the man, and the full meaning of the criticism can be arrived at only through a concurrent consideration of the poetry he actually writes and his emotional and intellectual history generally: the poet's total activity is only dimly and

[1] Trawick, p. 168.   [2] Ibid., pp. 161, 163.

partially—sometimes even inaccurately—perceived through his criticism. Clough's critical opinions yield important insights into his life as a poet and into the kind of artistic awareness he brought to his poetry, but unless we are to elevate these opinions into a tyrannical and omnipresent 'theory', it is essential to recognize them simply as starting-points, as a set of predilections, the relative emphases of which are not fixed but shift and alter with the shifting pressures of a responsive experience. Two examples will make this more clear. Clough's 'moralism' and 'realism' are commonplaces readily illustrated from his critical writings. Yet if we consider the wide dissimilarities in only three works, *The Bothie*, written in 1848, *Amours de Voyage*, begun in 1849, and *Dipsychus*, begun in 1850, the inadequacy of those terms becomes obvious. They offer only a beginning. The second example suggests the kind of area we might look into if we are to go any further. The review of 'Recent English Poetry' which Clough published in America betrays a significant uncertainty in delimiting moral and artistic merit. Clough is fully assured of Arnold's superiority as a poet, yet it is Smith whom he favours. The primacy he appears to concede to moral attitude here, gains significance from the biographical context, but it also reflects a less *ad hoc* judgement. Clough is a moral poet, literature for him is always a moral activity; the mode and content of his morality, however, his conception of what is moral, is a changing one, an integral part of his developing life, finding different modes of expression in his poetry. Further, this particular uncertainty in his essay reflects a kind of uncertainty which was widespread in Early-Victorian thinking about poetry. When Richard Chenevix Trench observed portentously, 'Tennyson, we cannot live in art',[1] he was really begging a twofold question—and Clough, like any poet, was involved in answering that question. The answers he proposed indicate both his participation in his age and his divergence from it, his conformity and his heterodoxy—and the unease that lies between the two extremes.

In the first two chapters of his book Houghton has traced the 'tradition of disparagement' which once surrounded Clough's poetry to the fact that the vast majority of his critics have judged him against the assumptions of Romantic and Symbolist poetics.

[1] [H. Tennyson], *Alfred Lord Tennyson, A Memoir*, 2 vols. (London, 1897), i. 118.

Further, Clough's realism and scepticism, his unevasiveness, his willingness to import the play of mind into poetry, his irony and ridicule, his exploration of doubt and anxiety and despair, became, under prevailing conditions of taste, liabilities, not strengths.[1] A brief survey of the prevailing conditions of taste before we look at Clough's own statements on poetry will help to clarify his relationship to his age, to indicate both his divergence from ruling preconceptions and the points of attachment to them which weaken his poetic heterodoxy as a heterodoxy.

Early-Victorian thinking about the place, nature, and function of poetry reflects, in its own terms, some of the larger intellectual and cultural predicaments and preoccupations of the age. The questions created in the active confluence in the poetics of the period of two traditions—the Romantic and idealistic and the empirical and rationalistic—mirror something of the wider unease and uncertainty of a society whose basic values, traditions, and assumptions were being massively called in question. The dominant critical tradition was, of course, a post-Romantic one. Primarily and overwhelmingly the critical effort, like the creative, was involved in consolidating the Romantic achievement and in asserting the prestige—usually conceived in Romantic terms—of poetry against the forces of utilitarianism, science, and the practical temper of an industrial and mercantile society. But there was also, as R. G. Cox pointed out several years ago,[2] a more submerged tradition, which is perhaps most characteristically represented by Sir Henry Taylor, particularly by the Preface to his *Philip van Artevelde*, which appeared in 1834. If the main tradition is post-Romantic, the affinities of this second tradition are with the eighteenth century. Opposed as the two traditions are in many important respects, there is between them also a shared ground that defines the special 'Victorianness' of both.

---

[1] As early as 1875, however, T. S. Perry commented on Clough's distinction as an artist in breaking away from conventional poetic attitudes and modes. T. S. Perry, 'Arthur Hugh Clough', *Atlantic Monthly*, xxxvi (Oct. 1875), 409–18.

[2] R. G. Cox, 'Victorian Criticism of Poetry: The Minority Tradition', *Scrutiny*, xviii (June 1951), 2–17. Cox traces a strong undercurrent of dissent from post-Romantic orthodoxy. This 'minority tradition' argued for greater thought, closer contact with contemporary life, and less subjectivism in poetry. Cox observes, however, that the voices of this minority were 'fairly strong in the early thirties, but from then on to mid-Victorian times there is a gradual but steady movement towards the acceptance of what we now consider to be the typical Victorian literary values' (15).

Between them they polarize elements which by their coexistence help to define the Victorianism of Victorian poetics.

Attacking the 'highly-coloured' poetry of the younger Romantics, Taylor wrote in his Preface:

> These poets were characterized by great sensibility and fervour, by a profusion of imagery, by force and beauty of language, and by a versification peculiarly easy and adroit and abounding in that sort of melody which, by its very obvious cadences, makes itself most pleasing to an unpractised ear. They exhibit, therefore, many of the most attractive graces and charms of poetry. . . .
> Yet their deficiencies were not unimportant. They wanted in the first place, subject-matter. A feeling came more easily to them than a reflection, an image was always at hand when a thought was not forthcoming. Either they did not look upon mankind with observant eyes, or they did not feel it to be any part of their vocation to turn what they saw to account. It did not belong to poetry, in their apprehension, to thread the mazes of life in all its classes and under all its circumstances, common as well as romantic, and seeing all things, to infer and to instruct: on the contrary, it was to stand aloof from everything that is plain and true; to have little concern with what is rational and wise; it was to be, like music, a moving and enchanting art, acting upon the fancy, the affections, the passions, but scarcely connected with the exercise of the intellectual faculties. These writers, indeed, had adopted a tone of language which is hardly consistent with the state of mind in which a man makes much use of understanding.[1]

There is much here that Johnson would have approved of. So would Wordsworth. So would Clough, in many ways a late perpetuator of this minority tradition. More significant for the immediate point is the fact that Tennyson, so obviously an heir of the later Romantics, so clearly important in his anticipation of the Symbolists, should have agreed with Taylor in 'most that he says of modern poetry', although he thought that 'the peculiar strength evolved by such writers as Byron and Shelley' was not taken 'sufficiently into consideration'.[2] This doubleness in Tennyson's response makes manifest a dilemma which, in one way or another, is pervasive in the poetics of the period.

---

[1] H. Taylor, *Works*, 5 vols. (London, 1877-8), i. v-vi.

[2] Quoted, *Victorian Poetry and Poetics*, ed. W. E. Houghton and G. R. Stange (Boston, 1959), p. 812 n. In my survey of the critical background I have not aimed at any kind of comprehensiveness. Rather, I have selected those elements which seem to have a special bearing on Clough's life as a poet.

The dilemma is an epistemological and ontological one, centred on the word 'fact', which leads outwards from poetics into the wider dilemmas of the age. How was a Romantically apprehended conviction of value to be adjusted to an increasingly intractable, insistent, and disturbing world of fact? Carlyle refused the dilemma by distinguishing between the fact of Dryasdust and the Fact, the Eternal Verity, which lay around for those who had eyes to see. In doing so he laid down the basic oppositional pattern, but not everyone could rest easily in it. Post-Romantic poetics can be seen as an effort in one specialized area to come to terms with that opposition.

M. H. Abrams has seen Wordsworth's dictum, 'Poetry is the spontaneous overflow of powerful feelings', as a convenient initial point marking the ascendancy of expressivist theory in the nineteenth century.[1] Expressivist elements enter, of course, into most theories of poetry, but by 1830 Wordsworth's statement, extended and pared of his important qualifications, had become elevated almost into an axiom. The nature of this extension and of some of the conclusions drawn from it are, fittingly, illustrated with especial clearness in the two essays on poetry which John Stuart Mill published in 1833—fittingly because this particular spokesman illustrates dramatically in his own experience the disintegration of the special object–subject synthesis achieved through Romantic, more particularly Coleridgean, theories of imagination and poetic cognition. As Mill recounted in his *Autobiography*, he turned to poetry not for philosophical truth but for the 'culture of the feelings' which the dry rationalism of his education had denied him. Poetry, Mill wrote, voicing what was rapidly becoming a dogma, is 'the expression or uttering forth of feeling'.[2] 'One may write genuine poetry, and not be a poet; for whosoever writes out truly any one human feeling, writes poetry. All persons even the most unimaginative, in moments of strong emotion, speak poetry. . . .'[3] Inevitably for Mill lyric poetry became 'more eminently and peculiarly poetry than any other'.[4] External objects in his poetics exist only for 'the generation of poetry',

[1] M. H. Abrams, *The Mirror and the Lamp*, paperback edn., (London, 1960), p. 21.
[2] 'What is Poetry?', *The Monthly Repository*, vii (Jan. 1833), 64.
[3] 'The Two Kinds of Poetry', ibid., vii (Nov. 1833), 715.
[4] Ibid., p. 719.

and even then 'the poetry is not in the object itself' but in 'the state of mind' in which the object is contemplated. When a poet describes a lion, he is 'describing the lion professedly, but the state of mind of the spectator really', and the poetry must be true, not to the object, but to the 'human emotion'. In a sentence which underlines the kind of cognitive surrender implied in this poetic, Mill continues his example, 'The lion may be described falsely or in exaggerated colours, and the poetry be all the better. . . .'[1]

A more genuinely Romantic variant of Mill's dismissal of the external world is his rejection of audience in any significant sense: the awareness of audience results not in 'poetry' but in 'eloquence'.[2] Shelley's poet-nightingale sitting in darkness and 'singing to cheer its own solitude', extracted from its revolutionary setting, finds an equivalent in Mill's doctrine, 'Poetry is feeling, confessing itself to itself, in moments of solitude. . . . All Poetry is of the nature of soliloquy.'[3]

In disengaging poetry from any essential connection with the external world—of objects or of audience—in insisting on poetry as utterance, and, further, on the distinction between 'poets born' and 'poets made', 'poets by nature' and 'poets by culture',[4] Mill tended to subordinate—if not positively repudiate—concern for poetry as art or craft. In doing so he not only reflected the attitudes of the majority of his contemporaries, but also laid down the lines in post-Romantic theory which converged to a concentrated attention on the figure and personality of the poet himself. Poetry became the utterance of genius ('A perfect poem is the perfect expression of a Perfect Human Mind'),[5] and what the poet expressed through the faculties of vision, intuition, imagination, intellect, and emotion was Reality itself. Romantic—and especially Shelleyan claims—were taken up and developed, particularly in Carlyle's transcendental poetic, into a conception of poetry as the apprehension and expression of beauty, reality,

---

[1] 'What is Poetry?', p. 63.   [2] Ibid., p. 64.   [3] Loc. cit.
[4] 'The Two Kinds of Poetry', 716. Cf. 'At least among painters of the present day, I feel myself more disposed to recognize spiritual beauties in those whose powers of execution are manifestly incomplete, than in artists whose hands are skilful and manner formed.' W. M. Thackeray, 'Men and Pictures', *Fraser's Magazine* (July 1841), quoted by M. Praz, *The Hero in Eclipse in Victorian Fiction*, trans. A. Davidson, p. 219.
[5] S. Dobell, *Thoughts on Art, Philosophy, and Religion* (London, 1876), p. 7.

truth, and goodness. The very interchangeability of these terms created a characteristic blurring in critical terminology. Since the end of art was 'Truth', truth absolute, unitary, and comprehensive, 'poetry' readily transformed itself into an inclusive term, applicable to any medium which might reveal a special kind of truth—religion, art, even action or a moral state. The poet proper was poet not by virtue of the form of his utterance, but because of the nature of his vision, because of his perception of the ideal in the actual, of the essence of beauty in the world which was identical with its truth. 'A talent for composition', John Newman declared, '. . . is no essential part of poetry, though indispensable to its exhibition. . . . [A]ttention to the language *for its own sake* evidences not the true poet but the mere artist.'[1] It was the perception and delineation of the ideal, he pointed out in his essay, 'Poetry, With Reference to Aristotle's Poetics', that rendered character, opinions, feelings, manners, and customs, 'poetical'. Dr. Arnold, we remember, had defined poetic inspiration as 'anything' which caused man to lift himself above his 'cold and selfish, and worldly' state of normal being into a *'poetical temper* and *poetical feelings'*.[2] We have arrived from a critical heritage of revolutionary idealism at more distinctively Early-Victorian positions with these specifically moralized versions of truth, of poetry, and of 'poetical feelings'. We are, in short, in the world of 'high seriousness' that looks askance at comedy and registers unease at the presence of satire.

It is this kind of transition which forms a Victorian substratum to the frequent Romantic assertions made on behalf of the Poet and his Vision. With typical vastness Carlyle declared,

The true Poet is ever, as of old, the Seer; whose eye has been gifted to discern the godlike Mystery of God's Universe, and decipher some new lines of its celestial writing; we can still call him a *Vates* and Seer; for he *sees* into this greatest of secrets, 'the open secret'; hidden things become clear; how the Future (both resting on Eternity) is but another phasis of the Present; thereby are his words in very truth prophetic; what he has spoken shall be done.[3]

[1] J. H. Newman, 'Poetry with Reference to Aristotle's Poetics', in *English Critical Essays: Nineteenth Century*, ed. E. D. Jones (London, 1934), p. 252. Newman's italics.
[2] T. Arnold, *Miscellaneous Works* (London, 1845), p. 253.
[3] T. Carlyle, 'Death of Goethe', *Works*, xxvii. 377.

Carlyle's vastness is exceptional; the expectancy of prophetic utterance, leadership, and elevation is not. F. D. Maurice, a leading spirit among the influential Cambridge Apostles, maintained, 'The mind of the poet of the highest order is the most perfect mind that can belong to man. . . . [H]e cannot be untrue, for it is his high calling to interpret those universal truths which exist on earth only in the forms of his creation.'[1] If there was an insistence on the poet as a being apart, it coexisted with an equal demand that he should be aware of shared manhood. God and Victorian man lived side by side in the shrine of poetry: Tennyson, who most nearly conformed to the dominant ideal, spoke of feeling like 'a priest who can never leave the sanctuary and whose every word must be consecrated to the service of Him who had touched his lips with the fire of heaven which was to enable him to speak in God's name to his age'.[2] Speaking to the age was an almost necessary condition of poetic being. Carlyle's titanic Poet Hero summed up the strengths of the Heroic Warrior, Politician, Thinker, Legislator, Philosopher, and made articulate and melodious the great heart of a nation: it was essential that he should recognize the greatness of that heart, and not stray into the dubieties of a *Maud* or an *Empedocles on Etna*—as Carlyle, again, put it, '[T]he true literary man' was 'the light of the world; the world's Priest;—guiding it, like a sacred Pillar of Fire, in its dark pilgrimage through the waste of Time.'[3] At its most crass the demand for leadership issued, in this age of victorious bourgeois enterprise, in reviews like the one with which *Blackwood's* greeted Matthew Arnold's first volume.

What would our friend be at? If he is a Tory, can't he find work enough in denouncing and exposing the lies of the League, and in taking up the cudgels for native industry? If he is a Whig, can't he be great upon sewerage, and the scheme of planting colonies in Connaught, to grow corn and rear pigs at prices which will not pay for the manure and the hogs'-wash? If he is a Chartist, can't he say so and stand up manfully with Julian Harney for 'the points', whatever may be their latest number?[4]

[1] [F. D. Maurice], 'Byron', *The Athenaeum*, i (1828), 351.
[2] Quoted from a reviewer of Hallam Tennyson's *Memoir*, H. Nicolson, *Tennyson* (London, 1923), pp. 16–17.
[3] T. Carlyle, *Heroes and Hero Worship*, in *Works*, v. 157.
[4] *Blackwood's Magazine*, lxvi (Sept. 1849), 346. Quoted L. Trilling, *Matthew Arnold* (London, 1949), p. 79.

Despite the doubts of a Macaulay,[1] it was still possible in the general cultural situation of the Early-Victorian period to conceive of poetry in traditional terms as an effective moral and social force. In fact, the concerted effort to maintain the traditional cultural emphasis is one of the salient characterizing features of the period. There might be disagreement about the immediate end of poetry, whether this was pleasure or beauty or truth, but as Alba Warren has pointed out, these post-Romantic theorists were in agreement about its ultimate end, especially about its relation to morals and to society.[2] The widely current instrumental view of intellectual activity in general and artistic activity in particular frequently led to doctrine which contradicted itself. The emphasis on the peculiar, essential privacy of the lyric poet was balanced by the role of public orator and guide which the age imposed on its singers. Sanctioning notions of poetry as prophecy and revelation, the age also inclined to insist that its poets should conform to law and fact. The prime test of poetic authenticity was feeling; yet the age displayed an exceptional quickness in pointing out the absence of moral or idea.

This element of ambivalence manifests itself in various ways in the criticism of the period. At one level it reveals itself, for instance, in the 'naturalist idealism' of John Ruskin, a neo-Aristotelian attempt to bring into consonance the idealistic and realistic impulses in art and refashion a synthesis between subject and object, between external reality and the mind of the artist. Ruskin's ideal is 'naturalist, because studied from nature, and ideal because it is mentally arranged in a certain manner'.[3] For him 'The work of [the] great idealists is . . . always universal; not because it is *not portrait*, but because it is *complete* portrait down to the heart, which is the same in all ages. . . .'[4] Not everyone was a Ruskin, however, and, if in the actual practice of ordinary criticism realism became equated with the fidelity of literalism (the history of Tennyson's 'ringing grooves of change' is symptomatic), in the hands of conventional critics the theory of 'natural idealism' underwent a characteristic insensitization. Shairp, who succeeded Sir Francis Doyle as Professor of Poetry

[1] Cf. especially the famous essay on Milton.
[2] A. Warren, *English Poetic Theory, 1825–1865* (Princeton, 1950), p. 20.
[3] J. Ruskin, *Modern Painters*, iii; *The Works of John Ruskin*, ed. E. T. Cook and A. Wedderburn, 39 vols. (London, 1902–12), v. 113.
[4] Ibid. 127–8.

at Oxford, attempted precariously and unsuccessfully to assert an autonomous view of poetry:

[P]oetry, as poetry, has nothing to do with conduct and action. Contemplation is its aim and end. It longs to see the vision of the beautiful, the noble, and the true; and that spectacle, when granted, suffices it. Beyond the contemplation of beauty and goodness it does not seek to go. Herein lie the weakness and the temptation not of actual poets only, but of all artistic persons. . . . A part of their being, their imagination and emotions, touches the ideal, but their will remains unaffected. . . . This, I suppose, is the moral of that early poem of the Laureate's *The Palace of Art*.

Shairp, clearly influenced by 'Tintern Abbey' in his distinctions, goes on in the same essay to trace the stages by which the poetry of nature ascends to its highest ideal. In the final sublime stage 'not merely moral qualities are suggested, but something more than these': 'In many persons, and not in poets only, a beautiful sunrise, or a gorgeous sunset, or the starry heavens in a cloudless night, create moral impressions, and something more; these sights suggest to them . . . the presence of Him from whom come both Nature and the emotions it awakens.'[1] The narrowing down of the Ideal to specific and traditional moral feelings is characteristic, as is the unease both about 'nature' and aestheticism. Moral conformism was written into much of the criticism of the period.

The preoccupation with feeling and insight, on the one hand, and, on the other, with moral and social teaching, resulted in some typical expressivist positions. The moral end of poetry was seen as necessarily flowering out of the 'moral centre' of the poet, the quality of his imaginative vision was linked indivisibly with his moral stature as a man. 'We do not hesitate to say', Newman declared, 'that poetry is ultimately founded on correct moral perception;—that where there is no sound principle in exercise there will be no poetry, and that on the whole (originality being granted) in proportion to the standard of a writer's moral character, will his compositions vary in poetical excellence.'[2] Ruskin asserted that 'He who habituates himself, in his daily life, to seek for the stern facts in whatever he hears or sees, will have these facts again brought before him by the involuntary

---

[1] J. C. Shairp, 'The Spiritual Side of Poetry', in *Aspects of Poetry* (London, 1881), pp. 69–70, 75.   [2] Newman, op. cit., p. 247.

imaginative power in their noblest associations; and he who seeks for frivolities and fallacies, will have frivolities and fallacies again presented to him in his dreams.'[1] The importance attached to the moral nature of the creative artist combined with the preference for subjective utterance in encouraging the widespread habit of using literature to illuminate biography. Poetry became the window into the poet's personality, style the literary expression of his moral qualities. Further, since words could be deceptive and attitudes feigned, it was necessary often to go behind the art-work to the biography in order to test the quality of the poet's imagination and of his moral centre. Matthew Arnold's essay on Shelley is an obvious example of such procedure.

Sincerity, therefore, became from this point of view a central test of value. Carlyle's Poet-Hero was a man 'in earnest with the Universe, though all others were but toying with it. He is a *Vates*, first of all, in virtue of being sincere';[2] the *Divine Comedy* was great because it was, 'at bottom, the *sincerest* of all Poems'.[3] Closely related to the criterion of sincerity was that of spontaneity. In distinguishing poets born, 'poets by nature', from poets made, 'poets by culture', Mill pointed out that natural poetry was identifiable because it was 'Feeling itself, employing thought only as the medium of its utterance'. On the other hand, the poetry of 'a cultivated but not naturally poetic mind' was written 'with a distinct aim', and in it thought remained the conspicuous component, however surrounded by a 'halo of feeling'.[4] Intellectualism, satire, wit, the play of mind, were not qualities which prevailing conceptions of poetry would admit easily into the precincts of the poetic.

Dulce et utile—we have looked at some of the distinctive definitions of *utile* in Early-Victorian criticism; *dulce* tended to be summed up in the single word 'beauty'. 'Beauty'—generally used as a final, undefined because indefinable, term—was regarded as the essence of all poetic utterance. As Arthur Carr put it, wittily and concisely,

The explanation [for Tennyson's dominance] is that the prevailing idea of poetry was his idea—how it should sound ('beautiful'), what it should utter ('wisdom'); in proportion as truth eluded, more beauty must be added. The Tennysonian style was dominant not because the

[1] Ruskin, op. cit., p. 124.   [2] Carlyle, *Works*, v. 81.
[3] Ibid., p. 91.   [4] Mill, 'The Two Kinds of Poetry', p. 717.

genius of Tennyson prevailed but because he was, for all his deficiencies, the 'heir of all the ages', the indubitable scion—perhaps the last—of the longest and most honoured traditions, descending from Spenser and Milton and, through them, from classical and Christian origins.[1]

Loading every rift with Keatsian ore, giving to utterance the golden colouring of fancy and imagination through the exploitation of verbal melody, the elaboration of exquisite images, the injection of beauty through the vocalic suggestiveness of the single rich word—such, in general, were the formal tasks and excellences expected of the poet.

Before turning to consider Clough's own critical statements it might be instructive to see how some of the traditional judgements of his poetry develop out of this background of critical preconceptions.[2] Sincerity is, quite overwhelmingly, the most frequently asserted of his virtues. J. A. Symonds made perhaps the strongest claims in his behalf on this basis:

> Clough had nothing of the self-conscious artist or of the ordinary *littérateur* about him. His poems are not flashes on the surface, occasional pieces, or set compositions upon given themes; but the very pith and marrow of a deeply thinking, deeply-feeling soul—the most heartfelt utterances of one who sought to speak out what was in him in the fewest and simplest words. His horror of artificial language was often carried to excess. His hatred of affectation betrayed him into baldness. But one thing you may be sure to find in him—sincerity and sense.[3]

With the exception of this single and, in itself, very dubious aesthetic virtue, Clough has been faulted on almost every count. He fails as a lyric poet, because, apart from his initially crippling suspicion of feeling, his work in this vein is hampered by 'the chronic state of introspective criticism on himself . . . [which] . . . necessarily diminishes the linearity and directness of the feeling expressed, refracting it, as it were, through media of very variable density'.[4] Alternatively, these 'dispersive influences' have been interpreted in religious terms. Faith, the writer of an article on 'Scepticism and Modern Poetry' asserts, is necessary at the lowest

---

[1] *Victorian Poetry: Clough to Kipling*, ed. A. J. Carr (New York, 1959), p. ix.
[2] Houghton's excellent examination of the 'tradition of disparagement' in the criticism of Clough's poetry makes it unnecessary to go into this area in any detail.
[3] J. A. Symonds, 'Arthur Hugh Clough', *Fortnightly Review*, x (Dec. 1868), 591.
[4] Review of *PPR*, *The Spectator*, xlii (11 Sept. 1869), 1073.

level for 'aesthetical reasons alone', since 'doubt disintegrates, disperses, repels. Faith attracts and knits together.' Clough, therefore, is seen as 'Perhaps the most striking illustration in modern times of the manner in which the poetical faculty may be overridden and paralysed by the action of doubt.'[1] A somewhat similar view was expressed in 1862 by R. H. Hutton: 'Suspense of mind is antagonistic to poetry. If you reserve your judgment as to either thought, faith, or fact, you have so far a vague and unrealized world—a world of misgivings and hesitations—instead of one from which the poet can glean its shapely pictures.'[2]

The extra-literary criteria frequently underlying these expressions of unease about a poetry which manifests doubt and hesitation instead of full-flowing faith, perplexity and ridicule instead of positive and heartening statement, blurring and intricate thought instead of clear, intensely unified emotion, are distinctly indicated, for instance, by Margaret Steede, who found the bitterness of irony and satire in 'The Latest Decalogue' and 'In the Great Metropolis' distressing, while the religio-moral poems of *Ambarvalia* were 'undoubtedly the best and most characteristic' of Clough's poems and the ones on which 'his claim to rank among the poets and thinkers of the century chiefly rests'.[3]

Dissatisfaction with the content of Clough's poetry is accompanied by equally repetitive assertions of his failings as an artist. 'Viewed critically, Clough's work is wanting in art . . . one feels a doubt whether in verse he chose the right vehicle, the truly natural mode of utterance', F. T. Palgrave wrote in 1862,[4] and in its most recent form the same charge was made in 1957 by H. N. Fairchild: 'It is perhaps unfortunate that Arthur Hugh Clough chose verse as the vehicle for his perplexities: although he desired to write "poetry" he was not sufficiently an artist to be much interested in making *poems*.'[5] The main source of dissatisfaction is that Clough's poetry lacks 'beauty', the perfect coherence of thought and expression, the aureate texture and

---

[1] [J. B. Brown], 'Scepticism and Modern Poetry', *Blackwood's Magazine*, cxv (Feb. 1874), 224, 229.
[2] [R. H. Hutton], 'Mr. Clough's Poems', *The Spectator*, xxxv (12 July 1862), 776.
[3] M. Steede, 'Arthur Hugh Clough', *Temple Bar*, cviii (May 1896), 42, 48.
[4] *Poems by Arthur Hugh Clough* (Cambridge and London, 1862), p. xi.
[5] H. N. Fairchild, *Religious Trends in English Poetry*, 4 vols. (New York, 1957), iv. 505.

musicality of true poetry, which should be 'simple, sensuous and passionate'. 'In one word, Clough was almost too grimly in earnest . . . for the fanciful play of the sheet-lightning of that fancy which—when not indulged too far—adds so much to the charm of the poet. His mind was always fixed on the real world.'[1] Stopford Brooke held that Clough's 'poetry itself is not of a high quality; its level is only a third of the way towards greatness; it is imaginative, but the imagination in it never soars and never is on fire, never at a white heat. . . . Art had not thrown her mantle over this man; the language does not enhance or uplift the thought; it rather depresses and lowers it. . . .'[2] Brooke's last sentence reveals a peculiar ambiguity in the attitude to language that underlies much of this kind of criticism. The somewhat vague demand for perfect fusion of form and content coexists curiously with an inorganic conception of language as an elevating, ennobling, generally 'poeticizing' element.

Perhaps the most magisterial pronouncement about Clough to issue out of the kinds of assumption we have been considering is that with which Osborne concluded his book. Clough, he said, suffered from one 'inescapable limitation': 'He was not sufficiently sensuous. He did the best he could with a nervous system that was simply not finely enough organized, not delicate enough, to delight and gloriously to succeed in creative effort.'[3]

If one detects in many of the traditional judgements of Clough's poetry the pressure of certain preconceptions, Clough's own views about poetry betray at points a doubleness about these assumptions which reflects itself in the uncertain, provisional, and heterogeneous nature of much of his work. On the whole, he diverged considerably from prevailing theory and, consequently, from the assumptions on which a great deal of the adverse criticism of his work is based. For much of the time, that is, he was not even trying to write the kind of poetry the critics wanted from him. But that divergence was neither complete nor fully comprehended; as Houghton has remarked, Clough was only partially aware of—and convinced about—his 'revolt',[4]

[1] R. H. Hutton, 'The Poetry of Arthur Hugh Clough', *Fortnightly Review* xxxix (June 1883), 794.
[2] S. A. Brooke, *Four Poets* (London, 1908), pp. 31, 41.
[3] J. I. Osborne, *Arthur Hugh Clough* (London, 1920), p. 191.
[4] Houghton, p. 15.

and it is as important to stress this area of uncertainty as it is to draw attention to his divergence.

His own critical statements are most rewardingly examined in conjunction with the acute and wide-ranging letters that Matthew Arnold wrote to him, and which constitute one half of what must have been a lively and extensive debate. Unfortunately, only one letter of Clough's—written from Rome in 1849—survives. The debate, therefore, as it exists, is wholly one-sided: one is thrown back on inference in attempting to interpret Clough's part in it. As far as Arnold himself is concerned, these letters are of crucial significance. In them one can see him working his way towards the attitudes and ideas that find finished expression in his classic 1853 Preface—and since his position there is emphatically anti-Cloughian, that general drift is of some importance for our purposes.

The first point to be made about the correspondence is the obvious one that it arose out of a friendship which was perhaps the closest and most meaningful of Clough's life, at the same time that it was the most uneasy, emotionally and intellectually. Without entering into the fluctuating and sometimes painful details, the broad outlines can be indicated briefly enough. Initially, in the years surrounding the summer of 1844, when Clough was coaching Arnold for the Final Schools and shaking his head doubtfully over his pupil's tendency to go off fishing when he should have been at his books (*Corr.* i. 134), he must have appeared as a monitorial embodiment of Rugby and the values which Arnold was attempting to resist. Gradually, however, the positions shifted. As the younger man began to find himself as a poet, he began to recognize in this friend (who, he privately maintained, 'had no vocation for literature')[1] a force antagonistic to his own life as a poet. He saw in him the restless, critical, analytical, disruptive drive of the nineteenth-century intellect which was fatal to the life of poetry as he saw it. But, as a kind of nostalgic and self-doubting undercurrent, he was also beginning to see in this friend's openness and inconclusiveness the youth that he himself was so pressingly aware of leaving further and further behind.[2] By the 1850s the initial

---

[1] *New Zealand Letters of Thomas Arnold the Younger*, ed. J. Bertram (Wellington, 1966), p. 136.

[2] Cf. 'The aimless and unsettled, but also open and liberal state of our youth we *must* perhaps all leave and take refuge in our morality and character; but with

positions had been reversed. It was Arnold, now possessed of his 'idea of the world', who was keeping an overseeing eye on the unsuccessful friend, urging him to exert himself and not waste his powers. The important point is that the tension and unease in the friendship involved two radically opposed standpoints on the question of how to live, fundamental standpoints from which both men derived their critical bearings regarding the nature and function of literature.

In February 1853 Arnold wrote a long and placating but courageous letter to Clough, obviously in reply to wounded accusations of neglect. It was true, he said, that at one stage, shortly after the publication of *The Bothie*, he had felt the necessity of secluding himself intellectually and 'barring out' all influences—including Clough's—which 'troubled without advancing' him. But this had been only a contemplated estrangement: in reality he was for ever linked to Clough, 'vitally connected' with him by intellectual bonds—those strongest of all bonds—since the period of his own development coincided so exactly with his friendship with him.

You ask me in what I think or have thought you going wrong: in this: that you would never take your assiette as something determined final and unchangeable for you and proceed to work away on the basis of that: but were always poking and patching and cobbling at the assiette itself—could never finally, as it seemed—'resolve to be thyself'—but were looking for this and that experience, and doubting whether you ought not to adopt this or that mode of being of persons qui ne vous valaient pas because it might possibly be nearer the truth than your own: you had no reason for thinking it *was*, but it *might* be—and so you would try to adapt yourself to it. You have I am convinced lost infinite time in this way: it is what I call your morbid conscientiousness— you are the most conscientious man I ever knew: but on some lines morbidly so, and it spoils your action.[1]

The attack is radical and, to the extent that Clough participated in this sense of truth as accretive and measurable along a deter-

most of us it is a melancholy passage from which we emerge shorn of so many beams that we are almost tempted to quarrel with the law of nature which imposes it on us.' Matthew Arnold to Jane Forster, 25 Jan. 1851. *Letters of Matthew Arnold, 1848–1888*, ed. G. W. E. Russell, 2 vols. (London, 1895), i. 14.

[1] Lowry, pp. 129–30.

mined line, pertinent. The accusations of 'morbid conscientious-ness', too, were ones he might well have levelled at himself in certain moods, particularly at this stage of his life—but they obscure a crucial point at issue, one which becomes fully clear only in Clough's poetry. At its most valuable, in its most sensitively articulated, most fully released form, the Cloughian experience of difficulty is not a slack inability to close off the options. It is, rather, a tough and scrupulous refusal to slur over for the sake of 'foundations' the encountered difficulties in one's attempt to identify truth, to simplify self-awareness for the sake of unity or progress, or regard as solid that which the act of inspection con-stantly reveals as profoundly self-modifying, arbitrary, accidental. Arnold and Clough are divided here, ultimately, by their sense of the nature of truth and identity. And yet the separation was neither simple nor clear. Both men were intensely aware, Clough in the form of aspiration and Arnold in that of temptation, of the possible validity of the other's stand, and this suppressed un-certainty sharpened even further the conflict between them. It accounts for the not infrequent and vehement exasperation of Arnold's letters. 'You certainly do not seem to me sufficiently to desire and earnestly strive towards—assured knowledge—activity —happiness. You are too content to *fluctuate*—to be ever learning, never coming to the knowledge of the truth. This is why, with you, I feel it necessary to stiffen myself—and hold fast my rudder.'[1]

As a response to history, Arnold's insistence on the absolute necessity of fixing and defining a purposive, 'ennobling', and 'animating'[2] centre of living issued in a repudiation of the forces of the '*Zeit Geist*'. '[W]hen one is trying to emerge to hard land it is irritating to find your friend not only persisting in "weltering to the parching wind" himself, but doing his best to pull you back into the Sea also', he wrote in October 1853.[3] From this angle he had attacked *The Bothie* five years earlier. Hearing the praise of friends like Sellar, who knew 'neither life nor themselves', embittered him—about them, about the poem, about Clough. But he had found strength in the inner assurance that he could, if the need arose, dispense with all of these, even with Clough, in order to possess himself. '[B]etter that, than be sucked for an hour even into the Time Stream in which they and he plunge and bellow.' Such a surrender to the immediate play of history was,

<hr>

[1] Ibid., p. 146.   [2] Loc. cit.   [3] Ibid., p. 144.

he thought, 'more English than European, . . . more American than English', and he fortified himself against Clough's '*Zeit Geist*' by taking up Obermann.[1] 'My dearest Clough', we find him fulminating again,

these are damned times—everything is against one—the height to which knowledge is come, the spread of luxury, our physical enervation, the absence of great *natures*, the unavoidable contact with millions of small ones, newspapers, cities, light profligate friends, moral desperadoes like Carlyle, our own selves, and the sickening consciousness of our difficulties: but for God's sake neither let us be fanatics nor yet chalf blown by the wind but let us be ὡς ὁ φρονιμος διορισειεν and not as any one else διορισειεν.[2]

The impulse towards isolated self-cultivation, towards moral withdrawal and self-sufficiency, which troubles Arnold's concept of culture, is already obvious. But this was, of course, only one terminal; the other, positive and outward-reaching, is hinted at in another letter which records the ambivalence of his attitude to the tempting and threatening ivory tower.

I am more and more convinced that the world tends to become more comfortable for the mass, and more uncomfortable for those of any natural gift or distinction—and it is as well perhaps that it should be so —for hitherto the gifted have astonished and delighted the world, but not trained or inspired or in any real way changed it. . . . I am sure however that in the air of the present times il nous manque d'aliment, and that we deteriorate in spite of our struggles—like a gifted Roman falling on the uninvigorating atmosphere of the decline of the Empire. Still nothing can absolve us from the duty of doing all we can to keep alive our courage and activity.[3]

This general philosophical attitude, this general historical sensitiveness, Arnold brought to his thinking about literature. Interpreted in literary terms, the restless, diverse, and divided nineteenth century became wholly antagonistic to the central, unitary, and luminous life of poetry. An awareness of its dispersive forces convinced one 'how deeply *unpoetical* the age and all one's surroundings are. Not unprofound, not ungrand, not unmoving:—but *unpoetical*.'[4] 'What a brute you were to tell me to read Keats' letters', he exploded in another letter,[5] and the violence of his reaction can be explained fairly easily, although

---

[1] Lowry, p. 95.   [2] Ibid., p. 111.   [3] Ibid., pp. 122-3.
[4] Ibid., p. 99.   [5] Ibid., p. 96.

that reaction itself was complex. Underlying the fastidious distaste at Keats's sensationalism and 'want of character' that Arnold later expressed in his essay on the poet was his antagonism to the basic intellectual and aesthetic proposition: '[T]he only means of strengthening one's intellect is to make up one's mind about nothing—to let one's mind be a thoroughfare for all thoughts, not a select party.'[1] But the enemy for Arnold was also an enemy within: the Strayed Reveller was a tempter who disturbed the clear and complete view of the Wise Bard. In the same letter to Clough he elaborated on the nature and consequences of Keatsianism:

> What harm he has done in English Poetry. As Browning is a man with a moderate gift passionately desiring movement and fulness, and obtaining but a confused multitudinousness, so Keats with a very high gift, is yet also consumed by this desire: and cannot produce the truly living and moving, as his conscience keeps telling him. *They will not be patient neither understand that they must begin with an Idea of the world in order not to be prevailed over by the world's multitudinousness*. . . .
> . . . But what perplexity Keats Tennyson et id genus omne must occasion to young writers of the ὁπλίτης sort: yes and those d——d Elizabethan poets generally. Those who cannot read Greek should read nothing but Milton and parts of Wordsworth: the state should see to it. . . .[2]

The strictures in the 1853 Preface against Shakespeare and the Romantics for concentrating on details of verbal and imagistic surface at the expense of clear, unified, central form and action spread extensive roots into the tissue of Arnold's convictions.

Despite the fact of a few incidental agreements, then, these two friends, neither of whom could adequately appreciate the other's excellences, were separated by fundamental moral, intellectual, and aesthetic differences which provide an essential context for Arnold's specific criticisms of Clough as a poet. Of almost equal significance is the reorientation in Arnold's own attitudes that these letters themselves reveal. The reorientation is implicit in Arnold's starting premisses about the nature of poetic form, but it amounts to a revision of emphasis radical enough to be almost a revision of theory. The earlier letters are untiring in their emphasis on the primacy of form and composition. The real truth

---

[1] *The Letters of John Keats, 1814–1821*, ed. H. E. Rollins, 2 vols. (Cambridge, Mass., 1958), ii. 213.　　　　　[2] Lowry, p. 97, my italics.

about Clough's poems 'in general' was that they were not '*natural*'.

Many persons with far lower gifts than yours yet seem to find their natural mode of expression in poetry, and tho: the contents may not be very valuable they appeal with justice from the judgement of the mere thinker to the world's general appreciation of naturalness— i.e.—an absolute propriety—of form, as the sole *necessary* of Poetry as such: whereas the greatest wealth and depth of matter is merely a superfluity in the Poet *as such*.

. . . The trying to go into and to the bottom of an object instead of grouping *objects* is as fatal to the sensuousness of poetry as the mere painting, (for, *in Poetry*, this is not *grouping*) is to its airy and rapidly moving life.

. . . You succeed best you see, in fact, in the hymn, where man, his deepest personal feelings being in play, finds poetical expression as *man* only, not as artist:—but consider whether you attain the *beautiful*, and whether your product gives PLEASURE, not excites curiosity and reflexion.[1]

The charges are three: Clough's poetry lacks naturalness of expression; it is overburdened by thought to the detriment of 'composition'; it is excessively concerned with the direct expression of this thought. The poetry, therefore, does not give that pleasure which is the immediate and essential end of poetry. One notices, however, that the 'pleasure' urged by Arnold is conceived wholly in terms of the 'beautiful', and, further, that the only criteria provided for a closer definition are 'sensuousness' and 'airy and rapidly moving life'. The charge of unmitigated subjectivism ('you poor subjective, you')[2] is constant in these letters. Arnold confesses to a 'growing sense of the deficiency of the beautiful' in his friend's poetry and to a conviction that this alone is 'properly *poetical* as distinguished from rhetorical, devotional and metaphysical'. Clough was only doubtfully an artist. He reminded one of Novalis 'in the way of direct communication, insight, and report'.[3] Seeing his friend's poetry as purely self-expressive, as 'thinking aloud', Arnold conceded to him the virtue of sincerity. Clough provided the 'spectacle of a writer striving evidently to get breast to breast with reality', but this, while it was 'always full of instruction and very invigorating', was not sufficient for poetry.[4]

[1] Lowry, pp. 98–9.   [2] Ibid., p. 89.
[3] Ibid., p. 66.   [4] Ibid., p. 86.

The authority of these strictures is weakened by the fact of their being based on special and limiting conceptions of the nature of poetic pleasure—but Arnold is too acute, too sensitive, a critic to be dismissed easily or entirely. He was unable to recognize the modes and procedures by which Clough's poetry at its finest achieves its distinction, but there remains, nevertheless, a considerable residue of validity in his case against his friend. Often Clough's scrupulousness, his conscientious watchfulness about disparities between experience and expression, operates in his poetry towards a direct, unmediated, and therefore unshaped precipitation into language. Often his suspiciousness of 'insincerity' translated itself into a suspiciousness about 'art' itself, and encouraged an excessive valuation of a poetry which wholly occupied itself with the bald writing-out of inner states. In his unsuccessful—or only half-successful—poetry one can detect, too, a responsiveness to the demand for a clear aspiration, a central message, a unifying emotion, which made him find in rhetoric or devotionality substitutes for the demanding discipline of art. But once these points are conceded, there remains the positive side of his uneven achievement.

Arnold's dissatisfaction with the formal qualities of Clough's poetry is intimately linked with his criticism of what he interpreted as the mode of that poetry: Clough was 'a mere d——d depth hunter in poetry'[1] attempting to '*solve* the Universe'.[2] Isobel Armstrong has met that charge with a penetrating observation: '[I]n accusing him of trying to solve the universe and in interpreting this as a sign of weakness, Arnold underrated Clough's self-consciousness and intelligence, failing to grasp that in these poems, reasoning is not only a procedure but a theme.'[3] Adopting argument, analysis, inspection as both material and procedure, Clough's poetry at its most accomplished, most alertly responsive, uncovers and confronts within itself a self-consciousness which resists Arnoldian formulations. Far from attempting to 'solve the universe', that poetry eloquently and with moving intelligence registers and articulates the minute play of consciousness attempting to realize itself, to identify self and experience. The frequently collapsing, introverted, deliquescent forms of this poetry are exact aesthetic images of a

[1] Ibid., p. 81.   [2] Ibid., p. 63.
[3] I. Armstrong, *Arthur Hugh Clough* (London, 1962), p. 20.

sense of time, truth, and structure, which is absolutely opposed to that which controls Arnold's demands.[1]

Arnold's assertion of classical form as a cure for the ills of his romantic contemporaries was flawed at its base, for he, too, was a romantic at heart, painfully aware of personal and social alienation and fragmentation, and looking impossibly for a poetry that was at once regulative, humanistic, and aesthetic. His insistence on form as a purely aesthetic entity was already crumbling in the letter he wrote to Clough early in March 1849:

. . . [T]here are two offices of Poetry—one to add to one's store of thoughts and feelings—another to compose and elevate the mind by a sustained tone, numerous allusions, and a grand style. . . . Nay in Sophocles what is valuable is not so much his contributions to psychology and the anatomy of sentiment, as the grand moral effect produced by *style*. For the style is the expression of the nobility of the poet's character, as the matter is the expression of the richness of his mind: but on men character produces as great an effect as mind.[2]

The expressivist-moral implications of his later definition of 'the Grand Style' are already emergent. The full consequence of this evolution is contained in his famous statement:

. . . [M]odern poetry can only subsist by its *contents*: by becoming a complete magister vitae as the poetry of the ancients did: by including, as theirs did, religion with poetry, instead of existing as poetry only, and leaving religious wants to be supplied by the Christian religion, as a power existing independent of the poetical power.[3]

The volte-face is complete; the claims about form have lost their impossibly disinterested artistic value. Previously poetic pleasure had been seen in terms of beautiful order and organization, now an instrumental criterion has been added. Form has been assimilated to content, and the two together have been mobilized towards the quasi-religious function, the insistence on which led Arnold to reject *Empedocles on Etna* on the grounds that it failed to 'inspirit and rejoice' the reader because in it 'suffering finds no vent in action'.[4] Arguing along the same lines in a letter to Clough

---

[1] In this connection see Barbara Hardy's excellent essay, 'Clough's Self-Consciousness', in *The Major Victorian Poets: Reconsiderations*, ed. Isobel Armstrong (London, 1968).

[2] Lowry, pp. 100–1.　　　　　　　　　　　　　　　　　　[3] Ibid., p. 124.

[4] Preface to *Poems* (1853), *The Poems of Matthew Arnold*, ed. K. Allott (London, 1965), pp. 591, 592.

written shortly after the 1853 Preface, he expressed his doubts about 'The Scholar Gipsy';

[W]hat does it *do* for you? Homer *animates*—Shakespeare *animates*—in its poor way I think Sohrab and Rustum *animates*—the Gipsy Scholar at best awakens a pleasing melancholy. But this is not what we want. . . . What . . . [men] . . . want is something to *animate* and *ennoble* them—not merely to add zest to their melancholy or grace to their dreams.[1]

'Only positive convictions and feeling are worth anything',[2] he had written two months earlier. One interesting point regarding this evolution in Arnold's critical attitudes, which is implied in his initial insistence on a firm centre, is that it accompanies a reverse evolution in Clough's poetry. Speaking generally, his development up to and including *Dipsychus* may be seen not merely negatively as a movement away from certainty but, positively, as a movement *towards* uncertainty and ambivalence. The weight of this movement is towards a more positive awareness of critical and sceptical attitudes, towards a tough acceptance of the multiple and problematic, and a firmer artistic control over it. And in this broad pattern of development the unfinished *Adam and Eve* may be seen as the link between the poetry of attempted statement and the poetry of process, which concerns itself with the ironies and ambiguities of 'character in the making, faith in the making, love in the making'.[3] Perhaps the parallel but counter evolutions are not entirely unrelated: one wishes that Clough's side of the debate had survived.

The clearly individualizing centre round which Clough formed his own literary judgements and values was his profound admiration and respect, wholly uncharacteristic of his period, for the eighteenth century. Matthew Arnold, although he held aloof from many contemporary critical trends, was at one with his age in his condemnation of the literary achievement of the 'age of prose and reason'. In general the 'poetic language of our eighteenth century' was for him 'language merely recalling the object as the common language of prose does'. In other words, because it tied itself too firmly to the factual object instead of committing

---

[1] Lowry, p. 146. [2] Ibid., p. 142.
[3] R. H. Hutton, 'The Unpopularity of Clough', *The Spectator*, lv (25 Nov. 1882), 1508.

itself to the life of imagination and feeling, it did not fulfil criteria for poetical creation such as those laid down by Mill. 'The evolution of the poetry of our eighteenth century is . . . intellectual; it proceeds by ratiocination, antithesis, ingenious turns and conceits. This poetry is often eloquent, and always, in the hands of such masters as Dryden and Pope, clever; but it does not give the emotion of seeing things in their truth and beauty.'[1] It is hardly surprising that with such preconceptions he should have found it difficult to admit the validity of Clough's poetry. Rephrasing the Coleridgean distinction between fancy and imagination, he made his final and immensely authoritative indictment of neo-classicism: 'The difference between genuine poetry and the poetry of Dryden, Pope, and all their school is briefly this: their poetry is conceived and composed in their wits, genuine poetry is conceived and composed in the soul.'[2]

In a lecture on Dryden Clough indicated concisely the relation of that 'true littérateur's' work to the larger meaning and achievement of his age. 'Dryden . . . simply reflects his epoch. The revolution he was intent upon was that of English verse composition. While Newton was balancing the earth, and Locke weighing the intellect, Dryden was measuring syllables. While Penn and Locke were venturing experiments in government, he was making them in prosody.'[3] At greater length he explored this connection in its historical and philosophical setting in another lecture. The 'proper manhood of the English nation dates . . . from the generation which rejected Milton', he declared. The returning Stuarts saw 'the joy and exultation of people at throwing off the yoke of an iron system of morals, proved by experience not co-extensive with facts, not true to the necessary exigencies and experiences of life'; the close of the seventeenth century witnessed the national mind forsaking 'the unsupported elevations of the speculative vision' and 'embarking . . . upon the seas of actual and positive experience'.[4]

In analysing the nature of this voyage Clough gave expression to some of his own most deeply felt attitudes towards life and reality. Anchoring his generalizations on eighteenth-century

[1] M. Arnold, 'Thomas Gray', in *Essays in Criticism, Second Series* (London and New York, 1891), pp. 95–6.
[2] Ibid., p. 95.
[3] 'Dryden and His Times, Lecture I', Trawick, pp. 92–3.
[4] 'The Development of English Literature', ibid., pp. 131–2.

literature to the parallel fertilizing and formative development of
the English mind in science and in mental and moral philosophy,
to the work of the Royal Society and Newton, of Locke and
Hume and Butler and Gibbon, he observed that the temper of the
prevailing philosophy was perhaps

> narrow and material; bent upon the examination of phenomena, it
> admitted only such as present themselves to the lower and grosser
> senses, to the notice of the higher and purer, it peremptorily refused
> its attention. . . . But it is certain also that without that matter of fact,
> nothing can be done, moreover and very little can be thought: pal-
> pable things, by divine right, by inevitable necessity, and intelligent
> ordinance, claim our habitual attention. . . . This austere love of truth;
> this righteous abhorrence of illusion; this rigorous uncompromising
> rejection of the vague, the untestified, the merely probable; this stern
> conscientious determination without paltering and prevarication to
> admit, if things are bad, that they are so; this resolute upright purpose,
> as of some transcendental man of business, to go thoroughly into the
> accounts of the world and make out once for all how they stand,
> such a spirit I may say, I think, claims more than our attention,—
> claims our reverence.
>
> We must not lose it, we must hold fast by it—precious to us as
> are Shakespeare's intellectual, or Milton's moral sublimities, while
> our eyes look up to them, our feet must stay themselves firmly here. . . .
> [T]he spirit of Newton and of Locke possesses us at least in as full
> measure as that of any one of their predecessors.[1]

That allegiance and that veneration defined the ground on which
Clough was willing and able to face both himself and his age:
'[T]here is a cogency in this resting upon only the lowest ground;
the winter-vitality of the moral convictions of Hume is worth
more than any summery exuberance of sentiment.'[2] 'Reconcile
what you have to say with green peas, for green peas are certain',
was how Walter Bagehot described Clough at his most wintry.[3]

This temperamental affinity with and respect for the general
mental culture of the eighteenth century gave Clough an insight,
exceptional in his time, into the real significance of the literary
effort of that age. He was scathing in his condemnation of Alexander Smith's stylistic excesses:

> He writes, it would almost seem, under the impression that the one
> business of the poet is to coin metaphors and similes. He tells them

out as a clerk might sovereigns at the Bank of England. So many comparisons, so much poetry; it is the sterling currency of the realm. Yet he is most pleased, perhaps, when he can double or treble a similitude; speaking of A, he will call it a B, which is, as it were, the C of a D. By some maturer effort we may expect to be thus conducted even to Z.[1]

The aetiology of this disease as Clough described it would have won Matthew Arnold's whole-hearted approval. 'Keats and Shelley, and Coleridge, perhaps, before them, with their extravagant love for Elizabethan phraseology, have led to this mischief. Has not Tennyson followed a little too much in their train?'[2] But the advocate of Greek and Milton and 'parts of Wordsworth' would have been rather less enthusiastic about the cure his friend recommended: 'To obtain a real command of the language, some familiarity with the prose writers, at any rate, of that period [between Milton and Burns], is almost essential; and to write out, as a mere daily task, passages, for example, of Goldsmith, would do a verse-composer of the nineteenth century as much good, we believe, as the study of Beaumont and Fletcher.'[3] Against what he saw as the exuberant over-elaborations of the Elizabethans and the Romantics Clough placed the achievement of Dryden, and in doing so indicated the qualities in language he himself prized most highly:

Our language before the restoration certainly was for the most part bookish, academical and stiff. . . . [The language of writers like Sidney, Taylor, Fletcher, Hooker and Bacon] is not an harmonious development of spoken words, but a copy of written words. We are set to study ornate and learned periods; but we are not charmed by finding our ordinary every day speech rounded with grace and smoothed into polish, chastened to simplicity and brevity without losing its expressiveness; and raised into dignity and force without ceasing to be familiar, saying once for all what we in our rambling talk try over and over in vain to say and saying it simply and fully, exactly and perfectly.[4]

The ideal written style, if it was to preserve cultural health, needed to fulfil certain definite conditions. It must approximate the idiom and texture of spoken, everyday speech; it must be definitive in its simplicity of exact, completely precipitated statement; it must be forceful without straining towards elevation.

[1] 'Recent English Poetry', Trawick, p. 165. [2] Ibid., p. 166.
[3] Ibid., p. 168. [4] 'Dryden and His Times, Lecture I', ibid., p. 94.

Since Clough has been so repeatedly charged with a neglect, or even unawareness, of style, his opinions on this subject demand an attentive hearing: they indicate, at the very least, the kind of artistic self-consciousness he brought to his own work. In a lecture on Wordsworth he said:

People talk about style as if it were a mere accessory; the unheeded but pleasing ornament; the mere put-on dress of the substantial being, who without it is much the same as with it. Yet is it not intelligible . . . that by a change of intonation, accent, or it may be mere accompanying gesture the same words may be made to bear most different meanings? . . . It may really be affirmed that some of the highest truths are only expressible to us by style,—only appreciable as indicated by manner.[1]

He attacked Browning's 'reckless, de-composite manner—dashing at anything and insisting that it would do' (*Corr.* ii. 514), and, in praising Wordsworth as a stylist, observed, 'Poetry like Science, has its final precision; and there are Expressions of Poetic Knowledge which can no more be rewritten than could the Elements of Geometry.'[2] He amplified his conception of 'final precision' as the quintessence of good style in an analogy which is his most important and illuminating single statement on the subject:

Conceive to yourselves a human being who discovered and had as it were a fully written out catalogue in his mind of all the multiple and intricate properties which we read of for example in the 3rd book of Euclid—but had never seen the geometric figure to which they belonged and in whose nature and essence they were combined. Conceive the problem, placed before a man's mind not as in our present geometry, given the figure to analyze and evolve the properties, but the converse, given a long array of facts and properties to invent a figure which shall contain them. Conceive a man *inventing* the Circle, and you will have an image of the effort which in the region of Nature's subtlest phenomena the Poet has to make, the Lyric Poet in a special sense, for producing what we look down upon as mere *style* and diction.[3]

The geometrical analogy affords a fascinating insight into Clough's conception of what was involved, ideally, in the poetic use of language: the correspondence with T. S. Eliot's notion of the 'objective correlative' need hardly be insisted on. Clough's 'formula' tends to be scientific, not magical. Aware of the richness

[1] 'Lecture on Wordsworth', ibid., p. 114.   [2] Loc. cit.
[3] Ibid., p. 115.

of connotative possibility in the English language, and often exploiting it for some of the most intricate dialectical effects in his poetry, he inclined, nevertheless, to prefer the precision and clarity of denotation to the richness of suggestiveness and implication. In an unpublished lecture 'On Language' he summarized the choices before anyone attempting to make a serious and considered use of words:

> The true rule for distinctness in the use of the vocabulary is to use such words as have been primo applied to visible or tangible objects or images and secundo in a single sense. To draw a tooth is [in the MS. 'maybe' pencilled above 'is'] a better expression than to extract a tooth; because to draw is more plainspoken than to extract. But it cannot be denied that extract is more precise, because the word draw has a host of applications. It is not one image, but a great many.[1]

This 'final Precision' of expression is integrally linked to a kindred one implied, again, in the geometrical analogy. The whole force of that analogy derives from the primacy of perfect, almost mathematically complete, possession of the poetic material, from the importance attached to holding a mental 'catalogue of the multiplex and intricate properties' of the state to be projected in the work of art. This basic necessity of poetry as he conceived it, formulated itself, following the pattern of his general outlook, as an insistence on the object, as an anti-romanticism deeply suspicious of the 'feeling' which so many of his contemporaries tended to regard as the sole proper province of poetry. On these grounds he attacked Wordsworth's 'sentimentality':

> [I]nstead of looking directly at an object and considering it as a thing in itself, and allowing it to operate upon him as a fact in itself, he takes the sentiment produced by it in his own mind as the thing; as the important and really real fact.—The Real thing ceases to be real; the

---

[1] Bodleian MS. Eng. Misc. d. 511, fol. 228. It is worth recalling in connection with Clough's declared preference for denotation Sir Henry Taylor's strictures on the vague, emotive, and associative use of language in the poetry of the Romantics. In this poetry words like 'wild', Taylor pointed out, became 'stockword[s] with those who have more of the feeling of poetry than of discrimination in the use of language, and [are] employed thenceforward with a progressively diminishing concern for [their] intrinsic significancy'. The word 'breathe', as conveying 'some vague impression of beauty and fervour' is for Taylor an example of the 'verb poetical' which carries every meaning except its primary one. H. Taylor, 'Essay on the Poetic Works of Mr. William Wordsworth', *Works*, 5 vols. (London, 1878–9), v. 1–52.

world no longer exists; all that exists is the feeling, somehow generated in the poet's sensibility.[1]

A glancing comment in a letter to Charles Norton on Macaulay's *History of England* further illuminates this aspect of his sensibility. Macaulay had referred to the 'oaks' of Magdalen: '[T]hey are *elms*', Clough wrote. 'There was no occasion to say anything but trees—but the temptation to say something particular was too strong' (*Corr.* ii. 513). Macaulay's search for romantic evocation had emptied words of all particular signification; he had tried to conjure up 'atmosphere' but had dissolved away the object. This attachment to the clear, defined object, not only in the world of things but of ideas, determined Clough's literary preferences. 'First and last', William Allingham wrote, 'Wordsworth was for him the chief among modern poets. He had also much liking for Crabbe, and but little for the rich aërial colourists, such as Keats and Shelley, being always uneasy when he felt his legs taken off the ground. He required a tangible intellectual basis, and was rather suspicious of sentiment and imagination.'[2]

Deeply as he respected the eighteenth century and the neo-classical achievement, Clough did not urge a regressive imitation of the excellences of Dryden and Pope. They were models to be used livingly, models from whom the nineteenth century could learn how to cope in literary terms with itself.

We have had a good deal of new experience, both in study and in action; new books and new events have come before us. But we have not yet in England, I imagine, had anyone to give us a manner suitable to our new matter. There has been a kind of dissolution of English; but no one writer has come to reunite and revivify the escaping components. We have something new to say, but do not know how to say it. . . . Have we anyone who speaks for our day as justly and appropriately as Dryden did for his?[3]

The evolution of his own work as a poet is essentially linked with this felt artistic need to find a historically adequate manner, to work out a linguistic method of articulating with sensitivity and precision a new and complex experience. In his review, 'Recent English Poetry', he further analysed the task before the

[1] 'Lecture on Wordsworth', Trawick, p. 121.
[2] [W. Allingham], 'Arthur Hugh Clough', *Fraser's Magazine*, lxxiv (Oct. 1866), 526–7.
[3] 'Dryden and His Times, Lecture I', Trawick, pp. 95–6.

contemporary poet. Where Matthew Arnold insisted that the perplexities, conflicts, and doubts of the nineteenth century needed to be refracted through the pure centrality of classical form, Clough, staking his claim on the solid reality of obvious, unchallengeable fact, asserted the need to confront directly the realities of present experience. Arnold was 'turning and twisting his eyes, in the hope of seeing things as Homer, Sophocles, Virgil, or Milton saw them'[1]—and if such attempts at the classical vision were both distorting and evasive, so was the romantic withdrawal into nature. What was needed was an art which engaged directly and fully with present actuality. The novel, Clough pointed out, was a more popular form because 'we do here feel an attempt to include these indispensable latest addenda —these phenomena which, if we forget on Sunday, we must remember on Monday—these positive matters of fact, which people, who are not verse-writers, are obliged to have to do with'.[2] Might it be possible therefore, he asked, that modern poetry

should deal, more than at present it usually does, with general wants, ordinary feelings, the obvious rather than the rare facts of human nature? Could it not attempt to convert into beauty and thankfulness, or at least into some form and shape, some feeling, at any rate, of content— the actual, palpable things with which our everyday life is concerned; introduce into business and weary task-work a character and a soul of purpose and reality; intimate to us relations which, in our unchosen, peremptorily-appointed posts, in our grievously narrow and limited spheres of action, we still, in and through all, retain to some central, celestial fact? . . . Might it not divinely condescend to all infirmities; be in all points tempted as we are; exclude nothing, least of all guilt and distress, from its wide fraternization; not content itself merely with talking of what may be better elsewhere, but seek also to deal with what *is* here?[3]

A healthy art could develop only in the context of its whole environment, spring from a comprehensive, uncensored, un-squeamish recognition of all aspects of human life; and, as Mrs. Armstrong has pointed out, his poem, 'O Land of Empire, art and love', ostensibly a satire on over-delicacy, develops this deliberately unsentimental and anti-romantic social theory of art.

---

[1] 'Recent English Poetry', Trawick, p. 160.   [2] Ibid., p. 145.
[3] Ibid., pp. 144–5.

The artistic perfection of the Corinthian column is fecundated and nourished by the totality of its surroundings—the squalid earth as well as the lustrous sky.[1]

One notices, however, a significant modulation in Clough's insistence on social realism as the essential foundation for a truly living modern poetry—and that modulation has important implications for his own life as a poet, since it hints at basic problems, problems of artistic confidence and purpose. The demand for fineness, clarity, and fullness in registering the distinctive texture of contemporary experience is balanced, in 1853, by a rather more coarse-grained assertion that 'general wants, ordinary feelings, the obvious rather than the rare facts of human nature' constitute the proper material of poetry. At his best Clough achieves an alert dialectic between the two, between psychological and analytical subtlety and a stubbornly solid sense of daily actuality, but the dialectic is difficult and vulnerable, threatened by polarizing forces—and, in 1853, we notice the movement towards such a polarization. Significantly, it occurs under the pressure of moral and instructional demand: the muse must become overtly a missionary among the alley-ways and sweat-shops of experience.

The tension about the moral end of poetry one detects here is closely related to that between the realist and the romantic in Clough's sensibility. Although he diverged widely from Matthew Arnold in his respect for the eighteenth-century achievement, he did detect in it deficiencies of a kind generally alleged by the Romantics. The literature of the eighteenth century as a whole was 'as deficient perhaps in force and fertility as it [was] remarkable for justness and propriety and elegance of diction'.[2] In fact, in his evaluation of poetic language Clough exhibits a bifurcation in his attitudes which, while it issues in some of his most complex poetic tonalities, is also important in explaining the unease and uncertainty, the often tentative mixture of modes and languages, in his poetry considered as a body. The preponderant weight of his approval is behind the conversational, the familiar, the easy, rather than the 'poetic' and strained: '[T]he charm of all really great poems is the ease and familiarity and closeness to common language with which they rise out of

---

[1] I. Armstrong, op. cit., pp. 13–15.
[2] 'Lecture on Wordsworth', Trawick, p. 111.

it and exceed and transcend common language.'[1] It is this quality
he admires in Dryden. And yet, 'after all what the littérateurs of
the day have to tell us does not amount to a great deal'; if their
manner is elegant, their matter is meagre.

This barrenness I ascribe in general greatly to that predominance
of the senses and understanding which prevailed naturally after the
high religious excitement. And in particular I think it acted forcibly
to the depression of literature by the tendency to scoff at all expression
of higher feeling or emotion. The British public has always in its
taste a considerable antipathy to sentiment.

But in the time of Charles II this proceeded rather from a disbelief
in the existence of virtues than from a fear of limiting or impairing
them by over-display. . . .

Toward the close of the life of Dryden the force of this anti-poetic
tendency began to be mitigated. Yet . . . how little expression of
personal and individual feeling do we find in the pages of Dryden.

We do not indeed find much direct expression of this in the pages
of Shakespeare: But contained, involved, implied in Shakespeare,
do we not find abundance? To meet our own individual feelings we
nowhere find so much. In the writers whose names succeed Dryden
you will not indeed find so rich a store for recognition as in Shakespeare, but expressions of personal feeling as personal will not any
longer be scanty, nor will those feelings be vulgar, trite or ordinary.[2]

While Clough praised the 'winter-vitality' of the post-Restoration
mind, he noticed the circumscribed reach of a factual empiricism
that excluded all 'intimations of the spiritual world'. 'You will
observe', he remarked,

that in the period commencing with the Restoration and continuing
through the Eighteenth Century—Literature, though gaining infinitely
in variety—loses in elevation; its predominant and characteristic
form is not, as hitherto, the highest, the poetical. What poetry does
exist, is by no means of the highest order, nor aims at the highest
objects. . . . What indeed the really instructive, the serious, and significant form of literature is, it were hard to say; it seems even doubtful
at times—whether it possesses at all any form deserving any such high
sounding epithets. . . .[3]

The charge of 'prose and reason' was not, after all, an entirely
unjustified one: Clough as an heir of the Romantics recognized

1 'Dryden and His Times, Lecture VI', Trawick, p. 101.
2 Ibid., p. 106.
3 'The Development of English Literature', ibid., p. 132.

fully the crucial value of the personal, the intuitive, the affective; but he was also a Victorian, and his remarks on Wordsworth indicate clearly the ways in which as a critic he tended to interpret 'the highest, the poetical'.

> A certain elevation and fixity characterize Wordsworth everywhere. ... To have attained a law, to exercise a lordship by right divine over passions and desires—this is Wordsworth's pre-eminence.
>
> .   .   .
>
> He did not, it is true, [like Byron] sweep away with him the exulting hearts of youth. ... He did not win the eager and attentive ear of high and low, at home and abroad in the entertainment of immortal Waverley novels; but to strive not unsuccessfully to build the lofty rhyme; to lay slowly the ponderous foundations of pillars to sustain man's moral fabric; to fix a centre around which the chaotic elements of human impulse and desire might take solid form and move in their ordered ellipses; to originate a spiritual stability—this was perhaps greater than sweeping over glad blue waters or inditing immortal novels.[1]

The ability to provide a moral basis of stability became a mark of the great poet and his highest claim to value. Further, it was the task of the modern poet to achieve this basis in and through the realities of modern existence, to infuse 'a sense of significance' into 'that often dirty, or at least dingy, work which it is the lot of so many of us to have to do'.[2] Wordsworth, for all his greatness, failed in this respect, especially in his later poetry:

> [H]is sphere was a small one, the objects he lived among unimportant and petty. Retiring early from all conflict and even contact with the busy world, he shut himself out from the elements which it was his business to encounter and to master. ... Perhaps it is only those that are themselves engaged in the thick of the struggle and conflict that rightly can cheer on or fitly can admonish their fellows, or to any good purpose assume the high moral tone.[3]

Clough's approximation to the Carlylean concept of the hero-poet is extremely close, and the stresses implicit in this personal and artistic ideal were intensified by the thoroughness with which he accepted some of the consequences of expressivist theory. Few would quarrel with the general proposition implied

---

[1] 'Lecture on Wordsworth', ibid., pp. 117, 118–19.
[2] 'Recent English Poetry', ibid., p. 145.
[3] 'Lecture on Wordsworth', ibid., pp. 119, 120.

in his lecture on 'The Development of English Literature' that Shakespeare and Milton wrote as they did because of the particularities of their separate natures. It is an entirely different matter when literature is linked morally to biography as it is in his discussion of Scott.

The profounder tones of Walter Scott's soul were never truly sounded until adversity and grief fell upon his latter days, and those old enjoyments in which he seemed to live and move and have his being—his natural and as it were predestined vocation, fell from him and were no more. The constancy, courage, and clear manly sense which, amid broken fortunes, severed ties, and failing health, spirits and intellect, the extracts from his journals given in Mr. Lockhart's Life evince, constitute a picture I think far more affecting than any to be found in Kenilworth or the Bride of Lammermoor. But the sports and amusements of Abbotsford, the riding and coursing and fishing and feasting and entertaining of guests, &c. &c.—these it appears to me a little disappoint, dissatisfy, displease, us; and make us really thankful, while we read, for the foreknowledge that so strong and capable a soul was ere the end to have some nobler work allotted to it, if not in the way of action, at any rate in that of endurance.[1]

The implications of such critical procedures for his own life and his activity as a poet are enormous: they were both liable to an identical kind of scrutiny.

The ideal poet provided dynamic moral example through the spiritual and intellectual stature, the capacious insight, which he expressed both in his life and in his art. As Clough put it in the first of the 'Letters of Parepidemus', 'Some function, indeed, higher than that of mere self-relief, we must conceive of for the writer. To sum up the large experience of ages, to lay the finger on yet unobserved, or undiscovered, phenomena of the Inner Universe, something we can detect of these in the spheric architecture of St. Peter's, in the creative touches of the Tempest.'[2] In 'Come, Poet, Come' (Poems, 107) he put his desire for the ideal prophet into the form of a poetic invocation to the singer who would, in the perfection of his art, read the riddle of the nineteenth century, interpret it and solve it as Homer and Shakespeare had done for their ages. This view of the significance and scope of poetic activity suggests one role which Clough aspired to himself in

[1] 'Lecture on Wordsworth', Trawick, p. 118.
[2] 'Letters of Parepidemus, Number One', ibid., p. 178.

certain moods as a poet and as a man. 'Somehow I fancy that a large experience and a decisiveness of character is necessary to attract the modern world to poetry. Shakespeare and Milton should meet together . . .', he wrote to William Allingham in December 1850 (*Corr.* i. 287). And yet decisiveness of the kind required by his age was precisely the quality that eluded him. The independence which he developed at Oriel was in many ways a privilege conceded to him as a pre-condition of leadership, and we have noticed a characteristic ambivalence in the attitude of the age towards its prophet-figures; sanctioning revelation and desiring it, it also required that prophecy, however critical about incidentals, should conform to existing moral and social law, should support and not subvert. Although Clough was often exasperated at the role which had devolved upon him, although he frequently rebelled against it, he was, in the final analysis, quite willing to accept it. In a letter to Tom Arnold, written during possibly the most depressed period of his life, he visualized himself as undergoing the preparative processes necessary to a final, effulgent activity: perhaps he was like the piece of coal in the fireplace that had to undergo aeons of imprisonment and compression before its final combustion into heat and light (*Corr.* i. 279). In a letter to Blanche Smith written two years later, after he had failed to obtain the Professorship in Sydney in hopes of which he had got engaged, he admitted that it was impossible, in his present condition, to fulfil the official requirement and legitimize himself.

What I had rather looked forward to originally in case of not going to Sydney, was unmarried poverty and literary work. . . . But I find myself utterly reluctant to enter on that sort of career quite independently of you. I do soberly think it replete with temptations and probable mischief for me, and that I am in no way called upon to talk to the world, (having nothing to say worth their serious attention) . . . (*Corr.* i. 303).

Obviously the strain of withholding and independence was beginning to tell; Blanche Smith appeared as a nostrum even for his literary ills. To persist in the course he had followed hitherto would be to perpetuate the 'mischief' his independence tempted him into.

For from the very outset Clough was acutely aware of the difficulties in the way of moral leadership. Unlike the more

confident prophets of his time, he was intensely conscious of the
danger of 'false or arbitrary positiveness'. As he said in his lecture
on Wordsworth,

> There is such a thing in Morals as in all Science, as drawing your
> conclusion before you have properly got your premises. It is desirable
> to attain a fixed point: but it is essential that the fixed point be the
> right one. We ought to hold fast by what is true; but because we hold
> wilfully fast it does not follow what we hold fast to is true. If you have
> got the truth, be as positive as you please; but because you choose to
> be positive, do not therefore be sure you have the truth.[1]

Such an awareness knocked the prophet's pedestal from under him;
the visionary stance became impossible to maintain.

Translated into literary terms the general ambivalence of
Clough's relationship with the accredited values of his age manifested itself as an uneasy awareness of the disparity between literary
ideal and actual performance. One result, very possibly, was the
uniformly deprecating tones in which he spoke of his own
work, a tone which can obviously be explained, in other terms,
by his shyness and reserve. But this shyness, as I remarked earlier,
was not a cause but a symptom of his personal uncertainty. His
shyness as a poet, similarly, grew out of the uncertainty of his
literary values. He was not entirely convinced of the literary
stature of his work; he was not entirely convinced of the modes
he employed or the attitudes he expressed. The polarity involved
in his literary life is most clearly seen, perhaps, if we place beside
'Come, Poet, Come' the unfinished poem beginning 'If to write,
rewrite, and write again' (Poems, 435), in which the doggerel
underlines the ironic absence of any fineness, elevation, or nobility
in the felt compulsion to write, and the claim to poetic stature is
reduced almost to vanishing point. Oscillating between these two
poles, Clough achieved the voice most congenial to modern
readers at the peak of his personal and intellectual independence,
when he most clearly broke away from prevailing literary
fashions. 'Like Bagehot,' V. S. Pritchett wrote,

> Clough is one of the few Victorians who seem to belong to our time
> rather than their own. The lack of the histrionic air, the lack of that
> invoked and obligatory sense of greatness, so characteristic of the
> chief . . . writers of the age, makes these two writers at once accessible

<hr>

[1] Trawick, p. 120.

to us. . . . [H]is unofficial manner, his truthfulness about personal feeling, his nonchalance, his curiosity, even his bitterness and his use of anticlimax, are closer to the poets of the Thirties than they were to his contemporaries. His line is clean. His lack of pretence is austere.[1]

But the finished artistry of this manner, which reached its brilliant best in *Amours de Voyage*, and rested on Clough's refusal to submit to the literary, intellectual, and spiritual pieties of his time, was the reticent—perhaps at points even reluctant—artistry of a man who was enough of a conformist to be exceptionally sensitive about his heterodoxy.

[1] V. S. Pritchett, 'The Poet of Tourism', *Books in General* (London, 1953), pp. 1, 6.

CHAPTER VI

Ambarvalia, Adam and Eve, The Bothie of Tober-na-Vuolich

I. AMBARVALIA

LINKING himself in poetic partnership with Burbidge, Clough published *Ambarvalia* in January 1849. Although *The Bothie of Tober-na-Vuolich* had been published a couple of months earlier, all his contributions to the later volume had been written before he embarked on his long narrative poem, and they include substantially (the only important omission is '*Epi-Strauss-ium*') all the shorter poems he wrote at Oxford. I have already commented on some of the undergraduate poetry in this volume; the later poetry calls for attention here. To speak generally—too generally, perhaps, since a poem like '*Qua Cursum Ventus*' so obviously resists such characterizations—the later poems originate in the same self-revelatory impulses as Clough's undergraduate poetry, but the emphasis shifts from immediate, relatively unmediated, emotional unburdening. They tend to be markedly more cerebral in coping with the fact and process of self-consciousness, more confidently intellectual and perplexed in both substance and procedure. Emotion does not evaporate: at times, as in a few of the more intense and direct love poems, it pours itself out nakedly; but, more typically, it exists interstitially, discovering and creating itself out of the frictions of analysis, encompassing, implying, transfusing itself through the act of inspection. The poetry is uneven—but one senses in that unevenness much more clearly than in any of the earlier poetry an active attempt at finding a true level. And that attempt itself is illuminating, since it mirrors so closely some larger issues and problems.

The lines beginning 'Why should I say I see the things I see not' (*Poems*, 21) indicate especially clearly the nature of some of these problems. The first section of the poem presents the intricate evolutions of a dance to loud and insistent music, as an image of conforming, untroubled, day-to-day life. The predicament of the poet is that of the dancer who is deaf to this music which fills everyone else's ears: should he conform meaninglessly or should he stop in his tracks, jeopardizing both himself and his partner? Perhaps his deafness is only temporary and soon to be broken by sudden perception and full engagement. But what if this music is only a deluding figment? Clough opens with four lines which have at least the virtue of freshness in their colloquial simplicity and vigour:

> Why should I say I see the things I see not,
>   Why be and be not?
> Show love for that I love not, and fear for what I fear not?
> And dance about to music that I hear not?

Then suddenly and sharply the strength disappears:

> Who standeth still i' the street
> Shall be hustled and justled about;
> And he that stops i' the dance shall be spurned by the dancers' feet,—
> Shall be shoved and be twisted by all he shall meet,
>   And shall raise up an outcry and rout;
>   And the partner, too,—
>   What's the partner to do?
> While all the while 'tis but, perchance, an humming in mine ear,
>   That yet anon shall hear,
>   And I anon, the music in my soul,
>   In a moment read the whole; . . .

The muscularity of 'hustled' and 'shoved' and 'twisted' becomes merely truculent in an academically 'literary' welter of alliteration and poetical locution.

The second section of the poem proposes a distinction between 'two musics'—that of the first section which is 'loud and bold and coarse' and 'only of fumes of foolish fancy bred', and another which is 'soft and low | Stealing whence we not know' (the inversion is characteristic of the strain in eking out metre and rhyme). To this second we are exhorted to give our attention. The third and final section confirms the reality of this elusive music, the existence of which is only tentatively proposed in the second. Beginning with a rhetorically flourishing 'Yea', it closes with an unequivocal intimation:

> So may the ear,
> Hearing, not hear,

Though drums do roll, and pipes and cymbals ring;
So the bare conscience of the better thing
Unfelt, unseen, unimaged, all unknown,
May fix the entrancèd soul 'mid multitudes alone.

The flabby ambiguities in the two 'mays' shuffle by under cover
of the show of confidence in the authoritative rhythms. The still,
small voice beneath the sounding brass is very still, very small,
and very complacent.

The rather odd title of Clough and Burbidge's joint volume
has been accounted for as 'a gesture of modesty'.[1] Two discarded
stanzas from an early draft of the poem we have been considering
suggest that possibly the authors were not actuated entirely by
this motive. Originally these stanzas were placed between the
first and second sections of the poem.

Age on age succeeding fast
From a far heroic past
      They went their rounds
      And beat the bounds
         Of old Imperial Rome
The Ambarvalian brothers Nine with hymns and sacred song
      That immemorial line along
      Of that august and holy home.

Even so Poets now
With more than priestly vow
Made separate from their birth
Walk the great world and mete the measures of the Earth
      And following on their feet
      Their acolytes withal
Who catching notes that haply fall
      From the great prophetic song
Tell them out loudly to the listening throng.

                                                    (*Poems*, 467.)

The insistent Victorian urge to strike prophetic attitudes, to see
visions and hear voices in poetry, could hardly be more clear, and
is causally related to the evolution of the final version. It pre-
scribes the quality of the assertions, the spurious timbre of the
language.

[1] I. Armstrong, *Arthur Hugh Clough* (London, 1962), p. 17.

Similar processes of failure can be observed in 'When Israel came out of Egypt' (*Poems*, 16). Contrasting primitive superstitious belief with modern scientific and mechanistic scepticism, Clough rejects both as unknowing constructs of reality. He exhorts his readers instead to 'Take better part, with manlier heart', to 'wait in faith | God's self-completing plan', which some 'chosen prophet-soul' will divulge to them from his communings with the deity 'Within the shroud of blackest cloud'. The verse is competent, heavily scored and insistently rhythmical, employing internal rhyme (a frequent device of Clough's) to speed up and tighten the metrical movement. But there is nothing exciting in it, no arresting nerve of thought, no sinew of emotional evolution—only inert and spurious assertion. The vagueness about the new revelation that is somehow to be achieved merely underlines the false oracular tone. To sustain that tone Clough once again falls back on poetic inversion, on derivation and imitation in his use of language, on an automatic and self-exhausted ventriloquism. To count the number of times he uses the Miltonic noun–adjective, adjective–noun–adjective collocation in a poem of 126 lines is instructive.

To place beside these two poems the well-known '*Qui Laborat Orat*' (*Poems*, 12) is to see at once the pernicious effect of this prophetic impulse. Dealing with a similar theme, the poem proves decisively, I think, that the subject of religion was not in itself, as some critics have implied, a necessary blight on Clough's poetry. Faith, equally firm if more humble, is presented here in an integrated, carefully discriminated evolution of thought and emotion.

> O only Source of all our light and life,
>   Whom as our truth, our strength, we see and feel,
> But whom the hours of mortal moral strife
>   Alone aright reveal!

The sheer economy and simplicity of the phrasing, familiar yet dignified, communicate without strain and with faultless precision the subtleties of content and response. 'Our truth, our strength'—two separate qualities, but by the juxtaposition strength also appears as a qualifying attribute of truth; 'mortal moral strife' again carries a multiple implication—human life is moral strife, moral strife is mortal in the sense of mortally serious, the nature of the moral strife we know on earth is limited by our mortality.

> If well-assured 'tis but profanely bold
>   In thought's abstracted forms to seem to see,
> It dare not dare the dread communion hold
>   In ways unworthy Thee, . . .

Stripped, unreverberative language is skilfully deployed to achieve a superb intellectual and emotional control in this rejection of the finite intellect. 'Profanely' in this fourth stanza links up with the 'mortal' of the first through 'earthly' in the third, and the negation of the thus-qualified mortality—partly because it is 'profane' and not admitted to the sanctum—follows with unhesitating exactitude: 'to seem to see, | It dare not dare'. The translatable 'content' of the poem is very similar to that of 'When Israel came out of Egypt'; the qualitative gap is enormous.

> Nor times shall lack, when while the work it plies,
>   Unsummoned powers the blinding film shall part,
> And scarce by happy tears made dim, the eyes
>   In recognition start.

> But, as thou willest, give or e'en forbear
>   The beatific supersensual sight,
> So, with Thy blessing blest, that humbler prayer
>   Approach Thee morn and night.

The faith is unshaken but the stridency has disappeared. The yearned-for revelation, described in the first of these two last stanzas, is reduced to a completely dependent possibility in the second, where the sudden metaphysical and technically abstract 'beatific supersensual' erupts into the true and enormous dimensions of the asked-for revelation when set beside the 'humbler prayer' of actual earthly labour.

Apart from the poems on religious and ethical subjects, the poems on love (a significant extension of Clough's themes) form the most important large group in his section of *Ambarvalia*, and in these he is, on the whole, more interested—and effective—in analysing and celebrating than in declaring personal emotion. Poems like 'My wind is turned to bitter north', "ὁ θεὸς μετὰ σοῦ", and "ἐπὶ Λάτμῳ" are emotional lyrics which suggest in their immediacy an actual living and impelling experience. As poems, however, their importance lies mainly in their revelation of an unexpected ardency in Clough. Much more fruitful is the poetry in which he brings the complexities of his self-consciousness to bear on the dissection of the phenomenon of love itself and its baffling paradoxes. If some of the shortcomings of his religious and ethical poems can be traced—when failure is not simply a matter of the insufficiency or irrelevance of inspiration—to a retreat into a particular interpretation of what was acceptable and expected, a similar uncertainty and failure of nerve can be detected in this love poetry. Clough attempts to be unfashionably intellectual and pretty at the same time.

> Ah, what is love, our love, she said,
>> Ah, what is human love?
> A fire, of earthly fuel fed,
>> Full fain to soar above.
> With lambent flame the void it lips,
>> And of the impassive air
> Would frame for its ambitious steps
>> A heaven-attaining stair.
> It wrestles and it climbs—Ah me,
>> Go look in little space,
> White ash on blackened earth will be
>> Sole record of its place.
>
> (Poems, 2.)

The effort to invest intellectual inquiry with liquidness of utterance ('With lambent flame the void it lips')[1] dissipates the force of the integrating image of an aspiring and yet self-consuming fire, just as the dramatic opening question contributes little apart from its female prettification. Clough resorts to exclamatory padding and decoration in an attempt to authenticate this poetry.

A much less inert poem, more confidently occupying itself with the abstract consideration of the nature of love and the difficulties in the right choice of a life-partner, is that beginning 'When panting sighs the bosom fill' (*Poems*, 4).[2]

> When panting sighs the bosom fill,
> And hands by chance united thrill

---

[1] The prettification is even more apparent in the draft additional lines printed by the Oxford editors (*Poems*, p. 458), in which a 'glorious band of Angel faces' keep watch from 'roseate clouds'.

[2] F. L. Mulhauser has shown how Clough originally started with a personal consideration of the best time for a man to marry, and moved through successive, and progressively less direct, versions to a completely impersonal philosophical consideration of the nature of love and its relation to reason. 'Clough's "Love and Reason"', *Modern Philology* (hereafter *MP*) xlii (Nov. 1945), 174–86.

> At once with one delicious pain
> The pulses and the nerves of twain;
> When eyes that erst could meet with ease,
> Do seek, yet, seeking, shyly shun
> Extatic conscious unison,—
> The sure beginnings, say, be these,
> Prelusive to the strain of love
> Which angels sing in heaven above?

This is not completely successful. The exaggerated decorum is at
first puzzling, and requires, perhaps, the reassuring confirmation
of light parody provided by the bantering triplets of earlier
versions.[1] Once the delicate ironies grafted into the language are
recognized, however, the tactic becomes clearer. The precise,
elaborately formal 'prelusive' sustains a stiff elevation which is
undercut by the sub-verbal smile lurking in the question posed by
the next stanza ('zest' is exact and subversive):

> Or is it but the vulgar tune,
> Which all that breathe beneath the moon
> So accurately learn—so soon?
> With variations duly blent;
> Yet that same song to all intent,
> Set for the finer instrument;
> It is; and it would sound the same
> In beasts, were not the bestial frame,
> Less subtly organised, to blame;
> And but that soul and spirit add
> To pleasures, even base and bad,
> A zest the soulless never had.

The long, easy sentences pattern themselves closely on informal
spoken rhythms, and counterpoint the strict presence of the
couplet. Turning on themselves, qualifying, expanding the
thought, the sentences are caught up at distant intervals by
syntactical connectives, and, by their satisfying completeness of
unhurried, intricate statement, make poetry out of logical
process. The sinew of intellection remains taut throughout the
poem: 'It may be ... But what if ... Yet ... For if ...'. And the
adequacy of this apparently loose discursiveness is not the only
pleasure the poem affords. Clough skilfully combines varying
poetic 'voices' to give particular shape to the altering contours of
the argument:

---

[1] See *Poems*, pp. 459–62.

> Let Reason first her office ply;
> Esteem, and admiration high,
> And mental, moral sympathy,
> Exist they first, nor be they brought
> By self-deceiving afterthought,—

The schoolroom voice, dusty, cautious, unconceding, is suddenly edged aside by the enraptured speculation of the devotee:

> What if an halo interfuse
> With these again its opal hues,
> That all o'erspreading and o'erlying,
> Transmuting, mingling, glorifying,
> About the beauteous various whole,
> With beaming smile do dance and quiver; . . .

But the rapture is cut short by another shift; the utterance of the enthusiast is countered by the cool dubiety of the sceptic:

> Yet, is that halo of the soul?—
> Or is it, as may sure be said,
> Phosphoric exhalation bred
> Of vapour, steaming from the bed
> Of Fancy's brook, or Passion's river?

This is the voice of the scientist basing his doubt on the intractable matter delivered by physics and chemistry. Interesting as these manœuvres are, however, they are interesting only as potentialities. 'When panting sighs' offers insights into possibilities in Clough's art, but is itself too tentative in its possession of those possibilities to be remarkably successful. The poem is more incipient than achieved.

In exploiting logical and argumentative process as he does, in the intellectualism of his figures, in the aliveness of his ratiocination, and in his occasional approximation to ordinary speech, Clough shows some affinities with the Metaphysical tradition,[1] just as in the ease and perspicuity of movement he sometimes achieves, in his generalizing tendency, in his preference for denotation and simile he reveals a kinship with Dryden, Cowley, and the eighteenth century. His frequently witty handling of serious material links him with both traditions; he is one of the few Victorian poets who can be serious without being solemn,

---

[1] For a good discussion of the Metaphysical element in Clough's poetry see Houghton, pp. 49–55.

handle poetry lightly without writing avowedly 'comic' verse. One of his earliest essays in this vein is the occasional poem, at least partly composed in 1845, beginning 'The Silver Wedding! on some pensive ear' (*Poems*, 19). In fifteen four-line stanzas he allows his mind engagingly relaxed play over the paradoxes growing out of the name of this particular anniversary. The silver of age looks back on golden youth and the golden day of the wedding twenty-five years ago; the years inevitably devalue the original, unsullied experience. And yet, the perfection implied in 'golden anniversary' attends maturest age, and if, in this time-flow, the silver of the present is later to be changed to gold, then the logic of this symbolism of value demands that the gold of the wedding day should be of less worth than the silver of the anniversary. The paradox is resolved through a closer examination of the gold of the wedding day. Its value was unrealized value,

> . . . its hopes, its joys were golden too,
>   But golden of the fairy gold of dreams:
> To feel is but to dream; until we do,
>   There's nought that is, and all we see but seems.

The contradiction is banished, the logical progression, fairy gold . . . silver . . . gold . . ., established, and Clough, throwing the thought forward in time to the day when the genuine silver of the present anniversary will be changed to pure gold, compares the processes of time and change to chemical transformation in two stanzas in which the scientific, neologistic conceit further confirms the sub-Metaphysical strain in his poetic sensibility. Through the artificial intricacies of conceit he manages to contain aesthetically some of his most profoundly disturbed perceptions about human life.

> Come years as many yet, and as they go,
>   In human life's great crucible shall they
> Transmute, so potent are the spells they know,
>   Into pure gold the silver of to-day.

> Strange metallurge is human life! 'Tis true;
>   And Use and Wont in many a gorgeous case
> Full specious fair for casual outward view
>   Electrotype the sordid and the base.

'*Natura Naturans*' (*Poems*, 36), the most remarkable poem in the whole volume, combines wit and intelligence with an astonishingly modern celebration of human sexuality as part of a cosmic vitalism. It is refreshing and startling also in its frank assault on a subject which Early-Victorians preferred on the whole to keep officially unexplored and unrecognized—especially in poetry.

The reviewer of *Ambarvalia* in the *Literary Gazette* declared 'Natura Naturans' 'trash', the very worst type of 'Cloughage'. 'The scene', he wrote scornfully,

is a second-class carriage on the railroad, where this unconscious inhaling takes place. . . . This casual youth informs us that 'her life was in him then' and that they 'fused in one', or something of that mysterious sort, and the circumjacent world began to partake of this wondrous influence, most alliteratively. . . . And then there is some nonsense about our first parents in Eden.[1]

When Blanche Clough came to edit her husband's poems, she found this one particularly distressing and fought tooth and nail against reprinting it. On 18 April 1862 she wrote to Charles Norton declaring her dislike: 'I do so dislike the Natura Naturans, and it was my impression that my husband did not intend it to be republished.' Her impression, as Norton pointed out, was a decidedly wrong one. Seven days later she wrote, 'The only thing I particularly desire is to leave out Natura Naturans which is abhorrent to me.' (In her first letter she had attempted also to proscribe 'The Latest Decalogue' from the American edition which Norton was preparing.) On 10 June she recurred to the offensive poem:

About the Natura Naturans I am sorry if you regret its absence, and if Mr. Emerson and Mr. Lowell do so. . . . Of course I feel it may to some people convey a poetic intuition; of course one is sorry to lose anything that is truly individual;—but—I do not feel, myself, that it is necessary to an understanding of his mind (Is not the same idea given in a passage of the Amours—'All that is Nature's is I')—while I do know that, at least in this country, it is liable to great misconception. Still what you say, with Mr. Lowell's and Mr. Emerson's opinion, backed by the fact that my husband intended it to reappear, cannot but have great weight. . . .[2]

Henry Sidgwick was an altogether less conventional person than Blanche Clough, yet he too, although he personally liked the poem, changed his mind about it and advised against its

---

[1] Review of *Ambarvalia*, *Literary Gazette*, lxv (21 Apr. 1849), 292–3.
[2] MS. letters in the Houghton Library, Harvard (1126, 1129, 1133).

publication in a selection: '[T]he unreserve of Natura is unique; and is something to which people in general are much less accustomed than they are to religious scepticism. I think I should leave it out in a selection.'[1] '*Natura Naturans*' was not republished in 1862.

The poem re-creates sudden, spontaneous, and unthinking sexual awareness in a railway carriage, and then proceeds to relate the experience of that awareness to the vital cosmic energy implied in the Spinozistic title. The first three stanzas record the strangely mutual sexual realization which, casually and insidiously as an odour, suddenly takes possession of both man and woman. The fourth stanza, resuming the initial situation, prepares, by its delicate irony, for the next major movement in the poetic evolution:

> As unsuspecting mere a maid
>   As, fresh in maidhood's bloomiest bloom,
> In casual second-class did e'er
>   By casual youth her seat assume;
> Or vestal, say, of saintliest clay,
>   For once by balmiest airs betrayed
> Unto emotions too too sweet
>   To be unlingeringly gainsaid: . . .

The casual everyday literalness of the third and fourth line deflates the outrageously stilted references to the girl, and, by playing an ironic thread into the linguistic texture, sharpens our reaction to 'saintliest clay'. The fifth stanza continues this finely adjusted tongue-in-cheek poise which gracefully includes subsidiary tensions and preserves a perfect literary tact.

> Unowning then, confusing soon
>   With dreamier dreams that o'er the glass
> Of shyly ripening woman-sense
>   Reflected, scarce reflected, pass,
> A wife may-be, a mother she
>   In Hymen's shrine recalls not now,
> She first in hour, ah, not profane,
>   With me to Hymen learnt to bow.

If 'dreamier dreams', along with its implications of faintness, confusion, and impermanence, tends to cast doubt on the reality of both love and simple sexual awakening, it also releases, by that

---

[1] Henry Sidgwick to Blanche Clough, 14 Mar. 1870. Bodleian MS. Eng. Lett. e. 84, fols. 62^v–63. Not included in Mulhauser's catalogue.

downward association of both, the possibility of the subsequent
upward revaluation of both: the *un*profaneness of the unackow-
ledged shrine is ironically established.

In the next stanza the particular sensation is widened into its
affinities with the whole pulsing world of organic nature:

> Ah no!—Yet owned we, fused in one,
>   The Power which e'en in stones and earths
> By blind elections felt, in forms
>   Organic breeds to myriad births;
> By lichen small on granite wall
>   Approved, its faintest feeblest stir
> Slow-spreading, strengthening long, at last
>   Vibrated full in me and her.

Once made, the connection is elaborated into a gigantic, hyper-
bolic fantasy of creative, evolutionary energy, the wild rankness
evoked is shot through with a wry humour which derives its
energy from the earlier play of irony in the poem:

> In me and her—sensation strange!
>   The lily grew to pendent head,
> To vernal airs the mossy bank
>   Its sheeny primrose spangles spread,
> In roof o'er roof of shade sun-proof
>   Did cedar strong itself outclimb,
> And altitude of aloe proud
>   Aspire in floreal crown sublime;
>
> Flashed flickering forth fantastic flies,
>   Big bees their burly bodies swung,
> Rooks roused with civic din the elms,
>   And lark its wild reveillez rung;
> In Libyan dell the light gazelle,
>   The leopard lithe in Indian glade,
> And dolphin, brightening tropic seas,
>   In us were living, leapt and played:
>
> Their shells did slow crustacea build,
>   Their gilded skins did snakes renew,
> While mightier spines for loftier kind
>   Their types in amplest limbs outgrew;
> Yea, close comprest in human breast,
>   What moss, and tree, and livelier thing,
> What Earth, Sun, Star of force possest,
>   Lay budding, burgeoning forth for Spring.

The heavily charged sexual imagery of the first of these stanzas is redeemed from simply foetid luxuriance by the sudden wild extravagance of alliteration, alternately crisp and liquidly full. Together with the packed rhythms and the impetuously pro- liferating images the alliterative compulsion enacts the helpless intensity of the creative dance. But it also—and simultaneously— writes a prodigal fantastic humour into the felt sensation, and prepares us for the last extravagance in which the second-class carriage is linked with the final immensities of space and the human pair becomes a microcosm of all creative force. The out- ward movement in space, through the whole range of matter, is replaced in the next stanza by a movement backward in time to the primal Garden, where man and woman walked and embraced sinlessly and unashamedly. The last stanza introduces a somewhat disappointingly conventional note, moralizing the poem and necessarily weakening it, since it denies what has been, in fact, achieved. Gathering together the imagery of growth and vernal abundance, it extends it through notions of futurity and con- sequence to the prospect of eventual fruition. We are reminded of the 'mystic love' which alone sanctions and transforms young desire, of the 'Spirit's Sun' which alone fructifies it.

In the short poems he wrote at Oxford Clough is more often disappointing than not. His earnestness, his drabness, his maimed technique, the frequent doubtfulness of his artistic concern, have been frequently enough insisted on. In recent years, however, we have been encouraged to recognize in some of these poems qualities which went insufficiently regarded before. We are learning to recognize his wit, his irony, his clarity, his intellectual and emotional toughness. Elegance, however, is not a quality we sufficiently acknowledge in him. And yet, as his letters reveal, he was capable of sharp deftnesses of social notation, often delicately turned on a single, understated, adroit epithet:

Brodie is going to be married. . . . To a Miss Thompson, daughter of . . . a titular Serjeant, living on his means, in Belgravia. Age, 21; he being 31; complexion dark, character, conjectured immature, but not quite decypherable to my informant; manners, lively; and indicative of intelligence; on the whole follows Mama rather than Papa, Papa being slightly Evangelical, Mama exclusively accomplishmentarian.[1]

[1] Letter to Tom Arnold, 31 Jan. 1848. *New Zealand Letters of Thomas Arnold the Younger*, ed. J. Bertram (Wellington, 1966), pp. 73–4.

The deft sensitivity which was to issue finally in the fastidious self-confidence of *Amours de Voyage* gives us in *Ambarvalia* the three delightful 'Commemoration Sonnets' (*Poems*, 7–9). Written on the occasion of the King of Saxony's visit to Oxford in 1844, they bring a delicate wit to bear on their observation of the social scene. In the second of these, for instance, Clough neatly evokes the ever-so-slight misjudgements in Oxford's entertainment of its royal visitor. The polka mania, incidentally, which gripped England in 1844, would have all the exciting novelty of the 'latest thing'.

> Thou whom thy danglers have ere this forgot,
> O Leonina! whether thou wert seen
> Waiting, upon the Isis' margent green,
> The boats that should have passed there and did not;
> Or at the ball, admiring crowds between,
> To partner academical and slow
> Teaching, upon the light Slavonic toe,
> Polkas that were not, only should have been;
> Or in the crowded gallery crushed, didst hear
> For bonnets white, blue, pink, the ladies' cheer
> Multiplied while divided, and endure
> (Thyself being seen) to see, not hear, rehearse
> The long, long Proses, and the Latin Verse—
> O Leonina! Thou wert tired, I'm sure.

The organization of the sestet in each of these sonnets is worth notice, especially when we remember that as a rule deftness in rhyming is not one of Clough's strong points. Here the use of rhyme to support and confirm nuance of implication is masterly. The pattern in the first sonnet, abbb aa, is changed in the second to aa bccb. The floating pattern is suddenly anchored in the final sonnet in three rhyming couplets which clinch the light mockery of the whole series:

> Uncrowned thou com'st, alone, or with a tribe
> Of volant varlets scattering jest and jibe
> Almost beside thee. Yet to thee, when rent
> Was the Teutonic Caesar's robe, there went
> One portion: and with Julius, thou to-day
> Canst boast, I came, I saw, I went away!

2. *ADAM AND EVE*

. . . and yet indeed 'tis true
E'en in my utmost impotence I find
A fount of strange persistence in my soul;
Also, and that perchance is stranger still,
A wakeful, changeless touchstone in my brain,
Receiving, noting, testing all the while
These passing, curious, new phenomena,
Painful, and yet not painful unto it.
Though tortured in the crucible I lie,
Myself my own experiment, yet still
I, or a something that is I indeed,
A living, central, and more inmost I
Within the scales of mere exterior me's,
I—seem eternal, O thou God, as Thou;
Have knowledge of the Evil and the Good,
Superior in a higher Good to both.

(*Adam and Eve*, Scene II, lines 30–45; *Poems*, 414–15.)

So Adam in *Adam and Eve*—and the shock is startling. Clough's earlier verse prepares us only in the most distant and occasional ways for this denuded, marvellously supple strength, this directness, this command, this fluidity. By July 1848 he had written enough of the dramatic poem to submit it to Matthew Arnold for his comments[1]—but the poem was far from complete. He continued to write additional scenes for it till 1850, but he neither completed nor published it and it remained untitled at his death. For its first publication in 1869 Mrs. Clough decided to call it *Fragments of the Mystery of the Fall*, although Clough himself had named the two notebooks in which he wrote the main drafts 'Adam and Eve Notebook 1' and 'Adam and Eve Notebook 2'. The Oxford editors called the poem simply *The Mystery of the Fall* (*Poems*, 410), but, as Houghton has pointed out,[2] this title has no warrant from Clough.

Fragmentary as it is, *Adam and Eve* is a crucial poem. Confidently centring itself in the labyrinthine interiors of psychological and intellectual process, it engages complexly and sensitively with the religious and ethical speculations which

[1] Lowry, pp. 86, 87.
[2] Houghton, p. 81. I have adopted Houghton's title but not his interpretative arguments in its favour.

Clough's whole experience at Oxford released. In doing so it initiates themes and techniques which are directly relevant to *Amours de Voyage* and *Dipsychus*. It simultaneously celebrates and scrutinizes the intellectual as hero, the intellectual not simply as intellectual but as artist, celebrator and victim of self-consciousness, the godlike, impiously daring player who creates in his perplexed play a precarious, intensely private and persistent reality, a non-attached, self-justified, and justifying world which, while it draws on human experience, repudiates time, space, and human limitation, and lies beyond ordinary formulas of good and evil. His first attempt at a long poem, *Adam and Eve* is also the first poem in which he exploits extensively the multiple, refracted, frequently introverted, perspectives of a form which exists between lyric and drama, to explore and encompass an elusive, continually self-modifying sense of reality. The incompleteness of the poem imposes severe limitations on its achievement, but even within these limitations Clough displays an impressive dramatic skill, objectivity, and alertness. The lines, for instance, with which I opened this discussion offer a splendid vindication of and insight into the psychology of the intellectual —and yet, a mere four lines later, here is Adam again:

> Really now, had I only time and space,
> And were not troubled with this wife of mine,
> And the necessity of meat and drink,
> I really do believe,
> With time and space and proper quietude
> I could resolve the problem on my brain.
>
> (II. 50–5.)

The delicate comedy of the intellectual's life, so godlike in its self-sufficient potentiality and yet so pitifully contingent, leaps into sudden vividness. Poor Adam, so deluded in his wistful earnestness as he trudges about his affairs! The short fourth line skilfully catches up the previous three (the naïvely ingenious 'reallys' tapping home in their conversational pseudo-precision the falsity of his dream), to pause in momentary suspense before the final swift dimensionless absurdity. This is the kind of doubleness of perception skilfully translated into language that later gives us the consummate figure of Claude in *Amours de Voyage*.

The arrestingly bare opening dialogue presents the opposed viewpoints of Adam and Eve in terms which are deceptively similar.

> *Adam*   Since that last evening we have fallen indeed!
> Yes, we have fallen, my Eve! O yes!—
> One, two, and three, and four;—the appetite,
> The enjoyment, the aftervoid, the thinking of it—
> Specially the latter two, most specially the last.
> There, in synopsis, see, you have it all:
> Come, let us go and work!
>   Is it not enough?
> What, is there three, four, five?
> *Eve*   Oh, guilt, guilt, guilt!
>   (I. 1–8.)

As Houghton has remarked, the opening speech read by itself would seem to belong to Eve rather than to Adam, and he has seen evidence here of what he calls Adam's 'dipsychan' nature, rejecting and yet attached to Christian guilt.[1] To some extent Adam is 'dipsychan', but perhaps this is not a complete account. Never in the whole poem does Adam deny a fall; it is on the question of whether it is a fall or a Fall that he differs from his wife—is it an inevitable access of self-consciousness resulting from unavoidable processes of growth, or is it, as Eve would have it, a religious and culpable alienation resulting from a punishable act of disobedience? In May 1847 Clough had written to his sister, 'The thing[s] which men must work at ... [are] ... philosophical problems of Grace and Free Will, and of Redemption as an Idea, not as an historical event' (*Corr.* i. 182). Two years later Prichard was writing to him, 'It did not need more than the little I have known of you the last year or two, to teach me that any doubts— or more—of the truth of the Xian System which you might feel, were grounded on what you say of its not satisfying your ideal of man's nature' (*Corr.* i. 239). Adam's conception of the fall is to be seen analogously as an attempt to extricate the notion of a fall from historical Christianity (with its machinery of religiously legislated Guilt, Punishment, Atonement), and to establish it as an eternal metaphysical fact generative of metaphysical shame and guilt. 'The appetite, the enjoyment, the aftervoid, the thinking of

---

[1] Houghton, p. 85.

it'—the processes of the fall are perpetual, inherent in the human condition, not necessarily attached to the transcendental consequence formulated in Christian eschatology. Adam's conception of the fall, complicated by his retreat in weaker moments into the terrors of traditional religious guilt, is so close to Eve's, and yet so different, that it becomes virtually impossible for them to speak to one another. He meditates aloud about his new-born son, Cain:

> This child is born of us, and therefore like us;
> Is born of us, and therefore is as we;
> Is born of us, and therefore is not pure;
> Earthy as well as godlike; bound to strive—
> Not doubtfully I augur from the past—
> Through the same straits of anguish and of doubt,
> 'Mid the same storms of terror and alarm,
> To the calm ocean which he yet shall reach,
> He or himself or in his sons hereafter,
> Of consummated consciousness of self.
> The selfsame stuff which wrought in us to grief
> Runs in his veins; and what to work in him?
>
> (III. 49–60.)

The statement drops stone-like into the committed pool of Eve's consciousness, disturbing her happiness in motherhood, setting up far-spreading ripples of religious implication:

> *Eve*   This child is born of us, and therefore like us—
>
> *Adam*   Most true, mine own; and if a man like me
> Externally, internally I trust
> Most like (his best original) to thee.
>
> *Eve*   Is born of us, and therefore is not pure—
>
> *Adam*   Did I say that? I know not what I said;
> It was a foolish humour; but, indeed,
> Whatever you may think, I have not learnt
> The trick of deft suppression, e'en the skill
> To sort my thoughts and sift my words enough.
> Not pure, indeed!—And if it is not pure,
> What is? . . .
>
> (III. 76–87.)

As the slow germinating thought begins to take shape in Eve's mind, shape, that is, in her terms of theological guilt and

impureness, of trespass and punishment, Adam's hurriedly molli-
fying words are actuated as much by the realization that his
meaning is being distorted, as they are by uxorious concern.

It is with these differences in mind that we must read the first
scene. Adam's reply to Eve's anguished cry of guilt is an acceptance of the dynamics of living, the inevitable, perpetual falling
away from the static Absolute—

> That which we were, we could no more remain
> Than in the moist provocative vernal mould
> A seed its suckers close, and rest a seed.
> We were to grow. Necessity on us lay
> This way or that to move; necessity, too,
> Not to be over-careful this or that,
> So only move we should.
>
> (I. 13–19.)

Eve's reiterated and suffering cries of 'Guilt!' provoke Adam into
a more forthright statement. By his 'living will' he rejects the
'guilt of [her] distracted fantasy' which invests the innocuous
apple with the significance of eternal punishment. He attributes
the 'mighty mythus of the Fall' to the 'thick fancies', originating
from Eve's 'teeming womb', which have been poured into the
'chance mould' offered by the sight of a snake and a dead lamb.
Forced by Eve into admitting that in his weaker moments, when
adversity and frustration weaken the will, he too has sometimes
been brought to near acceptance of Eve's terrifyingly real dream
of an outraged and all-present omnipotence,[1] Adam describes too
the sustaining Voice that has come to him at these moments. The
Voice carries the Goethean message of acquiescence in the patient
rhythms of nature's life, of hopeful work and purposeful labour.

> I hear a Voice, more searching, bid me, 'On!
> On! on! it is the folly of the child
> To choose his path and straightway think it wrong,
> And turn right back, or lie on the ground to weep.
> Forward! go, conquer! work and live!' Withal
> A Word comes, half-command, half-prophecy,
> 'Forgetting things behind thee, onward press
> Unto the mark of your high calling.' Yea,

---

[1] The rather overwritten beginning of Scene II shows Adam in the throes of
his struggle to maintain a rational metaphysic.

> And voices, too, in woods and flowery fields
> Speak confidence from budding banks and boughs,
> And tell me, 'Live and grow', and say, 'Look still
> Upward, spread outward. Trust, be patient, live.'
> Therefore, if weakness bids me curse and die,
> I answer, No! I will not curse myself
> Nor ought beside; I shall not die, but live.
>
> (I. 107–21.)

On the authority of this inner voice Adam rejects the feminine, accepting credulity of his wife. Intuitive apprehension must be tested by the 'wakeful, changeless touchstone' in his brain, which is equally a moral and an intellectual organ. Adam cannot accept the machinery of the doom-ridden apple and eternal punishment, because

> . . . God does not speak to human minds
> In that unmeaning arbitrary way;
> God were not God, if so, and Good not Good.
> Search in your heart, and if you tell me there
> You find a genuine Voice—no fancy, mind you—
> Declaring to you this or that is evil,
> Why, this or that I daresay evil is.
> Believe me, I will listen to the Word;
> For not by observation of without
> Cometh the Kingdom of the Voice of God:
> It is within us—let us seek it there.
>
> (IV. 50–60.)

Eve points out that she too has her Voices, which speak to her in equally authoritative tones. The problem, as Adam sees, becomes that of locating the central and divine moral imperative.

> God's Voice is of the heart: I do not say
> All voices, therefore, of the heart are God's;
> And to discern the Voice amidst the voices
> Is that hard task, my love, that we are born to.
>
> (IV. 63–6.)

From this angle, then, the poem becomes an investigation of these differing Voices, each incorporating an individual reading of the central mystery of the Fall, and, since each such reading involves a particular moral and spiritual commitment, the poem is also a study of these Voices as agents of alienation.

Abel's murder introduces a new, and morally less equivocal, element into the issue of man's disobedience. Scene VI centres on the figure of Abel, in whom the religious Voice of Eve has developed into an obsessed preoccupation, dividing him from his 'prayerless worldly' father and his brother who is 'overbearing, proud, and hard'. In a brilliantly dramatic passage Clough captures the authentic tones of the religion-drunk Elect, the voice of the 'justified' saint:

> They think not of the Fall: e'en less they think
> Of the Redemption, which God said should be;
> Which, for we apprehend it by our faith,
> Already is—is come for her and me.
> Yea, though I sin, my sin is not to death.
> In my repentance I have joy, such joy
> That almost I could sin to seek for it.
>
> . . .
>
> Yea, though the whole earth lie in wickedness, I
> Am with Thee, with Thee, with Thee evermore.
> Ah, yet am I not satisfied with this.
> Am I not feeding spiritual pride,
> Rejoicing over sinners, inelect
> And unadmitted to the fellowship
> Which I, unworthy, most unworthy, share?
> What can I do—how can I help it then?
> O God, remove it from my heart—pluck out,
> Whatever pain, whatever [wrench] to me,
> These sinful roots and remnants, which, whate'er
> I do, how high so e'er I soar from earth,
> Still, undestroyed, still germinate within.
> Take them away in Thy good time, O God.
>
> (VI. 10–16, 25–38.)

A passage like that, so confident in its casual clarity, so adroit in its nuancing of ambiguity, is emphatically not the work of a bungling craftsman; it can stand quite confidently beside Tennyson's 'St. Simeon Stylites'. The delicately and unostentatiously placed 'in Thy good time, O God' of the final line suddenly immobilizes and illuminates the shifting ambiguities of Abel's motivation. But the speech does not end on this shaft of sudden ironic penetration. For Abel, however snivelling his voice, is frighteningly sincere in his conviction, and the rest of his speech

expresses his struggle to preserve inviolate the rapturous intimations of his own inward Voice,

> . . . the sweet assurance of my soul
> That I am Thine, and Thou art mine, my God.
>
> (VI. 47–8.)

With Scene VII the focus shifts to Cain, in whom his father's
liberal and secularizing spirit is even further developed, just as his
mother's religious instinct issues in the extreme of Abel. He, too,
has his private Voice, an exultant, wondering awareness of his
magnificently unshared identity, which impels him to impress
himself, through action, on the surrounding world. Overwhelmed as he is by his sense of individuality, this becomes Cain's
imperative, driving him to the truth of self-realization through
self-expression.

> . . . for at times
> Ungovernable angers take the waves
> Of my deep soul and sweep them, who knows whither
> And a strange impulse, struggling to the truth,
> Urges me onward to put forth my strength,
> No matter how—Wild curiosity
> Possesses me moreover to essay
> This world of action round me so unknown;
> And to be able to do this or that
> Seems cause enough, without a cause, for doing it.
>
> (VII. 7–16.)

Peremptory, ungovernable, this impulsion makes Cain impatient,
fond as he is of his father, of Adam's tutelage. To be led by him
—or, for that matter, to be led at all—

> Is mere dissatisfaction: evermore
> Something I must do, individual,
> To vindicate my nature, to give proof
> I also am, as Adam is, a man.
>
> (VII. 21–4.)

The irony of his situation is that in attempting to prove his
exclusive possession he proves his co-partnership. In vindicating
his nature, he retraces a familiar pattern: he *is*, as Adam is, a man.

In Scene VIII Adam's forebodings about the superstitious
attitudes and ceremonies Eve has taught her children are cut short
by a fatal cry, and the next scene shows us Cain standing over

the body of his murdered brother. It is a brilliant scene, exploring
and interpreting at two simultaneous levels the birth of conscience
as a logical result of the murder. On the one hand, this birth is
viewed in the light of the traditional Christian myth. On the
other, it is viewed as part of the pattern of all human experience
discovered by Adam. Cain's first reaction is wondering recognition. The first murder brings knowledge, knowledge which
exists beyond moral consideration, knowledge to be savoured on
the palate.

> Dead is it then? O wonderful! O strange!
> Dead! dead! And we can slay each other then?
> If we are wronged, why, we can right ourselves;
> If we are plagued and pestered with a fool
> That will not let us be, not leave us room
> To do our will and shape our path in peace,
> We can be rid of him. There—he is gone;
> Victory! victory! victory! . . .
>
> (IX. 5–12.)

This, in Adam's scheme, is the stage of exultant 'enjoyment' to be
succeeded by the 'aftervoid' of disappointment, when the flavour
palls and the gap between achieved experience and ideal anticipation reveals itself. Clough rings these changes in response with
a fluently changing blank verse, grandly rhetorical in its opening,
dropping to an ordinary cadence of disappointment, quickening
to the pulse of ideally satisfying conflict, then fading again into
the unfulfilment of a deftly broken line:

> I stand upon the pinnacle of earth,
> And hear the wild seas laughing all about;
> Yet I could wish that he had struggled more—
> That passiveness was disappointing. Ha!
> He should have writhed and wrestled in my arms,
> And all but overcome, and set his knee
> Hard on my chest, till I—all faint, yet still
> Holding my fingers at his throat—at last,
> Inch after inch, had forced him to relax:
> But he went down at once, without a word,
> Almost without a look.
>
> (IX. 19–29.)

The 'aftervoid', to be followed by 'the thinking of it', and nascent
consciousness of responsibility moves uncertainly between

wrathful images of Eve's ethic of divine retribution and Adam's
conception of metaphysical loss:

> Ah hush! My God,
> Who was it spoke, what is this questioner?
> Who was it asked me where my brother is?
> Ha, ha! Was I his keeper? I know not!
> Each for himself; he might have struck again.
> Why did he not? I wished him to. Was I
> To strike for both at once? No! Yet, ah!
> Where is thy brother? Peace, thou silly voice;
> Am I my brother's keeper? I know not,
> I know not aught about it; let it be.
> Henceforth I shall walk freely upon earth,
> And know my will, and do it by my might.
> My God!—it will not be at peace—my God!
> It flames, it bursts to fury in my soul.
> What is it I have done?—Almighty God!
> What is it that will come of this? . . .

(IX. 29–44.)

Scenes X–XIII cover the reactions of Adam and Eve to Abel's
murder and the development of Cain's newly awakened conscience. After her initial response of undisguised loathing, Eve—
in many ways the Tractarian of the family—urges Cain to the
'rites and holy means of grace' ordained by God as the means of
forgiveness and atonement. Cain, however, finds it impossible to
accept her special view of the processes of atonement after guilt
incurred. He asks, instead, only for a constant, unfading awareness
of the fact of responsibility. The imperatives delivered by her
Voice are unheard by him:

> Alas! my mother,
> I know not; there are mysteries in your heart
> Which I profess not knowledge of: it may be
> That this is so; if so, may God reveal it.
> Have faith you too in my heart's secrets; yea,
> All I can say, alas, is that to me,
> As I now comprehend it, this were sin.
> Atonement—no: not that, but punishment.

(XI. 46–54.)

Adam urges acceptance, seeing Cain's act as part of the universal
law of necessity, under the shadow of which all human life is

lived. Repeatedly he advises, 'Be not over-scrupulous, my son.'
But Cain asks only for agonizing remembrance:

> Curse me, my father, ere I go. Your curse
> Will go with me for good; your curse
> Will make me not forget;
> Alas! I am not of that pious kind,
> Who, when the blot has fallen upon their life,
> Can look to heaven and think it white again—
> Look up to heaven and find a something [there]
> To make what is not be, altho' it is.
>
> (XIII. 7–14.)[1]

Cain's unflinching adherence to fact, and the memory of it, springs from his conviction

> That to forget is not to be restored;
> To lose with time the sense of what we did
> Cancels not that we did; what's done remains—
> I am my brother's murderer. . . .
> . . . No prayers to empty heaven,
> No vegetative kindness of the earth,
> Will bring back [warmth] into his clay again,
> The gentleness of love into his face.
>
> . . .
>
> But welcome Fact, and Fact's best brother, Work;
> Welcome the conflict of the stubborn soil,
> To toil the livelong day, and at the end,
> Instead of rest, re-carve into my brow
> The dire memorial of what still is.
> Welcome this worship, which I feel is mine;
> Welcome this duty—
>   —the solidarity of life
> And unity of individual soul.
> That which I did, I did, I who am here:
> There is no safety but in this; and when
> I shall deny the thing that I have done,
> I am a dream.
>
> (XIII. 35–42; 52–63.)

Torn by admiration and compassion, Adam can only urge his
old acceptance, his fragile wisdom of human endurance and

---

[1] Cf. the ironic short poem beginning, 'Blessed are they who have not seen'
(*Poems*, p. 91).

acquiescence, the virtue of self-tolerance. For him and his earnest but unruly son, at least, a stern hold on earthly actuality will also bring in time that certainty of things which, assimilating evil, sin, and death, is the nineteenth-century intellectual's characteristic quasi-Pauline consolation.

> That which your soul, in marriage with the world,
> Inbreeds in you, accept;—how can I say
> Refuse the revelations of the soul?
> Yet be not over scrupulous, my son,
> And be not over proud to put aside
> The due consolements of the circling years.
> What comes, receive; be not too wise for God.
> The past is something, but the present more;
> Will not it too be past?—nor fail withal
> To recognise the future in our hopes;
> Unite them in your manhood each and all,
> Nor mutilate the perfectness of life.
> You can remember, you can also hope;
> And doubtless with the long instructive years,
> Comfort will come to you, my son, to me,
> Even to your mother, comfort; but to us
> Knowledge, at least—the certainty of things
> Which, as I think, is consolation's sum.
>
> (xiii. 63–81.)

The final scene, an epilogue, is cast in the form of a vision. An elegiac tone replaces the dramatic, and the reader is prepared for the shift by the distanced cadences of this last speech of Adam's. In a tableau-like vision—'(We sat as in a picture people sit, | Great figures, silent, with their place content)'—Adam sees his two sons reunited in final realization, the figure of Abel saying to that of his brother,

> . . . 'Forgive me, Cain.
> Ah me! my brother, sad has been thy life,
> For my sake, all through me—how foolishly;
> Because we knew not both of us were right.'
>
> (xiv. 9–12.)

The vision continues into an eerie deliquescence and reabsorption. The sharp forms of Cain and of Abel, then of Eve, slowly melt and are drawn into the substance of Adam, which, in turn, undergoes this sad, lingering process of discreation, 'this fusion and mutation and return'. All that remains is the consciousness of untroubled, dreamless sleep.

Stepping out of the perimeter of his vision, Adam speaks the final fourteen lines that bring to a close this first long poem of Clough's. He is weary and longs for rest, but in spite of all sorrow and darkness life has been, and is, worth while.

> Yes, in despite of all disquietudes
> For Eve, for you, for Abel, which indeed
> Impelled in me that gaiety of soul—
> Without your fears I had listened to my own—
> In spite of doubt, despondency, and death,
> Though lacking knowledge alway, lacking faith
> Sometimes, and hope; with no sure trust in ought
> Except a kind of impetus within,
> Whose sole credentials were that trust itself;
> Yet, in despite of much, in lack of more,
> Life has been beautiful to me, my son,
> And if they call me, I will come again.
> But sleep is sweet, and I would sleep, my son.
> Behold, the words of Adam have an end.
>
> (XIV. 37–50.)

The tonalities of this speech, in fact of this whole scene, resemble strikingly the 'Biblical' poems which Clough wrote in 1850 and 1851,[1] and it is not impossible that this last scene was one of those written in 1850. Distancing and overlaying the dramatic conflict, exploiting unabashedly the emotive resonances of cadence and diction, the rather flabby and evasive consolations of the last five lines especially are a disappointing conclusion to the poem. Unable to endure or resolve the stark uncertainty and multi-valence of the poem, and lacking the traditional consolations of religious faith, Clough seems to have turned finally for his resolution to that space between actual and desired insight where sentimentality flourishes. That sentimentality cannot be discounted, but it stretches thinly across a profound lyric vision, profound because so fundamentally disturbed and disturbing, and also because it uncovers at the same time within itself irreducible strengths with which to confront its own disturbance. The visionary mode of the last scene is exact. Standing outside time,

---

[1] 'Genesis XXIV', 'Jacob's Wives', 'Jacob'. These poems are discussed below in Chapter VIII.

Adam's dream, which erases forms, cancels identities, reabsorbs and nullifies historical difference, is radically subversive. Its eroding fluidity dissolves away the large, reassuring meanings to be gleaned from the onward-rolling vistas of progressive history. *Amours de Voyage*, begun in 1849, is Clough's most sophisticated response to and portrayal of that collapse.

3. THE BOTHIE OF TOBER-NA-VUOLICH

That such an adept in the ways of introspection and doubt as Clough was should have written, in *The Bothie*, one of the most relaxed, ebullient, outgoing poems in the language is the kind of paradox which helps us to understand the tributes paid to his fascinating and abundant personality by his friends. He resigned his Oriel Tutorship at Easter in 1848. When he gave up his Fellowship in October, Oxford expected from him a weighty, probably theological, self-vindication. It was given instead the light-hearted hexameters of *The Bothie*, tossed out with a totally uncharacteristic absence of hesitation.[1] Humbert Wolfe described the poem as a 'school-boy shout on escaping from school into the air',[2] and the phrase, although it overlooks the coexisting seriousness, exactly matches the buoyant mood in which it was conceived and by which it is irradiated. Clough could afford to relax, to feel his muscles, to allow his mind expansive play, to be confident and hopeful, and tilt at solemn expectation in this first real summer of his life. Apart from everything else, *The Bothie* is a splendid commemorative gift to that engaging young idealist, Tom Arnold, who had sailed for New Zealand late in 1847.[3]

Set in the Highlands, the poem re-creates with a solid precision and extensiveness the feel and flavour of a mid-nineteenth-century University reading-party, the exuberant work and play of English

[1] *The Bothie* was composed in the autumn of 1848 in Clough's mother's house in Vine Street, Liverpool. *PPR* i. 37 says it was written in September. According to Clough's sister, it was written in October; B. A. Clough, *A Memoir of Anne Jemima Clough* (London, 1903), p. 68. See also *Corr.* i. 240. The poem was published before the year was out.

[2] H. Wolfe, 'Arthur Hugh Clough', in *The Eighteen-Sixties*, ed. J. Drinkwater (London, 1932), p. 36.

[3] The close parallels between Hewson's Antipodean decision and Tom Arnold's can be seen in the *New Zealand Letters of Thomas Arnold the Younger*, pp. 1–12 especially. The farewell gifts which Tom received obviously provided suggestions for the epic listing of gifts in his friend's poem.

youth, the dash and panache of Oxford undergraduates, their intelligent, puppyish wit, their in-group humour. That solid feeling of actuality derives in part from personal experience: the poem is warmed by affectionate memories of reading-parties Clough himself took to the Lake District and to Scotland, especially one to Drumnadrochit in the summer of 1847; as a *roman à clef* it is peopled by figures who, though disguised, re-distributed, composed, and transformed, begin their lives in personal acquaintance.[1] Even the singular misfortune of the original title seems oddly appropriate to this exuberant poem. When it was first published in November 1848, Clough called it *The Bothie of Toper-na-Fuosich*. He soon discovered that he had chosen unwisely. The *Literary Gazette*, correcting the spelling to *Tobair na Feosag*, pointed out that the name was, at the very least, inept.[2] It meant—so the *Gazette* maintained, although the etymology has since been challenged—'the hut of the bearded well', and was a Highland toast to the female organ of generation. Red-faced and embarrassed, Clough was nevertheless ribald enough to giggle delightedly over the appallingly ludicrous way in which he had introduced such unseemliness into 'all the drawing rooms and boudoirs (of course) of all the world' (*Corr.* i. 244). In revising the poem for the republication he did not live to see, he changed the title to its present innocuous, concocted, but sufficiently Gaelic-sounding, form.

Charles Kingsley, by this time an ardently muscular Christian Socialist, was delighted by *The Bothie* and in December 1848 he communicated his noisy approval to John Conington:

I am game to 'go in' fiercely against all Manicheans, Hermann-and-Dorothea formalists, and other unclean beasts, to prove that Clough knows best what he wants to say, and how; and that taking the poem inductively and not *à priori* (as the world, the flesh, and the devil take works of art), there is a true honest harmony, and a genial life

---

[1] See T. Arnold, 'Arthur Hugh Clough: A Sketch', *Nineteenth Century*, xliii (Jan. 1898), 108–9; W. Knight, *Principal Shairp and His Friends* (London, 1888), pp. 104–11; W. Tuckwell, *Reminiscences of Oxford*, 2nd edn. (London, 1907), p. 305; G. Rigaud, *Notes and Queries* (hereafter *NQ*), (17 Nov. 1877), p. 395; Mrs. H. Ward, *A Writer's Recollections*, 2nd edn. (London, 1919), p. 13; S. R. Gardiner, *The Academy*, xxii (Dec. 1882), 471; A. H. A. Hamilton, ibid., xxiii (Jan. 1883), 11, for accounts of the real-life background of *The Bothie* and attempts to identify the various characters.

[2] 'English Hexameters', *The Literary Gazette*, lxvi (18 Aug. 1849), 606.

in it, as of a man who seeing things as they were, and believing that God, and not 'taste', or the devil settles things, was not ashamed to describe what he saw, even to Hobbes's kilt, and the 'hizzies'' bare legs. All right; manly, more godly, too, in my eyes, than the whole moon-behowling school of male prude-pedants, who seem to fancy that God has left this lower world since 1688, and would, if they dared, arraign nature as indecent, because children were not born with shifts on. Carrion feeders, like the vultures,—they have a miraculous sense of smell—for the foul. . . . So if you will keep your trumpet for 'Ambarvalia', I will celebrate the birth of the 'Bothie' with penny whistle and banjo.[1]

He duly appeared in print in *Fraser's*, where, after some preliminary bullying thrusts at the Tractarians and at the 'deluge of milk-and-water from that perennial fount of bad verse', Oxford, he proceeded to his praise of Clough:

He found the sublime and the ridiculous hand-in-hand . . . and, like greater men than himself, he has not been ashamed to draw them in the same picture. . . . There runs all through the poem a general honesty, a reverence for facts and nature—a belief, that if things are here, they are here by God's will or the devil's, to be faced manfully, and not to be blinked cowardly; in short, a true faith in God—which makes Mr. Clough's poem, light as may seem the subject and the style, and coming just now, as it does, from noble old Oxford, anything but unimportant, because they indicate a more genial and manly, and therefore a more poetic and more godly spirit, than any verses which have come out from Oxford for a long time past.[2]

Strident and polemical though much of this review is, the doctrinaire, 'Fourieristic and Aesthetic' basis (*Corr.* i. 229) of Kingsley's praise is relevant. *The Bothie* is several other things as well, but at its core it is a poem with a thesis. It supplies and embodies Clough's justification for quitting Oxford: only it is not the religious apologia that might have been expected. The stubborn vein of advanced social thinking in the poem, the sociological realism, the final 'message' in which responsible sexual love vitalizes and validates theory—in short, all the elements which caused the poem to be declared 'indecent and profane, immoral and

[1] *Charles Kingsley: His Letters and Memories of His Life*, 2 vols., 2nd edn. (London, 1877), i. 191.
[2] [C. Kingsley], 'The Bothie of Toper-na-Fuosich', *Fraser's Magazine*, xxxix (Jan. 1849), 105.

(!) Communistic' (*Corr*. i. 240)—as well as the diffused but vividly communicated sense of release and expansion are interlinked aspects of Clough's vindication. Oxford's religious track was not only too narrow; it was irrelevant. Behind *The Bothie* lies the whole pattern of Clough's secular revolt.

Tackling contemporary social issues as it does, *The Bothie* is a thesis-poem also in its aesthetics. It is Clough's most combative version of the 'modern poem', the mere notion of which elicited such vehement protest from Matthew Arnold in his 1853 Preface.[1] We have already examined the rather Johnsonian terms in which Clough predicated the qualities of the 'modern' poem: it should approach the novel in its realism, it should embrace the whole compass of contemporary life, neglecting nothing, dealing with 'general wants, ordinary feelings, the obvious rather than the rare facts of human nature', and shaping into poetry the 'actual palpable things with which our everyday life is concerned'.[2] Fortunately the theoretic foundations of the poem—both the social message and the literary doctrine—are not frequently in naked view. When they do obtrude the poem suffers. Clough's insistence, for instance, on the faithful recording of actuality at times issues in a dogged sub-Wordsworthian literalness:

> Blank hill-sides slope down to a salt sea loch at their bases,
> Scored by runnels, that fringe ere they end with rowan and alder;
> Cottages here and there outstanding bare on the mountain,
> Peat-roofed, windowless, white; the road underneath by the water.
>   There on the blank hill-side, looking down through the loch to
>   the ocean,
> There with a runnel beside, and pine-trees twain before it,
> There with the road underneath, . . .
>
>   (Part VI, lines 7–13.)

As William Allingham remarked, 'His landscape painting is noteworthy for its truth and solidity. It is often too truthful to be good as art. . . . Something of the land-surveyor, one might say, mingles with the poet.'[3] In the same manner the theorist's

---

[1] For a brief historical discussion of the 'modern poem' in the mid-nineteenth century see Houghton, pp. 93–4. J. Killham, *Tennyson and 'The Princess'* (London, 1958) provides extensive and pertinent background material on the feminist movement. Chapters I, II, V, and VI are particularly illuminating.

[2] 'Recent English Poetry', Trawick, p. 144.

[3] *William Allingham, A Diary*, ed. H. Allingham and D. Radford (London, 1907), p. 143.

insistence that labour is attractive, that poetry, like the novel, should remember the 'phenomena which, if we forget on Sunday, we must remember on Monday',[1] translates itself into an unwavering attention in the love-scenes to the shifting fortunes of Elspie Mackaye's knitting—when she took it up, when she laid it in her lap, when she put it on the bench.

The device of exploiting the possibilities of a University reading-party as a theme, however, 'carries' much of the social theorizing, and provides, so to speak, a legitimizing and accommodating framework for the 'message' which, more than anything else, has dated the poem. The transplantation of Oxford into the Highlands affords endlessly fruitful material for a legitimate intellectualization of the lived experience of social difference and juxtaposition. Yet the central device only just carries the 'serious' elements: for the issues raised and the manner in which they are dealt with have only a period interest. What is perennial in the poem is the complex charm—that final unsatisfactory word on which all appreciative readers must fall back—with which it is interpenetrated, the sheer buoyancy, the fresh, exuberant vitality of invention and language. There is, first, the range of the material. In these lovingly—and often superbly—evoked Highlands we encounter a diverse, stratified, human society, richly assorted in its occupations. We are introduced to a spread of political and social ideas which, concentrating on problems of equality and feminism, are integrally related to the human encounters—social and personal—in the poem. We are continuously involved, as well, in an elaborate, varied game with literature itself, in which the detailed play of allusion and pun builds up the larger game of pastoral and mock-epic. This range of material is matched by an answering range of tone: the argumentative, the humorous, the tender, the passionate, the mock-heroic, the epic, the idyllic.[2] For the poem, we remember, is a 'Long-Vacation Pastoral', in which a fine Arcadian strain softens and transforms the combative, and rather repellent, vigour suggested by Kingsley's comments.

---

[1] 'Recent English Poetry', Trawick, p. 145.
[2] G. Tillotson, 'Clough's *Bothie*', in G. and K. Tillotson, *Mid-Victorian Studies* (London, 1965), is an enthusiastic recent discussion, valuable in drawing attention implicitly to the cross-fertilization between contemporaneity and tradition in the conventions which the poem establishes. The essay is particularly good in its discussion of Clough's exploitation of slang and classical epic conventions.

Range and variety of material, range and variety of tone: and the metre Clough selected for *The Bothie* is beautifully adapted to this profusion. As the prefatory note to the original version put it: 'The reader is warned to expect every kind of irregularity in these modern hexameters. . . .' Clough's attempts at the notoriously difficult English hexameter have been often and vigorously disparaged. Swinburne, who regarded English hexameters as 'at best . . . ugly bastards of verse',[1] thought they were merely rhythmical prose, while a writer in *The Academy* found the metre 'detestable' and not to be read 'without actual suffering'.[2] The judgement of metrical purists like Swinburne is based on the norm of the classical hexameter, but Clough's hexameters, as J. A. Symonds observed, 'are *sui generis*, unlike those of any other writer in any language'.[3] They are to be judged, if we are to make any sense of them, not by their approximation to the prosodist's abstraction, but by their effectiveness for the particular effects and purposes Clough had in mind. The game of hide-and-seek with classical echo and precedent which is such an engaging element in the mood and tone of *The Bothie* is also built into its metrical life.

The beginning of the nineteenth century saw a revival of interest, which had died with Elizabethan theorists and practitioners, in the hexametric form. The accentual hexameter, as distinguished from the quantitative classical one, was essayed first in Germany, by Klopstock and Voss, and then by Goethe and Schiller. England was soon infected and both Coleridge and Southey tried their hand at accentual hexameters. It was a reading aloud of Longfellow's *Evangeline* to his mother and sister, however, and a rereading of the *Iliad* that was the immediate impulse which set Clough on the hexametrical path to *The Bothie* (*Corr.* i. 241).

Many of the difficulties presented by the Cloughian hexameter, I find, disappear when one sees it as hovering between the principles of accent and quantity. Some of the lines ('With a mathematical score hangs-out at Inverary') show a clear reliance on accent, and Clough's freedom in handling accentual elements—his inversions, light beginnings, his skilfully varied

---

[1] A. C. Swinburne, *Essays and Studies* (London, 1895), p. 163.

[2] 'Clough and His Defender', *The Academy*, lii (Oct. 1897), 261.

[3] J. A. Symonds, 'Arthur Hugh Clough', *Fortnightly Review*, x (Dec. 1868), 617.

caesuras—makes for a variety and elasticity of movement which is far removed from Longfellow's sugary modulations. But to regard these hexameters as purely accentual is misleading. T. S. Omond, although he read the hexameters of both *The Bothie* and *Amours de Voyage* as accentual, noted that in his second 'Letter of Parepidemus' written in 1853,[1] Clough moved away from accent to quantity, and that in his later hexametric experiments (mainly in translations from the *Iliad*) he attempted to put this quantitative theory into practice. But as early as 1847 Clough had written on the subject of classical translation:

> Attempts . . . have usually gone on the theory, that while ancient metres were dependent on quantity, ours depend simply on accent. It would be more correct to say that all metre depends on both the one and the other. But with the ancients the accent of words in metre was, on the theory I subscribe to, independent of their colloquial accent, while with us the two are kept simply identical. The accent of words with us is fixed, with them was in metre arbitrary. So on the other hand, with them, the quantity was fixed and carefully observed; with us it is variable, and greatly neglected. Still there can be no question but that the discrimination of quantity enters largely into the modern art of versifying.[2]

Quantity, then, in Clough's view was an indispensable, though unobtrusive, element in the structuring of English verse, present as an elastic substratum beneath the more emphatic play of accent. The practical consequences on the reading and writing of verse are vividly illustrated in John Connington's account of a conversation with Clough:

> His 'Bothie' was just about to be published, and he gave me some account of it, particularly of the metre. He repeated, in his melodious way, several lines, intended to show me how a verse might be read so that one syllable should take up the time of two, or, conversely, two of one. The line which he instanced (altered, I think, from 'Evangeline') was this:—
>
> White/naked/feet on the/gleaming floor/of her/chamber.

This was new to me, as I had not risen beyond the common notion of spondees, dactyls, and the rest. So I asked for more explanation. He bade me scan the first line of the 'Paradise Lost'. I began, ' "Of man's:" iambus'. 'Yes.' ' "First dis—".' There I was puzzled. It

---

[1] 'On Translating Homer', Trawick, pp. 180–6.
[2] 'Illustrations of Latin Lyrical Metres', ibid., p. 76.

did not seem an iambus or a spondee: it was nearly a trochee, but not quite one. He then explained to me his conception of the rhythm. The two feet 'first disobe—' took up the time of four syllables, two iambic feet: the voice rested awhile on the word 'first', then passed swiftly over 'diso—', then rested again on 'be—', so as to recover the previous hurry. I think he went on to explain that in the next foot, 'dience and', both syllables were short, but that the loss of time was made up for by the pause required by the sense after the former of the two, and that finally the voice rested on the full-sounding word 'fruit'. Possibly this last impression may really be the result of my own subsequent use of the clue which he then gave me. But a clue it was in the fullest sense of the term: it gave me an insight into rhythm which I had not before, and which has constantly been my guide since both in reading and writing.[1]

In thus balancing quantity and accent Clough attempted an approach to the patterns of spoken speech. Though not always successful in practice, he attempted to build his 'Anglo-Savage' hexameters not on a rigid prosodic formula but on the living fluidities of natural utterance. Clough's line often suffers consequently *as a hexameter*, but the loss is amply compensated by the freedom and flexibility gained.

The choice of metre was a particularly felicitous one for *The Bothie*. Clough's line, as Henry Sidgwick pointed out,[2] is conscious of being a hexameter and is meant to be. It is learned but carries its learning with a certain wryness, always referring back sportively to the classical hexameter. The metrics chime in exactly with the ethos of a University reading-party; the academic (in the most un-pejorative sense of the word) wit, the faint burlesque, the gentle mockery, find ample scope for appropriate play within the compass of the educated line. Just as Clough did not take himself *too* seriously in the poem, neither does the metre. 'The *bizarrerie* of the subject', as Kingsley said, is 'charmingly expressed in the *bizarrerie* of the style'.[3] One further quality in Clough's hexameter invites comment. It is an elusive quality which has

[1] *PPR* i. 32–3.
[2] H. Sidgwick, 'The Poems and Prose Remains of Arthur Hugh Clough', *Westminster Review*, xcii (Oct. 1869), 381–2.
[3] [C. Kingsley], 'The Bothie of Toper-na-Fuosich', 105. The *bizzarerie*, as Kingsley calls it, of tone and treatment in Clough's poem suggests close parallels with the fantastic 'medley' in *The Princess*, Tennyson's first attempt at the long 'modern poem'. *The Princess* first appeared in 1847 and it might have had some influence on Clough.

been captured most successfully, perhaps, by Richard Hutton. Hutton is blatantly impressionistic, but, linking the metre as he does to an engaging vignette of Clough, he communicates an insight which might well elude pages of more rigorous methodology.

. . . Clough's genius . . . was, if I may say so, a genius for moving buoyantly under a great weight of super-incumbent embarrassment. . . . I remember . . . how, when I endeavoured, in twilight talks with him, to lay any of my youthful perplexities before him, he, in the kindliness of his heart and the extreme embarrassment of his intellect as to whether he should do more harm than good by his answers, would pick up with the tongs one little mite of coal after another from the grate and put it on the fire, as a mere physical relief to his perplexed and rather inarticulate feelings towards a junior whom he only half understood. . . . Well, this sense of embarrassment, this inertia about him, which was very real and constant, was bound to get some sort of expression in his more intellectual poetry; and he found in the English hexameter, varied, as he varied it, with frequent spondees . . . just the medium that he desired. For this metre expresses easily not only the resisting medium, but the buoyancy that makes itself felt through the resisting medium. I know no rhythm so effective as the rhythm of Clough's English hexameters for the purpose of expressing at once indomitable buoyancy of feeling and the inert mass of resistance which that buoyancy of feeling has to encounter. . . . It would be hardly possible, I think, to convey in any rhythm more effectually the impression of an eager, cordial, and embarrassed speech.[1]

★   ★   ★

The first section of the poem lays firm foundations for the succeeding eight—the relaxed and easy control of narrative, the economically deft notation of character, the elements of contrast and opposition (both those within the reading-party itself and the larger ones between gentry and peasant) later to be explored, the final light but pregnant reference to the resting-point towards which the whole adventure gravitates. The opening account of the Highland games, of the trials of skill and feats of strength, is succeeded by the elaborately wrought description (recalling in

---

[1] R. H. Hutton, 'The Poetry of Arthur Hugh Clough', *Fortnightly Review*, xxxix (June 1883), 797–8. G. Tillotson, op. cit., pp. 121–3, 138–48, is one of the most sympathetic, illuminating, and humane discussions of Clough's hexameters that has yet appeared.

delicious travesty the epic heroes' arming for battle) of the
University men's sartorial preparations for the festive dinner:

> Airlie descended the last, effulgent as god of Olympus;
> Blue, perceptibly blue, was the coat that had white silk facings,
> Waistcoat blue, coral-buttoned, the white-tie finely adjusted,
> Coral moreover the studs on a shirt as of crochet of women: . . .
>   (I. 39–42.)

The preliminary sketch, from which the characterization of
Philip Hewson is significantly withheld, introduces us, too, to
the racy University slang which is interlaced into the poem.
The mid-century-Oxford patois authenticates these young men
and the tonalities of their experience: these are real undergraduates,
really speaking to one another. But the implications of Clough's
exploitation of this area of language are more significant than
simple authenticity suggests. In an age which tended on the whole
to erect strict fences of decorum round the idea of poetic diction,
the slang of *The Bothie* is a casually daring assertion of a heterodox
poetic.

   The feast itself, where peasant and gillie and gamekeeper sit
in due subordination with their social and political betters, is
followed by the speeches, and Clough revels with classically
trained delight in his description of the mellow, asyntactic goodwill of after-dinner oratory. The health of the visiting reading-
party is drunk, and Hewson, the hero of the poem, is selected to
reply for the visitors—but with some misgiving, for Hewson is

> . . . a radical hot, hating lords and scorning ladies,
> Silent mostly, but often reviling in fire and fury
> Feudal tenures, mercantile lords, competition and bishops,
> Liveries, armorial bearings, amongst other matters the Game-laws: . . .
>   (I. 125–8.)

Obviously this impetuous young man has read his Carlyle;
obviously, too, he has much in common with his creator. But
he is held far enough away for the spirit of comedy to play
indulgently round his precocious theoretic fervour. The reader
is prepared for the tart political *double entendre*—lost on the bulk
of the audience but not on his friends—with which Hewson
concludes his speech, not only by the thumbnail sketch of
the speaker himself but also by the rapid notations of social

discrimination with which Clough had seasoned the *bonhomie* of the feast itself.

The second section picks up the threads the morning after, with lounging undergraduates retracing, over a lazy Victorian breakfast, the gaieties of the night before. Inevitably the talk turns to women, and Hewson, as impatient of impediment as a spirited colt, sweeps the company with the torrents of his conviction,

> Snorting defiance and force, the white foam flecking his flanks, the
> Rein hanging loose to his neck, and head projecting before him.
>
> (II. 71–2.)

Violently scorning conventional middle-class notions of feminine charm, he puts forward, instead, a special plea:

> Oh, if our high-born girls knew only the grace, the attraction,
> Labour, and labour alone, can add to the beauty of women,

and with the enthusiasm of the theorist he unhesitatingly draws out far-spreading economic consequences—

> Truly the milliner's trade would quickly, I think, be at discount,
> All the waste and loss in silk and satin be saved us,
> Saved for purposes truly and widely productive—
>
> (II. 25–9.)

But Hewson is not only a theoretician. He is a young man, and a young man whose democratic feminism is based equally on experience. The attractiveness of the working girls is for him an encountered fact:

> Never, believe me, I knew of the feelings between men and women,
> Till in some village fields in holidays now getting stupid,
> One day sauntering 'long and listless', as Tennyson has it,
> Long and listless strolling, ungainly in hobbadiboyhood,
> Chanced it my eye fell aside on a capless, bonnetless maiden,
> Bending with three-pronged fork in a garden uprooting potatoes.
> Was it the air? who can say? or herself, or the charm of the labour?
> But a new thing was in me; and longing delicious possessed me,
> Longing to take her and lift her, and put her away from her slaving.
> Was it embracing or aiding was most in my mind? hard question!
> But a new thing was in me, I, too, was a youth among maidens:
> Was it the air? who can say? but in part 't was the charm of the
> labour.
>
> (II. 39–50.)

Throughout the poem his ideas about love, work, womanhood, equality, are closely tied in with—and progressively ballasted by —his unfolding experience. Throughout, too, his sexual experience, like his theory, is coloured by the romantic idealization of womankind which nearly all the emancipatory radicalisms of the nineteenth century shared.

His ardent vision of a new—and proletarian—Eve in a new Paradise, advancing towards Adam as a helpmate, provokes the loud, insensitive hoots of his companions. The 'great Hobbes,'

> contemplative, corpulent, witty,
> Author forgotten and silent of currentest phrases and fancies,
> Mute and exuberant by turns, a fountain at intervals playing,
>
> (II. 124-6.)

is both more modish and more effective. Pouncing on a stray suggestion, he transforms his friend, because of his attempt at uniting 'use and grace', into a 'Pugin of women', fit author of

> a Treatise upon *The Laws of*
> *Architectural Beauty in Application to Women*;
> Illustrations, of course, and a Parker's Glossary pendent,
> Where shall in specimen seen be the sculliony stumpy-columnar,
> (Which to a reverent taste is perhaps the most moving of any,)
> Rising to grace of true woman in English the Early and Later,
> Charming us still in fulfilling the Richer and Loftier stages,
> Lost, ere we end, in the Lady-Debased and the Lady-Flamboyant:
> Whence why in satire and spite too merciless onward pursue her
> Hither to hideous close, Modern-Florid, modern-fine-lady?
>
> (II. 144-53.)

The Tutor, meanwhile, the 'grave man, nicknamed Adam', has gathered his purposes for a careful attempt to separate the sense from the exaggeration in his pupil's passionate outburst. Warning against the merely attractive, he urges Hewson to search out the good, good in Aristotle's terms, 'Not indeed absolute good' but 'that which is good for ourselves, our proper selves, our best selves'. Attacking the false view of equality on which much of the young man's argument rests, he points out that 'Nowhere equality reigns in all the world of creation, | Star is not equal to star, nor blossom the same as blossom (II. 183-4). This argument from 'nature', which sanctifies self-interest and the *status quo* by invoking intrinsic and ordained inequality, provokes Hewson into the scathing observation:

Ah! . . . Alas! the noted phrase of the prayer-book,
Doing our duty in that state of life to which God has called us,
Seems to me always to mean, when the little rich boys say it,
Standing in velvet frock by mama's brocaded flounces,
Eyeing her gold-fastened book and the watch and chain at her bosom,
Seems to me always to mean, Eat, drink, and never mind others.

(II. 202–7.)

There the discussion rests, interrupted by the other undergraduates' noisy plans for a break in the routine of reading and by their vigorously allusive, absurdly rhetorical farewell to the studies which have so long engaged their attention.

The third section opens with a picture of the studious two, Airlie and Hobbes, who have remained behind with their Tutor reading nine hours a day, of their quiet evening strolls, and of the corpulent Hobbes's more violent exercise when he,

. . . stung by the œstrum of some swift-working conception,
Ranged, tearing-on in his fury, an Io-cow, through the mountains,
Heedless of scenery, heedless of bogs, and of perspiration,
On the high peaks, unwitting, the hares and ptarmigan starting.

(III. 11–14.)

It then tells of the return of Lindsay and Arthur from their travels, of their meeting with the Tutor and his two conscientious pupils at the exquisite mountain pool which the party had discovered a month earlier, when in the course of their explorations they

Rounded a craggy point, and saw on a sudden before them
Slabs of rock, and a tiny beach, and perfection of water,
Picture-like beauty, seclusion sublime, and the goddess of bathing.
There they bathed, of course, and Arthur, the Glory of headers,
Leapt from the ledges with Hope, he twenty feet, he thirty;
There, overbold, great Hobbes from a ten-foot height descended,
Prone, as a quadruped, prone with hands and feet protending;
There in the sparkling champagne, ecstatic, they shrieked and shouted.

(III. 55–62.)

The brilliant bathing passages, like this one, scattered throughout the poem catch up in symbolic points the pure pervading ecstacy of youth, the idyllic, energetic enjoyment of these undergraduates in everything they do or say, their uncomplicated absorption in sensation, in 'the joy of eventful living'. In narrating the story of their travels—Lindsay 'to the great might-have-been upsoaring,

sublime and ideal', his more scrupulous companion 'to the merest
it-was restricting, diminishing, dwarfing'—the returned travellers bring strange (and for the Tutor, disturbing) tales of Hewson:
how he had egged them on to defy the gamekeepers in the forbidden glens of Mar and Athol, how he had flirted briefly with
a ferry-girl and then with a servant-girl at an inn, and, finally,
how he had been smitten by the golden-haired charms of Katie,
the youngest daughter of a farmer at Rannoch. There they had
left him, and he had been observed, Lindsay (nicknamed 'the
Piper') said,

> . . . in the ingle beside her
> Kneeling, picking the peats from her apron,—blowing together,
> Both, between laughing, with lips distended, to kindle the embers;
> Lips were so near to lips, one living cheek to another,—
> Though, it was true, he was shy, very shy,—yet it wasn't in nature,
> Wasn't in nature, the Piper averred, there shouldn't be kissing; . . .
>   (III. 205–10.)

He had last been seen helping the girl to put out the washing to
dry. The section, like the preceding two, ends with a reference
to the Bothie of the title, the *ultima Thule* of Hewson's wanderings.
Only now, for the first time, the place is connected with the
significant name of Elspie Mackaye.

The following section, as Houghton has observed, is not entirely
successful: the mode of Hewson's sexual guilt is too close to the
outdated Victorian vision of the prostitute as ruined maid, Adam's
lecture too much like a lecture from Clough himself.[1] The opening sweep of Highland landscape reveals the effectiveness of this
hexameter in compassing the 'weight' and the 'lift', the stubborn
yet strangely buoyant massiveness of time-worn patient mountains:

> There is it, there, or in lofty Lochaber, where, silent upheaving,
> Heaving from ocean to sky, and under snow-winds of September,
> Visibly whitening at morn to darken by noon in the shining,
> Rise on their mighty foundations the brethren huge of Ben-nevis?
> There, or westward away, where roads are unknown to Loch
>   Nevish,
> And the great peaks look abroad over Skye to the westernmost
>   islands?
>   (IV. 8–13.)

---

[1] Houghton, p. 103.

The figure of Hewson is picked out in these wide expanses, Hewson in the painfully ambivalent grip of guilt and longing, for he has deserted Katie and the farmhouse at Rannoch.

In a letter to his Tutor he explains what had caused this desertion and his subsequent fevered search for purgation in the wilds. It was a brief, penetrating glance from a passing girl, the still unknown Elspie, which revealed himself to himself, a glance of pure knowledge, the elaborate interpretation of which (IV. 135–44) is not only a 'skilful projection' of conscience,[1] but is supported by the Tutor's romantic, and anti-intellectual belief, shared by the pupil, that

. . . there is a power upon earth, seen feebly in women and children,
Which can, laying one hand on the cover, read-off, unfaltering,
Leaf after leaf unlifted, the words of the closed book under,
Words which we are poring at, hammering at, stumbling at, spelling.
(IV. 194–7.)

The Tutor repeats his former advice: choose the good and not the attractive, and choose it, if possible, in your own station. But even before the letter can be dispatched there is another surprise for the party from the seemingly inexhaustible Hewson: the scornful radical is now enveloped in the aristocratic pleasures of the Castle at Balloch.

Section v opens in quiet lyric expressiveness, evoking the slow changing pulse of deepening autumn in Highland glens. The passage clearly illustrates the combination of strength and delicacy in Clough's favourite stylistic device when well deployed, the Homeric iteration of phrase, the careful verbal echo which, as Kingsley observed, hints at 'an infinite hidden under the most trivial Finite, which must be felt for again and again'.[2] The hesitant accumulation of recurrence is like the slow charging of a battery; unhurriedly, protractedly, it builds a massive sense of unused, waiting power into the extended, pre-kinetic lines.

What if autumnal shower came frequent and chill from the
westward,
What if on browner sward with yellow leaves besprinkled
Gemming the crispy blade, the delicate gossamer gemming,
Frequent and thick lay at morning the chilly beads of hoar-frost,

---

[1] Houghton, p. 103.
[2] [C. Kingsley], 'The Bothie of Toper-na-Fuosich', p. 108.

Duly in *matutine* still, and daily, whatever the weather,
Bathed in the rain and the frost and the mist with the Glory of
headers

Hope. . . .

. . .

   Duly there they bathed and daily, the twain or the trio,
Where in the morning was custom, where over a ledge of granite
Into a granite bason the amber torrent descended;
Beautiful, very, to gaze-in ere plunging; beautiful also,
Perfect as picture, as vision entrancing that comes to the sightless,
Through the great granite jambs the stream, the glen, and the
mountain,
Beautiful, seen by snatches in intervals of dressing,
Morn after morn, unsought for, recurring; themselves too seeming
Not as spectators, accepted into it, immingled, as truly
Part of it as are the kine in the field lying there by the birches.
(v. 9–15; 20–9.)

The changing seasons and a changing hero. For Hewson, recoiling from his adventure with Katie, has turned with the exaggerated fervour of the doctrinaire to the elegant and aristocratic loveliness of the Lady Maria. Being who he is he erects a new theory—a rationalization rather—on this new fascination. The violence of the oscillation upsets certitude completely; even in the act of payment his homage is penetrated by his scepticism:

   And I find myself saying, and what I am saying, discern not,
Dig in thy deep dark prison, O miner! and finding be thankful;
Though unpolished by thee, unto thee unseen in perfection,
While thou art eating black bread in the poisonous air of thy cavern,
Far away glitters the gem on the peerless neck of a Princess,
Dig, and starve, and be thankful; it is so, and thou hast been aiding.
(v. 63–8.)

The uneasy, oscillating extravagance of the phrasing betrays the act of will. His command to the Lady Marias of society is impregnated with this same ambiguousness and irony, though the final injunction gives the whole a peculiarly Hewsonian twist:

   Often I find myself saying, in irony is it, or earnest?
Yea, what is more, be rich, O ye rich! be sublime in great houses,
Purple and delicate linen endure; be of Burgundy patient;
Suffer that service be done you,

. . .

Live, be lovely, forget them, . . . be beautiful even to proudness,
Even for their poor sakes whose happiness is to behold you;

Live, be uncaring, be joyous, be sumptuous; only be lovely,—
Sumptuous not for display, and joyous, not for enjoyment;
Not for enjoyment truly; for Beauty and God's great glory!

(v. 69–72; 75–9.)

Hewson has come round to something like his Tutor's philosophy of order, the 'wonderful order' of the beasts who live 'the one with another', 'one kind over another', but this too is shot through with doubt: 'it seems inspiration—of Good or of Evil!' As he says in the engaging conclusion of this letter to his Tutor, 'We can't know all things at twenty!' With his initial positiveness shattered, the young radical is obviously ripe for the final stage of his journeying.

Section VI brings us to the Bothie towards which the whole poem has moved and the end of Hewson's quest: for in Elspie he finds the 'good' and not merely the 'attractive'. In a letter to his Tutor he describes the wholly fortuitous yet destined accident which brought him to this final resting-place. The modern reader's response to the love-scenes in section VII and section VIII is inevitably mixed. Clough's frank, penetrating discernment of the mysteries of sexual feeling is marred by the pious sentimentalities of Victorian literary fashion. The figure of Elspie demands considerable suspension of disbelief. As James Froude commented (*Corr.* i. 235), the quality of finished and rounded articulateness in this simple Highland girl's speech jars against the realism of the other voices in the poem. Her domination over the intellectually and socially superior Hewson is to be understood only against the background of romantic primitivism, and the Victorian intellectual's need to find in women an embodiment of that potent simplicity of elemental nature which dissolves all contradiction and heals all difference.[1] This romantic idealization, however, coexists in *The Bothie* with a startlingly conversant psychological realism and fidelity in the evocation of sexual response. In '*Natura Naturans*' Clough had imaged awakening sexuality in the lily growing to 'pendent head'; Elspie compares her own emergent love to the new bridge over the burn:

---

[1] The recollection of Clough's relationship with his sister and his efforts to help her in her bid for independence, and the fact of his foward-looking interest in the 'woman question', should make us hesitate at least in identifying this mode of apprehending woman's capacities as his own. It corresponds nearly enough, however, to make it a vitally important factor in his relationship with Blanche Smith.

—this long time slowly with trouble
I have been building myself, up, up, and toilfully raising,
Just like as if the bridge were to do it itself without masons,
Painfully getting myself upraised one stone on another,
All on one side I mean; and now I see on the other
Just such another fabric uprising, better and stronger,
Close to me, coming to join me: and then I sometimes fancy,—
Sometimes I find myself dreaming at nights about arches and
bridges,—
Sometimes I dream of a great invisible hand coming down, and
Dropping the great key-stone in the middle: there in my dreaming,
There I feel the great key-stone coming in, and through it
Feel the other part—all the other stones of the archway,
Joined into mine with a strange happy sense of completeness. . . .
(VII. 60–72.)
</blockquote>

Elspie sees her love for Philip, as he does his for her, clearly as a Platonic completion, but it is also a completion in another sense. The strenuousness of the impulse and the effort—embodied in the effortful syntax and image—and the final melting fulfilment of her dream suggest clearly the sexual content. The keystone is phallic. It is also something more, for it brings with it (entirely appropriately in view of the spiritual reality of Elspie's love) echoes of the New Testament stone 'which the builders rejected'.[1] The ambivalences of sexual response are further explored by Elspie in another extended image, which re-creates perfectly the physical and breathless terror of imminent subjection and soilure and experience, the fear and the fascination, the over-whelming compulsion, the despair of identity:

<blockquote>
You are too strong, you see, Mr. Philip! Just like the sea there,
Which *will* come, through the straits and all between the
mountains,
Forcing its great strong tide into every nook and inlet,
Getting far in, up the quiet stream of sweet inland water,
Sucking it up, and stopping it, turning it, driving it backward,
Quite preventing its own quiet running: and then, soon after,
Back it goes off, leaving weeds on the shore, and wrack and
uncleanness:
And the poor burn in the glen tries again its peaceful running,
But it is brackish and tainted, and all its banks in disorder.
That is what I dreamt all last night. I was the burnie,
</blockquote>

---

[1] The association is strengthened in VII. 84: 'See the great key-stone coming down from the heaven of heavens!'

Trying to get along through the tyrannous brine, and could not;
I was confined and squeezed in the coils of the great salt tide, that
Would mix-in itself with me, and change me; I felt myself
                                                    changing;
And I struggled, and screamed, I believe, in my dream. It was
                                                    dreadful.
You are too strong, Mr. Philip!

                                                    (VII. 120–34.)

Hewson is stung with remorse, but when he promises to leave the
next day Elspie's feelings undergo a reversal. Forgetting her fears,
forgetting her shyness, she surrenders to her emotions, boldly
taking his hand and kissing his fingers. The reversal of feeling is
explored in a brilliant continuation of the image, the direction
of movement now reversed and the silvery feminine stream
searching out the ebbing masculine strength of the salt tide (VII.
154–65).

Elspie, in section VIII, is troubled by a new terror, a social not
personal one—that of 'deserting her station'. The discussion which
ensues repeats and expands the main social ideas of the poem—
equality (now between husband and wife), distaste for the arti-
ficialities of 'gentility', the importance of work, especially for
the woman, as a means to authenticity. Elspie's fears allayed, the
two decide to share the future, and, in true pastoral fashion, the
fruition of the relationship is embodied in an idyllic evocation of
the quiet maturity of a Highland autumn:

It was on Saturday eve, in the gorgeous bright October,
Then when brackens are changed, and heather blooms are faded,
And amid russet of heather and fern green trees are bonnie;
Alders are green, and oaks; the rowan scarlet and yellow;
One great glory of broad gold pieces appears the aspen,
And the jewels of gold that were hung in the hair of the birch-
                                                    tree,
Pendulous, here and there, her coronet, necklace, and ear-rings,
Cover her now, o'er and o'er; she is weary and scatters them from
                                                    her.
There, upon Saturday eve, in the gorgeous bright October,
Under the alders knitting, gave Elspie her troth to Philip.

                                                    (VIII. 44–53.)

Section IX covers the interval at Oxford during which Hewson
prepares himself for his examination and for his wedding.
Looking back on his vacation, his experience of both 'democratic'

peasant farms and aristocratic luxury, he, inevitably, extracts
from it a philosophy, a philosophy somewhat altered, still radical
but now tempered by experience. He admits inequality, but an
inequality based not on accidents of birth, but on the differentiated
fulfilment of individual potentiality in appropriate work. 'Only
let each man seek to be that for which nature meant him. . . . For
it is beautiful only to do the thing we are meant for' (IX. 17, 39).[1]
In his enthusiasm for Aristotle, he omits to investigate the meaning
either of 'nature' or of 'meant for'. But even this mild rebellion
is too much for the cautious Tutor, who repeats his plea for order.

> When the armies are set in array, and the battle beginning,
> Is it well that the soldier whose post is far to the leftward
> Say, I will go to the right, it is there I shall do best service?
> There is a great Field-Marshal, my friend, who arrays our
>   battalions;
> Let us to Providence trust, and abide and work in our stations.
>   (IX. 41–5.)

Eagerly his pupil pounces on the weakness in the conservative
argument—'Where does Circumstance end, and Providence
where begins it?' (IX. 49); when do we struggle, when accept?
Reluctantly, however, he admits that some order must be
respected, 'Still you are right, I suppose; you always are, and will
be; / Though I mistrust the Field-Marshal, I bow to the duty of
order' (IX. 55–6). And for the first time a sombre note of fundamental uncertainty creeps into Hewson's exuberance. For the
first time the poem's sunlight is obscured by a dark, uneasy
knowledge, a radical doubt, and we are confronted with the
Victorian dilemma:

---

[1] In the original 1848 version Hewson's radicalism had a sharper bite. The lines
quoted in the text were followed by an important passage on woman's place in
middle-class society:
> But they will marry, have husbands, and children, and guests,
>   and households—
> Are there then so many trades for a man, for women one only,
> First to look out for a husband and then preside at his table?
> Learning to dance, then dancing, then breeding, and entertaining?
> Breeding and rearing of children at any rate the poor do
> Easier, say the doctors, and better, with all their slaving.
> How many, too, disappointed, not being this, can be nothing!
> How many more are spoilt for wives by the means to become so,
> Spoilt for wives and mothers, and every thing else moreover!
>   (Poems, pp. 510–11.)

If there is battle, 'tis battle by night: I stand in the darkness,
Here in the mêlée of men, Ionian and Dorian on both sides,
Signal and password known; which is friend and which is foeman?
Is it a friend? I doubt, though he speak with the voice of a brother.

(IX. 51–4.)

The lights recede even further, the uncertainty deepens.

Yet is my feeling rather to ask, where *is* the battle?
Yes, I could find in my heart to cry, notwithstanding my Elspie,
O that the armies indeed were arrayed! O joy of the onset!
Sound, thou Trumpet of God, come forth, Great Cause, to array us,
King and leader appear, thy soldiers sorrowing seek thee.
Would that the armies indeed were arrayed, O where is the battle!
Neither battle I see, nor arraying, nor King in Israel,
Only infinite jumble and mess and dislocation,
Backed by a solemn appeal, 'For God's sake do not stir, there!'

(IX. 57–65.)

'Notwithstanding my Elspie'—and in his next letter the sunlight
breaks in again. The persistent, unsubduable vigour of the 'old
democratic fervour' is related to the vitalizing love of Hewson's
simple Highland girl and her primal beauty. In two magnificent
extended similes (IX. 73–109)—the first comparing Hewson's
political and social hope to the indomitable weight of the Atlantic,
the second his love for Elspie to the pure-breaking dawn over the
ugly desolations of nineteenth-century industrialism—Clough
illustrates once again the massive yet sensitive strength of these
hexameters.

The months pass, the dreaded Schools are successfully overcome (Hewson gets a First), and the Highland threads are picked
up once again as the next autumn ripens. Hewson had been
engaged to Elspie in the gold of autumn; in the gold of autumn
he marries her, the verbal echoes fulfil the pattern.

There in the bright October, the gorgeous bright October,
When the brackens are changed, and heather blooms are faded,
And amid russet of heather and fern green trees are bonnie,
Alders are green, and oaks, the rowan scarlet and yellow,
Heavy the aspen, and heavy with jewels of gold the birch-tree,
There, when shearing had ended, and barley-stooks were garnered,
David gave Philip to wife his daughter, his darling Elspie;
Elspie the quiet, the brave, was wedded to Philip the poet.

(IX. 130–8.)

Nature is rich in her benediction on these children of hers, who set out in hope and strength for the Antipodes, where, conquering complexity of intellect and difference of class, they will subdue the earth by their labour and build another Bothie of Tober-na-Vuolich.

The Bothie is a difficult poem to assess. It has been popular—especially in the nineteenth century—with a large number of Clough's readers. Edmund Gosse, no great admirer of Clough, considered it his 'most solid claim to immortality'.[1] The basic reason for this popularity is also given by Gosse: 'It is very crude and dull in some parts, but in others it has not merely a startling vividness and picturesqueness, but is sensuous and almost passionate. . . .'[2] In many respects *The Bothie* stands in complete isolation from the rest of Clough's work, coming closer than any other poem of his to simple, sensuous, impassioned utterance. In the scope of its attempt and in its vividly communicated sense of release and emancipation the poem is of enormous significance in Clough's personal and artistic development. It draws its enduring qualities precisely from this captured liberation—it is humorous, it is strong, it is benevolent, it is tender, it is untroubled. It is certainly successful as a romp, one of the finest in English literature, and this, in itself, is no mean achievement. The question is inevitable, though—is it merely a romp? Or, more accurately, is it satisfied with itself as a romp? The answer, in view of its doctrinaire basis, its effort at supplying a 'modern' need, is obviously 'no' in one sense, but the question can be approached from another angle.

The integration of disparate components is one of the major triumphs of *The Bothie*, but this very compositeness invites comment. How seriously does Clough take the several elements: how much weight, for instance, does he intend to give to the social and political arguments? To the love scenes? To the idyllic? To the realistic? How far, in other words, is Clough willing to go? The tone of the social and political discussion varies. Hewson and Adam are for the most part kept at a distance as separate artistic creations, but suddenly at intervals the debate acquires the urgent, troubled accents of the would-be leader of ideas, to be submerged once again in the carefree badinage of undergraduate

[1] E. Gosse, 'Arthur Hugh Clough', *Books on the Table* (London, 1921), p. 132.
[2] Loc. cit.

spirits. The playfulness, engaging as it is, is suspiciously like loss of nerve. Again, love is *the* solvent in this poem. From it originates the energy and hopefulness that leads to the happy conclusion in a far-away land, and brings to an end the displayed but otherwise unresolved debate between Adam and his pupil. A Utopian conclusion, perhaps, but not on that account to be dismissed, Utopia being the kind of proposition which cannot be proved either way this side of the grave. But when Utopia is placed round the corner, as it is in this poem, its credentials demand scrutiny. In *The Bothie* the vehicle to final triumph is love, the love of Hewson and Elspie, and that love is simply not sufficiently realized for the imposed task. We are given strikingly real and vibrant understandings of love between man and woman, but—is it again a failure of nerve?—the strength of these insights is countered, and in a sense denied, by the sentimental romanticism of the larger understandings of love. The poem, it can be urged, is a pastoral after all; but it is also sufficiently realistic to admit such questioning. The linearity and confidence of the pastoral fable are ironic, possibly; but that irony is avuncular and evasive.

The compositeness of the work, then, invites such suspiciousness. Is that compositeness, in other words, a position of strength or is it a refuge from uncertainty? Is the dawn which breaks over the raw mid nineteenth century merely a false dawn thinly veiling a recognized but unendurable vision?

> But as the light of day enters some populous city,
> Shaming away, ere it come, by the chilly day-streak signal,
> High and low, the misusers of night, shaming out the gas lamps—
> All the great empty streets are flooded with broadening clearness,
> Which, withal, by inscrutable simultaneous access
> Permeates far and pierces to the very cellars lying in
> Narrow high back-lane, and court, and alley of alleys:—
> He that goes forth to his walks, while speeding to the suburb,
> Sees sights only peaceful and pure; as labourers settling
> Slowly to work, in their limbs the lingering sweetness of slumber;
> Humble market-carts, coming-in, bringing-in, not only
> Flower, fruit, farm-store, but sounds and sights of the country
> Dwelling yet on the sense of the dreamy drivers; soon after
> Half-awake servant-maids unfastening drowsy shutters
> Up at the windows, or down, letting-in the air by the doorway;
> School-boys, school-girls soon, with slate, portfolio, satchel,

Hampered as they haste, those running, these others maidenly
tripping;
Early clerk anon turning out to stroll, or it may be
Meet his sweetheart—waiting behind the garden gate there;
Merchant on his grass-plat haply, bare-headed; and now by this
time
Little child bringing breakfast to 'father' that sits on the timber
There by the scaffolding; see, she waits for the can beside him;
Meantime above purer air untarnished of new-lit fires:
So that the whole great wicked artificial civilised fabric—
All its unfinished houses, lots for sale, and railway outworks—
Seems reaccepted, resumed to Primal Nature and Beauty:—
—Such—in me, and to me, and on me the love of Elspie!

(IX. 82–107.)

Unfortunate opposition when it could so nearly have been a
new interweaving! After the strength and courage of such
affectionate, though finally denied, knowledge it is difficult to
relapse into the old romantic and naturalistic schemes of value, to

> Forget six counties overhung with smoke,
> Forget the snorting steam and piston stroke,

as William Morris later adjured us to do in the Introduction to
The Earthly Paradise. By its very achievements, ironically, *The
Bothie* releases questions which infiltrate and disturb its manifold
successes.

CHAPTER VII

Rome and *Amours de Voyage*, 1849

I. APPOINTMENT AT UNIVERSITY HALL; MAZZINI'S ROME

This Hall was erected in commemoration of the passing of the Dissenters' Chapels Act in 1844, 7 & 8 Victoria, chap: 45, that statute being the first recognition by the legislature of the principle of unlimited religious liberty. Until that statute the law assumed all worship to imply the propagation of some special dogmas to be determined by itself if not declared by the founders.

The objects of the founders of this hall were

To provide for students of University College London the accommodation and social advantages of college residence

To provide a place where instruction without reference to creed should be permitted in theology and other subjects not taught or not wholly taught in University College and disavowing all denominational distinctions and religious tests to maintain the sanctity of private judgment in matters of religion.[1]

A JOINT venture between Presbyterians and Unitarians, University Hall was not quite ready in 1848 for its first students. Francis Newman was to have been the Principal but had resigned, and the Hall Council was on the lookout for fresh candidates. Clough's name was proposed in November and he seemed a likely man. Here was someone with an exceptional Oxford reputation who had thrown up his Fellowship because of his firm belief in the sanctity of private judgement in matters of religion. For Clough the prospect appeared a not inauspicious one. It is true that he disliked London generally and he had never been particularly careful about concealing his disdain for 'Stinkomalee', but the University Hall situation promised distinct, if modest, advantages. From the religious angle, the avowed aims of the founders seemed tailored exactly to his needs; the semi-collegiate character of the place—though a pallid compromise after Oxford—would have appealed to someone who set so much store by residence. Negotiations, however, turned out to be much more tangled than either party might have expected.[2] At one stage[3] the Council even

---

[1] Commemorative plaque in University Hall. Quoted, H. H. Bellott, *University College, London, 1825–1926* (London, 1929), pp. 299–300.
[2] G. P. Johari, 'Arthur Hugh Clough at Oriel and at University Hall', *PMLA* xvi (June 1951), 405–25, and Chorley, pp. 170–4, provide detailed accounts of these negotiations. [3] At a meeting on 11 Jan. 1849.

decided against the appointment, and it took the persistent efforts of Clough's supporters, particularly Henry Crabb Robinson and Walter Bagehot, together with the additional force of testimonials from James Martineau and Samuel Smith (who was later to become Clough's father-in-law), to swing the decision finally in his favour.

Unexpectedly—for the candidate at any rate—the difficulties centred on questions of religious belief and religious observance. As negotiations proceeded the pattern became depressingly familiar. For the past five years Clough had been compelled to scrutinize not only his personal religious position but also the compatibility of that position with his professional life. He had resigned his Fellowship in some hope that weary problems had finally been laid at rest, but now, after the briefest of respites, the old questions were reformulating themselves. Understandably, he rapidly became prickly and impenetrable. To judge from Bagehot's account, his interview with the inept subcommittee which had been appointed specifically to inquire into his religious views must have embarrassed and unsettled everyone present. 'There was a committee to see [Clough] composed of Bush, a chancery barrister, Le Bretton [sic] an amateur furniture broker, and Tagart. They came back with no end of blunders and said that nothing could be got out of Clough, and he would bind himself to nothing: and Tagart disgusted Clough by delivering fractions of bad sermons on general subjects.'[1]

Clough followed up this performance with a letter to Le Breton which crackled with positive conviction and with an uncompromising, even reckless, honesty. He needed the appointment badly. Both his own and his mother's finances were in a sorry state, and he needed, after his resignation, to reinstate himself in the estimation of a disapproving family;[2] yet he wrote to Le Breton:

I do not feel myself competent to undertake the conduct or superintendence of any prayers: nor can I in any way pledge myself to be present. Any attendance I might give would be that of a private person, in no way official; . . . it would be a matter of conformity, not of individual choice; . . .

Meantime I am sure I should feel every disposition to facilitate

[1] Quoted, A. Buchan, *The Spare Chancellor* (London, 1959), p. 51.
[2] B. A. Clough, *A Memoir of Anne Jemima Clough* (London, 1903), p. 68.

devotional arrangements. In fact I might be willing to admit that it would be better that your Principal should be one who could officially join in them; as indeed it might be *best*, could all your students be expected to do so. But, whether better or worse, I had conceived your institution to be one into which this element would not yet enter; that while it should offer a locus standi and home for theology and other subjects excluded from the College, and should look forward to and encourage the growth of moral and religious sympathy, it should nevertheless leave all this to a free spontaneous development. . . .

I need not of course say that I suppose I have on these subjects if not convictions, sentiments; not, assuredly, any definite theological creed, but undoubtedly what I imagine may be called distinctive religious views: views moreover which may very possibly prove in the end to be essentially different from those commonly entertained by Unitarians. . . .

I do not account myself to have made up my own mind, and should be shy of meddling with those of other people. At the same time what a man feels for himself can hardly fail to affect his communications with his neighbour: nor should I in any way hold myself bound to suppress because of the opinions of a young man's parents or friends anything which other reasons would not induce me to withhold (*Corr.* i. 230–1).

As, according to Crabb Robinson, he observed to Matthew Arnold, 'quitting Oxford because he will not conform, it would be absurd to become a Unitarian conformist'.[1]

These obstacles were removed, finally, by making a separate provision for 'some divine . . . to conduct the daily religious service . . . and to undertake some branch of theological instruction to be given to the students',[2] and Clough was given the Principalship. He was 'guaranteed £130 for the first two years', and for this he had to 'attend to the discipline and business of the house, and answer men's difficulties in classics and every thing but mathematics'.[3] Negotiations had at last ended, but neither side felt unalloyed satisfaction. On 27 January, Crabb Robinson wrote to his brother, '[T]he election of Mr. Clough, Fellow of Oriel Ox: has displeased a few of the shareholders of the Univ. Hall who wanted an out and out U[nitarian]. I quite

[1] *Henry Crabb Robinson on Books and their Writers*, ed. E. J. Morley, 3 vols. (London, 1938), ii. 684.
[2] Minutes of Council Meeting in Dr. Williams' Library. Quoted, Johari, 'Clough at Oriel and at University Hall', 422; Chorley, p. 173.
[3] W. Bagehot to R. H. Hutton, 1 Mar. 1849. Quoted, Buchan, op. cit., p. 50.

approve of what we have done and I was well aware that it would not be possible to choose a Principal that would be agreeable to all.'¹ The new Principal, too, had his doubts. 'I have accepted the Stincomalean position. I commence there in October. With a good deal of misgiving, it must be confessed; but on the whole I believe myself not wrong', he wrote to Tom Arnold in February (*Corr.* i. 242), and Anne, who had come to London to attend teachers' training school, wrote in her journal:

> People seem very fond of Arthur, and to think a great deal of him; but Arthur does not seem to mind much about people here; they don't seem to suit him exactly, and he gets wearied and worn out with the continual talking about religious matters; and I think, too, the pomp and grandeur trouble him. He does not appear at all to fancy coming to live in London. He says he prefers the North, and if he had a hundred a year, he would live in Liverpool with us.²

Gradually the consequences of his resignation were making themselves felt, undermining the hopefulness and the sense of achievement with which he had quitted Oxford and which had sustained the exuberance of *The Bothie*. On this ebbtide of personal hopefulness he set out, early in April, for Rome and the Italian holiday which was to occupy most of the interval till he actually took up his duties at University Hall.³

Italy, penetrated by echoes of 1848, was living through a critical stage in her struggle for unification and independence. Radetzky's Austrians had just crushed the Lombards and their Piedmontese supporters at Novarra. Joseph Mazzini's 'ideal' Republic in Rome had so far survived the threat from Austria, from Naples, and from her sister-republic, France, but when Clough arrived the storm was ready to break. The French under Marshal Oudinot were on their way, and the frail Roman defence rested on the heroic shoulders of Garibaldi. Yet, despite his republican sympathies, and though he stayed on to watch the struggle to its end, Clough remained curiously aloof. Contenting himself with a steady grumble against the French, his most passionate gesture of sympathy seems to have been the gift of some eau-de-Cologne

---

¹ Quoted, Johari, 'Clough at Oriel and at University Hall', p. 422.
² B. A. Clough, op. cit., p. 73.
³ Clough's Italian journal in the 1849 (Roma) Notebook gives the date of his departure from England as 4 Apr. He arrived in Rome on 15 Apr. after spending a few days in France. He left Rome on 17 July. Balliol MS. 441, fols. 14–15.

to the wounded in hospital (*Corr.* i. 262). It is true that a nagging edge of dismay at his own detachment sometimes creeps into his letters. It is true also that his attitude towards the Republic developed from an initial languidness to a real, if qualified, admiration—even to a kind of identification. But to explain this wholly in terms of a crippled psychology limping between engagement and withdrawal may be somewhat hasty.

Tom Arnold, although he admitted that Clough's letters from Rome gave no hint of it, believed that his friend passed through a profound crisis during this summer of 1849,[1] and it is through this fact of personal crisis that Clough's reactions to the Roman Republic should be viewed. For there was a crisis, a crisis of recognition and rebellion. Rebellion smoulders in Clough's intransigent correspondence with the University Hall authorities, it flares into the open in the poetry he wrote during the summer. Alone and free from custom and authority for the first time in his life, free, like Claude in *Amours de Voyage*, from 'All the *assujettissement* of having been what has been, / What one thinks one is, or thinks that others suppose one', he exploded into a new clarity. He saw himself clearly and honestly, he saw, too, the imprisoning self-definitions into which he had allowed himself to be guided by his responsiveness to the pressures of conformity.

The crisis of recognition which underlies this revolt is immediately connected with the problem of moral action and commitment, and this, in turn, with his recent experience of the University Hall authorities. In resigning his Fellowship he had acted with obstinate courage, but nothing had changed really. He was still on the same treadmill. In March 1849 (the month before he left for Rome) he wrote in the 1849 Roma Notebook:

The Wrong doctrine of habits is φιλικα ποιουντες φιλοι γιγνομεθα
By doing acts *like* those of love, we shall come to love.
It's all d——d virtue manufacture—not vital—but sham-vital.

Saith Jowett

There is something sacramental in an act—the spiritual reaction in the agent is transcendental.

Doubtless—to act commits us—this is true—chemical transformation has taken place—but to sham-to-act—to put hydrogen

[1] T. Arnold, 'Arthur Hugh Clough: A Sketch', *Nineteenth Century*, xliii (Jan. 1898), 111.

and oxygen together twenty times and say in the end they will turn to water![1]

Given such an outlook on action, one sees exactly where Clough's recurrent dread of the 'factitious' falls into place. Once action is invested with such stupendous—even sacramental—significance, it *matters* in a way difficult for a more casual age to understand. Dr. Arnold, Newman, Carlyle—all had inflated Action. Clough's notebook entry—like his hero's succinct question in *Amours de Voyage*, '*Action will furnish belief*—but will that belief be the true one?'—struck at two of the arguments with which these men effected their working conjunction with the Absolute: the Butlerian principle of acting on a strong probability as likely to be a certainty; and the principle, held by both Newman and Carlyle, of acting before thinking out, when the 'whole man' was straining at the leash—the principle, that is, of precipitating oneself into belief by an act of will. Seen in such contexts, Clough's suspiciousness about commitment appears not as an emasculate inability to decide but as an uncompromising adherence to the dictates of intellectual and moral honesty. *Amours de Voyage* is a skilful study of what happens when the genuinely critical modern intelligence attempts to achieve the Absolute through action which, at the same time, deftly and obliquely exposes the 'sham-vital' in contemporary *mores*.

This attitude of rebellion against 'd——d virtue manufacture' through arbitrary commitment is the real determinant of Clough's coolness towards the Republic. Katharine Chorley's comment, 'Clough, who had hurrahed the Revolutions of 1848 and had had a sonnet by Matthew Arnold dedicated to him as "A Republican Friend", ought surely to have approached the city in a mood of political fervour',[2] represents neatly the kind of compulsion he was resisting in Rome. Faced by one of *the* Romantic causes of the mid century, he was not going to permit himself to be stampeded into a 'sham-vital' enthusiasm—and not because of some perverse critical quirk either. Usually Clough has been seen as a clear, if cool, supporter of the Mazzinian Republic. Yet, apart from one unequivocally sympathetic passage in *Amours de Voyage* (Canto II, Letter i, 13–27)—which must necessarily be admitted, if at all, with extreme caution—the evidence points to a reserved response.

Balliol MS. 441, fol. 44ᵛ (rev.)-fol. 45 rev.   [2] Chorley, p. 187.

In his political and social attitudes, as we have seen, Clough presents a peculiar mixture of absolute, almost millennialist, demand and shrewd realism, of a somewhat naïve theoretical optimism and a vigilant practical scepticism; and if that balance left him open to quick despair, it also made for a sharp discriminating intelligence which put him on his guard against the deceptive slogan. He had certainly not been 'unconstrained' in 'hurrahing' the February Revolution in France, and his coolness had been justified by the actual nature and course of that revolution. Coming to rest in a bourgeois and bellicose nationalism, it had neither satisfied his political beliefs nor fulfilled his social hopes. In the same way his tepid reactions to the Mazzinian Republic can be traced to definitely held attitudes and positions. In the light, for instance, of his strong anti-Establishment sentiments and republican sympathies, his comment, 'Tell Blackett he really must defend S.P.Q.R. in the "Globe". It is a most *respectable* republic; it really (*ipse* dixit) thought of getting a monarch, but couldn't find one to suit' (*PPR* i. 144), takes on a patronizingly derisive colour.

Basically Clough may have been sympathetic towards the cause of Italian nationalism,[1] but his sympathy would have been qualified by his own singular lack of nationalistic fervour, and by the distrust of 'false patriotism' he had learnt under Dr. Arnold, as a schoolboy known to his fellows as 'Yankee Clough' (*Corr.* i. 5). The socialism he had absorbed at Oriel and the radical internationalistic sympathies he had acquired would tend even more strongly to qualify his sympathy.[2] Mazzini, although he made some magnanimous gestures to the poor, resolutely denied the 'right to work'—for that smacked of socialism, and of socialism he was an avowed enemy.[3] It is perhaps not without significance that the subject of socialism should have been a major

---

[1] In 1859 he declared that he was 'delighted' with Matthew Arnold's pamphlet, *England and the Italian Question*. *Letters of Matthew Arnold, 1848–1888*, ed. G. W. E. Russell, 2 vols. (London, 1895), i. 102.

[2] Houghton, p. 131, makes these points extremely well and provides further supporting references.

[3] In a series of articles entitled 'Thoughts upon Democracy in Europe', which ran in *The People's Journal* from Aug. 1846 to Apr. 1847, Mazzini attacked 'model republics', Utilitarianism, Saint-Simonianism, Fourierism, and Communism. What was necessary, he declared, was not the greatest happiness for all, but the highest nobleness possible. H. W. Rudman, *Italian Nationalism and English Letters* (London, 1940), p. 76.

topic in the half-hour interview Clough had with Mazzini on 22 April. Reporting the conversation to Palgrave, Clough wrote:

The feeling everywhere is, he says, simply political or national. Communism and Socialism are things undreamt of. Social changes are not needed; there are no manufacturing masses, and in the lands there is a métayer system. You have heard perhaps that they are going to divide Church lands among the peasants; this is true, but only of a portion, a surplus he called it, after provision is made for the carrying on of the services of each establishment (*PPR* i. 143–4).

One remembers his concern about the socialist programme in Paris, and especially about the question of organizing labour.

The anti-ecclesiasticism of the Republic, and its insistence on the separation of the Pope's spiritual and temporal powers, attracted Clough, but this was offset for him by the pertinacity of Catholic custom ('The religious customs seem to thrive still; they kissed away yesterday at St. Peter's toe as fast as they could have done in its best days' (*PPR* i. 144)), and by Mazzini's peculiar brand of moral idealism—that romantic religion of humanity with which he invested his conception of democracy. Reviewing Charles Eliot Norton's *Considerations on Some Recent Social Theories* in 1853, Clough wrote: 'The high doctrine proclaimed by the fervid Italian leader, of the supreme "authority of the People as the collective, perpetual interpreter of the will of God", finds but little favour with [the author]. . . . We cannot, indeed, any more than our author, soar to the high modern Mazzinian acceptation of the ancient maxim [i.e. *vox populi vox Dei*].'[1]

Although Lady Ashburton once wrote to Clough regretting that he was 'a *disciple* of Mazzini's' (*Corr.* i. 307), he appears on this visit to have been, in fact, extraordinarily suspicious of the Italian leader. Mazzini's power, like Garibaldi's, rested on a cult of devoted romantic enthusiasm, the 'fervid Italian leader' captured the heart and engaged the will, ultimately through personal *charisma*—and the critical intellect is notoriously suspicious of *charisma*. Something of Clough's suspiciousness about Mazzini—and something of his reservations about the Republic—can be detected in the letter he wrote to Tom Arnold in February:

Meantime the Great Powers are to restore the Pope! and crush the renascent (alite lugubri) Roman republic of which Joseph Mazzini

[1] Trawick, pp. 258–9.

has just been declared a citizen. The said J. M. has written two long letters in the Spectator attributing the Italian disaster entirely to the damper of the national enthusiasm caused by the Piedmontese inter-ference—which is possible, yet of course he would say so. I fear his own pets now dominant in Rome and Tuscany are not strong enough for the place. Yet some heroic deeds ought to come of them, if they are worth anything (*Corr.* i. 244).

It shows itself more clearly in his surprise at first meeting 'the said J. M.': 'He is a less fanatical fixed-idea sort of man than I had expected; he appeared shifty, and practical enough' (*PPR* ii. 142). The violent swing to 'shifty' suggests how deep-rooted Clough's suspicion was.

For Clough at any rate, then, Italian nationalism sounded no unequivocal summons. Although thoroughly disgusted with the French ('Unto this has come our grand Lib[erty], Eq[uality] and Frat[ernity] revolution!' (*Corr.* i. 256)), he was even unclear about the political rights and wrongs of the intervention. 'I consider', he wrote on 30 April when the French launched their attack, 'the invasion wholly outrageous—and yet I allow that if the Nea-politans were sure to come *and sure to* beat the Romans, the French might reasonably think themselves wanted' (*Corr.* i. 253). But he could respond unreservedly to the courage of the Romans and his letters reveal a growing admiration for the defenders of the Republic, and, in the end, even for Mazzini. At this level of sympathy for the fearless underdog, his identification was clear. 'Whether the Roman Republic will stand I don't know, but it has shown under Mazzini's inspiration a wonderful energy, and a glorious generosity: and at any rate has shaken to its foundation the Odillon–Barrot ministry, which I trust may yet go to its own place', he wrote to Tom Arnold on 24 May (*Corr.* i. 255); and on 3 June, when Oudinot attacked the outlying Roman Villas, '[T]hese blackguard French are attacking us again. May the Lord scatter and confound them' (*Corr.* i. 256). Incensed by the bias of the press, especially *The Times*, against the Republic, he took pains to include corrective eyewitness accounts in his letters, and when the *Journal des Débats* quibbled about the French bombardment—no bombs, it pointed out, had been used, only grenades—he sent off a sharp satirical attack on this equivocation to Palgrave.[1]

---

[1] Bodleian MS. Eng. Lett. d. 176, fol. 139.

The political and military conflict formed only part of Clough's Roman experience, however. For here he had his first real introduction to the world of art, a world which in its achieved perfection presented an ironic commentary on the struggling historical present. Rugby, intense, earnest, committed, left little time for such aesthetic pursuits—as Joshua Fitch remarked, Dr. Arnold had little interest in or appreciation of art to communicate to his pupils.[1] At Oxford Clough's energies had been occupied with religious controversy and with the problems of man's social, political, and economic life. Rome confronted him with the massively perennial evidences of man's aesthetic striving, with the timeless formulations in art of the meaning of civilization, and a new dimension was added to his sensibility. His sister noted the change: 'It seemed to me that the journey abroad, and his stay among the works of art, had given him a greater amount of taste, a stronger love of the beautiful, and a longing for something superior to what he had been accustomed to.'[2]

Initially, Clough was disappointed. 'St. Peter's', he wrote to his mother,

disappoints me: the stone of which it is made is a poor plastery material. And indeed Rome in general might be called a *rubbishy* place; the Roman antiquities *in general* seem to me only interesting as antiquities— not for any beauty. The Arch of Titus . . . is I could almost say the only one really beautiful relic, that I have yet seen. . . . I have seen two beautiful views since I came, one from San Pietro in Montorio, the other from the Lateran Church over the Campagna . . . (*Corr.* i. 252).

Once he had adjusted expectation and actuality, had shed some of his touristic cleverness—and his very English concern about fleas (*Corr.* i. 258)—however, he revised most of his early impressions. He devoted as much time as he could to the galleries, churches, and palaces. Some of his comments are, within the limits of a rather conventional taste, both independent and sensitive:

I live here studying chiefly Michael Angelo, specially in the Sistine Chapel: . . . I conceive myself to understand his superiority and Leonardo da Vinci's to Rafael, who is only natural, while they are intellectual. He produces with and they out of Nature.

[1] J. Fitch, *Thomas and Matthew Arnold* (London, 1897), pp. 112–13. On an earlier visit to the Continent he had found the countryside much more 'agreeable' than the galleries. *Corr.* i. 125.   [2] B. A. Clough, op. cit., p. 76.

The idea of St. Peter's has been wholly killed out of it, partly by the horrid internal ornaments, but still more completely by the change of the form from a Greek to a Latin cross, the latter belonging to Gothic which Michael Angelo rejects because he asserts *totality*—There! (*Corr.* i. 256.)

There was one opinion, however, which he did not revise. Moralizing his aesthetics in combatively Ruskinesque fashion, he remained unrelenting in his dislike of Baroque Rome. Noting in anxious detail the damage inflicted by French guns and listing the fortunate misses, he added maliciously, 'A bomb I am thankful to say has left its mark on the façade of the Gesù. I wish it had stirred up old Ignatius' (*Corr.* i. 264).

Repeatedly missing opportunities to leave—opportunities, probably, which he did not exert himself overmuch to take advantage of anyway—Clough lingered on in the beleaguered city until a fortnight after the military drama had played itself out: 'It is a sight to make one gnash one's very wisdom teeth to go about this fallen Jerusalem, and behold the abomination of desolation standing where it ought not', he exclaimed, finally touched by the inevitable collapse (*Corr.* i. 267). Living a life of Spartan frugality, he seems to have used every minute of his time in Rome. He returned again and again to his favourite haunts, especially the Sistine Chapel and the galleries of the Vatican, to visit which he had been given a special permit by Mazzini. He made new acquaintances, and in the company of the best known of these, Margaret Fuller, he visited the wounded in hospital. He filled his letters with some splendid first-hand reporting, which not only relayed the latest military and political news but communicated vividly the sharply observed sights and sounds of battle: 'I found a crowd assembled about 9 pm at the north-east corner of the Piazza Colonna, watching these pretty fireworks—Ecco un altro!—One first saw the "lightning"—over the Post Office, then came the missive itself, describing its tranquil parabola, then the distant report of the mortar, and finally the near explosion, which occasionally took place in the air' (*Corr.* i. 262). At times he paused in his letters to take a wry look at himself, sometimes to communicate the weary taste of non-engagement, 'Perhaps it will amuse you hereafter to have a letter commenced while guns are firing and, I suppose, men falling, dead and wounded. Such is the case on the other side the Tiber while I peacefully

write in my distant chamber with only the sound in my ears . . .'
(*Corr.* i. 253); sometimes to convey the strange ordinariness of
the tourist's view of violence, 'It is curious how much like any
other city a city under bombardment looks.—One goes to the
Ara Celi, or the Palatine to look at the firing; one hears places
named where shells have fallen; one sees perhaps a man carrying
a bit of one . . .' (*Corr.* i. 260); sometimes to record the outrageously timid futility of his own gestures of sympathy, 'This
morning I have been to the field of battle and looked at the
trenches. I condescended to speak with two Frenchmen, consoling
myself by an occasional attempt at sarcasm; . . . Last night I had
the pleasure of abandoning a café on the entrance of the French.
The Italians expect you to do so.—It was quite composedly
done—no bravado or hurry' (*Corr.* i. 266, 268). And all the while,
receptive, alert, sharply aware of himself and his surroundings,
he was shaping the clarity of his disengagement and his personal
insurrection into the hexameters of the 'Roman poem' which
John Addington Symonds called in 1868 'perhaps, the most highly
finished, various, and artistically complete of all his works'.[1]

2. *AMOURS DE VOYAGE*

In fact unity, agreement, is always silent, or soft-voiced; it is only discord that
loudly proclaims itself. So long as the several elements of Life, all fitly adjusted,
can pour forth their movement like harmonious tuned strings, it is a melody
and unison; Life from its mysterious fountains, flows out as in celestial music
and diapason. . . . Thus . . . in some languages, is the state of health well denoted
by a term expressing unity; when we feel ourselves as we wish to be, we say
that we are *whole*.   Thomas Carlyle, 'Characteristics'.

We constantly tend to think that discontinuities in nature are only *apparent*
and that a fuller investigation would reveal the underlying continuity. This
shrinking from a gap or jump in nature has developed to a degree which para-
lyses any objective perception, and prejudices our seeing things as they really
are. For an objective view of reality we must make use both of the categories
of continuity and discontinuity. Our principal concern at the present should be
the temper or disposition of mind which can look at a gap or chasm without
shuddering.   T. E. Hulme, *Speculations*.

The hero of *The Bothie* had gloriously triumphed over the
maladies of mid-nineteenth-century England. Pausing only to

[1] J. A. Symonds, 'Arthur Hugh Clough', *Fortnightly Review*, x (Dec. 1868),
601.

allow love to mature and to pick up his Oxford First, he had carried his Highland bride off on a flood-tide of conviction to an Antipodean farm. In his next long poem, begun (an early version was complete by the end of October 1849) in the independence of his first genuine holiday, Clough ignored his 'responsibilities' as a poet, refused to enter into any expected poetic transactions. Instead he produced a disturbingly unevasive, witty, and complex study of the psychology of the radically self-conscious intellectual. The toughly ironic yet deeply compassionate scrutiny of Claude (*claudus*, lame) in *Amours de Voyage* is a splendid testimony to the honesty and distinction of mind he achieved through this emancipation.

Claude has often been compared with Eliot's Prufrock. He has the same exquisite complexities of awareness, the same qualities of intelligence, the same sudden wrynesses of self-mockery—and he is, like Prufrock, an embodiment of futility, as much diminished as he is enlarged by his fastidious intelligence. Claude and Prufrock belong to the same family, but they are, in fact, separated by history. Claude, the inveterate doubter, inhabits a particular historical landscape, a middle-ground of the spirit where the traditional unities of experience and meaning have begun to disintegrate, where even the Romantic assertion has lost its potency as a principle of order, and where the escaping—*not escaped*—fragments mock both memory and desire. Claude anticipates Prufrock; he is also the descendant of Werther and Manfred and Childe Harold, of Rene and Obermann. He inherits from these ancestors his absurdly inflated, rather fashionable ego ('Rome disappoints me still; but I shrink and adapt myself to it'), but he also carries with him a radically subversive suspiciousness which makes any real faith in that ego impossible. His particular moment in history is that in which Evangelical introspection, secularized into intellectual liberalism, first faces a central dilemma: as Alfred de Vigny put it, 'In the universal shipwreck of beliefs, to what debris can generous hands still cling?'[1] The hero of Vigny's story finds certainty, finally, in an irreducible because absurdly co-opted idea of Duty, an unwavering commitment to the military code of honour: for Clough's hero there is no such resting-place:

---

[1] Alfred de Vigny, 'The Malacca Cane', in *Military Service and Grandeur*, trans. F. W. Huard (New York, 1919).

> . . . I tremble for something factitious,
> Some malpractice of heart and illegitimate process;
> We are so prone to these things with our terrible notions of duty.
> (II. xi. 273–5. Refs. are to Canto, letter no., and lines.)

Claude is a victim of his time, of 'the *maladie du siècle*—the
nondescript cachexy, in which aspiration mingles with dis-
enchantment, satire and scepticism with a childlike desire for
the tranquillity of reverence and belief—in which self-analysis
has been pushed to the verge of monomania, and all springs of
action are clogged and impeded by the cobwebs of speculation'.[1]
This unending oscillation is a central clue to Claude and his
ennui. He is dissociated not only from the community but from
himself. The affected Oxonian in him mocks at the naïve naturalist, the sceptic at the believer, the realist at the romantic idealist,
the wanderer at the pilgrim. He brings his sharp, often cynically
destructive intelligence to bear on cherished communal and
personal values—Art, Religion, Love, Heroism, Patriotism—and
they suffer under his devaluing scrutiny, but, obstinately, they
refuse to be dismissed entirely, insist uncomfortably on reassert-
ing, in however attenuated a form, their meaningfulness. Acutely,
widely, at times even preposterously sceptical, he is capable, too,
of the sudden unsettling enthusiasm, the sudden near-surrender
to the traditional and believing heart, and his languor is born of
the weariness of this inner conflict, his irony often becomes at
once self-protecting and self-despising:

> *DULCE* it is, and *decorum*, no doubt, for the country to fall,—to
> Offer one's blood an oblation to Freedom, and die for the Cause; yet
> Still, individual culture is also something, and no man
> Finds quite distinct the assurance that he of all others is called on,
> Or would be justified, even, in taking away from the world that
> Precious creature, himself.
> (II. ii. 32–7.)

Unable even to bring his bloodless love-affair to any kind of
conclusion, his futile sojourn in a Rome echoing with martial
conflict becomes a paradigm of the critical intellect's lonely,
private, and questioning progress through an age which set such
a high premium on public certitudes.

Claude, of course, shares many of his qualities and not a few
of his attitudes with his creator. We often suspect that the intel-

---

[1] J. A. Symonds, 'Arthur Hugh Clough', 602.

ligent, sceptical, hesitant voice is Clough's own, and the suspicion is not altogether unfounded in fact. Walter Bagehot, who came to know Clough well in London, wrote:

> The sort of conversation for which he was most remarkable rises again in the *Amours de Voyage*, and gives them to those who knew him in life a very peculiar charm. . . . He saw what it is considered cynicism to see—the absurdities of many persons, the pomposities of many creeds, the splendid zeal with which missionaries rush on to teach what they do not know, the earnestness with which most incomplete solutions of the universe are thrust upon us as complete and satisfying.[1]

One has only to compare some of the letters Clough wrote from Rome with *Amours de Voyage* to see how heavily he drew on personal experience and personal response in the poem. Claude clearly contains a great deal of Clough, and Clough of Claude— probably more than Clough himself allowed in his significantly over-emphatic rejoinder to John Shairp's suggestion that in the poem his 'nature' was 'ridding itself of long-gathered bile' (*Corr.* i. 275). 'Gott und Teufel, my friend,' he exploded, 'you don't suppose all that comes from myself!—I assure you it is extremely *not* so' (*Corr.* i. 276). To concede a closeness between Clough and his non-heroic hero, or to suspect, even, some element of dis- ingenuousness in Clough's explicit disclaimer, is not, however, to assume an identity between them. Apart from the dangers of biographical distortion, the assumption that Clough and Claude are inter-convertible obscures the really relevant and supremely important fact about *Amours de Voyage*: it is a made work of art, a work which fully earns by its achievement the right to be judged as such. It is useful to recall, too, that it is the work of a man who, however muddled his aesthetics might have been occasionally, could locate the superiority of Michelangelo and Leonardo da Vinci to Raphael in the fact that he was 'only natural', while they were 'intellectual', that 'He produc[ed] with and they out of Nature'.

   In a sensitive comparison of one of Clough's letters with one of Claude's, Houghton has shown how, by delicately rephrasing

---

[1] [W. Bagehot], Review of *Poems* (1862), *National Review*, xv (Oct. 1862), 325–6. In an anonymously published article C. E. Norton remarked: 'Had [Clough] been writing in his own name, he could not have uttered his inmost conviction more distinctly, or given the clue to his intellectual life more openly. . . . ' 'Arthur Hugh Clough', *Atlantic Monthly*, ix (Apr. 1862), 465.

his own letter and altering its emphases, Clough has underlined Claude's affectation, highlighted his self-conscious smartness, and given him an unmistakably 'other' life.[1] And this shifting, complex relationship between Clough and Claude is only one of the factors which contribute to the extraordinarily rich and complex range of intellectual and emotional responses that *Amours de Voyage* evokes. Claude is at least as much observed as he is expressed: by mingling self-portraiture with self-caricature Clough achieves an almost total impersonality and objectivity for a poem which begins, essentially, in the subjectivism of self-introspection. Claude the spokesman is also Claude the comic object.

Clough himself called his poem a 'tragi-comedy or comi-tragedy' (*Corr.* ii. 546). The composite, interchangeable epithets are fully justified by the delicate balance the work achieves. Claude exists on a perilous edge between counter-judgements. He is a fool, is recognized as such, recognizes himself as such— but he is also extremely intelligent. Vain, self-absorbed, opinion-ated, he is also pathetically vulnerable, touchingly humble and dependent. Hopelessly undignified, he can yet surprise us by the quiet dignity of his acceptance of failure and by the strength of his recommitment to the life of the intellect. This fine poise is maintained, of course, by the taut control of the containing ironic vision, and when this vision is translated into a structural and stylistic principle, that control involves itself in the total texture of the poem in all its developing meanings—from minor details of movement to larger and deeper significances. One preliminary example, perhaps the most inclusive in the poem, will make this clearer.

If *Amours de Voyage* advances any single positive value, that value resides in its vindication of the life of thought. This connects the poem immediately with *Adam and Eve*, and Claude with Adam. Yet if we place the opening prologue to *Amours de Voyage* against its final epilogue we see at once the immense advance over the sentimentalization of 'knowing' in the earlier work. 'Knowing' is now surrounded by a fine ironic awareness, which, far from being merely clever or destructively cynical, is deeply and sensitively responsible: 'Knowledge' here implies an altogether tougher ability to 'place' both the knower and the activity of knowing.

[1] Houghton, pp. 120-1.

Over the great windy waters, and over the clear-crested summits,
  Unto the sun and the sky, and unto the perfecter earth,
Come, let us go,—to a land wherein gods of the old time wandered,
  Where every breath even now changes to ether divine.
Come, let us go; though withal a voice whisper, 'The world that we live in,
  Whithersoever we turn, still is the same narrow crib;
'Tis but to prove limitation, and measure a cord, that we travel;
  Let who would' scape and be free go to his chamber and think;
'Tis but to change idle fancies for memories wilfully falser;
  'Tis but to go and have been.'—Come, little bark! let us go.

                                                            (I. 1–10.)

    So go forth to the world, to the good report and the evil!
      Go, little book! thy tale, is it not evil and good?
    Go, and if strangers revile, pass quietly by without answer.
      Go, and if curious friends ask of thy rearing and age,
    Say, 'I am flitting about many years from brain unto brain of
      Feeble and restless youths born to inglorious days:
    But', so finish the word, 'I was writ in a Roman chamber,
      When from Janiculan heights thundered the cannon of France.'

                                                            (V. 217–24.)

The two passages do not invite juxtaposition merely because they
occupy such significant positions in the poem; neither does the
relationship between them depend on simple, inert contrast.
Poetically the two passages are contiguous. The tension between
them is kept alive by an active traffic of poetic meaning, by an
ironically unbroken modulation into contrast. The imagery of
movement is the main connective. The emancipated outward and
upward impulse of the prologue's opening becomes more ample
with each succeeding line, the expanding sweep more ideal, till,
in the fourth line, aspiration frankly spills over into escape—
'every breath even now changes to ether divine'. This is the cue
for the weary voice of the disillusioned idealist. A contrary movement sets in, narrowing, compressing, down to the chamber,
and, ultimately, to the absolute arrestment of the eighth line—
''Tis but to go and have been'. Emptied of meaning, movement
has been reduced to mere motion. Travel has become the merest
tourism (Claude in one of his aspects is simply a creature of
Murray's *Guide*). It is into an uncertain, tossing in-betweenness
of meaning that the 'little bark' sets forth. The epilogue picks
up the image of movement at this point in the restless flitting of
lines 221–2 (the verbal link confirming the relationship between

the voyaging 'bark' and the 'little book'), and in the next two lines that restlessness resolves itself into the clear contrasts of the prologue, only now the movement is reversed. The life of the Roman chamber swells outward and upward to the splendid final comment of the French guns on the now achieved 'Janiculan heights'. What has happened, in fact, is that we have been wheeled round to the poem's beginning, and an ironic relationship has been established not only between the impossibly expansive aspiration and the sequestered whisper of doubt, or between that whisper and the full-throated engagement of the French cannon, but between all three. The committed cannons seem to get the best of this exchange—but only seem to, and the deceptiveness is important. For they are (the whole poem alerts us to the fact) the cannons of the oppressor, the commanding rhetoric which attaches to them is as fraudulent as their achievement. The impressive 'weight' of the two final lines is an integral part of the ironic and inspecting strategy.[1]

It is this kind of poetic craftsmanship, which can annex and revitalize a worn literary trope, coupled with the skilful and subtle anatomization of Claude, that gives to *Amours de Voyage* its distinction and completeness. It is a masterpiece flawed only by the occasional evidence of not fully convinced workmanship —the failure in narrative technique in some of Mary Trevellyn's letters, for instance,[2] or the odd passage where the hexameters, losing confidence in their own casual rejection of elevation, seek reassurance in a derived and obvious literary 'dignity'.[3] Clough himself had his qualms about this aspect of the poem. 'What I want assurance of', he wrote to Shairp, 'is in the way of execution rather than conception. If I were only half as sure of the bearableness of the former as I am of the propriety of the latter, I would publish at once. . . . However I believe that the execution of this is so poor that it makes the conception a fair subject of disgust' (*Corr.* i. 276). One must make allowances for Clough's character-

---

[1] The rhetoric of deflation in the poem is almost as varied as it is recurrent. III. iii. 68–73, and v. vi. 118–28, are two passages which indicate more obviously the variety and range of this movement of language and the multiple perspectives it can create.   [2] See especially Canto v, Letters i and iii.

[3] In referring to derived literary dignity I have in mind passages like v. v. 104–12, which, calling to mind as it does some of the speeches of Brutus (see especially *Julius Caesar*, IV. iii. 275 f.), leans heavily on Shakespearean rhetoric for its tonalities.

istic disparagement of his own poetry, but considering the absoluteness of the revolt which *Amours de Voyage* represents, what is surprising is not that he should have been dubious but that he should have written it at all. For the poem flouts nearly all conventional canons of the 'poetical'. Not only is its chief character a disturbing, witty, and mocking doubter, but the vacillating, introspective wretch does not even, as Walter Bagehot remarked uneasily, reflect in a 'very dignified or heroic manner'.[1]

Now supposing the French or the Neapolitan soldier
Should by some evil chance come exploring the Maison Serny
(Where the family English are all to assemble for safety),
Am I prepared to lay down my life for the British female?
Really, who knows? One has bowed and talked, till, little by little,
All the natural heat has escaped of the chivalrous spirit.
Oh, one conformed, of course; but one doesn't die for good manners,
Stab or shoot, or be shot, by way of a graceful attention.

(II. iv. 65-72.)

And if the non-hero lacks 'elevation', the poem itself makes no attempt to furnish it either. It comes to no clear moral decision or condemnation, offers no sustaining resolution: its sense of, and response to, reality remains stubbornly disturbing to the end. Even its low-keyed, casual idiom offers no atoning pleasure of mellifluousness. The nonchalant, iconoclastic verse makes little pretence to 'beauty' and the hexameter does not 'sing': as one reviewer, passing the expected judgement with exquisitely measured consideration, put it in 1862, 'It may be doubted whether what we may call the low domestic style in poetry is even in itself otherwise than a mistake.'[2]

Clough, never entirely at ease in the rebel's role, seems to have been fully aware of the extensive heterodoxy of *Amours de Voyage*. He took particular care over the final epilogue, discarding several versions before he arrived at the printed one.[3] Artistically his

---

[1] W. Bagehot, *Literary Studies*, 2 vols. (London, 1879), ii. 315. J. I. Osborne, too, found Claude falling short of 'the minimum of dignity desirable in the hero of a poem of this sort and length'. *Arthur Hugh Clough* (London, 1920), p. 120.

[2] [W. L. Collins], 'Clough's Poems', *Blackwood's Magazine*, xcii (Nov. 1862), 595. The review considers Clough's verse as a parallel with Patmore's in *The Angel in the House* and *Faithful Forever*.

[3] In Tom Arnold's opinion the final version of the Epilogue was written in 1858. 'Arthur Hugh Clough: A Sketch', p. 112. He is not a very trustworthy witness in these matters, however, since he maintained also that 'Say not the struggle nought availeth' was written during his friend's 'last illness'. Ibid., p. 115.

judgement was exact. The printed version is vastly superior to any of the extant earlier ones, but these latter shed an important light on his misgivings about the poem and the reception it was likely to get not only from a larger audience but from his expectant friends. To judge from these early versions his misgivings concerned both the substance and the manner of the poem. In one of them the first four lines read:

> So to the critical speech and yet more critical silence
>> Go, thine epithets earn morbid, imperfect, obscure.
> Go disappointment that will be to friends, disappointment already
>> Unto the labouring soul which hath conceived and borne.[1]

The editors of the Oxford *Poems* have printed an even more interesting possible alternative which Clough titled 'L'Envoi':[2]

> So to the critical speech go forth and the critical silence
>> Go; and if scrupulous souls ask of thy moral and end,
> What, if exclaim they, and wherefore, and how do we leave thee
>>> adjudging
>> Peace to the selfish and vain, grief to the beautiful soul,
> Nay, but rewrite, rearrange, bring it all in the ending to comfort,
>> Call things at least by their names; this is a good, this a bad;
> Say,—Am I God to make dead or alive, to repair the injustice,
>> Balance the pains, and undo all the vext ravel of life,
> Am I the Judge, say, Am I, of all the Earth to assign things
>> One name or other and give sentence to this or to that?
> Ah no! I am not such. I am but a poor foolish mirror
>> Helpless to judge or to act, faithful alone to reflect.
> Ah could a poor dumb glass, could a silvered plate make answer
>> Ah if a mirror could speak, angry perhaps it would say,
> There!—thou world! look, there! is the vile dirty face that you
>>> show me—
> Nay, but provoke not to speech, silence beseemeth it best.

The use of the mirror as image of both the poem and the poet's function is significant—especially when contrasted with Matthew Arnold's use of the same image in the 'wind-borne, mirroring soul' in *Empedocles on Etna*, a poem which Arnold was working on in 1849 and which provides some instructive and illuminating points of comparison and contrast, to Arnold's disadvantage I

---

[1] 1849 (Roma) Notebook, Balliol MS. 441, fol. 32.
[2] *Poems*, p. 527. The editors have queried this as an 'alternative'. It is not clear what other possibility they might have had in mind.

think, with *Amours de Voyage* in matters of structure, language, and vision. Here the mirror analogy emphasizes Clough's non-expressive aims, his interest in language as a lucidly responsive, discriminating, and therefore valuable recorder. It strengthens, too, his clear inversion of the role of Romantic-Victorian Poet-Prophet-Lawgiver-and-Sage. The vehement explicitness of this inversion, and of his repudiation of conventional moral simplicities, makes it tempting to conjecture that this 'L'Envoi' was written after the poem had had its taste of criticism.

For in the event, Clough's apprehensions were completely justified. Shairp was one of the first to see an early draft (*Corr.* i. 274), and his comments were exactly predictable.

> The state of soul of which it is a projection I do not like. It strikes me as the most Werterish (not that I ever read Werter) of all you have yet done. There is no hope, nor strength, nor belief in these;— everything crumbles to dust beneath a ceaseless self-introspection and criticism which is throughout the one only inspiration. The gaiety of manner where no gaiety is, becomes flippancy. In the Bothie . . . there was strength and something positive in the men's characters and the Highland Hills—but here this fresh element is wanting and blasé disgust at men and things rampant. The Ambarvalia, if Werterish, was honest serious Werterism—but this is Beppoish or Don Juanish (If I remember them right). The Hexameters still do not go down with me. They give me a sense of Travestie—which is their place I think. The snatches of longs and shorts are very nice, but they would not do to be more than snatches. One page or two of the Hexameters rise into music—that 'Falling Falling still to the ancient Lyrical cadence' and that about the statues on the Monte Cavallo. But I need not go on to enumerate minor things which I liked. No, I would cast it behind me and the spirit from which it emanates and to higher, more healthful, hopeful things purely aspire (*Corr.* i. 275).

In a sentence which reads like a caricature of the immediate ethos Clough was forced to contend with, Shairp added, 'I won't flatter; but you were not made, my dear Clough, to make sport before The Philistines in this way, but for something else.' Clough remained unshaken. 'You're a funny creature, my dear old fellow—If one don't sing you a ballant or read you a philosophic sermonette, if one don't talk about the gowans or faith— you're not pleased' (*Corr.* i. 276). When Shairp repeated his criticisms in his next letter, adding that the 'execution too [was]

wanting in dramatic power, scenes, and scenery' (*Corr.* i. 277),
Clough replied with a refreshing near-rudeness which veiled
under its light-heartedness a serious criticism of the cult of
natural description in poetry: '. . . I am not sure that Scenes and
Scenery, after which you always go awhoring, would exactly
improve the matter. . . . Your censure of the conception almost
provoked me into publishing—because it showed how washy
the world is in its confidences. There is a Roland for your Oliver,
—my boy.—But I probably shan't publish for fear of a row with
my Sadducees.'[1] His 'Sadducees' were the Unitarians who controlled University Hall. Nonconformity, even in poetry, demanded extraordinary circumspection.

Apart from the comments—somewhat politely enthusiastic—
made by American friends when *Amours de Voyage* was first
published in serial form in the *Atlantic Monthly* in 1858,[2] Shairp's
is—with one important exception—the only criticism of the
poem which survives in the letters. Matthew Arnold, the friend
whose opinion Clough valued most highly, wrote: 'We will
not discuss what is past any more: as to the Italian poem, if I
forbore to comment it was that I had nothing special to say—
what is to be said when a thing does not suit you—suiting
and not suiting is a subjective affair and only time determines, by
the colour a thing takes with years, whether it *ought* to have
suited or no.'[3] This was in March 1853, when Arnold was attempting to reassure Clough that any impression of coolness he might
have created by his behaviour in the past had been wholly un-
intended. How long was it since he had seen the poem? The
'critical silence' which the poem had to face was even more

---

[1] *Corr.* i. 278. It is possible that Clough was influenced in his scorn for natural
description by Carlyle's comments on 'View-hunting' in literature (cf. 'Characteristics', in *Works*, xxviii. 24).

[2] See *Corr.* ii. 536–7 (Lowell), 544 (Lowell), 548 (Emerson). Although Lowell's
comments are the more appreciative, Emerson's stand out because of his complaint about the poem not ending happily. The 'whimper' with which *Amours
de Voyage* appears to end caused considerable discomfort to nineteenth-century
readers. K. Graham, *English Criticism of the Novel, 1865–1900* (Oxford, 1966),
pp. 53–4, is useful in showing how the demand for a satisfying ending, even in
novels, influenced the reaction to realism quite late in the century.

[3] Lowry, pp. 131–2. In Aug. 1855, however, Arnold wrote apropos of Tennyson, 'From the extracts I have seen from Maud, he seems in his old age to be
coming to your manner in the Bothie and the Roman poem. That manner, as
you know, I do not like: but certainly, if it is to be used, you use it with far
more freedom vigour and abundance than he does.' Ibid., p. 147.

damning than the 'critical speech' of people like Shairp. One sees
why Clough never published *Amours de Voyage* in England.
One sees, too, why he offered it with noticeable diffidence[1]
to the *Atlantic Monthly* nine years after its composition. That he
published it at all reveals a tenacious faith in the poem.

Although *Amours de Voyage* has never been popular, it has had,
since its first publication in England in 1862, a steady and sometimes distinguished support, and we are beginning to recognize
its claims as one of the finest, most profoundly original poems of
its time.[2] As A. Alvarez put it, incisively:

Clough's genius was to see that, whatever pressure to conform his
age and friends exerted on him, his unique brand of touchy, choosy
sophistication couldn't be expressed in the language of mid-nineteenth-
century romanticism. Like Henry James's intimations of morality,
his own needle-fine responses required a subtly polished language of
manners. Through that casual formality alone he could catch what he
called, in one of his best similes,

> . . . in a stream when the wave of the tide is
> Coming and not yet come—a sort of poise and retention.

This critical poise and retention of sensibility is given perfect form
only in *Amours*. . . . [I]n that, I think, he wrote better than any Victorian poet apart from Hopkins.[3]

The implied judgement of Victorian poetry is tendentious, but
the association with Hopkins is apt. *Amours de Voyage* breaks new
and significant poetic ground. Showing up the weaknesses, the
falsities, the opacities of the conventions of Victorian-Romantic
poetic language, the 'casual formality' of its hexameters anticipates
some of the characteristic qualities of the twentieth-century
poetic voice and manner.[4] In isolating this distinctive idiom for
attention and praise, however, it is easy to overlook the poem

---

[1] Cf. 'If you see or write to Lowell, tell him to postpone my hexameters sine
die if he likes—I don't think they would be popular and have not any great
affection or even esteem for them.' Clough to C. E. Norton, *Corr.* ii. 535.

[2] See especially John Goode's fine essay, '*Amours de Voyage*: the Aqueous
Poem', in *The Major Victorian Poets: Reconsiderations*, ed. Isobel Armstrong
(London, 1969), pp. 275–97.

[3] A. Alvarez, 'Convictions of Excellence', *New Statesman*, 3 Feb. 1962, 163–4.

[4] The affinities between Clough and poets like Eliot were first pointed out by
Michael Roberts in his Introduction to the *Faber Book of Modern Verse* (London,
1936), pp. 11–14. They have been more elaborately indicated in F. Bowers,
'Arthur Hugh Clough: The Modern Mind', *Studies in English Literature* (hereafter
SEL) vi (Autumn 1966), 709–16.

itself, to lose sight of the fact that this 'casual formality' is only a part of a brilliantly organized, brilliantly analytical, poetic whole, that it is one component only in Clough's originality.

To put it with the pure simplicity of cliché, *Amours de Voyage* is concerned with the search for meaning. Its aims are twofold: first, to create the figure of Claude as a particular, historically rooted instance of the hypersensitive intelligence, quick to see through conventional values and detect the throttling simplifications on which they rest; second, to observe him in the act of criticism and analysis, also attempting to convert perception into meaning and re-establish a syntax of experience—to recognize 'this' and 'that' and put the two together. The modified dramatic form of the poem is exactly fitted to these aims. Claude writes nearly all the letters. Those written by the Trevellyn girls provide only an occasional change of perspective—a necessary one, since both Georgina's fussy, utterly mindless conventionality, and Mary's subdued suggestions of a more enduring substantiality and worth, help to locate Claude. The drama, after all, is wholly his, the only real dialogue is 'of the mind with itself'. And yet the drama is not exactly the drama of interior monologue: Claude is defined by the personal letter, that oblique and yet most self-conscious of verbal forms. His existence is inseparable from his capacity for considered verbalization, his capacity to find the exactly answering, discriminating phrase. He is at once the text and the gloss: he is the creature, not of spontaneous utterance, but of the deliberate, inevitable, afterthought. The letter form, approaching the intimacy and directness of private self-revelation, can place us sufficiently close to the cutting-edge of Claude's consciousness to involve us in the involutions, the hesitations, the revisions, and the circuits, of his responses:

Yet it is pleasant, I own it, to be in their company; pleasant,
Whatever else it may be, to abide in the feminine presence.
Pleasant, but wrong, will you say? But this happy, serene coexistence
Is to some poor soft souls, I fear, a necessity simple,
Meat and drink and life, and music, filling with sweetness,
Thrilling with melody sweet, with harmonies strange overwhelming,
All the long-silent strings of an awkward, meaningless fabric.
Yet as for that, I could live, I believe, with children; to have those
Pure and delicate forms encompassing, moving about you,
This were enough, I could think; and truly with glad resignation

Could from the dream of romance, from the fever of flushed
                                                  adolescence,
Look to escape and subside into peaceful avuncular functions.
                                                  (I. ix. 168–79.)

Intimidated by the directness of the first statement, the mind
burrows hastily into qualification—'pleasant, whatever else it
may be'—and into the safe, comfortably abstract, and un-
localized 'feminine presence'. Issuing forth once more to grapple
with felt experience, the statement strengthens from 'meat and
drink' to 'life', from the minimum of the necessary to the plenitude of the essential, and from mere 'coexistence' to the 'over-
whelming' reciprocity of musical harmony. Once again the
affirmation has been pushed too far, and the mind, withdrawing
to the refuge of the safely asexual, adds a new motive to the
general fear of illusion ('the dream of romance') in Claude's
uneasiness about his association with Mary Trevellyn. In this
letter Claude enforces an inward view; he can equally impose a
distance, and, by holding himself far enough, elicit and record an
almost wholly critical response to his own idling mind, moving
aimlessly back and forth along itself, outrageously, comically,
resolute only in its refusal to engage with experience, trapped in
and isolated by its awareness of miscellaneousness and indeterminacy.

So we stand in the sun, but afraid of a probable shower;
So we stand and stare, and see, to the left of St. Peter's,
Smoke, from the cannon, white,—but that is at intervals only,—
Black, from a burning house, we suppose, by the Cavalleggieri;
And we believe we discern some lines of men descending
Down through the vineyard-slopes, and catch a bayonet gleaming.
Every ten minutes, however,—in this there is no misconception,—
Comes a great white puff from behind Michael Angelo's dome, and
After a space the report of a real big gun,—not the Frenchman's?—
That must be doing some work. And so we watch and conjecture.
   Shortly, an Englishman comes, who says he has been to St. Peter's,
Seen the Piazza and troops, but that is all he can tell us;
So we watch and sit, and, indeed, it begins to be tiresome.—
All this smoke is outside; when it has come to the inside,
It will be time, perhaps, to descend and retreat to our houses.
                                                  (II. v. 117–31.)

Moving between two such contrary potentialities the form
becomes a subtly controlling and directing instrument.

All this, however, is only on the outskirts of the poem's existence. The centre is the poetry itself and in this the Roman background is inseparably involved. At an obvious level the heroic defence of the Mazzinian Republic provides an ironic commentary on Claude's fastidious hesitancy, but the setting penetrates much further into the poem's life and creates much more profoundly significant ironic patterns. For underlying this undetermined Rome of present political violence, there is another Rome felt as an organic presence—Rome as the Eternal City, the seat of civilization, the embodiment of achievement and culture, where the tides of history have been stilled into the poised and mythic tranquillity of art. The evidences of this Rome are everywhere and they bring memories of wholeness and of meaningful continuities which mock the perspiring, inchoate, distracted, and dislocated present. Once he has shed his initial languidly clever superiority, Claude responds positively to the community of meanings and values which this Rome represents; only, he is a fragment in a fragmented world and history separates him from that community. 'Once', as Heine wrote, 'the world was whole, in antiquity and the Middle Ages; despite external conflicts there was an all-embracing unity, and the poets were also whole. We are ready to honour these poets and take delight in them; but all imitation of their wholeness is a lie, which the healthy eye detects and which cannot escape derision.'[1] The poetry which re-creates Claude's often ludicrous, often tragic attempt to achieve meaning displays a precise awareness of the crisis in culture that gives to his attempt a relevance extending beyond the purely personal. Without an explicit historical insistence *Amours de Voyage* achieves through the integrated movement of structure and language a scope, density, and precision which shows up the pallidness of *Empedocles on Etna*.[2]

[1] *Die Bader von Lucca, Kapitel IV*: Einst war die Welt ganz, im Altertum und im Mittel-alter, trotz der äusseren Kampfe gab's doch noch immer eine Welteinheit, und es gab ganze Dichter. Wir wollen diese Dichter ehren und uns an ihnen erfreuen; aber jede Nachahmung ihrer Ganzheit ist eine Lüge, eine Lüge, die jedes gesunde Auge durchschaut, und die dem Hohne dann nicht entgeht. (H. Heine, *Prosa* (Munchen/Zurich, 1961), pp. 157–8).

[2] It is relevant to recall here Clough's strictures on Matthew Arnold's poetry: 'Not by turning and twisting his eyes, in the hope of seeing things as Homer, Sophocles, Virgil, or Milton saw them; but by seeing them, by accepting them as he sees them, and faithfully depicting accordingly, will he attain the object he desires.' 'Recent English Poetry', Trawick, p. 160.

Unwittingly Shairp laid his finger on something basic in the poetic structure and method of *Amours de Voyage* when he excepted from his general condemnation the 'snatches of longs and shorts' and the 'page or two' of the hexameters which 'rise into music'. For two distinct kinds of poetry are immediately discernible in the poem, and the active, complexly ironic relationship between them is centrally important in creating the sensitive and mobile wakefulness which distinguishes the work as a whole. The elegiacs that frame each canto have a consistent and clearly recognizable poetic life, which consciously recalls the ideal past and is permeated by it.

> Is it illusion? or does there a spirit from perfecter ages,
>   Here, even yet, amid loss, change, and corruption abide?
> Does there a spirit we know not, though seek, though we find,
>   comprehend not,
>   Here to entice and confuse, tempt and evade us, abide?
> Lives in the exquisite grace of the column disjointed and single,
>   Haunts the rude masses of brick garlanded gayly with vine,
> E'en in the turret fantastic surviving that springs from the ruin,
>   E'en in the people itself? is it illusion or not?
>
> (II. 1–8.)

Saturated in the Rome of Antiquity and controlled by its presence, this self-possessed voice, which gives to that Rome its high imaginative valency, translates Claude's hesitant, self-conscious wanderings and perplexed conflicts into an ironically distanced, recognizably 'poetic' experience.

> Yet to the wondrous St. Peter's, and yet to the solemn Rotonda,
>   Mingling with heroes and gods, yet to the Vatican walls,
> Yet may we go, and recline, while a whole mighty world seems above us
>   Gathered and fixed to all time into one roofing supreme;
> Yet may we, thinking on these things, exclude what is meaner around us;
>   Yet, at the worst of the worst, books and a chamber remain;
> Yet may we think, and forget, and possess our souls in resistance.—
>   Ah, but away from the stir, shouting, and gossip of war,
> Where, upon Appenine slope, with the chestnut the oak-trees immingle,
>   Where amid odorous copse bridle-paths wander and wind,
> Where under mulberry-branches the diligent rivulet sparkles,
>   Or amid cotton and maize peasants their water-works ply,
> Where, over fig-tree and orange in tier upon tier still repeated,
>   Garden on garden upreared, balconies step to the sky,—

Ah, that I were, far away from the crowd and the streets of the city,
  Under the vine-trellis laid, O my beloved, with thee!

                                                                    (III. 1–16.)

Clearly the ironic traffic runs both ways. If these gracefully
finished, traditionally accomplished elegiacs mock at the sprawl-
ing libertinage of the hexameters, the exceptional openness of
the hexameters, their receptiveness to process, exposes, in turn,
the illusory and unreal quality of this kind of loveliness. The
two kinds of poetry, in fact, organize two radically different
modes of experience. Their confrontation dramatizes the crisis in
meaning.

Yet, opposed as these two kinds of poetry are, they are not
discontinuous. The hexameters and the elegiacs are linked by a
common pattern of imagery which, in drawing them together,
only emphasizes the absolute difference between them. The
language of the hexameters seems to reach out to that of the
elegiacs and to the kind of rest which that language organizes;
the attempt, ironically, proves its own impossibility. Two main
classes of image predominate in *Amours de Voyage*, and their
centrality in a poem concerned so fundamentally with the search
for meaning and integrity and with the discrimination of historical
continuity will be immediately apparent. To describe them in
their most general and inclusive aspect, these are the continually
recurring images of solidness and fixity and of fluidity and movement. Most frequently they appear as images of land and water,
but they appear in many other forms as well—as images of voyaging and travel, of arrival and departure, the flow of a crowd,
the fixity of a relationship, the flow of emotions: the list can be
expanded quite easily. In themselves the images are important,
of course, but even more important is the difference in their
treatment and function in the two kinds of poetry, and the emotional significance with which they are invested.

In the elegiacs these leading images are absorbed into serenely
balanced, ideally harmonious landscapes from which they derive
an unobtrusive stability and completeness of meaning:

Therefore farewell, ye hills, and ye, ye envineyarded ruins!
  Therefore farewell, ye walls, palaces, pillars, and domes!
Therefore farewell, far seen, ye peaks of the mythic Albano,
  Seen from Montorio's height, Tibur and Æsula's hills!

Ah, could we once, ere we go, could we stand, while, to ocean descending,
*   Sinks o'er the yellow dark plain slowly the yellow broad sun,*
Stand, from the forest emerging at sunset, at once in the champaign,
*   Open, but studded with trees, chestnuts umbrageous and old,*
E'en in those fair open fields that incurve to thy beautiful hollow,
*   Nemi, imbedded in wood, Nemi, inurned in the hill!*

(III. 293–302.)

There is a city, upbuilt on the quays of the turbulent Arno,
*   Under Fiesole's heights,—thither are we to return?*
There is a city that fringes the curve of the inflowing waters,
*   Under the perilous hill fringes the beautiful bay,—*
Parthenope do they call thee?—the Siren, Neapolis, seated
*   Under Vesevus's hill,—are we receding to thee?*

(V. 1–6.)

Exempt from the press and complexity of particulars, this poetry
of evocation accumulates its pictures into a perfect poise and
simplicity of meaning—sea balances land, mountain plain, nature
civilization, movement stillness. The harmony of the landscape
is the outward and visible sign of an inner grace of uncomplexity
—love is sure here and totally convinced, travel is purposeful,
even loss has meaning.

In the elegiacs the poetic significance of these images of solidness and fluidity is stabilized by their poetic context. Significantly,
it is primarily when Claude responds most simply and unreservedly to the spell of Roman antiquity that the hexameters
approach most nearly the poetic quality of the elegiacs, and, in
doing so, sustain a similar kind of equilibrium in these images.

Ye, too, marvellous Twain, that erect on the Monte Cavallo
Stand by your rearing steeds in the grace of your motionless
                                                movement,
Stand with your upstretched arms and tranquil regardant faces,
Stand as instinct with life in the might of immutable manhood,—
O ye mighty and strange, ye ancient divine ones of Hellas,
Are ye Christian too? . . .
    And ye, silent, supreme in serene and victorious marble,
Ye that encircle the walls of the stately Vatican chambers,
Juno and Ceres, Minerva, Apollo, the Muses and Bacchus,
Ye unto whom far and near come posting the Christian pilgrims,
Ye that are ranged in the halls of the mystic Christian Pontiff,
Are ye also baptized? are ye of the kingdom of Heaven?

(I. x. 186–91; 194–9.)

Tibur is beautiful, too, and the orchard slopes, and the Anio
Falling, falling yet, to the ancient lyrical cadence;
Tibur and Anio's tide; and cool from Lucretilis ever,
With the Digentian stream, and with the Bandusian fountain,
Folded in Sabine recesses, the valley and villa of Horace:—
So not seeing I sang; so seeing and listening say I,
Here as I sit by the stream, as I gaze at the cell of the Sybil,
Here with Albunea's home and the grove of Tiburnus beside me;
Tivoli beautiful is, and musical, O Teverone,
Dashing from mountain to plain, thy parted impetuous waters!
Tivoli's waters and rocks; and fair under Monte Gennaro
(Haunt even yet, I must think, as I wander and gaze, of the shadows,
Faded and pale, yet immortal, of Faunus, the Nymphs, and the Graces),
Fair in itself, and yet fairer with human completing creations,
Folded in Sabine recesses the valley and villa of Horace: . . .

(III. xi. 214–28.)

Normally this kind of stability is as foreign to the hexameters as
is the lucid, contemplating, Horatian voice, for the characteristic
idiom of the hexameters and the mode of being out of which
that idiom emerges provide no such continuously supporting and
equilibriating context. Claude can no more find absolute rest in
the 'positive, calm, Stoic-Epicurean acceptance' (I. iv. 76) of
Classical and Renaissance humanism than he can free himself
completely from the stark, neurotic dualisms of Protestantism,

With its humiliations and exaltations combining,
Exaltations sublime, and yet diviner abasements,
Aspirations from something most shameful here upon earth and
In our poor selves to something most perfect above in the heavens,—
(I. iv. 66–9.)

or exorcize himself of the anguishing injunction, 'Except ye be
converted, and become as little children, ye shall not enter into
the kingdom of heaven': his desire for the safe, sinless, and asexual
company of children (I. ix. 175–80) acquires wicked ironic point
from being interposed between his rejection of 'the Martyrs,
and Saints, and Confessors, and Virgins, and children' in favour
of the 'mightier forms of an older, austerer worship' (I. viii.
159–60), on the one side, and, on the other, his apostrophe to the
'immutable manhood' of the Horse Tamers on the Monte Cavallo.
Normally the implications and the emotional equivalents of
the leading images of fixity and fluidity are in a constant state of

transformation in the hexameters. Images of fixity are used, for instance, to represent the strangling effect of civilization on the natural life (I. ii), the tyranny of regimented devotion (I. v), the closed, limpet-like life of selfish withdrawal (II. ii), the safe familiarity of the present and the near at hand (II. iv), the rest and steadiness of achieved human relationship (II. xi), the serene contemplation of the spectator withdrawn from any relationship (II. xii), an escape from the flux of living (III. vii), a hard and naked rock to which to cling amid loss and change (v. v). Images of fluidity can represent the wandering, chaotic seas of theological controversy, historically disastrous because their invasion denies and perverts pure growth (I. v), the transformation of a peaceful crowd into a violent mob (II. ix), the life of primitive organisms in the Aqueous Ages of the world (III. ii), the limitless ocean of possibility when one is freed from the circumscription of action (III. vi), the ebb and flow of love's fortunes (IV. iii). This crudely descriptive and merely illustrative list is useful only quantitatively in indicating something of the range and pervasiveness of these sliding significances. Only the poetry itself gives us the experience of these transformations in meaning:

But I am in for it now,—*laissez faire*, of a truth, *laissez aller*.
Yes, I am going,—I feel it, I feel and cannot recall it,—
Fusing with this thing and that, entering into all sorts of relations,
Tying I know not what ties, which, whatever they are, I know one
                                                            thing,
Will, and must, woe is me, be one day painfully broken,—
Broken with painful remorses, with shrinkings of soul, and
                                                    relentings,
Foolish delays, more foolish evasions, most foolish renewals.
But I have made the step, have quitted the ship of Ulysses;
Quitted the sea and the shore, passed into the magical island;
Yet on my lips is the *moly*, medicinal, offered of Hermes.
I have come into the precinct, the labyrinth closes around me,
Path into path rounding slyly; I pace slowly on, and the fancy,
Struggling awhile to sustain the long sequences, weary, bewildered,
Fain must collapse in despair; I yield, I am lost, and know nothing;
Yet in my bosom unbroken remaineth the clue; I shall use it.
Lo, with the rope on my loins I descend through the fissure; I
                                                        sink, yet
Inly secure in the strength of invisible arms up above me;
Still, wheresoever I swing, wherever to shore, or to shelf, or

Floor of cavern untrodden, shell-sprinkled, enchanting, I know I
Yet shall one time feel the strong cord tighten about me,—
Feel it, relentless, upbear me from spots I would rest in; and though
                                                                    the
Rope sway wildly, I faint, crags wound me, from crag unto crag re-
Bounding, or, wide in the void, I die ten deaths, ere the end I
Yet shall plant firm foot on the broad lofty spaces I quit, shall
Feel underneath me again the great massy strengths of abstraction,
Look yet abroad from the height o'er the sea whose salt wave I
                                                    have tasted.
                                            (I. xii. 227–52.)

The rate and density of change are dizzying; the images of fixity
and movement, of solidness and fluidity, draw together, interpenetrate, fall apart, change emotional colour and even actual
reference. This oscillating, helplessly open poetry places us at the
vertiginous centre of consciousness, where meaning is in constant
process, solidifying, dissolving, re-forming into new shapes, and
where large significances have to be painfully extracted from an
unremitting flux.

   This tension and ambiguity in meaning is achieved through—
and regulated by—Clough's deceptively casual hexameters. Spill-
ing more frequently into enjambement and running to longer
verse-paragraphs, infinitely more subtle in movement than the
hexameters of *The Bothie*, these long, untwisting lines achieve a
remarkable range and flexibility of expressiveness and a delicate
command over pause and cadence. Without the least strain they
can rise to a quiet understated lyricism, drop to the informal
rhythms of natural colloquial speech, or record deftly the empty
talkativeness of Georgina Trevellyn's letters. What distinguishes
them most clearly, however, is their brilliant syntactical strategy.

   So, I have seen a man killed! An experience that, among others!
   Yes, I suppose I have; although I can hardly be certain,
   And in a court of justice could never declare I had seen it.
   But a man was killed, I am told, in a place where I saw
   Something; a man was killed, I am told, and I saw something
                                            (II. vii. 164–8.)

      Great is Fate, and is best. I believe in Providence partly.
      What is ordained is right, and all that happens is ordered.
      Ah, no, that isn't it. But yet I retain my conclusion.
                                            (V. viii. 176–8.)

The punctuation is not heavily grammatical. It reproduces, rather, the rhythmic patterns of reflective speech, and the loosely strung phrases reach out to one another through these light pauses, each phrase picking up the meaning at the point at which it has been deposited by the preceding one and pushing it—comically in the first example, pathetically in the second—one unexpected stage further. The curiously open syntax, delicately following every curve and nuance of response, gently—and ironically— disconnects 'this' from 'that' and disperses statement into non-statement. In this deftly controlled, fastidiously self-inspective poetry of afterthought even the single line can become the subtle record of ambivalence:

> I am in love, you say: I do not think so, exactly.
>
> (II. x. 265.)

This sensitive syntactical fidelity to the tentative and the provisional in human response not only enables the hexameters to hold meanings and rhetorics in suspense and observe their incipience and dissolution, but gives to Claude's recognitions, when he does arrive at them, a movingly precise, exact, veracity:

> She goes,—therefore I go; she moves,—I move, not to lose her.
>
> (II. xiii. 291.)

It is this rhetorically validated veracity, this minimal utterance, which ensures that Claude emerges from the poem as something more than a mere fool or an absolute failure. The story of his love ends 'in smoke' (*Corr.* ii. 538) and he loses Mary Trevellyn. Unable to relate himself to himself or, through decision, to the world which surrounds him, he submits to the rule of necessity;

> Ah, the key of our life, that passes all wards, opens all locks,
> Is not *I will*, but *I must*. I must,—I must,—and I do it.
>
> (v. viii. 154–5.)

Mainly because of his interminable speculativeness, his incessant 'fiddle-faddling' (IV. iii. 38), partly because he is genuinely, as Clough called him, an '*unfortunate* fool' (*Corr.* i. 278, my italics) and the victim of circumstances, two lives lose an opportunity for what might have been mutual enrichment. But something valuable is not merely rescued but born out of loss and futility and misunderstanding and personal failure, something deeper, less spectatorial than his once threatened allegiance[1] to the life of the

---

[1] Cf. *Amours de Voyage*, III. x. 206–13.

intellect, and quite distinct from his 'wilful unmeaning acceptance' (v. v. 65) of necessity. We see it forming in the fifth letter
of the last Canto, when, reduced to an almost complete degradation by his recognition of loss and failure, Claude yet refuses
the strangely moving consolation offered by a homely symbol
of all that is simple and familiar, conventional and reassuring—a
barrel-organ grinding out an English psalm-tune.

> What with trusting myself and seeking support from within me,
> Almost I could believe I had gained a religious assurance,
> Found in my own poor soul a great moral basis to rest on.
> Ah, but indeed I see, I feel it factitious entirely;
> I refuse, reject, and put it utterly from me;
> I will look straight out, see things, not try to evade them;
> Fact shall be fact for me, and the Truth the Truth as ever,
> Flexible, changeable, vague, and multiform, and doubtful.—
> Off, and depart to the void, thou subtle, fanatical tempter!
>   (v. v. 95–103.)

The toughened movement of the verse, the purposive, abrupt,
accumulating syntax, enacts the strengthening resolve in the face
of realized inadequacy. In despair of meaning, yet refusing to be
overwhelmed by his desire for meaning, Claude is, like his hexameters, shortening his syntactic reach. The process is completed
when he comes to rest in his final crippled but splendid affirmation:

> Not as the Scripture says, is, I think, the fact. Ere our death-day,
> Faith, I think, does pass, and Love; but Knowledge abideth.
> Let us seek Knowledge;—the rest may come and go as it happens.
> Knowledge is hard to seek, and harder yet to adhere to.
> Knowledge is painful often; and yet when we know, we are
>   happy.
> Seek it, and leave mere Faith and Love to come with the chances.
> As for Hope,—to-morrow I hope to be starting for Naples.
>   (v. x. 197–203.)

Claude has come to terms with syntax: he has begun to acquire
'the temper or disposition of mind which can look at a *gap* or
chasm without shuddering'. The hexameters no longer reach out
to one another in search of meaning.

> As for Hope,—to-morrow I hope to be starting for Naples.

In the wintry finality of that utterance *Amours de Voyage* faces
unflinchingly the human consequences of Claude's bleak commit-

ment. The poem ends with the French guns of the closing epilogue and their comment on the individual failure which yet seems so akin to victory.

The superbly original artistry of these hexameters, restlessly alive with implication beneath their off-hand surface, is, of course, the most immediately striking single achievement of *Amours de Voyage*. As V. S. Pritchett has put it, 'in an age of professional trumpets, [Clough] engaged the dubious, the personal, the inquiring, the definite but conversational flute'.[1] It seriously diminishes both the hexameters themselves and the poem as a whole, however, if we lose sight of the larger artistic strategy which contains this new and exciting poetic voice. For by playing off what we might call the poetry of the background against that of the foreground Clough establishes an intricate structure of ironic and poetic relationships which creates the whole point of the hexameters, and establishes the validity of the artistic revolt they represent. It is only when we put this local idiom back into its validating framework that we can begin to take the measure of Clough's achievement, of the depth and complexity of the poem and its scrutiny of contemporary history and contemporary values.

3. THE SHORTER POEMS OF 1849

The shorter poems that Clough wrote in 1849, many of them during his Italian holiday, confirm and extend our insight into the extraordinary release of creative energy which he shaped into his masterpiece. Purely quantitatively the poetry he wrote in the course of this single year is remarkable. Even more impressive is its quality. Among these poems are some of the finest he ever wrote; taken together as a body they reveal a distinguishing consistency of craftsmanship when compared with his earlier work. Not all the poems are equally good, of course. One or two sink far below the others. But on the whole there is comparatively little dead wood here, little of the fumbling hesitancy which mars so much of that earlier verse. The conclusion is almost irresistible: for the first time in his life Clough seems to have been in continuous possession of himself as a poet. With equal assurance he moves from the demandingly precise argumentative structure

---

[1] V. S. Pritchett, *Books in General*, p. 3.

of a poem like 'Uranus' to the explosive control of 'Easter Day.
Naples, 1849', from the light seriousness of 'O land of Empire,
art and love!' to the subtle gravity of syntactical, rhythmic, and
responsive balance in 'Say not the struggle nought availeth'.

The energy and assurance which inform this varied output are
intimately connected with the clarity of Clough's self-recognitions
during this period of his life, a clarity that finds its supreme expression in *Amours de Voyage*. Skilfully channelled into a *persona*
in the long poem, his revolt finds a more direct expression in
several of these short poems which gave explicit strength to
positions implicit in the longer work. A negligent flick of Claude's
intelligence had, for instance, exposed the oppressive monolith
of 'our terrible notions of duty'. 'Bethesda. A Sequel' brings this
particular rebellion out into the open. It is a direct rejoinder to
'The human spirits' which Clough had written in 1844 and which
had appeared in January 1849 as the first poem in his section of the
Ambarvalia. This earlier poem had asserted the all-sufficiency of
duty as a guiding principle in life. 'Bethesda'—which suffers as
poetry by its association with the heavy didacticism and the rather
gratuitous allegorical mode of its predecessor—aims a sledge-
hammer blow at that assertion:

> And I beheld that on that stony floor
> He too, that spoke of duty once before,
> No otherwise than others here to-day
> Foredone and sick and sadly muttering lay.
> 'I know not, I will do—what is it I would say?
> 'What was that word which once sufficed alone for all,
> 'Which now I seek in vain, and never can recall?'
> 'I know not, I will do the work the world requires
> 'Asking no reason why, but serving its desires;
> 'Will do for daily bread, for wealth, respect, good name,
> 'The business of the day—alas, is that the same?'
>
> (*Poems*, 53–4.)

Once before, in 1840, significantly, the period of his most profound unsettlement as an undergraduate, Clough had written
in this vein.[1] Now, in 1849, the break-up of what Symonds called
the 'criterion of Duty'[2] is complete—duty merely leads to the

---

[1] Cf. 'Duty—that's to say complying', *Poems*, p. 27.
[2] J. A. Symonds, 'Arthur Hugh Clough', *Fortnightly Review*, x (Dec. 1868),
615.

'world' and to a convenient conformity. This ethical recognition feeds one of the most important currents in the poetry Clough wrote during this year and in the years immediately following— the witty, sardonic, satiric exposure of shoddy, self-seeking, comfortably prudential Victorian virtue.

Of all these poems, 'Easter Day. Naples, 1849' gives us perhaps our deepest understanding of the complex sub-structure of Clough's rebellion, and of some of the deep-buried personal tensions which reveal themselves clearly only later on in his life in his relationship with Blanche Smith. This magnificent, fluently perfect ode stands quite apart from the rest of Clough's poetry. It triumphs not by the austere precision of poetic ratiocination or the cerebral play of ironic wit but by the intensity and firmness of communicated emotion. It is not a simple poem, but its complexities and ambivalences develop more from the interaction and conflict of opposed emotional responses than from the intricateness of intellectual argument—even its ironic use of phrases from the New Testament and from the Burial Service depends for its effectiveness on an emotional rather than an intellectual apprehension of disjunction. Passionate but carefully structured, the relentlessly reverberating rhythms of its vast, reiterated negatives hammer home the meaning of religious crisis, the appalling significance of a universe deprived by science and by Biblical criticism of the sustaining Christian myth.

> Is He not risen, and shall we not rise?
>   Oh, we unwise!
> What did we dream, what wake we to discover?
> Ye hills, fall on us, and ye mountains, cover!
>   In darkness and great gloom
> Come ere we thought it is *our* day of doom,
> From the cursed world which is one tomb,
>   Christ is not risen!
>
>   . . .
>
> Eat, drink, and play, and think that this is bliss!
>   There is no Heaven but this!
>   There is no Hell;—
> Save Earth, which serves the purpose doubly well,
>   Seeing it visits still
> With equallest apportionments of ill

> Both good and bad alike, and brings to one same dust
> > The unjust and the just
> > > With Christ, who is not risen.
>
> > > > > *(Poems, 56–7.)*

As Doris Dalglish has remarked, 'The vehemence with which [Clough] paints the universal effects that follow from a denial of the Resurrection is the vehemence springing from abhorrence of a world unprotected by that holy fact.'[1] The need for protection presses in on us through these desolating negations of the first two sections: man needs this protection because he is sinful, because virtue is weak and wickedness powerful. This tormented consciousness of the reality of sin and corruption is the emotional centre of these two sections; it penetrates even the flaming rebelliousness of the opening lines:

> Through the great sinful streets of Naples as I past,
> With fiercer heat than flamed above my head
> My heart was hot within me; till at last
> My brain was lightened, when my tongue had said
> > Christ is not risen!
>
> > > > > *(Poems, 54.)*

The radical ambivalence in this 'emancipation' which is poised on the edge of despair has an actual correspondence in Clough's personal life. Even the values which guide the most independent, most iconoclastic, most questioning movements of his intellect are anchored, ultimately, in an ineradicable Christian guilt; when he is finally defeated by the values of his age, his crucial surrender is to this irreducible, non-rational, emotionally apprehended reality instilled into him by his rigorous upbringing.

These considerations anticipate the future, however. At the time when he wrote 'Easter Day'—more widely the period of '*Natura Naturans*', *Adam and Eve*, *Amours de Voyage*, '*Sa Majesté très Chrétienne*', and *Dipsychus*—Clough was far from submission. In fact, looking into himself, remembering his earlier life and the spiritual spasms of the 'Blank Misgivings' period, he was holding up the phenomenon of exacerbated guilt for ironic contemplation, and the final section of 'Easter Day' makes clear the positive foundation on which he constructed his irony. For the poem

---

[1] D. N. Dalglish, 'Arthur Hugh Clough: The Shorter Poems', *Essays in Criticism*, ii (Jan. 1952), 42–3.

does not collapse in despair. It refuses to be overwhelmed by its appalling denial, or by its vision of universal death, of the 'foul engendered worm' which 'Feeds on the flesh of the life-giving form | Of our most Holy and Anointed One'. The emphasis of anguish customarily seen in the repeated negatives of the last stanza of the poem, is, as Houghton has remarked,[1] an emphasis which has been read into them by readers who *wanted* to read Clough in a particular way.

> Here on our Easter Day
> We rise, we come, and lo! we find Him not;
> Gardener nor other on the sacred spot,
> Where they have laid Him is there none to say!
> No sound, nor in, nor out; no word
> Of where to seek the dead or meet the living Lord;
> There is no glistering of an angel's wings,
> There is no voice of heavenly clear behest:
> Let us go hence, and think upon these things
> In silence, which is best.
> Is He not risen? No—
> But lies and moulders low—
> Christ is not risen.
>
> *(Poems, 58–9.)*

This is exactly what it is meant to be, firm and precise though tinged with regret. It is a careful and deliberate cutting-off of escape—either into the traditional comfort of the historical Jesus or, more important, into the moral nihilism of the refrain—

> Ashes to ashes, dust to dust;
> As of the unjust, also of the just—

which chimes through the first two sections but does *not* occur in the third. For the whole emotional direction of the poem is altered at the beginning of this third section, as the focus shifts from the historical past, now shown to be fictitious, and the appalled present to the future. The anguish of discovery settles into the firmness of positive conclusion; emotionally the tremendous denial has been assimilated.

> And oh, good men of ages yet to be,
> Who shall believe *because* ye did not see,
> Oh, be ye warned! be wise!
> No more with pleading eyes,

---

[1] Houghton, p. 66.

And sobs of strong desire,
  Unto the empty vacant void aspire,
Seeking another and impossible birth
That is not of your own and only Mother Earth.
But if there is no other life for you,
Sit down and be content, since this must even do:
        He is not risen.

  One look, and then depart,
    Ye humble and ye holy men of heart!
And ye! ye ministers and stewards of a word
Which ye would preach, because another heard,—
    Ye worshippers of that ye do not know,
    Take these things hence and go;
        He is not risen.

                                          (*Poems*, 58.)

More strongly than the sense of disillusionment, there is in these
lines a positive emotional conviction in the asserted 'here and now'
which verges, at the end of the second of these stanzas, on outright
exasperation.[1] And that is why this last section of 'Easter Day'
succeeds as a counter-statement where 'Easter Day II', important
as it is as a statement of Clough's positive religious beliefs, fails.
For it opposes the torrential despair of the first two sections with
an emotionally convinced resolve, not with an abstract statement
of the Straussian positive of the eternal, although unhistorical,
Christ-fact in man: emotion is met with emotion to create a
poetically live balance. In fact the only point at which the otherwise pale 'Easter Day II' rises to its counterpart is the only point
in it at which a tough, internalized apprehension invests the
positive assertion:

  Sit if ye will, sit down upon the ground,
  Yet not to weep and wail, but calmly look around.
      Whate'er befell,
      Earth is not hell;
  Now, too, as when it first began,
  Life yet is Life and Man is Man.

                                          (*Poems*, 60.)

  [1] The assertion is made clearer in an early draft. After the sixth line of the first
of these stanzas (line 130 of the poem), Clough wrote:

        Spasmodically strive to attain those ambient skies
        To attain which great Nature's law denies
        Wherefore the unseen choose
        And the plain fact refuse?   (*Poems*, p. 479.)

'Easter Day'—with its counterpart 'Easter Day II'—is obviously a major landmark in the history of Clough's spiritual life. Its balance of desolation and resolve contains the germs both of his personal revolt and of his ultimate capitulation. More immediately relevant to the poetry he wrote in 1849 is the way in which most of the important short poems of this year seem to grow out of this central one. The denial of the Resurrection provides the starting-point for the unfinished poem beginning 'I dreamed a dream' which was titled 'The Shadow' in the 1869 *Poems and Prose Remains.*[1] The deft, incisively colloquial verse develops, in this poem, a bitterly sardonic attack on the 'Great World' and on an entrenched Church which would cling to a useful myth for the sake of order, decorum, plain financial gain, and possible death-bed consolation, even if the dead Jesus appeared to testify to its falseness. The pragmatic recognition in the two Easter poems that 'Life yet is Life and Man is Man' provides the containing conviction for Clough's best-known poem, 'Say not the struggle nought availeth', where an adult and clear-eyed possession of confidence in the face of contrary possibilities finds perfect, sensitive expression for itself, though an unfortunate currency has tended to debase it into something like a tub-thumping companion to 'Invictus'.

In a different way that same recognition inspires 'O land of Empire, art and love!', which Clough titled in one manuscript 'Resignation—to Faustus', obviously with Matthew Arnold's 'Resignation: To Fausta' in mind.[2] Clough's poem locks with Arnold's at several points. It redefines and deals in its own way with Arnold's contrast between work-bound, impatiently questing achievers and 'milder natures and more free', and with Arnold's romantic despair at the 'something that infects the world'. Clough's poem begins with 34 lines—suppressed for obvious reasons by early editors, and published for the first time in 1951—of delightfully ironic and outspoken mimicry of the accents of fastidious sensibility:

> O land of Empire, art and love!
> What is it that you show me?

[1] *Poems*, p. 406. I adopt Katharine Chorley's conjectural date for the poem. Chorley, p. 201.

[2] Cf. *Poems*, p. 481. Arnold's 'Resignation' had appeared in 1849 as the last piece in *The Strayed Reveller and Other Poems*.

> A sky for Gods to tread above,
>   A soil for pigs below me!
>
>   .   .   .
>
> Though oft the meditative cur
>   Account it small intrusion
> Through that great gate to quit the stir
>   Of market-place confusion,
> True brother of the bipeds there,
>   If Nature's need requireth,
> Lifts up his leg with tranquil air
>   And tranquilly retireth:
> Though priest think fit to stop and spit
>   Beside the altar solemn,
> Yet, boy, that nuisance why commit
>   On this Corinthian column?
>
>   (*Poems*, 64.)

It is at this point that the earlier printed versions begin and the witty play on 'soiled' and 'sunned' on which the whole poem turns shows how much it had lost through editorial emasculation:

> O richly soiled and richly sunned,
> Exuberant, fervid, and fecund!
>   Are these the fixed condition
> On which may Northern pilgrim come
> To imbibe thine ether-air, and sum
>   Thy store of old tradition?
> Must we be chill, if clean, and stand
> Foot-deep in dirt in classic land?
>
>   (*Poems*, 65.)

And here Clough hints at a theory of the nature of poetry and the poet which counters the romantic specialness conferred by Arnold's '*Those gipsies . . . Are less, the poet more, than man*':

> So is it: in all ages so,
> And in all places man can know,
> From homely roots unseen below
> In forest-shade in woodland bower
> The stem that bears the ethereal flower
> Derives that emanative power;
> From mixtures fetid foul and sour
> Draws juices that those petals fill.
>
>   (Ibid.)

From this conviction of a common and indivisible source for the whole of life Clough's poem goes on to combat the darkness of 'Faustus' Arnold's knowledge, vouchsafed through a special exemption from 'action's dizzying eddy', of the absolute dominion of aimless change and of the vanity of all existence.

> What dies already, look you, lives;
> In such a clime, who thinks, forgives;
> Who sees, will understand; who knows,
> In calm of knowledge find repose,
> And thoughtful as of glory gone,
> So too of more to come anon,
> Of permanent existence sure,
> Brief intermediate breaks endure.
> O Nature, if indeed thy will,
> Thou ownest it, it is not ill!
>
> (*Poems*, 66.)

This attitude of acceptance and affirmation of 'nature', of growth and decay, provides a very relevant and necessary background to 'Sa Majesté très Chrétienne'. First published in 1951, this poem is one of Clough's most accomplished, most caustic achievements. It is also a key document in his biography. Although she seriously distorts the poem, and draws some dangerously simplified psychological conclusions from this distortion, Katharine Chorley is undoubtedly right in detecting in the monologue a central clue to Clough's life.[1] Because of its importance to an understanding of Clough I have adopted a somewhat different, more straightforwardly biographical approach to *Sa Majesté très Chrétienne* than I have used in discussing most of Clough's poetry. In fact, my discussion of all the short poems of 1849 and my emphasis on their content have been directed towards the correct biographical, 'placing' of this crucial work; for it is essential that we should try to interpret whatever personal relevance it has as accurately as possible.

---

[1] See Chorley, pp. 201–6, 353–4. Her recklessly selective *mélange* of quotations out of context from published and unpublished sources, and her theory of poetry as a direct transcript of psychological states, reduce the poem to straightforward self-revelation. Under her treatment the poem reveals, quite simply, a poet, not a *persona*, reduced to utter impotence through moral paralysis. See R. M. Gollin, 'Clough Despite Himself', *Essays in Criticism*, xii (Oct. 1962), 433, for a criticism of her treatment of the poem.

Of the two surviving manuscripts of the poem—in the 1849 (Roma) Notebook and in the 1849-50 (Lamech) Notebook— the editors of the Oxford *Poems* have, quite rightly, followed the second, a later and somewhat altered fair-copy. Since, however, they have printed no readings from the early draft, the reader must depend wholly on Katharine Chorley's selections for any guidance these can give. I reproduce here, by collating the 1849 (Roma) Notebook version[1] with that printed by the Oxford editors, roughly what the poem might have looked like had Clough persisted in his original intention. Open parentheses indicate passages interpolated from the 1849 (Roma) Notebook; folio references for these are given beside the text for convenient reference. I have italicized (and, where necessary, corrected) the manuscript readings printed by Katharine Chorley. In the left-hand margin of the 1849 (Roma) Notebook (fol. 22) is written, transversely, 'L.XV'. As the Oxford editors have suggested (*Poems*, p. 484), this may stand for 'Louis XV'. The identification provides an illuminating dramatic context for the poem.

fol. 23 (Papers to sign and documents to read
         (Letres [*sic*] de cachet,—and [2 illegible words]
         (*So many things to do I cannot do*
         (*To think of*—*to decide, my acts they say*
         (*And yet they never mean that I should act*
         (*Nor dream I sho*[*ul*]*d decide. . . . And yet my acts*
         (*My acts, they say*—Ah you are come, my girls
         (My children, my flowers of Paradise
         (My darling ones, and what have you been doing
         (Playing all day and I, poor King, the while
         (So tired, so tired.—Come round me, play with me
         (Would I had mouths as berries on a bush
         (For all of you at once to pick in kisses
         (Ninon, your fingers here in mine—[Fanchetta?]
         (Is it not you sweet [rogue?] with thee?
         (Come play awhile, and then we say our prayers
         (E'en as in holy Church together all
         (Say prayers—and then—which shall it be, you ask.
         (Ah which—shall we draw lots? the Lutheran
         (And Calvinistic heretics repeat
         (Hour-long thanksgivings ere they set to dinner
         (E'en so, prayers done by lot? [or] choose in the dark?

                    [1] Balliol MS. 441, fol. 23-fol. 29.

(Ah but you are not heretics, my girls.
(Louise, you/who came from pestilent Auvergne
(You are sound, [I trust?], my child;—I'd have you so
(We will all go you know at last to heaven,
(Confess our naughty deeds, repent, receive
(The wafer and the Unction of the Church
fol. 23ᵛ (And so—through Purgatory pass to heaven:
(And Purgatory also is not long,
(But much like penance upon Earth: ye say
(The seven penitential psalms: repeat
(Eight or nine/A course of prayers with holy meditations
(And so washed white, and clad in virgin robes
(The good kind God receives us to himself.
(You laugh, my pet ones—Ah I mean it, though,
(Yes and tomorrow—I will not forget
(I'll bring with me the Catechism of Trent
(And test you in your faiths, my little ones.
(Ah but you'll all be dutiful and learn
(And docilely believe the Church's word
(Keep safely all in union blest with her
(Sinners as we are we shall yet join
(The happy Saints who in their heavenly seats
(Pity us in poor sad ways below.
(Come
(The blinds are closed, the curtains drawn; put out the lights
(We'll fold each other in each other's arms
(Forget the uproarious world and dream of the day
(When we shall all be [mingled?] into Heaven.[1]

★　　★　　★

'Tis true, Monseigneur, I am much to blame;
But we must all forgive; especially
Subjects their King; would I were one to do so
What could I do? and how was I to help it?
'Tis true it should not be so; true indeed,
I know I am not what I would I were.
I would I were, as God intended me,
A little quiet harmless acolyte,
Clothed in long serge and linen shoulder-piece,
Day after day

---

[1] At this point an early version of lines 1–26 of *Sa Majesté très Chrétienne*
follows on a fresh page (fol. 24) of the 1849 (Roma) Notebook. The lines are
headed 'XV'. I reproduce the text of the later version printed in *Poems*.

To pace serenely through the sacred fane,
Bearing the sacred things before the priest,
Curtsey before that altar as we pass,
And place our burden reverently on this.
There—by his side to stand and minister,
To swing the censer and to sound the bell,
Uphold the book, the patin change and cup—
Ah me—
And why does childhood ever change to man?
Oh, underneath the black and sacred serge
Would yet uneasy uncontented blood
Swell to revolt? Beneath the tippet's white
Would harassed nerves by sacred music soothed,
By solemn sights and peaceful tasks composed,
Demand more potent medicine than these,
Or ask from pleasure more than duty gives?[1]

fol. 25 *(Ah yes: but who is to blame for this? I wonder,/You found me*
(You found me
(Not you, but some one of your bold/bad/filthy kith and kin
(You found me
(A little foolish innocent ignorant Prince
(Awkward and sheepish, bashful and devout
(A silent shrinking, somewhat overgrown child
(Who at the coarse-tongued age of [illegible word] 15
(Knew not his sister differed from himself
(Save in her frock and fashion of her hair
(You found me and you told me—oh kind saints
(What was it that you told me then and [how?]!—
(But I remember that you left me weeping
(The wicked world was real to me and Heaven
(Which had the Substance been was Shadow now.[2]

                          Ah, holy father, yes.
Without the appointed,
Without the sweet confessional relief,
Without the welcome all-absolving words,
The mystic rite, the solemn soothing forms,
Our human life were miserable indeed.

[1] The fifteen lines which follow are written on a fresh page in the 1849 (Roma) Notebook and are headed 'XV'.
[2] Some apparently unrelated passages of verse follow at this point in the 1849 (Roma) Notebook. The poem continues again on fol. 26ᵛ at the line beginning 'Ah, holy father, yes . . .' (line 27 of the Oxford text) and is once again headed 'XV'.

And yet methinks our holy Mother Church
Deals hardly, very, with her eldest born,
Her chosen, sacred, and most Christian Kings.
To younger pets, the blind, the halt, the sick,
The outcast child, the sinners of the street,
Her doors are open and her precinct free:
The beggar finds a nest, the slave a home,
Even thy altars, O my Mother Church—
O *templa quam dilecta.* We, the while,
Poor Kings, must forth to action, as you say;
Action, that slaves us, drives us, fretted, worn,
To pleasure, which anon enslaves us too;
Action, and what is Action, O my God?
Alas, and can it be
In this perplexing labyrinth I see,
This waste and wild infinity of ways
Where all are like, and each each other meets,
Quits, meets, and quits a many hundred times,
That this path more than that conducts to Thee?
Alas, and is it true
Ought I can purpose, say, or will, or do,
My fancy choose, my changeful silly heart
Resolve, my puny petty hand enact,
To that great glory can in ought conduce
Which from the old eternities is Thine?
Ah never, no!
If ought there be for sinful souls below
To do, 'tis rather to forbear to do;
If ought there be of action that contains
The sense of sweet identity with God,
It is, methinks, it is inaction only.
To walk with God I know not; let me kneel.
Ah yes, the livelong day
To watch before the altar where they pray:
To muse and wait,
On sacred stones lie down and meditate.
No, through the long and dark and dismal night
We will not turn and seek the city streets,
We will not stir, we should but lose our way;
But faithful stay
And watch the tomb where He, our Saviour, lies
Till his great day of Resurrection rise.

Yes, the commandments you remind me, yes,

The Sacred Word has pointed out the way,
The Priest is here for our unfailing guide;
Do this, not that, to right hand and to left,
A voice is with us ever at our ear.
Yes, holy Father, I am thankful for it;
Most thankful I am not, as other men,
A lonely Lutheran English Heretic;
If I had so by God's despite been born,
Alas, methinks I had but passed my life
In sitting motionless beside the fire,
Not daring to remove the once-placed chair,
Not stir my foot for fear it should be sin.
Thank God indeed,
Thank God for his infallible certain creed.
Yes, the commandments, precepts of good life,
And counsels of perfection and the like,—
'Thou knowest the commandments'—Yes, indeed,
Yes, I suppose. But it is weary work;
For Kings I think they are not plain to read;
Ministers somehow have small faith in them.
Ah, holy father, would I were as you.
But you, no less, have trials as you say;
Inaction vexes you, and action tempts,
And the bad prickings of the animal heats,
As in the palace, to the cell will come.

fol. 28   (*Alas—and why*
       (*Why in that blessed and baptismal/regenerative rite*
       (*When pain is small and small the sense of sin*
       (*Could/should not the holy and preventive hand*
       (*With one short act, decisive for all time*
       (*By sharp excision pluck the unsprouted seed/sever the seed of ill*
fol. 28ᵛ (*There are the Scripture tells us who have done it*
       (*Origen was not orthodox, you say,*
       (*In this in least was not his heresy:*
       (*You holy priests who do all else for us*
       (*What he did for himself might do for us.*[1]

Ah, well a day!
Would I were out in quiet Paraguay,
Mending the Jesuits' shoes!—

---

[1] The last five lines of this passage in the 1849 (Roma) Notebook are cancelled. Clough's bracketing in the left-hand margin suggests that the three lines which follow—and which are identical in this MS. and the printed version—were intended to replace them.

You drive us into action as our duty.
Then action persecutes and tortures us.
To pleasures and to loving soft delights
We fly for solace and for peace; and gain
Vexation, Persecution also here.
We hurry from the tyranny of man
Into the tyranny yet worse of woman.
No satisfaction find I any more
In the old pleasant evil ways; but less,
Less, I believe, of those uneasy stirs
Of discontented and rebellious will
That once with self-contempt tormented me.
Depraved, that is, degraded am I—Sins,
Which yet I see not how I should have shunned,
Have, in despite of all the means of grace,
Submission perfect to the appointed creed,
And absolution-plenary and prayers,
Possessed me, held, and changed—yet after all
Somehow I think my heart within is pure.

Obviously Clough started with two separate but related monologues,[1] both by the same speaker and both wickedly ironic. The first, which ends with the opening passage from the 1849 (Roma) Notebook, is about the most blackly sardonic— and the most deliberately outrageous—thing he ever wrote. Almost unbelievable in 1849, we have to wait for the ending of Huxley's *Point Counter Point* and the spectacle of Burlap and Beatrice romping in the bath together for a comparable exposure of obscene 'innocence'. The subtlety of the psychological penetration and the finely honed and unobtrusive dexterity with which Clough exposes the full range of ambiguities—comically naïve, salaciously sophisticated, pathetic—in the King's regressive withdrawal from the world of action and decision make much of Browning's psychologizing look crude and immature. The

---

[1] On the basis of the first of what I have called apparently unrelated passages of verse in note 2, p. 332, *Catalogue* (p. 18) suggests that perhaps Clough was 'moving away from dramatic monologue towards a possible drama'. The passage, which appears at the bottom of fol. 25, reads:

'Tis curious too
These fits of eloquence that come upon him
He will go dozing, mumbling/maundering [month on month?]
And if you [four illegible words]
And then at last if something touches him
Comes out with words like these.

second monologue is set in the confessional. Clough exploits to
its limits his mastery of tone and of ironic syntax to expose
obliquely the morally impotent King who, having obviously
put his epicene manhood to some use, refuses to accept either his
manhood or the responsibility for his act. Instead, overwhelmed
by the enormity of the world and filled with the comic despair
of his initiation into sexual knowledge, he seeks refuge in the
ritualistic machinery of an infallible Church and comes to rest in
the superbly comic whine—'Somehow I think my heart within
is pure.'

Manifestly, then, the monologues are comic, witty, and completely ironic—we know, for instance, what Clough thought
about the infallible Church and about the Resurrection. The
passages, too, which Katharine Chorley has selected for quotation from the 1849 (Roma) Notebook—especially the one about
initiation into sexual knowledge and the one about the desirability of castration as a preventive against contamination—are,
in their context, wholly ironical. Any interpretation of their
biographical implications which does not take into account
Clough's extremely sophisticated art in these sardonic studies of
fact-denying 'purity' is, I think, bound to be not only inadequate
but positively misleading.

Ultimately, these two passages—like the monologues—must be
connected with the jotting in the 1849 (Roma) Notebook, part
of which I have already quoted.

What used to disgust me so was the sight of a man looking up in
this way into . . . vacuum, seeking and claiming spiritual en-rapportité
with Angels and Archangels and all the company of heaven at the same
time that his nether parts were not en-rapportité only but in actual
active combination with Elementa terrestria vel pudendi prima. This
is the hypocrisy hated of Men.

What is the meaning of Prayer of looking up to heaven in this case?
. . . Is it to obtain juxta-position—en-rapportité with a vacuum.[1]

This awareness of the 'nether parts of man', which makes itself
so insistently and so extensively felt in Clough's writings,
provides, perhaps, the most important single clue to his whole
career. Seen from this angle his mature life is a continual attempt
to answer the question: 'What kind of recognition are we to give

[1] 1849 (Roma) Notebook, Balliol MS. 441, fol. 39 (rev.)–fol. 38ᵛ (rev.).

to the phenomenon of man's sexuality?' And it is essential to remember that for Clough the problem was not an abstract philosophical and academic one. The weight of sin under which his early, directly lyrical, spiritually lacerated poetry totters is evidence enough of a prolonged and painful adolescence; the scattered—sometimes ribald, sometimes bitter and tormented— pieces of scatology in his maturer writings point, among other things, to the effects of a protracted celibacy. As a human animal he was directly and painfully involved in this question, and his answers to it, either explicit or only implicit, determine his relationship to his age at various stages of his life. For any answer to such a question implies not only a conception of 'sin' but a definition of man, and a structure of values which either conforms or does not to the prevailing, officially endorsed definitions and values upheld by the larger society. Necessarily, too, that answer has—or can have—a real if indirect bearing on poetry, for it can determine what kinds of experience are to be recognized and what concerns and attitudes are to be admitted. The whole question of realism is at issue.

Clough's development up to 1849 reveals, broadly speaking, two opposed attitudes towards this central question, which, between them, polarize the forces of conformity and revolt. The first and earlier attitude is, as we have seen in the chapters on Rugby and Balliol, clear, unambiguous, rigidly Christian, and traditional. It rests on an emotionally grounded apprehension of the absolute separation of spirit and flesh. It reveals itself in the pervasive guilt and the longing for purity of the earlier poems. Its *locus classicus* in this poetry, and the only point at which it breaks through directly, is the two lines:

> Yea, the first kiss that by these lips was set
> On any human lips, methinks was sin.

This view of sex as irredeemably sinful, and as the blackest stain on fallen man, can be traced to the powerful, emotion-charged influence of his mother, to the even more powerful and almost equally emotion-charged influence of Dr. Arnold, to the impact of the Tractarian ideal of immaculateness. The second attitude, relying for its strength on the full resources of Clough's independent intellect, draws on all the emancipating influences to which he had exposed himself at Oriel. Growing out of his whole secular revolt, this second attitude towards sex is, in contrast to the first, essentially humanistic, heterodox, and modern. Instead of outright denial it sees human sexuality as part of a cosmic vitality, as a fact of existence to be admitted and to be assimilated somehow into man's moral life. The development of this attitude, most succinctly expressed perhaps in the play on 'soiled' in 'O Land of Empire, art and love!', can be traced through poems like 'Natura Naturans', the franker passages of The Bothie, and the general interest in the 'rehabilitation of the flesh' which Clough, in his Oriel years, appears to have shared with Burbidge. It is this impulse of acceptance, coupled with Clough's rejection of traditional, institutionalized Christianity, which provides the positive basis for the satire in Sa Majesté très Chrétienne; and the primary significance of the two draft passages that Katharine Chorley has printed is in the sharp clarity with which they reveal the satiric chasm, created by the critical intellect, which separates the Clough of 1849 from the Clough of earlier years.

Yet the very sharpness of this revelation indicates the ambivalence in the satire: the savageness displays a man deeply committed to purity. The passage from this early draft of Sa Majesté très Chrétienne which refers to Origen conveniently defines the ambivalence which permeates all Clough's thinking on the subject. Roughly, the ironic statement in this passage can be translated: the only way in which a Church pretending to take care of all man's spiritual needs can really perform this function is by castrating him—that is, by making him (as the whole poem makes clear) other than, and less than, man. Sex as a metaphor of manhood is also a metaphor of sin, and the acceptance of sex as a condition of being does not necessarily imply that it thereby loses its sinfulness. The ambivalence and its implications are worth examining at some length, for, besides their importance as central themes in Clough's next long poem, Dipsychus, they are absolutely essential to an understanding of the next major development in Clough's personal life—his relationship with Blanche Smith.

To describe this ambivalence in Clough's sense of the animality of the human condition as a tension between emotional apprehension and intellectual conviction is useful only as long as we recognize the limiting simplifications in such a description.

Although he struggled against the 'spectre of sin' he could never declare himself completely emancipated. Obviously his early and sustained grounding in an ethic of purity is mainly responsible for the strength and persistence of his emotional adherence to the traditional scheme of good and evil. What is less obvious, perhaps, is the way in which this adherence, by being contained in the intellectual positives of his revolt, weakens that revolt from within. This last point is crucial if we are to understand why and how it was that, having moved so far from conformity, he ended in a submission so nearly complete. Even intellectually, Clough never erased sin—he merely redefined it and, in some ways, limited its province. Implicit in his positive belief in the philosophical, as against the historical, truths of Christianity— Incarnation, Redemption, Atonement—is an acceptance of the doctrine of Sin. *Adam and Eve*, his most ambitious and explicit treatment of the subject, attempts not to reject the Fall but to absorb it into a more secular view of Man and divest it of its traditional eschatology. The conviction of the reality of sin, then, —and the ethic of purity which follows from it—forms a subtle, reactionary, emotionally based fifth-column in the theoretical structure of Clough's revolt. It is at this point, in other words, that his revolt *as an attitude of mind* is most vulnerable. Meshed into his whole attempt to recognize and to assert his own authentic nature against the weight of defining authority is an inescapable conviction of the need to perfect that nature through Grace. It was this profound ambivalence—most sharply experienced in the phenomenon of sexual nature—and the search for a perfecting, emotionally satisfying Grace which finally defeated Clough.

In April 1848 his diffident but tenacious sister, Annie, recently arrived in London to carry her personal struggle one stage further by attending teacher-training college, was seeing as much as she could of her adored Arthur. She was meeting his friends, greedily drinking in his conversation, poring over his *Ambarvalia* poems, and talking them over with him. She was also confiding her thoughts to her painstaking journal, and, as always, they bore the impress of her brother's attitudes and interest. 'People seem to be shocked', she wrote,

at some of Burbidge's poems. I cannot say I have ever thought a great deal about them, but I did not discover the shocking part of them. It seems to me that people have yet to learn what real purity is. The indulgence of feelings and desires that are the natural offspring of our hearts, that grow up everywhere, in the savage and in the refined breast, cannot be said to be impure. As refinement increases, the spiritual part of our nature increases also. To those who are in a lower stage the bodily presence is almost a necessity, but to those who have risen higher, this, it appears to me, may become of less importance. And surely, as woman begins to take a more prominent part in the duties of life, this will be acknowledged and practised. The woman will no longer leave the business she has entered upon to go after her husband. . . . In a holy and beautiful communion she lives with her chosen one, but each walks alone in a round of duties, and the days of union are the Sabbaths of rest, the foretaste of a better life. Then will they go forth to their work refreshed and strengthened. They will surely seek to keep themselves pure, to aspire after what is best, for the thought of the absent one will be constantly present. . . .

. . . Surely married life too often becomes dull and hard. People enter into close intercourse too suddenly. We all know well enough that we are often disgusted with ourselves, and in this light must we appear to others; therefore it is a great relief sometimes to hide ourselves, so that we may wash off the stains and again look bright. . . .

Yes, and this holy love shall clothe our work and common occupations with an atmosphere all golden. Then shall we learn truly to pray, for we shall aspire, and it is when we aspire, when we feel our weakness, that we pray. . . .

Some [sic] of these days perhaps I shall say this is all nonsense and untrue, but at least I shall have recorded that once I did thus dream of love, and that this dream has helped me to live. . . . I would not say that the being who has called forth my affections, has made me wish to live this spiritual life, is imaginary. No; far from it. My brother Arthur has been in a great measure all this to me. . . .[1]

Annie had not travelled very far from her brother's boyhood dream of a quiet vicarage where the two of them could spend their uncomplicated days together.[2] But in many ways, infinitely more complex and sophisticated though he was, neither had her brother, and her journal entry sheds a curiously prophetic light on his future.

[1] B. A. Clough, op. cit., pp. 74–5. [2] *Corr.* i. 7.

CHAPTER VIII

London: University Hall, 1849–1852

I. UNIVERSITY HALL

ON 31 August 1849 Mrs. Brookfield had some Council Office men to dinner. One of them brought along a friend who appeared to have some acquaintance with Thackeray. He behaved most oddly throughout the evening. Not saying very much, and sitting at the foot of his hostess's sofa with a 'keen expression of investigation' on his face, he stared at her with eyes which 'cut one through, twenty times sharper than Sir Alexander Duff who [had] that way of scrutinising one'. Poor Mrs. Brookfield did her brave best: she decided that the man was 'merely ununderstandable' and determined 'not to mind'.[1]

The friend, of course, was Clough, and the evening at Mrs. Brookfield's set the pattern for what was later described by his wife as 'the dreariest, loneliest period of his life'. It was a period during which 'he became compressed and reserved to a degree quite unusual with him, both before and afterwards. He shut himself up, and went through his life in silence.'[2] The letters and reminiscences of friends frequently recur to this baffling and often boorish uncommunicativeness of Clough's. Even Carlyle, that insistent advocate of silence, was driven to complaints about the 'stinginess' of the young man's speech.[3] Henry Crabb Robinson, who in his own bumbling way took a kindly interest in Clough, was at first attracted by his reticence. 'He is modest and amiable', he confided to his journal, 'as well as full of talent, and I have no doubt that we have made a very good choice in him of a Principal for University Hall. . . . Clough does not announce his opinions on religion, and is wise.'[4] Less than six months later the new Principal's silentness was awakening some misgiving.

---

[1] *The Letters and Private Papers of William Makepeace Thackeray*, ed. G. N. Ray, 4 vols. (London, 1945–6), ii. 578.

[2] *PPR* i. 39.

[3] F. Espinasse, *Literary Recollections and Sketches* (London, 1893), pp. 363–4.

[4] *Henry Crabb Robinson on Books and their Writers*, ed. E. J. Morley, 3 vols. (London, 1938), ii. 692. Entry dated 4 Oct. 1849.

'Clough is a great deal too silent. There is a danger lest the faculty which never appears should be denied.'[1] A few days after making this journal entry, when he took Clough along to meet old Samuel Rogers, he discovered that he had to nudge his companion into greater communicativeness with a well-placed hint or two.[2] Before long the garrulous old diarist, notoriously shaky about names, was regularly referring to Clough as 'that admirable and accomplished man. You know whom I mean. The one who never says anything.'[3]

Richard Hutton and William Allingham are particularly illuminating on this subject of Clough's reserve. As Vice-Principal of University Hall, Hutton came to know Clough well. He remarked that when Clough 'was happy and at ease, there was a calm and silent radiance in his face, and his head was set with a kind of stateliness on his shoulders, that gave him almost an Olympian air; but this would sometimes vanish in a moment into an embarrassed taciturnity that was quite uncouth'.[4] After spending a few days with Clough in London in the autumn of 1851, Allingham wrote to Emerson, '[H]e is secret as an oyster: opens a little at certain times of the tide, but snaps to again in a jiffy if touched, and maybe bites your finger.'[5] The range and violence of the oscillation suggested by this combined testimony is significant. The highly unstable blend of serenity, of brittle sensitiveness, and of aggressively irritable impatience in the personality which Clough presented to the outside world is indicative of a crucial uncertainty and unsettlement during these two complex and critical years in London.

Mulhauser has drawn attention to the general similarity of this period of Clough's life to the years 1839–40[6] and the comparison is a useful one. Once again Clough found himself in a strange environment, this time one unequivocally alien and uncongenial. Once again, because of the recent 'martyrdom' of his resignation, he brought with him a 'reputation' as 'troublesome'—and limiting—in its way as his Rugby fame had been. Once again he was thrown back on his own resources, but now he was an adult,

---

[1] *Henry Crabb Robinson on Books and their Writers*, ii. 695.
[2] Ibid., pp. 695–6.
[3] W. Bagehot, *Literary Studies*, 2 vols. (London, 1879), ii. 332.
[4] Prefatory Memoir, ibid. i. xxxv.
[5] *Letters to William Allingham*, ed. H. Allingham and E. Baumer Williams (London, 1911), p. 47. [6] *Corr*. i. xx-xxi.

and he brought with him a considered, though only partially
advertised, dissidence of outlook. He was also past thirty, he
had achieved nothing of all that had been hoped for him, and
multiplying failures in London were to test the depth and stamina
of his independence.

From the outset Clough tended to adopt a languidly belittling
attitude towards his University Hall position. 'My "young men" ',
he observed to Shairp in a short note written in October 1849,
'are only 11 in number; an Iscariot is expected next Term.—
Some of them wear jackets—and talk of papa.'[1] His off-hand
manner concealed serious misgivings. He wrote to Tom Arnold
a few days later:

Here, I take it, I shall remain for some little time, though even as you
talk of coming over here, so I, believing that in the end I shall be kicked
out for mine heresies' sake, and doubtful of success in literary doings,
have sometimes looked at my feet and considered the Antipodes, . . .
As I say I have no confidence in my own tenure. For intolerance, O
Tom, is not confined to the cloisters of Oxford or the pews of the
establishment, but comes up like the tender herb—partout. And is
indeed in manner indigenous in the heart of the family man of the
middle classes. . . .
A Sadducee, which is to say, an Unitarian, comes every morning
to read prayers here. I, who declined having any concern in it, submit
to this and condescend to be present. To such base compromise may
we come. . . . Do we not work best by digging deepest? By avoiding
polemics, and searching to display the real thing? . . . Emerson is an
example and also Matt. And in his kind Carlyle. . . . Let Froudes delight
to bark and bite, if indeed God has made them so (*Corr.* i. 273–4).

Clough's recent Italian holiday gives a private point to this
recognition of 'heresy' which is sharper than the one Tom would
have recognized. Yet, as his willingness to compromise in the
matter of daily prayers suggests, and his reference to Froude
makes clear, he was unwilling to bring his heterodoxy out into
the open. It seems from this letter that he deliberately set out to
drive his 'heresy' underground, not surrendering it but cultivating it and re-examining it beneath the public surface of social
and professional relationships. He was, as he said, still 'digging',
and if he had not relinquished his 'heresies', he had certainly
not relinquished those hopes for himself which matched the

[1] *C.* 16 Oct. 1849. Bodleian MS. Eng. Lett. d. 176, fol. 156ᵛ (386).

expectations of his friends. The brief, expansive Italian summer was over.

Such strategies for living are, of course, more forced on people than deliberately worked out by them, and this particular deployment of personality should be seen as part of a total and multi-dimensional response to London. The Principalship was an unmitigated disaster for Clough, and his sudden dismissal at the end of 1851—for this is what it amounted to—was the logical end of what had gone before.[1] Occasions of friction multiplied inevitably in a situation in which limits of authority were not clearly defined and in which a prickly and sensitive Principal found himself confronted with a watchful, often over-zealous, Committee of Management and a Council which was rather less than unanimously approving. Clough found his overseers quick to interfere; they found him increasingly casual and apathetic about his duties. Evidently the authorities took their duties with a somewhat pompous and not infrequently small-minded solemnity. Evidently, too, Clough was apt to take a high disdainful line towards what he interpreted as their middle-class anxiousness and their neglect of elementary points of professional courtesy.[2] Whatever value Clough placed on success at University Hall, it must have been abundantly clear to him that he was failing miserably. Neither does he seem to have been an outstanding success as Professor of English Literature at University College, a post, impressive only in its title, to which he had been elected in 1850 at a salary of £30 a year.[3]

Professional failure shaded off into the wider unhappiness and insecurity of London generally, a personal unhappiness which confirmed and nourished—as it was nourished by—his distrust of the city. While he was in Rome, Clough had toyed with the idea of having his mother and his sister to stay with him permanently in London,[4] but by April 1850 he had experienced enough of his new life to set him definitely against such an arrangement.

[1] See G. P. Johari, 'Arthur Hugh Clough at Oriel and University Hall', *PMLA* lxvi (June 1951), 405–25, and Chorley, pp. 212–29, for fuller accounts of Clough's career at University Hall.

[2] Both aspects are brought out clearly in the acid letter, dated 30 Oct. 1850, in which Clough vented his feelings, but which he probably never sent. See Chorley, p. 224.

[3] See *Henry Crabb Robinson on Books and their Writers*, ii. 720; *Letters and Journals of W. Stanley Jevons*, ed. H. A. Jevons (London, 1886), p. 22.

[4] Letter of 27 May 1849, quoted Chorley, p. 216.

Partly he was influenced by the realization that his hold on the Principalship was uncertain at best, partly by the quality of his life in London. 'I very much doubt', he wrote to his mother,

whether you will find it agreeable. I myself have experienced that friends who used to be very eager to see me when I used to come up for three or four days now that they can see me at any time, do not care much about seeing me at all. Dull and dismal as Liverpool is, and little as you may care about people whom you know there, still London is drearier to those who have no old acquaintance in it; and after 30 as I find, one is not very quick at forming new ones. People would call on you no doubt, but some would be Unitarians, and some might be rather fine ladies. It would take some time before you would feel much at ease with either sort. . . (*Corr.* i. 282).

The distant whisper of proud yet diffident Charleston isolation which mingles with personal pique in this dingy letter comes as a useful reminder at this point. Beneath Clough's sluggishness, beneath his unwillingness or incapacity to assert himself, lay, somewhere, the habit of withdrawal as a family characteristic, one strengthened by the family history of shamefaced financial decline. Confronted by the 'bustling miscellaneous external life of London',[1] his first impulse was to look back to the comfortable, enclosed years of Oxford, when his life had rested easily on an assured basis of recognized merit. Instinctively he turned to old friends for reassurance—but they had their own concerns and he was perhaps oversensitive where he suspected neglect. As Katharine Chorley has pointed out, it was not as if there was any real dearth of new and interesting social and intellectual contacts in London,[2] and Clough was invited out frequently enough. He did make valuable friends—notably Carlyle, who in some ways appreciated him more than many older friends did, and Lady Ashburton, who was to be enormously helpful in paving the way for his return from America. If Clough had wanted to— perhaps more accurately, if he had been capable—he could have made a place for himself in the intellectual and social life of the metropolis. But, as he laconically remarked, 'A loneliness relieved by evening parties is not delightful' (*Corr.* i. 278).

Sometimes, rarely, life could seem almost like old times. A group of four students from University College with whom he

<hr>

[1] *PPR* i. 39.   [2] Chorley, pp. 216–19.

read the *Nicomachean Ethics* in 1850 certainly gave some genuine satisfaction; as he himself admitted later, he got on 'famously' with them (*Corr*. ii. 410). The small group offered exactly the kind of informal and personal situation in which Clough excelled as a teacher, and two members of the group who later achieved some eminence, Sir Edward Fry, the Chancery Judge, and Thomas Hodgkin, the historian, left enthusiastic reports of his teaching.[1] Both remembered these classes as, possibly, the most stimulating and enriching experience of their University years. Sir Edward Fry recalled how avidly the whole group 'devoured' their teacher's poems, and how excited he himself used to be when Clough invited him to the breakfast parties at which he entertained his Oxford friends. Above all, to mitigate the barrenness of London, there was Matthew Arnold, with whom he breakfasted twice in an average week. But bachelor friends have an unsettling tendency to break familiar patterns. By July 1850 Matt was 'deep in a flirtation with Miss Wightman, d[aughte]r of the Judge' (*Corr*. i. 286). Tom Arnold, to whom he was writing, was even further on the road to matrimony in far-away Hobart, and Clough reflected gloomily, 'I myself begin to think I shall be a last rose of summer, werry faded' (ibid.). Very faded and very disconsolate; a year later Matthew's marriage was imminent, and Clough wrote to the now married Tom: '[T]o a certain extent even at this distance, old friends have to make their graceful withdrawal, so it seems to me with Matt at any rate on this side the water, and I consider Miss Wightman as a sort of natural enemy. How can it be otherwise—shall I any longer breakfast with Matt twice a week?' (*Corr*. i. 290.) As they grew older, the two friends drew further and further apart. The differences between the failure who had once promised to shine with unparalleled lustre and the seemingly unreclaimable dandy who achieved greatly and brilliantly spread wide and deep. But the connecting threads of personal affection between them were never entirely dissevered. They were friends, often uncomfortable and exasperated friends, and that basic, uneasy fact of friendship coloured all their wider disagreements. Certainly personal pique had some hand in writing to Blanche Smith in January 1852, 'The Strayed Reveller you won't like. It had a great effect on me though, it and its

---

[1] A. Fry, *A Memoir of Sir Edward Fry* (Oxford, 1921), p. 42; L. Creighton, *Life and Letters of Thomas Hodgkin* (London, 1917), pp. 19–20.

writer, but it is over I hope, and I don't mean to let it have any more'.[1]

Profoundly conscious of his isolation, oppressed by and yet cherishing proudly the sense of himself as an Ishmael, Clough reverted to his old broodings about himself, his place, his function, the direction and purpose of his life. Early in January 1850 he wrote to his most unwavering friend, Tom Arnold:

Of what use is paedagogy? Some, I suppose; and as much probably as any other earthly occupation one is in the way of getting harnessed to. Cast therefore thy Syntax on the waters—but in the meantimes εἴσελθε εἰς τὸ ταμιεῖόν σου, καὶ κλείσας τὴν θύραν σου κ.τ.λ.[2]

There is a great blessing, I sometimes think in being set down amongst uncongenial people—for me at least who am over provocable. Consider the coal upon the fireplace, how it came to blaze thus: was it not concealed or compressed for long world-ages, etc., etc.—never expected to see the light again, far less that in its own self there was light, heat and joyfulness—had no sort of imagination that it ever should be transmuted into—or shall we say wooed by, wedded and incorporated with the subtle atmosphere itself? Consider, I say, my dear Tom, the long preparations of this strange marriage of coal and oxygenic air, and say if you can, moreover, when was their most real worthiness of existence—in the grimy or the blazy period,—in the imprisonment or deliverance of the gases—the incarnation or apotheosis—the suppression or expression etc., etc., etc. (Corr. i. 278-9.)

The self-dramatization, which recalls that earlier and rather more flattering picture of himself as a volcanic force barely restraining itself from 'pouring a flood of lava boiling-hot amidst the flowery ecclesiastical fields and parterres of Oxford', introduces one of Clough's dominant self-images during these 'grimy' years in London, just as the analogical opposition between 'coal' and 'air' and the problem of uniting them into a radiant marriage outlines his major preoccupation. In moods like this he embraced his loneliness;[3] to adapt the New Testament Greek in his letter, he entered his closet and shut the door behind him, opening it from time to time in order to hurl admonitory messages at his friends. 'It continues to strike me', he observed to Shairp in June 1850,

how ignorant you and I and other young men of our set are. Actual

<hr/>

[1] Corr. i. 301. Chorley, pp. 221-2, is a good discussion of this aspect of Clough's friendship with Matthew Arnold.

[2] Matt. 6: 6.   [3] Cf. Corr. i. 278, 285.

life is unknown to an Oxford student, even though he is not a mere Puseyite and goes on jolly reading parties—Enter the arena of your brethren and go not to your grave without knowing what common merchants and sollicitors, much more sailors and coalheavers, are well acquainted with. Ignorance is a poor kind of innocence. The World is wiser than the wise and as innocent as the innocent: and it has long ago been found out what is the best way of taking things. 'The Earth', said the great traveller, 'is much the same wherever we go': and the changes of position which women and students tremble and shilly shally before, leave things much as they found them. Caelum non animum mutant. The Winter comes and destroys all, but in the spring the old grasses come up, all the greener.

Let us not sit in a corner and mope and think ourselves clever for our comfort, while the room is full of dancing and cheerfulness. The sum of the whole matter is this. Whatsoever your hand findeth to do, do it without fiddle faddling; for there is no experience, nor pleasure, nor pain, nor instruction nor anything else in the grave whither thou goest. When you get to the end of this life, you won't find another ready made in which you can do without effort what you were meant to do with effort here (*Corr.* i. 283–4).

A month later he was writing to Tom Arnold about Tasmania, 'Your population of course won't be very beautiful and attractive but all the truer to facts in general for having plenty of alloy: that is a comfort to a certain extent; earthly paradises being mostly milk-and-watery and not long to last' (*Corr.* i. 285).

These two letters, following one another so closely, and written shortly before Clough set off for the holiday in Italy during which he began *Dipsychus*, are directly relevant to the satiric treatment of the over-tender conscience in that poem. Clearly, the acceptance of 'fact' and the 'world' grows out of the positive positions in Clough's independence. At the same time, the manifest desire for engagement, the expressed need for going ahead and *doing* something in the letter to Shairp, resurrects a familiar anxiety. The awareness of 'fact' can be a toughening presence in a larger and multi-dimensional complex of recognitions; isolated into a doctrine of practical morality, it is, potentially, constricting. The desire for action, in Clough's case, begins increasingly to control the impulse of recognition, creating a new definition for that impulse and narrowing it down ultimately to the arid and blindfold conception of duty which seems to have been his final resting-point.

One can, of course, relate the final emergence of duty as a moral criterion to a number of influences, and point towards certain wider affiliations. At one level it represents the triumph of one aspect of the Evangelical work ethic. At another, it represents a logical conclusion to the influence of Arnoldism. At another, perhaps more interesting, level, since it clearly focuses the issue as that of providing objective sanctions and bases for transcendental insights and convictions, one could point to Carlyle—and beyond Carlyle to the 'categorical imperative' of Kant, the ethical idealism of Fichte, the 'conscience' of Butler. These larger implications are important and relevant, but they should always be measured against the reducing fact of Clough's 'Service' to Florence Nightingale. Biography here imposes its limits on intellectual history. Duty, for Clough, was a dead-end, not an expanding and forceful solution.

For an intensely scrupulous person like Clough, a half-romantic whose whole life can be regarded as an effort to arrive at some stable, satisfying, and not wholly subjective source of epistemological and ontological authority, the liberating impulse of self-enlargement through self-acknowledgement ended inevitably in the sense of a moral *impasse*. For such a person the gradual emergence of duty as an objective-seeming and at the same time inner-dictated moral criterion was, one might venture, almost predictable. During these critical years in London, Clough developed even further his philosophy of realism, and, in taking it to its furthest daring limits, initiated frustrating counter-forces within himself which led to his 'submission'. The beginnings of this dual movement are best examined in the somewhat scanty prose of these years—scanty, that is, if we discount the not immediately relevant lectures on English Literature.

In his public prose[1] Clough once again reverted to the posture and the rhetoric of the Carlylean idol-breaker that fitted in so well with the igneous images of himself he cultivated in his

---

[1] I use the term 'public' to describe the 'Letter on Socialism', the review of Francis Newman's *The Soul*, and the 'Paper on Religion'. This last piece has been assigned tentatively to a period between 1852 and 1853 (Trawick, p. 350). The draft which appears in the 1850 (Venice) Notebook (Bodleian MS. Eng. Poet. d. 133, fol. 84^v–fol. 83^v) is strong evidence in support of an earlier date. Although none of these pieces seem to have been published by Clough, their manner and tone are unmistakably public. In calling this prose 'public' I attempt to distinguish it from pieces like 'A Sunday Morning Contemplation' and 'An ill world . . .', which are as obviously private and ejaculatory.

most officially heterodox moments; and, in the review of Francis Newman's *The Soul*, which he wrote most probably in 1850, he declared his discipleship explicitly.[1]

The review itself is a key document in Clough's spiritual history. The attitudes he adopts and the positives he advances are ones which any attentive follower of his development would expect, only now they are given a new and emphatic explicitness which makes the review as a whole part of the essential background to *Dipsychus*. Perhaps the single most arresting aspect of the review is its strongly anti-'Methodistical' tone: as Clough puts it in his penultimate sentence, '[I]n the name of the Past and of the Future . . . let us have done with Methodism.'[2] What this anti-Methodism amounts to is indicated in his highly significant comments on the sense of sin, which endorse Newman's views and, incidentally, also take the debate about action one stage further.

> One could almost fancy that in the Spiritual as in the Intellectual Region there are *Antinomies*. It is needful to believe that between the doing and the not doing of a given act there is a difference simply infinite—it is needful also to believe that it is indifferent. . . . Is it perhaps that in our times the conscience has been over-irritated? . . . [A]t present for young minds there is at least as much harm as good in calling things *very* wrong. Be strict, if you please, be severe, be inflexible. . . . But meddle not rashly, O pedagogue, with the conscience. . . . Give a dog a bad name and hang him: give a boy a bad name, and he will hang himself. . . . But it is in Education and the Young that this mischief is mostly prevalent. Few persons perhaps pass the age of 30, very few males reach it, without having some how or other . . . quieted their conscience, and brought their minds to the comfortable conclusion that they must get on as best they may. . . . As the great Traveller said, the World is much the same everywhere.[3]

It is hard to believe, especially remembering the prose Epilogue to *Dipsychus*, that Clough is not glancing here at his own experience at Rugby.[4]

---

[1] Cf. Trawick, p. 286.   [2] Loc. cit.   [3] Ibid., pp. 280–1.
[4] A single word in Clough's description of a visit to Laleham, where Dr. Arnold taught private pupils before going to Rugby, makes the connection almost irresistible. 'We also looked in at the church window and made out the pulpit whence he used to fulminate', he wrote to Blanche Smith in June 1852 (*Corr.* i. 319). 'Fulminate' hardly seems the word he would have used about his headmaster fifteen years before.

He also enthusiastically endorses Newman's rejection of the historical and dogmatic basis of Christian faith: '[T]he abiding revelation is written not on hard tables of legal, historic, or dogmatic stone but on the fleshly tablets of the human heart and conscience.'[1] He doubts, however, if Newman has been entirely successful in developing a 'religious Ontology' from this funda-mental axiom. Although he sidesteps, with lofty disingenuous-ness,[2] some of the fundamental questions which must be resolved before a trust in the individual soul can become viable religious doctrine, he is quite explicit about one aspect of religious sub-jectivism. Severely critical of Newman's chapter on the 'Sense of the Personal relation to God', he attacks that uncontrolled religious sense which surrenders itself entirely to the devotional instinct, and is totally overwhelmed by its own sense of the noumenon.

Be it far from either the present or any other reviewer to speak lightly or otherwise than reverently of the mysterious instinct of prayer. . . . But there is some truth as well as some extravagance—more pertinence we think than impertinence in the question which a young man once put, . . . How long can I love God without having seen Him? Love implies a sensible consciousness of an Object; is it safe to ascribe an objective actual character to any picture of our imagination even in highest moments of beatitude? . . .
. . . [In the case of pure devotionality] the religionist simply ignores the exterior world—all that is done is merely mechanical—absorption in the contemplation of the Deity is the whole life. . . . [T]his is the one thing needful with which Martha must not interfere, however much Mary be needed for the many things of service. . . .
But obliged as most people must be to mix with things earthly and be cumbered and careful and troubled,—they have to settle the question of reconciling the world and the spirit, they have to make themselves holy friendships out of the unrighteous Mammon—to serve God in the world and in their generation. For the solution of this problem so little information is apparently derivable from devotional habits, so alien on the contrary are they, to the cultivation of plain sense and worldly wisdom—that those who indulge in them are usually forced to take refuge in a position either of mere fantastical caprice or of hard unmeaning formalism.[3]

Accepting individual conscience as the sole basis for authentic religious knowledge, and yet rejecting the excesses of unregulated

[1] Trawick, p. 279.   [2] Cf. loc. cit.   [3] Ibid., pp. 281-3.

subjectivism, Clough urges the indubitable here and now as the only reliable external guide. ' "The kingdom of God is within us", but it is also without us.' 'We are here, however we came, to do something—to fulfil our *ergon* to live according to Nature, to serve God. The World is here, however it came here, to be made something of by our hands. Not by prayer, but by examination; examination not of ourselves, but of the world, shall we find out what to do, and how to do it.'[1]

At their best, when allowed to regulate but not dominate, such positives can create a tough astringency of outlook; at their worst, if embraced too purposefully, they can lead to an indiscriminating and bankrupt acquiescence. Nature is an oracle only to those who are capable of committing themselves to her more thoroughly than Clough ever was; the given 'world'—as he was well aware— can be morally very shoddy indeed. Further, the intimations of morality delivered by nature and those delivered by the 'world' do not frequently coincide: there are further choices to be made before one discovers a moral principle.

The intensification—under an insistent activist pressure—of the stresses in Clough's whole attempt at welding untuited spiritual reality with the world of empirically derived fact can be observed even more clearly in the 'Paper on Religion'. The first half of the paper is a vindication of the religion 'whose revelation is to be what Religion so-called calls Irreligion. It is, shall we say, Silence.'[2] Clough is caustic about worshippers of the First Cause, because of their too ready identification of Divinity in a universe of continually receding boundaries. 'We touch the line which we thought our horizon. . . . We approach, and behold, leagues away, and receding and receding yet again beyond each new limit of the known a new visible unknown. You have found out God, have you? Ah my friends! let us be—*Silent.*'[3] The histrionic air suggests consecration, not vindication. Silence provides the vestments and Clough seems hereby to be ordained one of his own 'Priests, to vindicate the unknown'.[4] As so often with Clough's public prose, the manner seriously undermines the position.

Since the second part of the paper as it appears in the draft has not been published, I reproduce it here in its entirety.

---

[1] Trawick, p. 285.   [2] Ibid., p. 287.
[3] Ibid., p. 288.   [4] Loc. cit.

But there is yet again another religion miscalled irreligion whose watchword—a simpler one—is action. Thank heaven there are many 1000's in Israel who, unknown of Elijah, [would?] not the knee [*sic*] to Baal, but worship—*thus!*—Oh, my pious friend—they don't pray—at least it isn't made out they do so—in public: nay in private they are sleepy: they at it are not regular at church—their prayer books and hymn books are dusty outside and inside unbethumbed— they sleep at sermons—and are indeed—religious people tell me— unconverted. I have heard them swear—and been told of their getting drunk. Yes, they do fall into real contamination —they lie, they cheat —they run after pleasures, ambitions, money-makings—they are any- thing but good—and we do well assuredly to rebuke and revile, and avoid, and in the end put them down.

But—they confront the World and do not shirk it—But they go to the Vineyard, and set themselves one way or other to work— they stand not—in childish or indolent [piety?] at their Father's side, saying I go Sir and go not.—

I confess this appears to me to be the natural tendency of good sense and commonsense. My employer sends me on an errand; let me not think about him, but about his errand. I am set a sum—don't let me fidget about what my teacher wants or wishes but work at my figures —the multiplication table goes further than Sentiment: and twice- two-make-four is more to the purpose than rivers of tears of tenderness.[1]

The needle-fine responses of the alert dialectical intelligence which gave us *Amours de Voyage* have been dulled into a single, inert antithesis of two complementary but self-circumscribed and virtually non-communicating 'religions'—the practical and the speculative. As the continuation of the draft in the 1850 (Venice) Notebook makes clear, a resolution of this kind, so obviously fashioned by the pressure of Clough's desire for a firm basis, has, potentially at least, important effects on his literary values and attitudes.

If literature call off the youth of a nation from the latter of these Services or Worships, which is of necessity the ordained Service or Worship of the most,—if it paralyse and may I say decompose the Action of a People—if it become a dilettante thing—it is irreligious. Yet it is difficult—it does seem to go ag[ains]t it &c. . . .

The other religious tendency which I have spoken of, it assists all the least [observed?], least registered or classified, all the subtlest and least manipulated, least retainable phenomena.

[1] Bodleian MS. Eng. Poet. d. 133, fol. 82ᵛ–fol. 81ᵛ (rev.).

In the limits of the ascertained system it is conscious of unexplainable perturbations—and when Science has said Uranus is the last it has already the data of some further [two illegible words] of Neptune.[1]

Adumbrated here, despite a flicker or two of hesitation, is a return to standards like those implied in Shairp's criticisms of *Amours de Voyage*, which approved only a poetry that was positive and outward-looking, or, if at all introspective or dubious, was at least 'honest serious Werterism'. It is not irrelevant that the two alternatives should have a rough correspondence to the polarity of *Dipsychus*.

Since there will be no occasion to deal at any length with Clough's religious views in later chapters, it may be as well to include at this point a brief discussion of the 'Notes on the Religious Tradition', although it is likely that these notes fall outside the immediate period. According to Mrs. Clough the notes probably belong to the 'last period' of her husband's life.[2] Both Houghton and Trawick, however, have tentatively ascribed them to a period between 1852 and 1853, since the manuscript appears in the 1852–3 (A) Notebook.[3] The existence of a very sketchy draft in the 1851 (C) Notebook[4] introduces the possibility of an even earlier date—at least for the leading ideas in these notes.

Reflecting clearly the dilemma about the utilitarian position into which he had been led by his commitment to fact,[5] the 'Notes on the Religious Tradition' grow out of the 'Paper on Religion', just as this, in turn, draws out some of the implications of the review of *The Soul*. Any critical response to these notes, one of Clough's most moving pieces of prose, is likely to be an ambivalent one. The purity of its tone, the grave and unpretentious precision of its language and argument, the manifest humility of its attempt to get face to face with and formulate real, irreducible conviction, disarm criticism. More than any other piece of Clough's prose these notes give us an insight into the profound respect which he could inspire by sheer strength and nobility of character. And yet it is difficult to resist the suspicion that the

[1] Bodleian MS. Eng. Poet. d. 133, fol. 81–fol. 80ᵛ (rev.).
[2] *PPR* i. 421 n.   [3] *Catalogue*, p. 54, and Trawick, p. 350.
[4] Bodleian MS. Eng. Poet. d. 123, fol. 22–fol. 21ᵛ (rev.).
[5] On the inside back cover of the 1852–3 (A) Notebook in which Clough made these notes he wrote: 'Do you believe in Political Economy? Of course; do not *you* believe in the Multiplication Table, $2+2$ are of course 4. $2a+2a = 4a$. —Therefore of course 2 soul$+2$ soul $= 4$ soul.' Bodleian MS. Eng. Poet. d. 140.

service of truth has become little more than a routine gesture—particularly when it is at once so narrowly channelled and so rampantly eclectic, so rigid and so collapsed. For, given the uncertain historicity of Christianity, Clough's guiding 'Religious Tradition' is to be found

Everywhere.—But above all in our own work, in life, in action, in submission so far as action goes, in service,—in experience,—in patience and in confidence. I would scarcely have any man dare to say that he has found it, till that moment when death removes his power of telling it. . . .

The Religious Tradition—as found everywhere, as found not only among clergymen and religious people, but among all who have really tried to order their lives by the highest action of the reasonable and spiritual will. I will go to Johnson, I will go to Hume, as well as to Bishop Butler. . . .

Everywhere—to India if you will and the ancient Bhagvad Gita and the laws of Menu, to Persia and Hafiz, to China and Confucius; to the Vedas, and the Shasters; the Koran;—to Pagan Greece and Rome; to Homer; to Socrates and Plato; to Lucretius; to Vergil, to Tacitus. . . .[1]

It would be a difficult task to defend this infinitely absorptive

> . . . rationalistic
> Half-puritano-semitheistic
> Cross of Neologist and Mystic

against the charge of religious 'dram-drinking' which has been levelled at him.[2] More fruitful in the final analysis, perhaps, would be something very much easier: to note quite simply the massive, unchannelled, continually replenishing sense of reverence in this sceptical, unconceding, testing personality. Intellectually, there is little to distinguish this sense of reverence from the most blatant religiosity; emotionally and psychologically, it presents us with one of the central facts about Clough without which it would be impossible to understand his later life.

Perhaps it is only an ironically appropriate accident of survival that Clough's prose should mirror so dramatically his renewed interest in the theological and religious questions which he seems to have almost entirely given up at one stage. At any rate the 'Letter on Socialism' is the only paper devoted to social questions,

[1] Trawick, pp. 291–2.
[2] *Poems of Arthur Hugh Clough*, with an Introduction by Charles Whibley (London, 1913), p. xv.

and its curiously baffled quality gives us an insight, wider and more illuminating in many ways, into the consequences for Clough of the attitudes he advocated so energetically in his review of *The Soul*. Written with the conviction that 'earthly paradises' are 'mostly milk-and-watery', the 'Letter' also betrays Clough's inability to forgive such paradises for being what they are. Coloured by the disappointment of his 'radical' hopes both in France and in Italy, it exposes also the lack of stamina in his social thinking.

The advertised satirical intent of the 'Letter' is, really, part of a fairly elaborate ruse. Clough has left himself too many escape routes. Describing himself as a sympathetic observer and signing himself 'Citoyen', he ventures to say 'something' on the 'other side' in this intolerably condescending letter to the Christian Socialists. But he also suggests that the whole argument is set up really in order that it may be knocked down.[1] The 'Letter' is, in fact, an extended and very puzzled prose doodle in which Clough finds himself led into positions which he can neither accept nor vacate. The *ad hoc* satirical postures are part of the tactic of his uncertainty.

Since Clough uses common sense for his sights, and since the target is Christian Socialism, some good marksmanship is inevitable. Questioning the Christian Socialist assumption of the identity of Christianity and Socialism, he points out that it is naïvely unrealistic to believe that in a morally imperfect world moral regeneration will result from political, social, or economic reorganization.

[B]ecause you are good, will there be no more bad men? Because tailors divide profits equally, will there be no more fools and brutes? Because shoemakers have a common purpose, will spirituous liquors cease to tempt, and wanton women to allure?—And if scavengers should only cooperate would there be no more dirt? Soberly, you must give me leave to doubt whether a highly imperfect-Christian population can be got to do its necessary work entirely for the love of the brotherhood unassisted by the (imperfect-Christian) love of getting-on.[2]

Few would demur at such obvious facing of reality or with Clough's further recognition that human nature is often vicious, that there is much dirty and degrading work which has to be done,

---

[1] Trawick, pp. 243 and 248.   [2] Ibid., p. 245.

that there is necessarily an element of inequality between man and man.[1] But recognition of the world rapidly transforms itself into a wholesale invasion, and it certainly does not increase one's respect for Clough as a social thinker when he mobilizes the Psalmist, 'who tells us that no man can save his brother and that it is very well if he can save himself', in order to conclude that 'Each man is to look out for himself: and if he doesn't, must learn to do so. Competition is not naturally wrong: it is merely one way, and the most efficient yet known . . . for teaching men this great law of a sadly uncelestial world . . ., for if everybody were to see to somebody else, what an increase of trouble it would cause!'[2] In his newly found enthusiasm for the world Clough has led himself into a position which can be supported only by his most muscular flourishes of moral vigour.

And suppose in this race of competition a man beats me!—how has it happened? by his own superiority, by luck, or by trickery. In the first case, Eternal Justice is pleased, and so ought I to be; in the second case, I must hope for a better chance next time, in the third—I must take care and keep a better look out. . . .
O dear! It would be nicer certainly if nobody ever cheated us, or injured us, or insulted us, or despised us, or was unkind to us or rough to us or did anything we didn't like to us! But whether it would be better for us, in the end is really quite another question.[3]

The position is, of course, one that Clough cannot accept, and the rest of the 'Letter' is an acrobatic attempt at extricating himself which ends only in a confused tangle, betraying his inability to bring the argument to any satisfactory conclusion. Adopting an outrightly satirical stance, he offers the conventional religious sop to those who come off badly in the struggle:

If thou wilt be perfect in fraternity, say thou to the rich ones in their carriages, 'I am poor and you are rich; but mine is thine, and thine is mine; and if you enjoy, I enjoy with and for you. Blessed be God.—'
'Rejoice with them that do rejoice' 'Are we not members one of another?' With such a thought let even the scavenger (of a reflective turn) console his unsavouriness! For oh just heavens, in this worm also there is a butterfly; and though it is by no means the doctrine of . . . Christian Socialism that Dives goes to the Gulf and Lazarus (the Scavenger) to Abraham's bosom, still in another world, if he has been faithful here in his dirty things, some cleaner things, one would hope,

[1] Loc. cit.   [2] Ibid., p. 246.   [3] Loc. cit.

(perhaps a real carriage and homes and everything handsome to match) may at last turn up for him![1]

Clough had 'a habit', Bagehot wrote, 'of putting your own doctrine concisely before you, so that you might see what it came to, and that you did not like it'.[2] In collapsing inward upon itself in the way it does, the 'Letter on Socialism' reveals the precariousness of this *modus operandi*. It, too, could become an automatic response, embracing confusion instead of exposing it, blunting rather than sharpening the intellect. The wearied expression of a man burdened and bowed down by the insoluble mysteries of the universe, which so forcibly struck those who knew him in his later life,[3] was already forming in the University Hall years. Hutton thought Emerson had Clough in mind when he remarked, '"Ah," says my languid Oxford gentleman, "nothing new, and nothing true, and no matter"',[4] and in his own correspondence Clough confirms that he was no stranger to moods in which the circle merely came round and the world did little more than travel 'about the Sun, round and round, and round and round, in the old foolish fashion'.[5] It is only a short step from the 'Letter on Socialism' to the fatigued worldly wisdom of the review of Charles Eliot Norton's *Considerations on Some Recent Social Theories* which Clough wrote in America, and in which the sense of the actual and palpably present, once a powerful co-operating force in his criticism of the given, comes to rest in an exhausted submission. It is a short step—but Clough had not yet taken it in the University Hall Years. He needed Blanche Smith to complete the exhaustion of his radicalism. Richard Hutton was both perceptive and succinct when he described the University Hall period as one during which

Clough . . . wandered in the wilderness into which Carlyle had led him—lonely, perplexed, at odds with the society with which he lived, tinged with a Carlylian scorn for the conventional, and yet profoundly conscious of the fitness of the frame in which convention sets a great deal of our social life, desiring to fraternise with those who denounce the conventional but not finding it very easy.[6]

[1] Trawick, p. 247.   [2] W. Bagehot, *Literary Studies*, ii. 321.
[3] Ibid., p. 316; H. Spencer, *An Autobiography*, 2 vols. (London, 1904), ii. 62.
[4] Prefatory Memoir to W. Bagehot, *Literary Studies*, i. xxxv.
[5] *Corr.* i. 289, 290. See also *Corr.* ii. 411.
[6] R. H. Hutton, 'The Poetry of Arthur Hugh Clough', *Fortnightly Review*, xxxix (June 1883), 795–6.

The prose, as we have seen, mirrors these wanderings, and, undistinguished as it is in its over-all content, it gives us a valuable insight into the frustration of the would-be rebel. In attempting to arrive at a simple formula for his purposive role—to legitimize, so to speak, his heterodoxy—Clough was working against the grain of his intelligence. Instead of allowing his intellect to remain dialectically alert and unengaged, and so continuously freshen and activate the moral sense, he was pressing it into the service of an attitude not so very far removed, ultimately, from that expressed by the worried Provost of Oriel in 1848, 'In truth you were not born for *speculation*. . . . [W]e are sent into this world not so much to speculate as to serve God and serve man' (*Corr*. i. 198).

As an attempt to provide a set of answers and furnish a basis for living, the prose of the University Hall years is inadequate and facile. The meagreness of the conclusions reflects the uncongeniality of the attempt, and betrays, too, Clough's serious limitations as a thinker—limitations which an excessively flattering reputation did not encourage him to recognize. His inability to construct can (if one leaves out the more general factor of his tendency to be easily discouraged)[1] be related directly to his inability to sustain any single line of inquiry or, as in his political and social thinking, to make distinctions and choices sharply and decisively enough to enable him to do so: repeatedly moral, religious, political, and social considerations overlap and interpenetrate confusingly rather than productively. Perhaps more important in accounting for the impoverished and unsatisfying nature of Clough's positive positions is the fact that their relevance and their validity are so clearly limited by the orbit of his personal dilemmas and anxieties, that they are so often and so patently directives to himself. In generalizing from himself he limited the relevance and validity of his positives; in generalizing away from himself he deprived them of the full resonance of their meaning.

For, viewed as a collection of attitudes rather than a set of answers—attitudes towards morality, towards the religious instinct, towards the world, and towards human nature—the same body of prose displays a local toughness and intelligence which makes Bagehot's admiration for Clough as a destroyer of 'earnestness' understandable.[2] Self-impoverishing when it

[1] Prefatory Memoir to W. Bagehot, *Literary Studies*, i. xxxiv.
[2] Ibid. p. xxxv.

masquerades as a solution, Clough's 'realism' is of value only as a contributing attitude, as one element in a living dialectic. 'Clough', Hutton wrote,

was an idealist, but an idealist always pressing for greater reality in life. . . . Once, I remember, when I praised to him some book with a mystical turn in it, he spread out his hand and called my attention to the fact that his fingers widened, instead of tapering towards the ends, remarking that men whose fingers taper are disposed to symbolism and mysticism, but that men with fingers like his cannot rest on anything but broad and homely fact.[1]

In restoring Clough's positives to the dialectic from which they had been extracted in the prose, the poetry of the University Hall years gives us our other insight into the frustrated rebel.

2. THE SHORTER POEMS

Individual poems cut across the chronological division, the fact that Clough was working over many of the earlier poems blurs that division, but comparing the poems written in 1850 and 1851 with those written in 1849, one cannot help being struck by a shift in quality and emphasis. For one thing, the pressure of personal unhappiness and uncertainty seems to have reopened—often to the detriment of the poetry—that vein of direct reportage from inner life which had been so prominent in his earlier work. More generally, as a body the poems of the University Hall period confirm the impression, created by the prose, of a general attempted reordering—and in some ways, shrinkage—of personality. *Dipsychus*, the obvious exception, stands out like a rebellious Triton—and it is significant that it, too, should have been conceived during a holiday away from England. The quantity of poetry Clough wrote at University Hall suggests that he was working seriously at it in search of the fulfilment that was denied him elsewhere; its quality—with very few exceptions —suggests that he was cultivating assiduously a poetic identity which conformed more closely to the ideas and expectations of his contemporaries.

Immediately following the draft of the poem beginning 'If to write, rewrite, and write again' in the 1851 (A) Notebook, Clough wrote, in a careful, printed hand,

[1] R. H. Hutton, *Fortnightly Review*, xxxix. 797.

> Go thou that seek'st thy worldly gain
> Go seek it not from me.

The two lines, foreign as they are to the light-hearted banter of
the poem, really restate in a graver key much that is implicit in
its playful self-irony, and they express a recurrent mood of these
years. The renunciation of the world as a personal end recalls
immediately the Balliol period, and is explored as a simple
terminal attitude in such directly self-revelatory poems as 'These
vulgar ways that round me be' or 'Go foolish thoughts and join
the throng'. But that attitude, either simply as a withholding or,
more positively, as an implicit or explicit assertion of extra-
worldly values and realities, establishes too the tension with the
sense of the world as a present and even moral positive, which,
in one way or another, informs some of the most successful
poetry of the University Hall years and gives it its particular
contour of emotion. Setting up the tension, the renunciation
also creates the serenity necessary to maintain its balance, and the
artistic problem in these poems defines itself as that of translating
this serenity from a state of mind into an aesthetic fact, of finding
an equivalent in artistic form to either contain or resolve, without
violence, the two opposed senses of the world. Inherent in his
dialectical sensibility, the problem is not, of course, a new one for
Clough. Two factors, however, co-operate to give it a new kind
of relevance. As it appears in these University Hall poems the
dialectic acquires a new simplicity and sharpness of definition:
the schizophrenic structure of *Dipsychus* is its most exact image.
Secondly, in turning to new—and in many ways more conventional—poetic modes, Clough committed himself to a fresh
beginning. Why the dialectic should have acquired this new
simplicity and this new, almost antithetical, sharpness is a question
for which one can propose only tentative answers. One could
argue that the simplification is an unavoidable result of the comparatively inflexible moulds in which Clough elected to cast his
University Hall poems, and at one level the argument is complete
and valid. A truer view, probably, and one which the prose
supports, would be that his choice of poetic moulds is as much a
symptom as it is a cause, that, in other words, the sharpened and
simplified polarities correspond to developments within Clough's
sensibility itself under the strains and pressures of self-definition.

As attempts to solve the aesthetic problems posed by these polarities, the shorter poems, although in terms of chronology they straddle *Dipsychus*, give us some valuable insights into the workings of Clough's most ambitious—and complex—attempt to cope with two antagonistic valuations of the world.

The poems on Biblical subjects—'The Song of Lamech', written early in 1849, 'Genesis XXIV' and 'Jacob's Wives', written in 1850, 'Jacob', written in 1851, and 'Repose in Egypt', which can only tentatively be ascribed to the same period—clearly isolate themselves into a group. With the exception of 'Genesis XXIV' which is really little more than an academic exercise, the themes of all these poems lie close to the personal and introspective centre of Clough's life. Even 'Jacob', which has been regarded traditionally, on the basis of a fancy of Anne Clough's,[1] as inspired by Clough's father and his experience of commercial life, can be quite validly seen as a treatment of Clough's own feelings about the moral compromises involved in growing up from the innocence of youth and the sheltering single-mindedness of one's teachers into an imperfect and demanding world.[2] Turning to the Bible for objectifying myth, probably on the impulse of *Adam and Eve*, and sharing the same 'patriarchal' atmosphere, as it has been aptly called,[3] these poems all explore basically the same highly self-conscious poetic in their search for impersonal form.

[1] B. A. Clough, *A Memoir of Anne Jemima Clough* (London, 1903), p. 21.

[2] It is instructive to compare Clough's poem with a passage from a sermon on 'The Christian Standard of Good and Evil' which Dr. Arnold preached in Rugby Chapel on 28 Oct. 1838:

'To Christian men, looking at Jacob's life, with the faults recorded of it, it is sometimes strange that he should be spoken of as good. But it seems that in a rude state of society, where knowledge is very low, and passion very strong, the great virtue is to be freed from the dominion of the prevailing low principle, to see and resolve that we ought and will live according to knowledge, and not according to passion and impulse. The knowledge may be very imperfect, and probably is so: the practice may in many respects offend against knowledge, and probably will do so: yet it is a great step taken,—it is *the* virtue of man, in such a state of society,—to follow, though imperfectly, principle where others follow instinct, or the opinion of their fellows. It is the great distinguishing mark, in such a state of things, between the good and the evil. . . .' (T. Arnold, *Sermons*, iv. 65–6.)

Like the moralized and Victorianized Cain who recurs in Clough's poetry, Jacob is a figure who embodies both the guilt and the self-vindication of his creator.

[3] Houghton, pp. 78–9. The closeness between Clough's 'Biblical' manner and the 'Nazarene'-influenced primitivism of William Dyce is striking. I suspect some connection here.

'The Song of Lamech', which focuses on the figure of Cain, comes closest to *Adam and Eve*, particularly to the last scene in which the whole drama had been distanced and overlaid with a vaguely nostalgic hopefulness and serenity in Adam's dream. Cain's guilt and his alienation of himself despite the remonstrances of his parents, the contrary realities of terror and confidence in his inner life, and the promise of eventual reconciliation are handled in the form of a recitative in which the opening lines set the mood and define the poetic quality.

> Hearken to me, ye mothers of my tent;
> Ye wives of Lamech, listen to my speech;
> Adah, let Jabal hither lead his goats,
> And Tubal Cain, O Zillah, hush the forge;
> Naamah her wheel shall ply beside, and thou
> My Jubal, touch, before I speak, the string.
>
> Yea, Jubal, touch, before I speak, the string.
> Hear ye my voice, beloved of my tent,
> Dear ones of Lamech listen to my speech.
>
> (*Poems*, 50, ll. 1-9.)

It is a poetic, essentially, of the 'speaking picture', and the visual images of the 'song' repeat and emphasize the pictorial qualities of the initial grouping:

> For Cain replied not. But, an hour more, sat
> Where the night through he sat, his knit brows seen,
> Scarce seen, amidst the foldings of his limbs.
> But when the sun was bright upon the field
> To Adam still and Eve still waiting by
> And weeping, lift he up his voice and spake.
>
> (ll. 21-6.)

The broad, simple strokes that create this tableau-like effect of carefully arranged and mutely eloquent stillness correspond to the marmoreal simplicity of the emotional states successively blocked out in the poem. That the simplicity is, in fact, not simple, that it is highly artificial and contrived, is not automatically self-condemning. The tension between the apparent bareness of the language, on the one hand, and its actual rhetorical elaborateness, on the other, is an essential part of the reconciliatory ritual—but a closer look at the nature of the elaboration reveals it as the essential weakness of this kind of poetry.

> Cain said, The sun is risen upon the Earth;
> The day demands my going; and I go.
> As you from Paradise, so I from you;
> As you to exile, into exile I:
> My Father and my Mother, I depart.
> As betwixt you and Paradise of old,
> So betwixt me, my Parents, now and you
> Cherubims I discern and in their hand
> A flaming sword that turneth every way, . . .
>
> (ll. 27–35.)
>
> For Adam laid upon the head of Cain
> His hand, and Cain bowed down, and slept and died.
> And a deep sleep on Adam also fell,
> And in his slumber's deepest he beheld,
> Standing before the gate of Paradise
> With Abel, hand in hand, our father Cain.
>
> (ll. 90–5.)

The artful simplicity of the emphatic rhythmic recurrences, the equally emphatic verbal repetitions and parallelisms, and the archaizing pseudo-Biblical remoteness, is controlled by a thoroughly—and exclusively—emotive aesthetic. Alexander Smith identified it perfectly when he observed,

'My son Absalom' is an expression of precisely similar import to 'my brother Dick' or 'my uncle Toby'. . . . It would be difficult to say that 'oh! Absalom, my son, my son' is not poetry; yet the grammatical and verbal import of the words is exactly the same in both cases. The interjection 'Oh,' and the repetition of the words 'my son,' add nothing whatever to the meaning; but they have the effect of making words which are otherwise but the intimation of a fact, the expression of an *emotion* of exceeding depth and interest. . . .[1]

In being spread with such even deliberation over the whole poem the 'emotion of exceeding depth' becomes something extrinsic and superadded. Lamech summoning his family, Cain embracing his solitude or confessing his terror, Adam's vision of his reconciled sons, even the reminders about the accompanying music with which Lamech intersperses his recitative—all equally evoke a mellow sigh of regret. The formula is too indiscriminatingly

---

[1] 'The Philosophy of Poetry', *Blackwood's Edinburgh Magazine*, xxxviii (1835), 830. Quoted, M. H. Abrams, *The Mirror and the Lamp* (paperback edn., London, 1960), p. 153.

effective; the artfulness is that of an art which does not wear
very well.

The unsuitedness of this kind of poetry—and this kind of
sentimentalized serenity—to anything like a dialectic is heavily
underlined in 'Jacob's Wives', where the conflict between measur-
ably fruitful but calculated duty, and spontaneous but un-
productive impulse whose only justification is itself, is allegorized
in the figures of Rachel and Leah. Like 'The Song of Lamech',
the poem displays, in its own terms, considerable skill and
craftsmanship. The pastoral opening is very similar in pictorial
and tonal quality to the earlier poem:

> These are the words of Jacob's wives; the words
> Which Leah spake and Rachel to his ears,
> When in the shade at eventide he sat
> By the tent-door, a palm tree overhead,
> A spring beside him, and the sheep around.
>
> (*Poems*, 80, ll. 1–5.)

The introduction of the two wives is a minor triumph of
compressed characterization.

> And Rachel spake and said, The nightfall comes;
> Night, which all day I wait for, and for thee.
>
> And Leah also spake, The day is done;
> My lord with toil is weary, and would rest.
>
> (ll. 6–9.)

The four lines 'contain' all of Rachel and Leah and the essential
emphasis of their debate; the rest of the poem is only amplifica-
tion. The debate, although it yields some good lines and at least
one splendid image (ll. 56–9), is, necessarily, since Rachel and
Leah are placed in absolutely non-communicating opposition,
largely repetitive. The closing lines complete the frame by recalling the opening, and they cut off arbitrarily what is, on the
evidence of the poem, endless.

> These are the words of Jacob's wives, who sat
> In the tent door, and listened to their speech,
> The spring beside him, and above the palm,
> While all the sheep were gathered for the night.
>
> (ll. 122–5.)

The closing sigh is a desperate exhalation which succeeds only
in sentimentalizing the continuing mutter of female dispute.

The artistic resolution is, if anything, even weaker than the argumentative one. For although Leah is given the last word,

> And Leah, ended, Father of my sons,
> Come, thou shalt dream of Rachel if thou wilt,
> So Leah fold thee in a wife's embrace,
>
> (ll. 119–21.)

the poem invites us (ll. 89–97) to look outside it to the birth of Joseph, the Child of Promise. One can hope, at least, that that argument, though deferred, is conclusive.

'Repose in Egypt' is Clough's single indisputable success among these 'Biblical' poems,[1] and it is perhaps significant that the meditated scene should so closely parallel Goethe's 'Heilige Familie', which Clough translated.[2] His own poem is worth quoting in full.

> O happy mother, while the man wayworn
> Sleeps by his ass and dreams of daily bread,
> Wakeful and heedful for thy infant care,
> O happy mother, while thy husband sleeps,
> Art privileged, O blessed one, to see
> Celestial strangers sharing in thy task,
> And visible angels waiting on thy child.
>
> Take, O young soul, O infant heaven-desired,
> Take and fear not the cates, although of earth,
> Which to thy hands celestial hands extend.   10
> Take and fear not: such vulgar meats of life
> Thy spirit lips no more must scorn to pass;
> The seeming ill, contaminating joys,
> Thy sense divine no more be loth to allow.
> The pleasures as the pains of our strange life
> Thou art engaged, self-compromised, to share.
> Look up, upon thy mother's face there sits
> No sad suspicion of a lurking ill,
> No shamed confession of a needful sin.
> Mistrust her not, albeit of earth she too.   20
> Look up! The bright-eyed cherubs overhead
> Strew from mid air fresh flowers to crown the feast.

---

[1] Even 'Jacob', a relatively adroit psychological study of the man who has made his way in the world, but only, as he is too well aware, by deserting the values of his fathers, suffers from its hybrid nature, part ode, part realistic self-revelation. See Houghton, pp. 73–8, for a discussion of the poem.

[2] *Poems*, p. 455.

Look! Thy own father's servants these, and thine,
Who at his bidding and at thine are here.
In thine own word was it not said long since
Butter and honey shall he eat, and learn
The evil to refuse and choose the good?
Fear not, O babe divine, fear not, accept.
O happy mother, privileged to see,
While the man sleeps, the sacred mystery.   30

Eschewing *ersatz* simplicity, the ceremonious, richly connotative texture generates a reverence which is controlled by the
clarity—and strength—of the visual image. The poem translates
the repose of the title—and by extension of the Incarnation—
into itself as it explores, elaborates, redefines, and equilibriates
the relationships in that image, and its real distinction is in its
masterly treatment of Joseph, the structural frame Clough seems
to have been so fond of in these 'Biblical' poems. Far from being
sentimentally decorative, he is an organic part of the poem's
reality and meaning. The 'man wayworn', sleeping by his ass and
dreaming of 'daily bread', is locked in the incognizant harmonies
and necessities of earthly being, eternally separated from the
central mystery. But 'wayworn' fills in the background to the
repose, and 'daily bread' spreads tentacularly into the body of
the poem, becoming the 'cates' of divine ceremony and paralleling the hinted transformation of Eve into the Virgin (ll. 17–20).
When we return to him, the man, his sleep, and his earthbound
dreams, emerge in the last line as unwitting participants in the
miracle. Caught in the repose between eternal separateness and
eternal participation, the poem is as much about Joseph as it is
about Mary and the Child. The 'Egypt' of the title, like 'Repose',
acquires a new significance; the poem is about being human, and
in its carefully modulated distinctions of language it emphasizes
the enormous difference between a poetic apprehension and a
prose statement of Clough's positives.

Accomplished as it is, 'Repose in Egypt' is an incidental
achievement, and lies outside the main line of Clough's development as a poet. On the whole the 'Biblical' is a stylistic cul-de-sac,
which he entered in his conscious search for a more conformist
aesthetic—perhaps in response to Matthew Arnold's repeated
demands for 'beautiful' remoteness and impersonality. Although
certain of its presuppositions can be traced in some of his later

work—particularly in the mock-naïve conventions which govern the *Mari Magno* tales—Clough never reverted again to this style. Comparatively inelastic as a poetic mode and too easily acquiring a factitious serenity, it not only denies him his true distinction and strength but emphasizes the weaker elements in his sensibility.

He is more characteristically present in those short poems in which he attempts a more directly expressive form instead of relying on an imported formula for poetic serenity. The failures in this much more precarious attempt are disastrously obvious in comparison with the poems on Biblical subjects, which, even at their worst, are at least innocuously pleasing to the ear. The fear of the insincere and the less-than-exact which, as a positive refusal of the vague, the pretentious, or the merely emotional, gives Clough's poetry its individual curve and precision, also results in some very shoddy verse when it becomes an artistically valueless impulse to get one's thoughts down on paper merely because one has thought them and they happen to be not un-edifying. Metrical moralizings like 'Old things need not be therefore true' take several cubits off Clough's stature as a poet. Sentimental self-dramatizations like 'Ah, blame him not because he's gay!' or slack, self-pitying pleas like 'O tell me, friends, while yet we part' merely show him fingering half-sharpened moods with that idle earnestness which critical tradition once identified as the characteristic Cloughian note. The utmost that critical intercession can do with such versified spiritual vapours is to point out that perhaps the fact that many of them were never completed should be counted on the credit side.

When, however, the full pressure of his concentration is brought to bear on the poem, the result, however modest, is in-imitable and impressive. Two short poems stake out the limits of his range in this kind of poetry; they also polarize what Houghton has identified as the neo-classical and romantic elements in his poetic nature.[1] The first of these is the well-known 'It fortifies my soul to know', where, in three iambic tetrameter couplets, Clough achieves a pentagrammatic tightness and subtlety.

> It fortifies my soul to know
> That, though I perish, Truth is so:
> That, howsoe'er I stray and range,
> Whate'er I do, Thou dost not change.

[1] Houghton, pp. 38–49; 55–68.

I steadier step when I recall
That, if I slip, Thou dost not fall.

(Poems, 75.)

Stripped to its ligaments, the language is alive in every cell—not a single word or rhythm is thrown away. The poem uses all of itself to enact itself. The couplet form, the firmly maintained and continually restated antithetical structure, the regular metrical pattern, give the poem an immobility which imitates the fixity and strength of its 'Truth'. But beneath this simplicity and playing against it is a continuous undercurrent of subtly varied movement. The caesural pattern created by the skilful weaving in of subordinate clauses breaks up the metrical regularity and, at the same time, is in itself a deft combination of unity and diversity. The second couplet separates itself quite distinctly from the first and third which appear to be identical in movement—but only appear to be. The light pause after the sixth syllable in the first line shifts to the fourth syllable in the fifth line, the heavier grammatical pause after the fifth syllable of the second line shifts to the fourth syllable in the sixth and releases the counterbeat of 'Thou dost not fall', which echoes that of 'Thou dost not change' in the fourth line and links the last two couplets together, the first two being connected by their grammatical continuity. This variation in rhythm and pace is matched by the deftly managed slip and clutch of the vowels and consonants. The subtlety of these verse harmonics, achieved primarily by playing the speaking voice against the metrical mould, is not exceptional for Clough, and it gives point to the satire on 'identical recurrences' in the wry prose Prologue to *Dipsychus*.[1] Further, this subtlety is related integrally to the meaning of the poem.

A casual reading would tend to dismiss the poem as a simple, if neat, opposition between Truth and self. Actually the poem is rather more subtle. 'Fortifies' standing out against 'perish', as it does in the first couplet, suggests that the 'I' and the 'soul' are not interchangeable though clearly related. There are, in fact, three terms, not two: the 'I', the 'soul', and 'Truth', and each makes its particular connection with the others within the poem.

---

[1] It has been suggested that these six lines are, in fact, the 'six more verses' referred to in the prose Epilogue to *Dipsychus* (*Poems*, p. 296). See J. Bertram, 'The Ending of Clough's *Dipsychus*', *RES* vii (Jan. 1956), 59–60.

The straying and ranging 'I' of the third line refers obviously to the perishable 'I' of the second, the 'Thou' of the fourth line seems to refer equally obviously to 'Truth' —except that the change of address is puzzling. The easy movement of the verse impels us towards a single simple connection; the grammar casts a doubt on that connection. Somewhere in the shifting rhythms a link seems to have been dropped—or been made. The 'Thou' of the sixth line confirms our hesitation. It seems to refer to 'Truth', but it also—and very strongly—suggests a reference to the 'fortified' soul which does not 'fall'. The ambiguity is central to the meaning and the movement. By its knowledge the 'soul' participates in the immovable stability of 'Truth', and becomes itself a source of strength, infusing that stability and strength into the more inclusive 'I' which is now both steady and liable to err, subject to change and immutable. The mimetic aliveness of the verse translates the process from argument into experience. The balance of firmness and fluidity *is* the poem.

The other poem requires much less close scrutiny. Placed in the category of unfinished poems by the Oxford editors, it has the self-complete yet mysteriously open quality peculiar to the romantic fragment, and perhaps it owes something to the German poets—especially to the more gnomic and fragment-like short poems of Goethe.

> But that from slow dissolving pomps of dawn
> No verity of slowly strengthening light
> Early or late hath issued; that the day
> Scarce-shown, relapses rather, self-withdrawn,
> Back to the glooms of ante-natal night,
> For this, O human beings, mourn we may.
>
> (*Poems*, 395.)

The heavily orchestrated, self-consciously melancholic impressiveness of this blank verse, and the deliquescent copiousness of the language, can easily blind one to the more substantial qualities in the fragment—if it is a fragment. Briefly, these qualities can be located in the single word 'verity' in line 2. Not denying light but distinguishing between a true and a false one, it keeps a firm grip on what might have been otherwise a merely diffusive impressiveness. Revaluing downward—and eliciting the exactness of—the 'pomps of dawn', it also looks forward into the poem and gives precision to the paradox of 'self-withdrawn' day.

In themselves these lines are, like 'It fortifies my soul to know', minor, but they acquire importance when they are seen as a stage in the development of Clough's pentameter line. To generalize, and to use categories which are neither precise nor mutually exclusive, the emphasis shifts from a lyrical or, more characteristically, dramatic, movement to a more purely meditative one. The 'Seven Sonnets' (*Poems*, 396)—which, as Paul Veyriras pointed out, need to be read in Clough's original order rather than the one selected by Mrs. Clough—give us a further insight into Clough's attempt at creating a rhetoric of contemplation out of the pentameter line. In these unfinished meditations the mind discovers itself in the effortless, inwardly resonant gravity with which it moves through complex syntactical and emotionally responsive structures, as it circles on its own sense of mystery, evanescence, incompleteness, of nascence and relapse. Its delicate forward-reaching movement is matched exactly by an unpretentious, marvellously muted adequacy of language and verse-movement, which places the voice precisely at the still, contemplative point, detached, fulfilled, remote, but warmed into intimacy by the candour and directness of the personal accent.

> That children in their loveliness should die
> Before the dawning beauty, which we know
> Cannot remain, has yet begun to go;
> That when a certain period has passed by,
> People of genius and of faculty,
> Leaving behind them some result to show,
> Having performed some function, should forego
> A task which younger hands can better ply,
> Appears entirely natural. But that one
> Whose perfectness did not at all consist
> In things toward forming which time could have done
> Anything,—whose sole office was to exist—
> Should suddenly dissolve and cease to be
> Calls up the hardest questions. . . .
>
> (*Poems*, 396–7.)

The precise note is an entirely new one in Clough's poetry (indeed, in Victorian poetry), although it has antecedents in parts of *Adam and Eve* and *Amours de Voyage*. Its pure, effortless, solid timbre sounds again in some of the finest contemplative passages of *Dipsychus*.

The inner shape of Clough's University Hall years as presented in his letters, his prose, and the bulk of his short poems is altered considerably—although not completely—by the fact of *Dipsychus*. He must have devoted a great deal of his spare time after the summer of 1850 to elaborating and revising this major work, and this accounts largely, no doubt, for the meagreness, numerically, of the short poems in which he exploited irony and wit as means of encompassing his apprehensions of morality and the world. His efforts in this vein show up quite clearly the diminution involved in his unwillingness to trust more confidently in this irreverent faculty of his. 'The Latest Decalogue', that sharp and well-known satire on contemporary society, belongs most certainly to these years. The last four lines, which Mrs. Clough obviously found too distasteful to print,[1] clinch the poem with a devastatingly sardonic finality, as they turn to and pervert the New Testament commandments.

> The sum of all is, thou shalt love,
> If any body, God above:
> At any rate shall never labour
> *More* than thyself to love thy neighbour.
>
> (*Poems*, 61.)

The sheer cleverness, the metrical verve, the deft pause, and the shocking swing in themselves create a delight and a participation which is an essential part of the obliqueness. The mixture of jauntiness and subtlety (the speaker, after all, is strictly doing no more than restate the New Testament) is inseparable from the acidness. A similar use of metre, this time to create a morally quite uninvolved observer, gives its particular effectiveness to the gaily jingling 'In the Great Metropolis' (*Poems*, 91), with its Carlylean refrain 'The devil take the hindmost, o!'[2]

This exploitation of metre and rhythm as an oblique presence in the total poem is, of course, a key technique in *Dipsychus*. In a very small group of short poems—dealing mainly with the themes of middle-age, the disturbing intimations of irrepressible sexual nature, and, sometimes, with the fatiguing aridness of the intellec-

---

[1] On 18 Apr. 1862 she wrote to Charles Eliot Norton declaring her dislike of the poem. MS. letter in the Houghton Library at Harvard. The last four lines were first printed in 1951.

[2] The poem appears to have been written early in 1852 and so does not fall within the University Hall period strictly.

tual and practical life[1]—the same technique, basically, is explored more subtly. Metre, and in some poems a deliberately tilted diction, is slanted away slightly from referential meaning to create a wittily ironic depersonalization. Sometimes, as in 'Dance on, dance on, we see, we see', the middle-aged *persona* adopted by Clough becomes embarrassingly avuncular in tolerant, self-pitying contemplations of a sentimentalized and stereotyped youthful gaiety. In the lines beginning 'On grass, on gravel, in the sun', however, which Clough sent off to Tom Arnold as a memento in March 1851, he hits an exact and delicate note. The last two stanzas are a good sample:

> O odours of new-budding rose,
>   O lily's chaste perfume,
> O sweetness that didst first unclose
>   The young creation's bloom!
> Ye hung around me, while, in sun
>   Anon, and now in shade,
> I watched in pleasant Kensington
>   The footman and the maid.
>
> Ah! years may come, and years may bring
>   The truth that is not bliss,
> When will they bring, or how, the thing
>   That can compare with this?
>
> (Poems, 390.)

Essentially, the technique is the same as that of 'Natura Naturans'. The slight but unmistakable 'lift' in the diction,[2] and the light, lilting rhythm play an awareness of evanescence (the word 'bloom' is exact, like 'odour') and delicate pastoral unreality into the lyricism, and give the whole poem an ironic finesse which recalls, in its very minor way, the fastidious art of the *Amours de Voyage*. One of Clough's most dexterous efforts in this kind, and more complex because it also exploits his mastery of different poetic voices within the same poem, is the poem entitled 'Solvitur Acris Hiems' (*Poems*, 405). Left in a more incomplete state than

---

[1] Moods of frustration and fatigue are frequent in the poems Clough wrote in this period. Cf. 'Go, foolish thoughts, and join the throng', 'To spend uncounted years of pain', 'Say, will it, when our hairs are grey'.

[2] See also 'July's Farewell', where diction is even more extravagantly, almost parodically, handled, and is matched by the exuberant extravagance of double and triple rhymes.

'On grass, on gravel, in the sun', its full but still unpolished text has only recently been put together by Evelyn Barish.[1] Her excellent analysis makes any comment here ungrateful. One might be forgiven, however, for quoting two stanzas from this 'inane geniality', as Clough called it,[2] to which its author 'seldom condescend[ed]' at University Hall.

> Youth is pretty and the song.
> But the pleasure lasts not long
> And we mustn't do what's wrong
> > Oh no, Eva,
> It's a trifle, much I doubt it,
> Carnal—we were well without it
> And the world wo[ul]d talk about it
> > Ah yes Eva.

On that note we can turn to *Dipsychus*.

[1] E. Barish, 'A New Clough Manuscript', *RES* xv (May 1964), 168–74.
[2] Ibid., p. 170. Letter to Shairp enclosing the lines and dated 2 Jan. 1850.

CHAPTER IX

Dipsychus

A PASSAGE from an early draft of one of Claude's letters in *Amours de Voyage* makes explicit the dilemma which, though basic, is only implicit in the finished poem:

It is the virtue of man to know and to love the ideal,
It is the wisdom of man to accept and love the real
But if he know that first ah say can he love the second
If unto this he consent, can he live,
Can he in this acquiescing abide in his sight of the other?
Yet as the law of our nature is eating and drinking; and victual
Fails to habituate mortal made stomachs to living [on] nothing . . .[1]

Unable to break out of his sense of unbridgeable gaps between different orders of value and different levels of being, Claude comes to terms with his quandary by refusing all activity and all meaning except 'knowing'. *Dipsychus*, portraying in a loose dramatic form the 'conflict between the tender conscience and the world', is Clough's most comprehensive and detailed attempt to deal with precisely the same dilemma. The main emphasis is on the question of purity and the problem of action, but the poem ranges widely as it explores, in its exhaustive, peculiarly diffuse and yet single-minded fashion, the relationships and antagonisms between virtue and wisdom, ideal and real, vision and appetite, soul and body. Sex, love, religion, the individual's relation to society, questions of social justice and social conscience, even the claims of antithetical poetics and aesthetics as interpretations of human reality—these are some of the areas touched on. The range of subject-matter is matched by an almost equal range of method, style, and tone. At points the poem approaches naturalistic dialogue, at others it progresses almost completely through antiphonal and opposing lyrics, at others it settles into lengthy meditative soliloquies. The tone oscillates between satire which can be marvellously and wittily comic or cruelly sardonic, earnest argumentation, and straight lyricism. This

[1] 1849 (Roma) Notebook. Balliol MS. 441, fol. 29^v.

extraordinary multiplicity and fullness makes *Dipsychus* the most elusive of all Clough's poems: there is always something more to be said about it—and then qualified.

Perhaps this elusiveness is best approached indirectly. Even a cursory sampling of critical opinion about the poem indicates the nature of the problems posed. The most obvious disagreements are about the two speakers themselves. The nineteenth century leans heavily towards Dipsychus, who is usually seen as the pure idealist:

Dipsychus has a yearning for what is good, and the Spirit is the vulgar, sneering, ironical mood which is one of the results of excessive mental culture.[1]
The Evil Spirit . . . is this low worldliness, this ignoble prudence, this cynicism, the demon of a *saeculum realisticum*, who draws men down to hell.[2]

The same emphasis, moderated by a willingness to concede positive value to the Spirit's qualities of wit and honesty, continues into the twentieth century. For Isobel Armstrong the Spirit is 'callous', a 'cheerfully insensitive philistine' who 'subjects all major questions—sex, class, religion—to a coarse irony',[3] and Houghton endorses Dipsychus' own descriptions of the Spirit: he is the 'Enemy', 'The Power of this World! hateful unto God!'[4] H. W. Garrod, on the other hand, virogously declared himself in the opposite camp. 'The moper and the mocker, Mephistopheles and the Muff, Dullness and the Devil—these are the two souls in one person to which the poem owes its title. All along the Devil has the best of the argument, and the sympathy of the reader. . . .'[5] More recently, the Spirit has been seen as the 'spur',[6] and as 'a helpful and sagacious soul' who is 'quite simply the spirit of Action goading a morally and emotionally paralysed hero to decision and commitment, to that "more life and fuller", as the speaker in [Tennyson's] "The Two Voices" would call it'.[7]

    [1] T. S. Perry, 'Arthur Hugh Clough', *Atlantic Monthly*, xxxvi (Oct. 1875), 416.
    [2] E. Dowden, *Studies in Literature, 1789–1877* (London, 1892), p. 80.
    [3] I. Armstrong, *Arthur Hugh Clough* (London, 1962), p. 28.
    [4] Houghton, p. 170.
    [5] H. W. Garrod, *Poetry and the Criticism of Life* (Cambridge, Mass., 1931), p. 125.
    [6] Chorley, p. 251.
    [7] M. Miyoshi, 'Clough's Poems of Self-Irony', *SEL* v (autumn 1965), 697.

Interpretations of the poem—which depend, obviously, on one's reaction to the two speakers—vary as widely. John Addington Symonds saw *Dipsychus* as a tragedy:

There is nothing . . . tragic (melodramatically speaking) in the final concession of Dipsychus. But beneath the ironical sneers of the one, and the helpless struggles of the other, lurks the deep and subtle tragedy of human life and action—of free souls caged, and lofty aspirations curbed—a vulgar and diurnal tragedy over which no tears are shed in theatres, but which, we might imagine, stirs the sorrow of the angels day by day as they look down upon our world.[1]

Houghton concurs with Symonds, whom he quotes approvingly. For him, too, the poem is a tragedy, although in a qualified sense, since he is aware of Clough's divided sympathies.[2] Alternatively, the poem has been seen as 'one of the few truly humorous poems of the Victorian era'.[3] *Dipsychus* is Clough's 'gentle' satire on himself, on the anguish which he suffered during the process of growing up, and on Romantic metaphysics generally. There is, it has been pointed out, no question of defeat or triumph at the end for either Dipsychus or the Spirit, since the poem closely follows the pattern of *Sartor Resartus*, Dipsychus achieving his 'Everlasting Yea' through his acceptance of a necessary world.[4]

The interesting point about this representative spread of critical opinions is that each of these readings has a valid, indisputably present basis in the poem—even though many of them, in fact, cancel one another out. Equally—and this is the obvious corollary—each is subsequent, a reordering of abstracted emphases involving its particular suppressions and simplifications of the total fact of *Dipsychus*. This may seem an unnecessarily round-about way of saying that the poem is complex and that it presents serious problems of tone and emphasis. There is no reason why *Dipsychus* should yield to any single description or interpretation; few poems of comparable length do. In Clough's own work, *Amours de Voyage*, to cite the most outstanding example, is in its way as elusive. The issue is really not the complexity of *Dipsychus* but its comprehension of complexity: elusiveness is only one of the marks of sophisticated art.

[1] J. A. Symonds, 'Arthur Hugh Clough', *Fortnightly Review*, x (Dec. 1868), 614–15.
[2] Houghton, pp. 206–7.
[3] C. de L. Ryals, 'An Interpretation of Clough's *Dipsychus*', *Victorian Poetry*, i (Aug. 1963), 188.　　　　　　　　　　　　　　　　[4] Ibid., pp. 182–8.

The 'complexity of modern experience' has been invoked in approval of the multiplicity and variety of *Dipsychus*,[1] and, despite the fact that in many ways the poem is decidedly unmodern in the sensibility it displays, the justification is attractive. At least it draws attention to the collage-like, colliding, and collapsing qualities of the form, which can, otherwise, be easily overlooked. Evaluatively, however, 'modern experience' is far too vague and permissive a criterion to be of much use: poetry not only renders experience but orders it, and *Dipsychus* must be judged not only by the complexity of its material but the adequacy of its discovered order. The two judgements are indivisible and, in the end, identical. The question posed by *Dipsychus* is whether the problem of its variations in tone, emphasis, and mood reflects a skilfully controlled and complex vision or a desperate attempt to have the best of all possibilities. The decision between these two alternative descriptions of the many-sidedness of the poem involves a judgement about its stature.

*   *   *

To begin with basic affiliations, *Dipsychus* is a lyric drama conceived along the lines of *Faust*, and although Clough later claimed that he had never read this work 'properly',[2] his poem presents some illuminating parallels and contrasts with it. In the early drafts he called his two speakers Faustulus and Mephistopheles, the diminutive, doubtless, to underline the irony in the invited comparison. The conception of Dipsychus himself as the two-souled man—particularly when we interpret the Spirit as he has been interpreted traditionally (though not with complete accuracy), as a projection into explicitness of the unideal underside of Dipsychus' consciousness—is akin to the twofold personality which Faust declares to Wagner as his own: a fleshbound self craving for sensual pleasure and experience, together with another self that aspires continually to a lofty spiritual heritage.[3] Mephistopheles' description of Faust in the 'Prologue in Heaven' fits Dipsychus as neatly:

> Indeed, lord, a retainer strange and fervent.
> From any earthly victuals he'll refrain,

[1] Houghton, p. 158.
[2] Letter to Blanche Smith. Quoted, Chorley, p. 251.
[3] *Faust: Part One*, trans. P. Wayne (Penguin Books, 1949), p. 67.

> His fever drives him to a loftier plane,
> In madness, half-suspected on his part,
> He hankers after heaven's loveliest orbs,
> Demands from earth the choicest joy and art,
> And, far and near, what pleases and absorbs,
> Still fails to satisfy his restless heart.[1]

Clough's Spirit taunts his victim in exactly the same vein:

> To move on angels' wings were sweet;
> But who would therefore scorn his feet?
> It cannot walk up to the sky;
> It therefore will lie down and die.
> Rich meats it don't obtain at call;
> It therefore will not eat at all.
>
> (Scene x, lines 171–6.)

Comparisons with Goethe are even more illuminating in the case of Clough's Spirit. Like Goethe's Mephistopheles, he is an incorrigible mocker, and in the Hudibrastic verse he speaks he takes over the jingling, reductive idiom of his literary ancestor. More important, in him the dualistically conceived *function* of Goethe's Devil is developed into a thoroughly equivocal *characterization*. Mephistopheles is unmistakably evil, he is the tempter and perverter, the antagonist. But, in Goethe's vision of cosmic truth, he performs a necessary function in the evolution of fully developed moral and spiritual being. Questioned by Faust about his identity in a manner which is recalled by the last scene in Clough's poem, he declares himself

> Part of a power that would
> Alone work evil but engenders good.[2]

At least once in *Dipsychus* the Spirit suggests that he might not be only an instrument but a manifestation of God:

> The Devil oft the Holy Scripture uses,
> But God can act the Devil when He chooses.
>
> (xi. 63–4.)

A discarded passage—most probably from this same scene—is worth salvaging at this point. No speech headings are given, but the speakers identify themselves obviously.

---

[1] Ibid., p. 41.   [2] Ibid., p. 75.

Off, devil, leave me!
                    Devil oh!
And how the devil can you know
Whether I am a devil or no.
Some of you think I'm told, there's [none?]
How should you think that I am one.
Why, le bon dieu, who when all's done
Like other people likes his fun
In black his angels often dresses
Which much all tender souls distresses
That daren't for anything act or [progress?]
They stop, they [lacuna], they whine, while he
Sits chuckling up above to see.
How can your qualms so chill and shivering
Prove I'm not a ['cherubs' written above lacuna] out
                                        of [illegible word].
For ought your silly conscience knows
Arch-Angel Gabriel in plain clothes.
O by their fruits you know them. Well
Are you so sure that you can tell
What in fact are the good fruits—Eh
The sacred scriptures surely say
The second person of the Trinity
When living here not en divinity
By every Jewish godly liver
Was thought a glutton and wine bibber.
                    .   .   .
    Indeed so bad was his behaviour
Beelzebub they called our Saviour
Much as occasionally you please
To call [lacuna] Mephistopheles.
Pray can you swear I'm not your soul,
The nether half if not the whole. . . .[1]

To dismiss this lively and outrageously irreverent speech as a
typically coarse piece of mockery on the Spirit's part would both
distort *Dipsychus* and diminish the force of what has been called
Clough's 'positive naturalism',[2] his sense that more of the human
fact, including a great deal that is traditionally disparaged as evil,
should be given positive moral weight and recognition. It is
instructive, in this connection, to compare the Spirit's mocking

    [1] 1850 (Venice) Notebook. Bodleian MS. Eng. Poet. d. 133, fol. 63.
    [2] M. Timko, *Innocent Victorian* (Athens, Ohio, 1966).

irreverence with Clough's original version of a passage in the
poem beginning 'To think that men of former days'.

> The commonplace, whom daily we
> In our dull streets and houses see,
> To think of other mould than these
> Were Solon, Cato, Socrates,
> Or Mahomet or Confutzee,
> This also is a vanity.

(Poems, p. 396.)

In the 1851 (B) Notebook the tentative alternatives are:

> Were Paul or John or . . .
> Or Antonine, or . . . or he
> Who preached about in Galilee.[1]

The angle is different but the basic perception is the same.
Dipsychus contains enough explosive elements within it to explain
the intensity of Clough's guilt-feelings in later years, and the
panic with which he reacted to Blanche Smith's distress when she
dipped into the poem while he was in America.

The fact remains, however, that the Spirit's account of himself
as, possibly, a manifestation of God is placed in a dramatic context. It can no more be taken at face value than Dipsychus'
continual denigrations of him. The only external and dramatically
uninterested interpretation is provided by the Epilogue—and that
playfully casts us back into the poem: 'perhaps he wasn't a devil
after all' (*Poems*, 294). The 'perhaps' is crucial. In *Dipsychus*
there is no clear metaphysic, no clear moral hierarchy, into which
the manifold dialectic can fit. The poem is in the fullest sense
investigative. It begins and ends in a 'perhaps', and is sign-
posted only by a thoroughly relativist dialogue. The failure of
Dipsychus lies in its unwillingness to admit wholeheartedly to its
explosive 'perhaps'.

The best introduction to the two speakers in the poem, to the
basic disposition of ideas and attitudes, and to the ambivalence
and tensions within these, is provided by a long note in the
1850 (Venice) Notebook which also contains the earliest drafts
of *Dipsychus*. The note follows directly, and is most probably
a continuation of, the early version of the 'Paper on Religion',

[1] Clough's dots.

which puts forward the idea of two complementary religions, that of Silence and that of Action.

When you are set your examination papers, will it do (with whatsoever felicitous variation of phrase) to write in your answer to each question—Dear Mr. Professor, I admire you most extremely—will that pass you in the first or even in the second division, will that bring books and certificates, does that indicate knowledge or ignorance, diligence or indiligence, common sense or uncommon want of sense [?]

Centrip[etal] and Centrif[ugal]

(silence)
New Centrip[etal] = sense of illusion
   Scepticism   world = o

(works)
New Centrifu[gal] = the sense of actuality
   Positivism   God = o

Common-sense

He who labours, serves
He who studies, worships
He who teaches, both.—

['or neither' written in in ink, probably as an afterthought].

Is this all then!—the Bibles and Prayer-books and hymn book[s], and the aspirations of saints and the intuitions of the pious, and the inward experiences and agonies of consolations and [illegible word] trials—the [illegible word] and martyrdoms of 1800 years to be brought to this. Ah but the dreams of which this is the dissipating daylight! The sick man's hallucinations of which this new health will retain no record.

This I am in no way called upon or prepared to say[1]—I know too little of life—too little even of my own self to let me utter so large a proposition—

There may be yet a more excellent way which Apostles can show and which martyrs have trod—I meantime follow but the precept to walk according to that which I have attained. Till I learn better, let me abide by what I have learnt—I deny nothing—I am silent, and I work. In silence and in work, in [illegible word] and in commonsense and in confidence shall be your strength.

[1] In his review of *The Soul*, however, Clough was prepared to visualize himself as 'the new convalescent' recalling 'sick room phenomena', and dwelling once again 'among the details of pathology and morbid anatomy', when he discussed the 'devotional' instinct and the perniciousness of an attachment to an exclusively inward spiritual reality. Trawick, p. 282.

Let us go home, eat our suppers and go to bed with our wives. For the evening star is not a bodily angel, nor the setting sun a messenger of God. I cannot eat golden clouds, nor have I organs for digesting the moon reflected in the Lake, If I am given worse meats, shall I refuse to eat; shall I put them away because I can imagine what is delicate [?][1]

Dipsychus writes out these reflections in more sensitive and extensive detail. The bias here, supported by most of Clough's University Hall prose, is strongly in favour of the Spirit and his rationalistic worldliness, and he must be credited, in the terms (the only relevant ones) of Clough's morality, with much more positive moral and epistemological value than he is frequently allowed. Rather like the people who neither pray nor go to Church, who lie, swear, cheat, and get drunk, who 'run after pleasures, ambitions, money-makings', but who 'go to the vineyard, and set themselves one way or other to work',[2] he is justified in the doctrine of works. One does not have to dig very deeply, however, to discover the unease and evasiveness beneath the confident surface of these jottings. The basic antagonism is not so much between action and knowledge as between two different kinds of knowledge, drawing on two different sets of data and leading to two different interpretations of moral and spiritual reality. The falseness in the show of stoical confidence with which a vague common sense is asserted as a *via media* is betrayed in the bitter ambivalence of the final reflection: 'Let us go home, eat our suppers and go to bed with our wives. For the evening star is not a bodily angel. . . .' The nature of the antagonists, their stature, and the level at which their conflict is engaged admit, at best, a highly unstable compromise.

The problem—Clough's problem and that which *Dipsychus*, of all his poems, attempts to face most squarely—is that both kinds of knowledge are legitimized by the self, the only touchstone for truth he was willing to recognize. His distinction as a thinker and as a man lies in the singular honesty and searchingness with which he looked into himself. His dilemma, as a thinker and as a man, lies in his inability to deny what he saw or to reject either of the contrary logics which grew out of his self-scrutiny. This is why the usual Evangelical formula of being *in* the world and not *of* it,

[1] Bodleian MS. Eng. Poet. d. 133, fol. 79ᵛ–fol. 76ᵛ (rev.).
[2] Ibid., fol. 82.

or the notion of necessary evil which is ultimately productive of good, are inadequate accounts of Clough's case: he questioned both the wickedness of the world and the evilness of evil. His predicament is more deeply rooted. It is that of a man who asserts the goodness of man, of nature, of the flesh and the world, and in the same tortured breath confesses their contaminating corruptness: both assertions begin in and are validated by the self. A poem like 'Repose in Egypt' stands out as clearly as it does from the rest of Clough's work because it works in terms of an icon which is firm enough and clear enough to assimilate the counter-assertions into a productive co-operation. More usually, Clough has no icons outside himself—'self-wrung, self-strung, sheathe-and shelterless, thoughts against thoughts in groans grind': there is always an alternative against which to grind.

The 'perhaps' which inevitably precedes either view of moral and spiritual reality in *Dipsychus* renders partial and inadequate any attempt to treat it as a Faustian Drama tracing the hero's evolution through experience to a fuller and deeper moral principle and a Goethean 'many-sidedness' of integrated personality. The poem belongs, as J. H. Buckley pointed out some years ago,[1] in the large category of nineteenth-century poems which derive from *Faust* or resemble it, and have as their theme the conversion of the isolated romantic egotist. Ryals is right, too, in seeing a parallel with Carlyle's archetypal account of conversion.[2] Like Teufelsdröckh, Dipsychus begins in the despair of lost religious faith (he quotes some of the most desolated lines of 'Easter Day') and sees around him a world sold to unbelief. His protest is perfectly imaged in the lonely and aspiring Campanile thrusting upward from the thronged Venetian evening:

> The whole great square they fill,
> From the red flaunting streamers on the staffs,
> And that barbaric portal of St. Mark's,
> To where, unnoticed, at the darker end,
> I sit upon my step. One great gay crowd.
> The Campanile to the silent stars
> Goes up, above—its apex lost in air.
> While these—do what?

(I. 42–9.)

---

[1] J. H. Buckley, *The Victorian Temper* (New York, 1952; paperback edn. 1964), pp. 107–8.
[2] 'An Interpretation of Clough's *Dipsychus*', pp. 183–4, 186–7.

Like Teufelsdröckh, he is made to adjust his infinite longings to the actual and the finite and to emerge out of his metaphysical isolation. But spiritual conversion implies a total commitment. It engulfs and penetrates the whole being. It is a re-selving, a synthesis, a weaving together which leaves no ends dangling. Teufelsdröckh's 'Everlasting Yea' reverberates out of a passionate, pitying and unifying love:

With other eyes, too, could I now look upon my fellow man: with an infinite Love, an infinite Pity. Poor, wandering, wayward man! . . . O my Brother, my Brother, why cannot I shelter thee in my bosom, and wipe away all tears from thy eyes!—Truly the din of many-voiced Life, which, in this solitude, with the mind's organ, I could hear, was no longer a maddening discord, but a melting one. . . . The poor Earth, with her poor joys, was now my needy Mother, not my cruel Stepdame; man with his so mad Wants and so mad Endeavours, had become the dearer to me; and even for his sufferings and his sins, I now first named him Brother.[1]

The gulf which separates such regeneration from Dipsychus'

> O man, behold thy wife, th' hard naked world;
> Adam, accept thy Eve
>
> (XII. 69–70)

is simply unbridgeable.[2] A 'conversion' which cannot dissociate itself from echoes of the Crucifixion and the Fall is surely one of the strangest in all history. And, since the Victorians showed such a *penchant* for achieving this state in literary experience, this radical ambivalence makes *Dipsychus* a unique document in cultural history. For, essentially, it does not—perhaps cannot is more precise—believe in conversion. Its characteristic vision is antithetical and polar. At best it presents a loose amalgamation of unreconciled perceptions.

It is significant, in this connection, that Clough should have remarked about Alexander Smith's turgid rendition of the converting and fulfilling power of love in his *A Life Drama*, '[I]t is really what I have had in my own mind' (*Corr.* ii. 414). This was in 1853, and while the remark throws some light on what may possibly have been the intention of *Dipsychus*, it reveals more clearly Clough's awareness of *not* having written his poem of

---

[1] T. Carlyle, *Sartor Resartus*, in *Works*, i. 150–1.
[2] See Buckley, loc. cit., for some excellent comments on the frustrated impulse of conversion which historically distinguishes *Dipsychus*.

conversion. When he made the remark, he had passed beyond *Dipsychus*. He was making his muddle-headed and, in many ways, pathetic discovery of the restorative power of love.

★   ★   ★

'Clough's poetry', H. N. Fairchild observed, 'is the record of a hopeless struggle to be simultaneously religious, romantic, rational, and realistic. In *Dipsychus* the conflicting elements are juxtaposed but not harmonised.'[1] The comprehensive judgement is unjustly dismissive. A great deal of Clough's poetry is much more than a record of any struggle. Neither was his attempt to reconcile disparate and even antithetical elements within his own sensibility always unsuccessful. At least once, in *Amours de Voyage*, he had achieved a language subtle, flexible, and various enough to get a whole complex self talking. As a particular judgement on *Dipsychus*, however, Fairchild's comment is, I think, impossible to controvert. The general outlines of the poem are clear enough. Man, if he is to live effectively, must bring his intuited ideal into line with the experienced actual, and learn to subordinate the rule of contemplation to the more pressing rule of action. But the multiplicity of meanings, attitudes, and emphases created by *Dipsychus*, as it moves through its wide variety of mood and manner, renders this crude and rather obvious proposition almost entirely meaningless as an account of its content. The shifting lights in which both the 'tender conscience' and the 'world' are seen in the course of the poem result in a wholly ambiguous conclusion. A decision about the precise moral value of living 'effectively' is, in fact, left floating, and the resolution of the conflict is deferred to an indefinite future. The Spirit brings the poem to its only possible ending:

> But time, my friend, has yet to show
> Which of us two will closest fit
> The proverb of the Biter Bit. . . .

> Come, come, don't maunder any longer,
> Time tests the weaker and the stronger; . . .
>
> (XIII. 53–5, 77–8.)

The poem begins and ends in a 'perhaps'.

---

[1] H. N. Fairchild, *Religious Trends in English Poetry*, 4 vols. (New York, 1957), iv. 508–9.

In themselves, of course, the equivocal conclusion and the ambivalent attitudes toward the 'tender conscience' and 'the world' do not constitute artistic failure. Rather, the particular conception and rendering of the conflict lay the poem open to charges of failure and evasiveness, and make the appeal to 'experience', as a justifying principle of ambivalence, much less convincing than it is, for instance, with *Amours de Voyage*. For *Dipsychus*, in contrast to the earlier poem, does not believe unreservedly in ambivalence—either as a state of mind or as a state of art. Clough's vision in the earlier poem had been wholly and uncompromisingly ironic. Its superb tranquillity rested on its willingness to contemplate rather than resolve, to display experience rather than place it. *Dipsychus*, on the other hand, comes to be dominated by an ethic of action, not knowledge, which is not only intolerant of the ambiguous but, more positively, presses towards a kind of resolution that the executed poem cannot offer. What it does offer instead is a pseudo-resolution, imposed on, rather than elicited from, the poem. As a whole work *Dipsychus* is simply not conceived or executed firmly enough to carry the weight and complexity of its material. Clough the man is too closely involved in the debate, his allegiances are too mobile. The poem has the restlessness of *Amours de Voyage* without the tranquillity.

For a variety of reasons the 'failure' of *Dipsychus* is a difficult charge to allege or discuss. In the first place, the charge must be qualified in several ways if it is to be fairly asserted. The historical importance of the poem, the range and penetration of some of its insights, the sheer interest of its content, and the not infrequent excellences of execution—sporadic and unsustained though they are—must rescue it from outright dismissal. In the second place, the intrusive personal relevance of the poem presents something of a critical problem. The central conflict is insufficiently distanced from Clough's personal conflicts and bewilderments: to ignore these biographical implications would be needlessly and obtusely rigoristic; to dwell on them too closely would be to lose sight of *Dipsychus* as a poem. Finally, the failure of *Dipsychus*, like the bursting of an overstuffed hold-all, is a multiple, diffused, and interacting phenomenon. Almost everything in the poem, even its excellences, one might suggest, contributes to its disintegration as a totality.

Basically, that failure results, on the one hand, from Clough's choice of a form which imposes particular restrictions on his sensibility and, on the other, from his inability to work within those restrictions or exploit them positively. In so far as they are spokesmen for opposed selves within a single consciousness, Dipsychus and the Spirit divide between them perceptions which are basically and paradoxically continuous. The dramatic, or, more strictly, duologue, form imposes a limiting simplicity and polarity on what is essentially dialectical and complex: it can render the oppositions more easily than the continuities, intimations of moral reality tend to become alternately, not simultaneously, 'this' and 'that'. Emphasizing the conflict (as no doubt Clough intended it to), the form also entices us into taking sides, into identifying with one or other of the speakers—and here the poem begins to move against itself. For 'identification' in this sense is not an abstract moral allegiance the reader renders to the 'good' character.[1] Where identification is a moral process at all it arises out of and operates within the moral terms created by the poem. There is no 'given' outside the poem itself and the sanctions and codes of its language, structure, and action. The language of *Dipsychus* calls for more extensive treatment, but these other aspects can be briefly remarked on here. Since neither the Spirit nor Dipsychus is 'right' in the poem's terms, and since intelligence and penetration are divided between them, the reader cannot adopt either's as an adequate report on moral reality. Nor is there any clear action, either as plot or as internal development, to guide our sympathies or substantiate a resolution. The structure of *Dipsychus* is more like a series of variations on a single broad theme than a sequence, either cumulative or evolving, in terms of action or character. Neither of the speakers is presented fully or coherently enough to allow significant development or, indeed, to be regarded as dramatic characters in any meaningful sense. Each is a loose amalgam of uttered—and not always consistent—attitudes to which our response is determined largely by local texture. But to say that the poem does not permit us to align ourselves behind either speaker, and see the conflict through his eyes, is not to say that there is no carry-over from scene to scene. *Dipsychus* is

---

[1] The tendency to moralize the two speakers affects a good deal of the criticism of *Dipsychus*. The chapter on the poem in Houghton is a recent example.

not really paratactical in structure, and there are enough elements of continuity and connection in it for attitudes created and insights gained in one scene or one particular exchange to colour subsequent ones. There is at once too little and too much mortar in the poem. This last point leads us to what is—apart from the question of the language, with which it is in some ways related—the single most important source of weakness and uncertainty. The juxtaposition of satire and straight lyricism imposes a strain on the poem that it is not resilient enough to support. Clough attempts to make the best of two worlds, satirizing and vindicating —or attempting to vindicate—the tender conscience. In fact, the way in which the poem divides itself into two broadly differentiated emphases suggests that he attempted, perhaps half-consciously, to realign the energies of the poem. This shift is a matter which must be looked at in greater detail, but the net result is a self-defeating movement towards revision. The savage effectiveness of the Spirit's satire on Dipsychus' idealistic visions, particularly in the earlier scenes, makes the latter's lyricism and his declarations of confidence difficult to take at their face value: his terms have become suspect, his protestations of strength and courage in the final scene ring hollow. Inevitably the mewling prig devalues the noble idealist. There is not elasticity or strength or precision enough in his language to recover his bona fides or enforce his moral vision.

These criticisms of one of the most important poems of its period are harsh—especially in view of the status which has recently been accorded to it.[1] They need to be substantiated by a closer and more careful scrutiny.

* * *

Dipsychus has been seen in terms of a twofold division, Scenes I–VII forming one part, and Scenes VIII–XIII the other.[2] Another

[1] Houghton, p. 156, calls *Dipsychus* Clough's 'masterpiece'. The poem has also been hailed as 'Clough's most successful long work'. M. Timko, op. cit., p. 152.

[2] Houghton, p. 177 *passim*. Since Clough never shaped *Dipsychus* into final form it is unfair, in a sense, to scrutinize the poem too closely, or, for that matter, to regard it as a complete work. The unfinished state of *Dipsychus* should perhaps be given more weight in judging it than has been customary. For a general discussion of the textual problems involved, and a description of the manuscripts, see *Poems*, pp. 528–30. In referring to the manuscripts, I have adopted, as throughout this study, the designations of the Oxford editors. For a criticism of the Oxford text, particularly of the somewhat careless treatment of Scene IIA, see

possible division, and perhaps a more illuminating one, is three-fold: Scenes I–III, Scenes IV–VII (the weakly organized central scenes), and Scenes VIII–XIII. The separation into one unit of the first three scenes, at least, has some warrant from Clough himself since in MS. I he pencilled in, at the close of Scene III, 'End of Act I'.[1] Opening with a short introductory scene, this first section concentrates quite strictly on the question of Dipsychus' 'purity' and his efforts at preserving uncontaminated the integrity of a 'higher' self. Scenes II and IIA explore the subject of sexual purity. Scene III concentrates on the relationship of the 'pure' individual to society, and the cynical equation implied by the Spirit in diverting attention from the Venetian street-walker provides the link between the two subjects:

> If the plebeian street don't suit my friend,
> Why he must try the drawing room, one fancies,
> And he shall run to concerts and to dances!
>
> (III. 15–17.)

Scenes VIII–XIII focus on the necessity for action and the choice of a profession, and culminate in Dipsychus' 'submission' to the world. This last section is connected with the first by a clever ironic manipulation of thematic imagery and reference. Scene VIII begins with Dipsychus contemplating two pictures:

> A modern daub it was, perchance;
> I know not; but I dare be sure
> From Titian's hues no connoisseur
> Had turned one condescending glance
>
> Where Byron, somewhat drest-up, draws
> His sword, impatient long, and speaks
> Unto a tribe of motley Greeks
> His pledge word unto their brave cause.
>
> Not far, assumed to mystic bliss,
> Behold the ecstatic Virgin rise!
> Ah wherefore vainly to fond eyes
> That melt to burning tears for this?
>
> (VIII. 1–12.)

R. M. Gollin, 'The 1951 Edition of Clough's Poems: A Critical Re-Examination', *MP* lx (Nov. 1962), 120–7.

[1] Cf. *Poems*, p. 537.

In turning reluctantly, and with a sneer he cannot help ('somewhat drest up' and 'motley Greeks' are obviously significant), from the contemplation of the Virgin to that of Byron and the life of noble deeds, Dipsychus signalizes his farewell to the kind of aspiration towards innocence which had dominated him in the first three scenes. The reference to the Virgin recalls Scene II, set on the Feast of the Assumption (II. 15-16). It also recalls a pattern of reference which runs through these early scenes. Dipsychus, exposed to the taunts of the Spirit, sees himself in the situation of the unfallen Eve (II. 35-6), he invokes the angelic purity of womankind to centre his thoughts more firmly on the chastity he struggles to preserve (IIA. 1-10). The Spirit, too, draws on the same range of references, but with exactly opposite intent. 'O Joseph and Don Quixote!' he exclaims in blasphemous derision of Dipsychus' chastity (IIA. 55), and, later in the same scene, draws attention to the portrait of the Madonna over the prostitute's bed (IIA. 111).

In terms of the threefold division I have suggested, Scenes V–VII form a transitional middle section, which deals with Dipsychus' exposure to the world in a more discursive fashion than either the first section or the last, but shares some of the qualities of both. With the exception of Scene VII, the weakest and most tentative in the whole poem, all the scenes grow out of or relate to some specific activity, setting, or incident: the ride in a gondola, the excursion to the Lido, the insult. In this respect this section resembles the first three scenes much more than the last six, where the dialogue is almost completely detached from locating incident or setting. On the other hand, Dipsychus occupies more of the centre than he had done in the first section. The wide-ranging and not always satisfactorily integrated debate, too, is much less pressingly personal, much more speculative, in its quality. Both features draw these scenes closer to the final section.

One advantage of this threefold division is that it draws attention to the changing centre of gravity in the poem. More important, it brings into clear focus the alteration in the Spirit's function and significance. The distinctions here are, obviously, relative and of emphasis only. In the first section, which concentrates on purity, the Spirit's voice is the voice of experience. His is the gospel of knowledge.

I know it's mainly your temptation
To think the thing [i.e. sexual initiation] a revelation,
A mystic mouthful that will give
Knowledge and death—none know and live!

(IIA. 20–3.)

In the last section, however, he is the voice of action, relentlessly
tugging at Dipsychus' unmoving 'contemplation'. In a sense
this second aspect is a specialization of the first. The realization
that one must act is a form of knowledge. But equally this second
aspect works against the first. Action militates against knowledge.
Between them the two faces of the Spirit, as knowledge and as
action, determine the ambiguous and shifting lights in which the
poem views the relationship between 'ideal' and 'actual', 'virtue'
and 'wisdom'. The 'common sense' which the Spirit unceasingly
urges is at once the most subversive and the most conformist
of faculties, the most acute and the most obtuse. *Dipsychus* is
a desperate and ultimately futile attempt to put this unruly faculty
into clear perspective.

The shift in emphasis from the world as a principle of knowledge to the world as a principle of 'practical' living has far-
reaching and disruptive implications. If the Spirit in the first
section is not quite the same as in the rest of the poem, neither is
Dipsychus, or, in fact, the poem itself. A cancelled passage from
Scene IIA as it appears in the Second Revision is directly relevant
here.

Dipsychus: Oh heaven—to yield a treasured innocence
            To fetid fondling and a forced caress,
            To heavy kisses, and the plastery speech
            Of a would-be but can't be sentiment.

Spirit: Ah / Well I like sentiment—he! he!
            'T should have been you instead of me,
            When t'other day just after noon
            Having got up a little soon,
            Tiring of cafes, quays, and barks
            I turned for shade into St. Mark's.
            I sit awhile—studying mosaics
            (Which we untheorizing laics
            Have leave to like)—a girl slips by—
            And gives the signal with her eye.
            She takes the door; I follow out:
            Curious, amused, but scarce in doubt

While street on street she winds about,
Heedful at corners, but au reste
Assured, and grandly self-possessed,
Trips up a stair at last, and lands me
And to a little chamber hands me.
No would–be-pretty hesitation
No farce of female expectation
Most business-like in her vocation
She but the brief half instant lingers
That strikes the bargain with five fingers.
'Twas well enough—I do not mean
Voluptuous, but plain and clean;
Doctors perhaps might recommend it,
You step and do the thing and end it.

Dipsychus: Myself / Ah Well, I like a mild impression
Of something bordering on illusion.
To dream and dreaming know one knows
That as the dream comes, so it goes,
You know that feeling I suppose.[1]

The Spirit is never quite as coarse in the poem as we have it as he is in this discarded passage,[2] and yet the whole weight of the criticism is on Dipsychus. He, not the Spirit, is the one who is exposed. He is quite explicitly the pious hypocrite and his 'idealism' is a refined and sybaritic self-indulgence.

I have reproduced this cancelled passage at length because it isolates with unmistakable clarity the satiric emphasis in the whole of the first section. Rarely can the Dipsychus of these scenes be taken seriously as a spokesman for the ideal. Usually he is either an insufferable prig or a complete neurotic:

Ah me, me!
Clear stars above, thou roseate westward sky,
Take up my being into yours; assume
My sense to own you only; steep my brain
In your essential purity. Or, great Alps,

[1] Bodleian MS. Eng. Poet. d. 136, fol. 29^v–30.
[2] In an earlier draft of the same passage he was even more foul-mouthed:

Trips up a stair at last, and lands me;
Up with her petticoats, and hands me
Without one thought of hesitation
Much as one might a pot de chambre
The vessel that relieves le membre.

(1850 (Venice) Notebook. Bodleian MS. Eng. Poet. d. 133, fol. 61^v.)

That wrapping round your heads in solemn clouds
Seem sternly to sweep past our vanities,
Lead me with you—take me away; preserve me!
—Ah, if it must be, look then, foolish eyes—
Listen fond ears; but, oh, poor mind, stand fast!

(II. 54–63.)

Let it be enough
That in our needful mixture with the world,
On each new morning with the rising sun
Our rising heart, fresh from the seas of sleep,
Scarce o'er the level lifts his purer orb
Ere lost and sullied with polluting smoke—
A noonday coppery disk. Lo, scarce come forth,
Some vagrant miscreant meets, and with a look
Transmutes me his, and for a whole sick day
Lepers me.

(III. 66–75.)

The more nasal Dipsychus is in his protestations, the more extravagantly outrageous the Spirit becomes. The satiric wit flashes from colliding extremes: the excesses of the virtue-and-purity-invoking prig against those of the out-and-out materialist who takes a cynical delight in rubbing his companion's fastidious nose in sordid fact.

The state of the manuscripts renders any inferences from them more tentative that one might wish, but if Clough's revisions reflect his intentions accurately, they do suggest that he made some attempt—inevitably ineffective because of the 'scissors and paste' method—to soften not only the outspokenness but the satire of these early scenes. The omission of Scene IIA from his third—and, as far as may be judged, final—revision was dictated mainly, no doubt, by the shocking coarseness of the Spirit's speeches.[1]

---

[1] In revising this scene Clough pruned away some of its most rank passages. The lines quoted in the preceding note provide one example. Another is the continuation of the lines which, in the notes to the Oxford edition, read:

> Fiddle di diddle fal lal lal!
> By candle light they are pas mal;
> Better and worse of course there are,—
> Star differs (with the price) from star.

(Poems, p. 535.)

[Footnote cont. on p. 395.

More striking is the omission from the same revision of the
deliciously sly final lines (68 ff.) of Scene II in which Dipsychus,
urged by the Spirit to follow up a prostitute's invitation, hovers
in comical irresolution between his sexual desire and his feelings
of sexual incompetence. For the reader an insight like this gives
authority to the Spirit's diagnosis when he sardonically dismisses
Dipsychus' earnest defences of 'conscience' in Scene IIA;

> Ah, just what I was going to say;
> An Angel met you in the way!
> Cry mercy of his heavenly highness—
> I took him for that cunning shyness.

(IIA. 75–8.)

The attempt—if that is what is is—to take some of the edge off
the satire is significant. Perhaps Clough realized that these early
scenes pull too strongly against the rest of the poem, especially
the closing scenes. For although the view of Dipsychus does not
cease to be critical and qualified, the quality of the poem alters
—at points radically enough to suggest a complete reversal of
intention. Beginning with Scene IV, *Dipsychus* changes from an
abrasive exposure of whining and not entirely unhypocritical
priggishness, to a more equal debate between, on the one side,
the idealist trying genuinely, if muddle-headedly, to live to a
higher reality and, on the other, the representative of worldly
common sense. Losing the confidence of its daring obliqueness,
the poem becomes fairminded, more obviously and earnestly
'ambitious'—and, in the end, even something like a straight
declaration of belief about the posited antagonism. The Spirit
still has some brilliant satiric thrusts, his candour and his honesty
can still win respect, but as the emphasis in his common sense
shifts from knowledge to an advocacy of sensible—that is, re-
spectably normal—activity, Dipsychus grows in stature. It is the

A loose sheet in the Second Revision contains a cancelled version which continues:

> I found it hard I must confess
> To answer a small Frenchman to say yes
> Who told me, in a steamer talking,
> That one can pick up in one's walking
> In the Strand Street in London town
> Something nice for half a crown.
> But in the dark what comes amiss
> Except bad breath and syphilis.

(Bodleian MS. Eng. Poet. d. 133.)

victim who seems to have most of the knowledge and nearly all of the strength when he declares in the last scene:

> Oh, your sole chance was in the childish mind
> Whose darkness dreamed that vows like this could bind;
> Thinking all lost, it made all lost, and brought
> In fact the ruin which had been but thought.

(XIII. 28–31.)

But the poem provides little support for this Dipsychus. In the balance of the whole his assertion lacks any proven weight. Both he and the Spirit have been scrutinized too closely.

A fuller sense of the complexity and profusion of *Dipsychus*, and of the problem which Clough set himself in it, can be gained from a closer examination of the two speakers. The most insistent questions raised by the poem relate to basic conceptions. Who are the two speakers? How are they connected? An answer can start confidently enough. Dipsychus is the central figure, unquestionably real. The Spirit is a kind of exteriorized *alter ego*, who brings to Dipsychus' attention those worldly perceptions and attitudes he struggles to deny. When, in Scene IX, Dipsychus speaks of

> These pitiful rebellions of the flesh,
> These caterwaulings of the effeminate heart,
> These hurts of self-imagined dignity,

(153–5)

his words have meaning only if we ascribe to an opposing self the Spirit's part in the earlier scenes which are here referred to. Dipsychus himself suggests some such explanation for the Spirit's voice.

> What is this persecuting voice that haunts me?
> What? whence? of whom? How am I to detect?
> Myself or not myself? My own bad thoughts,
> Or some external agency at work,
> To lead me who knows whither?

(II. 17–21.)

From Dipsychus' point of view an element of uncertainty is essential. For him the poem is a journey of moral and spiritual discovery in an unknown and disturbing territory. It is a rather different matter when this necessary uncertainty is reflected in structural inconsistencies within the poem. The further details about the Spirit which Dipsychus gives in a later scene do not have the warrant of actual execution behind them.

> I have scarce spoken yet to this strange follower
> Whom I picked up—ye great gods, tell me where!
> And when! for I remember such long years,
> And yet he seems new come. I commune with myself;
> He speaks, I hear him, and resume to myself;
> Whate'er I think, he adds his comments to;
> Which yet not interrupts me.
>
> (VIII. 28–34.)

The account is accurate only in its general outlines. At least once— in Scene III—Dipsychus had taken his cue from the Spirit. He has engaged several times in lively debate with him, and often in their exchanges, as Houghton has pointed out, it is impossible to attribute the Spirit's utterances to any 'side' of Dipsychus.[1] They have the independent life of an external voice. To resolve this difficulty as Houghton, possibly taking a hint from the Epilogue, has done, by saying that 'we need not attribute these speeches to an external agency in the literal sense' and that the Spirit's speeches, if they 'are not what Dipsychus would say, . . . are what he can imagine the world would say',[2] does not really meet the case fully. It is not entirely convincing, for instance, to ascribe the detail and vivacity with which the Spirit describes a prostitute's room (Scene IIA) to the vividness of Dipsychus' imagination. Cavilling as these points may seem, they have important consequences, which become more apparent when we attempt to explore the characters, as distinguished from the conception, of the two speakers.

The idealist–materialist opposition is only the most modest of beginnings here. Broadly, Dipsychus is a nineteenth-century romantic idealist whose rebellion consists in the assertion of soul as the supreme and ultimate reality. He is the man trying to live to a transcendental idea and realize absolute determinations of self, seeking only for that action which is

> In its kind personal, in its motive not;
> Not selfish as it now is, nor as now
> Maiming the individual.
>
> (IX. 149–51.)

---

[1] Houghton, pp. 171–2.
[2] Ibid., p. 172. Cf. '[T]he Spirit in my poem may be merely the hypothesis or subjective imagination, . . .' (*Poems*, p. 294).

His definition of 'natural' self oscillates between, on the one hand, the Rousseauistic creature of noble impulse and, on the other, the near-animal of Christian-idealist tradition. The Spirit's affinities, by contrast, are with the Enlightenment and with the forces of nineteenth-century rationalism. His rebellion consists in the denial of soul as a useful or even valid category. His 'natural' self is a compound of reason, good sense, and perfectly legitimate animality. For him the measure of all value, truth, and reality is objective and indisputable fact. Dipsychus, attempting to add up his apprehensions of spiritual and moral reality, is for ever haunted by hints of a 'More beyond', for ever rebuked by a sense of the incomplete,

> Of a completion over-soon assumed,
> Of adding up too soon.

> (x. 31–4.)

For the Spirit the 'beyond' has no meaning. His finite arithmetic admits only one ineluctable answer (XII. 88–91): the facts are given and demonstrable and they must be recognized and added up. 'Why', he asks Dipsychus,

> Why will you walk about thus with your eyes shut,
> Treating for facts the self-made hues that float
> On tight-pressed pupils, which you know are not facts?
> To use the undistorted light of the sun
> Is not a crime; to look straight out upon
> The big plain things that stare one in the face
> Does not contaminate; to see pollutes not . . .

> (XI. 124–30.)

The contrast of optics is a key image in an antagonism which involves so basically questions of epistemology. Dipsychus knows subjectively and intuitively. His knowledge images itself in elusive half-lights, in interpenetrating and shifting shadows and dissolving outlines, through which plays the flickering 'reality' of a romantic metaphysic.

> The south side rises o'er our bark,
> A wall impenetrably dark;
> The north the while profusely bright.
> The water—is it shade or light?
> Say, gentle moon, which conquers now
> The flood, those massy hulls, or thou?

> (IV. 238–43.)

For the Spirit this kind of thing, like the interfused glories of 'Tintern Abbey', is 'but moonshine after all' (IV. 263). Inclining towards factual empiricism in his philosophy, in his aesthetics he upholds the standards of neo-classicism and applauds the clarity of Palladian serenity.[1]

> Come, leave your Gothic, worn-out story,
> San Giorgio and the Redemptore;
> I from no building, gay or solemn,
> Can spare the shapely Grecian column.
>
> . . .
>
> Maturer optics don't delight
> In childish dim religious light,
> In evanescent vague effects
> That shirk, not face, one's intellects; . . .

(IV. 204–7; 216–19.)

In the terms of the Spirit's detached intelligence, emotion is a suspect avenue to truth—'Emotions', after all, 'are so slippery' (X. 128). As in religion, so in all things, he interdicts what he calls 'vague emotion' (VIII. 67–8):

> Devotion, and ideas, and love,
> And beauty claim their place above;
> But saint and sage and poet's dreams
> Divide the light in coloured streams,
> Which this alone gives all combined,
> The *siccum lumen* of the mind
> Called common sense: and no high wit
> Gives better counsel than does it.
> Submit, submit!
>
> To see things simply as they are
> Here, at our elbows, transcends far
> Trying to spy out at midday
> Some 'bright particular star', which may,
> Or not, be visible at night,
> But clearly is not in daylight;
> No inspiration vague outweighs
> The plain good common sense that says,
> Submit, submit!

(IX. 164–81.)

[1] This is not strictly true. At one point, at least, the Spirit declares the mixture of 'Gothic' and 'Grecian' in the arcade of the Doge's Palace, 'Singularly to [his] liking' (*Dipsychus*, VII. 1–7).

The paradox of the Enlightenment could not be more succinctly put. At once limiting and liberating, denying and asserting the value and range of human existence, the Spirit's naïve yet sophisticated belief in seeing things as they are contains a wide variety of implications.

At one extreme it is in genuine though cynically expressed revolt against traditional moral and spiritual—and social—sanctities.

> O yes, you dream of sin and shame—
> Trust me, it leaves one much the same.
> 'Tisn't Elysium any more
> Than what comes after or before:
> But heavens! as innocent a thing
> As picking strawberries in spring.
>
> (IIA. 12–17.)

This is not quite as plainly the incitement to libertinage it has sometimes been made out to be. For, running through the Spirit's urgings towards sexual experience, there is a moral awareness which is not the less moral for being untraditional.

> 'Try all things'—bad and good, no matter;
> You can't till then hold fast the latter. . . .
> Briefly—you cannot rest, I'm certain,
> Until your hand has drawn the curtain.
> Once known the little lies behind it,
> You'll go your way and never mind it.
> Ill's only cure is, never doubt it,
> To do—and think no more about it.
>
> (IIA. 30–1; 36–41.)

The 'Tempter' has at least Apostolic, if not Gospel, authority behind him, without anything of the baffling Apostolic circularity.[1]

At the other extreme, taking things 'simply as they are' is the classic argument for conformity. In his religion, the Spirit, as is his wont, takes the eighteenth century for his guide. Airily urging Dipsychus to take 'larger' views, in a voice reminiscent of the caustically observed 'world' of the poem beginning 'I dreamed a dream', he scoffs at his companion's frittering away

---

[1] 'Prove all things: hold fast that which is good. Abstain from all appearance of evil . . .', 1 Thessalonians, 5: 21–2.

his time on the speculative niceties of a 'critical hair-splitter'
like Strauss. Since, as Butler observed, nothing can be explained,

> Why should you fancy you know more of it
> Than all the old folks that thought before of it?
> Like a good subject and wise man,
> Believe whatever things you can.
> Take your religion as 'twas found you,
> And say no more of it—confound you!
>
> (VII. 60–5.)

Religion, in his view, is really a matter of observing expected
decencies and limiting inconveniences of doctrine and belief to
the minimum.[1] All his fervour he channels instead into the forms,
the ceremonies, the meanings, of social convention (cf. Scene III).
Manners for him are easily equated with morals, and he can rise
to an appropriate occasion with all the eloquence of passionate
banality:

> O Lord! and walking with your sister,
> If some foul brute stept up and kissed her,
> You'd leave that also, I dare say,
> On account for the judgement day.
>
> (VI. 41–4.)

But if we are to call the Spirit a conformist, what are we to make
of Dipsychus himself?

---

[1] It is not improbable that in the whole of this section of *Dipsychus* (VII. 16–67)
Clough had at the back of his mind J. A. Froude's description of Markham's
ordination in *The Nemesis of Faith*, as well as his memory of his dealings with
Hawkins.

'I was ordained deacon privately a fortnight before Christmas, and priest yesterday—the Sunday after it. Exquisite satire on my state of mind!—I was compli-
mented publicly on my examination, as having shown myself possessed of so much
well-digested information, and on being so prudent in avoiding extremes.... I
was told privately that I had only to persist in such sensible moderation, and that
with my talents, in these trying times, I should be an ornament to the Church,
and that its highest places might be open to me. But above all, my admonition
concluded—"Be extreme in nothing—you do not require me to remind you of
Aristotle's caution. Puseyism is the error on one side, German rationalism on
the other. Walk steadily in the position which our own admirable Church has
so wisely chosen, equidistant between these two. Throw yourself into her spirit
and, with God's grace, you may rise hereafter to be one of those strong lights
which is her highest honour and her highest witness to have nurtured." I felt so
sick, Arthur. So I may live to be like Burnet, or Tillotson, or Bishop Newton,
or Archdeacon Paley—may I die sooner!' (*The Nemesis of Faith* (Chicago, 1879),
pp. 59–60).

O welcome then, the sweet domestic bonds,
The matrimonial sanctities; the hopes
And cares of wedded life; parental thoughts,
The prattle of young children, the good word
Of fellow men, the sanction of the law,
And permanence and habit, that transmute
Grossness itself to crystal.

(IIA. 79–85.)

It is the 'speculating brain' (in this context, the Spirit), we
remember, which prevents him from resting in such comforting
stabilities (IIA. 85–7).

The conflict displayed in *Dipsychus* has been described as that
between the intellectual and his materialistic, morally degenerate
society.[1] The description has the attractive simplicity of half truth.
Certainly the Spirit is coarse, materialistic, cynical. His realism,
at its best a refusal to evade facts, too often displays itself as an
eagerness to reduce life to its lowest common denominator.
Perhaps his most reprehensible trait, exactly and delightfully
re-created in the bluff energy of his atrocious rhymes, is the
insensitive hedonism with which he dismisses all idealism and all
conscience. As he reminds Dipsychus in Scene IV, the gondolier
does not mind being made the slave of a fellow human-being.
He knows his station and he gets paid: a gondola-ride is a gondola-
ride, and life, although it may not correspond exactly to such
a ride, can, with a little judicious callousness, be made a near-
enough approximation (IV. 1–120 *passim*). With his next long
lyric[2] the Spirit, who is more characteristically a fastidious snob,
assumes the voice and manner of the most vulgar provincial
parvenu—and moral judgements become much less easy. Is he,
we ask ourselves, being entirely serious in this outrageous celebration of lucre? Is he being altogether unserious? The subtlety
and poise of Clough's wit deride simple decisions. As far as I
am aware, his dexterity here in creating and manipulating multiple
satiric perspectives has not been fully recognized. For behind the
lyric, controlling its movement and creating much of its 'point',
is one of Isaac Watts's better-known 'Divine Songs', 'The
Sluggard'. The last two of Watts's five stanzas provide adequate
comparisons for our purposes:

I made him a Visit, still hoping to find
He had took better Care for improving his Mind:

---

[1] Armstrong, op. cit., pp. 27–8.   [2] 'As I sat at the café . . .'

He told me his Dreams, talk'd of Eating and Drinking:
But he scarce reads his Bible, and never loves thinking.

Said I then to my Heart, 'Here's a lesson for me;
That Man's but a Picture of what I might be:
But thanks to my Friends for their Care in my Breeding,
Who taught me betimes to love Working and Reading.[1]

Needless to say, Watts's incorrigible was on his visible way to a very bad end indeed, his clothes falling apart, his garden turning into a mess, his money wasting away. By deftly reversing the coin the Spirit manages to make some very pertinently waggish comments on such dingy Evangelical morality. Neither is the outrageously exuberant raffishness of his parody entirely facetious. In its dramatic context the lyric is *also* a deliberately mordant comment on the world as it is. Dipsychus has just expressed his despair at the lack of noble and inspiring example in modern life (IV. 122–7). The Spirit's retort is actually a rephrasing, infinitely more effective because of its ironic obliqueness, of the same perception. The method, in fact, is his customary one of rubbing Dipsychus' nose in the dirt of present reality.

For beneath the Spirit's cynicism there is frequently a moral irony which betrays him as a disillusioned idealist. Alert for disparities between profession and actuality, he can take sardonic note of the paintings of the Last Supper and the Madonna which hang in the prostitute's room (IIA. 109–12). After declaring himself the most tepid of religionists, conforming with effortless discretion and easy tolerance to the forms of a bland religion, he breaks into a polished satire on contemporary religious life

---

[1] In this adroit reworking of Watt's poem Clough may have been developing a hint lodged in his mind by Froude.

'[The English Church] was a worldly Church: yes there was no doubt of it; and, being so, it early began to scent danger, to cry out and anathematize the new teachers who prescribed a severer doctrine; who were trying to shame the clergy into a more consistent life by reminding them of the dignity of their office. Newman had dared to tell them that their armour was pasteboard; the oil dying out of their lamps; that a tempest was rising which would scatter them like chaff before it. . . . And what was his reward? He was denounced as a Cassandra prophet; bid, go get him gone, shake the dust from off his feet, and depart to his own place. He took them at their word, and left the falling house, not without scorn. A little more slumber, a little more sleep. It was the sluggard's cry. Let them find the sluggard's doom.' (*The Nemesis of Faith*, p. 171).

For evidence of Clough's use of Watts see also P. G. Scott, 'The Text and Structure of Clough's "The Latest Decalogue" ', *NQ* ccxii (Oct. 1967), 378–9.

and the secular, self-regarding motivations of belief—if not exactly in God, in 'something very like Him' (v. 156–85). It is the Spirit, again, who caustically recalls Dipsychus to the initial and crucial problem when the latter appears, while out bathing, to be losing himself in his own regenerative symbol.

> But you—with this one bathe, no doubt,
> Have solved all questions out and out.
> 'Tis Easter Day, and on the Lido
> Lo, Christ the Lord is risen, indeed, O![1]
>
> (v. 232–5.)

And he can applaud Dipsychus' sense of a world emptied of significance and value, because deprived of God (v. 7–132), since there is, at the centre of his hedonism, a dark and bitter knowledge:

> Well; people talk—their sentimentality.
> Meantime, as by some sad fatality
> Mortality is still mortality;
> Nor has corruption, spite of facility,
> And doctrines of perfectibility
> Yet put on incorruptibility, . . .
>
> (Poems, p. 536.)

The Spirit eludes any coherent and circumscribing description, because there is, quite simply, no unifying idea or attitude to organize his presence and activity in the poem.

That *Dipsychus* should fall back on a visionary chorus (xɪɪ. 8–31) to lend an air of authority to its 'hero' in the closing scenes, and to create some semblance of direction, is symptomatic of its desperation. It is also characteristic of its compulsive—and pointless—honesty that, just as it attempts to retract the vindication of its protagonist in the witty Epilogue, it should question the reliability of the vision at the moment of enlisting its support:

> I had a vision; was it in my sleep?
> And if it were, what then? But sleep or wake,

[1] For Dipsychus, the sea, like the Campanile in the first scene, is a symbol of the eternal and the infinite, its slow, majestic swell contrasting with the unknowing sleep and ruffled activity of human life:

> On her still lake the city sits,
> Where bark and boat about her flits,
> Nor dreams, her soft siesta taking,
> Of Adriatic billows breaking.
>
> (v. 197–200.)

I saw a great light open o'er my head;
And sleep or wake, uplifted to that light,
Out of that light proceeding heard a voice
Uttering high words, which, whether sleep or wake,
In me were fixed, and in me must abide.

(XII. 1–7.)

One way of extricating oneself from the tyranny of a 'perhaps'
is to entrench oneself in a 'nevertheless', and consolidate one's
position by appealing to an order of experience which admits no
argument and recognizes no proof: nowhere else in his poetry
does Clough come so close to the Tennysonian 'I have felt' of
In Memoriam. Signalizing the breakdown of normal modes of
discourse—normal, that is, in terms of Clough's elected form—
the *deus ex machina* of the hymn-like chorus, and the genu-
flectory response it appeals to, are virtually admissions of defeat.
The multiplicity of detailed meanings in the poem is matched
by no corresponding alertness and sensitivity of structure and
language:

Not for thy service, thou imperious fiend,
Not to do thy work, or the like of thine;
Not to please thee, O base and fallen spirit!
But One Most High, Most True, whom without thee
It seems I cannot.

(XII. 32–6.)

Dipsychus' words have no more than the willed relevance conferred by his vision: he is speaking at an arbitrarily co-opted
antagonist, not to the complex and multivalent Spirit who
inhabits the poem.

Nor is this an isolated instance of such vaguely directed
language. In an earlier scene, for instance, Dipsychus declares,

Yes, it is beautiful ever, let foolish men rail at it never.
Yes, it is beautiful truly, my brothers, I grant it you duly.
Wise are ye others that choose it, and happy ye all that can use it.
Life it is beautiful wholly, and could we eliminate only
This interfering, enslaving, o'ermastering demon of craving,
This wicked tempter inside us to ruin still eager to guide us,
Life were beatitude, action a possible pure satisfaction.

(IV. 63–9.)

In their context, these lines—adapted from *Amours de Voyage*—[1]

---

[1] See *Amours de Voyage*, III. viii.

have little discoverable meaning. What is this 'demon of craving', this 'wicked tempter'? Surely not the social conscience which disrupts the contemplative-aesthetic tranquillity imaged in Dipsychus' gondola-ride? We sense that the abuse somehow includes the Spirit; it is impossible to be more specific.

Thrusting through the dialogue, these sudden outcroppings of wilfully declarative verse are indications of the uncontained seismic pressures in this most ambitious and also most subjective of Clough's long poems. The ambitiousness and the subjectivism weave inseparably into one another, and it is impossible to take the full measure of the first without recognizing the implications of the second. *Dipsychus* is ambitious not only because it attempts to portray and to reconcile the contention of two incompatible apprehensions of the world, the flesh, and the Devil, but also because it attempts to render, in effect, a total, encyclopedic account of self. It is at once an anatomy and a testament, informed and controlled by the evolving and emergent dynamics of self-scrutiny, self-discovery, self-declaration. The three processes are related but not identical. Each involves its different version of truth and sincerity, its different set of determining values, judgements, and purposes, its different accommodation between awareness and admission. And it is the tension and interplay of these diverse, frequently conflicting impulses which explains, I think, the unregulated polymorphousness of *Dipsychus*, its air of groping toward, without ever arriving at an idea of, or language for, itself. The poem, in short, uncovers a crisis it cannot cope with, a crisis in identity which involves the whole of Clough, the man as much as the poet.

It is not purely a quasi-biographical quirk to see *Dipsychus* as Clough's most elaborate and complex attempt to view himself *sub specie aeternitatis*, and so give the displayed consciousness a representative significance. The self is the starting-point of romantic lyric-drama, and the writing out of self, under whatever alias, is a basic strategy. What distinguishes *Dipsychus* within this broad literary category is the absence from it of any decisively elected idea of or attitude towards self, or, to put it in another way, of any clearly organized disguise for the autobiographical presence. In a more literal sense than is usually implied in the commonplace about all introspective writing, the process of self-discovery is inseparable from that of self-revelation: the writing out is the finding out. Further, the poem comes to be governed by an impulse of sincerity which is intolerant of the subterfuges and approximations of a disguise. It aspires to tell the truth, the whole truth, and nothing but the truth.

This desire for truth, basically moral rather than artistic, although it necessarily involves different, frequently conflicting versions of artistic truth, is ultimately self-defeating. It poses a problem which the poem cannot solve: sincerity and truth of what? of self-discovery or of self-declaration?—and, if of the latter, which self and which kind of declaration? *Dipsychus* attempts several kinds of truth, but fails to find the formula, the language, to bring its various purposes together.

At one level the biographical significance of *Dipsychus* has been adequately commented on. The poem has been seen as Clough's most determined attempt to place in a stable and ordered perspective the thoughts on religious faith, on love, on the problem of action, which had occupied him over several years. It has further been argued that in making this attempt he was responding fairly directly to his immediate circumstances. With an arid year at University Hall behind him, possibly, too, having recently made the acquaintance of Blanche Smith, it is natural that he should have felt the necessity of rethinking his attitudes and his positions during the summer of 1850. One can also understand why *Dipsychus* should be so clearly and so extensively occupied with dilemmas—like those connected with love and the choice of a profession—which have such obvious personal relevance.[1] But the biographical fact is both broader and deeper, more inwardly woven into the artistic fact, than such limited—and ultimately superficial—connections suggest. Similarly, it includes but extends beyond the patent self-portraiture in the figure of Dipsychus himself—a self-portraiture which is largely, but not wholly, ironic.[2] A truer sense of the biographical significance of

---

[1] P. Veyriras, *Arthur Hugh Clough, 1819–1861* (Paris, 1964), p. 366.

[2] The scope of the self-portraiture and self-irony can be deduced from the 'Equator Letters' written by Tom Arnold in Nov. 1847 and Jan. 1848. Addressed to J. C. Shairp, these letters are an analytical account of the history of Tom's mind and its development to the time of his decision to emigrate, which illuminates, since it so closely parallels, Clough's own development over roughly the same chronological period. See *New Zealand Letters of Thomas Arnold the Younger*, ed. J. Bertram (Auckland, 1966), Appendix A, pp. 207–19. Although addressed to Shairp, the letters were intended for the whole 'Clougho–Matthean circle', and Clough not only read the letters but found them 'remarkable' (ibid.,

Dipsychus and its relation with the content, structure, and style of the poem suggests itself when, viewing the poem from this angle and attempting to isolate Clough's presence in it, we see this as a matter more of protean shifts and readjustments within an inclusive dialogue than as one of specific identities. Clough is both Dipsychus and the Spirit—and he is neither. He is also the acute self-diagnostician of the Epilogue who traces Dipsychus' *malaise* to the early influence of 'mamma', to a conscience over-excited by the religious revival beginning in the eighteenth century and culminating in Puseyism, and, possibly, to the in-fluence of Arnoldian earnestness. Ultimately, these disparate selves relate to the central ambiguity of the poem: its double vision of the world and of the relationship between the actual and the ideal. An attempt to investigate this ambiguity would take us to the core of *Dipsychus* both as a poem and as a document in a personal history.

Clearly such an attempt, if undertaken with any pretence to adequacy, would introduce perspectives which lie beyond our immediate concern at this point. For *Dipsychus*, as basically a poem about the Fall, stands at a special critical point in a curve

p. 207 n.). A passage from the second of the three letters is of particular interest as far as *Dipsychus* is concerned:

'Take but one step in submission, and all the rest is easy: persuade yourself that your reluctance to subscribe to Articles which you do not believe is a foolish scruple, and then you may take orders and marry, and be happy; satisfy yourself that you may honestly defend an unrighteous cause, and then you may go to the Bar, and become distinguished, and perhaps in the end sway the counsels of the State. . . . All this is open to you; while if you refuse to tamper in a single point with the integrity of your conscience, isolation awaits you, and unhappy love, and the contempt of men; and amidst the general bustle and movement of the world you will be stricken with a kind of impotence, and your arm will seem to be paralysed, and there will be moments when you will almost doubt whether truth indeed exists, or, at least, whether it is fitted for man. Yet in your loneliness you will be visited by consolations which the world knows not of; and you will feel that, if renunciation has separated you from the men of your own generation, it has united you to the great company of just men throughout all past time; nay, that even now there is a little band of Renunciants scattered over the world, of whom you are one, whose you are, and who are yours for ever' (ibid., pp. 215–16).

The specific relevances here to the debate in *Dipsychus* are immediately obvious. Of special interest, however, is Tom Arnold's use of the word 'submission'—which becomes a key term in Clough's vocabulary. *Dipsychus*, in fact, can be regarded as an attempt to redefine 'submission'. The passage from Tom Arnold's letter is even more interesting when we recognize its relevance to *Dipsychus Continued*, which redefines 'submission' one stage further, in a reverse direction, as it were, back to the sense in which Tom had used it.

described through poems like 'Natura Naturans', 'Sa Majesté très Chrétienne', 'O Land of Empire, art and love!', 'Easter Day', and, of course, *Adam and Eve*. The attempt to unfold the ambivalent understandings of the Fall in *Dipsychus* involves, really, both an account of and some explanation for the redistribution of values, attitudes, and purposes at this particular stage of Clough's life. At the risk of assuming much that has yet to be substantiated, it is wiser perhaps to defer these more extensive considerations to the next chapter, to suggest a general weakening of confidence and a loss of that expensively achieved ironic poise which enabled Clough to comprehend his multidimensional apprehensions, and to concentrate here on the problem as a problem of poetic identity specifically.

The nature and scope of this problem are conveniently sketched out in a letter to William Allingham written in December 1850, shortly after the vacation during which *Dipsychus* was begun. 'Somehow I fancy', Clough wrote, 'that a large experience and a decisiveness of character is necessary to attract the modern world to poetry. Shakespeare and Milton should meet together as Rousseau and Voltaire have in Goethe and in Beranger' (*Corr.* i. 287). It is hard to believe that when Clough made this remark he did not have in mind the work he had so recently embarked on himself. The mention of Goethe is an obvious clue; and what are Rousseau and Voltaire but rough analogues for Dipsychus and the Spirit, the conjunction between them but the general aim of the poem as a whole? In its way, too, the association of Shakespeare and Milton is as illuminating. As types, respectively of the morally uncommitted and committed poet, they summarize a central dilemma in *Dipsychus*—the dilemma, that is, of deducing 'a decisiveness of character' from 'a large experience of the world', an experience which includes both Rousseau and Voltaire, but concedes to neither a supremacy in insight or moral concern. The dilemma can be described another way. It is that of converting introspection into declaration, the multiplicity of personality into the declared unity of character.

The problem in *Dipsychus*, then, is that of bringing into co-operative alliance identities and outlooks which normally tend to be antagonistic. Fundamental, of course, is the epistemological antagonism between the idealist and the empiricist. It underlies the contention between the romantic and the realist and between the religious believer and the sceptic. Similarly it lies at the basis of the conflict between the earnest lyricist and the satirist whose irony—complicating the conflict still further—can be engaged equally against and on behalf of the claims of here-and-now actuality. Further multiplication of these basic descriptions is pointless, since they are valuable mainly in indicating the range of implication in that broad movement of reorientation which begins in Clough's University Hall years. Beginning in self-despair, in frustration, and—catalysed by Blanche Smith—in the sense of somewhere having severed the tap-root of spiritual vitality, this reorientation involves, briefly, an attempt to revise the habits of being and vision in which Clough was beginning to feel he had indulged too carelessly and too extensively: the habits of irony and mockery, of scepticism, analysis, and intellectuality, and, most important of all, the habit of facing up to the necessary animality of the human condition. In the uncertainty of his standards he was beginning to recognize as his own the predicament which, as early as 1839–40, he had envisaged for the would-be satirist:

Neither must we forget, that, though this [i.e. the awakening of the moral sense] be the legitimate and genuine development of satire, it is but seldom that the weapon is wielded by a Horace or a Juvenal, and it may happen not infrequently to be employed in very opposite service. As Satire descends lower and lower in the regions of Comedy, the value of its moral effects becomes proportionally less and less. Ridicule in the mouth of Horace and Juvenal becomes Satire in its best form. Satire as employed by the Unworthy is degraded into mere vulgar Ridicule: and is likely to be oftener exercised against what is noble and excellent than against what is shameful and debasing.[1]

The world which this most unworldly of men had so confidently asserted in his prose becomes a treacherous and unruly principle under the sustained scrutiny of *Dipsychus*. Caught between two incompatible logics, one reducing the world, the other, God, to zero, and alarmed at the temerity of its satire, the poem dis-integrates into a series of adjustments dictated by an anxiety to declare some kind of truce between warring selves, to establish some general concluding moral principle, to certify itself as the work of a 'serious' moral poet. As the swansong of the satirist, *Dipsychus* enacts the death which it signalizes.

[1] 'The Moral Effects of Works of Satire', Trawick, pp. 64–5.

This unresolved turmoil manifests itself stylistically as an unassimilated heterogeneousness of poetic texture and quality. At its two most successful extremes *Dipsychus* contains some of Clough's most accomplished writing. The assurance of its light-hearted satire, mixing high-toned mimicry with slangy colloquial, rapidly outrageous verse, is matched in another key by the lyrical firmness and lucidity of the later blank verse soliloquies.

> There have been times, not many, but enough
> To quiet all repinings of the heart;
> There have been times, in which my [tranquil] soul,
> No longer nebulous, sparse, errant, seemed
> Upon its axis solidly to move,
> Centred and fast; no mere chaotic blank
> For random rays to traverse unretained,
> But rounding luminous its fair ellipse
> Around its central sun.
>
> (x. 1–9.)

Reverie here becomes luminous in its continual translation into a manifoldly organized, sensuous solidity. Essentially similar rewards of clarity and solidness are offered by this verse when, modulating into a more effortful, slightly starker movement, it gives us a passage like the following:

> What we call sin,
> I could believe a painful opening out
> Of paths for ampler virtue. The bare field,
> Scant with lean ears of harvest, long had mocked
> The vext laborious farmer. Came at length
> The deep plough in the lazy undersoil
> Down-driving; with a cry earth's fibres crack,
> And a few months, and lo! the golden leas,
> And autumn's crowded shocks and loaded wains.
> Let us look back on life. Was any change,
> Any now blest expansion, but at first
> A pang, remorse-like, shot to the inmost seats
> Of moral being?
>
> (x. 34–46.)

As a poet of contemplation, detached, subdued, completely fulfilled in the condition of beholding, of taking and holding and ordering on the brain

>   The faces, and the voices, and the whole mass
>   O' the motley facts of existence flowing by,
>
>   (x. 28–9.)

Clough stands out conspicuously among his contemporaries.

The provenance of the particular manner—Shakespeare felt through the Miltonic tradition—declares itself, of course, in every line, and as a manner it is especially effective in the later exchanges, where it plays off against the utilitarian astringency of the Spirit's more 'modern' language:

>   Will you go on thus
>   Until death end you? if indeed it does.
>   For what it does, none knows. Yet as for you,
>   You'll hardly have the courage to die outright;
>   You'll somehow halve even it. Methinks I see you,
>   Through everlasting limbos of void time,
>   Twirling and twiddling ineffectively,
>   And indeterminately swaying for ever.
>
>   (XI. 181–8.)

As this relentless realism penetrates more and more brutally into the softer, elaborate, often movingly intimate cadences of the reflective manner, Dipsychus and his dilemma approach an almost tragic significance. But only at moments; Dipsychus' language is too precariously arrived at to sustain consistently the stature of an Everyman.

At the simplest level, it lapses too frequently into inert derivativeness:

>   Contamination taints the idler first.
>   And without base compliance, e'en that same
>   Which buys bold hearts free course, Earth lends not these
>   Their pent and miserable standing-room.
>   Life loves no lookers-on at his great game,
>   And with boy's malice still delights to turn
>   The tide of sport upon the sitters-by,
>   And set observers scampering with their notes.
>
>   (IX. 85–92.)

Automatic, unendingly extensible, poised continually on the edge of cliché ('base compliance' is symptomatic),[1] this Shakespeare-Parnassian—to adapt Hopkins's term—offers little besides the consolation of having covered some ground.

---

[1] It occurs, significantly, also in an earlier and similar passage. See VIII. 21–7.

Occasionally, however, this verse displays a special kind of vigour, the implications of which reach further.

> How much soe'er
> I might submit, it must be to rebel,
> Submit then sullenly, that's no dishonour.
> Yet I could deem it better too to starve
> And die untraitored. O, who sent me, though?
> Some one, and to do something. O hard master!
> To do a treachery. (XII. 50–6.)

'Untraitored' leaps out from its sparse verbal environment with an utterly pointless athleticism. Leading nowhere and connected to nothing, it merely attracts attention to the violent wrench of its un-Englishness. One encounters this linguistic over-supply in extended passages too:

> To herd with people that one owns no care for;
> Friend it with strangers that one sees but once;
> To drain the heart with endless complaisance;
> To warp the unfashioned diction on the lip,
> And twist one's mouth to counterfeit; . . .
>
> (III. 34–8.)

> Heaven! to pollute one's fingers to pick up
> The fallen coin of honour from the dirt—
>
> . . .
>
> To enter the base crowd and bare one's flanks
> To all ill voices of a blustering world, . . .
>
> (VI. 88–9; 94–5.)

It is not altogether clear how one would go about baring one's flanks to voices—ill or otherwise. The general vagueness underlines the merely postural qualities of the language. Like the hyperactivity, the grape-shot verbality corresponds to the absurd overcharge in the fear of pollution. The language reflects the absence of any significant grasp of spiritual or human reality.

It is in this area, where structural and stylistic failure penetrates to root questions of sensibility and grasp, that the disintegration of *Dipsychus* is most significant. The failure manifests itself in two main ways. An examination of the lyric beginning 'O let me love my love unto myself alone' indicates one of these.

> O let me love my love unto myself alone,
> And know my knowledge to the world unknown;

No witness to the vision call,
Beholding, unbeheld of all;
And worship thee, with thee withdrawn, apart,
Whoe'er, whate'er thou art,
Within the closest veil of mine own inmost heart.

Better it were, thou sayest, to consent,
Feast while we may, and live ere life be spent;
Close up clear eyes, and call the unstable sure,
The unlovely lovely, and the filthy pure;
In self-belyings, self-deceivings roll,
And lose in Action, Passion, Talk, the soul.

Nay, better far to mark off thus much air
And call it heaven, place bliss and glory there;
Fix perfect homes in the unsubstantial sky,
And say, what is not, will be by-and-by;
What here exists not, must exist elsewhere.
But play no tricks upon thy soul, O man;
Let fact be fact, and life the thing it can.

(IV. 82–101.)

One could say a good deal about this dingy verbal smudge, about its impoverished poeticisms, about the adjectival insistence of 'closest . . . mine own inmost', about the empty, unlocated importance of the capitals, about the hysteria of 'In self-belyings, self-deceivings roll'. More to our point is the way in which this lyric mirrors the general aimlessness of the central scenes. The appearance of an antithetical and dialectical structure, and the clinching firmness of the last two lines, suggest an intellectual control and arrival which is, on examination, as utterly spurious as the poeticism. The final declaration bears no relation to the data offered by the lyric. As an exhortation it is vigorous enough: but what does it mean? It neither illuminates the lyric nor is illuminated by it. What the lyric has done is to run through a series of emotional reactions and paroxysms—the preachy 'resolution' being only the last in the series.

This inability to focus, to relate, to choose finally and find an adequate language, appears at its most disruptive in the second major manifestation of a failure of grasp. In the earlier scenes, where the weight of the satire is thrown clearly on Dipsychus, his 'Spasmodic' excesses are easily assimilated into the total texture. We cannot take him very seriously: the mimicry in the language given to him, together with the lively mischievousness of the Spirit, is enough to assure us. As the weight of the poem begins to shift, however, as the sense of the conflict becomes more turbid and uneasy, and as the debate begins to develop into a direct, un-comic encounter between 'purity' and 'worldliness' in their customary acceptations, our responses become less certain. The inflated rhetoric of 'idealism' persists—but without the firm counter-statement of ironic wit. Insulted by a soldier and egged on by the Spirit to vindicate his honour, Dipsychus declares:

> By heaven, it falls from off me like the rain
> From the oil-coat. I seem in spirit to see
> How he and I at some great day shall meet
> Before some awful judgement-seat of truth;
> And I could deem that I behold him there
> Come praying for the pardon I give now,
> Did not I think these matters too, too small
> For any record on the leaves of time.
>
> (VI. 33–40.)

It is impossible to judge what kind of assent lies behind this absurdity. We hope that Clough is not behind it—we fear that he is. The impulses of self-declaration and self-attestation have begun to dominate. Increasingly we encounter in the poem a ponderous and worried moralist more anxious to establish his bona fides than to produce a work of art or of intelligence.

> O the misery
> That one must truck and practise with the world
> To gain the vantage-ground to assail it from;
> To set upon the giant one must first,
> O perfidy! have eat the giant's bread.
> If I submit, it is but to gain time
> And arms and stature: 'tis but to lie safe
> Until the hour strike to arise and slay:
> 'Tis the old story of the adder's brood
> Feeding and nestling till the fangs be grown.
>
> (XII. 36–45.)

This fustian rings pathetically like the desperate cry of a man intent on justifying his course and his purposes to a judging world. One final passage should be cited here:

> And am not I, though I but ill recall
> My happier age, a kidnapped child of Heaven,

Whom these uncircumcised Philistines
Have by foul play shorn, blinded, maimed, and kept
For what more glorious than to make them sport?
Wait, then, wait, O my soul! grow, grow, ye locks,—
Then perish they, and if need is, I too.

(XII. 77–83.)

It is ironical that this regression to the worst excesses of Clough's
'Blank Misgivings' period should also echo so clearly the letter
which Shairp wrote to him about the *Amours de Voyage*: '[Y]ou
were not made, my dear Clough, to make sport before The
Philistines in this way. . . .' The irony, when we remember the
distinction Clough had once achieved as a poet, is tragic. It both
measures the gap between *Dipsychus* and the art of *Amours de
Voyage* and suggests an explanation for it.

CHAPTER X

Blanche Smith, America, Marriage, Florence Nightingale, and *Mari Magno*, 1850–1861

The grand unparallelled peculiarity of Teufelsdröckh is, that with all this Descendentalism, he combines a Transcendentalism, no less superlative; whereby if on the one hand he degrade man below most animals . . . he, on the other, exalts him beyond the visible heavens. . . .

Thomas Carlyle, *Sartor Resartus.*

> Then love: I scarce can think
> That these be-maddening discords of the mind
> To pure melodious sequence could be changed,
> And all the vext conundrums of our life
> Prove to all time bucolically solved
> By a new Adam and a second Eve
> Set in a garden which no serpent seeks.
> And yet I hold heart can beat true to heart: . . .
>   . . . But love, the large repose
> Restorative, not to mere outside needs
> Skin-deep, but throughly to the total man,
> Exists, I will believe, but so, so rare,
> So doubtful, so exceptional, hard to guess; . . .

Dipsychus, IX. 14–21; 30–4.

Poets have always had a genius beyond their fellows for irritating the feminine devotee by their ineptitude in pairing themselves; to judge by the wingless widow, Clough, Arthur Hugh carries off the cake in this respect.

The Diary of Alice James.

Tom Arnold recalled an occasion in 1858 when he was dining in a restaurant with his brother, Matthew, and with Clough. Matthew was in fine spirits and 'talked incessantly', Clough was morose and said very little. At one point in the conversation Voltaire's name cropped up, and Matthew, gesturing airily, declared, 'As to the coarseness or sensuality of some of his writings, that is a matter to which I attach little importance.' Clough's retort was quick and blunt: 'Well, you don't think any better of

yourself for that, I suppose.'[1] The prim reproof is startling in the
mouth of the man who had written 'Natura Naturans', Sa Majesté
très Chrétienne', and Dipsychus. Yet, oddly, there is about it a simultaneous sense of expectation fulfilled: one had, in spite of—or
perhaps because of—those poems, been anticipating that particular
asperity. Clough's relationship with the woman who was to
become his wife makes sense of our contradictory reactions.
Retrospectively, that relationship illuminates the crisis of identity
out of which Dipsychus was created. It also explains a great deal
about his life in America and his years at the Education Office.

Clough first met Blanche-Smith, it appears, in 1850 in Fryston
Lodge in Yorkshire, the home of Richard Monckton Milnes, and
Florence Nightingale seems to have played an important part in
bringing them together.[2] Blanche Smith's father, Samuel Smith,
was an Examiner of Private Bills. From her mother's side she was
a first cousin of Florence Nightingale's. Her family lived amply at
Combe-Hurst—at the time a country-house—near Kingston in
Surrey, and she had been brought up in the conventional, leisurely,
rather aimless female ways of Victorian well-to-do-ism. To judge
from her letters, she had grown naturally and deeply into the loyalties and affections of the close-knit family that was in time to stand
generously, if with somewhat uncertain comprehension, behind her
decision to marry the odd and failing man she had chosen. She also
seems to have been educated into a truly remarkable sensitiveness
and delicacy: at one point she remarked to her future husband, 'Is it
necessary for men to coarsen their imaginations? It is curious, how
very seldom you read any poems—any book of any kind that does
not in some degree offend.'[3] One can infer from her letters, too,
that she inherited from her mother—the 'Aunt Mai' who sacrificed
so much for Florence Nightingale, and was in time cast off by
her—something of a taste for the life intellectual, especially for
abstract metaphysical speculation.

The few glimpses we have of her life subsequent to Clough's
death furnish some details with which to fill out a preliminary
acquaintance. She was quite obviously utterly devoted to her

[1] T. Arnold, 'Arthur Hugh Clough: A Sketch', The Nineteenth Century, xliii
(Jan. 1898), 115.
[2] G. Levy, Arthur Hugh Clough, 1819–1861 (London, 1938), pp. 129–30 n.,
and C. Woodham-Smith, Florence Nightingale (London, 1951), p. 109.
[3] Blanche Smith to Clough, 4 Mar. 1853, Bodleian MS. Eng. Lett. d. 179,
fol. 153ᵛ (653).

husband and admired him immensely. She loved him lavishly and to the point of adoration. In everything that pertained to him she acted from the best motives and according to the best light of her understanding: it is hardly her fault that we today are very likely to concur with John Addington Symonds's unkind estimate of her as a 'thick-sighted woman'.[1] Symonds judged with some authority—he had come to know her very well through his collaboration in the 1869 edition of Clough's works. Blanche Clough's anxious memoir is only the most obvious indication of her concern for her husband's reputation. She frequently carried her battle on his behalf into the camp of the reviewers, pointing out to them the errors and inadequacies in their estimate of her husband—particularly of his religious views. In 1869 Henry Sidgwick found it necessary to write apologetically to her about the unflattering valuation of the *Mari Magno* stories in his *Westminster Review* article.[2] Six years earlier R. H. Hutton had written to her apropos his piece in the *Spectator*,

> I am very sorry you think that I put the sceptical side of Mr. Clough's intellect too much forward. To me everything you say is strictly true and I think was more or less implied in the article. All I meant to say was that while his mind was essentially religious, his intellect was quite dissatisfied with even the most simple forms in which our faiths are *stated*. Had I asked him for instance whether he held with me that God is in the highest sense a *person*, I think he would have replied with Goethe and many of the greatest intellects of modern times, that personality is probably a human conception which may or may not be consistent with real infinitude and that he thought it an insoluble problem. That he looked to the future world with hope and peace, and towards the world above us in faith I know and hoped I had strongly expressed. But I think his doubts went far enough to disturb his own peace and to unsettle many who were greatly influenced by him. . . . I know well how much larger his intellect was than my own, —but in describing the general effect of his poetry upon me it would be impossible to ignore it.[3]

In 1866 John Addington Symonds, with the permission of Blanche Clough, published an article, based on the privately circulated 1865 edition of Clough's *Letters and Remains*, in the *Cornhill*.

---

[1] Quoted, P. Grosskurth, *John Addington Symonds* (London, 1964), pp. 150–1.

[2] A. S[idgwick] and E. M. S[idgwick], *Henry Sidgwick, A Memoir* (London, 1906), p. 216.

[3] R. H. Hutton to Blanche Clough, 17 Nov. 1863, Bodleian MS. Eng. Lett. d. 178, fols. 98–9 (1154).

In his article Symonds, who tended to see something of his own
state in his subject, stressed Clough's reluctance to come to firm
conclusions and his inability to express himself adequately because
of his open-mindedness, and he drew a parallel with De Musset.
Blanche Clough took up her pen. She wrote to Symonds saying
that he had come to his conclusions without a sufficient knowledge
of his subject's life. Symonds, making his apologies for 'underestimating' and 'misrepresenting' her husband, added in his reply,
'Might I suggest that if you believe there is a prevalent misconception of the life of Mr. Clough, it would be well to directly
combat it? I almost think such an elucidation of his true aspect
of [sic] thought and opinion might have been included in the
memoirs.' Clough's poems, he pointed out, gave little of the
impression she considered was the true one.[1] The reply placated
Blanche and subsequently she and Symonds grew into a fairly
close friendship. At Jowett's suggestion he became her chief
helper in preparing the 1869 *Poems and Prose Remains*. Symonds
was fascinated by Clough's life, which he felt sure, he wrote to
Graham Dakyns, had been 'in some sense mutilated', and he
felt that this should be communicated in the memoir.[2] He also
believed—perhaps with a slightly easy youthful courage—that
the new edition should withhold nothing; but, as he put it in the
same letter to Dakyns, '[Mrs. Clough] is very timid and very
desirous of suppressing points here and there.'[3] To his co-editor he
wrote, 'Of course you have always known, and I have, I think,
always reminded you that you must in publishing be prepared
to risk somewhat; to face the opinion of the world to a certain
extent. . . . Either do the whole thing or nothing.'[4] Not many
people held such views. Among Clough's friends, John Gell, for
instance, had written to Blanche in 1862 when the first collection of Clough's poems was being prepared, 'I should think it
a great triumph of biographical skill to make the world know why
we loved Clough.'[5] John Shairp—along with several others—had
been especially anxious about the contents of this first collection:
'If I may venture to say as much there are one or two very
powerful poems written but withheld by your husband during

[1] Quoted, M. Symonds, *Out of the Past* (London, 1925), p. 109.
[2] Quoted, Grosskurth, op. cit., p. 132.   [3] Quoted, ibid., p. 133.
[4] Quoted, loc. cit.
[5] J. P. Gell to Blanche Clough, 11 Feb. 1862, Bodleian MS. Eng. Lett. d. 178,
fol. 41 (1116).

his life, which I hope will not appear now. I allude especially to one he read me, written in Naples, of deepest most condensed feeling, but very painful. And it would give much pain to many persons if published now.'[1] We have already seen how passionately Blanche herself fought with Charles Norton over the 'abhorrent' 'Natura Naturans', and the dislike she expressed for 'The Latest Decalogue'. The 1869 edition, when it appeared, was—not surprisingly—a carefully censored one.

The proper disposition of her husband's literary remains did not occupy all Blanche Clough's attention, however. She frequently wrote to Symonds—and sometimes to Jowett—about her own inactivity, her lack of adequate occupation, her inability to fulfil herself. Symonds set her to the task of analysing Shakespeare's sonnets. 'The analysis of the gradual improvement in stability and elevation of feeling', he commented about the resulting manuscript, 'is very good.'[2] But Shakespeare's sonnets were only a stopgap. In January 1869 we find him expostulating, 'You complain of two rather contradictory things—of not having time enough for study and yet of being insufficiently occupied.'[3] His correspondent obviously was nettled, for a few days later he wrote again to make somewhat stern amends. 'You say you never complained of want of occupation. Perhaps not exactly. But you are always asking for something to do. You say that Jowett in spite of his many avocations will find time 'to give you something to do!' I hardly see how anyone is exactly to prescribe a task for another person.'[4] He went on to propose that she should undertake a book along the lines of Besant's work on the early French poets, or a 'Golden Treasury' of Italian Poetry. In 1869 T. H. Green, at the prompting of Symonds and Jowett, had proposed that she should collaborate with him in a translation of Baur, but the project never came to fruition.[5] In 1873, finally, she found some kind of fulfilment: John Murray published her translation of Jacob Burckhardt's The Cicerone.

Such, then, was the very conventional, very earnest, and very persistent woman who wrote of her husband's life after marriage:

For the next seven years he lived quietly at home; and during this time

[1] J. C. Shairp to Blanche Clough, 31 Aug. 1862, ibid. fol. 53 (1123).
[2] Quoted, M. Symonds, op. cit., p. 121.
[3] Quoted, ibid., p. 123.   [4] Quoted, ibid., p. 124.
[5] T. H. Green to Blanche Clough, 12 Dec. 1859, Bodleian MS. Eng. Lett. e. 76 (1250) and M. Symonds, op. cit., p. 120.

three children were born to him, who formed his chief and unfailing delight. No events of any moment marked this period; but it was one of real rest and contentment. . . . After his marriage there was nothing of [the previous] enforced and painful communing with self alone. . . . All the new duties and interests of domestic happiness grew up and occupied his daily thoughts. The humour which in solitude had been inclined to take the hue of irony and sarcasm, now found its natural and healthy outlet. The practical wisdom and insight into life, for which he was distinguished, were constantly exercised in the service of his friends; and the new experience which he was daily gathering at home made many perplexed questions, both social and religious, clear and simple to his mind. In this way, though he did not cease to think about the problems which hitherto had occupied his leisure, he thought about them in a different way, and was able, so to speak, to test them by the facts of actual life, and by the intuitions and experience of those whose character he valued, instead of submitting them only to the crucible of his own reflection. The close and constant contact with another mind gave him fresh insight into his own, and developed a new understanding of the wants of other people, so that the results of many years of meditation grew distinct and solid.[1]

One might be justifiably exasperated at this complacent picture of fulfilled domesticity; one might disagree emphatically with the implied valuations of Clough's earlier life and activity; but the portrait of these years is not an untruthful one. It is more than probable that Clough himself would have concurred in his wife's judgement, although a closer look at these years—especially at the 'service' to Florence Nightingale and the strange *Mari Magno* stories—might suggest that the comforts and certainties of domesticity were not quite so comprehensively and effectively emollient. The important point, however, is not these inaccuracies in detail, or even Blanche Smith's very limited understanding of her husband. It is, rather, the fervour and completeness with which Clough himself embraced domesticity. Blanche Smith's conventionality and her pedestrian intellect are pertinent, but the finally significant questions can be answered only from Clough's side. How did she come to be such an important influence? What was he looking for, what did he find in her? What, in other words, was he creating in his relationship with her? What authority was he investing her with? The answers must

[1] *PPR* i. 44–5. I have ascribed the memoir to Blanche Clough on the basis of a letter from J. A. Symonds. Grosskurth, op. cit., p. 133.

circle widely over Clough's life, and they bring that life to a particular psychological focus. In that cruelly clear focus alone can we learn to recognize his desperate and solitary strength.

Clough met Blanche Smith sometime in 1850 and, although there was no formal engagement, by the end of 1851 he was more or less officially recognized as the man she was going to marry. These were months also during which his own isolation and lack of success were beginning to take a severe toll: psychologically he was becoming more and more vulnerable. It is difficult to see how he could have avoided feeling utterly stranded as far as his professional life was concerned. In December 1851 he resigned from his position in University Hall, expecting an appointment to the Classical Chair at University College, Sydney. On 2 January 1852 he heard from Sir John Herschel, chairman of the electing board, that Dr. Woolley had been given the position.[1] The news must have been demoralizing. As Clough's dealings with the University Hall authorities and his private dreams for the future with Blanche Smith show,[2] he had invested a great deal of trust and confidence in the Sydney possibility. In a dispirited mood he began casting about for alternative openings. The chance of an Examinership in the Council Office—for which he had the valuable backing of Lady Ashburton and, through Matthew Arnold, of Lord Lansdowne—was spoilt when Lord Derby's Conservative government replaced the Liberals in February. Rather dubiously— and unsuccessfully—Clough next put in for a Roman Catholic Inspectorship. The Regius Professorship in Humanities at Aberdeen seemed a more likely possibility, but he withdrew when he learned that subscription to the Westminster Confession was obligatory. It was only after he had canvassed these prospects at home that he turned his gaze across the seas once again, this time toward America. The 'stigma of the abjured xxxix articles', as he called it in a letter to Blanche (*Corr.* i. 312), was rapidly becoming in his eyes the mark of Cain.

More serious was the sterility within, of which this outer

---

[1] A letter which Clough drafted (in Dec. 1851?), possibly to the electing Committee for the Sydney Professorship, suggests that he was uneasy about the religious issues which might stand in the way of his appointment. In his letter he said that he was willing to answer any questions the Committee might have. He also pointed out that he always tried to avoid wounding anyone's religious feelings by speaking out his own opinions. Bodleian MS. Eng. Lett. d. 177 (430).

[2] Cf. Clough to Blanche Smith, [17?] Jan. 1852, *Corr.* i. 303.

barrenness seemed a mocking reflection. His nonconformity had led him into an utterly 'inactive useless hopeless life' from which he longed to escape.[1] 'I, like you,' he wrote to Tom Arnold in May 1851, 'have jumped over a ditch, for the fun of the experiment and would not be disinclined to be once again in a highway with my brethren and companions. . . . Nothing is very good, I am afraid, anywhere. *I* could have gone cracked at times last year with one thing or another, I think—but the wheel comes round' (*Corr.* i. 290). Beneath his exhortations to his friends to shed their timidity and go out boldly into life, to mingle with coalheavers and merchants and solicitors, there lurked the devastating sense of his own isolation. While he wrestled pointlessly and alone, life and achievement were steadily slipping by. The spiritual and intellectual exhaustion involved in his ceaselessly testing, proving, measuring scrutiny is brought out dramatically in a prose piece entitled 'A Sunday Morning Contemplation', which, it seems likely, he wrote while he was at University Hall.

O for heaven's sake, a little fun, a little release, a little freedom and expansion. Shall we write a romance—At any rate let our watch run down, let us cease to know hours. That twice two has been four so many times and still will be so many times in all possible sums and tradesmen's accounts, is it not a thing almost insupportable[?]. That ['Goodge' cancelled] St. is still Goodge St. at right angles to Berners St., that go where I will and how many times soever as I may, this angular positivity abides and is positive, is it not a thing to drive a man to distraction[?]. Blessed be God Almighty, of whose only gift it cometh that when I awake in the night I know not which way I am lying, and can rest uplifted for a few minutes even from the region of fixed position—But alas it is at the utmost for a few minutes only. Released from the pressing finger the needle of the soul sways round according to her essential attractions—but alas the finger is soon down again on her elective affinities. Oh facts that are not facts and never merit to be, and yet must needs for victual and for drink's sake be pro tempore held for such—for God's sake let me for a little interval get rid of you—and write a romance! But where then, out of your sphere of gravitation?—To what strange land? Patagonia is known and the latitude and longitude of all the towns of Madagascar. Of New Guinea the Admiralty has adequate surveys, and the rivers of Oregon are fixed to their courses in Wyld and Arrowsmith. Between China and California who shall dare to solace himself with Flanfasnic and Bulnibari? The very air, enslaved to telescopes, cannot pass off any make-belief Laputa.

---

[1] Clough to Blanche Smith, 31 Dec. 1851. Quoted, Chorley, p. 235.

Tentanda via est

After 40 days travelling under a burning sun through the sandy deserts of central Kamkatcka amongst the Creoles, finding myself suddenly on the rocky shore of the straits of Babelmandeb, without means of transit, I resolved to turn southeastwards to Bucharest and the Yellow Sea and take the passage boat from the port of Cenchrea to the great North German settlement of [Seunam?]. Meeting however with a Chinese Indian passing that way from Valparaiso to Malabar I was induced to spend the night at Erz-rum, in full view of that remarkable Volcano, to which the early Dutch navigators gave the singular name of Mont Blanc. The Carpathians in the nearer foreground and the graceful Dofrefeldt sweeping in Southwest distance formed a panorama I had never seen equalled except on one crowning occasion when from the summit of the lofty Irkutsk-Kou I looked abroad northward over the vast expanse of the island spotted Pacific, and southward up the Euxine and the Categat, while westward over the extreme horizon rose the Gothic towers of Ispahan, and eastward the eye found repose in the rich and populous plains of Otaheite and the upper Orinoco. The following week I arrived by the easy stages of Parana, Trieste, St. Kitts, Nova Zembla and Fernando Po at—

In nomine Patris et filii—[At this point Clough has drawn a diagram (a diagonal cross intersected by transverse lines) representing a bene-dictional sign of the cross] are we yet emancipated? If not let me recommend a diagram as above—and as near as possible a reproduction of it by the bodily members.

O thou deep engrained disease art thou in me still?

How shall I exorcise thee? Books! oh heaven; are not these that I look on, those I have looked on for I know not how many many yester-days?—Novels from the Circulating Library—Oh Powers! As Berners St. enters Oxford St., so doth Maddox St. come into Regent St;—even so is the difference of modern Novels. A little excursive quotation, however, by the way—a lenitive if no more!

Peritisque necesse est Multa diu concreta modis inolescere miris.

That is to the purpose, doubtless, but only too much so—What we want is what is to no purpose with anything or at cross purposes with everything—that won't do—

μὴ νῦν περὶ σαυτὸν εἶλλε τὴν γνώμην ἀεί,
ἀλλ' ἀποχάλα τὴν φροντίδ' ἐς τὸν ἀέρα
λινόδετον ὥσπερ μηλολόνθην τοῦ ποδός.[1]

Too germane to our matter—much—much.

Quod in [humum?] venerit

[1] Aristophanes, Clouds 762-4.

Of man's first disobedience and the fruit

Arma virumque cano

μῆνιν ἄειδε θεά

Nel Mezzo del cammin di nostra vita / Mi recontrava in una oscuro selva [*sic*]

—O qui me!—

[Pueri fortes?]

Spercheiusque et virginibus bacchata Laecanis

[illegible word] y geta

Le Donne, I cavalier, l'âme, gliamori

My father had a small estate in Nottinghamshire. I was the third of five sons. He sent me to Emanuel College in Cambridge at 14 years old where etc.

Ludimus interea Celeri nos ludimur [*sic*] hora

There is upon the west side of Itaille

Downe at rote of Vesulus the cold

A lustre plaine habundant of vitaille

Where many a town and towr thou maist beholde

The former treatise have I made O Theophilus

ποικιλόθρον' ἀθανάτ' ἀφρόδιτα

Abdul Kadur Gilanee was asked when he was sick what his heart desired. He replied only this that it may not desire anything. When the stomach is oppressed and the belly suffering pain, there is no benefit in having all the things in perfection. Wherefore O Arjoon resolve to fight. For indeed as Dr. Johnson sensibly observed to Mrs. Piozzi, oh shades of Authors, are not these things also in all reviews? together with the Servian [*sic*], Kurdish, Czech and Bulgarian poetry—they lie in the [hull?] like sheep. Now the best of the acts of Jeremiah, and all that he did, and his might and the ivory house that he made, and all the cities that he built, are they not written in the book of Chronicles of the King of Israel. Very probably. O Ye fanatic flames in Alexandria, but after all ye did as much good as harm—Butyrum et mel comedet. Confutzee, it is recorded—

Are we not yet released? is not the tyranny yet overpast? Is the fastening finger yet upon our compass needle?

Ah could I only recal my own past self; could I only re-image what I was of old at school, and in the holidays with my cousins here and my other cousins there. What I was when I was a little thing with my nurse learning to talk, and a scarcely bigger thing with my mother learning sums—wouldn't that do! But it is early days yet to write

memoirs—and perhaps a trifle mawkish at anytime—Well write something. Only see it a'n't grammar. Shall us? O dear won't us forget him
cursed Syntax! Won't that do I and you a much deal of good!—
them rules and they concords and what you call! Alas me, that won't
go very far neither. En dernier [resort?] for indeed it is the Sabbath
morn shall us go to Church and learn of the devout rustic who to the
clergyman encomiastic of his Church-going regularity took up his
parable ('for our own instruction') and yes, sir, made answer, I works
hard all the week, and on Sunday why I goes to Church; and I lays
up my legs; and I thinks of nothing. O fortunatos nimium sua si
bona norint!

Oh blissfully re-rendered all Church-Service-long to the reparative
upper magnetic or is it even dia magnetic influences and visited of restorative quick-changing [unrealities?] or lost at least in restorative
vacuities. O happy in great nature's maternal lap—O blessed of the
clergyman—Shall not we go and do likewise! If we can only! But
thou O Preacher, Temper then thy discourse to our too unsomnolent
town-nerves—let thy speech distil as the poppy, and thy words as the
breath of Morpheus. Enough. Fiat Voluntas! Andiamo. Venez donc.
Ja Wohl![1]

The 'Contemplation' endeavours to become a verbal talisman
of total abandonment. It strains towards an absolute release, a
sustained repudiation and suspension. Through a cancellation of
the logic-contracts of time, space, language, numbers, of the
'angular positivity' of 'facts'—the bedrock on which Clough
struggled to base certainty—it reaches out to total irresponsibility.
It cancels identity, in order, paradoxically, to achieve the fullness
of true identity, an identity which is full and true because so
completely undetermined. At first glance it might appear that the
'elective affinities' which the soul seeks are to be interpreted in
traditional terms—the soul seeking itself in its proper realm of
higher spiritual reality. In fact, however, such categories are
themselves included in the dissolution. The fantasy, at one level,
obliterates soul and body as it obliterates mind; at another, it
casts back a mocking image of the perplexity which 'facts' lead
to: the sacred invariably encounters its grimacing parody; even
while it is being made, the gesture of consecration transforms itself
into a gesture of desecration. Even in the flight to fantasy there is
no true release from the burden of self-consciousness. The body,
however religiously the limbs are arranged, remains recalcitrant.

[1] Bodleian MS. Eng. Misc. d. 512, fols. 154–62.

At some point, possibly in 1847 and almost certainly not later than 1852, Clough composed a fragment of prose entitled 'An ill world . . .', which leads us to the centre of the agonizing problem of embodiment.[1]

An ill-world indeed, Apemantus! An ill-world—a most pestilent, miasmatic, Epidemic-breeding atmosphere. Ah mother Eve, Father Adam, ye two between ye let out a most pernicious gas amongst us— a most concentrated transcendental sulphuretted hydrogen. That which of Cholera is not true, say the doctors, is saith Apemantus in the moral world axiomatic—The air that I inhale, and this pellucid, sincere-seeming element that recreates me—these things are replete with fungoids that once in the human venter do generate, not one way nor two, but many, by composition and by division, by coitus and by [lacuna], by ordinary methods and methods extraordinary. O ye foul subtle infusoria how shall we escape you, how live if we do not. For to walk about one mass of engendering fungoids, to be the brothel and public bedchamber for the perpetual copulation and re-copulation of the progeny of a close-stool—such is our lot O my brother.

Have respect therefore unto dunghills—which in comparison of us are respectable—to the dry innocuous horse dung and round [uncompromising?] sheep-droppings—how much better are these than thou, my good lord, or I?

Yet indeed shall no man [deprecate?] nor deodorize, which is indeed but smooth hypocrisy, [nor?] appoint sewage or Sanitary Commissioners upon us. He that endureth to the end—For indeed God would have his angels strong-minded. Butter and honey shall he eat—ordure and compost shall he smell, and submit himself to be engendered upon of zoophyta that he may through much tribulation of nose, enter into the Kingdom of good smells, having learnt to abjure the evil and choose the good, or having done otherwise maybe probation into the olfactories of saints yet to come. For indeed God is also glorified in them that perish at [Endor?] or elsewhere and become as the dung of the Earth.—Have patience therefore O thou semifungoidified

<hr>

[1] E. Barish, 'The Morals of Intellect: A Study of Arthur Hugh Clough's Political and Religious Prose, 1837–1853' (unpublished Ph.D. thesis, New York University, 1966), pp. 196–7, assigns 'An ill-world . . .' to 1847 on the basis of the references to cholera, the handwriting, and the fact that the paper on which it is written is identical with that on which Clough wrote the fragmentary letter on the 'Rights of Property'. Miss Barish's contention, that 'An ill-world . . .' is a piece of social criticism inspired by the cholera epidemic and directed against the resistance to Chadwick's sanitary reforms, seems to me misleading. Clough's Oxford journals show that as an undergraduate he suffered frequent attacks of what he called 'cholera'. Presumably there was some authority for his diagnosis, since he was under professional medical care.

Apemantus—for indeed is there an objectivity of smell—and the copulation of infusoria is it not as the combining of grapes or the working
of thy own cerebral . . .[1]

Fascination and loathing weave indistinguishably into one
another as the self confronts its involvement in the vileness of the
body. The 'excremental vision'[2] is almost unendurable, leading
an appalled imagination to the verge of collapse—but it is also
a radically penetrative act of insight. Sardonically obliterating
'higher' and 'lower' and projecting the Devil's lineaments on to
the face of God, that insight carries us to the brutal, intractable
basics from which new sanities of moral and artistic order can
be formed. As a perception of the ground of human reality it is
potentially as subversive and as luminous as St. Augustine's
inter urinas et faeces nascimur, Lear's recognition on the heath,
Swift's savagery, Baudelaire's vision of Paris, Genet's understanding of depravity. But Clough's vision is only potential: he never
achieves comprehension of these dimensions and only fitfully
suggests it in his realism. He is too deeply entrenched in conventional understandings of purity and too deeply committed
to conventional versions of transcendence. For him the excremental vision is merely the agonizing reflection of his own
guilt. It reveals to him that gap between 'self' and the 'world'
(including his 'body') which he copes with chiefly in two ways—
either through the self-eliminating, sometimes gay and often
bitter, manœuvres of the ironist, continually creating and cancel-
ling attitudes, moods, and *personae*, or through an ethical didacticism which openly avows its allegiance to 'true' spirituality and
purity. The satirist often supports the conventional didacticist,
but sometimes pulls in a contrary direction: they can be connected,
as we have seen in *Dipsychus*, through a process of action and
reaction, the didacticist sternly calling to order the unregenerate
energies of the satirist. It is the conventional didacticist who
finally triumphs.

In a specialized form the anguished doubleness of this excremental vision invades Clough's awareness of sex and of womankind.
At the basis of this awareness stands the repellent and tempting
figure of the prostitute on which all the forces of unredeemed

[1] Bodleian MS. Eng. Misc. d. 512, fols. 163–4.
[2] I have adopted the term which N. O. Brown took over from J. Middleton
Murry for his discussion of Swift in *Life Against Death* (New York, 1959).

carnality converge. At the summit, arrived at through progressive stages of romantic idealization and transcendence, stands the 'Beatifica', as he called Jenny Lind.[1] It is Blanche Smith as the 'Beatifica' that we are concerned with.

A brief general summary of the more obviously relevant aspects of Clough's psychological development is helpful at this point, since it furnishes us with a kind of lexicon to the intensely private and symbolic language of his relationship with Blanche. A key image round which to construct such a summary is that of the solitary, gradually darkening study in the School House at Rugby in which Clough sat quietly struggling to understand and subdue his disappointment and jealousy at Simpkinson's friendship with the elder Walrond. Capable of strong emotional attachments, pathetically in need of them, he had had to learn at an early age to suspect them, to withhold himself and become self-sufficient. When he was nine years old he had been sent away from home: his mother had withdrawn herself, emotionally he was left to fend for himself in a puzzling and alien world. Lonely and insecure, he had tried to find a clear identity. He strained to live up to his mother's spotless ideals, he slaved at his books, and he earned the satisfaction of Dr. Arnold's approval—but always and inescapably he was conscious of 'never being . . . among those who I [am] sure love me' (*Corr.* i. 24). Early in life watchfulness and responsibility had become wearisome psychological necessities: were the attachments he formed, the relationships he entered into, 'really real'? The ontological insecurity[2] which manifests itself throughout Clough's life and provides the psychological energy behind his search for truth and assurance, was created out of the emotional deprivations of his childhood. The insulation of his true inner self from the false selves which entered into relational transactions was a procedure dictated by his sense of his own vulnerability. That inner self was precious as well as precarious and it had to be protected from invasion by the outer world. It had to be withheld from others, partly for the sake of preserving their autonomy, mainly for the sake of personal survival.

---

[1] *The New Zealand Letters of Thomas Arnold the Younger*, ed. J. Bertram (Wellington, 1966), p. 3.

[2] I have used the term 'ontological insecurity', like 'reality' in the next paragraph, in the empirical sense in which R. D. Laing has used it in *The Divided Self* (London, 1960). I am extensively indebted to Laing for the substance of this paragraph and the following one.

This bifurcation between true and false selves—which Clough as an adult tried so heroically to transform into unity—also trapped him in the schizoid dilemma. Since the authentic self was excluded from direct relationships with reality, reality itself dissolved into an endless recession. Neither the world within nor the world without were trustworthy. Action, too, became a mere simulacrum since it was not 'genuine', not vitally connected with the true self. And yet the unremitting introspection which the inner self enjoined became a parching glare which killed all spontaneity, all life, constantly depleted and reified the emotions, the relationships, the responses, which this self hungered for. One became, in Matthew Arnold's words, 'Nothing but a de-vouring flame of thought'. Paradoxically the inner self, if it was to remain alive, both refused and demanded relation, action, 'reality'. 'Reality' could kill it, but without 'reality' it withered into deadness: 'reality' was both suicide and salvation.

Clough's earlier letters to Blanche Smith are some of the strangest—and in their own way some of the most splendid—love-letters ever written. Reckless, inconsiderate, even cruel, these unyielding letters disclose the frankness and the suspiciousness of a man who stubbornly refuses to allow his feet to be swept from under him, who tries to catch the exact truth of the 'facts' in this relationship which he craves and fears—but who is patheti-cally unconscious of the inability of 'facts' to encompass that relationship. The self is threatened ('[M]en too are timid-hearted —not girls only—there is an instinct of girlish isolation even in the man no longer young', he wrote on his thirty-third birthday),[1] and it attempts continually to fly to unembodied realizations, to its own uniqueness, its higher allegiances and prior commitments —to truth, to honour, to justice, to service. As so often when he is confused, Clough preaches hard ethics: 'What was the true apple? do you know? I believe its true name was "Love is everything." . . . Love is not everything, Blanche; don't believe it, . . . "*Service*" is everything' (*Corr.* i. 300).

'Your heart is a priceless treasure.' No I tell you *it is not*. . . . I ask no girl to be my friend that we may be a fond foolish couple together all in all each to the other. If one that has dreamt of such unreality will open her eyes and look about her and consent to be what alone

[1] Quoted, Chorley, p. 235.

in plain fact she can be, a help-mate—that is a different thing. I will ask no one to put off her individuality for me; nor will I, weak and yielding as I am, if I can help it, put off mine for anyone. We are companions—fellow-labourers—to the end of our journey here, and then it will have not been in vain; we shall still be something, I think, to each other. But as for everlasting unions, and ties that no change can modify, do not dream of them—God knows, he only; it is no evidence for them that the exacting hearts of girls would fain believe in them, and make their lovers (mostly) pretend to do so. There, that is my creed; expect no other of me, even though in my weakness I belie myself.[1]

I am more 'odious' I fear than ever than [*sic*] in your eyes—but—*it is best it should be so.* I was very nearly saying by mischance instead of this—*I don't care. If* I don't care, it is because I feel a belief that you are taking me for worse than I am (far far better this than that you should take me for better—far far more acceptable to me) and because I think that, if I have not the love to offer you which your heart deserves, still I have something which I do not wrong you by offering you, nor would you wrong yourself by condescending to.—You will wait, will you—You believe in better things than this miserable mere companionship—do so—wait, and heaven be with you—there are Souls to whom this is allotted; but there are other souls also to whom it seems impiety against the Highest—ah, well, you will not understand, so I will not go on. Believe me however that if I quit you (which by my act, seems utterly unlikely to me) you would still be more to me than any human being that I can think of, parent or brother or sister or friend or teacher has been yet.[2]

In February 1852—before, that is, he left for America and actual separation tested his sentiments—he declared with lofty unlovely austerity, ' "Marriage", says the wise man, "is a discipline." That is not the way that everybody looks at it. *If* Marriage, how much more, years before marriage!'[3] Stern ethical imperatives which dictated a doctrine of effort and endurance together with undeniable 'facts'—these were the only grounds of certainty. Further, Blanche had to know the whole truth, she had to be fully acquainted with the multiplicity of selves, hesitant, cynical, tender, she was dealing with. She had to know about the realistic 'devil' who mockingly pointed out the dishonest role-player

---

[1] *Corr.* i. 301. The first two sentences are quoted from Chorley, p. 237.

[2] Clough to Blanche Smith, 1 Jan. 1852, Bodleian MS. Eng. Lett. e. 77, fols. 23ᵛ–24ᵛ, Clough's italics.

[3] Clough to Blanche Smith, [Feb. 1852?], ibid., fol. 103.

in him, the actor who 'blarneyed' this 'simple girl' as if he cared 'a fig about it'; she also had to know about the sentimentalist who kissed the paper on which the letter was written—by which self?[1] 'Fortified by bread and cheese', this strange man wrote the next day,

> I return and rise to the sublime . . . here in this dim deceitful misty moonshiny night-time of existence we grope about and run up against each other, and peer blindly but enquiringly into strange faces, and sooner or later (for comfort's sake for the night is cold you see and dreary) clasp hands and make vows and choose to keep together and withdraw again sometimes and wrench away hands and seize others and do we know not what.[2]

Like Claude, Clough was bewildered by himself, was 'fusing with this thing and that', 'tying [he] knew not what ties', and 'bread and cheese' were becoming less and less fortifying, less capable of accounting for the love and the sense of relationship which were actually invading his life.

The inconsiderate honesty of these letters was for Clough an imperative: only through total confession, total self-display, could he make the contact which he longed for, commit at last the 'genuine' act. He could no longer remain invisible.

> It may be true as you say that there is something in me that makes you think at times that I am nothing to you nor you to me—I wish I could make out what it means. I can ascertain nothing. To a certain extent it seems to me that the whole world is apt to wear a mere pictorial aspect to me, and that it must be by an effort that I accept anything as fact. This is the meaning of what I have often told you, that 'I believe in you'. I do not think I can say the same to anyone else, though I can with less effort or with no effort talk and get on with old familiars, understand and be understood; but if I am to make a choice, to act . . . I cannot turn, I think, except to you. There has never been in my whole life I may say *any act* of mine, sealing either friendship or love, up to this time. It has seemed a great thing (a thing that at times I doubt the truth of myself) to have done this at all. . . .
> But it has seemed to me that this scepticism is the mere occasional visitation of a malady which is not inherent in me, and which I could easily shake off; would circumstances only favour—that a little time would melt away the stone which it may be true now exists. On the

---

[1] See Clough's letter of 30 Dec. 1851, quoted, Chorley, pp. 234–5.
[2] Quoted, Chorley, p. 235.

whole I did not believe I was imperilling your happiness in seeking to give substance to my poor existence.[1]

Blanche was mystified, flattered, and distressed. 'I do hope I might make your life happier and more real at least, as you put it. ... You most certainly are not stone; ... [Y]ou shall teach me what you will, let it be good, and I will bring you back into the real warm life you were meant for' (*Corr.* i. 307–8). 'Let it be good'— the condition strikes an ominous note.

If it was necessary to expose—and, as it were, catalogue—all one's conflicting selves in order to arrive at this saving sense of reality, it was also necessary to strip that duplicity down to a single, central integer. The disguises had to be displayed only in order that they might be discarded. 'People who have got at all used to write as authors', Clough wrote in February 1852,

are so incapable of writing or even speaking except 'in character', and will run through a whole list of dramatis personae as occasion occurs without giving you a chance of seeing what they really are— in themselves—off the stage—if they try to be sincere it often makes bad worse. There—is one of the mischiefs and miseries of authorship which deter me. . . . I have been rather spoilt by somewhat *over*-quick sighted *men*—and thus (unfortunately for making myself understood by you—which straightforward view I *much prefer*) have got into a perverse habit of 'hiding'.[2]

The most important determining influence on the identity which emerged from its years of 'hiding' through this encounter with 'reality' was the complex symbolic value with which Clough invested Blanche Smith.

Quite clearly innocence and purity were primary values in the 'reality' to which Clough was reaching out in Blanche. He was trying to find in her absolution for his own besmirched self. He cast Blanche in the role of the child—the 'dear child of 12' —and as Katharine Chorley has pointed out,[3] she played up to the role: she was the little girl who sadly needed teaching and reforming. But Clough, too, was the 'dear boy'—'the appellation dearest to me in the whole world of appellations', he once

[1] Clough to Blanche Smith, Feb. 1852, Bodleian MS. Eng. Lett. e. 77, fols. 123–5. Quoted in part, Chorley, p. 234.
[2] Clough to Blanche Smith, 19 Jan. 1852, Bodleian MS. Eng. Lett. e. 77, fols. 61ᵛ–62ᵛ. Printed in part, *PPR* i. 173.
[3] Chorley, p. 238.

declared[1]—and when he was in America he constantly envisioned his fiancée as a maternal, totally restorative presence: 'I could think my dear love that even now I was resting my head upon you and getting cured of everything and restored for I know you would do it, if you were here.'[2] To be seen as a child, to feel as if he were a child (cf. *Corr.* i. 308), was to relinquish the weariness, the watchfulness, the responsibility, that life had so relentlessly imposed on him. Through Blanche he could recover the innocence he had had to surrender in his wanderings. To him she was a sister, to her he was a brother—two children attempting to cope with an ungiving world. 'Yet I feel . . . that we are like two little children and that we don't properly know what is to come in the end—brother and sister may have to part . . .', he wrote from America.[3] The symbolism of purity is not confined to this concentrated and uniformly asexual range of family reference. Anyone who goes through Blanche's letters—published and unpublished—to Clough can hardly avoid connecting her with flowers: snowdrops, azaleas, primroses, daffodils, rhododendrons, bluebells—letter after letter refers to a little memento.

What can I say? All these flowers surely cannot be meant for me! . . .
You really must send me no more of these beautiful flowers—they are a great deal too beautiful for me—and I a great deal too unbeautiful for them.—They are far more fitly placed in your own rooms at Combe—where henceforth I will imagine them.[4]

Like Faust's Margaret, like Maud, like Teufelsdröckh's Blumine, Blanche was inseparable from the green world of gardens. She was the living, Victorian-domestic, embodiment of the prelapsarian myth: 'You . . . seemed so much in your right place in the gardens and the walks', Clough wrote to her from America.[5]
Innocence and 'real warm life', the two principal symbolic motifs in this Blanche of Clough's, coalesce in the submerged

[1] Clough to Blanche Smith, [June? 1852], Bodleian MS. Eng. Lett. e. 78, fols. 140ᵛ–141.
[2] Clough to Blanche Smith, 22 Jan. [1853], Bodleian MS. Eng. Lett. e. 80, fol. 105ᵛ.
[3] Clough to Blanche Smith, 1 Apr. 1853, Bodleian MS. Eng. Lett. e. 81, fol. 115ᵛ (668).
[4] Clough to Blanche Smith, [May 1852], Bodleian MS. Eng. Lett. e. 78, fols. 107, 109.
[5] Clough to Blanche Smith, [11 Jan. 1853], Bodleian MS. Eng. Lett. e. 80, fol. 99 (623).

resurrectional imagery that can sometimes be detected in his letters. Twice while he was on his way to America on board the *Canada* he referred to the 'visits' she paid him in his little 'coffin' of a berth (*Corr.* ii. 322, 328). For, ultimately, she was a religious symbol, a Beatrice to be approached in reverence and purity, the child-guide to truth and light. In April 1853 he wrote, in an unpublished letter:

These dear people are all in Church, and I've locked the door, and taken out your picture, and the new picture and Aunt Julia's picture out of the drawing room window—Only your picture, my dearest, is half right or at most only half true. . . . The Picture wouldn't look at me; so I took her and shut her up—however I've left the slippers and the waistcoat and the blue and green neck-wrapper—all on the sofa, where they were put with the pictures—(no, not the waistc[oa]t, that's not there)—Goodbye my own Blanche—God bless you for ever and ever, my own dear one—I shall go out I think for my little walk—having kept my little festival here.[1]

Robert Browning's Elizabeth Barrett and John Stuart Mill's Harriet Taylor provide rough analogies to put this idealizing devotion into historical perspective, but the closest parallel I can think of is Leslie Stephen's equally moving letter to *his* guardian-angel, Julia Duckworth. 'You must let me tell you that I do and always shall feel for you something which I can only call reverence as well as love. *Think* me silly if you please. . . . You see, I have not got any saints and you must not be angry if I put you in the place where my saints ought to be.'[2] The friends in America who thought that Coventry Patmore's anonymously published *The Angel in The House* had been written by Clough were not making quite as 'disconcerting' a judgement as Katharine Chorley believed.[3]

[1] Clough to Blanche Smith, 19 Apr. 1853, MS. Eng. Lett. e. 81, fol. 159 (676).
[2] Quoted, N. L. Annan, *Leslie Stephen* (London, 1951), p. 75.
[3] Chorley, p. 300. An unpublished letter from Mrs. Ticknor (a member of the high-Boston set whom Clough did not even like very much) indicates that he was in the habit of making his feelings for Blanche known quite openly—and, it would seem, lugubriously—to his American acquaintances. Mrs. Ticknor wrote,

I felt your kindness in showing me that most expressive and interesting countenance and while looking at it, the perception of the loneliness and dreariness of your [home?] which is always very distinct to me, rather oppressed and absorbed me, and so I came away without any words at all, I believe.
I have had half a mind to write a note to Miss Smith, to thank her for aiding

The nature of the conversion effected through this pilgrimage to fresh sanctity was determined by the combined workings of Clough's own guilt-stricken conscience and the prudish and uncomprehending reformist determination of Blanche. As I have suggested in discussing the University Hall years generally and *Dipsychus* especially, Clough had become both confused and alarmed by himself. His recoil from the flesh and the 'world' is the most obvious indication of that alarm. 'Believe me', he wrote to Blanche in January 1852,

that, as in the first instance I ventured to look forward to your aid in my little *enterprise* [i.e. the Sydney project], so since the chance of it has passed away I have seen no course of life open to me which I could *permanently* believe true and good except one in which my vagabond imaginations should be steadied by——.
... What I had rather looked forward to originally in case of not going to Sydney, was unmarried poverty and literary work. . . . But I find myself utterly reluctant to enter on that sort of career quite independently of you. I do soberly think it replete with temptations and probable mischief for me . . . (*Corr.* i. 303).

The 'vagabond imaginations' which had developed his realism, his sardonicism, his sense of the value of natural and even fleshly impulse—his 'Descendentalism', in short, as Carlyle would call it—had released demons which he would gladly be rid of.

To judge from the important letter which James Martineau sent to Blanche in October 1851 (*Corr.* i. 291–4), Clough had tried to introduce her at a relatively early stage of their acquaintance to some of his ideas about religion and morality, and she had written to Martineau about the disturbing points he had raised. Did formulated religion as it existed in England permit an adequate and true expansion of human faculties? Were there no imperatives to be discovered in the spontaneity of nature and impulse? Was the Rule of Conscience trustworthy or sufficient? For Blanche's commonplace and irretrievably conventional mind these questions were only dim and academic ones: they never seriously impinged on her values or her sense of morality, although they flattered some of her pretensions. At times she

you in giving me such a pleasure the other day, and to tell her how really glad we should all be to add in any way to your success. . . . [18 June 1853], Bodleian MS. Eng. Lett. d. 177, fols. 199ᵛ–200 (723).

inclined to see herself in terms of rebellious upheaval as a kind of counterpart to her husband-to-be: since they were companions, they were companions in 'doubt' as well. 'I feel such a humbug. I pretend to be good and calm, outside when I am full of storms and unbelief in any kind of good.'[1] She provided some details about these hidden fires in other letters.

I don't feel very good this morning, and sometimes it seems such humbug, when I have been cross with other people to come and be sentimental. Do you know I am not really so good as I should be with Beatrice [her sister]. She puts me out with being dawdling and all that and I am too sometimes and then it clashes [sic] and then she looks so wretched at little things, and I get provoked. Indeed—but I will try—but really I find it extremely difficult to be good, I am afraid it is not at all natural to me.[2]

This evening Alfred came down and has been reading Villette aloud. I meantime, as I had read it, read the 2nd vol to myself, for wh[ich] piece of unsociableness A[un]t Joanna rewarded me with a few allusions at the end. Do you know I can't do civil things easily and give up little things to others and be on the look out to be kind. . . .[3]

She clung bravely, nevertheless, to her ideals. 'Do you know I respect your realism so much. I think almost too much for a certain portion of idealism keeps people above water. . . .'[4] 'I really do think you do not always believe in the best. . . . I cannot bear to have my ideals hunted down.'[5]

For Clough, Blanche's 'delicacy' was an integral aspect of her value and he made a determined effort to suppress anything in himself that might give offence. Writing from Boston about *The Bothie*, which he had seen lying about on drawing-room tables and had reread, he assured her that he found it 'innocent enough, which indeed believe me my dear child it really is— a little boyish of course—but really childishly innocent' (*Corr.* ii. 338). Once he made a mild joke about Mrs. Howe's *décolletage*, but hurried to add, 'don't be shocked, Blanche dear, but [Mrs. Howe's shoulders] distress me' (*Corr.* ii. 356). All the while, however, there was his past self waiting to be discovered—and

---

1 Blanche Smith to Clough, 14 Jan. 1853, Bodleian MS. Eng. Lett. d. 179, fol. 81ᵛ. (625).
2 Blanche Smith to Clough, 15 Apr. 1853, ibid., fol. 248 (674).
3 Blanche Smith to Clough, 30 Apr. 1853, ibid., fol. 279 (682).
4 Blanche Smith to Clough, Bodleian MS. Eng. Lett. e. 79, fol. 125.
5 Blanche Smith to Clough, ibid., fols. 73ᵛ–74ᵛ.

judged—in the Pandora's box of manuscripts he had left behind
in England. In December 1852 Blanche asked his permission to
read *Dipsychus*. Clough was agitated: 'Dear Blanche, please don't
read *Dipsychus* yet—I wish particularly not. You shall see it
sometime—but now, not, please—dear, I beg not, please' (*Corr.*
ii. 350). In March 1853, finally, the blow struck. Blanche had
dipped into *Dipsychus* and into some of his letters.

> It is strange those peeps and reminders of your old times and thoughts
> and your other sides always upset me—I believe I am unjust. Now I
> am writing to you, it seems to come back to a more usual state, but it
> is horrid—they seem to me full of honest coarse strength and per-
> ception. I don't mean to blame, but I don't like it. I don't like men in
> general; I like women—why was not the world made all women—
> *can* there not be strength without losing delicacy. . . . I did hardly
> know that good men were so rough and coarse. I mean not that they
> prefer evil, but they consider of it so much.—I do not mean anything
> about you—you always give me the impression of being good, very
> good (*Corr.* ii. 402–3 n.).

Two days later she took up her letter again,

> I feel I am wrong and yet I cannot come back to you quite as before—
> and still it is not your fault—I cannot tell why this made such an im-
> pression on me. It is because I do not understand nor know what to
> believe, what things in general. . . . It seemed to me I saw the reason
> why men's love was so much less personal and less enduring, less
> spiritual and depending more on juxtaposition, and that feeling made
> me hate the idea of all men—not you especially, but it seemed such
> a fall. . . .[1]

By the time Clough received that letter he was hopelessly
entangled in Blanche and in the obscure workings of his own
self-revulsion. Her voice was authoritative. It bore the credentials
of that 'instinctive' knowledge which his romantic distrust of
intellect conferred on her. Bent on committing intellectual
suicide, he was in no condition to recognize her inanities. All he
saw was his child-saint withdrawing herself, the implacable angels
of retribution waving wrathful brands before the gates of Eden.
He saw himself cast out once more into the lonely, impoverished,
unreal, paths of the homeless. In an agony of anxiety, desperation,

---

[1] Blanche Smith to Clough, 4 Mar. 1853, Bodleian MS. Eng. Lett. d. 179,
fol. 156 (651).

and self-pity he wrote a letter which ran to three versions and 5,300 words:

I do not know quite, what it is that repelled you so—I can only say that I am ready to give up everything rather than do any force to your feelings in this respect—You must do what you think right about it—I do not claim or ask or feel to deserve anything from you—
. . . I could almost conceive that it might be wrong for me to go on with you—
Yet, if I do not the least say that you have to trust me in the past, *still in the future*—However upon my word I could really believe that you had better withhold yourself—I have deserved that you should—And I will work on and not ask for happiness which is too much for me. . . .
You are above me—better than me. I am soiled—why should I therefore try and come near you. I did wrong perhaps ever to do so.—
. . . [Y]ou may cast me off forever if you please and you may seek someone in a better and more innocent sphere than mine—There are such believe me—. . .
I have been wrong, I know, yet it was partly I think in trying to be right—I repeat it again—You may if you please look rigidly into the past—read all the papers and letters—*and then choose better—dismissing me*—or be content with the hopes that surely do exist for the future—I have not as the world would say gone far wrong even in the latest time of exclusion and hopelessness but—I don't say that I may not have disqualified myself for you. . . .
It is perfectly true you see that feelings of the kind which repel and revolt you, did (for lack of better) possess me more or less for some time between 20 and 34—At the same time it was the necessity of facing things and doing work that led to it—
Nor do I think that you have any occasion to believe that I ever so far settled in them as to make it likely I should recur to them—. . .
As for being unsoiled in the past, it were mere deception to claim anything like it—I believe I went on in everything in the hope, amidst a great deal of perplexity, of finding the right way, even though it were by trying what might prove the wrong—for how else could one hope to find it—. . .
You must, please, look to the future—and help me, please, to look to it. . . . And I hope you believe for the future that I am capable of being restrained above any feelings that you would in any sense or kind felt [*sic*] the remotest approach to being revolted at. I am ready to go rather than do anything of that kind—. . .
But we will, please, look forward and hope. . . .
But meantime, please, aid me to look forward—it is so sadly easy to look back and down—

O please, my dear child do not you turn my eyes in that direction—
well, I will try and keep them well away. . . . Oh my dear Blanche,
I hope without taking one step downward you will be able to reach
out your hand to me. . . . I hope so, must hope so.[1]

The note of personal reconstruction becomes explicit and persistent in the letters which follow. Early in April, Clough wrote:

Believe me however my own dear Blanche, that you may fix your
thoughts as high as you please I will never (again) tempt you to lower
them. I think I am not too earthly or worldly or matter of fact or
whatever else—to rise—a good way:—and indeed I can surely some-
way support you even if it be only to seek what is better. . . . I am
getting much better, I do hope, in that way; am getting rid of what
you disliked in me. . . .
    To go home again would be a sort of youthful new happiness to
look forward to which it would be nice to keep before us would it not?
We would go back to Embley [the Nightingales' home in Hampshire],
and you should be the same dear girl whom I came to, out on the lawn
in the year 1852 in July was it, or June—June I think . . . do you remember that sudden funny call on me to come down [?] and we would go
and walk once again to the rhododendrons. . . .[2]

Ten days later he wrote again, 'Yes, stay as high as you please—
I am not going to pull you down.'[3] Blanche was gratified. On
14 May 1853 she wrote:

I thought among other things in church that really I had improved
you very much—don't think it presumptuous, please love, for I
don't think it was *me*, but you are much improved. . . . I do think
somehow you have a higher idea of what things ought to be—and
perhaps more respect for me, not as me, than you seemed formerly
to have—you never shock me now.[4]

Clough had indeed changed. In September 1854 he wrote to
F. J. Child about the latter's prospective edition of Chaucer:

I don't quite see what you should do about the Miller's and the Reve's
[*sic*] tales. I think explanation might be a little retrenched there, so as to

---

[1] *Corr.* ii. 402–4, with additions from Bodleian MS. Eng. Lett. e. 81, fols.
127^v, 130.
[2] Clough to Blanche Smith, 5 Apr. 1853, Bodleian MS. Eng. Lett. e. 81, fols.
127^v, 130 (670).
[3] Clough to Blanche Smith, 15 Apr. 1853, ibid., fol. 143 (675).
[4] Blanche Smith to Clough, 14 May 1853, Bodleian MS. Eng. Lett. d. 179,
fol. 304 (693).

leave them in the 'decent obscurity of a learned language'. . . . They are just what would be relished to this day in public-houses in farming districts, but I can't say that I could wish them upon any palate that does not already fancy them, and I don't much admire the element in the English character that does relish them (*PPR* i. 220).

Katharine Chorley has demonstrated conclusively that *Dip-sychus Continued* was written in America.[1] This sketchy sequel (which can be not unfairly described as an embarrassingly bad poetic version of Millais's picture, *The Retribution*) can now be seen as the act of contrition and self-repudiation it is. The action is set thirty years later. Dipsychus, who obviously succumbed to the Spirit's tempting and tasted of forbidden sexual fruit at the end of the original poem, has made his pact with the world and has risen to eminence as Lord Chief Justice. He administers the world's laws with enviable, but nevertheless soul-wearying, sagacity. The woman of thirty years ago—now an accusing and be-draggled angel of doom—suddenly reappears. Vainly Dipsychus pleads,

> It was not I
> That took your innocence; you spoilt me of mine.
> (*Poems*, 298; Scene II, ll. 16–17.)

He cannot stay to hear what she has to say, since the nation's business calls, and she leaves threatening that she is going to die. Before she goes, however, she leaves two distressing reflections behind: Dipsychus' success is founded on her body; her name, which for him was 'Pleasure' at one time, is now 'Guilt'. Dipsychus, presumably through a paroxysm of conscience, suffers a seizure and has to resign his office. The last scene displays him ruminating over the woman's words, 'Once Pleasure and now Guilt'. Perhaps because he has now relinquished the world, he also hears dimly another word which he cannot quite make out. Is it a word of hope? We never find out.

Blanche found some cause for satisfaction in this sequel. In September 1866 she wrote to the Revd. Percival Graves of Dublin:

I cannot think that [in *Dipsychus* Clough] meant the feeling of religion in one sort or another to succumb, but that he did think there must be a time of dearth, so to speak, in a practical life, especially to a mind somewhat overfed in youth. I grieve so much that he did not live to

---

[1] Chorley, pp. 264–6.

do more, because I think he would have done differently later. He did change enough to make me think he would have gone further, and this also makes me shrink from giving out anything which might *look* as if it were the final result at which he had attained. I think the Continuation 30 years after, tho' most unsatisfactory, was a sort of returning to commonplace views as having a degree of truth in them.[1]

Withdrawing his imagination from its 'vagabond' ways, Clough fell back on his identity as a moralist and as a religious thinker. 'I do hope, Arthur, you will be in some degree my religious instructor, indeed you sometimes are now indirectly', Blanche wrote,[2] and the role of teacher and guide flattered and fulfilled. It offered him true scope for the expansion of his idealism and the development of the ethical imperatives he cherished— work, self-denial, and service. 'My dear child,' he wrote from America in 1853, 'about being religious—the only way to become really religious is to enter into those relations and those actualities of life which demand and create religion' (*Corr.* ii. 392). With the settled resoluteness of one whose Arnold-and-Carlyle-fostered convictions had had to live through the hag-ridden night of unrestrained speculation, he addressed himself to the realization of 'practical Christianity'. 'All things, my dear Blanche,' he declared, 'become clear by work more than by anything else. Any common drudgery will help me out of the most uncommon either sentimental or speculative perplexity. The attitude of work is the only one in which one can see things properly' (*PPR* i. 174). Clough was in no mood to pause and examine the intellectual or moral adequacy of 'drudgery'—its reality was substantive and indubitable. He included Blanche in his programme of self-application. In a manner which recalls his supervision of his sister's education, he set her to the task of improving herself. They were to be fellow servants, companions in labour. 'I hope you will work, at Guizot, Plato, Music, everything. . . . Work, please, I beg of you: in every case this can do no harm. We have been sadly lazy since January', he wrote in late January or February 1852.[3]

---

[1] Blanche Smith to the Revd. Percival Graves, 2 Sept. 1864, typewritten copy, Bodleian MS. Eng. Lett. d. 178, fols. 100–01 (1156).

[2] Blanche Smith to Clough, 12 Apr. 1853, Bodleian MS. Eng. Lett. d. 179, fol. 237 (672).

[3] Clough to Blanche Smith, [Jan.–Feb.?] 1852, Bodleian MS. Eng. Lett. e. 77, fols. 71–2. Cf. 'Do work, my dear child,—*drudge, slave,—submit:*—So it must be—.' Ibid., fol. 84ᵛ.

A postscript to the same letter reads, 'There I have been looking over her Guizot and I beg to tell her she has *skipped* absolutely the whole law of the Vizigoths—8 important pages at the end of Lecture X!!'[1] Poor Blanche was not altogether to blame when in later life she peppered Jowett and Symonds with complaints about having nothing to do.

As far as religion and religious truth were concerned, Clough adopted towards Blanche an oracular, hectoring stance:

> Lay not your hand upon the veil of the inner sanctuary, to try and lift it up; go, thou proselyte of the gate, and do thy service where it is permitted thee. Is it for nothing, but for the foolish souls of men to be discontented and repine and whimper at, that He made this very tolerably beautiful earth, with its logic and its arithmetic, and its exact and punctual multifarious arrangements, &c &c? . . . Was it ordered that twice two should make four, simply for the intent that boys and girls should be cut to the heart that they do not make five? Be content, when the veil is raised, perhaps they will make five! who knows? (*PPR* i. 175).

The doctrine of acceptance and realism is familiar, but the fires have dampened, the attack and urgency have vanished. The tired liberal acceptance of externals is of the same kind as that which we encounter, in another region of inquiry, in the review of Charles Norton's *Recent Social Theories*.

The content of Clough's religious beliefs undergoes no marked change in these later years of his life. He had given up historical Christianity, but believed—with increasing firmness[2]—that Christianity was the highest form of religion man had achieved. What does change, however, is his attitude towards his own religious position. A new acerbity and touchiness manifest themselves in the years of his 'engagement' to Blanche. Having yielded up so many of his heterodoxies, he clung tenaciously and with an intensified self-consciousness to this final one. It seems as if this new emphasis resulted from the interaction of diverse pressures —the need to redefine himself, the compensatory thrust of individuality against the wider movement of submission, the impulse of self-justification against the awareness of failure. Some

---

[1] Clough to Blanche Smith, [Jan.–Feb.? 1852], ibid., fol. 74ᵛ.
[2] See especially the fragment to Margaret Clough, Jan. 1852, *Corr.* i. 304. See also Clough's remarks on the religions of India in his letter to C. E. Norton, 31 Oct. 1857, *Corr.* ii. 534.

of these points become more clear when we consider his visit to America.

★　　★　　★

On 19 June 1852 Clough wrote to Blanche, 'My dear child, I kept your birthday by writing to the great American transcendentalist [i.e. Emerson].'[1] Blanche failed to see the significance of what he had done; she wrote back saying that she was glad that he had done this, but also felt at times that he was 'missing chances' in England by not exerting himself sufficiently.[2] Clough wrote again. 'My dear child . . . Don't you perceive that I did it *all* ['all' underlined six times] of myself (I mean writing to E[merson]) in the prettiest manner possible, on your birthday.'[3] It is imperative that we should recognize the private and totally superstitious symbolic signals if we are to understand the strange mixture of asserted activist confidence and actual passiveness demonstrated in Clough's life in America. For Clough the 'American Hegira', as Emerson called it (*Corr.* i. 315), and the idea of Blanche were indivisibly connected aspects of a single, integrated commitment. Going to America, making the break, appears to have been for him the self-sufficient act which rendered further decisions about a career supererogatory. He had cast himself on the sea and on Blanche—Blanche and the sea would take care of him.

Clough's experience of America is not simple, but its essential outlines can be readily discerned. Emerson's reply to his exploratory letter was not only encouraging but enthusiastic. Pupils would be easy to come by, opportunities for work and for intellectual activity were abundant, his talents would be appreciated and there was ample room to expand. Congratulating Clough on his domestic prospects, Emerson added, 'But, first, you must come out and climb Pisgah alone' (*Corr.* i. 317). He also urged Clough to take the first boat out. It was impossible, however, to sail before the end of October and Clough filled in the interval visiting friends and saying his goodbyes. Among the friends he visited was James Froude, with whom he spent a month in Plas Gwynant in North Wales. Froude remembered the visit: '[Clough] was looking forward to great things which he was yet

---

[1] Clough to Blanche Smith, [19 June 1852], Bodleian MS. Eng. Lett. e. 78, fol. 185.
[2] Blanche Smith to Clough, [June 1852], ibid., fol. 189.
[3] Clough to Blanche Smith, [June 1852], ibid., fol. 194.

to accomplish; yet he was struggling with a half consciousness that little more could come out of him. On the day he left us, he said to me: "I mean to wait till I am forty, and if I can't do it then, I will cobble shoes." [1]

We should never lose sight of this ambitiousness of Clough's —now troubled, as Froude affirmed, by a gradually developing sense of failure. Much of the difficulty he experienced in settling down in America can be explained by his restless, unformulated, but cherished conviction of some true vocation which was larger and more worthy of himself than that embodied in any actual possibilities that presented themselves. In the beginning he thought of America in terms of private pupils and some literary work of his own. On the voyage out, however, James Russell Lowell, a fellow passenger, recommended that he start a school. These were the only two avenues Clough explored while he was in America, and while—with exasperating indecisiveness—he blew alternately hot and cold about each, fundamentally he disliked both almost equally. 'I am content to do this till I am 40', he remarked to Blanche in November 1852 about both these modes of earning a living (*Corr*. ii. 339). He did make a very considerable effort, however. He lived in what must have appeared to him a veritable social whirl, he conversed easily (Crabb Robinson noticed how his tongue had been loosened in America),[2] he displayed a wholly uncharacteristic circumspection in threading his way through the rivalries and animosities of Boston society, he even went to church with the Nortons during the earlier weeks of his stay. But sometimes he rebelled,

Will you think it wrong of me towards you—if I do what I think is best in itself—even if it don't seem the quickest way to unite us. . . . It seems to me sometimes as if I must not trifle away time in anything which is not really a work to some purpose—and that any attempt to be happy except in doing that would be mere failure even if apparently successful.

. . . Believe me, my own beloved—there would be small good in our living together a few short years here—providing merely for our own daily subsistence, or making that our object and business. . . .

. . . It may be the sanguine atmosphere of a new country has filled

---

[1] W. H. Dunn, *James Anthony Froude*, 2 vols. (Oxford, 1961–3), i. 173.

[2] *Henry Crabb Robinson on Books and their Writers*, ed. E. J. Morley, 3 vols. (London, 1935), ii. 735.

me with a vain confidence of there being really something in me to be done beyond mere subsistence. In London I felt myself pretty well helpless to effect anything (*Corr.* ii. 380).

Three days later, and after a talk with Emerson, he dismissed such talk as 'rhadomontade', and declared himself quite reconciled to the idea of buckling down to mere 'subsistence' (ibid., 381, 382). It is unnecessary to point out, perhaps, that Clough was hopelessly unfitted to the specific purpose of his American visit—to make enough money to get married on.

The overridingly important point about this visit, however, is that there is no real evidence to indicate that the New World made any decisive impact on him. He formed some important, interesting, and valued friendships and he kept in touch with his new friends throughout the remainder of his life. He was cultivated—and in a modest way fêted—by some of the most distinguished circles in Boston and its environs. He won wide respect for himself. But apart from the single issue of religion, he remained almost totally aloof. He often expressed enthusiasm for the hopefulness and energy of the young Continent, and contrasted it with the weary, overcrowded, tradition-bound ways of Europe, but these expressions are couched in such large and general terms that they amount to little more than sincere commonplaces. He wrote some vigorous articles for the magazines, but their vigour derives largely from a moralistic and hortatory (and frequent condescending) rhetoric. He wrote several short poems, especially about love and separation, duty and hopefulness, but, apart from one or two (particularly the magnificent 'Upon the water, in the boat'), these poems rarely rise above an embarrassing ladies'-album banality. Several of them have, fortunately, not yet struggled into the light of publication.[1] He embarked on a translation of the *Iliad*, and on the mammoth task of revising the translation of *Plutarch's Lives* which Ticknor and Fields commissioned, and which was to occupy him until 1858: 'It is odd', he observed to Blanche, 'how much better I like this Plutarch than I do anything which requires distinct statement of opinion or the

---

[1] The first two lines of one such set of verses Clough enclosed in a letter to Blanche Smith of 10 Dec. 1852 should provide a sufficient sample:

Come to me through the air above
Come hither to my breast, my love . . .

(Bodleian MS. Eng. Lett. e. 80, fol. 48 (606).

like' (*Corr.* ii. 376). The drug of drudgery was becoming insidiously attractive. His letters home, both to Blanche and to his friends, communicate nothing more than the alert curiosity of the interested bystander. There is, of course, much that is familiar in this spectatorial Clough—but there is one important distinguishing feature. The whole experience of America was subordinate to and coloured by the reality of Blanche. To put it very baldly, above all what he wanted from America, all he was looking for, was to get married to Blanche. Once he was united with her everything else would fall into place, the world would become finally real.

The regularity with which he wrote to Blanche is astonishing. He scarcely missed a day during the entire period of his separation from her. Repeatedly he counted up the days, weeks, months since he had last seen her. He drew up an incredibly detailed list of the dates of the letters which passed between them, together with the name of the ship which carried each one. From the beginning he looked forward to his return to England in the summer of 1853— if only for a visit (cf. *Corr.* ii. 340). Almost his first thought when he began to look into the prospect of a school was the rather impractical one of having Blanche come out straight away and join him (*Corr.* ii. 348). His American acquaintances had all spoken confidently about opportunities, but somehow they failed to materialize. At the end of December he still had only one pupil, and his fits of despondency became more frequent.

My dear girl, I fear I am living a very idle useless life here; for my pupil doesn't come at present and I do very little but write to you. ... [H]owever, Blanche dearest, I hope if you were to live with me and help me, I should get on better, and be better too—I get wrong with people and have nobody to be quite right with—never had so far as I know. I don't know that you would always understand exactly what my little troubles might be, my dear good child, but I think I should be right with you; and there is no one else, that I can say so of.... So you must come, dear, come, come, come—and make me happy which is not so much matter perhaps but sounder-minded and better (*Corr.* ii. 355-6).

'I have been longing, longing, longing for you so, these last 3 days and nights', he cried out in another letter (*Corr.* ii. 369).

America, then, was a land viewed distantly through the pain of longing and homesickness. With the enthusiasm of a man who had lived nearly all of his life in celibate institutions Clough soaked his mind in the comforting trivia of domestic detail:

I think this country would suit you all remarkably well—even Papa, though he would not get everything quite as nice as at home—so far as I can see yet, but then I have not been in the best houses to stay. Longfellow's library and Ticknor's d[itt]o and Prescott's d[itt]o are very nice rooms, and the Abbot Lawrence's drawing room pretty well. . . . But I can't say much yet about domestic doings (*Corr.* ii. 334).

Oh, Pianos!—that was what I wanted to tell you. The air here is so dry that English-made pianos spoil in it. The best maker in the U.S. is Chick[k]oring here at Boston, who is said to be very good . . . (*Corr.* ii. 340).

In another letter—the one in which he made his little joke about Mrs. Howe—he recounted how he had spent his time at a ball 'observing young ladies' dresses for the benefit of [his] young lady far away' (*Corr.* ii. 356). And beyond ladies' dresses there was the dream of the modest and undemanding home, the still point of peace and rest. 'My dear love, I think we could make each other happy here, in some small house—Do you not think it would be really possible somehow for you to come out?—then we would go back after a while together: and see the old places, and people' (*Corr.* ii. 384). Unfortunately sad realities interposed—and the demands of his future father-in-law, who required assurance that his daughter would be taken adequate care of.

An important point about the letters Clough wrote to Blanche is that they are, in their way, totally confessional. She was to share all his tribulations, be part of all his moods. How else can one account for letters like the following?

8 o'clock, Saturday, [16 April]

. . .

Dear girl—please don't think about those old matters so very very much—indeed there's no need. We cannot see right through the future, but the more we hope, and work towards that hope, the more real hope and prospect of union there will be—don't you think that? I do. Hope, hope, hope—and believe—though don't say one is sure when one isn't, that's all—but hope, hope, hope—toujours hope. . . .

8 am Sunday, [17 April]

. . . I have had doubts in abundance between this place and England—but though there are plenty of things to be said against this, on the whole I can feel sufficient advantages to make me content I think—they are very stupid and unintellectual I think, and a little rude and wanting in refinement (*Corr.* ii. 416).

O dear I am very tired of being without you—and I shall have to go again presently to Ethics, and the printers and then to Lowell's and then to Child (the Profr) perhaps, and tomorrow into town, and the next day to Emerson . . . (*Corr.* ii. 449).

Over and over again we witness in these letters the transformation from weary giant to querulous child.

Blanche, quite understandably, was alarmed at Clough's transparent display of indecision and passiveness, but her response was neither imaginative nor sympathetic. When her fiancé said, 'I don't think I shall ever do much hard work until you help me —not from laziness, but really from not having a proper rest to go to after it' (*Corr.* ii. 345), she saw merely a man who was contracting out of his responsibilities. She was deeply concerned, too, that he should not waste his powers—it is hardly fair to blame her for being, unintentionally and unknowingly, the chief cause and agent of his collapse. 'I will be ambitious, and I will have my dear boy do his utmost . . . for indeed I believe the chief purpose of me is to make you work', she declared,[1] and she set about her vocation with a determination and a practical common sense which become repellent at times. 'I do think you rather lazy, rather apt if you cannot do a great deal—to do nothing— (By the way, *will* you *please* go on with the Iliad when you have time. I do wish you would). I do think you do hardly sufficiently consider things for yourself but are willing to throw responsibility on others.'[2] Frequently she recurred to her injunctions. Clough was to work and not be lazy, to better himself, to do things and make progress—she had, after all, learnt the lesson of hard work from her fiancé. In her desperation she began to nag and manage, and Clough, on his side, was both hurt and annoyed:

As soon as ever you had begun to say kind things, you infallibly—when I as it were had opened my heart—went off to complaint of the past or urgent injunctions about beginning school, which were like little—daggers I might almost say—I don't think you need ever *drive* me at all. I am very tolerably easy to lead—but the other does not do (*Corr.* ii. 434).

[1] Blanche Smith to Clough, 20 May 1853, Bodleian MS. Eng. Lett. d. 179, fol. 324ᵛ (696).   [2] Quoted, Chorley, p. 287, Blanche Smith's italics.

Blanche maintained an unrelenting pressure, however. She was determined that the man she had chosen should make something of himself.

> The worst fear has been of your losing yourself in inactivity.—You see you hardly do anything till you are driven to it by outward pressure —at least you are very apt to wait for that before making up your mind and that *does* make it harder for those who have to deal with you. . . . I may have put it too strongly, but is there not a sort of laziness in you, that shrinks from taking the initiative and [putt]ing the burden on others? . . . But, if you choose the England . . . do resolve to work on and up. You *must* succeed; you must not give way to inertia. You must work through perhaps disagreeable work to success and if you give yourself to it, not be stopping to think it is not your vocation and that you would not have chosen it (*Corr.* ii. 443 n.).

The problem of earning a livelihood and settling down to a profession assumes comic proportions during Clough's sojourn in America, as doubts, stipulations, resentments, and misunder-standings tangle across the Atlantic. His future parents-in-law tended to discount the discouraging reports he sent, and to trust the more optimistic versions of American prospects which they were given by occasional visitors. For some reason they seem to have been bent on keeping him on the other side of the Atlantic. Clough, on the contrary, wanted to return home. Without ex-ception his friends, too—including relatively recent ones like Carlyle and Lady Ashburton—considered America, if not a mistake, a stopgap at the very most. His proper sphere was in England.

After an initial period of confidence, he lapsed into a resentful sense of loneliness.

> [I]t is only sheer necessity that drives me to undertake a school—and . . . I cannot and will not engage *to go on* keeping it. . . . [T]here is not a soul in Boston who is [in] any sense a friend or eager congenial companion, though I like people well enough, no doubt (*Corr.* ii. 434).

> Yes, my dear—it is horribly stupid here—the people are good and dull as I don't know what. I am sick to death of it.[1]

> I certainly should much like to come home if it were but for two or three years and then to settle here. I am often desperately sick of country,

---

[1] Clough to Blanche Smith, May 1853, Bodleian MS. Eng. Lett. e. 80, fol. 193^v (692).

people, and everything: above all however of the climate . . . (*Corr.* ii. 439).

One sometimes wonders whether Blanche ever paid careful attention to what he wrote. Even after letters like these, she wondered, '[Temple] advocates your coming home but on the ground that you do not like and will not succeed in America (why, have you told him so). . . .'[1]

Grudgingly enough, Clough tried to reconcile himself to the idea of staying in America for several years, and either taking private pupils or opening a school—he was never quite sure which. A letter from Carlyle introduced a fresh complication in February. Lord Derby's government had been replaced by one under Lord Aberdeen, and there were distinct possibilities that something could be secured for him by Lord Granville, whom Lady Ashburton had lost no time in approaching. Clough's response to Carlyle's letter is significant:

You will see how Carlyle talks about coming back, and Lady Ashburton too in the scrap, which Carlyle sends, of a note to him from Mrs. C. Which don't show. *But I don't like thinking about them, so I want you just to do so, and tell me what I had better think.* Literary and pupillizing work would pay better than there, and are more my vocation I think. Yet one's country is one's own, no doubt; though it be true that there is something more of freedom in America (*Corr.* ii. 367, my italics).

The canvassing of all sides of the question becomes more elaborate, more microscopically thorough, more academic almost, as possibilities begin to multiply.

In May, Carlyle informed him of the almost certain offer of an Examinership in the Education Office. The salary was modest—only £300—and he would have to wait twelve years before it rose to £600, the amount Blanche's father had stipulated as the minimum before he and Blanche could marry. There was, of course, the prospect of promotion to an adequately paid Inspectorship, but this was wholly contingent. Two days after Carlyle, Frederick Temple, at the time Principal of Kneller Hall, a teacher-training college, also wrote to say that Francis Palgrave, who was his Vice-Principal, had applied for a transfer to the Education Office. Temple offered the Vice-Principalship to Clough. The post was worth £400, with free board and lodging, and the

---

[1] *Corr.* ii. 442 n., with additions from Bodleian MS. Eng. Lett. d. 179.

chances of moving to an Inspectorship from it were as good as
they would be from an Examinership. The residence requirements
were something of an obstacle for a man intending to get married,
but Clough felt sure that 'the Kneller Hall plan might be so
arranged as to suit' (*Corr.* ii. 439). He wrote to Blanche's father
cataloguing all the prospects, begged him not to overestimate
prospects in America, and added firmly enough, 'Upon the whole
I have no great difficulty in deciding, so far as I am concerned,
in favour of the Kneller Hall proposal.' He added, further, that
he left the matter in Mr. Smith's hands and that he would be
satisfied with any decision made in consultation with Temple
(*Corr.* ii. 437–8). This washing his hands of the whole business
was, of course, totally unacceptable, and perhaps it is unpardon-
able. It is not impossible to understand.

Almost every letter Clough received made it clearer to him that
he was not being regarded with much trust, and that his own
wishes and feelings about a profession were of little moment.
Not only was he not exerting himself nearly enough in the eyes
of Blanche and her parents, they also seemed to have ideas about
how his life should be ordered. He vented some of his annoyance
in a letter to Blanche written probably on the same day as the
one to her father: '. . . I greatly fear that nothing but their own
pet plan will satisfy your dear Papa and Mama. I sometimes feel
a little vexed at their "adhesiveness" but I cannot absolutely rebel
against it, because it may really be right—or so nearly right as to
be accepted for it' (*Corr.* ii. 439). The choices confronting him
were not easy. As Temple pointed out (*Corr.* ii. 441), if he turned
down the Examinership he would in all probability be cutting
himself off for life from prospects in England. On the other hand,
the salary offered fell far short of what was required—and
Clough had no desire to wait. There were chances of more re-
munerative work in America—but they were only chances and
might not materialize. But, again, Mr. Smith offered financial
assistance if he remained in America, and, in June, he also
offered to let Blanche come over and gave them permission to
get married whenever they decided. Not unreasonably, Clough
concluded that Mr. Smith and Temple had decided in favour of
America, and he declared himself quite satisfied. Nothing had,
in fact, been decided. Nothing could be decided. Temple sent
a sharp summons calling him back to England to decide for

himself. Emitting several grumbles and declaring that as far as he could make out everything had been settled for America, Clough hurriedly packed his bags. He sailed from New York at the end of June. When he got home he discovered that Mr. Smith had changed his mind. He now made the same offers, even if Clough stayed on in England. There really was no question of choice. Clough decided on the Examinership.

If Clough displayed an astonishing unwillingness to commit himself and an equally astonishing eagerness to disclaim any responsibilities for his professional life, he also believed that demands were being made on the fulfilment of which depended his marriage to Blanche. Throughout he tried—often resentfully, and always ineffectively, because so passively—to throw himself into the professional posture which Blanche's parents would find acceptable; as he said to Charles Norton, he 'simply wished to do what they liked' (*Corr.* ii. 454). The notion of a career was not only subordinate to Blanche, it had become unimportant. Once again his behaviour restates the values and the priorities which determined his surrender.

The single subject on which Clough seems to have displayed any kind of positiveness at all while he was in America was religion. In December 1852 he wrote to Blanche, 'Theodore Parker has been preaching some very infidelical sermons, they say—proclaiming disbelief in Miracles and all that—by which the genteel Boston mind is a good deal disturbed, poor thing—I am told. And Mr. Peabody, the genteel Unitarian minister, has preached an answer, very satisfactory to the genteel Boston mind— I am told' (*Corr.* ii. 354–5). Is it unfair to detect in the heavy sardonicism an effort to maintain some vestige of his old rebellious self? The religious question had become more prominent during Clough's years at University Hall and his association with Blanche drew it further to the forefront. Faced by the failure and the self-doubt of America, he seems almost instinctively to have taken up the cross of his heterodoxy. His friends were proving poor correspondents and he was beginning to feel that he was dropping out of their lives, silently lapsing into unimportance. Not all his friends were careful to avoid lecturing him. In the first letter he wrote (late in January 1853) John Shairp sent a well-meant but entirely unprovoked sermon on the necessity of Christian belief (*Corr.* ii. 367–8). About a fortnight later, without waiting for a reply, Shairp, returned 'to the charge', as he put it, and expressed his fervent hope that his friend would arrive at a simple faith of heart rather than head, as he himself had done (*Corr.* ii. 377). Clough's reply does not survive, but, to judge from Shairp's third letter (*Corr.* ii. 400), it must have been outspoken, completely rejecting historical Christianity and accusing Shairp of hypocrisy and self-deception. Rather sanctimoniously, since he himself had opened a correspondence of this kind, Shairp concluded, 'Therefore as we do not agree, let's write no more of this. It will do neither of us any good and will only cause pain. Please, No more of this!' (ibid.). But Clough was incensed. He charged Shairp with attempting to muzzle him. 'Don't let us wrangle any more across the wide Atlantic', Shairp pleaded (*Corr.* ii. 444).

Meanwhile Clough was sending disturbing accounts of the religious position in Boston to Blanche.

[T]he Ticknors are exclusive, but not grand. The Nortons are neither grand nor exclusive—very kind-hearted and good but perhaps a trifle too Unitarianish. Emerson is *very* wrong in the eyes of Ticknors and Nortons. (Don't tell Papa nor Mama but) I do fear that it will be, some day, rather difficult to keep quite right with the Unitarianism. I don't go to church—that contents me—but they are so awfully rococo in their religious notions that were I much in the way of hearing them expressed I should infallibly speak out and speak strongly. That may be some difficulty, but we won't anticipate—but there's no good rushing into controversy, but I know you won't wish me to be a time-server—will you, my dear child? (*Corr.* ii. 360.)

Two weeks later he recurred to the question of religion, this time to the offending Theodore Parker, whose rationalistic but absolute divinity Clough was in sympathy with.

I do indeed sometimes think that my course is one that must be walked alone and that it is altogether too unpleasant and poverty-stricken for married happiness. I sometimes, when I have heard people here for example talk of Theodore Parker as if he were the scum of the earth, think that it will not do to keep silence. I have no particular love for Th[eodore] P[arke]r, but he is so manifestly more right than these people who despise him.—I cannot, I think, in right altogether remain silent and acquiesce. Indeed I don't think it will continue to be possible (*Corr.* ii. 365-6).

Despondency tended to make him think of himself as a martyr. Emotionally, Blanche's response was satisfying:

What you say about the Unitarianism makes me think and be rather anxious, but I shall say nothing to anyone: and I can't begin about that seriously now; I could, do, I believe, wish you could refrain at present; would it do any good now to martyr yourself? I have always had a feeling you must write, but now when your influence is less than it will be, and when you have often said you did not feel entirely prepared to write, is it necessary? I sometimes hope it is something of a morbid sensitiveness to truth that makes you think the opprobrium and the necessity for speaking greater than they are. . . .

My dear, dear Arthur I can't get the Unitarianism out of my head. I don't know what to say. I feel as if you need not martyrise yourself. I hope too that the effect would not be so bad as you think. Whatever you do, do not talk of being solitary, for I must be with you. If you must disburthen your heart, you shall, but I hope you will not think it necessary at least yet. Wait for me, is that wrong Dear? . . .

. . . Dear boy, don't talk anymore of being alone, in your heresy. I don't know what to say: but I don't believe things are as bad as you say. I believe you might speak out, at any rate to some degree, and not be injured if you only get yourself valued first. The Lyells [Sir Charles Lyell, the geologist, and Lady Lyell had recently returned from Boston] say Theodore Parker is considered only *odd*. If we were but together I believe we could manage them. . . .[1]

Her fiancé did not, in fact, break his silence. Silence of a certain kind was to become habitual with him.

*   *   *

Much of the work in which Clough found himself involved as an Examiner, on his return to England, was routine. His chief task was to advise on reports sent in by Inspectors, and to scrutinize the marks they sent in after examining student teachers so that they should conform to a standard. But, as he wrote to Emerson after a year at it, such employment had its compensations. It was a relief after years of teaching Greek, and it did not draw him into the religious questions which were unavoidable in any other career in education (*Corr.* ii. 485). For several months after his return he entertained vague hopes of going back to America, and in his letters to his friends there he often expressed regret at having had to leave their confident young country, but he was settling down contentedly enough. He had found his modest berth in life. As the years passed his work became more varied and more interesting. In 1856 he was examining candidates

---

[1] *Corr.* ii. 381 n., with additions from Bodleian MS. Eng. Lett. d. 179.

for the Royal Engineers and the Royal Artillery in English composition and literature and in history. That autumn he spent
three months touring military schools in Prussia, Austria, and
France as secretary to a Commission which, as a result of the
Crimean experience, had been appointed to inquire into the
education of officers. Two or three years later he became private
secretary to Robert Lowe, who had been made Vice-President
of the Privy Council Committee on Education.

He was married to Blanche at Embley—the Nightingales'
home—on 13 June 1854, and, after a honeymoon at Lea Hurst
in Derbyshire—the Nightingales' other home—they set up house
in St. Mark's Crescent in Regent's Park. They stayed there till
1859, when they moved to Campden Hill Road, Kensington.
Their first child, a boy, was born in April 1855 but died a few
hours after birth. Their eldest daughter, Florence, was born in
1858, their son, Arthur, in 1859, and Blanche Athena (who,
following in Anne Clough's footsteps, became in time Principal
of Newnham College) in 1861, while Clough was abroad on
sick-leave. He did not live to see this daughter.

On the surface, at least, there is a derived placidity in Clough's
life after his marriage. He picked up the threads of old friendships, although he found that most of his former friends had
grown too 'churchy' for his liking (*Corr.* ii. 460). He made
several new friends, notably Tennyson. He kept up a faithful
correspondence with the friends he had made in America. Apart
from these transatlantic letters of his, and the occasional one to
friends nearer home, his life over these years remains almost
completely opaque. The inescapable impression this correspondence creates is of a man who has made his treaty with himself
and with the world. His letters to America are totally anonymous
as far as the inner life is concerned. Charles Norton once complained humorously,

Seriously, I wish you were here again for I think I may have grown
brighter since [your last visit], I should not have to force you to in-
telligibility as I used to, at any rate I should like to see. Your letters
are very plain and I begin to be afraid that you think it right to lower
them to the standard of my comprehension. Do not be afraid, however,
and let me have as much of yourself in each one of them as you would
if you were on the couch in my room under that engraving of
Washington which you remember.—But now let us come to a serious

seriously,—do write me a little more of yourself,—your letters contain everything I want to know but how you are and what you are doing beside office work, and this they never tell me.[1]

The letters continue as impenetrably full of information about externals as before. Clough retailed news of the latest literary and political doings, identified the authors of anonymous and pseud-onymous articles in the most recent reviews and magazines, commented distantly on the passing scene. Occasionally he gave revealing glimpses of his own intellectual life.

There's a book called the Plurality of Worlds, by Whewell I believe, which some people are praising. It professes to prove that there are, most probably, no inhabitants in any of the planets, stars, or other bodies. I fear I read nothing myself—except an occasional newspaper . . . (*Corr.* ii. 473).

The great literary success of the last twelve months *has* been Buckle's History of Civilisation or whatever it is called—Really it is wonderful what numbers of people have read this thick volume and what a reputation its author has gained by it—I cannot say I have any desire to read it . . . (*Corr.* ii. 546).

By the way, are your people reading Darwin on Species, published by Murray; it is a very remarkable book I believe (*Corr.* ii. 574).

Clough had withdrawn to the sidelines. Even his most loyal friend, Tom Arnold, remarked how his once 'marvellous' intelligence had become 'dulled' in later life.[2] Marriage and stability had turned his eyes away from the creative fissures and anxieties and conflicts of his earlier life.

He kept himself busy enough. He worked steadily at the Plut-arch, and when it was completed he prepared a shorter edition of eight *Lives* which Longmans had commissioned. Early in 1854 Charles Norton proposed an American edition of his poems, and he slowly set about revising and arranging his 'weaved-up follies', as he called them (*Corr.* ii. 477), but he died before the volume materialized. He revised *Amours de Voyage* for its appearance in the *Atlantic Monthly*, and was delighted when he made some money through its publication—the first time he had done so with any of his poetry. In 1859 he was considering

---

[1] C. E. Norton to Clough, 20 Dec. 1853, Bodleian MS. Eng. Lett. e. 74, fol. 27 (761).

[2] T. Arnold, 'Arthur Hugh Clough: A Sketch', p. 105.

collaborating with Tom Arnold on a series of 'Lives' of English poets, along the lines of Johnson's, and beginning roughly where Johnson left off. The same year he published in *Fraser's* a review of the *Poems and Ballads of Goethe* translated by Aytoun and Martin, which contains some perceptive and important remarks on the problems involved in translation.[1] Not once, however, did he venture into fresh original work.

It is difficult to see this withdrawal from intellectual and creative effort as anything but a capitulation. Life and his restless intellect had exhausted him and he was willing to drift. It is more than likely, however, that Clough himself saw, not capitulation, but affirmation. He was living out the gospel of Silence and Action he had arrived at. According to his wife, his 'mind in these years turned more and more to action as its natural relief' (*PPR* i. 47). We have already seen how thoroughly Clough embraced Silence, how completely he surrendered 'speculation'. His connection with Florence Nightingale illuminates the creed of Action.

Florence Nightingale had been an important ally in the early months of his association with Blanche. She had worked out elaborate sums to arrive at the absolute minimum on which they could get married. Her arithmetic had been characteristically thorough: in her calculations she took into account the arrival of children, using the national birth-rate as a predictive index. Armed with her figures she had persuaded Aunt Mai to consent to her daughter's engagement.[2] Some early references to her in Clough's letters to Blanche suggest that he did not greatly care for her initially. She was too hard, too cold, too 'arithmetical' —in many respects too much like himself.[3] Possibly he was comparing her unfavourably with Blanche. By the end of 1856, however, he was almost totally engulfed by her. He had accompanied her to Calais in August 1854, on her way to Scutari, and when she returned she was rapidly becoming a living public

---

[1] Cf. Trawick, pp. 187–202.

[2] C. Woodham-Smith, op. cit., p. 109.

[3] Cf. *Corr.* i. 307. In an unpublished part of this letter Clough wrote, 'Shall I tell you something? I like your mama much better than her friend [i.e. Florence Nightingale] . . .' (Bodleian MS. Eng. Lett. e. 77, fol. 121ᵛ). In an earlier letter he had written rather unfeelingly, 'Hilary, as well as Florence, is more sensible and practical (and indeed! more generally intelligent) than B.M.S.S. It is odd decidedly her superiors as they are that anybody should feel it possible to be to her what he could not so far as he sees be to either of those two very superior cousins of hers.' Ibid., fol. 116.

legend. As a member of the family Clough had a much more intimate and inward sense of her heroic temper, of the bitter struggle she had to wage against the opposition and animosity of her own immediate family. He became in time the slave of this imperious, austere, unyielding woman. No task was too menial for him. He proof-read her huge volume of *Notes on Matters Affecting the Health, Efficiency, and Hospital Administration of the British Army*, suggested rearrangements in the text, and supervised its passage through the press. He was appointed secretary to the Nightingale Fund, he tied up parcels, he looked up timetables, he acted as her courier. When her health broke down in 1857 and she moved into the Burlington Hotel, he became, with Aunt Mai, a guardian of the inner sanctum. He spent all the time he could spare with her, doing whatever work needed doing. Blanche and the children had to live with her father (who himself had been deserted by his wife for the same Cause) for a year, while he remained in London to fulfil his service.[1] At times Aunt Mai and her son-in-law felt as if they were working against the clock. Florence was going to die, and the work needed to be finished. At times there were morbid little rituals in the shadow of impending death. One day Florence discussed with Clough the full details of her funeral; on several occasions she 'promised' to die before he did. Several times she drew up wills for Clough to witness—and in one of them she left him all the money that would come to her on the death of her parents, with the proviso that he should pay back with compound interest whatever he had been given out of the Nightingale Fund.[2] In this highly charged atmosphere of mortality she and Aunt Mai and Clough discussed points of faith and philosophy which arose out of the *Suggestions for Thought to the Searchers for Truth among the Artizans of England*. The volume was printed privately and anonymously in 1860. Clough sent a copy to Jowett for his comments, and thus paved the way for one of the most important attachments in the lives of both the author and her reader.

Florence Nightingale's absorption of Clough is a complex

[1] C. Woodham-Smith, op. cit., p. 330. In a rare moment of insight Blanche Smith had once written to him in America, 'I am afraid you will not be satisfied with me, or you will use me as a [pillar?]—heaven knows I do long to be a comfort to you, but I can't be quite made into an instrument.' Bodleian MS. Eng. Lett. d. 179, fol. 196.

[2] Nightingale Papers, vol. lvii. British Museum Add. MS. 45795, fol. 9.

phenomenon. At an obvious level he was performing his life-work, acting—however modestly. As he might have put it, he was willingly transforming himself into an 'operative' and 'cobbling shoes' for a cause which was unmistakably good, unmistakably a 'correlative of the soul'. It is hardly credible, however, that he was emotionally uninvolved—he had, after all, defined love as 'fellow-service'. One need not suggest a romantic attachment in the customary sense, but it is not entirely fanciful to suggest that in this asexual, completely self-abnegative relationship with an immensely authoritative woman he was fulfilling obscure and profound psychological impulsions, delivering himself of himself.

He was, of course, seriously overworking himself and the strain was beginning to tell. His health had never been robust and an attack of scarlatina in the winter of 1859 left him seriously debilitated. His life from then on was to be a succession of ill-nesses which necessitated progressively more lengthy periods of sick-leave. In the autumn of 1860 he was alone in Malvern taking the water-cure for two months. Six weeks at Freshwater with his family followed and during this period he became a good friend of the Tennysons. The doctors next advised him to go abroad, and he set out with a courier, but from Marseilles he went on alone to Greece, Constantinople, and Scutari. In June he returned to England and stayed for a fortnight with his family in Derbyshire. Returning to London, he tried to do a little work, but very quickly overtaxed himself. Once again he was advised to go abroad and he resumed his solitary wanderings, this time never to return. He went first to Paris and then to Auvergne and the Pyrenees, where he met the Tennysons. He went back to Paris to meet Blanche, who had recently had her baby, and together they made their way to Florence. There, on 13 November, he died. His sister, Anne, who had come out three days earlier, was with Blanche at his bedside.

The months of enforced loneliness while Clough travelled in search of health released for the last time the creative forces which had remained dormant for so many years. In 1861, while he was abroad on the Continent, he wrote the *Mari Magno* stories. Some of the old questions—about morality, love, guilt, redemption—were reopened by solitude, but he now saw them in a different light. Hindsight is dangerous and easy, but it is difficult to see these verse tales in terms other than those of a final summing-up—especially when we remember his compulsive effort to get down on paper 'The Lawyer's Second Tale', the last 248 lines of which he dictated to Blanche when his fingers became unable to guide the pencil firmly. There is about the whole poem an air of revisitation. The first two stories take us back to the troubled, uncomprehended world of childhood, adolescence, and young manhood, when life seems so complicated, when the over-active brain and moral sense lead one away from the simple and obvious paths, when impulse and spontaneity arrive only after their moment has passed. It is a world which resembles unmistakably that in which Clough himself grew up, and the narrative passes judgement on an earlier self. The framework of the voyage to Boston, which provides the occasion for the storytelling, clearly recalls Clough's own voyage in 1852.[1] Imaginatively and thematically, some of the stories revisit scenes and situations he had dealt with in his earlier poetry. 'The Lawyer's Second Tale' is patently a reworking of *The Bothie* situation; somewhat less obviously 'The Lawyer's First Tale' recalls the missed opportunity of *Amours de Voyage*. The past blends into the present in *Mari Magno*. The diaristic 'My Tale' has its genesis in the locale—and possibly the situations—in which Clough was actually living when he wrote it; the initial situation in 'The Clergyman's Second Tale', that of a man consigned to the loneliness of hotels in a foreign land for reasons of health, is drawn from first-hand experience. The important point is the extensive pressure of personal relevance in *Mari Magno*. The mood of self-understanding, usually quiet though sometimes deeply distressed, is throughout uppermost.

Critical opinion has been sharply divided over *Mari Magno*. Several critics in the nineteenth century saw it as Clough's best work, as the mellow product of a deepened imagination. Following the tradition laid down in the Memoir of 1869, they saw it as a work of ripened wisdom, a foretaste of the fruits that might have followed if Clough had not died so early, although, in the words of the Memoir, 'We find in [these stories] rather a freedom

---

[1] A. M. Turner, 'A Study of Clough's *Mari Magno*', *PMLA* xliv (June 1929), 569–89, is an interesting study of some of the autobiographical elements in the poem, and especially of the resemblances between Clough's storytellers and his fellow passengers on his trip to Boston in 1852.

from disturbance than a positive expression of belief.'¹ High valuations of the poem are not confined to the nineteenth century. H. W. Garrod maintained that *Mari Magno* could not be called Clough's masterpiece only because it was an unfinished and hurried work. Nothing else in Clough, Garrod maintained, gives the same evidence of a 'nature genuinely poetical'.² As early as 1862, however, when only three of the stories ('The Lawyer's First Tale', 'My Tale', and 'The Clergyman's Second Tale') were published, a reviewer declared that they 'had better have remained unpublished'.³ In 1869 Henry Sidgwick said that in *Mari Magno* Clough's 'genius of twaddle' prevailed, and compared the stories to the worst aspects of Patmore.⁴ More recently Morchard Bishop held that it would be best to draw a veil over this 'most embarrassingly dreadful long poem of the nineteenth century'.⁵ It is difficult to envisage readers today who will quarrel violently with this last judgement. Yet the poem does represent a new departure, and, although it does not repay extended examination, it has considerable importance as Clough's final resting-point.

All the stories in *Mari Magno* relate to a single subject, the relationship between man and woman, and each one illustrates a particular aspect of the love relationship which is usually but not always connected with marriage. Clough is indebted to Chaucer for the frame situation, in which shipboard companions meet on deck each night to tell their illustrative stories, and the

---

¹ *PPR* i. 48. T. S. Perry's verdict is typical of the kind of critical favour the poem has received in its time:

'[*Mari Magno*] gives evidence of [Clough's] tardily-attained maturity. It seems as if at length he had found his place in life, as if he had passed safely through the experiences which make up so much of his earlier poems and as if while sympathizing with others he had found firm ground under his feet, from which he could examine what went on about him, without losing himself in wonder . . . They serve to show what it would have been fair to expect from him if he had lived longer; but that is not all: they are, though brief and few, good models of narration, by means of both their simplicity and seriousness' (T. S. Perry, 'Arthur Hugh Clough', *Atlantic Monthly*, xxxvi (Oct. 1875), 417–18).

² H. W. Garrod, *Poetry and the Criticism of Life* (Cambridge, Mass., 1931), p. 122.

³ [W. L. Collins], 'Clough's *Poems*', *Blackwood's Magazine*, xcii (Nov. 1862), 597.

⁴ [Henry Sidgwick], 'The Poems and Prose Remains of Arthur Hugh Clough', *Westminster Review*, xcii (Oct. 1869), 385.

⁵ M. Bishop, 'Thyrsis; or the Importance of Not Being Earnest', in *The Pleasure Ground*, ed. M. Elwin (London, 1947), p. 72.

whole collection can be seen, too, as a nineteenth-century equivalent of the 'Marriage Group' in *The Canterbury Tales*. As they
unfold, these stories canvass nearly all the understandings of this
central human relationship which we encounter in Clough's
earlier works; the desires, the anxieties, the half-understood
impulsions and hesitations which must somehow be accommodated. We see love defined as fellow-service and as juxtaposition, we see the workings out of guilt and final redemption.

The most striking departure is the verse manner itself, which
owes something to Chaucer, but even more to Crabbe, whose
realism—'There is no one more purely English (in the Dutch
manner)' (*Corr*. ii. 522)—Clough endeavours to emulate. He
lacks Crabbe's toughness and solidity, but occasionally he ap-
proximates Crabbe's flat earthiness—as in this description of a
journey in a *banquette*:

> Close-packed we were, and little at our ease,
> The *conducteur* impatient with the squeeze;
> Not tall he seemed, but bulky round about,
> His cap and jacket made him look more stout;
> In *grande tenue* he rode of *conducteur*;
> Black eyes he had, black his moustaches were,
> Shaven his chin, his hair and whiskers cropt;
> A ready man; at Ussel when we stopt,
> For me and for himself, bread, meat, and wine,
> He got, the *courier* did not wait to dine;
> To appease our hunger, and allay our drouth,
> We ate and took the bottle at the mouth;
> One draught I had, the rest entire had he,
> For wine his body had capacity.
>
> ('My Tale', ll. 29–41; *Poems*, 344–5.)

In MS. A these lines were expanded, but the additions were
cancelled:

> A dog he had; that squatted at his side
> And barked at every other dog he spied—[1]

This depressed prosaism of externals sometimes brings off,
through implication, effects which are deft even in the portrayal
of human situations. In 'The Lawyer's First Tale', for example,
the young boy, visiting his girl cousins, strays from the rest with
his unacknowledged love, Emily.

[1] Bodleian MS. Eng. Poet. d. 145, fol. 12.

> Looking into a sort of cave
> She stood, when suddenly a wave
> Ran up; I caught her by the frock,
> And pulled her in, and o'er a rock,
> So doing, stumbled, rolled, and fell.
> She knelt down, I remember well,
> Bid me where I was hurt to tell,
> And kissed me three times as I lay;
> But I jumped up and limped away.
> The next was my departing day.
>
> (1, ll. 140–9; *Poems*, 315.)

The manner, however, is not outstandingly successful. The literalism becomes trivial. In the first of these passages the strain of the heroic couplet is evident in the broken-backed lines and the unnatural locutions. In the second the octosyllables topple *naïveté* into puerility. Yet Clough does use the manner with considerable success in the two stories I have quoted from. Significantly, they are stories in which the realism of the manner is matched by the realism of the treatment as a whole. 'My Tale', strictly not a tale at all, perfectly answers the depersonalized verse style. We are presented with a succession of scenes and activities, two generalized lyrics, a series of human figures observed in a landscape. Life is presented *currente calamo* and left at that. In 'The Lawyer's First Tale'—the only one of the stories, apart from 'My Tale', which is told in the first person—we view through the eyes of experience a precocious, eager, but awkward young boy's slow growth into the realization that he is in love. But the realization comes too late; the cousin he almost speaks out his love to is already married by the time he brings himself to the point of utterance. It is a moving and well-told story, in which the imagery of travel is neatly handled—but it comes to no conclusion.

Before turning to the other stories a few more observations about Clough's verse manner in this poem should be made. If the octosyllabic and heroic couplets recall Crabbe, they also recall Coventry Patmore, whom Clough read with approval. The realism of *Mari Magno* is a domesticated and mid-Victorian realism. One can indicate another affinity which is especially strong in 'The Clergyman's Second Tale': Tennyson's *Enoch Arden*. A consideration of Clough's manner leads us to wider questions of sensibility. Some of the areas of sexual morality into which he enters in these stories are daring enough; it is the manner in which those areas are imaginatively invested that is at issue here.

In his review, 'Recent English Poetry', Clough had written:

[The true and lawful haunts of poetry are], if anywhere, in the blank and desolate streets, and upon the solitary bridges of the midnight city, where Guilt is, and wild Temptation, and the dire Compulsion of what has once been done—there with these tragic sisters around him, and with Pity also, and pure Compassion, and pale Hope, that looks like Despair, and Faith in the garb of Doubt, there walks the discrowned Apollo, with unstrung lyre. . . .[1]

One might suspect in this Gustave Doré vision the pressure of personal anxiety on poetic doctrine. At any rate, the two stories in *Mari Magno* in which an illustrative conclusion is not perfunctorily imposed—'The Clergyman's Second Tale' and 'The Lawyer's Second Tale'—attempt to fulfil this poetic function. The plots of both these stories are depressingly novelettish and melodramatic, and, in their different ways, both exhibit an affinity with the inflamed sentimentality of *Dipsychus Continued*.

'The Lawyer's Second Tale' is the better executed of the two. It is a fantasy of redemption and trust after misunderstanding. Philip, an Oxford Tutor, lingers on in the Highlands after his reading-party has broken up. He enters into a liaison with Christie, a maid at the inn where he is staying. For a week the lovers continue their clandestine affair, but then Philip has to leave on account of the College Audit. He takes Christie to Glasgow and leaves her there with an aunt who is married to a grocer. This first part of the story is done with a delicacy, honesty, and strength of detail which one misses in the idealized portrayals of *The Bothie*. There is little democratic illusion here. Christie is a simple, unquestioning servant-girl, attractive and limited, her kinsfolk are stupid, distrustful, human. The real love and tenderness of the two people involved are brought out movingly because of this fidelity—they love, in spite of as well as because of, one another. The story continues, unfortunately. When he leaves Glasgow, Philip promises to return and marry Christie, but mischance and meddling relations intervene. When he does return he discovers that the girl has left for Australia with her aunt and uncle. Philip thenceforth leads a spotless life, and in time rises in

[1] Trawick, p. 146.

the world. He also marries a wealthy and well-connected widow, but his marriage is childless. He knows, however, from an earlier visit to Australia in search of Christie, that he has an illegitimate son there, although he has lost track of both mother and boy. One day at a ball the almost impossible happens: Christie reappears. Shaken by recognition, Philip leaves immediately, and his wife, the completely understanding Lady Mary, makes the overture. Christie, in fact, nurses no bitterness. She is now married herself and has several children, but she loves and trusts Philip still. She leaves her first son with his father, and in a tender letter she explains how it was that, quite against her will, she had been separated from the man she loves. Philip himself is moved to tears—he has found his true love at last, but too late.

The moral imagination which creates and controls 'The Clergy-man's Second Tale' is more specifically affiliated with the neurotic and perfervid conventionality which produced *Dipsychus Continued*. Nowhere else in his poetry does Clough exhibit such a complete abnegation of sanity. The strange tension between the equable, 'wise', and rather tired surface of *Mari Magno* and the undertow of pain and anxiety we sometimes encounter in these stories is nakedly in view in this last accounting with guilt. The sin is monstrously real; it can be expiated only through horrified recoil. What we have in this tale is a Victorian understanding of, and verdict on, the 'other Victorians'.

Edward and Jane were happily married for nine years. 'Nothing beyond their home they sought or craved.' He had worked for nine years in an insurance office when suddenly his health failed. He took three months' sick-leave and went abroad by himself. As a boarder in a hotel he lived miserably, homesick, 'helpless and alone'. He wrote home before his leave expired saying that he was better and would like to go back. His wife wrote back urging him to stay out his full term for his own sake, for hers, and for the children's. Edward gave way, but as his health improved and he began to take more interest in the people around him, he began to notice a dark, attractive young girl who used to look at him in the dining-room. She appeared innocent but in reality

all the arts she had
With which some dreadful power adorns the bad,—
(ll. 98–9; *Poems*, 359.)

Silently, covertly, she challenged and tempted him. The glances they exchanged grew more prolonged. In his solitude Edward struggled, but one day he met her on the stairs as she stood at her half-open bedroom door.

> A sudden madness mounted in his blood
> And took him in a moment to the place;
> He stooped, and seeking swift the half-hidden face
> There, with the exultation of a boy,
> Read in her liquid eyes the passion of her joy;
> And went in with her at the fatal door
> Whence he reissued innocent no more.
>
> (ll. 129–35; *Poems*, 360.)

For two days he lived in the 'flame' of this illicit love. On the third a letter from his wife arrived, and with it a note, scrawled in a child's hand, from his daughter. In a remorseful frenzy Edward rushed from his room. Returning, he swiftly packed, and by the time evening fell he was a hundred miles from the scene of his shame. Four days later a haggard, dishevelled, and greying figure arrived at a little provincial town in France, wrote and posted some letters. ''Twas Edward four days from his fall.' One of the letters was to his wife, to whom he confessed everything—but he did not ask, could not accept, forgiveness. He could not desecrate the home and so would take lodgings near his office. Once a quarter he would meet his wife and hand over his earnings. He would meet her only; his children would not see his sinful face. For a full year he lived out his penance, living in unfriendly lodgings and dining in dingy chop-houses. Every quarter-day he met his wife at dusk in the 'green lane' beside her mother's home where they used to walk in happier days. Then one evening he returned to his lodgings to discover a telegram saying that his daughter was dangerously ill. He hurried home and found her delirious and asking for him. He arranged for another spell of leave, nursed his child back to health, and in the process was restored to the bosom of his family.

There is one crucial point in the story I have omitted in my retelling. On the evening Edward received the telegram he had been followed on the way back to his lodgings

> By a poor flaunting creature of the town
> In crumpled bonnet and in faded gown
> With tarnished flowers and ribbons hanging down.
>
> (ll. 235–7; *Poems*, 363.)

Slowly he came to recognize in this 'hapless thing of woe' the 'occasion of his shame twelve months ago', now transported to her proper sphere where gas-jets glared balefully as in 'the flaming streets of hell'. It is only after he recognizes himself as 'an unblest wanderer in hell', and resists the temptation which is once more offered, that Edward is ready to receive the redemptive summons of the telegram. By the painful, ironic circuit of almost a whole life we are brought to an understanding of moral reality which has advanced little beyond a poem like the 'Lines'[1] which Clough had composed while he was at Rugby.

Ostensibly in *Mari Magno* Clough has finally surfaced, has achieved the tranquillity of the ocean's face. The great sea—that subtle and profound symbol of bewilderment, indeterminacy, flux, and chance which dominates his poetry—now lies beneath him and the depths no longer trouble. Yet, if one looks closely, the sea remains uncertain and unmastered. The stories simply present dissociated viewpoints and unrelated perspectives; occasionally they give us a glimpse of the still-threatening gulfs. The tranquillity of the surface is not the tranquillity of achievement; it is, rather, the quiescence of surrender. Clough is unwilling and unable to submerge himself. His wisdom is simply the specious wisdom of a tonality. Tennyson reported that when they were together at Bagnères de Luchon and Luz in 1861, Clough read him *Mari Magno*, and broke down and 'cried like a child' over it.[2] He could not have read the whole poem, since some of it was not yet written, certainly not 'The Lawyer's Second Tale'. According to Mrs. Clough, her husband wrote 'The Clergyman's Second Tale' in one night while he was with the Tennysons in the Pyrenees (cf. *Poems*, 469). Was this one of the poems he read? What did the tears of this lonely, reserved, and stoical man mean? Were they caused by the pain of revisitation, by the possibilities, hopes, and guilts which pass under review in *Mari Magno*? Did they lament wrong turnings taken and a promise that was once bright? Or did they merely express a self-pitying recognition of his own plight in the ailing and exiled Edward? The tears perhaps are totally unimportant, but I would still like to know their secret.

[1] *Poems*, p. 439. See above, pp. 56–7.
[2] [H. Tennyson], *Alfred Lord Tennyson, A Memoir*, 2 vols. (London, 1897), i. 475 n.

Notebook Labelled 'Essays—1841'

I GIVE here extracts and summaries that illustrate the nature of the contents of this notebook which, possibly, Clough used in his last year at Balliol. I have silently normalized some of the punctuation. Double strokes (//) indicate line-breaks. On the inside front cover is written 'Adam Smith's New Patent//Self-Acting Producer//Coleridge's approved distributor', and possibly this has some bearing on the Latin with which the notebook opens.

fol. 1

De Tib. et C. Gracchorum virtutibus et vitiis
Multa ferociter multa imprudenter egisse Gracchos tum Tib[erium] tum Caium nemo fortasse non libenter agnoscat: qui ex omni parte facta eorum defendat plane deest. Illud in primis pessimi apud posteros exempli et malorum plurimorum in re publica quasi fontem fuisse notandum est, quod tribunatum plebis, rem in primis quidem civitatis Romanae [saeculis?] omnium utilissimam, iis subsidiis firmaverint, et in eam vehementiam assueverint ut Senatui Populoque Romano solus imperaret ille Magistratus leges, senatus consulta, dignitatem consularem, quicquid sanctum quicquid venerandum erat pro suo arbitrio violaret, verteret, ageret.

fol. 2

'The science of the laws which regulate the production, accumulation, distribution and consumption of those articles or products which are necessary, useful, or valuable to Man and which at the same time possess exchangeable value (i.e., wealth). An Art[icle] or Prod[uct] is said to be possessed of exch[angeable] val[ue] when there are persons disposed to give a certain quantity of labour or of some other article or product obtainable only by means of labour in exchange for it. . . .'

Insert between fol. 2ᵛ and fol. 3

'Political Economy has for the object of its researches the increase of the stock of wealth existing in a Nation; with the distribution of that stock among the members of the community it has no concern except so far as the means used for the better regulation of that distribution interfere with the machinery it employs for its own particular object. It has no concern whatever with public provision for the Poor.'

v. of insert

'... Luxury//sho[ul]d a rich man burn wax or tallow?//i. Should there be any unnecessary consumption of Wealth.//i. for the benefit of national Wealth/ii. for the better distribution of Wealth.//Is it a good thing to have labour cheap?—i.e., Wages low—'

fol. 3

'Part of the Science treating of Prod[uctio]n of Wealth resolves itself into discussion of the Means by which labour may be rendered most efficient or by which the greatest amount of necessary, useful and desirable products may be obtained with the least possible labour.'

Transversely across the bottom of the page Clough has drawn a diagram representing 'Security of Property', 'Division of Labour—1. Skill 2. Time 3. Invention' and 'Accumulation of Capital' as the three pillars supporting the 'Self Interest Principle'.

fol. 3ᵛ–fol. 4

'... Must there in any case, be a class of people labouring hard with their bare sustenance for Wages?... But [the] happiness of [a people] does not depend on their being more or less densely peopled, upon their Poverty or their riches, their youth or their age, but on the Proportion which the Population and the food bear to each other. Malthus cf. M[c]C[ulloch], 224'

fol. 4ᵛ

'Is there anything to be got to serve the purpose of the 'luxury stimulus'?—

M'Culloch [*sic*] makes the only use of Profuse Consumption to be this of stimulation, consumption for consumption's sake—(and therefore Johnson's green peas in Feb[ruar]y (?)) he allows to be wholly prejudicial.— ...'

fol. 5ᵛ

'... M[c]C[ulloch], p. 379//In fact there are no means whatever by which the comm[an]d of the lab[our]ing classes over the necessaries and conveniences of life can be enlarged other than by accelerating the incr[ease] of cap[ital] as comp[are]d with Pop[ulatio]n or by retarding the increase of Pop[ulatio]n as comp[are]d with Cap[ita]l: and every Scheme for improving the cond[itio]n of the labourer which is not bottomed on this Principle, or wh[ich] has not an incr[ease] of ratio of cap[ita]l to P[opulatio]n for its object must be completely nugatory and ineff[ectua]l.'

fol. 6

'Int[eres]t of Labourer—as high wages as are consist[en]t with the

increase of Cap[ita]l//[Interest] of C[apital]ist Slave-trade-slavery?
//Wages, in superficial variations regulated by ratio of Cap[ital]:
Pop[ulation]—(M[ar]ket) but (Nat[iona]l) ultimately and permanently by cost of support—the labourer's price = a decrease of
productiveness if it last long enough, by agency of more-dying and
fewer-begotten principle, raises this price; incr[ease] vice versa;—
Conti[nuation] of high m[ar]ket Wages raises the labourer's standard
and of low vice versa. Abs[tract] fr[om] McC[ulloch].
　　Profit 1. Total surplus of produce produced by labour and capital;
　　　　　(2. Whole produce remaining for capitalists' share)
　　　　　　3. Surplus falling to the cap[italists' share—'

fol. 6ᵛ

'Profits (3) depend not on proportion to Wages but to capital invested. . . .'

fol. 7

Clough here considers Mill's distinction between the laws of Mind and
those of Matter. Political Economy 'takes for granted that the physical
p[ar]t of the process takes place somehow—It then inquires what are
the phenomena of Mind wh[ich] are concerned in the production and
distribution (consumption only as affecting these) of those objects [of
value as produced by labour]; it borrows from the pure science of the
Mind the laws of those phenomena and enquires what effects follow
from these mental laws acting in concurrence with those physical ones.'

fol. 7ᵛ

'The science wh[ich] treats of Pr[oduction] and D[istributio]n of
Wealth so far as they dep[en]d upon the laws of H[uma]n Nature:—
or//[The science] relating to the Moral or Psychological laws of the
Production and distribution of Wealth'

　　At this point Clough has drawn a chart to show 'Political Economy'
under the 'Moral Sciences' as a study 'of man as actuated by the desire
of wealth abstracting all other desires and passions except those
wh[ic]h may be reg[ar]ded as perpetually antagonizing Principles to
this desire of w[ea]lth, viz. aversion to labour and desire for the present
enjoyment of costly indulgence.' As such, Political Economy is a
branch of the Moral Sciences which is distinct from that concerned
with 'laws of mere intellect' and 'purely self-regarding desires' because
it is social, but which is again, in turn, different from that which concerns 'conscience, affections, love of approbation, the science on which
ἠθική τέχνη is founded.'

fol. 8

'(This exam[inatio]n of the result of particular motives Mill approves—

(cf. Sartor Res[artus]?)) . . . Complete def[initio]n then—//"The science which traces the laws of such of the Phenomena of Society as arise from the combined operations of Mankind for the Production of Wealth in so far as these phenomena are not modified by the pursuit of any other object." '

fol. 8ᵛ

'Q. 2. That P[olitical] E[conomy] is a Priori and must be//. . . Useful-ness of the Posteriori Method, i.e., requiring specific experience// Exceptions belong to Rules not to Laws, to Art, not Science.'

fol. 9

' "It is built upon hypotheses strictly analogous to those which under the name of def[initio]ns are the f[oun]d[atio]ns of the other abstract sciences. Geometry presupposes an arbitrary def[initio]n of a line . . . Just in the same way does P[olitical] E[conomy] presuppose an arbitrary def[initio]n of man as a being who invariably does that by which he may obtain the greatest amount of necessaries, conveniences and luxuries with the smallest quantity of labour and physical self-denial with which they can be obtained in the existing state of knowledge. "— p. 16.'

fol. 9ᵛ–fol. 10

'Coleridge//When shall we return to a sound conception of the right to property, namely, as being official, implying and demanding the performance of commensurate duties. Nothing but the most horrible perversion of Humanity and Moral Justice under the specious names of P[olitical] E[conomy] co[ul]d have blinded men to this truth as to the possession of land—the law of God having connected indissolubly the cultivation of every rood of Earth with the maintenance and watch-ful labour of man. But Money, Stock, Riches by Credit, transferable and convertible at will are under no such obligations; and unhappily it is from the Selfish, Autocratic possession of such Property, that our land-holders have learnt their present theory of trading with that which was never meant to be an object of Commerce.' p. 135, vol. 2.

'What they truly state they do not truly understand in its ultimate gr[oun]ds and causes and hence they have sometimes done more mischief by their ½ right ½ sophistical reasonings ab[ou]t and deduc-tions from well founded Positions than they could have done by the promulgation of positive error. This particularly applies to their famous ratio of increase between Man and the Means of his Subsistence.'

fol. 10ᵛ (in pencil)

'Arnold Dec[embe]r 6th//Benefit of the exertion of rising in the World //Benefit of Wealth//. . . Coleridge on Property . . . //Cap[ital] and

lab[our] rel[atio]ns he acknowledges to be bad// . . . That we must
take the new machine [Political Economy] and moralize it.'

fol. 23ᵛ [the pages between fol. 12 and this are blank]
'P[olitical] E[conomy] positions are not those of justice but of ex-
pediency; and we must beware of regarding them as of the former.
There is, for instance, in the relation of Capitalist and labourer, a system
of barter carried on in which the labourer always makes the house and
gets the pair of shoes. We must indeed let it be so till some system of
Money is invented to give hands, as it were, to this as yet impotent
Justice; till then let the Capitalist remember his unscored yet not therefore less real account with his easily defrauded brother . . .'

fol. 24
'. . . Temptations of the Palpable (especially perhaps in all Na[tiona]l
questions), where, of course, a balance must be made of the obj[ec]t
of P[olitical] E[conomy] with others.'

fol. 24ᵛ
'Corrective Postulates//That these producers do not produce for themselves, but the whole body, just as foragers forage not for themselves
but all the Army.'[1]

  [1] Sources of quotations in this notebook are identified in the index under
Coleridge, McCulloch, and Mill.

Notes on Religion in the 1849 (Roma) Notebook

THE notes which follow are headed in pencil, 'Grasmere '45'. I have used double parentheses to represent Clough's own square brackets. The italics are Clough's.

fol. 2

Miracles

Hume:—

Belief is regulated by Experience—

We experience false testimony, but not breach of order of Nature—

———

Channing:

1. If experience or Nature include ((Knowledge of)) God's existence miracles are no breach
2. Proves too much—goes ag[ain]st a miracle we ourselves saw [Pencilled exclamation mark in the left-hand margin preceding '2']
3. The conviction of the narrator is a fact to be accounted for.

Effect→Cause?

———

Can any event be proved to be a breach of the laws of Nature, and not an effect of some hitherto unknown Cause?—

Combination of Miracles with Doctrine—A prophet rests the issue on ... Elijah and the fire on Carmel.—Moses—cf. Ols[hause]n on Matt. VIII who makes Goodness its own evidence—but miraculous power its corroboration—the Goodness proves the miraculous agent to be good —the miracles then prove the Good teacher to be inspired.

fols. 4ᵛ, 5ᵛ

A divinely *ordained* ((example of the)) *conquest over Evil*—((in the Temptation and in the Passion)) *effected by divine humanity.*—How far then is that human nature identical with the divine?—How far is human nature in us dependent for its divine strength on the acts of this divine humanity?—are they an actus causati[v]us of our divine grace? Are we dependent on it—is it an actus causati[v]us to us for anything else? If in either respect we do so depend on it can it [be] no more divine than ourselves? And apart from these questions remains another, viz., How does human Nature conquer Evil—in its own strength or in God's strength. [Is?] God's strength given to it from the first, or by a regeneration?—Is this a real or only a verbal or impressional distinction?—

Is there anything in the notion of a Fall and a Redemption which is not conveyed in the common philos[ophical] expressions. So Atonement and Grace.—

And 2dly. If so, = is it essential to connect these truths of human Nature with the historical phenomena of Christ, and his life. May not Adam and Christ and their stories be but a Time-Effigiation of the Untemporal Truth? Or is there a special benefit for us in seeking div[ine] aid thro' Xt.—in consciously uniting ourselves to him; distinct even from any benefit which he may have done us once for all and which is ours whether we know him and his history or not—If so don't we get the Ch[ristian] System!

Cf. Prosp[ective] Rev[iew] No. III on Xtn. Fellowship in re. Theod[ore] Parker.

fol. 5

Moral Will Supreme

Ontol[ogical] Law or Idea

Phenomenal   Physical Uniformity—Moral Imperative.

De Wette ass. Pr.

Chr[ist] (whether h((uman)) or d((ivine)) attained such a state of the Will as to command Nature; and in that State we in him in the moral side participate.

Schl[egel?] ibid that by his passage thro' humanity he renewed it for all men.

Pr. that there is a lack acc[ording] to our conscience of some compensation for sin—and to that transcendent need the transcendent reality of Xt's death corresponds.

(Balliol MS. 441.)

Select Bibliography

FOR an extended Bibliography see Richard M. Gollin, Walter E. Houghton, and Michael Timko, *Arthur Hugh Clough: A Descriptive Catalogue* (New York Public Library, n.d.).

I. PRIMARY MATERIALS

A. *Manuscript and Special Collections:*

Clough MSS. in Balliol College, Oxford.
Clough MSS. in the Bodleian Library, Oxford.
Clough MSS. in the possession of Miss Katharine Duff.
Clough MSS. in the Houghton Library, Harvard.
Clough MSS. in Oriel College, Oxford.
Clough Collection in the Temple Reading Room, Rugby School.
Correspondence and Minutes of Meetings, Dr. Williams Library, London.

B. *Published Materials:*

[Arthur Hugh Clough], *The Close of the Eighteenth Century: A Prize Poem Recited in Rugby School, Wednesday, April 22, 1835* (Rugby, Rowell and Sons, 1835).

Clough's contributions in prose and verse to *The Rugby Magazine*, 2 vols., July 1835–Nov. 1837 (London, William Pickering, n.d.).

Plutarch's Lives: The Translation called Dryden's, corrected from the Greek and revised by A. H. Clough, 5 vols. (Boston, Little, Brown, 1859).

Greek History from Themistocles to Alexander, in a series of Lives from Plutarch, revised and arranged by A. H. Clough (London, Longmans, 1860).

Poems by Arthur Hugh Clough, with a Memoir by F. T. Palgrave (Cambridge, Macmillan, 1862).

Poems by Arthur Hugh Clough, with a Memoir by C. E. Norton (Boston, Ticknor and Fields, 1862).

Letters and Remains of Arthur Hugh Clough (for private circulation only; London, Spottiswoode, 1865).

The Poems and Prose Remains of Arthur Hugh Clough, with a selection from his Letters and a Memoir, ed. by his wife, 2 vols. (London, Macmillan, 1869).

Poems of Clough, ed. H. S. Milford (London, Henry Frowde, 1910).

Plutarch's Lives: The Dryden Plutarch, revised by Arthur Hugh Clough, 3 vols. (Everyman Library, London, J. M. Dent; New York, E. P. Dutton, 1910).

Poems of Arthur Hugh Clough, with an Introduction by Charles Whibley (London, Macmillan, 1913).

The Poems of Arthur Hugh Clough, ed. H. F. Lowry, F. L. Mulhauser, and A. L. P. Norrington (Oxford English Texts, The Clarendon Press, 1951).

The Correspondence of Arthur Hugh Clough, ed. F. L. Mulhauser, 2 vols. (Oxford, The Clarendon Press, 1957).

Selected Prose Works of Arthur Hugh Clough, ed. Buckner B. Trawick (Alabama, University of Alabama Press, 1964).

The Poems of Arthur Hugh Clough, ed. A. L. P. Norrington (Oxford Standard Authors, The Clarendon Press, 1967).

A Selection from Arthur Hugh Clough, ed. John Purkis (London, Longmans, 1967).

A Choice of Clough's Verse, selected, with an Introduction by Michael Thorpe (London, Faber and Faber, 1969).

See Greenberger, Evelyn B., ' "Salsette and Elephanta": An Unpublished Poem by Clough', *Review of English Studies*, xx (Aug. 1969), 284–305.

Greenberger, Evelyn B., 'Clough's "The Judgement of Brutus": A Newly-Found Poem', *Victorian Poetry*, viii (Sept. 1970), pp. 127–50.

Some Clough material is also to be found in:

The Letters of Matthew Arnold to Arthur Hugh Clough, ed. Howard F. Lowry (London, Oxford University Press, 1932).

The New Zealand Letters of Thomas Arnold the Younger, ed. James Bertram (Wellington, Auckland University Press, 1966).

II. SECONDARY MATERIALS

Armstrong, Isobel, *Arthur Hugh Clough* (London, Longmans, Green, for the British Council and the National Book League, 1962).

Bagehot, Walter, *Literary Studies*, 3 vols. (London, Longmans, Green, 1895).

Barish, Evelyn, 'A New Clough Manuscript', *Review of English Studies*, xv (May 1964), 168–74.

Bertram, James, 'Clough and His Poetry', *Landfall*, xvii (June 1963), 141–55.

Bishop, Morchard, 'Thyrsis; or the Importance of Not Being Earnest: A Study of Arthur Hugh Clough', in *The Pleasure Ground: A Miscellany of English Writing* (London, Macdonald, 1947).

Brooke, Stopford A., *Four Poets: Clough, Arnold, Rossetti, Morris* (London, Duckworth, 1908).

Chorley, Katharine, *Arthur Hugh Clough, The Uncommitted Mind: A Study of His Life and Poetry* (Oxford, The Clarendon Press, 1962).

Coulling, Sidney B., 'Matthew Arnold's 1853 Preface: Its Origin and Aftermath', *Victorian Studies*, vii (Mar. 1964), 233–63.

Dalglish, Doris N., 'Arthur Hugh Clough: The Shorter Poems', *Essays in Criticism*, ii (Jan. 1952), 56–61.

Dowden, Edward, *Studies in Literature, 1789–1877* (London, Kegan Paul, Trench, Trübner, 1892).

Dowden, John, 'Arthur Hugh Clough', *Contemporary Review*, xii (Dec. 1869), 513–24.

Emerson, Ralph Waldo, Review of 'The Bothie of Toper-na-Fuosich', *Massachusetts Quarterly Review*, ii (Mar. 1849), 249–52; reprinted in *Uncollected Writings*, ed. Charles C. Bigelow (New York, 1912).

Gollin, Richard M., 'Arthur Hugh Clough's Formative Years: 1819–1841' (unpublished Ph.D. dissertation, University of Minnesota, 1959).

Goode, John, '*Amours de Voyage*: the Aqueous Poem', in *The Major Victorian Poets: Reconsiderations*, ed. Isobel Armstrong (London, Routledge and Kegan Paul, 1968).

Guyot, Edouard, *Essai sur la formation philosophique du poète Arthur Hugh Clough: Pragmatisme et intellectualisme* (Paris, 1913).

Hardy, Barbara, 'Clough's Self-Consciousness', in *The Major Victorian Poets: Reconsiderations*, ed. Isobel Armstrong (London, Routledge and Kegan Paul, 1968).

Harris, Wendell V., *Arthur Hugh Clough* (New York, Twayne Publishers, 1970).

Heath-Stubbs, John, *The Darkling Plain* (London, Eyre and Spottiswoode, 1950).

Houghton, Walter E., *The Poetry of Clough: An Essay in Revaluation* (New Haven and London, Yale University Press, 1963).

Hutton, R. H., *Essays Theological and Literary*, 2 vols. (London, Macmillan, 1871).

Hutton, R. H., *Criticisms on Contemporary Thought and Thinkers*, 2 vols. (London, Macmillan, 1894).

Jump, J. D., 'Clough's *Amours de Voyage*', *English*, ix (summer 1953), 176–8.

[Kingsley, Charles], 'The Bothie of Toper-na-Fuosich', *Fraser's Magazine*, xxxix (Jan. 1849), 103–10.

Levy, Goldie, *Arthur Hugh Clough, 1819–1861* (London, Sidgwick and Jackson, 1938).

Lucas, F. L., *Ten Victorian Poets* (Cambridge, Cambridge University Press, 1940).

Lutonsky, Paula, *Arthur Hugh Clough* (Wiener Beitrage zur Englischen Philologie, Bd. xxxix; Wien, W. Braumuller, 1912).

Masson, David, 'The Poems of Arthur Hugh Clough', *Macmillan's Magazine*, vi (Aug. 1862), 318–31.

Miyoshi, Masao, 'Clough's Poems of Self-Irony', *Studies in English Literature*, v (autumn 1965), 691–704.

Mulhauser, Frederick, Jr., 'Clough's "Love and Reason"', *Modern Philology*, xlii (Nov. 1945), 174–86.

Norton, C. E., 'Arthur Hugh Clough', *North American Review*, cv (Oct. 1867), 434–77.

Osborne, James Insley, *Arthur Hugh Clough* (London, Constable, 1920).

Patmore, Coventry, *Principle in Art* (London, Bell, 1912).

Pritchett, V. S., *Books in General* (London, Chatto and Windus, 1953).

Rossetti, W. M., 'The Bothie of Toper-na-Fuosich', *The Germ*, i (Jan. 1850), 36–48.

Ryals, Clyde De L., 'An Interpretation of Clough's *Dipsychus*', *Victorian Poetry*, i (Aug. 1963), 182–8.

Sidgwick, Henry, *Miscellaneous Essays and Addresses* (London, Macmillan, 1904).

Symonds, John Addington, *Last and First*, ed. Albert Morrell (New York, N. L. Brown, 1919).

Tillotson, Geoffrey, 'Clough's *Bothie*', in G. and K. Tillotson, *Mid-Victorian Studies* (London, The Athlone Press, 1965).

Timko, Michael, *Innocent Victorian: The Satiric Poetry of Arthur Hugh Clough* (Columbus, Ohio University Press, 1966).

Veyriras, Paul, *Arthur Hugh Clough, 1819–1861* (Paris, Didier, 1964).

Waddington, Samuel, *Arthur Hugh Clough: A Monograph* (London, Bell, 1883).

Williams, David, *Too Quick Despairer: A Life of Arthur Hugh Clough* (London, Rupert Hart-Davis, 1969).

Wolfe, Humbert, 'Arthur Hugh Clough', in *The Eighteen-Sixties*, ed. John Drinkwater (Cambridge, Cambridge University Press, 1932).

Woodward, Frances J., *The Doctor's Disciples: A Study of Four Pupils of Dr. Arnold of Rugby* (London, Oxford University Press, 1953).

Note: I read Evelyn Barish Greenberger's, *Arthur Hugh Clough: The Growth of a Poet's Mind* (Cambridge, Mass., Harvard University Press, 1970) when it became generally available in England after my own book had gone to press.

INDEX

Aberdeen, Lord, 452

Abrams, Meyer H., 203

Academy, The, 268

Allingham, William, 227, 233, 266, 342, 409

Alvarez, Alfred, 303

Angelo, Michael, 301

Annan, Noel Gilroy, 2, 131

'Apostles, The', 83, 206

Aristotle, 74, 274, 282; *Nicomachean Ethics*, 346

Armstrong, Isobel, 219, 228, 238, 376, 402

Arnold, Matthew, 5, 112, 124, 135 n., 137, 139, 146, 147, 151–2, 163, 166, 170, 175, 178, 180, 184, 195, 197, 198, 199, 200, 209, 221–2, 224, 228, 229, 250, 289, 293 n., 306, 308, 309 n., 327, 328, 329, 346–7, 367, 417, 423, 431; letters to A. H. C., 213–21; 1853 Preface, 213, 217, 266; *Empedocles on Etna*, 206, 220, 306, 312; 'Resignation: to Fausta', 327; 'The Scholar-Gipsy', 146, 221; 'Thyrsis', 146

Arnold, Dr. Thomas, the prophet as schoolmaster, 13; sense of the relevant, 14; scope of his educational aims, 15; and Evangelicalism, 15–16; and the Noetics, 16; on the limitations of intellect, 16–19; distinction between truth and good, 16–17; and conscience, 17–19; nature and significance of his historical vision, 18–21; as analyst of his times, 20–4; awareness of change and crisis, 21; attitude towards class and property, 22, 23; anti-Tory sentiments, 22; on Jacobinism, 22–3; and Political Economy, 23; the responsibility of the middle-classes, 23–4; the aristocracy and the Church, 24; Church and State, 24–5; Rugby as miniature Arnoldian State, 25; reality and omnipresence of Evil, 25–6; boyhood and manliness, 26–7; enthusiasm, 27–8; the ethic of punishment, 28; earnestness, 28–30; and the sixth-form, 30–1; as a

teacher, 31; limitations of Arnoldism, 16–17, 44–5, *see also*, 43; on poetry, 49; moral response to literature, 49–50, *see also*, 54; attitude to the Oxford Movement, 61–2; 63–4, 67, 75, 77, 78, 84, 91, 93, 94, 100, 105; his death, 111; 114, 115, 122, 132, 135, 156–7, 158, 163, 164, 177, 205, 292, 293, 296, 337, 349, 349 n., 362 n., 408, 430, 442

Arnold, Mrs. Thomas, 32

Arnold, Thomas (Tom), 32, 61, 91, 110, 122, 123, 125, 133 n., 134, 137, 146, 153, 154, 164, 170, 175, 195, 196, 233, 263 and n., 264 n., 290, 291, 294, 305 n., 343, 346, 347, 373, 407 n., 417, 424, 458, 459

Ashburton, Lady, 294, 345, 423

Ashley, Lord, 164

Athanasian Creed, The, 114–15

Atlantic Monthly, The, 308, 458

Augustine, Saint, 429

Aytoun, William Edmonstone, 45

Bagehot, Walter, 65, 189, 223, 288, 301, 305, 358, 359

Barbés, Armand, 172

Barish, Evelyn (*see also*, Evelyn Barish Greenberger) 374, 428 n.

Baudelaire, Charles, 429

Baur, Ferdinand Christian, 132; *Untersuchungen über die sog. Pastoral briefe des Apostels Paulus*, 134

Benn, Alfred William, 60 n., 138 n.

Bentham, Jeremy, 63, 115

Bertram, James, 184, 187 n., 369 n.

Besant, Sir Walter, 421

Bhagvad-Gita, The, 135 n.

Bishop, Morchard, 113, 463

Blackwood's Magazine, 206, 305 and n.

Blanc, Louis, 171

Blanqui, Auguste, 172, 173

Bowdler, John, 15

Bowers, Frederick, 309 n.

Boyle, George David, 71

Breton, Philip Le, 228

British Critic, The, 100